'09   BE   2⁵⁰

2008 Index
of Economic Freedom

D1567512

Contributors

Ambassador Terry Miller is Director of the Center for International Trade and Economics at The Heritage Foundation.

Kim R. Holmes, Ph.D., is Vice President for Foreign and Defense Policy and Director of the Kathryn and Shelby Cullom Davis Institute for International Studies at The Heritage Foundation.

Edwin J. Feulner, Ph.D., is President of The Heritage Foundation.

Mary Anastasia O'Grady is a member of the Editorial Board of *The Wall Street Journal* and Editor of the *Journal*'s "Americas" column.

William W. Beach is Director of the Center for Data Analysis at The Heritage Foundation.

Paul A. Gigot is Editor of *The Wall Street Journal* Editorial Page.

Anthony B. Kim is a Policy Analyst in the Center for International Trade and Economics at The Heritage Foundation.

Daniella Markheim is Jay Van Andel Senior Trade Policy Analyst in the Center for International Trade and Economics at The Heritage Foundation.

Stephen L. Parente is Associate Professor of Economics at the University of Illinois at Urbana–Champaign.

James M. Roberts is Research Fellow for Economic Freedom and Growth in the Center for International Trade and Economics at The Heritage Foundation.

Carl J. Schramm is President and CEO of the Ewing Marion Kauffman Foundation.

Guy Sorman is a French journalist and author.

Caroline Walsh is a Research Assistant in the Center for International Trade and Economics at The Heritage Foundation.

Tim Kane, Ph.D., is former Director of the Center for International Trade and Economics at The Heritage Foundation.

2008 Index of Economic Freedom

Kim R. Holmes, Ph.D.

Edwin J. Feulner, Ph.D.

Mary Anastasia O'Grady

with Anthony B. Kim, Daniella Markheim, and James M. Roberts

THE WALL STREET JOURNAL.

Copyright © 2008 by The Heritage Foundation and Dow Jones & Company, Inc.

The Heritage Foundation
214 Massachusetts Avenue, NE
Washington, DC 20002
(202) 546-4400
heritage.org

The Wall Street Journal
Dow Jones & Company, Inc.
200 Liberty Street
New York, NY 10281
(212) 416-2000
www.wsj.com

Cover images by iStockphoto, World Bank
ISBN: 978-0-89195-276-3
ISSN: 1095-7308

Table of Contents

Advisory Board

The following members of the Advisory Board for the *2008 Index of Economic Freedom* were consulted as part of the ongoing review of the methodology used in this year's edition. Their advice, insights, and critiques, as well as the efforts of many others who participated in the review process, are gratefully acknowledged.

William W. Beach, *The Heritage Foundation*

Maria Sophia Aguirre, *Catholic University of America*
Axel Dreher, *ETH Zurich, KOF Swiss Economic Institute*
Douglas Holtz-Eakin, *Economist, Washington, D.C.*
Tim Kane, *Economist, Washington, D.C.*
Mordechai "Max" Kreinin, *Michigan State University*
Philippe Lacoude, *Economist, Paris and Washington, D.C.*
Richard Roll, *University of California, Los Angeles*
Friedrich Schneider, *University of Linz*

Foreword

I don't know who first used the word "globalization," but he was probably no friend of capitalism. The word is bureaucratic and implies that the world economy is subject to the control of some vast, nefarious force beyond human influence. The reality is that the world economy is enjoying its strongest run of prosperity in 40 years thanks to the greater ability of billions of individuals to make free choices in their own self-interest. The *Index of Economic Freedom* has been encouraging this trend for 14 years, and at the end of 2007, we can happily say it continues.

The world economy extended its multiyear run of 5 percent or so annual GDP growth this year, notwithstanding an American slowdown due mainly to the housing correction. As I write this, the U.S. economy seems to have survived the August credit crunch related to the collapse of the sub-prime mortgage market. The summer squall showed once again how interrelated financial markets have become, with sub-prime losses popping up around the world and even causing an old-fashioned bank run at Northern Rock in the United Kingdom.

The episode is naturally leading to soul-searching about the stability of this brave new world of global finance—including the spread of asset securitization, the rise of hedge funds, and an explosion in derivatives. This introspection ought to be healthy. The sub-prime fiasco has, at the very least, exposed the need for more careful vetting by investors, but regulators and bankers are also sure to examine the rules for transparency and capital requirements to prevent the spread of problems throughout the financial system. The event also shows the need for more careful driving by America's Federal Reserve, whose easy-money policy in the first half of this decade was the root cause of the housing boom and bust. The good news is that, at least so far, there hasn't been a regulatory overreaction that could stymie growth.

The irony of the year has been the shifting economic policy trends in America and France, of all places. The U.S. political debate is moving in a negative direction as "fairness" and income redistribution replace growth as the policy lodestar and proposals for tax increases proliferate. The Bush tax cuts of 2003 were crucial to kicking the economy out of its post-9/11, post-dot.com doldrums. But they expire after 2010 and are in serious jeopardy. The free-trade agenda has also stalled as bilateral pacts with Latin America and South Korea face heavy going on Capitol Hill. The 2008 election will be as much a referendum on economic policy as on foreign policy.

Perhaps the rest of the world will have to teach America a policy lesson or two. As the *Index* shows, Europe overall has moved in a freer direction this decade. This is due in large part to reform in the former Eastern Europe, as well as to the policy competition caused by the success of the euro. With capital and people free to move and governments no longer able to inflate their way out of fiscal difficulty, the trend has been toward lower tax rates and labor market liberalization.

Miracle of miracles, even France has been mugged by this reality. Nicolas Sarkozy made the revival of the French economy a main theme of his successful campaign for president, and he has followed with proposals for what he called "a new social contract founded on work, merit and equal opportunity." We should all hope he

succeeds—not merely to compensate for any slowdown in America, but for its own sake to help Europe break away from its self-imposed sense of diminished expectations. In any event, this policy churning in Europe shows how the ability to move capital freely across borders imposes a price on bad government decisions.

The larger point is that if we step back from the daily turmoil, we can see that we live in a remarkable era of prosperity and spreading freedom. Hundreds of millions of people are being lifted out of poverty around the world as global trade and investment expand and countries like India and China liberalize parts of their economies. The International Monetary Fund reported in early 2007 that every country in the world, save for a couple of small dictatorships, was growing. This prosperity can itself create discontent due to the rapidity of change, and it certainly poses a challenge to political leaders who are obliged to explain and manage its consequences. The *Index of Economic Freedom* exists to help in that explanation, and we hope readers continue to find it a source of comparative policy wisdom.

Paul A. Gigot
Editorial Page Editor
The Wall Street Journal
October 2007

Preface

Our confidence in freedom as a liberating moral force and the foundation of true democracy has never been stronger. The victory of political freedom as a universal ideal advances and continues to drive revolutionary change throughout the world. Now, as we progress into the 21st century, more countries understand the importance of adopting institutional frameworks to enhance their citizens' economic freedom. The link between economic freedom and prosperity has never been clearer. People around the world are demanding that their governments support and maintain economic environments that provide the best chance for economic growth and the creation of wealth.

A country's level of economic freedom reflects the ability of ordinary citizens to make economic decisions on their own. It includes the freedom to choose a job, start a business, work where one chooses, borrow money, and use a credit card. It ranges from buying a house to having a choice in health care, from being fairly taxed to being treated justly by the courts. The higher the economic freedom in a country, the easier it is for its people to work, save, invest, and consume.

Yet the struggle for economic freedom faces determined opposition. Tariffs are just one example of protectionism that never lacks champions, and those who want special privileges will always pressure societies to expand the size and weight of government intervention. Special privileges for the few mean less prosperity for the many.

The *Index of Economic Freedom* has documented the link between economic opportunity and prosperity with research and analysis for 14 years. Published jointly by The Heritage Foundation and *The Wall Street Journal*, the *Index* has painted a global portrait of economic freedom and established a benchmark by which to gauge a country's prospects for economic success. It follows a simple tenet: Something cannot be improved if it is not measured. Tracing the path to economic prosperity, the annual *Index* continues to serve as a critical tool for students, teachers, policymakers, business leaders, investors, and the media. The findings of the *Index* are clear and straightforward: Countries with an enduring commitment to economic freedom enjoy greater prosperity than do those with less economic freedom.

The 2008 *Index*, covering 162 countries, shows that economic freedom worldwide continues to advance steadily, albeit at a slower rate than one might hope. In this 14th edition, most of the 20 freest countries from last year are still ranked among the freest, while others in the middle of the pack have experienced some shuffling as a result of varying efforts at reform.

Europe, Asia, and the Americas are the three freest regions. Asia has both the world's freest economy and its least free economy. More than half of the top 20 freest countries are found in Europe, and the Americas are home to some of the richest and most dynamic countries in the world.

For countries pursuing sustainable prosperity, the *Index* reveals that both policy direction and commitment to economic freedom matter. For example, the erosion of economic freedom in the Americas reflects some countries' reversals of free-market policies and stalled pursuit of economic freedom. Venezuela, in particular, is risking long-run economic failure as President Hugo Chávez takes the country further down an anti–free market path.

The 2008 *Index* contains three notable guest chapters written by outside scholars. A chapter by Carl Schramm, President and CEO of the Ewing Marion Kauffman Foundation, highlights the importance of economic fluidity and how it fosters innovation and entrepreneurship as a crucial element of economic freedom. Professor Stephen Parente of the University of Illinois at Urbana–Champaign documents the necessity of dismantling barriers to economic catching-up so that all economies can have the chance to flourish in the 21st century. Guy Sorman, a French journalist and author, reminds us of six major characteristics of the globalization that we enjoy today and of the potential threats to it.

This edition also contains a chapter analyzing each of the five geographic regions—a focus that matters for local competition. And, of course, this edition includes our traditional country pages with new charts highlighting the changes in each economy's economic freedom and detailed explanations analyzing each of the freedoms.

As our *Index* has demonstrated again in this edition, economic freedom is the key to creating an environment that allows a virtuous cycle of entrepreneurship, innovation, and sustained economic growth to flourish. Leaders who commit to expanding economic freedom will realize the fruits of their labor. For citizens living in such a country, increased economic freedom will improve their standard of living, make their daily lives more stable, and help to ensure a bright future for their families.

Edwin J. Feulner, Ph.D., President
The Heritage Foundation
November 2007

Acknowledgments

We wish to express our profound gratitude to the many individuals, especially those at The Heritage Foundation, who have made such valuable contributions to this 14th annual edition of the *Index of Economic Freedom*. The Heritage Foundation's Center for International Trade and Economics (CITE) produces the *Index*, an effort that this year involved CITE Director Terry Miller and Anthony Kim, Daniella Markheim, and James Roberts, as well as Research Assistant Caroline Walsh. Former Director of CITE Tim Kane and former Research Assistant Andrew Peek made significant contributions to the 2008 *Index*.

Others at The Heritage Foundation also made invaluable contributions to this year's edition. We are particularly grateful to Center for Data Analysis Director William Beach for his continued support and for his contributions to the methodology chapter.

In the Douglas and Sarah Allison Center for Foreign Policy Studies, a division of the Kathryn and Shelby Cullom Davis Institute for International Studies, Ariel Cohen and James Phillips wrote introductory paragraphs and provided their expertise. We are also grateful once again for the many insights provided by Helle C. Dale, Director of the Allison Center and by Kathy Gudgel, Assistant to the Vice President, and Janice A. Smith, Special Assistant to the Vice President, The Kathryn and Shelby Cullom Davis Institute for International Studies.

In the Asian Studies Center, Director Walter Lohman and Lisa Curtis, Bruce Klingner, and John J. Tkacik, Jr., wrote country backgrounds and provided assistance. Likewise, in the Margaret Thatcher Center for Freedom, Sally McNamara and Brett Schaefer wrote country backgrounds, and Director Nile Gardner offered valuable guidance. In the Information Technology Department, invaluable help was provided by Vice President of Information Technology Michael Spiller and Michael Smith. We are grateful for their professionalism.

In Publishing Services, Director Therese Pennefather and Elizabeth Brewer were responsible for all aspects of the production process, including the design and layout that make this 14th edition the most readable and accessible yet published, as well as for developing the world and country maps and formatting the charts and tables.

We are grateful to Director of Online Communications Ted Morgan, Tosan Ogharaerumi, and the other IT staff for placing the entire *Index* on the Heritage Web site (*www.heritage.org/ index/*). We also thank Bridgett Wagner, Mike Franc, Rebecca Hagelin, Alison Fraser, James Dean, and Todd Gaziano for their insightful contributions and support.

We once again gratefully acknowledge the continuing efforts of Senior Editor Richard Odermatt, who is responsible for final review of the completed text, and Senior Copy Editor William T. Poole, who bears the primary responsibility for editing the entire book. Each year, their professionalism, commitment, and attention to detail have been crucial in maintaining consistency of tone and making the *Index* a reality. We are likewise grateful to Editor Jon Rodeback, who carefully reviewed every one of the many charts and tables included in the book. In addition, the dedicated research of CITE interns Caroline DuMond, Christopher Grau, Joseph Lawler, Celeste Le Roux, Jay Soley, and Samantha Soller did much to make the specialists' in-depth analysis possible.

Countless individuals serving with various accounting firms, businesses, research organizations, U.S. government agencies, foreign embassies, and other organizations again cooperated by providing us with the data used in the *Index*. Their assistance is much appreciated. As always, we acknowledge our enduring debt to Heritage Trustee Ambassador J. William Middendorf II, who originally encouraged us to undertake such a study of global economic freedom.

Finally, we would like to express our appreciation to the many people who, year after year, either praise or criticize the *Index of Economic Freedom* so enthusiastically. The support and encouragement of people in all parts of the world continue to inspire The Heritage Foundation and *The Wall Street Journal* in their ongoing collaboration on this important work. We hope this year's effort once again matches the expectations of our supporters, as well as the thoughtful critics who so often have provided the insights that enable us to continue to improve the *Index*.

Kim R. Holmes, Ph.D.
Edwin J. Feulner, Ph.D.
Mary Anastasia O'Grady
November 2007

What's New in the 2008 *Index*?

Every year, the editors evaluate the *Index of Economic Freedom* and consider ways to improve the product. This year's edition of the *Index* continues the substance and style of the 2007 edition with a renewed emphasis on a more scientific and objective methodology coupled with an accessible format. There are few dramatic changes in the 2008 *Index*, but there are a number of important refinements.

These changes continue the Heritage Foundation/*Wall Street Journal* tradition of year-by-year improvement. For example, changes in the methodology were instituted in 2000, 2002, 2004, 2006, and 2007 to enhance the robustness of one or more of the 10 factors that are used to measure overall economic freedom. Each time, the entire time series is revised so that all scores are as consistent as possible, dating back to 1995. Our goal is to make the *Index* a resource that is credible, usable, and relevant to a changing world, with new data and knowledge, while also consistent with our heritage.

A more detailed explanation of what has changed, as well as what has not changed, in the 2008 *Index* follows:

- **Free Downloads at *www.heritage.org/index*.** The *Index* Web site has been revised to include free downloads of each chapter and even each individual country page. These can be used for briefing books, student handouts, or anything else that readers find useful. The Web site also has new audio and video presentations by *Index* scholars, as well as all of the raw data and related research papers.
- **Non-Tariff Barrier Penalty.** The *Index* methodology is consistent with the revisions made in 2007, measuring the same 10 economic freedoms in each economy and using exactly the same underlying data. The only change is a set of refinements in the equations used for three of the 10 freedoms. One of these refinements is in trade freedom, which has always included a penalty for non-tariff barriers (NTBs). Until now, it has been a binary penalty equal to a reduction of 20 percentage points in the trade freedom

score as calculated by tariffs, and thus a reduction of 2 percentage points in a country's total score. The change is that the NTB penalty now ranges in increments of 5 percentage points, up to a 20-percentage point maximum penalty. As a result, a country with moderate import restrictions will have 10 percentage points subtracted from its trade freedom score. This change was also applied retroactively so that previous penalties of 20 percentage points dating back to 1995 were largely reduced to 15 or 10 percentage points. The effect has been to raise overall scores, since the vast majority of countries utilize NTBs and had the penalty in place. This is an improvement in the level of detail that the *Index* provides, allowing greater differentiation and fairness in reflecting economic policies across countries.

• **Taxes and Expenditures.** The introduction of a new methodology in 2007 produced some results that could not be anticipated until grading was completed. One surprise was that average scores for each of the 10 freedoms varied widely. The "best" score was fiscal freedom, which averaged 82.8, but this sent the unintended signal that the area least in need of reform was taxation. Regrettably, tax reform is badly needed in almost all countries, and the creeping size of government taxation and expenditure is a signature reason for the existence of the *Index*. In fact, most economists would agree that the primary area of success in economic governance has been the rise of stable prices and low inflation, largely as a result of independent central banking, implying that the "best" score on average should be in monetary freedom. To remedy the balance among the 10 economic freedoms in the *Index*, an adjustment was made to two equations with no change in the underlying data. Since the equations to calculate scores for financial freedom and government size were producing overly generous scores, the coefficients were tightened in each case. The same equation is used to calculate scores through the entire time series back to 1995, so these changes were made retroactively and seamlessly in past scores. The effect was to lower scores for every country. The overall effect of the higher average scores for trade freedom and lower average scores for fiscal freedom and government size was neutral.

• **New 10 Freedoms Chart.** Each country page includes two charts. The first shows how the country's overall economic freedom score has changed from 1995 to the present. The second shows, numerically and graphically, the score of each of the 10 freedoms. New this year, this second chart also includes an "up-or-down arrow" that signals the change during the most recent year. For example, you can see that the United States worsened in four freedoms, improved in one other, and is unchanged in the remaining three freedoms. The overall effect was under a full percentage point decline, but these new arrows help to identify exactly what areas are causing the score to slip.

We hope the changes in the *Index* make it an even better research tool and a more accessible policymaking guide. Whatever changes may be made from year to year, however, our goal remains constant: to advance human freedom. We believe that today's *Index* might even make the transition to a better world faster and surer.

One of the editors' paramount concerns is that the *Index* always remains a useful tool for researchers. This means that the integrity of the current-year scores is crucial. During a period of aggressive improvements, there undoubtedly will be mistakes in the scores, based on our errors and errors in source data. We cannot promise perfection, but we do promise objectivity: Our methods and modifications will always be transparent and duplicable by other scholars.

Moreover, even though the *Index* itself is published in January, based on policies and data available as of the previous June, we remain committed to providing the most accurate and up-to-date measures online and will make any needed corrections in that source file immediately. For researchers who want to weight the *Index* or consider individual components in statistical analysis, the 10 freedoms and even the raw data are also available transparently online. Revised scores of individual factors for all years are available for download at *www.heritage.org/Index*.

Executive Summary

This is the 14th edition of The Heritage Foundation/Wall Street Journal *Index of Economic Freedom*. Over the past years, the *Index* has documented the link between economic opportunity and prosperity, researching and analyzing economic policies in countries around the world. That trend continues in the *2008 Index*, which paints a portrait of economic freedom around the world and establishes a benchmark by which to gauge a country's chances of economic success.

The idea of producing a user-friendly "index of economic freedom" as a tool for policymakers and investors was first discussed at The Heritage Foundation in the late 1980s. The goal then, as it is today, was to develop a systematic, empirical measurement of economic freedom in countries throughout the world. To this end, the decision was made to establish a set of objective economic criteria that, since the inaugural edition in 1995, have been used to study and grade various countries for the annual publication of the *Index of Economic Freedom*.

Economic theory dating back to the publication of Adam Smith's *The Wealth of Nations* in 1776 emphasizes the lesson that basic institutions that protect the liberty of individuals to pursue their own economic interests result in greater prosperity for the larger society. Perhaps the idea of freedom is too sophisticated, as popular support for it seems constantly to erode before the onslaught of populism, whether democratic or autocratic. Yet modern scholars of political economy are rediscovering the central fact that "free institutions" are essential to rapid long-term growth. In other words, the techniques may be new, but they reaffirm classic truths. The objective of the *Index* is to catalogue those economic institutions in a quantitative and rigorous manner.

Yet the *Index* is more than a simple ranking based on economic theory and empirical study. It also identifies the variables that comprise economic freedom and analyzes the interaction of freedom with wealth.

The *2008 Index of Economic Freedom* covers 162 countries across 10 specific factors of economic freedom, which are listed below. Chapter 4 explains these factors in detail. High scores approaching 100 represent higher levels of freedom. The higher the score on a factor, the lower the level of government interference in the economy.

The 10 Economic Freedoms
- Business Freedom
- Trade Freedom
- Fiscal Freedom
- Government Size
- Monetary Freedom
- Investment Freedom
- Financial Freedom
- Property Rights
- Freedom from Corruption
- Labor Freedom

Taken together, these 10 freedoms offer an empirical depiction of a country's degree of economic freedom. A systematic analysis of the 10 freedoms has demonstrated again this year that economic freedom is the key to creating an environment that allows a virtuous cycle of entrepreneurship, innovation, and sustained economic growth and development to flourish. Economies with higher levels of economic freedom enjoy higher living standards.

HIGHLIGHTS FROM THE 2008 INDEX

Global economic freedom continues to hold steady while progressing more slowly than one might hope. The global economic freedom score is 60.3 percent, essentially the same as last year. In the years since the *Index* began in 1995, world economic freedom has improved by 2.6 percentage points. Overall, each region's economic freedom holds steady,

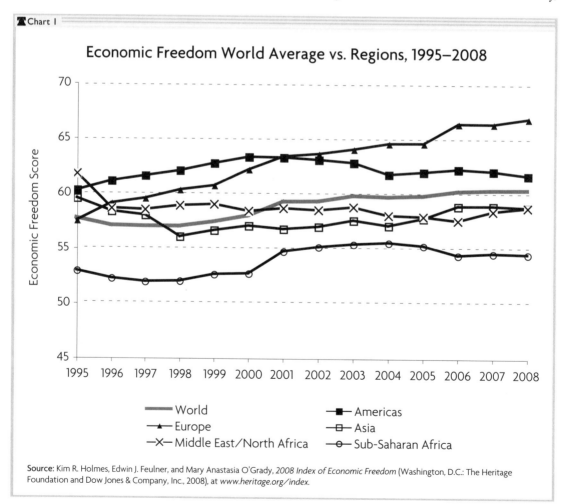

Chart 1

Economic Freedom World Average vs. Regions, 1995–2008

Legend:
- World
- Europe
- Middle East/North Africa
- Americas
- Asia
- Sub-Saharan Africa

Source: Kim R. Holmes, Edwin J. Feulner, and Mary Anastasia O'Grady, *2008 Index of Economic Freedom* (Washington, D.C.: The Heritage Foundation and Dow Jones & Company, Inc., 2008), at *www.heritage.org/index*.

but varying degrees of commitment to economic freedom over the past decade have resulted in mixed trends in individual regions' pursuit of greater economic freedom.

Former British colonies in Asia continue to lead the world in economic freedom. Hong Kong has the highest level of economic freedom for the 14th straight year. Singapore remains close, ranked second in the world, and Australia is ranked fourth-freest, which means that the Asia–Pacific region is home to the three of the world's top five freest economies.

While every region has at least one of the top 20 freest economies, half of them are European. A majority of the freest economies are in Europe, led by Ireland, Switzerland, the United Kingdom, and Denmark. Five are in the Asia–Pacific region, and three are from the Americas: the United States, Canada, and Chile. One country (Mauritius) is from the sub-Saharan Africa region, and one (Bahrain) is from the Middle East/North Africa region.

Economic freedom is strongly related to good economic performance. The world's freest countries have twice the average per capita income of the second quintile of countries and over five times the average income of the fifth quintile. The freest economies also have lower rates of unemployment and lower inflation. These relationships hold across each quintile, meaning that every quintile of less free economies has worse average rates of inflation and unemployment than the preceding quintile has. (See "The Impact of Economic Freedom.")

In pursuing sustainable prosperity, both the direction of policy and commitment to economic freedom are important. Across the five regions, Europe is clearly the most free using an unweighted average (66.8 percent), followed at some distance by the Americas (61.6 percent). The other three regions fall below the world average: Asia–Pacific (58.7 percent), Middle East/North Africa (58.7 percent), and sub-Saharan Africa (54.5 percent). However, trends in freedom are mixed across regions. Consistently scoring above the global average, Europe has continued to advance its economic freedom because of policy improvements, such as tax cuts and other business cli-

mate reforms, adopted by many of the region's individual economies as they compete with one another to attract more investment.

On the other hand, the Americas, while also maintaining a level of economic freedom higher than the global average during every year covered by the *Index*, has experienced some regional deterioration in economic freedom in recent years. The erosion of economic freedom in the Americas reflects reversals of free-market policies and lack of perseverance in pursuing economic freedom in some countries. Venezuela, in particular, is tempting long-run decline as President Hugo Chávez takes the country further down an anti-democratic and anti–free market path. Asia–Pacific countries have the highest variance within their region, which means that there is a much wider gap between the heights of freedom in some economies and the lows in others that is nearly twice as variable as the norm. Economic freedom in sub-Saharan Africa and the Middle East/North Africa region has somewhat stagnated over the life of the *Index*, but those regions have been moving slowly toward higher economic freedom in recent years.

The methodology for measuring economic freedom is further strengthened. The methodology introduced in the 2007 *Index*, using a scale of 0–100 rather than the 1–5 brackets of previous years when assessing the 10 component economic freedoms, was refined slightly, particularly in assessing non-tariff barriers, taxes, and government spending. The modifications allowed the methodology to be tightened. The methodology has been vetted with an academic advisory board and should now even better reflect the details of each country's economic policies. In order to compare country performances from past years accurately, scores and rankings for all previous years dating back to 1995 have been adjusted to reflect the refinements.

As shown in Chart 2, of the 157 countries graded numerically in the 2008 *Index*,[1] only

---

1   Five countries (the Democratic Republic of Congo, Iraq, Serbia, Montenegro, and Sudan) were suspended from grading again this year because of questions about the accuracy of the data or about whether the data truly reflect economic

seven have very high freedom scores of 80 percent or more, putting them into the "free" economies category (the highest). The next 23 countries are in the 70 percent range, placing them in the "mostly free" category. This means that only 30 countries, or less than one-fifth of all countries surveyed, have economic freedom scores higher than 70 percent. The bulk of countries— 103 economies—have freedom scores of 50 percent–70 percent. Of those, about half are "moderately free" (scores of 60 percent–70 percent), and half are "mostly unfree" (scores of 50 percent–60 percent). This year, 24 countries—a slight increase from last year's 20 countries—have "repressed economies" with scores below 50 percent.

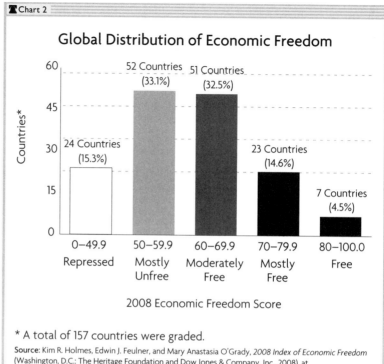

Chart 2

Global Distribution of Economic Freedom

*Countries**

- 52 Countries (33.1%)
- 51 Countries (32.5%)
- 24 Countries (15.3%)
- 23 Countries (14.6%)
- 7 Countries (4.5%)

| 0–49.9 Repressed | 50–59.9 Mostly Unfree | 60–69.9 Moderately Free | 70–79.9 Mostly Free | 80–100.0 Free |

2008 Economic Freedom Score

* A total of 157 countries were graded.

Source: Kim R. Holmes, Edwin J. Feulner, and Mary Anastasia O'Grady, *2008 Index of Economic Freedom* (Washington, D.C.: The Heritage Foundation and Dow Jones & Company, Inc., 2008), at *www.heritage.org/index.*

The typical country has an economy that is 60.3 percent free, essentially the same as last year. Improved scores in business freedom, fiscal freedom, government size, and investment freedom were offset by worsened scores in monetary freedom, freedom from corruption, and labor freedom. The trade freedom and property rights scores were unchanged. Notwithstanding the absence of dramatic improvement in global economic freedom this year, it is gratifying to note that the past two editions of the *Index* have recorded the two highest global scores ever achieved, so the overall trend continues to be positive.

circumstances for most of the country. Data for suspended countries are reviewed annually to ascertain whether the situation has improved. The Democratic Republic of Congo and Sudan were suspended from grading in the 2008 *Index* because, in each case, civil unrest or anarchy indicated that official government policies did not apply to large portions of the country. Serbia, Montenegro, and Iraq were suspended because reliable data were not available.

THE IMPACT OF ECONOMIC FREEDOM

There are clear relationships between economic freedom and numerous other cross-country variables, the most prominent being the strong relationship between the level of freedom and the level of prosperity in a given country. Previous editions of the *Index* have confirmed the tangible benefits of living in freer societies. Not only is a higher level of economic freedom clearly associated with a higher level of per capita gross domestic product, but those higher GDP growth rates seem to create a virtuous cycle, triggering further improvements in economic freedom. Our 14 years of *Index* data strongly suggest that countries that increase their levels of freedom experience faster growth rates.

Chart 3 shows a strong relationship between the level of economic freedom in 2008 and the logarithmic value of the most recent data for per capita GDP using 157 countries as data points.

Charts 4–7 illustrate four different relationships using a quintile framework. The top quintile of countries is composed of those that

THE 10 ECONOMIC FREEDOMS: A GLOBAL GUIDE

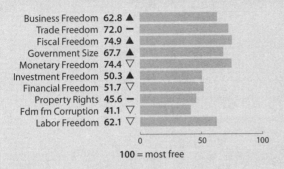

Business Freedom 62.8 ▲
Trade Freedom 72.0 —
Fiscal Freedom 74.9 ▲
Government Size 67.7 ▲
Monetary Freedom 74.4 ▽
Investment Freedom 50.3 ▲
Financial Freedom 51.7 ▽
Property Rights 45.6 —
Fdm fm Corruption 41.1 ▽
Labor Freedom 62.1 ▽

0   50   100

100 = most free

BUSINESS FREEDOM — 62.8%

Business freedom measures how free entrepreneurs are to start businesses, how easy it is to obtain licenses, and the ease of closing a business. Impediments to any of these three activities are deterrents to business and therefore to job creation. Globally, starting a business takes an average of 43 days, while getting necessary licenses takes an average of 19 procedures and 234 days. Bankruptcy proceedings take an average of three years.[1]

TRADE FREEDOM — 72%

Tariffs are the primary obstacle to free trade among nations, but non-tariff barriers (NTBs) such as quotas and bureaucratic delays are also significant impediments. The overall trade freedom score is composed of these two elements. The first component is a score calculated from each country's weighted average tariff rate and ranges from 0 to 100 percent. The higher the score, the lower the tariff rate. The mean worldwide tariff rate is 11.1 percent. A country with that rate would receive a score of 80 percent. Depending upon the severity of a country's NTB barriers, a penalty of 5, 10, 15, or 20 percentage points is subtracted from the weighted average tariff rate score to arrive at each country's overall trade freedom score. The global average trade freedom score for 2008 is 72 percent.

FISCAL FREEDOM — 74.9%

The top tax rate on individual income averages 31 percent, and the top tax rate on corporate income averages 26 percent. There are also many other types of taxes that governments use to raise revenue, and total tax revenue from all forms of taxation averages 21 percent of country GDP. Mixing the three scores together is the basis of the fiscal freedom score. Using a quadratic cost function that penalizes higher taxes with a higher penalty, the average score is 74.9 percent.

GOVERNMENT SIZE — 67.7%

Government size is defined to include all government expenditures, including consumption and transfers. Ideally, the state will provide only true public goods with an absolute minimum of expenditure. The average level of government spending as a portion of GDP is slightly over 30 percent.[2] Using a non-linear quadratic cost function that

downgrades higher government spending with a higher penalty, the world average score for government size is 67.7 percent.

MONETARY FREEDOM — 74.4%

The worldwide average of the weighted average inflation rates per country from 2004 to 2006 is 10.6 percent, an increase over last year's weighted average of 7.9 reflects in part Zimbabwe's hyperinflation, which climbed to over 1,000 percent. Price stability explains most of the monetary freedom score, although there is a penalty of up to 20 percentage points for countries that use price controls. The average price control penalty was 10.3 points this year.

INVESTMENT FREEDOM — 50.3%

Only 17 countries enjoy high investment freedom with scores of 80 percent and higher. These countries impose few or no restrictions on foreign investment, which promotes economic expansion and enhances overall economic freedom. Meanwhile, more than one-third of countries significantly lack investment freedom with scores of less than 50 percent.

FINANCIAL FREEDOM — 51.7%

The more that banks are controlled by the government, the less free they are to engage in essential financial activities that facilitate private sector–led economic growth. Regrettably, most countries continue to impose a heavy burden of bank regulation on the private sector, reducing opportunities and restricting economic freedom. About 80 countries' financial freedom scores are between 50 and 70.

PROPERTY RIGHTS — 45.6%

Progress toward stronger property rights is still gradual and slow. With scores above 80, many Western economies (along with Hong Kong and Singapore) benefit from secure protection of property rights, but more than half of the world's countries score below 50.

FREEDOM FROM CORRUPTION — 41.1%

Little progress has been made since last year, and corruption is still perceived as widespread in many countries. Scores for only 16 countries are 80 percent or higher, while 114 countries' scores are below 50. Freedom from corruption remains the lowest average score among the 10 factors.

LABOR FREEDOM — 62.1%

Labor market flexibility is essential to enhancing employment opportunities and overall productivity growth. The rigidity of hiring and firing a worker creates a risk aversion for companies that would otherwise employ more people and grow. The world average of labor freedom is 62.1 percent, reflecting wage, hour, and other restrictions. Only 25 countries have notably flexible labor market policies with scores above 80, while 35 countries score below 50 as a result of their rigid labor market regulations.

---

1   The global average is based on data for 146 countries that are graded by both the *Index of Economic Freedom* and the World Bank's *Doing Business 2008.*
2   In general, the government size indicator looks

at general government expenditure data that combine all levels of government such as central or federal, state or provincial, and local. In countries for which general government spending data are not available, central government expenditure data are used for grading.

Chart 3

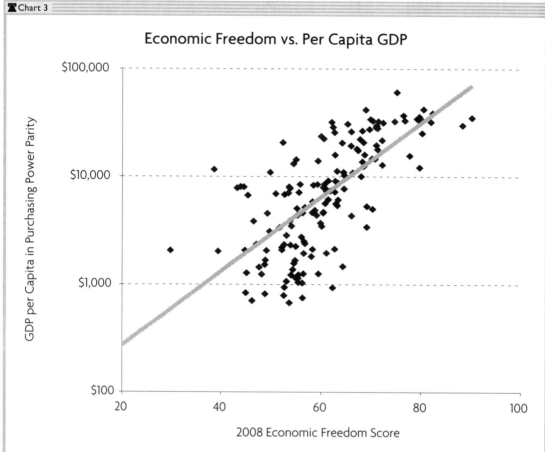

Economic Freedom vs. Per Capita GDP

GDP per Capita in Purchasing Power Parity

$100,000

$10,000

$1,000

$100

20   40   60   80   100

2008 Economic Freedom Score

Sources: World Bank, World Development Indicators Online, at *http://publications.worldbank.org/subscriptions/WDI* (September 5, 2007; subscription required); Central Intelligence Agency, *The World Factbook 2007*, at *www.cia.gov/library/publications/the-world-factbook/index.html* (September 5, 2007); International Monetary Fund, World Economic Outlook Database, April 2007, at *www.imf.org/external/pubs/ft/weo/2007/01/data/index.aspx* (September 5, 2007); and Kim R. Holmes, Edwin J. Feulner, and Mary Anastasia O'Grady, *2008 Index of Economic Freedom* (Washington, D.C.: The Heritage Foundation and Dow Jones & Company, Inc., 2008), at *www.heritage.org/index.*

are ranked from 1 to 31 globally (Hong Kong to Spain), and each subsequent quintile includes the next group of countries. Quintiles are not the same as categorical groups (free, mostly free, etc.) and are used here because each quintile is comparable based on about the same number of countries.

Chart 4 shows that four of five quintiles have roughly equal populations, but the fourth quintile alone contains half of the world's population. This is due to the presence of China and India together.

This fact suggests that when China and India further open their economies to globalization so that internal economic freedoms are strengthened, the rise in global prosperity will be spectacular.

Chart 5 is another look at the relationship

between economic freedom and average per capita incomes. The quintiles with higher economic freedom have dramatically higher incomes per person.

Chart 6 and Chart 7 show that unemployment rates are higher for each quintile of lower economic freedom. Likewise, on average, inflation rates rise as economic freedom declines.

The lesson from these charts is simple: Economic failure is a predictable consequence of economic repression. Countries that reflect the desires of their people for better lives will adopt economic freedom, and countries that repress their people for political reasons will cause economic suffocation.

In other words, any populist who claims that the suspension of economic freedom is done for the good of the people is no longer credible.

Chart 4

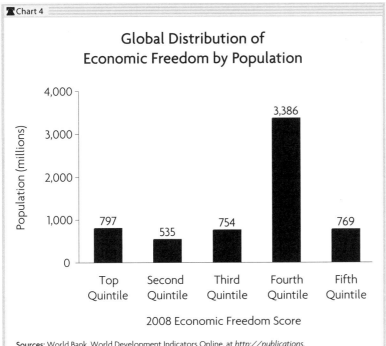

Global Distribution of Economic Freedom by Population

Population (millions)

Top Quintile	797
Second Quintile	535
Third Quintile	754
Fourth Quintile	3,386
Fifth Quintile	769

2008 Economic Freedom Score

Sources: World Bank, World Development Indicators Online, at *http://publications. worldbank.org/subscriptions/WDI* (September 5, 2007; subscription required); Central Intelligence Agency, *The World Factbook 2007*, at *www.cia.gov/library/publications/the-world-factbook/index.html* (September 5, 2007); International Monetary Fund, World Economic Outlook Database, April 2007, at *www.imf.org/external/pubs/ft/weo/2007/01/data/index.aspx* (September 5, 2007); and Kim R. Holmes, Edwin J. Feulner, and Mary Anastasia O'Grady, *2008 Index of Economic Freedom* (Washington, D.C.: The Heritage Foundation and Dow Jones & Company, Inc., 2008), at *www.heritage.org/index.*

Chart 5

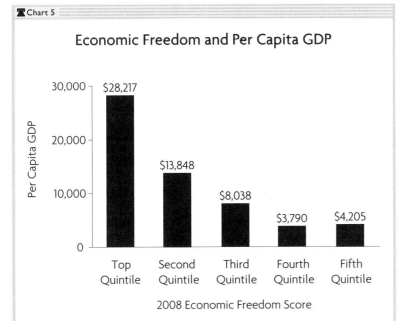

Economic Freedom and Per Capita GDP

Per Capita GDP

Top Quintile	$28,217
Second Quintile	$13,848
Third Quintile	$8,038
Fourth Quintile	$3,790
Fifth Quintile	$4,205

2008 Economic Freedom Score

Sources: World Bank, World Development Indicators Online, at *http://publications.worldbank.org/ subscriptions/WDI* (September 5, 2007; subscription required); Central Intelligence Agency, *The World Factbook 2007*, at *www.cia.gov/library/publications/the-world-factbook/index.html* (September 5, 2007); International Monetary Fund, World Economic Outlook Database, April 2007, at *www.imf.org/external/pubs/ft/weo/2007/01/data/index.aspx* (September 5, 2007); and Kim R. Holmes, Edwin J. Feulner, and Mary Anastasia O'Grady, *2008 Index of Economic Freedom* (Washington, D.C.: The Heritage Foundation and Dow Jones & Company, Inc., 2008), at *www.heritage.org/index.*

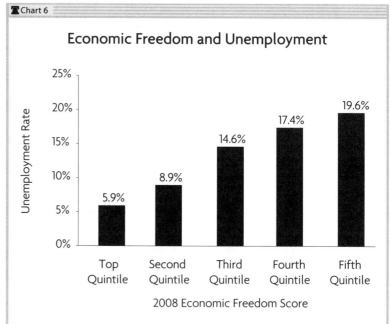

Chart 6

Economic Freedom and Unemployment

Unemployment Rate

- Top Quintile: 5.9%
- Second Quintile: 8.9%
- Third Quintile: 14.6%
- Fourth Quintile: 17.4%
- Fifth Quintile: 19.6%

2008 Economic Freedom Score

Sources: World Bank, World Development Indicators Online, at *http://publications. worldbank.org/subscriptions/WDI* (September 5, 2007; subscription required); Central Intelligence Agency, *The World Factbook 2007,* at *www.cia.gov/library/publications/the-world-factbook/index.html* (September 5, 2007); International Monetary Fund, World Economic Outlook Database, April 2007, at *www.imf.org/external/pubs/ft/weo/2007/01/data/index.aspx* (September 5, 2007); and Kim R. Holmes, Edwin J. Feulner, and Mary Anastasia O'Grady, *2008 Index of Economic Freedom* (Washington, D.C.: The Heritage Foundation and Dow Jones & Company, Inc., 2008), at *www.heritage.org/index.*

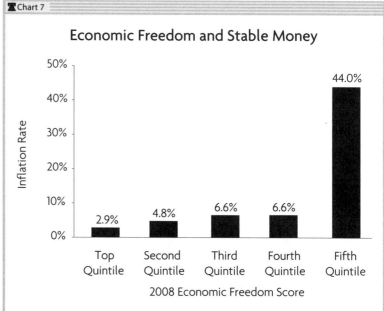

Chart 7

Economic Freedom and Stable Money

Inflation Rate

- Top Quintile: 2.9%
- Second Quintile: 4.8%
- Third Quintile: 6.6%
- Fourth Quintile: 6.6%
- Fifth Quintile: 44.0%

2008 Economic Freedom Score

Sources: World Bank, World Development Indicators Online, at *http://publications. worldbank.org/ subscriptions/WDI* (September 5, 2007; subscription required); Central Intelligence Agency, *The World Factbook 2007,* at *www.cia.gov/library/publications/the-world-factbook/index.html* (September 5, 2007); International Monetary Fund, World Economic Outlook Database, April 2007, at *www.imf.org/external/pubs/ft/weo/2007/01/data/index.aspx* (September 5, 2007); and Kim R. Holmes, Edwin J. Feulner, and Mary Anastasia O'Grady, *2008 Index of Economic Freedom* (Washington, D.C.: The Heritage Foundation and Dow Jones & Company, Inc., 2008), at *www.heritage.org/index.*

Index of Economic Freedom World Rankings

World Rank	Country	Overall Score	Change from 2007	Business Freedom	Trade Freedom	Fiscal Freedom	Government Size	Monetary Freedom	Investment Freedom	Financial Freedom	Property Rights	Freedom from Corruption	Labor Freedom
1	Hong Kong	90.3	-0.3	88.2	95.0	92.8	93.1	87.2	90	90	90.0	83.0	93.3
2	Singapore	87.4	0.2	97.8	90.0	90.3	93.9	88.9	80	50	90.0	94.0	99.0
3	Ireland	82.4	-0.2	92.2	86.0	71.5	64.5	84.9	90	90	90.0	74.0	80.4
4	Australia	82.0	1.0	89.3	83.8	59.2	62.8	83.7	80	90	90.0	87.0	94.2
5	United States	80.6	-0.3	91.7	86.8	68.3	59.8	83.7	80	80	90.0	73.0	92.3
6	New Zealand	80.2	-0.8	99.9	80.8	60.5	56.0	83.7	70	80	90.0	96.0	85.5
7	Canada	80.2	2.1	96.7	87.0	75.5	53.7	81.0	70	80	90.0	85.0	82.9
8	Chile	79.8	0.8	67.5	82.2	78.1	88.2	78.8	80	70	90.0	73.0	90.0
9	Switzerland	79.7	1.6	83.9	87.2	68.0	61.6	83.6	70	80	90.0	91.0	82.0
10	United Kingdom	79.5	-0.5	90.8	86.0	61.2	40.1	80.7	90	90	90.0	86.0	80.7
11	Denmark	79.2	2.2	99.9	86.0	35.0	19.8	86.5	90	90	90.0	95.0	99.9
12	Estonia	77.8	-0.2	84.5	86.0	86.0	62.0	82.0	90	80	90.0	67.0	50.3
13	Netherlands, The	76.8	1.9	88.0	86.0	51.6	38.2	86.9	90	90	90.0	87.0	60.5
14	Iceland	76.5	-0.2	94.5	85.0	73.6	46.3	74.8	60	70	90.0	96.0	75.0
15	Luxembourg	75.2	-0.1	76.9	86.0	65.4	44.8	79.8	90	80	90.0	86.0	53.1
16	Finland	74.8	0.6	95.2	86.0	64.3	29.1	88.5	70	80	90.0	96.0	48.8
17	Japan	72.5	0.3	88.1	80.0	70.3	56.2	94.3	60	50	70.0	76.0	79.8
18	Mauritius	72.3	3.1	81.6	80.6	92.1	81.4	75.7	70	60	60.0	51.0	70.6
19	Bahrain	72.2	1.0	80.0	80.8	99.7	80.3	74.3	60	90	60.0	57.0	40.0
20	Belgium	71.5	-0.9	93.7	86.0	43.9	17.9	80.4	90	80	80.0	73.0	69.9
21	Barbados	71.3	1.4	90.0	58.8	71.3	62.2	74.0	60	60	90.0	67.0	80.0
22	Cyprus	71.3	-0.4	70.0	81.0	78.2	43.0	85.0	70	70	90.0	56.0	70.0
23	Germany	71.2	-0.4	88.9	86.0	58.4	34.0	81.4	80	60	90.0	80.0	52.8
24	Bahamas, The	71.1	-0.9	80.0	32.0	96.2	86.4	76.3	40	70	80.0	70.0	80.0
25	Taiwan	71.0	0.8	70.7	86.7	75.9	87.8	83.3	70	50	70.0	59.0	56.9
26	Lithuania	70.8	-0.7	83.2	86.0	86.3	68.3	78.5	70	80	50.0	48.0	57.6
27	Sweden	70.4	1.4	94.8	86.0	32.7	3.9	82.8	80	80	90.0	92.0	62.0
28	Armenia	70.3	1.0	81.3	85.0	89.0	86.4	84.6	70	70	35.0	29.0	73.1
29	Trinidad and Tobago	70.2	-1.1	64.1	79.0	81.1	81.7	72.6	70	70	65.0	32.0	86.9
30	Austria	70.0	-0.2	80.6	86.0	51.2	25.3	81.4	70	70	90.0	86.0	59.2
31	Spain	69.7	-0.2	77.5	86.0	54.5	56.2	78.1	70	80	70.0	68.0	56.7
32	Georgia	69.2	-0.1	85.0	71.0	90.7	81.2	71.4	70	60	35.0	28.0	99.9
33	El Salvador	69.2	-0.6	58.6	76.6	83.4	88.7	76.8	70	70	50.0	40.0	78.0

Index of Economic Freedom World Rankings

World Rank	Country	Overall Score	Change from 2007	Business Freedom	Trade Freedom	Fiscal Freedom	Government Size	Monetary Freedom	Investment Freedom	Financial Freedom	Property Rights	Freedom from Corruption	Labor Freedom
34	Norway	69.0	0.6	89.1	86.2	50.3	46.3	76.1	60	50	90.0	88.0	53.9
35	Slovak Republic	68.7	0.3	69.3	86.0	89.4	53.9	76.9	70	80	50.0	47.0	64.9
36	Botswana	68.6	0.1	68.7	67.6	76.4	61.8	69.7	70	70	70.0	56.0	75.9
37	Czech Republic	68.5	0.8	63.9	86.0	71.3	45.6	80.3	70	80	70.0	48.0	70.2
38	Latvia	68.3	0.1	74.3	86.0	83.4	59.2	73.8	70	70	55.0	47.0	64.6
39	Kuwait	68.3	1.7	68.5	81.0	99.9	74.6	73.8	50	50	55.0	48.0	82.1
40	Uruguay	68.1	-0.7	59.8	83.0	85.9	76.6	74.2	60	30	70.0	64.0	77.3
41	Korea, South	67.9	0.7	84.0	66.4	71.1	77.3	80.1	70	60	70.0	51.0	49.0
42	Oman	67.4	1.4	55.8	83.6	98.5	60.7	74.7	60	60	50.0	54.0	77.2
43	Hungary	67.2	2.8	73.9	86.0	70.0	26.5	77.2	80	70	70.0	52.0	66.8
44	Mexico	66.4	0.1	82.6	79.0	83.4	83.7	77.7	50	60	50.0	33.0	64.3
45	Jamaica	66.2	0.2	82.0	70.4	74.9	59.6	74.3	80	60	50.0	37.0	73.3
46	Israel	66.1	1.5	68.4	86.6	55.9	35.1	81.8	80	60	70.0	59.0	64.0
47	Malta	66.0	-0.1	70.0	86.0	61.3	29.1	79.8	50	70	90.0	64.0	60.0
48	France	65.4	2.5	87.1	81.0	53.2	13.2	81.2	60	70	70.0	74.0	63.8
49	Costa Rica	64.8	0.2	59.7	81.8	82.9	87.4	67.9	70	40	50.0	41.0	66.8
50	Panama	64.7	0.1	72.8	76.2	83.0	89.1	80.2	70	70	30.0	31.0	44.4
51	Malaysia	64.5	0.1	69.0	76.2	82.2	80.8	78.6	40	40	50.0	50.0	78.7
52	Uganda	64.4	0.7	56.3	72.0	80.5	86.0	78.5	50	70	30.0	27.0	93.9
53	Portugal	64.3	-0.2	79.6	86.0	61.3	32.6	79.4	70	50	70.0	66.0	48.0
54	Thailand	63.5	-1.3	72.1	75.2	74.7	90.7	66.7	30	50	50.0	36.0	89.6
55	Peru	63.5	1.0	64.5	73.4	80.2	91.8	85.9	60	60	40.0	33.0	45.8
56	Albania	63.3	0.9	55.6	75.8	90.3	76.0	80.4	70	70	30.0	26.0	59.3
57	South Africa	63.2	-0.2	71.2	74.2	69.5	76.8	77.2	50	60	50.0	46.0	57.5
58	Jordan	63.0	-0.5	55.4	74.8	83.7	53.2	80.4	50	60	55.0	53.0	64.8
59	Bulgaria	62.9	0.9	67.5	86.0	82.7	56.0	73.7	60	60	30.0	40.0	73.2
60	Saudi Arabia	62.8	1.2	72.5	76.8	99.7	69.1	76.7	30	40	50.0	33.0	80.6
61	Belize	62.8	-0.4	76.3	64.6	69.3	74.8	77.3	50	50	50.0	35.0	80.9
62	Mongolia	62.8	3.0	71.1	81.4	85.0	71.7	78.2	60	60	30.0	28.0	62.4
63	United Arab Emirates	62.8	-0.1	47.9	80.4	99.9	80.2	70.9	30	40	40.0	62.0	76.2
64	Italy	62.5	-0.2	76.8	81.0	54.3	29.4	80.6	70	60	50.0	49.0	73.5
65	Madagascar	62.4	1.3	56.0	79.6	80.9	86.4	72.2	70	50	50.0	31.0	47.9
66	Qatar	62.2	-0.7	60.0	70.8	99.8	72.1	69.4	30	50	50.0	60.0	60.0

Index of Economic Freedom World Rankings

World Rank	Country	Overall Score	Change from 2007	Business Freedom	Trade Freedom	Fiscal Freedom	Government Size	Monetary Freedom	Investment Freedom	Financial Freedom	Property Rights	Freedom from Corruption	Labor Freedom
67	Colombia	61.9	2.3	72.5	70.8	72.8	71.2	71.4	60	60	40.0	39.0	61.4
68	Romania	61.5	0.3	74.1	86.0	85.6	70.8	72.5	60	50	30.0	31.0	55.3
69	Fiji	61.5	0.9	69.7	74.2	74.5	75.3	78.9	30	60	30.0	40.0	82.7
70	Kyrgyz Republic	61.1	0.8	60.4	81.4	93.9	76.1	75.6	50	50	30.0	22.0	72.0
71	Macedonia	61.1	0.5	65.1	83.4	88.1	61.6	85.5	50	60	30.0	27.0	60.7
72	Namibia	61.0	-2.1	73.8	87.4	67.9	71.0	76.8	30	50	30.0	41.0	82.4
73	Lebanon	60.9	-0.5	55.4	77.4	91.4	69.5	77.8	30	70	30.0	36.0	71.2
74	Turkey	60.8	2.5	67.9	86.8	77.7	68.3	70.8	50	50	50.0	38.0	48.0
75	Slovenia	60.6	0.4	73.0	86.0	62.4	33.2	79.5	60	50	50.0	64.0	47.7
76	Kazakhstan	60.5	1.4	56.5	86.2	80.1	84.7	71.9	30	60	30.0	26.0	80.0
77	Paraguay	60.5	1.6	57.6	78.4	96.6	90.8	76.6	50	60	35.0	26.0	34.2
78	Guatemala	60.5	-0.8	54.1	78.4	79.9	95.9	72.9	50	50	30.0	26.0	67.9
79	Honduras	60.2	-0.2	59.5	78.0	84.5	82.6	73.7	50	60	30.0	25.0	59.0
80	Greece	60.1	1.8	69.5	81.0	65.6	57.8	78.5	50	50	50.0	44.0	54.3
81	Nicaragua	60.0	-2.0	56.4	79.2	79.0	77.6	70.6	70	50	25.0	26.0	65.7
82	Kenya	59.6	-0.4	65.3	75.0	78.2	84.8	72.2	50	50	35.0	22.0	63.2
83	Poland	59.5	2.1	54.1	86.0	68.6	43.5	82.3	60	60	50.0	37.0	53.5
84	Tunisia	59.3	-0.2	79.2	71.8	76.4	77.1	77.6	30	30	50.0	46.0	55.3
85	Egypt	59.2	4.0	59.7	66.0	90.8	73.0	69.9	50	40	40.0	33.0	69.1
86	Swaziland	58.9	-1.7	69.0	69.0	71.4	62.4	76.0	50	40	50.0	25.0	75.7
87	Dominican Republic	58.5	0.9	62.2	73.0	80.4	88.8	69.3	50	40	30.0	28.0	63.6
88	Cape Verde	58.4	1.3	55.1	41.2	66.2	60.5	78.7	60	50	70.0	40.0	62.3
89	Moldova	58.4	-0.8	68.5	79.2	83.0	56.9	67.6	30	50	50.0	32.0	66.6
90	Sri Lanka	58.3	-1.0	71.5	69.6	73.5	81.7	65.4	30	40	50.0	31.0	70.5
91	Senegal	58.2	0.1	54.5	71.6	65.2	82.3	81.4	50	50	50.0	33.0	43.6
92	Philippines, The	56.9	-0.1	53.0	78.8	75.8	90.2	73.8	30	50	30.0	25.0	61.9
93	Pakistan	56.8	-1.7	70.8	65.2	79.1	90.1	72.2	40	30	30.0	22.0	69.1
94	Ghana	56.7	-0.7	53.1	63.0	83.7	71.5	68.0	50	50	50.0	33.0	44.2
95	Gambia, The	56.6	-0.8	57.1	62.6	72.5	72.8	73.9	50	50	30.0	25.0	72.1
96	Mozambique	56.6	0.7	53.0	72.8	78.1	85.2	73.6	50	50	30.0	28.0	45.0
97	Tanzania	56.4	-0.4	47.9	73.2	80.5	79.9	75.4	50	50	30.0	29.0	48.1
98	Morocco	56.4	-0.8	75.8	62.6	65.4	73.2	79.8	60	40	35.0	32.0	40.2
99	Zambia	56.4	-0.8	62.4	71.2	72.6	80.3	62.9	50	50	40.0	26.0	48.2

Index of Economic Freedom World Rankings

World Rank	Country	Overall Score	Change from 2007	Business Freedom	Trade Freedom	Fiscal Freedom	Government Size	Monetary Freedom	Investment Freedom	Financial Freedom	Property Rights	Freedom from Corruption	Labor Freedom
100	Cambodia	56.2	0.1	43.0	52.2	91.4	94.2	80.9	50	50	30.0	21.0	49.1
101	Brazil	55.9	-0.2	53.6	70.8	68.6	55.5	75.7	50	40	50.0	33.0	61.9
102	Algeria	55.7	0.6	72.7	68.8	77.0	74.6	80.2	40	30	30.0	31.0	52.3
103	Burkina Faso	55.6	0.6	49.8	66.6	77.5	85.9	78.8	40	50	30.0	32.0	45.7
104	Mali	55.5	0.8	41.9	68.6	69.3	81.5	79.9	50	40	30.0	28.0	66.0
105	Nigeria	55.5	-0.5	52.6	63.4	84.4	68.1	73.8	30	40	30.0	22.0	90.6
106	Ecuador	55.4	-0.2	58.1	67.6	86.4	82.3	74.1	40	50	30.0	23.0	42.4
107	Azerbaijan	55.3	0.5	61.6	78.4	80.3	82.9	76.5	30	30	30.0	24.0	59.2
108	Argentina	55.1	0.1	63.2	69.6	70.5	80.9	65.0	50	40	30.0	29.0	52.9
109	Mauritania	55.0	1.5	38.9	70.2	75.4	66.3	77.1	60	50	30.0	31.0	51.2
110	Benin	55.0	0.1	47.7	65.2	67.5	86.4	77.5	40	60	30.0	25.0	50.8
111	Ivory Coast	54.9	-1.0	47.0	59.8	52.3	88.1	80.7	40	60	30.0	21.0	70.5
112	Nepal	54.7	-0.4	60.0	61.4	86.5	92.0	78.5	30	30	30.0	25.0	53.4
113	Croatia	54.6	0.7	58.1	87.6	68.8	28.0	78.8	50	60	30.0	34.0	50.5
114	Tajikistan	54.5	0.7	43.4	77.8	89.3	84.1	65.8	30	40	30.0	22.0	62.1
115	India	54.2	0.1	50.0	51.0	75.7	73.5	70.3	40	30	50.0	33.0	68.6
116	Rwanda	54.1	1.7	51.8	70.6	76.9	75.6	73.3	40	40	30.0	25.0	58.2
117	Cameroon	54.0	-1.4	39.9	57.0	71.8	93.6	72.3	50	50	30.0	23.0	52.5
118	Suriname	53.9	-0.5	41.7	65.0	68.0	72.8	69.2	30	30	50.0	30.0	82.1
119	Indonesia	53.9	-0.1	48.8	73.0	77.5	89.7	68.2	30	40	30.0	24.0	57.5
120	Malawi	53.8	-0.2	52.1	64.6	70.2	44.3	69.9	50	50	40.0	27.0	70.1
121	Bosnia & Herzegovina	53.7	-0.6	56.1	79.8	73.7	48.3	76.6	50	60	10.0	29.0	53.7
122	Gabon	53.6	-0.6	52.8	56.4	61.7	85.6	74.6	40	40	40.0	30.0	54.6
123	Bolivia	53.2	-1.1	58.6	79.0	87.8	68.1	76.5	20	60	25.0	27.0	30.5
124	Ethiopia	53.2	-1.2	58.3	63.0	77.2	80.9	69.4	40	20	30.0	24.0	69.5
125	Yemen	52.8	-0.4	53.7	66.4	83.2	58.5	62.9	50	30	30.0	26.0	67.7
126	China	52.8	1.0	50.0	70.2	66.4	89.7	76.5	30	30	20.0	33.0	62.4
127	Guinea	52.8	-1.7	44.9	59.6	70.1	88.7	54.3	40	50	30.0	19.0	71.1
128	Niger	52.7	-0.4	36.0	64.4	66.4	89.3	86.0	50	40	30.0	23.0	42.2
129	Equatorial Guinea	52.5	-1.6	47.1	52.2	75.4	82.0	81.1	30	50	30.0	21.0	56.2
130	Uzbekistan	52.3	0.3	67.8	68.4	88.0	68.3	57.5	30	20	30.0	21.0	72.1
131	Djibouti	52.3	-1.2	37.5	28.2	80.8	57.8	78.3	50	60	30.0	30.0	70.6
132	Lesotho	51.9	-1.2	56.9	56.4	67.2	46.8	75.4	30	50	40.0	32.0	64.0

Index of Economic Freedom World Rankings

World Rank	Country	Overall Score	Change from 2007	Business Freedom	Trade Freedom	Fiscal Freedom	Government Size	Monetary Freedom	Investment Freedom	Financial Freedom	Property Rights	Freedom from Corruption	Labor Freedom
133	Ukraine	51.1	-0.6	44.3	82.2	79.0	43.0	69.9	30	50	30.0	28.0	54.3
134	Russia	49.9	-2.5	52.8	44.2	79.2	69.5	64.4	30	40	30.0	25.0	64.2
135	Vietnam	49.8	0.4	60.0	62.8	74.3	78.0	67.4	30	30	10.0	26.0	59.5
136	Guyana	49.4	-5.0	56.4	65.8	67.3	16.1	73.9	40	40	40.0	25.0	69.1
137	Laos	49.2	-0.0	60.8	57.0	71.0	92.1	73.0	30	20	10.0	26.0	52.3
138	Haiti	48.9	-2.4	35.7	67.0	77.8	93.2	65.3	30	30	10.0	18.0	62.4
139	Sierra Leone	48.9	1.3	49.4	60.2	81.0	81.8	74.4	30	40	10.0	22.0	40.3
140	Togo	48.8	-0.9	36.1	69.2	53.9	88.8	78.2	30	30	30.0	24.0	48.2
141	Central African Rep.	48.2	-2.1	40.7	51.4	65.5	91.6	72.5	30	40	20.0	24.0	46.7
142	Chad	47.7	-2.3	34.6	60.0	49.9	94.9	73.6	40	40	20.0	20.0	44.2
143	Angola	47.1	1.9	36.5	73.0	85.2	72.8	57.8	20	40	20.0	22.0	44.1
144	Syria	46.6	-1.5	52.9	54.0	86.2	60.3	66.2	30	10	30.0	29.0	47.1
145	Burundi	46.3	-0.7	35.5	50.2	72.1	59.4	74.7	30	30	30.0	24.0	57.4
146	Congo, Republic of	45.2	0.8	45.3	54.6	60.1	83.1	73.0	30	30	10.0	22.0	44.0
147	Guinea–Bissau	45.1	-1.7	24.8	56.8	88.4	56.5	75.7	30	30	20.0	10.0	58.5
148	Venezuela	45.0	-2.9	51.4	54.6	74.5	79.7	60.6	20	40	10.0	23.0	35.8
149	Bangladesh	44.9	-3.1	55.3	0.0	84.0	93.2	68.9	20	20	25.0	20.0	62.8
150	Belarus	44.7	-1.8	58.6	52.2	81.0	55.5	66.2	20	10	20.0	21.0	62.0
151	Iran	44.0	-0.1	55.0	57.4	81.1	84.5	61.3	10	10	10.0	27.0	43.8
152	Turkmenistan	43.4	0.3	30.0	79.2	90.6	85.3	66.4	10	10	10.0	22.0	30.0
153	Burma (Myanmar)	39.5	-1.5	20.0	71.0	81.7	97.0	56.5	10	10	10.0	19.0	20.0
154	Libya	38.7	1.6	20.0	39.6	81.7	63.5	74.9	30	20	10.0	27.0	20.0
155	Zimbabwe	29.8	-2.0	41.0	55.4	57.8	24.1	0.0	10	20	10.0	24.0	56.0
156	Cuba	27.5	-1.1	10.0	60.8	54.8	0.0	64.6	10	10	10.0	35.0	20.0
157	Korea, North	3.0	0.0	0.0	0.0	0.0	0.0	0.0	10	0	10.0	10.0	0.0

Source: Kim R. Holmes, Edwin J. Feulner, and Mary Anastasia O'Grady, *2008 Index of Economic Freedom* (Washington, D.C.: The Heritage Foundation and Dow Jones & Company, Inc., 2008), at *www.heritage.org/index*.

Chapter 1

Economic Fluidity: A Crucial Dimension of Economic Freedom

Carl J. Schramm

A brief glance at the preceding seven years of thoughtful essays in the *Index of Economic Freedom* reveals a steady evolution of focus from macro-level to, more recently, micro-level issues. The former include the constitutional rule of law, global free trade, property rights, and terrorism. Indisputably, these are all important structural elements to consider in pursuing economic freedom and growth, and economists have performed important research into how they shape economic action.

In the past two years, however, essays on entrepreneurship and labor freedom have evinced a growing recognition that developments on the micro level are centrally important to economic freedom. Without entrepreneurship—what Joseph Schumpeter called the "fundamental impulse" of a free-market system—an economy will stagnate, and without the requisite labor mobility, a society's workers will not feel secure enough to launch an entrepreneurial venture. Economist William Baumol has helped to bring the entrepreneur back into economic analysis, and some economic historians have highlighted the role of entrepreneurs in continuously renewing economic growth and freedom.

The importance of these microeconomic elements points up a crucial dimension of economic freedom: fluidity. The degree of economic freedom (and, thus, of economic growth) in any society will reflect the amount of fluidity in the institutional, organizational, and individual elements of the economy. Every economy evolves based on the interactions within and between these elements, but the *rate* of evolution is determined by the level of fluidity and corresponding degree of interaction, which allows the mixing of ideas and generation of innovation. This might be viewed as the "meso" level of economic analysis.

HISTORICAL EXAMPLES

For example, the growth of cities in late medieval Europe raised the level of economic freedom and helped to drive increasing economic growth. On the Italian Peninsula—the most urbanized part of Europe—most cities enjoyed similar levels of freedom and trade. It was Florence, however, ahead of the others, that achieved exponential growth, giving rise to early capitalism and the Italian Renaissance. Why did this occur exclusively in Florence? Why, if most Italian cities had comparable levels of economic freedom, did all the cities not experience such a leap?

We face a similar paradox when we look at Chicago's brilliant rise in the 19th century. Other cities, notably St. Louis and Cincinnati, enjoyed a head start over Chicago in terms of trade and transportation. Chicago also did not possess superior geographical advantage (and even faced a great disadvantage considering climate and seasonal variation). Most American cities in the 1830s and 1840s were economically free, and cities in the western part of the country battled among themselves to be the most attractive to business. Yet by 1900, Chicago stood as the grand mid-continental city, the true gateway to the Pacific. Why?

The answers to the riddles of Florence and Chicago are complex; it would be a historical disservice to boil an analysis down to one single element or mechanical formula. Yet the two cities do appear to share something relevant to our purposes: economic fluidity, which increased the rate of interaction inside the cities, raising the amount of entrepreneurial energy and speeding the cities' economic evolution.

INNOVATION AND ECONOMIC GROWTH

Before turning to the historical details of these two cities, we must first define what is meant by "fluidity." To do that, however, we must say a few words on the nature of economic growth. It is now well established in economics that innovation and entrepreneurship—distinct yet related concepts—are absolutely central to development, growth, and enhanced well-being.[1] From Henri Pirenne and

Joseph Schumpeter to Paul Romer and William Baumol, economists and historians have seen disruption and renewal, and not simply incremental continuation, as key to increasing human welfare.

Schumpeter observed that the "fundamental impulse that sets and keeps the capitalist engine in motion comes from the new consumers' goods, the new methods of production or transportation, the new markets, the new forms of industrial organization that capitalist enterprise creates."[2] These are all forms of innovation. Professor Baumol, moreover, points to innovation as the source of the "enviable growth record" of capitalism: "the most critical attribute of the free-market economy" is "its ability to produce a stream of applied innovations and a rate of growth in living standards far beyond anything that any other type of economy has ever been able to achieve for any protracted period."[3]

---

[1] See, for example, William J. Baumol, Robert E. Litan, and Carl J. Schramm, *Good Capitalism, Bad Capitalism, and the Economics of Growth and Prosperity* (New Haven, Conn.: Yale University Press, 2007).

[2] Joseph A. Schumpeter, *Capitalism, Socialism and Democracy* (New York: Harper Perennial, 1975), p. 83.

[3] William J. Baumol, *The Free-Market Innovation Machine: Analyzing the Growth Miracle of Capitalism* (Princeton, N.J.: Princeton University Press, 2002), p. viii. Pirenne offered an earlier explanation of what Baumol describes as "recurring industrial revolutions." In a 1914 article, Pirenne theorized of economic history in general: "I believe that, for each period into which our economic history may be divided, there is a distinct and separate class of capitalists. In other words, the group of capitalists of a given epoch does not spring from the capitalist group of the preceding epoch. At every change in economic organization we find a breach of continuity. It is as if the capitalists who have up to that time been active, recognize that they are incapable of adapting themselves to conditions which are evoked by needs hitherto unknown and which call for methods hitherto unemployed. They withdraw from the struggle and become an aristocracy.... In their place arise new men, courageous and enterprising, who boldly permit themselves to be driven by the wind actually blowing and who know how to trim their sails to take advantage of it, until the day comes when, its direction changing and disconcerting their manoeuvres, they in their turn pause and are distanced by new craft having fresh forces and new directions." Henri Pirenne, "The Stages in the Social History of Capitalism," *American Historical Review*, Vol. 19 (April 1914), pp. 494, 495. Romer, too, sees innovation as the key to

Innovation—the creation of new knowledge and the useful applications that flow from it—drives growth and improvement in standards of living, but what determines or produces innovation? This is a disputed question, and the partial answer offered here is that economic fluidity is a principal determinant of a society's level of innovation. Fluidity, then, is that condition of a loose yet stable alignment of institutions, organizations, and individuals that facilitates the exchange and networking of knowledge across boundaries. This fosters both innovation and its propagation through entrepreneurship.

This must not be confused with the often chimerical notion of equilibrium in economics. It bears more resemblance, instead, to the idea in complexity science of the "edge of chaos," the estuary region where rigid order and random chaos meet and generate high levels of adaptation, complexity, and creativity.[4] How adaptive is a society's economic structure, and how well does it absorb beneficial adaptations?

The notion of economic fluidity, however, goes beyond merely the generation and diffusion of ideas and technology within the existing economic structure. Substantial research indicates that it is those ideas on the margins, challenging the status quo, that lift the trajectory of an economy's performance.[5] Psychologist Howard Gardner, for example, highlights the role of "asynchrony...a lack of fit, an unusual pattern, or an irregularity," in generating creative ideas and innovation.[6]

Such innovations are often referred to as "disruptive," but this is accurate only to the extent that the innovations are absorbed and propagated. Marginal and potentially disruptive innovations likely exist in every society at every point in history. They become productive, however, only when the alignment—the dialogue—among institutions, organizations, and individuals is fluid enough that the innovations become part of that co-evolution and shift the trajectory of economic performance to a higher level. Such absorption and propagation are determined by the level of economic fluidity.

LEVELS OF FLUIDITY

At an institutional level, fluidity signals a society's capacity to adapt to changing circumstances, its ability to absorb adaptations productively, and its openness to new ideas. Institutions are here taken to mean "durable systems of established and embedded social rules that structure social interactions."[7]

---

growth: "Economic growth occurs whenever people take resources and rearrange them in ways that are more valuable. A useful metaphor for production in an economy comes from the kitchen. To create valuable final products, we mix inexpensive ingredients together according to a recipe. The cooking one can do is limited by the supply of ingredients, and most cooking in the economy produces undesirable side effects. If economic growth could be achieved only by doing more and more of the same kind of cooking, we would eventually run out of raw materials and suffer from unacceptable levels of pollution and nuisance. Human history teaches us, however, that economic growth springs from better recipes, not just from more cooking. New recipes generally produce fewer unpleasant side effects and generate more economic value per unit of raw material." Paul Romer, "Economic Growth," in *The Concise Encyclopedia of Economics*, at *www.econlib.org/library/enc/EconomicGrowth.html*.

4   See, generally, Stuart Kauffman, *At Home in the Universe: The Search for the Laws of Self-Organization and Complexity* (New York: Oxford University Press, 1995); M. Mitchell Waldrop, *Complexity: The Emerging Science at the Edge of Order and Chaos* (New York: Simon & Schuster Touchstone, 1992); and John H. Holland, *Hidden Order: How Adaptation Builds Complexity* (New York: Perseus Books, 1995).

5   "This historic and irreversible change in the way of doing things we call 'innovation' and we define: innovations are changes in production functions which cannot be decomposed into infinitesimal steps. Add as many mail-coaches as you please, you will never get a railroad by so doing." Joseph A. Schumpeter, "The Analysis of Economic Change," *Review of Economic Statistics*, May 1935, pp. 2, 4.

6   Howard Gardner, *Creating Minds: An Anatomy of Creativity Seen Through the Lives of Freud, Einstein, Picasso, Stravinsky, Eliot, Graham, and Gandhi* (New York: Basic Books, 1993), pp. 40–41.

7   Geoffrey M. Hodgson, *The Evolution of Institutional Economics: Agency, Structure and Darwinism in American Institutionalism* (London and New York: Routledge, 2004), p. 14: "According to this definition, systems of language, money, law,

According to Nobel laureate Douglass North, these include both formal (rules, laws, constitutions) and informal (norms of behavior, conventions, self-imposed codes of conduct) constraints, as well as "their enforcement characteristics."[8] If the laws and conventions of a society—and the regulations and habits of economic activity—fail to account for a changing reality, the society will become frozen.

Obversely, if the institutions do not maintain a measure of stability and permanence, a society will neither absorb adaptations nor be able to adapt in the first place. As Heraclitus observed, "On those stepping into rivers staying the same other and other waters flow." For example, American universities have continuously adapted themselves as the needs and demands of society have changed, yet they have also maintained a level of institutional permanence. Adaptation and absorption require openness to those marginal ideas that often form the foundation of economic progress.

Organizationally, fluidity means minimal bureaucracy. Though necessary and perhaps inevitable to some degree, bureaucracy is, in its essence, "a means of communication whose purpose is to reduce risk. Within organizations, the risk-averting dialogue is articulated in rules that bound the behaviors of people and control processes."[9]

In terms of economic growth, bureaucracy often hinders progress because it seeks predictable, low-risk outcomes—notions that are antithetical to dynamic, entrepreneurship-driven growth. Rules and structure, however, are inevitable and even desirable because they can help to propagate new ideas and innovations. Within a business firm, a facilitative bureau-

cratic structure can increase the "technology adoption investment" that is key to growth.[10] Problems and barriers arise when bureaucracy—in a firm, in government, in a university—sees its goal as perpetuation of the status quo rather than adaptation. The fluidity of a society's organizations—their ability to minimize bureaucracy and adapt their structure—is often a prime determinant of economic growth.[11]

The third level of economic fluidity is that of the individual: the ability of individual economic actors to freely decide their line of work, move between jobs, and, crucially, start new businesses. In last year's *Index of Economic Freedom*, Johnny Munkhammar highlighted constrictive labor laws that continue to hamper economic growth even in Europe.[12] Similarly, the most recent Nobel laureate in economics, Edmund Phelps, has done extensive research into how the "corporatist" economic structure of Western Europe limits individual mobility: "high corporatism is strongly correlated with stifled entrepreneurship and obstructive job protection."[13] Here, a nation's bankruptcy laws, ease of business formation, tax treatment

10   Stephen L. Parente and Edward C. Prescott, "Barriers to Technology Adoption and Development," *Journal of Political Economy*, Vol. 102 (April 1994), pp. 298, 318.

11   Others view organizational fluidity more expansively, in terms of the institutional context: "Organizations are central to all aspects of social order…. [B]ecause cooperation and coordination directly affect productivity, the ability to support complex, sophisticated organizations is central to economic growth…. Open access societies support open access to organizations…. Creative destruction depends critically on open entry and support for organizational forms." Douglass C. North, John Joseph Wallis, and Barry R. Weingast, "A Conceptual Framework for Interpreting Recorded Human History," National Bureau of Economic Research *Working Paper* No. 12795, December 2006.

12   See Johnny Munkhammar, "The Urgent Need for Labor Freedom in Europe—and the World," Chapter 2 in *2007 Index of Economic Freedom* (Washington, D.C.: The Heritage Foundation and Dow Jones & Company, Inc., 2007), pp. 27–36.

13   Edmund Phelps, "The Dynamism of Nations," Project Syndicate, December 2003, at *www.project-syndicate.org/commentary/phelps4*.

weights and measures, traffic conventions, table manners, firms (and all other organizations) are all institutions."

8   Douglass C. North, "Economic Performance Through Time," Nobel Prize Lecture, December 9, 1993, at *www.nobelprize.org*.

9   Carl J. Schramm, "Entrepreneurial Capitalism and the End of Bureaucracy: Reforming the Mutual Dialog of Risk Aversion," paper presented at annual meeting of the American Economics Association, January 6, 2006, at *www.aeaweb.org/annual_mtg_papers/2006/0107_1015_0304.pdf*.

of capital gains, and, informally, receptivity to new ideas are all important.

FLUIDITY IN OPERATION

None of these three levels of fluidity is independent; they interact with and determine each other's degree of fluidity. Moreover, there is likely no "optimal" state of fluidity toward which an economy's institutions, organizations, or individuals should gravitate. The desirable level for innovation and its propagation will vary because of the ceaseless march of economic change.

The ubiquity of uncertainty and change in human systems makes fluidity itself necessary. As North observed, "conditions of uncertainty…have characterized the political and economic choices that shaped (and continue to shape) historical change."[14] Rigidity at any level—institutional, organizational, or individual—hinders adaptation and, thus, the ability to improve living standards. This does not mean, of course, that a society should throw itself open to any and all adaptations; the result would be chaos. The corollary of fluidity is the ability to make salutary changes "stick," to institutionalize them. Returning to the examples of Florence and Chicago, we see these two sides of fluidity at work.

- In Florence, economic growth created scores of "new men," made rich from trade and banking, who challenged the old landholding aristocracy. What set Florence apart from other Italian cities was the level of mixing and interaction between the two groups, which prevented aristocratic ossification. (Much of this mixing involved political calculation on both sides, but that doesn't change the fact that it occurred.) At the same time, the artisan and craftsmen guilds in Florence remained more open than in other cities—accepting, for example, silk weavers driven from nearby Lucca. This openness also reflected the movement of the Florentine economy up the value chain. Artisans were continually able to upgrade their skills, and there was much

interaction between the artisans and the upper classes, which increasingly displaced the Church as artistic patrons. This intermingling helped to drive the rebirth of artistic creativity that subsequently spread across Europe.

- We find a similar story in Chicago, where successive waves of settlers, investors, and entrepreneurs constantly remained open to change and new developments. Though Chicago enjoyed water access, the city quickly capitalized on the innovation of the railroad. Meanwhile, its rival St. Louis resisted this advancement, and its commercial institutions failed to adapt quickly to changes wrought by railroads. The growing institutions of Chicago, by contrast, resisted ossification and continuously evolved. One measure of this fluidity is that Chicago simultaneously experienced the fastest rate of wealth creation in the country and the highest turnover of citizens. The level of entrepreneurial energy, facilitated by near-liquid fluidity, pushed the city at an incredible clip.

This notion of fluidity parallels the work done by other economists and economic historians in recent years. Phelps has examined the importance of "economic dynamism" in explaining the difference in economic performance across countries. According to Phelps:

[Dynamism reflects] how fertile the country is in coming up with innovative ideas having prospects of profitability, how adept it is at identifying and nourishing the ideas with the best prospects, and how prepared it is in evaluating and trying out the new products and methods that are launched onto the market.[15]

Phelps is absolutely correct that economic dynamism is "a crucial determinant of [a] country's economic performance."[16] Yet even the level of dynamism is determined by other factors, as Phelps recognizes:

---

14   North, "Economic Performance Through Time."

15   Edmund S. Phelps, "Entrepreneurial Culture," *The Wall Street Journal*, February 12, 2007, p. A15.
16   *Ibid.*

A country's economic model determines its economic dynamism.... There are two dimensions to a country's economic model. One part consists of its economic institutions.... The other part of the economic model consists of various elements of the country's economic culture.[17]

The contention of this essay is that unless there is *a priori* fluidity in that "economic model," the character of the institutions and culture will matter less. There must be fluidity for the development of a co-evolutionary process among institutions, organizations, and individuals. "Economic dynamism" emerges from that process and the fluidity that facilitates it.

Put differently, it is not the existence of a specific set of institutions *per se*, but how fluid they are. Many European countries have a start-up rate just as high as that of the United States; ideas and potential innovations, however, cannot break into the prevailing economic model. The proper institutions and organizations appear to exist, but they are not fluid. Recent research suggests that a high rate of entrepreneurship may be necessary but not sufficient to stimulate dynamism and high performance.[18]

Others have looked at the incentive structure of an economy and how it allocates economic activity. Baumol has analyzed entrepreneurial activity in terms of the "reward structure in the economy" at any given time:

[I]t is the set of rules and not the supply of entrepreneurs *or the nature of their objectives* that undergoes significant changes from one period to another and helps to dictate the ultimate effect on the economy via the *allocation* of entrepreneurial resources.[19]

Similarly, Robert Hall and Charles Jones posit that economic performance is almost exclusively determined by the "infrastructure," the context of economic activity:

Our hypothesis is that an important part of the explanation lies in the economic environment in which individuals produce, transact, invent, and accumulate skills.... A successful infrastructure encourages production. A perverse infrastructure discourages production in ways that are detrimental to economic performance.[20]

The scholar whose work is perhaps most reflected in this essay is North. By refocusing economic research on the importance of institutions, he has added rich insight into how we view our economies and societies: "It is the interaction between institutions and organizations that shapes the institutional evolution of an economy. If institutions are the rules of the game, organizations and their entrepreneurs are the players."[21] Moreover, for North, "the

---

17   *Ibid.* "A transformation of the economy to one of dynamism, thus the teamwork to implement it and to adapt well to it, can be obtained only if the economic culture and possibly other 'background conditions' are conducive, not just the institutional machinery." Edmund S. Phelps, "Economic Culture and Economic Performance: What Light is Shed on the Continent's Problem?" paper presented at conference, "Perspectives on the Performance of the Continent's Economies," Venice Summer Institute, July 21–22, 2006.
18   See Robert Fairlie, "Entrepreneurship in Silicon Valley During the Boom and Bust," Report for Small Business Administration, Office of Advocacy, March 2007. See also William J. Baumol, *The Free-Market Innovation Machine: Analyzing the Growth Miracle of Capitalism* (Princeton, N.J.: Princeton University Press, 2002), p. viii, emphasizing the importance of "the way in which the market mechanism—together with institutional arrangements—influences, not the creation, but the *allocation* of entrepreneurship between productive and unproductive (rent-seeking) pursuits.... Rather, [entrepreneurs] can be and are reallocated by economic conditions and circumstances

into (or out of) activities that appear not to be entrepreneurial because the preconception that enterprising activity is necessarily productive."
19   William J. Baumol, "Entrepreneurship: Productive, Unproductive, and Destructive," *Journal of Political Economy*, Vol. 98 (October 1990), pp. 893, 894. Emphasis in original.
20   Robert E. Hall and Charles I. Jones, "Levels of Economic Activity Across Countries," *American Economic Review*, Vol. 87 (May 1997), pp. 173, 174–175.
21   North, "Economic Performance Through Time."

most fundamental long run source of change is learning by individuals and entrepreneurs of organizations."[22]

CONTEXT AND ECONOMIC GROWTH

Much of the research referenced here appears to point toward a common idea: Context matters greatly for economic growth. This, too, is one premise of the *Index of Economic Freedom*. The contention of this essay is merely that context is important for growth to the degree that it is fluid enough to promote that growth—fluidity determines the rate of learning.[23]

This ostensible tautology can be resolved by pointing out that the proper context of economic success is not a Goldilocks point of equilibrium at which conditions are "just right." The notion of a stable equilibrium to which all countries must converge is often a mirage,[24] and there is nothing inevitable or automatic once a country achieves a threshold level of economic freedom. A society can maintain economic freedom—freedom to start a business, to choose one's occupation, to own property—yet still slide toward ossification due to a lack of fluidity. As North writes: "In fact most societies throughout history got 'stuck' in an institutional matrix that did not evolve."[25]

For example, in the 1970s and early 1980s, the U.S. economy faltered; the economic structure that the author calls "bureaucratic capitalism" stultified American economic performance.[26] Yet this economic structure, the context, was not "wrong." The United States still possessed the ostensibly proper infrastructure and institutions for growth. It simply became too rigid. It lacked fluidity. It did not lack for adaptations: Many would have adapted the American economy toward central planning, and, indeed, several changes in this era did eventually come together to produce entrepreneurial capitalism.[27] But bureaucratic capitalism lacked the capacity to generate, absorb, or propagate beneficial adaptations such as innovation. It was not fluid enough.

As noted above, Edmund Phelps has analyzed the economic woes of Western Europe in analogous terms. These two examples demonstrate that threats to fluidity are omnipresent. Even the "proper" institutional context cannot guarantee against stagnation.[28] Even today, in the advanced economy of the U.S., we confront developments that could easily have a deleterious impact on fluidity.[29]

---

22   *Ibid*.
23   Furthermore, a high level of fluidity can itself serve as a stimulus for innovation and entrepreneurship because it helps maintain the requisite "vibrancy and sense of excitement" and "energy and optimism" that can spark entrepreneurship and growth. Baumol, Litan, and Schramm, *Good Capitalism, Bad Capitalism, and the Economics of Growth and Prosperity*, p. 33.
24   "What redeems their system in Continental eyes is its stability and job security. But recent history suggests vulnerability, not stability.... Europe is learning that when economic shocks hit, policies that rigidify wage rates and protect existing jobs can only slow—not lessen—the fall of total employment.... By delaying restructuring, such policies may aggravate the fall in profitability, share prices, and the currency, worsening unemployment." Edmund Phelps, "European Myths, European Realities," Project Syndicate, November 2002, at *www.project-syndicate.org/commentary/phelps4*.
25   North, "Economic Performance Through

Time." See also Lewis Mumford, *The City in History: Its Origins, Its Transformations, and Its Prospects* (New York: Harcourt, Brace and World, 1961), pp. 5, 110–111: Any organism can become "sessile...overadapted to a fixed position and lose the power of movement.... Groups of organisms may occupy a common environment and make use of each other's activities without any one organism reaching its fullest growth, or achieving its maximum potentialities for development. As a matter of fact, they may live together for a long time while undergoing a steady deterioration.... Survival by itself indicates nothing about the development or rank of the organism that survives."
26   See, for example, Carl J. Schramm, *The Entrepreneurial Imperative* (New York: HarperCollins, 2006).
27   *Ibid*.
28   See also Terence Kealey, *The Economic Laws of Scientific Research* (New York: Palgrave Macmillan, 1996).
29   See, for example, Schramm, *The Entrepreneurial Imperative*, pointing to creeping regulatory strictures as well as the institutional rigidity of American universities.

By the same token, however, fluidity does not mean change for the sake of change, which can be just as detrimental to economic performance: "There is no guarantee that the beliefs and institutions that evolve through time will produce economic growth."[30] It means instead that degree of looseness and stability that permits successful adaptation through the rapid generation, absorption, and propagation of innovation.

A key point to keep in mind is that a society's economic structure or "economic model" likely cannot be created *de novo* through government action. Government policy certainly is important, but it is only one factor in determining economic performance and, indeed, can often work to hinder growth. The level of economic fluidity at any given moment will reflect a co-evolutionary process of individuals, organizations, and institutions over time. Evolution and change do not cease, but neither do they guarantee progress and improved human welfare:

As social scientists we often associate change with movement and progress.... But a great deal of change in history is simply change. In every society the balance among political, economic, religious, military, and educational organizations is in continual flux.[31]

The level of economic fluidity determines how much a society can absorb beneficial adaptations and incorporate them into a self-reinforcing process of increasing economic performance.

Economic freedom continues to be a goal of surpassing importance, but we must recognize that it contains several dimensions, one of which is economic fluidity. To reach and maintain economic freedom in any society, whether advanced or developing, we must ensure that institutions, organizations, and individuals remain fluid enough to facilitate growth.

This essay argues that whether the economic infrastructure is "successful" or "perverse" and whether the "reward structure" is conducive to innovation and entrepreneurship rests on the degree of economic fluidity. Without constant mixing across boundaries, without the creation and testing of ideas, and without learning and adaptation, the specific character of the institutional structure matters little. Fluidity determines whether or not the structure will be successful in facilitating growth.

---

30   North, "Economic Performance Through Time."

31   North, Wallis, and Weingast, "A Conceptual Framework for Interpreting Recorded Human History."

Chapter 2

Narrowing the Economic Gap in the 21st Century

Stephen L. Parente

Today, huge differences in living standards exist across countries. Even after adjusting for differences in relative prices, gross domestic product (GDP) per capita, the best proxy for a country's living standard, is reportedly 50 to 60 times greater in the richest industrial nations than in the poorest countries. Interestingly, substantial differences such as these are a recent phenomenon. Up until about 1700, differences between nations were on the magnitude of a factor of 2 or 3. Thus, in the past 300 years, the gap between the world's richest and poorest countries has widened tremendously.

If an increasing disparity between rich and poor is a reality of modern times, what then lies ahead over the next century? Will differences continue to widen, or will they narrow to a lesser factor, similar to the situation observed prior to 1700? My answer to this question—drawing heavily on my own work with Edward C. Prescott over the past decade, as well as rel-evant work of other scholars,[1] and taking into consideration a number of complex issues—is that differences between rich and poor will not widen significantly in the future, though it is far less clear whether they will return to their 1700 equivalent levels.

We know that differences in living standards between rich and poor countries can be eliminated in rather short periods. Several poor countries have been able to catch up to the industrial leaders in terms of income levels by experiencing more rapid growth. However, we know from the limited number of success stories that catching up is not easily accomplished. Political stability, while necessary, is insufficient. Rather, catching up requires certain economic reforms—reforms that are likely

---

1   Stephen L. Parente and Edward C. Prescott, "A Unified Theory of the Evolution of International Income Levels," in Philippe Aghion and Steven Durlauf, eds., *The Handbook of Economic Growth* (Amsterdam: North-Holland, 2005), pp. 1371–1416.

Chart 1

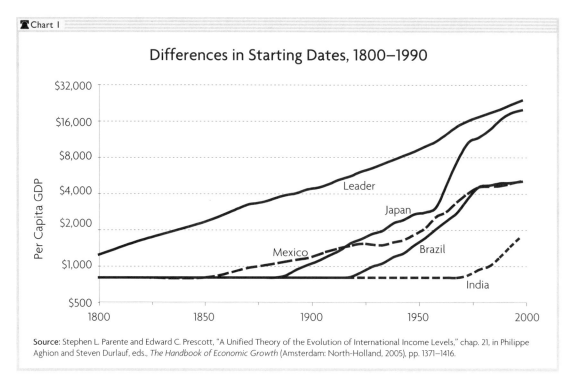

Differences in Starting Dates, 1800–1990

Per Capita GDP

$32,000
$16,000
$8,000
$4,000
$2,000
$1,000
$500

Leader

Japan

Mexico

Brazil

India

1800   1850   1900   1950   2000

Source: Stephen L. Parente and Edward C. Prescott, "A Unified Theory of the Evolution of International Income Levels," chap. 21, in Philippe Aghion and Steven Durlauf, eds., *The Handbook of Economic Growth* (Amsterdam: North-Holland, 2005), pp. 1371–1416.

to be opposed vigorously by certain societal groups who rightly or wrongly believe these reforms will be to their detriment. Weakening and countering this opposition will be key to catching up in the next century.

THE EVOLUTION OF INTERNATIONAL INCOMES

Different Starting Dates. The widening income disparity that has occurred since the 18th century reflects the fact that some countries began to experience economic growth before others. Prior to 1700, there was little to no increase in the living standard of any country. This all changed in 1700 when England began to experience sustained increases in its per capita output. Soon thereafter, Western Europe and the ethnic offshoots of England began to develop. At first, increases in these early starters were modest and irregular. However, since the beginning of the 20th century, these increases have been larger and more regular, with income doubling roughly every 35 years—a phenomenon that Simon Kuznets labeled *modern economic growth*.

Over time, more and more countries have come to accomplish this feat of increasing their per capita output. Chart 1 shows the paths of

per capita GDP for a selected number of countries since 1800, as well as that for the leader, which was the Netherlands from 1800 to 1820, the United Kingdom from 1820 to 1890, and the United States subsequently. Starting dates differ substantially across countries: Mexico started to grow around 1860; Japan, around 1870; Brazil, around 1920; and India, around 1970.

The implication of these different starting dates for the world income distribution is depicted in Chart 2, which plots per capita GDP for four major regions relative to the leader's level between 1700 and 1990. With the exception of Africa, the gap between each region and the leader stopped increasing once the region began modern economic growth. Africa's gap has continued to widen because, although almost every African country has become richer in the past 50 years, the increases have been modest and highly irregular.

The Advantage of Being a Late Starter. Experiences of regions have varied subsequent to initiating economic growth. Latin America, which started modern economic growth around 1900, has subsequently maintained an income level that is 25 percent of the industrial leader's. Asia, which started economic growth around 1950, has eliminated a large part of its

Chart 2

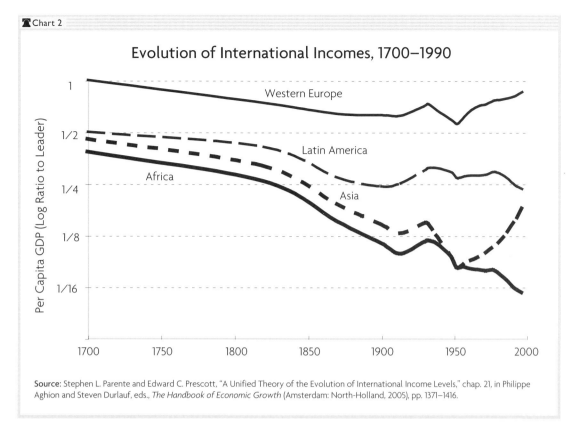

Evolution of International Incomes, 1700–1990

Per Capita GDP (Log Ratio to Leader)

Western Europe

Latin America

Africa

Asia

1
1/2
1/4
1/8
1/16

1700   1750   1800   1850   1900   1950   2000

Source: Stephen L. Parente and Edward C. Prescott, "A Unified Theory of the Evolution of International Income Levels," chap. 21, in Philippe Aghion and Steven Durlauf, eds., *The Handbook of Economic Growth* (Amsterdam: North-Holland, 2005), pp. 1371–1416.

gap, having outperformed the United States, which continued to grow at its historical rate of 2 percent per year.

The rapid growth subsequent to 1978 in China, with 20 percent of the world's population, played an important role in Asia's catching up, as did the dramatic growth experiences in a number of other Asian countries: Japan went from 21 percent to 87 percent of the U.S. level between 1950 and 1993; South Korea went from 11 percent to 43 percent between 1960 and 2000; Singapore went from 16 percent to 80 percent between 1960 and 2000; and Taiwan went from 8 percent to 55 percent between 1952 and 1995. Such experiences are seen as development miracles.

These growth miracles are a recent phenomenon and are limited to countries that were well behind the industrial leader at the time the miracle began. No record exists of a poor country prior to 1950 doubling its per capita GDP in a decade or less as Japan, South Korea, Taiwan, Singapore, and China all have done, and at no point in history has the industrial leader accomplished this feat. Whereas all of

these countries are located in Asia, not every country that has realized large increases relative to the leader is located in this part of the world. As a matter of fact, China's catching up is not all that different from that of the African country Botswana, which increased its living standard from 8 percent to 21 percent of the U.S. level between 1970 and 1999.

As can be seen from these Asian and African examples, rapid growth is possible. In fact, it seems that the farther behind the industrial leader a country is, the greater its potential for rapid growth and catching up is. That is, late developers have been able to double their incomes in less time than early developers.

Chart 3 illustrates this point. It plots the number of years it took a country to double its income from $2,000 to $4,000 (in 1990 prices) against the year it first achieved a per capita income of $2,000. Rich countries such as England, the United States, and France, which achieved this level of income roughly 200 years ago, took around 45 years to double their incomes to $4,000. Countries that achieved this minimum level of income after 1950, such as

Years for Income per Capita to Grow from $2,000 to $4,000 (in 1990 U.S. dollars)

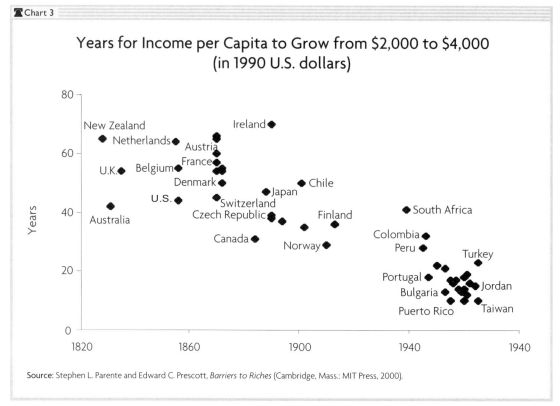

Source: Stephen L. Parente and Edward C. Prescott, *Barriers to Riches* (Cambridge, Mass.: MIT Press, 2000).

Taiwan and Portugal, took only 15 years to double their incomes. These results are robust to the starting income level. That is, whether we use $500, $1,000, or $2,000 as the initial level, countries achieving these levels after 1950 have been able to double their incomes in far less time than countries achieving these levels earlier in history.

THEORIES OF INTERNATIONAL INCOMES

What explains this evolution of incomes, characterized by its huge disparity and rapid catching up by a handful of late developers? Today, there is widespread consensus that differences in resources—that is, a country's land, workforce, and capital—play only a small part in this explanation. Instead, macro and micro evidence suggests that differences in *Total Factor Productivity (TFP)*—that is, the efficiency at which a society uses its resources to produce goods and services—play the primary role.

Macro Evidence. A prime determinant of a country's capital stock is its savings rate—the amount of output not consumed. A prime determinant of a country's labor resource is the

education of its population. Casual inspection of international savings rates and educational attainments over the post–World War II period suggests that neither resource is important for understanding the evolution of international incomes. Savings rates are not substantially different between rich and poor countries. According to the International Monetary Fund, both rich and poor countries on average invested about 20 percent of their GDPs. Educational differences are more pronounced, but the fact that many poor countries succeeded in eliminating part of their educational gaps with the rich countries over the past 50 years while failing to eliminate any part of their income gaps suggests that this resource is not critical.

A rigorous examination of the contribution of these resources for international income differences was undertaken by Peter Klenow and Andres Rodriguez-Clare in 1997[2] and by Robert E. Hall and Chad Jones in 1999.[3] This exami-

2   Peter Klenow and Andres Rodriguez-Clare, "Economic Growth: A Review Essay," *Journal of Monetary Economics*, Vol. 40 (1997), pp. 587–617.
3   Robert E. Hall and Chad Jones, "Why Do Some Countries Produce So Much More than

Table 1

Implied Differences in Total Factor Productivity, 1988

Country	Per Worker Output	Relative TFP
United States	100	100
West Germany	82	91
France	82	113
United Kingdom	73	101
Japan	59	66
South Korea	38	58
Portugal	37	75
Malaysia	27	37
Thailand	16	76
Philippines	13	22
India	9	27
Kenya	6	17

Source: Robert E. Hall and Chad Jones, "Why Do Some Countries Produce So Much More Than Others?" *Quarterly Journal of Economics*, Vol. 114 (1999), pp. 83–116.

These studies have the advantage of examining easily observable features of the production process: technology, capital, land, and labor. In the past two decades, an increasing number of such studies have been carried out, and the McKinsey Global Institute (MGI) has been instrumental in this regard.

Since 1990, MGI has examined the nature of production at the firm level for a set of representative industries in 13 countries that include rich, middle-income, and poor nations. Findings indicate that output-per-worker productivity differs considerably across countries. Even among the rich countries, productivity can vary by a factor of 3. Additionally, productivity rankings by country vary across industries. No country is the most productive in all industries; for example, whereas the United States is the most productive country in the service industries, Japan is more productive in several manufacturing industries.

In examining production of individual businesses operating in a given industry in each country, MGI concluded that the main source of output-per-worker differences was TFP, not worker skills or the amount of machinery and equipment. Rather, less productive countries in a given industry failed to apply the best-practice technology used in the most productive country. Moreover, in many cases, less productive countries failed to maximize efficiency in their given technology. For example, MGI estimated that India's modern industries could increase their productivity from 15 percent to 45 percent of their U.S. counterparts simply by changing the way production was carried out.

nation, which takes the form of an accounting exercise, begins by postulating that a country's GDP is a function (F) of its physical capital (K) and human capital (H) multiplied by its TFP, or efficiency (A):

$$GDP = A \, F(K,H)$$

Measures for K and H are then constructed for each country, and these measures, together with each country's GDP, are used with the aggregate production function to impute each country's efficiency. The finding of both studies is that efficiency is strongly and positively related to the level of development. Hall and Jones, for example, report a correlation coefficient between the log of output per worker and the log of TFP equal to 0.89.

Table 1 displays a representative sample of their findings for a set of rich, middle-income, and poor countries. As can be seen, TFP is, for instance, more than five times higher in the United States than in Kenya.

Micro Evidence. More support for the efficiency-based theory and against the resource-based theory of international income differences comes from industry and firm-level studies.

BARRIERS TO TECHNOLOGY ADOPTION

Why then do poorer countries use inferior technology and in many instances operate them

Others?" *Quarterly Journal of Economics*, Vol. 114 (1999), pp. 83–116.

below their full potential? The answer is not that poorer countries have a smaller stock of knowledge to access. The stock of useable knowledge is essentially the same for each country, as ideas do not obey international borders; there is a tremendous amount of knowledge that is publicly available, and even knowledge that is proprietary can be accessed through licensing agreements or foreign direct investment.

This means that poor countries do not need to spend resources on reinventing ideas, but rather can tap into an international knowledge base. And because this base continues to grow, late starters have an advantage. This is why late developers have been able to double their incomes in far shorter periods than early developers and, hence, why countries that begin to develop in the future will also benefit from existing world knowledge and experiences.

While it is true that poor countries have access to the same stock of knowledge as rich countries, it is also a fact that they use far less of it because they impose far more constraints, or barriers, on their technology choices. The barriers take many forms. In the end, each constraint limits competition and in consequence deters entry by domestic and foreign firms making use of more efficient technologies. In some cases, public safety or the environment justifies the constraint; but in most cases, the barrier exists to protect a group with interests vested in the status quo. Because of these special-interest groups, removing barriers is not easily accomplished. However, when they are eliminated, large gains in efficiency typically follow.

Examples of Barriers. Some constraints, such as work rules, affect how a given technology can be used. A work rule, which specifies how inputs can be used, leads to overstaffing and underutilization of machines. For example, in Brazil and New Jersey, government regulation requires that all gas stations be full-service. In Australia, a work rule in the beer industry specifies that individual forklifts cannot be operated by different people.

Besides barriers on how technology can be used, other constraints affect which technology is used. Regulation that effectively outlaws the use of a certain technology is one example of this type of constraint. Such constraints can be found in many countries, including the rich ones, in the form of zoning laws that prevent large retailing formats. In India, for instance, a law called the Small Scale Reservation prevents large-scale plants from being built.

Often, constraints on technology are less explicit than zoning laws yet equally effective. For example, bureaucracy and bribes constitute very effective constraints on the technology choice of firms. Hernando de Soto showed exactly how these types of barriers work to lower efficiency. He pointed out that the huge costs associated with bureaucracy and bribes in Peru cause many people to operate illegally.[4] Such informal firms, however, are not efficient because, to avoid detection, they tend to operate older and smaller-scale technologies.

Peru is not alone in this respect. Simeon Djankov and his co-authors have shown that the bureaucratic cost of establishing a firm is strongly and positively correlated with the level of a country's development.[5] For example, they find that in 1999, the average cost of bureaucracy in the 25 richest countries in their sample of 100 countries was 20 percent of GDP, whereas the average cost of the 25 poorest countries was an astounding 134 percent of GDP.

Another type of barrier relates to government involvement in business. For example, preferential treatment of firms in the form of taxes, subsidies, and awards of government contracts also works to reduce efficiency. MGI found that such preferential policies are common, for example, in Russia. These constraints keep inefficient firms afloat and prevent efficient businesses from entering since they cannot compete successfully with privileged incumbent firms.

Moreover, state-owned enterprises are notoriously inefficient. In India, for instance, output per worker in government enterprises in

---

4   Hernando de Soto, *The Other Path: The Invisible Revolution in the Third World* (New York: Harper and Row, 1989).
5   Simeon Djankov, Rafael La Porta, Florencio Lopes-de-Silanes, and Andrei Shleifer, "The Regulation of Entry," *Quarterly Journal of Economics,* Vol. 117 (2002), pp. 1–37.

power generation, telecommunications, and retail banking is around 10 percent of the average U.S. level of output in those industries. In contrast, private-sector Indian firms operating in those same industries achieve 40 percent of the U.S. level.

Prohibitions on international trade constitute other important constraints. Quotas, tariffs, multiple exchange rate regimes, and restrictions on repatriation of profits have the effect of lowering the price elasticity of demand for goods. This is important because a higher price elasticity of demand translates into a larger percentage increase in revenues following a 1 percent decline in the good's price, hence increasing the profitability of innovation. Imperfect enforcement of debt contracts also reduces efficiency. That is, when debt contracts are not fully enforceable, individuals are not able to obtain the financing they need to adopt best-practice technologies.

Overall, as poor countries impose numerous constraints on the economic choices of their citizens, differences exist in quality as well as quantity. That is, the type of barriers and the number of barriers imposed vary from one poor nation to another. The MGI studies provide some information on the prevalence of various barriers in different countries.

However, a far more comprehensive picture of the mix of barriers across countries is provided by the annual *Index of Economic Freedom* published jointly by The Heritage Foundation and *The Wall Street Journal*. Since 1995, the *Index* has assigned a score for each country on 10 different categories of barriers, or economic freedoms to use the language of Milton Friedman. These categories include constraints on international trade (trade freedom); restrictions on foreign investment (investment freedom); bureaucracy (business freedom); and corruption (freedom from corruption).

Barriers Matter. How do we know that barriers to technology adoption are the main reason for low TFP in poor countries? There are two bodies of support, one empirical and the other theoretical.

The empirical support takes the form of industry studies that document the changes in productivity associated with an increase or a decrease in barriers. Paul Romer,[6] William Lewis,[7] and Harold L. Cole et al.[8] document large productivity increases following the elimination of barriers in a variety of industries and countries.

The theoretical support entails economic models that examine technology choices of firms. These theoretical models provide systematic explanations for the empirical finding that barriers give rise to the differences in TFP and income. For instance, when Edward Prescott and I inserted the bureaucratic cost estimates of Djankov *et al.* into such a theoretical model of technology adoption, we found that the model accurately predicted the current differences in TFP and living standards between the world's richest and poorest nations.

Reasons for Barriers. If constraints prevent firms from reaching a higher economic potential, why do societies put economic barriers in place, and why are they maintained? Industry and firm-level data suggest that these constraints often exist to protect specialized factor suppliers and corporate interests, which rightly or wrongly believe they will fail to benefit from the introduction of more productive technology.

Consider the following illustrative example, documented by Merritt Fox and Michael Heller, involving the Segezhabumpron Paper Mill, one of Russia's largest pulp and paper mills, located in Karelia, Russia. After acquiring a majority stake in the mill in the early 1990s, Assidoman of Sweden put forth a $100 million modernization plan. The investment plan, however, raised the fear that jobs would be eliminated.

6   Paul Romer, "Two Strategies for Economic Development: Using Ideas and Producing Ideas," in Lawrence Summers and Shekhar Shah, eds., *Proceedings of the World Bank Annual Conference on Development Economics 1992* (Washington, D.C.: World Bank, 1993), pp. 63–91.

7   William Lewis, *The Power of Productivity: Wealth, Poverty, and the Threat of Global Stability* (Chicago: University of Chicago Press, 2004).

8   Harold L. Cole, Lee Ohanian, Alvaro Riascos, and James A. Schmitz, Jr., "Latin America in the Rearview Mirror," *Journal of Monetary Economics*, Vol. 52 (2004), pp. 69–107.

Because of this fear, the plant's employees and local government officials undertook a number of actions that effectively ran the Swedes out of town, including a judicial challenge on the legality of Assidoman's initial purchase of shares, threats of violence, and a refusal by the regional government, the minority owner of the mill, to provide the working capital needed to keep the plant open.[9]

THE CHALLENGE OF ELIMINATING BARRIERS

Currently poor countries will catch up to the industrial leaders if existing constraints on efficient production are eliminated and an arrangement is set up to ensure that barriers will not be re-erected in the future. That is, the removal of constraints is a necessary condition for catching up to be possible. But this is easier said than done, because technological change does not benefit everyone equally in society. Some people lose, or at least believe that they will lose, since technological change may eliminate jobs and destroy economic rents. These groups will fiercely resist attempts to eliminate constraints in their industries.

What then, if anything, can be done? Despite the inherent problems with removing barriers, some societies have managed to do just that. To understand the specific circumstances under which barriers to efficient use of technology were successfully reduced, it is instructive to examine the record on catching up in greater depth.

Successes

Several success stories of economic catching up exist. The United States, Western Europe, and parts of Asia provide some clear examples. In examining the experiences of these countries, Prescott and I came to the conclusion that the success of many countries is the result of being a free-trade club or a member of such a club. In our definition of a free-trade club, two conditions need to be met: Member states cannot impose tariffs and other restrictions on the import of goods and services from other member states, and member states must have a considerable degree of economic sovereignty apart from the collective entity.

A free-trade club reduces both a group's ability and its incentive to obtain the government's support in erecting barriers. It reduces a group's ability because as no single state is able to block the movement of goods between states, and as the collective entity cannot block the adoption of a superior technology in one of its member states, a group wanting the barrier must lobby each individual state's government. This increases the cost of erecting the barrier. It reduces the group's incentive because, as the size of the market and the price elasticity of demand for an industry's product are increased, the adoption of a more productive technology results in larger percentage increases in industry revenues and output. This means that employment and earnings of factor suppliers are less likely to be adversely affected by the adoption of a more productive technology.

The United States and Western Europe. The United States caught up with and surged past the United Kingdom in the 1865–1929 period because the United States was and continues to be a free-trade club. The individual state governments have a considerable degree of sovereign power over the federal government. Additionally, the Interstate Commerce Clause of the U.S. Constitution gives the federal government the right to regulate interstate commerce and prevent individual states from imposing tariffs and other restrictions on the import of goods and services.

Western Europe caught up with the United States in the 1973–1993 period because, with the creation of the European Union (EU), it became an equally important free-trade club. In fact, EU states enjoy even greater sovereignty than do U.S. member states. For instance, the German state cannot block Toyota's introduction of just-in-time production in Wales even though German politicians would do so if they could in response to domestic political pressure. If Toyota starts to gain market share, it

9   Merritt B. Fox and Michael A. Heller, "Corporate Governance Lessons from Russian Enterprise Fiascos," *New York University Law Review*, Vol. 75 (2000), pp. 1720–1780.

will not be long before the auto industry throughout Europe adopts the superior technology and, as a consequence, productivity in the automobile industry increases. This is competition at work.

The positive effect of belonging to a free-trade club can be seen in the labor productivity of EU and non-EU countries over time. Table 2A reports labor productivity, defined as output per work hour, for the original members of what became the EU and the labor productivity of members that joined in the 1970s and 1980s. Productivities are reported for an extended period before the EU was formed as well as for the period subsequent to its creation.

One striking fact is that prior to forming the EU, the original members had labor productivity that was only half that of the United States. This state of affairs persisted for over 60 years with no catching up. However, in the 36 years after forming what became the EU, the countries that signed the Treaty of Rome caught up with the United States in terms of labor productivity. As Prescott demonstrates, the factor leading to this catching up was an increase in the efficiency with which resources were used in production, not changes in capital/output ratios.[10] EU countries that joined the union in 1973 also caught up significantly in terms of productivity subsequent to joining.

Perhaps even more striking is the comparison between the original EU members and the set of Western European countries that either joined in 1995 or still have not joined. This latter set, labeled "Others" in Table 2B, consists of Switzerland, Austria, Finland, and Sweden. The important finding is that the original EU countries and the "Others" were equally productive in the pre–World War II period. However, in the 36 years from 1957 to 1993, the "Others" fell from 1.06 times as productive as the original EU countries to only 0.81 as productive. This constitutes strong empirical evidence that membership in a free-trade club fosters higher productivity.

Asia. The reasons for catching up in Asia are slightly more varied than the reasons for Europe. Countries such as South Korea, Taiwan, and Japan were forced to adopt policies that did not block efficient production as a condition for support from the United States. The recent catching up by China, however, is primarily a result of its having become a free-trade club.

The rapid development of China began in 1978 when the Chinese government became more decentralized, with much of the centralized planning system dismantled. Although the central government gave more power to regional governments, it did not give them the right to restrict the flow of goods across regions. In fact, as Alwyn Young reports, when individual regions attempted to erect trade barriers in the late 1980s and early 1990s, the central government immediately took steps to restore the

---

T Table 2A

EU Labor Productivity

Year	Original* EU Members (Percentage of U.S. Productivity)	Joined in 1973** (Percentage of U.S. Productivity)
1870	62%	-
1913	53%	-
1929	52%	-
1938	57%	-
1957	53%	57%
1973	78%	66%
1983	94%	76%
1993	102%	83%
2002	101%	85%

* Belgium, France, Italy, Luxembourg, Netherlands, and Germany.
** Ireland, United Kingdom, and Denmark.

Source: Stephen L. Parente and Edward C. Prescott, "What a Country Can Do to Catch Up to the Leader," in Leszek Balcerowicz and Stanley Fischer, eds., *Living Standards and the Wealth of Nations: Successes and Failures in Real Convergence* (Cambridge, Mass.: MIT Press, 2006), pp. 17–40.

---

10   Edward C. Prescott, "Prosperity and Depression," *American Economic Review,* Vol. 92, No. 2 (2002), pp. 1–15.

free flow of goods and services.[11] The resulting competition between businesses in different Chinese provinces led to rapid growth in living standards.

Failures

Russia. China's spectacular performance since its transition to capitalism stands in stark contrast to Russia's dismal performance since its transition to capitalism, going from 30 percent to 22 percent of U.S. income between 1985 and 1998. Unlike China, Russia does not belong to a free-trade club, as it remains economically isolated from Western Europe and its federation of states fails to comprise a free-trade club.

Local and regional governments in Russia have the power both to discriminate against producers from other member states operating within their borders and to restrict the flow of goods and people into and out of their regions. This power of local governments has been exercised quite frequently. They have, for example, prohibited exports of food goods from their regions and put in place price ceilings for many of those items. Additionally, they have used federal funds to subsidize inefficient producers in their regions and they have prevented the conversion of non-industrial structures for new commercial activity.

Latin America. Latin America has failed to catch up to the industrial leader, despite starting modern economic growth 100 years ago, because, like Russia, it has failed to develop into a free-trade club. There has been no free movement of goods and people between the set of relatively sovereign states.

The Washington Consensus, which is viewed by many participating countries as a failure, did not turn Latin America into a free-trade club. While the Washington Consensus did advocate liberalization and privatization as part of its 10-point plan, it did not bring about a significant reduction in barriers. According to the MGI, significant barriers still are in place in Brazil, for example. Furthermore, Sebastian

---

Table 2B

Labor Productivity of Other Western European Countries

Year	Other Countries* (Percentage of Original EU Members' Productivity)
1900	103%
1913	99%
1938	103%
1957	106%
1973	96%
1983	85%
1993	81%

* Switzerland, Austria, Finland, and Sweden.

Source: Stephen L. Parente and Edward C. Prescott, "What a Country Can Do to Catch Up to the Leader," in Leszek Balcerowicz and Stanley Fischer, eds., *Living Standards and the Wealth of Nations: Successes and Failures in Real Convergence* (Cambridge, Mass.: MIT Press, 2006), pp. 17–40.

Etchemendy documents that in Argentina, the government had to grant special-interest groups certain privileges to obtain concessions.[12]

Moreover, recent political developments, most notably in Venezuela, Ecuador, Argentina, and Brazil, seem to bear out that Latin America's desire to reform and increase competition was not serious. Unless reforms are seen as being permanent in nature, firms will not make the necessary investments to adopt more productive technology.

CONCLUSION

Will today's poor countries catch up with the industrial leaders, or will they forever lag behind? The answer is that *all* countries have the potential to become rich. Rapid catching up is possible; we have seen a number of countries do it in the past 50 years. China, for instance, is well on its way to becoming a rich industrialized country, and India is another country that has made important gains. Given that a third of the world's population lives in these two countries, their rapid economic success signals a

---

11   Alwyn Young, "The Razor's Edge: Distortions and Incremental Reform in the People's Republic of China," *Quarterly Journal of Economics*, Vol. 115 (2000), pp. 1091–1135.

12   Sebastian Etchemendy, "Constructing Reform Coalitions: The Politics of Compensation in Argentina's Liberalization," *Latin American Politics and Society*, Vol. 43, No. 3 (2001), pp. 1–35.

positive future. The admission of 12 new countries to the European Union is another positive development.

Yet the recent surge in anti-globalization and anti-trade sentiment and the return to state-owned enterprises in some countries are reasons to doubt that many nations will eliminate the gaps between themselves and the leaders any time soon. Regrettably, special-interest groups in numerous countries have succeeded in convincing the larger populace that greater integration in the world economy will make the national economy worse off.

There is absolutely no empirical support for this belief. On the contrary, empirical evidence supports integration as well as elimination of barriers as a way for rapid economic growth to occur in today's world. Allowing barriers in the form of work rules, zoning laws, government subsidies, international trade quotas, and other policies and regulations means continued unacceptable living standards for large numbers of people and ultimately a more divided and unequal world.

To eliminate such disparate relationships, poor countries need to embrace international competition in business and trade. As a first step toward this goal, unnecessary barriers that constrain technology and production processes need to be eliminated. Only then can all nations have the opportunity to flourish.

Chapter 3

Globalization Is Making the World a Better Place

Guy Sorman

What we call "globalization," one of the most powerful and positive forces ever to have arisen in the history of mankind, is redefining civilization as we know it. This is one of my hypotheses. To be more specific, I will try to describe what globalization is, its impact on world peace, and the freedom it brings from want, fear, and misery.

Globalization has six major characteristics: economic development, democracy, cultural enrichment, political and cultural norms, information, and internationalization of the rule of law.

ECONOMIC DEVELOPMENT

Usually, globalization is described in terms of intensified commercial and trade exchanges, but it is about more than just trade, stock exchanges, and currencies. It is about people. What is significant today is that through globalization many nations are converging toward enhanced welfare.

This convergence is exemplified by the 800 million people who, in the past 30 years, have left poverty and misery behind. They have greater access to health care, schooling, and information. They have more choices, and their children will have even more choices. The absolutely remarkable part is that it happened not by accident but through a combination of good economic policy, technology, and management.

Of course, not all nations are following this path, but since the fall of the Berlin Wall, more and more are coming closer. Only Africa's nations have yet to join, but who would have hoped and predicted 30 years ago that China and India, with such rapidity and efficiency, would pull their people out of misery? There is no reason why Africa, when its turn comes, will not do the same. Convergence should be a source of hope for us all.

DEMOCRACY

In general, since 1989, the best system to improve the welfare of all people—not only economically, but also in terms of access to equality and freedom—appears to be democracy, the new international norm. As more and more countries turn democratic or converge toward democratic norms, respect for other cultures increases.

Democracy has guaranteed welfare far better than any dictatorship ever could. Even enlightened despots cannot bring the kind of safety democracy is bringing. Sometimes a trade-off between economic allotment and democracy occurs. Sometimes the economy grows more slowly because of democracy. Let it be that way. Democracy brings values that are as important for the welfare of the human being as economy is.

After all, as history shows, the chance of international war diminishes step by step any time a country moves from tyranny to democracy, as democracies do not war against one other. That more and more nations are turning democratic improves everyone's way of life.

CULTURAL ENRICHMENT

Critics of globalization frequently charge that it results in an "Americanization of culture" and concomitant loss of identity and local cultural values. I would propose a more optimistic view, and that is that globalization leads to never-ending exchange of ideas, especially through popular culture, since it affects the greatest number of people.

Through popular culture, people from different backgrounds and nations discover one another, and their "otherness" suddenly disappears. For example, a popular Korean television sitcom now popular in Japan has shown its Japanese viewers that, like them, Koreans fall in love, feel despair, and harbor the same hopes and fears for themselves and for their children. This sitcom has transformed the image Japanese have of the Korean nation more profoundly than any number of diplomatic efforts and demonstrates that globalization can erode prejudices that have existed between neighboring countries for centuries.

Furthermore, this process of better understanding allows us to keep our identity and add new identities. The Koreans absorb a bit of the American culture, a bit of the French, a bit of other European societies. Perhaps they have become a different sort of Korean, but they remain Korean nonetheless. It is quite the illusion to think you can lose your identity. And it goes both ways. When you look at the success of cultural exports out of Korea—this so-called new wave through music, television, movies, and art—Korea becomes part of the identity of other people.

Now, as a Frenchman, I am a bit Korean myself. This is how globalization works. We do not lose our identity. We enter into the world that I call the world of multi-identity, and that is progress, not loss.

POLITICAL AND CULTURAL NORMS

One of the most significant transformations in terms of welfare for the people in the globalized world is the increased respect given to the rights of women and minorities. In many nations, to be a woman or to belong to a minority has not been easy. In the past 30 years, however, women and minorities everywhere have become better informed and have learned that the repression they suffered until very recently is not typical in a modern democracy.

Let us consider India, where a strong caste system historically has subjugated women and untouchables. Thanks to the globalization of democratic norms, these minorities are better protected; through various affirmative action policies, they can access the better jobs that traditionally were forbidden to them. This transformation has positive consequences for them, of course, and also creates better outcomes for their children's welfare and education. We are entering into a better world because of their improved status, thanks to the cultural and democratic exchanges generated by globalization.

INFORMATION

Through legacy media and, more and more, through the Internet and cellular phones, everyone today, even in authoritarian countries, is better informed. For one year, I lived in the poorest part of China, and I remember well how a farmer, in the most remote village, knew exactly what was happening not only in the next village, but also in Beijing and New York because of the Internet and his cellular phone. No government can stop information now. People know today that, as they say, "knowledge is power."

Now let us imagine if the genocide in Darfur had happened 20 or 30 years ago. The Darfur population would have been annihilated by the Sudanese government, and no one would have known. Today we all know about the genocide. The reason why the international community has been forced to intervene is because of the flood of information. Knowledge is proving to be the best protection for oppressed minorities and, thus, one of the most vital aspects of globalization.

INTERNATIONALIZATION OF THE RULE OF LAW

Internationalization of rule of law, of course, has limitations. The institutions in charge of this emerging rule of law, whether the United Nations or the World Trade Organization, are criticized. They are not completely legitimate. They are certainly not perfectly democratic, but you cannot build a democratic organization with non-democratic governments. It becomes a trade-off.

In spite of all the weaknesses of international organizations, the emergence of a real international rule of law replaces the pure barbarism that existed before, which had consisted of the most powerful against the weak. Even though globalization cannot suppress war, it is remarkably efficient at containing war. If you examine the kinds of wars we have today, compared to the history of mankind, the number of victims and number of nations involved are very few. We are all safer because of both this emerging rule of law and the flow of information provided by globalization.

INVENTED BY ENTREPRENEURS

We also need to remember that globalization is not some historical accident but has been devised and built by those who wanted it. Diplomats did not invent it. Entrepreneurs did.

Let us look at Europe. After World War II, the Europeans discovered that they had been their own worst enemies. For 1,000 years, we were fighting each other. Why? We do not remember very well. Every 30 years, we went to war. The French killed the Germans. The Germans killed the French. When you try to explain this history to your children, they cannot understand. Diplomats and politicians from the 18th century onward unsuccessfully made plans to avoid this kind of civil war within Europe.

Then, in the 1940s, a businessman came along named Jean Monnet. His business was to sell cognac in the United States, and he was very good at it. The idea Jean Monnet had was that perhaps the unification process of Europe should not be started by diplomats. Maybe it should be started by business people. He proceeded to build the European Union on a foundation of commerce. He started with coal and steel in 1950, and it was through the liberation of that trade that he conceived the unification of Europe, which has played a crucial role in the globalization process.

Monnet's guiding principle was that commercial and financial ties would lead to political unification. The true basis of European solidarity has come through trade. Through this method, all of the benefits of globalization have been made possible, because free trade has been at the root level. An attack on free trade is an attack on both globalization and the welfare of the peoples of the world, so we must be very cautious when we discuss trade, as it is the essential key allowing the rest to happen.

None of this is to imply that trade is easy. In the case of Europe, it was made easier because all of the governments were democratic. It is much more complicated to build free trade with non-democratic governments, but because globalization starts with the construction of this materialistic solidarity, ideals must come afterwards.

TWO THREATS TO GLOBALIZATION

Perhaps what I have presented so far is too optimistic a picture of globalization, but I believe we have good reason to be upbeat. However, there are two threats to globalization that may be taken too lightly today.

Global epidemics. In terms of health care, we are more and more able to cope with the current illnesses of the world. Though Africa still poses a problem, through global efforts it will be possible in the years to come to reduce the major epidemics there: AIDS and malaria.

But new epidemics are threatening the world. If we remember what happened in China some years ago with the SARS epidemic, which was very short, and then the avian flu threat in 2005, you understand that there are new threats somewhere out there and that the modern world is not really prepared. One of the consequences of globalization is that people travel more, which means that viruses travel more and adapt.

Therefore, I think globalization should require the international community to develop ever more sophisticated systems to detect and cure the new epidemics that have been a negative consequence of globalization.

Terrorism. Although wars these days are more limited, new forms of warfare have emerged, which we call terrorism. Terrorism today can seem like a distant menace somewhere between the United States and the Middle East. Because of the global progress of the rule of law, however, violent groups know that it is no longer possible to wage war in the traditional way; therefore, people driven by ideological passions are increasingly tempted by terrorist methods as a way of implementing their agenda.

Those are the true negative aspects of globalization: epidemics and terrorism. Regretfully, we are too focused on the traditional problems like free trade. We are not focused enough on the future threats.

I wish globalization were more popular, but it is our fault if it is not. Perhaps we should use different words. "Globalization" is ugly. We should find a better word, and we should try to explain to the media and students that we are entering into a new civilization of welfare, progress, and happiness, because if they do not understand the beauty of globalization, they will not stand up for it when it is threatened.

Chapter 4

Methodology: Measuring the 10 Economic Freedoms

William W. Beach and Tim Kane, Ph.D.

The *Index of Economic Freedom* is a simple average of 10 individual freedoms, each of which is vital to the development of personal and national prosperity. For centuries, great philosophers of liberty such as Locke and Montesquieu have recognized the fundamental right of property as a bulwark of free people. Over time, scholars and practitioners have likewise recognized many other pillars of economic liberty, including free trade, investment rights, and labor freedom.

As the first comprehensive study of economic freedom ever published, the 1995 *Index of Economic Freedom* defined a method of measuring and ranking such vastly different places as Hong Kong and North Korea. Some of the 10 freedoms are external in nature, measuring the extent of an economy's openness to investment or trade. Most are internal in nature, assessing the liberty of individuals to use their labor or finances without restraint.

Since 1995, the *Index* has grown and improved as other, similar studies have joined the effort. Each cross-country study offers a unique and profound contribution that has helped to shape the world being measured.[1]

DEFINING ECONOMIC FREEDOM

Economic freedom is that part of freedom that is concerned with the material autonomy of the individual in relation to the state and other organized groups. An individual is economically free who can fully control his or her labor and property. This economic component of human liberty is related to—and perhaps a necessary condition for—political freedom, but it is also valuable as an end in itself.

The authors of the *Index* perceive economic freedom as a positive concept, recognizing that

---

1   See, for example, James D. Gwartney and Robert A. Lawson with Russell S. Sobel and Peter T. Leeson, *Economic Freedom of the World, 2007 Annual Report* (Vancouver, B.C., Canada: Fraser Institute, 2007), and Richard E. Messick, *World Survey of Economic Freedom: 1995–1996* (New Brunswick, N.J.: Transaction Publishers, 1996).

its traditional definition as an *absence of government coercion or constraint* must also include a sense of liberty as distinct from anarchy. Governments are instituted to create basic protections against the ravages of nature so that positive economic rights such as property and contract are given social as well as individual defense against the destructive tendencies of others.

The definition of economic freedom therefore *encompasses all liberties and rights of production, distribution, or consumption of goods and services. The highest form of economic freedom provides an absolute right of property ownership; fully realized freedoms of movement for labor, capital, and goods; and an absolute absence of coercion or constraint of economic liberty beyond the extent necessary for citizens to protect and maintain liberty itself.* In other words, individuals are free to work, produce, consume, and invest in any way they please, and that freedom is both protected by the state and unconstrained by the state.

All government action involves coercion. Some minimal coercion is necessary for the citizens of a community or nation to defend themselves, promote the evolution of civil society, and enjoy the fruits of their labor. This Lockean idea is embodied in the U.S. Constitution. For example, citizens are taxed to provide revenue for the protection of person and property as well as for a common defense. Most political theorists also accept that certain goods—what economists call "public goods"—can be supplied more conveniently by government than through private means. Of particular interest are those economic freedoms that are also public goods, such as the maintenance of a police force to protect property rights, a monetary authority to maintain a sound currency, and an impartial judiciary to enforce contracts among parties.

When government coercion rises beyond the minimal level, however, it becomes corrosive to freedom—and the first freedom affected is economic freedom. Logically, an expansion of state power requires enforcement and therefore funding, which is extracted from the people. Exactly where that line is crossed is open to reasoned debate.

Throughout history, governments have imposed a wide array of constraints on economic activity. Constraining economic choice distorts and diminishes the production, distribution, and consumption of goods and services (including, of course, labor services).[2] The establishment of a price control is perhaps the clearest example of the distortionary effect of state coercion because of its well-known disruption of the equilibrium of supply and demand.

The 10 Economic Freedoms. Overall economic freedom, defined by multiple rights and liberties, can be quantified as an index of less abstract components. The index we conceive uses 10 specific freedoms, some as composites of even further detailed and quantifiable components. A detailed discussion of each of these factors and their component variables follows this overview.

- **Business freedom** is the ability to create, operate, and close an enterprise quickly and easily. Burdensome, redundant regulatory rules are the most harmful barriers to business freedom.
- **Trade freedom** is a composite measure of the absence of tariff and non-tariff barriers that affect imports and exports of goods and services.
- **Fiscal freedom** is a measure of the burden of government from the revenue side. It includes both the tax burden in terms of the top tax rate on income (individual and corporate separately) and the overall amount of tax revenue as a portion of gross domestic product (GDP).
- **Government size** is defined to include all government expenditures, including consumption and transfers. Ideally, the state will provide only true public goods, with an absolute minimum of expenditure.
- **Monetary freedom** combines a measure of

2   "The property which every man has in his own labour, as it is the original foundation of all other property, so it is the most sacred and inviolable." Adam Smith, *An Inquiry into the Nature and Causes of the Wealth of Nations* (New York: The Modern Library, 1937), pp. 121–122; first published in 1776.

price stability with an assessment of price controls. Both inflation and price controls distort market activity. Price stability without microeconomic intervention is the ideal state for the free market.

- **Investment freedom** is an assessment of the free flow of capital, especially foreign capital.
- **Financial freedom** is a measure of banking security as well as independence from government control. State ownership of banks and other financial institutions such as insurer and capital markets is an inefficient burden, and political favoritism has no place in a free capital market.
- **Property rights** is an assessment of the ability of individuals to accumulate private property, secured by clear laws that are fully enforced by the state.
- **Freedom from corruption** is based on quantitative data that assess the perception of corruption in the business environment, including levels of governmental legal, judicial, and administrative corruption.
- **Labor freedom** is a composite measure of the ability of workers and businesses to interact without restriction by the state.

Equal Weight. In the *Index of Economic Freedom*, all 10 factors are equally weighted in order not to bias the overall score toward any one factor or policy direction. As described earlier, economic freedom is an end in itself. The ability of economic freedom to establish a foundation for the rapid development of wealth for the average citizen explains contemporary interest, but it is not a valid rationale to weight some components over others. Nor would it be proper to weight the *Index* in a manner that caused the relation between democracy and economic freedom to be statistically stronger.

This is a common-sense approach. It is also consistent with the purpose of the *Index*: to reflect the balanced economic environment in every country surveyed. The *Index* has never been designed specifically to explain economic growth or any other dependent variable; that is ably done by empirical econometricians elsewhere.

Nor is it clear how the 10 economic freedoms interact. Is a minimum threshold for each one essential? Is it possible for one to maximize if others are minimized? Are they dependent or exclusive, complements or supplements? These are valid questions, but they are beyond the scope of our more fundamental mission. The *Index*, then, offers a simple composite based on an average of the 10 freedoms. It also offers the raw data for each factor so that others can study and weight and integrate as they see fit.

The Grading Scale. Each one of the 10 freedoms is graded using a 0 to 100 scale, where 100 represents the maximum freedom. A score of 100 signifies an economic environment or set of policies that is most conducive to economic freedom. The grading scale is continuous, meaning that scores with decimals are possible. For example, a country could have a trade freedom score of 50.3. Many of the 10 freedoms are based on quantitative data that are converted directly into a score. In the case of trade, a country with zero tariffs and zero non-tariff barriers will have a trade freedom score of 100. This will often be described using percent terminology.[3]

Period of Study. For the current *Index of Economic Freedom*, the authors generally examined data for the period covering the second half of 2006 through the first half of 2007. To the extent possible, the information considered for each factor was current as of June 30, 2007. It is important to understand, however, that some factors are based on historical information. For example, the monetary freedom factor is a three-year weighted average rate of inflation from January 1, 2004, to December 31, 2006.

Sources. In evaluating the criteria for each factor, the authors have used a range of authoritative sources. All sources are indicated in the narrative where appropriate. Because it would be unnecessarily cumbersome to cite all the sources used in scoring every single variable of each factor, unless otherwise noted, the major sources used in preparing the country

---

3   For detailed guidance on how the data in the *Index* can be used in statistical research, see *http://www.heritage.org/research/features/index/downloads.cfm#methodology*.

summaries may be found below, in the introduction to the country pages in Chapter 6, and in the list of Major Works Cited.

METHODOLOGY FOR THE 10 ECONOMIC FREEDOMS

Freedom #1: Business Freedom

Business freedom is a quantitative measure of the ability to start, operate, and close a business that represents the overall burden as well as the efficiency of government regulations. Regulations are a form of taxation that makes it difficult for entrepreneurs to create value.

Although many regulations hinder businesses, the most important are associated with licensing new companies and businesses. In some countries, as well as many states in the United States, the procedure for obtaining a business license can be as simple as mailing in a registration form with a minimal fee. In Hong Kong, for example, obtaining a business license requires filling out a single form, and the process can be completed in a few hours. In other countries, such as India and countries in parts of South America, the process involved in obtaining a business license requires endless trips to government offices and can take a year or more.

Once a business is open, government regulation does not always subside; in some cases, it increases. Interestingly, two countries with the same set of regulations can impose different regulatory burdens. If one country, for instance, applies its regulations evenly and transparently, it lowers the regulatory burden because it enables businesses to make long-term plans more easily. If the other applies regulations inconsistently, it raises the regulatory burden by creating an unpredictable business environment. Finally, regulations that make it difficult and expensive to close businesses are disincentives for entrepreneurs to start them in the first place.

Methodology. The business freedom score for each country is a number between 0 and 100 percent, with 100 equaling the freest business environment. The score is based on 10 components, all weighted equally, based on

objective data from the World Bank's *Doing Business* study:

- Starting a business—procedures (number);
- Starting a business—time (days);
- Starting a business—cost (% of income per capita);
- Starting a business—minimum capital (% of income per capita);
- Obtaining a license—procedures (number);
- Obtaining a license—time (days);
- Obtaining a license—cost (% of income per capita);
- Closing a business—time (years);
- Closing a business—cost (% of estate); and
- Closing a business—recovery rate (cents on the dollar).[4]

Each of these raw components is converted to a 0 to 100 scale, after which the average of the converted values is computed. The result represents the country's business freedom score. For example, even if a country requires the highest number of procedures for starting a business, which yields a score of zero in that component, it could still receive a score as high as 90 based on scores in the other nine components.

Norway, for example, has a business freedom score of 89.1 percent. Norway receives scores of 100 in seven of the 10 components.

Each component is converted to a 100 percent scale using the following equation:

$$Component\ Score_i = 50 \frac{component_{average}}{component_i}$$

which is based on the ratio of the country data for each component relative to the world average, multiplied by 50. For example, on average worldwide, there are 18.89 procedures to close a business. Norway's 14 procedures is a component value better than the average, resulting in a ratio of 1.349. That ratio multiplied by 50 equals the final component score of 67.4 percent. The average country will receive a component score

---

4   The recovery rate is a function of time and cost. However, the business freedom factor uses all three subvariables to emphasize closing a business, starting a business, and dealing with licenses equally.

of 50 percent, whereas a country's maximum component score is limited to 100 percent.

For the 11 countries that are not covered by the World Bank's *Doing Business* study, the business freedom factor is scored by looking into business regulations based on qualitative information from reliable and internationally recognized sources.[5]

The method for business freedom dates to 2006. From 1995–2005, we used a subjective assessment with a score of 1–5. Those earlier scores have been converted with a simple formula to make them comparable. Observations with the top score were converted to 100, the next best to 85, and so on. This conversion formula is different from the one used for other subjective factors because those other factors are not bridging to a new, data-driven methodology.

Sources. Unless otherwise noted, the authors used the following sources in determining business freedom scores, in order of priority: World Bank, *Doing Business 2008*; Economist Intelligence Unit, *Country Report* and *Country Profile*, 2004–2007; and U.S. Department of Commerce, *Country Commercial Guide*, 2004–2007.

Freedom #2: Trade Freedom

Trade restrictions can take the form of taxes on imports and exports (known as tariffs), quotas or outright bans on trade, and regulatory barriers. The degree to which government hinders access to and the free flow of foreign commerce can have a direct bearing on the ability of individuals to pursue their economic goals.

Tariffs increase the prices that local consumers pay for foreign imports, and these price distortions change incentives, often pulling producers away from specializing in some goods and toward the blocked goods. By interfering with comparative advantage, trade restrictions impede economic growth. Also, tariffs make local citizens poorer by raising prices. In many cases, trade limitations put advanced-technology products and services beyond the reach of local people, limiting their own productive development.

Methodology. The trade freedom score is based two inputs:

- The trade-weighted average tariff rate and
- Non-tariff barriers (NTBs).

Different imports entering a country can, and often do, face different tariffs. The weighted average tariff uses weights for each tariff based on the share of imports for each good. This is calculated by dividing the country's total tariff revenue by the total value of imports. Weighted average tariffs are a purely quantitative measure and account for the basic calculation of the score using the following equation:

$$TF_i = \frac{Tariff_{max} - Tariff_i}{Tariff_{max} - Tariff_{min}} - NTB_i$$

where Trade Freedom$_i$ represents the trade freedom in country i, Tariff$_{max}$ and Tariff$_{min}$ represent the upper and lower bounds for tariff rates, and Tariff$_i$ represents the weighted average tariff rate in country i. The minimum tariff is naturally zero, and the upper bound was set as 50 percent. An NTB penalty is then subtracted from the base score. The penalty of 5, 10, 15, or 20 percentage points is assigned according to the following scale:

- **20%**—NTBs are used extensively across many goods and services and/or act to impede a significant amount of international trade.
- **15%**—NTBs are widespread across many goods and services and/or act to impede a majority of potential international trade.
- **10%**—NTBs are used to protect certain goods and services and impede some international trade.
- **5%**—NTBs are uncommon, protecting few goods and services, and/or have very limited impact on international trade.
- **0%**—NTBs are not used as a means to limit international trade.

We determine the extent of NTBs in a country's trade policy regime using both qualitative and quantitative information. Restrictive rules

---

5   Eleven countries are not covered by the World Bank's *Doing Business* study: Bahamas, Bahrain, Barbados, Burma, Cuba, Cyprus, North Korea, Libya, Malta, Qatar, and Turkmenistan.

that hinder trade vary widely, and their overlapping and shifting nature makes it difficult to gauge their complexity. The categories of NTBs considered in our penalty include:

- Quantity restrictions—import quotas; export limitations; voluntary export restraints; import–export embargoes and bans; countertrade; etc.
- Price restrictions—antidumping duties; countervailing duties; border tax adjustments; variable levies/tariff rate quotas.
- Regulatory restrictions—licensing; domestic content and mixing requirements; SPSS; safety and industrial standards regulations; packaging, labeling, and trademark regulations; advertising and media regulations.
- Investment restrictions—exchange and other financial controls.
- Customs restrictions—advance deposit requirements; customs valuation procedures; customs classification procedures; customs clearance procedures.
- Direct government intervention—subsidies and other aids; government industrial policy and regional development measures; government-financed research and other technology policies; national taxes and social insurance; competition policies; immigration policies; government procurement policies; state trading, government monopolies, and exclusive franchises.

As an example, France received a trade freedom score of 81 percent, based on the weighted average tariff of 2.6 percent common to all EU countries. The tariff yields a base score 96 percent, but the existence of significant French NTBs reduces the nation's trade freedom score by 15 percentage points.

Gathering data on tariffs to make a consistent cross-country comparison can be a challenging task. Unlike data on inflation, for instance, countries do not report their weighted average tariff rate or simple average tariff rate every year; in some cases, the most recent time a country reported its tariff data could have been as far back as 1993. To preserve consistency in grading the trade policy factor, the authors have decided to use the most recently reported weighted average tariff rate for a country from our primary source. If another reliable source reports more updated information on the country's tariff rate, the authors note this fact and may review the grading of this factor if there is strong evidence that the most recently reported weighted average tariff rate is outdated.

The World Bank produces the world's most comprehensive and consistent information on weighted average applied tariff rates. When the weighted average applied tariff rate is not available, the authors use the country's average applied tariff rate; and when the country's average applied tariff rate is not available, the authors use the weighted average or the simple average of most favored nation (MFN) tariff rates.[6] The data for customs revenues and total imports may not be consolidated in just one source. In addition, in the very few cases in which data on duties and customs revenues are not available, the authors use data on international trade taxes instead.

In all cases, the authors clarify the type of data used and the different sources for those data in the corresponding write-up for the trade policy factor. Sometimes, when none of this information is available, the authors simply analyze the overall tariff structure and estimate an effective tariff rate.

Sources. Unless otherwise noted, the authors used the following sources to determine scores for trade policy, in order of priority: World Bank, *World Development Indicators 2007* and *Data on Trade and Import Barriers: Trends in Average Tariff for Developing and Industrial Countries 1981–2005*; World Trade Organization, *Trade Policy Reviews*, 1995–2007; Office of the U.S. Trade Representative, *2007 National*

---

6   The most favored nation tariff rate is the "normal," non-discriminatory tariff charged on imports of a good. In commercial diplomacy, exporters seek MFN treatment; that is, the promise that they will be treated as well as the most favored exporter. The MFN rule requires that the concession be extended to all other members of the World Trade Organization. MFN is now referred to as permanent normal trade relations (PNTR).

Trade Estimate Report on Foreign Trade Barriers; World Bank, *Doing Business 2008*; U.S. Department of Commerce, *Country Commercial Guide*, 2004–2007; Economist Intelligence Unit, *Country Report*, *Country Profile*, and *Country Commerce*, 2004–2007; and official government publications of each country.

Freedom #3: Fiscal Freedom

A government can impose fiscal burdens on economic activity by generating revenue for itself, primarily through taxation but also from debt that ultimately must be paid off through taxation. Fiscal freedom is a quantitative measure of these burdens in which lower taxation translates as a higher level of fiscal freedom. The *Index* methodology includes the top marginal tax rates on individual and corporate income, as well as a measure of total tax revenue as a portion of GDP.

The marginal tax rate confronting an individual is, in effect, the price paid for supplying the next economic effort or engagement in an entrepreneurial venture. What remains after the tax is subtracted are the rewards of the effort. The higher the price of effort or entrepreneurship, the lower the rewards—and the less often such effort will be undertaken. Higher tax rates interfere with the ability of individuals to pursue their goals in the marketplace.

While individual and corporate income tax rates are important to economic freedom, they are not a comprehensive measure of the tax burden. First, they do not include the many other taxes such as payroll, sales, and excise taxes, tariffs, and the value-added tax (VAT). One way to capture all taxation is to measure total government revenues from all forms of taxation as a percentage of total GDP.

Methodology. Fiscal freedom is composed of three quantitative components in equal measure:

- The top tax rate on individual income,
- The top tax rate on corporate income, and
- Total tax revenue as a percentage of GDP.

In scoring the fiscal freedom factor, each of these numerical variables is weighted equally as one-third of the factor. This equal weighting allows a country to achieve a score as high as 67 percent based on two of the components even if it receives a score of 0 percent on the third.

The economics of public finance are unambiguous on the effect of taxation, using simple supply and demand. A doubling of the tax rate quadruples the economic cost to society of lost market activity. This is known as deadweight loss because it is not value gained by government, but simply prosperity that is destroyed. This happens because the price wedge created by taxation separates optimal supply and demand and diminishes the quantity of goods exchanged. In the extreme, raising tax rates will decrease tax revenue itself, as famously demonstrated by the Laffer curve.

Therefore, the scoring of fiscal freedom is calculated with a quadratic cost function. Each of the component pieces of data is converted to a 100-point scale using this quadratic equation:

$$FF_{ij} = 100 - \alpha \left(Component_{ij}\right)^2$$

where Fiscal Freedom$(FF)_{ij}$ represents the fiscal freedom in country i for component j; Component$_{ij}$ represents the raw percentage value (a number between 0 and 100) in country i for component j; and α is a coefficient set equal to 0.03. The minimum score for each component is zero, which is not represented in the printed equation but was utilized because it means that no single high tax burden will make the other two components irrelevant.

As an example, the Bahamas has no tax on individual or corporate income, so two of the components equal 100. However, overall tax revenue from other forms of taxation are sizable. As a portion of GDP, tax revenue in the Bahamas is 19.6 percent, or 0.196, yielding a revenue component score below 86.4. When the three component freedoms are averaged together, you get the Bahamas' overall fiscal freedom score of 96.2 percent, one of the world's best fiscal freedom scores.

Sources. Unless otherwise noted, the authors used the following sources for information on taxation, in order of priority: Ernst & Young, *The Global Executive* and *Worldwide Corporate Tax*

Guide, 2006–2007; Deloitte, *Country Snapshot*, 2006–2007, and *Corporate Tax Rates at a Glance*; International Monetary Fund, Staff Country Report, *Selected Issues and Statistical Appendix*, 2004–2007; investment agencies; and other governmental authorities (embassy confirmations and/or the country's treasury or tax authority).

For information on tax revenue as a percentage of GDP, the authors' primary sources were Organisation for Economic Co-operation and Development data (for member countries); African Development Bank; International Monetary Fund, Staff Country Report, *Selected Issues and Statistical Appendix*, 2004 to 2007; Asian Development Bank, *Key Indicators of Developing Asian and Pacific Countries 2006*; official government publications of each country; and individual contacts from government agencies and multinational organizations such as the IMF and World Bank.

Freedom #4: Government Size

The burden of excessive government is a central issue in economic freedom, both in terms of generating revenue (see fiscal freedom) and in terms of expenditure. This factor considers the level of government expenditures as a percentage of GDP. Government expenditures, including consumption and transfers, account for the entire score. Due to the inconsistent quality and availability of data on revenue generated by state-owned enterprises, that variable is no longer considered, and previous years' scores were adjusted to reflect this methodological refinement.

Government expenditures are often justified in terms of "public goods" that are provided efficiently by the state rather than by the market. There is also a justification for correcting market failures through government action. Economists recognize another kind of systemic failure as well: a tendency for government failure whereby the state becomes inefficient, bureaucratic, and even harmful to productivity. Government expenditures necessarily compete with private agents and interfere in market prices by overstimulating demand and potentially diverting resources through a crowding-out effect. In extreme cases, governments can coerce goods and capital out of markets altogether, driving up interest rates and inflation. Distortions in markets occur whenever the purpose of the government's expenditure is to acquire resources for the government's own purposes (government consumption) or for transfer payments.

It is understood that some level of government expenditures represents true public goods, implying an ideal level greater than zero. However, identifying that ideal level seems too arbitrary, static, and difficult to apply universally. For these reasons, the methodology treats zero government spending as the benchmark. Moreover, governments that have no public goods will be penalized by lower scores in the other factors (such as property rights and financial freedom).

The scale for scoring government size is non-linear, which means that government spending that is close to zero is lightly penalized, while levels of government exceeding 30 percent of GDP receive much worse scores in a quadratic fashion (e.g., doubling spending yields four times less freedom), so that only really large governments receive very low scores.

The government's appetite for private resources affects both economic freedom and economic growth. Even if a state-managed economy achieves fast growth through heavy expenditure, it diminishes freedom in the process and can create long-term damage to a country's growth potential.

Methodology. Scoring of the government size factor is based on government expenditures as a percentage of GDP. The following non-linear quadratic cost function is used to calculate the expenditures score:

$$GE_i = 100 - \alpha \left(Expenditures_i \right)^2$$

where GE_i represents the government expenditure score in country I; $Expenditures_i$ represents the total amount of government spending at all levels as a portion of GDP (between 0 and 100); and α is a coefficient to control for variation among scores (set at 0.03). The minimum component score is zero.

In most cases, general government expenditure data include all levels of government:

federal, state, and local. In cases where general government spending data are not available, data on central government expenditure are used instead.

Sources. Unless otherwise noted, the authors used the following sources for information on government intervention in the economy, in order of priority: World Bank, *World Development Indicators*, 2006 and 2007, and *Country at a Glance* tables; official government publications of each country; Economist Intelligence Unit, *Country Report* and *Country Profile*, 2004–2007; Organisation for Economic Co-operation and Development data (for member countries); African Development Bank, *Selected Statistics on African Countries 2007*; International Monetary Fund, Staff Country Report, *Selected Issues and Statistical Appendix*, 2002–2007; Asian Development Bank, *Key Indicators 2006*; and U.S. Department of Commerce, *Country Commercial Guide*, 2005–2007.

Freedom #5: Monetary Freedom

Monetary freedom is to market economics what free speech is to democracy. Free people need a steady and reliable currency as a medium of exchange and store of value. Without monetary freedom, it is difficult to create long-term value.

A country's currency is controlled largely by its government's monetary policy. With a monetary policy that endeavors to maintain stability, people can rely on market prices for the foreseeable future. Investment, savings, and other longer-term plans are easier to make, and individuals enjoy greater economic freedom. Inflation not only confiscates wealth like an invisible tax, but also distorts pricing, misallocates resources, raises the cost of doing business, and undermines a free society.

There is no singularly accepted theory of the right monetary institutions for a free society. At one time, the gold standard enjoyed widespread support, but this is no longer the case. What characterizes almost all monetary theorists today, however, is support for low inflation and an independent central bank. There is a powerful consensus among economists that price controls corrupt market efficiency and

that measured inflation in the face of widespread price controls is essentially impossible since the price signal can no longer equate supply and demand.

Methodology. The score for the monetary freedom factor is based on two components:

- The weighted average inflation rate for the most recent three years and
- Price controls.

The weighted average inflation rate for the most recent three years serves as the primary input into an equation that generates the base score for monetary freedom. The extent of price controls is then assessed as a penalty of up to 20 percentage points subtracted from the base score. The two equations used to convert inflation into the policy score for a given year are:

$$WAI_i = \Theta_1 Inflation_{it} + \Theta_2 Inflation_{it-1} + \Theta_3 Inflation_{it-2}$$

$$MF_i = 100 - \alpha\sqrt{WAI_i} - PC_i$$

where θ_1 through θ_3 (thetas 1–3) represent three numbers that sum to 1 and are exponentially smaller in sequence (in this case, values of 0.665, 0.245, and 0.090, respectively); $Inflation_{it}$ is the absolute value of the annual inflation rate in country i during year t as measured by the consumer price index; α represents a coefficient that stabilizes the variance of scores; and the PC penalty is an assigned value of 0–20 percentage points based on the extent of price controls. The convex (square root) functional form was chosen to create separation among countries with low inflation rates; 128 of 161 countries had weighted average inflation under 10 percent in absolute value. A concave functional form would essentially treat all hyperinflations as equally bad, whether they were annual price increases of 100 percent or 100,000 percent, whereas the square root provides much more gradation. The α coefficient is set to equal 6.333, which converts a 10 percent inflation rate into a freedom score of 80.0 and a 2 percent inflation rate into a score of 91.0.

Sources. Unless otherwise noted, the authors used the following sources for data on monetary policy, in order of priority: International Monetary Fund, *International Financial Statistics On-line*; International Monetary Fund, *2007 World Economic Outlook*; and Economist Intelligence Unit, *Country Report*, 1999–2007, and *Country Profile*, 2004–2007.

Freedom #6: Investment Freedom

Restrictions on foreign investment limit the inflow of capital and thus limit economic freedom. By contrast, the presence of few or no restrictions on foreign investment enhances economic freedom because foreign investment provides funds for economic expansion. By its nature, capital will flow to its best use where it is most needed and the returns are greatest. State action to redirect the flow of capital is an imposition on both the freedom of the investor and the people seeking capital. For this factor, the more restrictions a country imposes on foreign and domestic investment, the lower its level of economic freedom.

Methodology. This factor scrutinizes each country's policies toward foreign investment, as well as its policies toward capital flows internally, in order to determine its overall investment climate. The authors assess all countries using the same rubric.

Questions examined include whether there is a foreign investment code that defines the country's investment laws and procedures; whether the government encourages foreign investment through fair and equitable treatment of investors; whether there are restrictions on access to foreign exchange; whether foreign firms are treated the same as domestic firms under the law; whether the government imposes restrictions on payments, transfers, and capital transactions; and whether specific industries are closed to foreign investment.

The following criteria are used:

- **100%**—Foreign investment (FI) is encouraged and treated the same as domestic investment, with a simple and transparent FI code and a professional, efficient bureaucracy. There are no restrictions in sectors related to national security or real estate. No expropriation is allowed. Both residents and non-residents have access to foreign exchange and may conduct international payments. Transfers or capital transactions face no restrictions.
- **90%**—Same as above with the following exceptions: There are very few restrictions on FI in sectors related to national security. There are legal guarantees against expropriation of property. Transfers or capital transactions are subject to virtually no restrictions.
- **80%**—Same as above with the following exceptions: A transparent FI code is subject to minimal bureaucratic or other informal impediments. There are very few restrictions on foreign exchange. Transfers or capital transactions are subject to very few restrictions.
- **70%**—Same as above with the following exceptions: There are some restrictions on FI through general rules or in a few sectors such as utilities, natural resources, or national security. There are a few restrictions on access to foreign exchange or the ability to conduct international payments.
- **60%**—Same as above with the following exceptions: FI is generally encouraged but may not receive equal treatment in a few sectors. The FI code is somewhat non-transparent, and/or FI faces bureaucratic impediments. Expropriation of property is highly unlikely, and the government guarantees compensation. Transfers or capital transactions are subject to some restrictions.
- **50%**—Same as above with the following exceptions: Foreign investors face restrictions on their ability to purchase real estate. All investors face bureaucratic impediments and corruption. Residents and/or non-residents face some restrictions on access to foreign exchange or their ability to conduct international payments. Transfers or capital transactions are subject to obvious restrictions.
- **40%**—Same as above with the following exceptions: FI is somewhat restricted, the FI code is somewhat discriminatory, and FI is restricted outright in some sectors. Expropriation of property is rare. Transfers and capital transactions are subject to significant restrictions.

- **30%**—Same as above with the following exceptions: FI is significantly restricted, the FI code is discriminatory, and foreign investors may purchase real estate only in limited circumstances. All investors face significant bureaucratic impediments and corruption. Residents and non-residents face strict restrictions on access to foreign exchange, and the government imposes many controls on international payments.
- **20%**—Same as above with the following exceptions: FI is discouraged and prohibited in many sectors, the FI code is discriminatory, and the approval process is opaque and subject to widespread corruption. Few sectors are open to FI. Expropriation of property is common. The government imposes extensive controls on international payments, transfers, and capital transactions.
- **10%**—Same as above with the following exceptions: Foreign investors may not purchase real estate. The government controls or prohibits most international payments, transfers, and capital transactions.
- **0%**—Same as above with the following exceptions: FI is prohibited, foreigners may not own real estate, and the government prohibits international payments, transfers, and capital transactions.

Sources. Unless otherwise noted, the authors used the following sources for data on capital flows and foreign investment, in order of priority: International Monetary Fund, *Annual Report on Exchange Arrangements and Exchange Restrictions*, 2006 and 2007; official government publications of each country; Economist Intelligence Unit, *Country Commerce*, *Country Profile*, and *Country Report*, 2005–2007; Office of the U.S. Trade Representative, *2007 National Trade Estimate Report on Foreign Trade Barriers*; and U.S. Department of Commerce, *Country Commercial Guide*, 2005–2007.

Freedom #7: Financial Freedom

In most countries, banks provide the essential financial services that facilitate economic growth. They lend money to start businesses, purchase homes, and secure credit for the purchase of durable consumer goods, and they furnish a safe place in which individuals can store their savings. Greater direct control of banks by government is a threat to these functions because government interference can introduce inefficiencies and outright corruption. Heavy bank regulation reduces opportunities and restricts economic freedom; therefore, the more a government restricts its banking sector, the lower its economic freedom score will be.

It should be noted that virtually all countries provide some type of prudential supervision of banks and other financial services. This supervision serves two major purposes: ensuring the safety and soundness of the financial system and ensuring that financial services firms meet basic fiduciary responsibilities. Ultimately, this task falls under a government's duty to enforce contracts and protect its citizens against fraud by requiring financial institutions to publish their financial statements and relevant data, verified by independent audit, so that borrowers, depositors, and other financial actors can make informed choices.

In a free banking environment, the marketplace should be the primary source of protection through such institutions as independent auditors and information services. Such oversight is distinguished from burdensome or intrusive government regulation or government ownership of banks, both of which interfere with market provision of financial services to consumers. It is such government intervention in the market, not the market itself, that limits economic freedom and causes a country's grade for this factor to be worse than it might otherwise be.

Increasingly, the central role played by banks is being complemented by other financial services that offer alternative means for raising capital or diversifying risk. As a result, the authors take related non-banking financial services, such as insurance and securities, into consideration when grading this factor. As with the banking system, aside from basic provisions to enforce contractual obligations and prevent fraud, increased government intervention in these areas undermines economic freedom and inhibits the ability of non-banking financial services to contribute to economic growth. If the government intervenes in the stock market, it contravenes the choices of millions of individuals by interfering with the pricing of capital—the most critical function of a market economy. Equity markets measure, on a continual basis, the expected profits and losses in publicly held companies. This measurement is essential in allocating capital resources to their highest-valued uses and thereby satisfying consumers' most urgent requirements. Similarly, government ownership or intervention in the insurance sector undermines the ability of providers to make available those services at prices based on risk and market conditions.

Methodology. The financial freedom factor measures the relative openness of each country's banking and financial system. The authors score this factor by determining the extent of government regulation of financial services; the extent of state intervention in banks and other financial services; the difficulty of opening and operating financial services firms (for both domestic and foreign individuals); and government influence on the allocation of credit. The authors use this analysis to develop a description of the country's financial climate and assign it an overall score between 0 percent and 100 percent.

The following criteria are used in determining a country's score for this factor:

- **100%—Negligible government influence.** Independent central bank supervision and regulation of financial institutions are limited to enforcing contractual obligations and preventing fraud. Credit is allocated on market terms. The government does not own financial institutions. Financial institutions may engage in all types of financial services. Banks are free to issue competitive notes, extend credit and accept deposits, and conduct operations in foreign currencies. Foreign financial institutions operate freely and are treated the same as domestic institutions.
- **90%—Minimal government influence.** Same as above with the following exceptions: Independent central bank supervision and regulation of financial institutions are minimal but

may extend beyond enforcing contractual obligations and preventing fraud.
- **80%—Nominal government influence.** Same as above with the following exceptions: Independent central bank supervision and regulation are straightforward and transparent but extend beyond enforcing contractual obligations and preventing fraud. Government ownership of financial institutions is a small share of overall sector assets. Financial institutions face almost no restrictions on their ability to offer financial services.
- **70%—Limited government influence.** Same as above with the following exceptions: Credit allocation is slightly influenced by the government, and private allocation of credit faces almost no restrictions. Foreign financial institutions are subject to few restrictions.
- **60%—Significant government influence.** Same as above with the following exceptions: The central bank is not fully independent, its supervision and regulation of financial institutions are somewhat burdensome, and its ability to enforce contracts and prevent fraud is insufficient. The government exercises active ownership and control of financial institutions with a significant share of overall sector assets. The ability of financial institutions to offer financial services is subject to some restrictions.
- **50%—Considerable government influence.** Same as above with the following exceptions: Credit allocation is significantly influenced by the government, and private allocation of credit faces significant barriers. The ability of financial institutions to offer financial services is subject to significant restrictions. Foreign financial institutions are subject to some restrictions.
- **40%—Strong government influence.** Same as above with the following exceptions: The central bank is subject to government influence, its supervision and regulation of financial institutions are heavy, and its ability to enforce contracts and prevent fraud is weak. The government exercises active ownership and control of financial institutions with a large minority share of overall sector assets.
- **30%—Extensive government influence.** Same as above with the following exceptions:

Credit allocation is extensively influenced by the government. The government owns or controls a majority of financial institutions or is in a dominant position. Financial institutions are heavily restricted, and bank formation faces significant barriers. Foreign financial institutions are subject to significant restrictions.

- **20%—Heavy government influence.** Same as above with the following exceptions: The central bank is not independent, and its supervision and regulation of financial institutions are repressive. Foreign financial institutions are discouraged or highly constrained.
- **10%—Near repressive.** Same as above with the following exceptions: Credit allocation is controlled by the government. Bank formation is restricted. Foreign financial institutions are prohibited.
- **0%—Repressive.** Same as above with the following exceptions: Supervision and regulation are designed to prevent private financial institutions. Private financial institutions are prohibited.

Sources. Unless otherwise noted, the authors used the following sources for data on banking and finance, in order of priority: Economist Intelligence Unit, *Country Commerce*, *Country Profile*, and *Country Report*, 2005–2007; official government publications of each country; U.S. Department of Commerce, *Country Commercial Guide*, 2005–2007; Office of the U.S. Trade Representative, *2007 National Trade Estimate Report on Foreign Trade Barriers*; and World Bank, *World Development Indicators 2007*.

Freedom #8: Property Rights

The ability to accumulate private property is the main motivating force in a market economy, and the rule of law is vital to a fully functioning free-market economy. Secure property rights give citizens the confidence to undertake commercial activities, save their income, and make long-term plans because they know that their income and savings are safe from expropriation. This factor examines the extent to which the government protects private property by enforcing the laws, as well as the extent

to which private property is safe from expropriation. The less protection private property receives, the lower a country's level of economic freedom and the lower its score.

Methodology. This factor scores the degree to which a country's laws protect private property rights and the degree to which its government enforces those laws. It also assesses the likelihood that private property will be expropriated and analyzes the independence of the judiciary, the existence of corruption within the judiciary, and the ability of individuals and businesses to enforce contracts. The less certain the legal protection of property, the lower a country's score; similarly, the greater the chances of government expropriation of property, the lower a country's score.

The authors grade each country according to the following criteria:

- **100%**—Private property is guaranteed by the government. The court system enforces contracts efficiently and quickly. The justice system punishes those who unlawfully confiscate private property. There is no corruption or expropriation.
- **90%**—Private property is guaranteed by the government. The court system enforces contracts efficiently. The justice system punishes those who unlawfully confiscate private property. Corruption is nearly nonexistent, and expropriation is highly unlikely.
- **80%**—Private property is guaranteed by the government. The court system enforces contracts efficiently but with some delays. Corruption is minimal, and expropriation is highly unlikely.
- **70%**—Private property is guaranteed by the government. The court system is subject to delays and is lax in enforcing contracts. Corruption is possible but rare, and expropriation is unlikely.
- **60%**—Enforcement of property rights is lax and subject to delays. Corruption is possible but rare, and the judiciary may be influenced by other branches of government. Expropriation is unlikely.
- **50%**—The court system is inefficient and subject to delays. Corruption may be present,

and the judiciary may be influenced by other branches of government. Expropriation is possible but rare.

- **40%**—The court system is highly inefficient, and delays are so long that they deter the use of the court system. Corruption is present, and the judiciary is influenced by other branches of government. Expropriation is possible.
- **30%**—Property ownership is weakly protected. The court system is highly inefficient. Corruption is extensive, and the judiciary is strongly influenced by other branches of government. Expropriation is possible.
- **20%**—Private property is weakly protected. The court system is so inefficient and corrupt that outside settlement and arbitration is the norm. Property rights are difficult to enforce. Judicial corruption is extensive. Expropriation is common.
- **10%**—Private property is rarely protected, and almost all property belongs to the state. The country is in such chaos (for example, because of ongoing war) that protection of property is almost impossible to enforce. The judiciary so corrupt that property is not protected effectively. Expropriation is common.
- **0%**—Private property is outlawed, and all property belongs to the state. People do not have the right to sue others and do not have access to the courts. Corruption is endemic.

Sources. Unless otherwise noted, the authors used the following sources for information on property rights, in order of priority: Economist Intelligence Unit, *Country Commerce*, 2005–2007; U.S. Department of Commerce, *Country Commercial Guide*, 2005–2007; U.S. Department of State, *Country Reports on Human Rights Practices*, 2005–2007; and U.S. Department of State, *Investment Climate Statements 2007*.

Freedom #9: Freedom from Corruption

Corruption is defined as dishonesty or decay. In the context of governance, it can be defined as the failure of integrity in the system, a distortion by which individuals are able to gain personally at the expense of the whole. Political corruption is a sad part of human history and manifests itself in many forms such as bribery, extortion, nepotism, cronyism, patronage, embezzlement, and (most commonly) graft, whereby public officials steal or profit illegitimately from public funds.

Corruption infects all parts of an economy unless the market is allowed to develop transparency and effective policing. As a general rule, a higher level of corruption equates to a greater corrosion of economic freedom, although this may not hold in extreme cases. "In some circumstances," notes Harvard economist Robert Barro, "corruption may be preferable to honest enforcement of bad rules. For example, outcomes may be worse if a regulation that prohibits some useful economic activity is thoroughly enforced rather than circumvented through bribes."[7]

Many societies, of course, outlaw such activities as trafficking in illicit drugs, but others frequently limit individual liberty by outlawing such activities as private transportation and construction services. A government regulation or restriction in one area may create an informal market in another. For example, a country with high barriers to trade may have laws that protect its domestic market and prevent the import of foreign goods, but these barriers create incentives for smuggling and an informal market for the barred products.

Methodology. This factor relies on Transparency International's Corruption Perceptions Index (CPI), which measures the level of corruption in 152 countries, to determine the freedom from corruption scores of countries that are also listed in the *Index of Economic Freedom*.

The CPI is based on a 10-point scale in which a score of 10 indicates very little corruption and a score of 1 indicates a very corrupt government. In scoring freedom from corruption, the authors convert each of these raw CPI data to a 0 to 100 scale by multiplying the CPI score by 10. For example, if a country's raw CPI data score is 5.5, its overall freedom from corruption score is 55.

---

7   Robert J. Barro, "Rule of Law, Democracy, and Economic Performance," Chapter 2 in Gerald P. O'Driscoll, Jr., Kim R. Holmes, and Melanie Kirkpatrick, *2000 Index of Economic Freedom* (Washington, D.C.: The Heritage Foundation and Dow Jones & Company, Inc., 2000), p. 36.

For countries that are not covered in the CPI, the freedom from corruption score is determined by using the qualitative information from internationally recognized and reliable sources. This procedure considers the extent to which corruption prevails in a country. The higher the level of corruption, the lower the level of overall economic freedom and the higher a country's score.

Sources. Unless otherwise noted, the authors used the following sources for information on corruption, in order of priority: Transparency International, *Corruption Perceptions Index*, 2002, 2004, 2005, and 2006; U.S. Department of Commerce, *Country Commercial Guide*, 2004–2007; Economist Intelligence Unit, *Country Commerce, Country Profile*, and *Country Report*, 2004–2007; Office of the U.S. Trade Representative, *2007 National Trade Estimate Report on Foreign Trade Barriers*; and official government publications of each country.

Freedom #10: Labor Freedom

Labor policy has been a key variable in the *Index of Economic Freedom* since its inception in 1995 as part of the wages and prices factor as well as the regulation factor. However, coverage of labor market flexibility in the previous methodology was limited by the lack of data on labor regulation that were available across countries in a consistent manner.

In light of the growing importance of labor market flexibility in today's economy and the increased availability of consistent labor policy data across countries, the 2007 *Index* adopted an independent labor freedom factor that is designed to measure countries' labor market regulations more adequately.

Methodology. The labor freedom factor is a quantitative factor based on objective data from the World Bank's *Doing Business* study. It provides reliable cross-country data on regulations concerning minimum wages, laws inhibiting layoffs, severance requirements, and measurable regulatory burdens on hiring, hours, and so on.

Specifically, four quantitative components are equally weighted as 25 percent of the labor freedom factor:

- Minimum wage,
- Rigidity of hours,
- Difficulty of firing redundant employees, and
- Cost of firing redundant employees.

The minimum wage component is basically a single quantitative measure: each country's mandatory minimum wage as a percentage of the average value added per worker. A higher minimum wage makes hiring unskilled workers more difficult.

Rigidity of hours is an index measure, calculated by *Doing Business*, that includes five components:

(i) whether night work is unrestricted; (ii) whether weekend work is unrestricted; (iii) whether the workweek can consist of 5.5 days; (iv) whether the workweek can extend to 50 hours or more (including overtime) for 2 months a year; and (v) whether paid annual vacation is 21 working days or fewer.[8]

Difficulty of firing is also an index measure calculated by *Doing Business*. It represents a simple issue: whether employers have the legal authority to lay off workers efficiently, or whether that act has to be justified to the government or third parties. It has eight components:

(i) whether redundancy is disallowed as a basis for terminating workers; (ii) whether the employer needs to notify a third party (such as a government agency) to terminate 1 redundant worker; (iii) whether the employer needs to notify a third party to terminate a group of more than 20 redundant workers; (iv) whether the employer needs approval from a third party to terminate 1 redundant worker; (v) whether the employer needs approval from a third party to terminate a group of more than 20

---

8   World Bank, *Doing Business 2007: How to Reform*, p. 81.

redundant workers; (vi) whether the law requires the employer to consider reassignment or retraining options before redundancy termination; (vii) whether priority rules apply for redundancies; and (viii) whether priority rules apply for reemployment.[9]

The cost of firing is a composite of three quantitative subcomponents related to dismissals: the legally mandated notice period, mandatory severance pay, and a penalty the employer must pay when dismissing a worker.

In constructing the labor freedom score, each of the four components is converted to a 0 to 100 scale, based on the following equation:

$$Component\ Score_i = 50\frac{component_{average}}{component_i}$$

where country i data are calculated relative to the world average and then multiplied by 50. The average country will receive a component score of 50 percent, whereas a country's maximum component score is limited to 100 percent. The four component scores are then averaged for each country, yielding a labor freedom score.

As an example, the imaginary country Indexia has an average minimum wage as a ratio of the average wage of 0.62, which is almost double the average of 0.32 globally, yielding a component score of roughly 25 percent. Yet Indexia's overall score is 44 percent, because the other three components scored much better.

The simple average of the converted values for these four variables is computed for the country's labor freedom score. For example, even if a country has the worst rigidity of hours in the world, with a zero score for the component, it could still get a score as high as 75 based on the other three components.

For the 11 countries that are not covered by the World Bank's *Doing Business* study, the labor freedom factor is scored by looking into labor market flexibility based on qualitative

information from other reliable and internationally recognized sources.[10]

Sources. Unless otherwise noted, the authors relied on the following sources for data on labor freedom, in order of priority: World Bank, *Doing Business 2008*; Economist Intelligence Unit, *Country Report* and *Country Profile*, 2004–2007; and U.S. Department of Commerce, *Country Commercial Guide*, 2004–2007.

CONTINUITY AND CHANGE

With over a decade's experience measuring freedom in over 100 nations annually, two issues regularly challenge our methodology.

The first challenge has to do with outdated data. Country data in the most up-to-date sources are often behind by years. Also, countries often make policy changes during the year of grading. Sometimes the policy changes are not reflected in official data, and sometimes the changes are proposed but not made law, or are made law but not enforced. Additionally, a country can experience a violent conflict or catastrophe that interrupts all efforts to measure the economy.

The second challenge is the balance between quality and consistency of the *Index* itself. The authors aim for methodological consistency from one year to the next, balanced against opportunities to incorporate new data and methods that improve the quality of the current year's scores.

Most Current Information. Analyzing economic freedom annually permits the authors of the *Index* to include the most recent information as it becomes available country by country. A cutoff date is utilized so that all countries are treated fairly. As described above, the period of study for the current year's *Index* considers all information as of the last day of June of the previous year (June 30, 2007). Any changes in law effective after that date have no positive or negative impact; nor do new constitutions, election results, or democratic initiatives.

Occasionally, because the *Index* is published several months after the cutoff date for evaluation, recent economic events cannot be factored

---

9   *Ibid.*

10   See note 5.

into the scores. In the past, such occurrences have been uncommon and isolated to one region of the world. The Asian financial crisis, for example, erupted at the end of 1997 just as the *1998 Index of Economic Freedom* was going to print. The policy changes in response to that crisis therefore were not considered in that year's scoring, but they were included in the next year's scores.

Changes in government policy are occurring at a rapid rate in many less-developed countries. The *Index of Economic Freedom*, because it is published each year, enables readers around the world to see how recent changes in government policy affect economic freedom in specific countries. Each country page includes a time-series graph of the country's overall score for each year from the present back to 1995.

Continuity. Ideally, the methodology used for the *Index of Economic Freedom* should not change over time. Instead, the scores for various countries would improve as the institutions of freedom improved as measured against a constant standard of measurable liberty. However, the increased quality of data available allows researchers to create more detailed measures of institutions as well as economic performance. The happy consequence of progress is an enhanced ability to measure progress.

Over time, therefore, the *Index of Economic Freedom* has been continually revised and improved; but we also aim for continuity, so each time a methodology change is implemented, we also attempt to make the scores continuous back to 1995. In this way, country performance from one year to the next is comparable.

Nevertheless, there are still some cases for which new data are not available going back to the first year, at least not in the same level of detail. There is a natural tension between the quality of the *Index* and the continuity of the *Index*. It would be easy to maintain perfect continuity if no changes were ever made, or vice versa, but we are committed to incorporating innovations into the methodology to optimize both the quality and continuity of the *Index* rather than simply maximizing one at the expense of the other.

It is important to remember that the *Index* has been an effort to quantify subjective factors, not the measure of a singular, natural data-generating process (such as temperature). It is a policy tool with uses for current-year analysis and time-series analysis.

This year, changes in the *Index* methodology include:

- **Rescaling** the business freedom scores from 1995–2005 in order to make them comparable as a time series with the new methodology in place for 2006–2008;
- **Revising** last year's business freedom and labor freedom scores to reflect revisions to the World Bank *Doing Business* data;
- **Enhancing** the detail and process used to measure non-tariff barriers (NTBs) and extending that approach back to 1995;
- **Updating** the coefficients used in the equations for two factors—government size and fiscal freedom—to align them with each other and with the other eight freedoms; and
- **Adding** new data from Transparency International for earlier years back to 1997.

All of these changes are minor and aim simply to improve the internal and time consistency of the *Index*.

Chapter 5

Economic Freedom in Five Regions

James M. Roberts and Anthony B. Kim

The average global economic freedom score is 60.3, according to our 2008 *Index* assessment. In the years since the 1995 *Index*, global economic freedom has improved by 2.6 percentage points and has held steady despite slow progress in the past few years. The varying degrees of commitment to economic freedom over the past decade in the five major regions of the world have resulted in mixed trends within individual regions' pursuit of greater economic freedom.

This chapter provides snapshots of economic freedom indicators at the aggregated regional level for each of the five geographic regions.

☎ Table 1

2008 Economic Freedom and Performance by Region

	Average Economic Freedom Score		Population	GDP per Capita (PPP)*	GDP 5-Year Growth Rate*	Unemployment Rate*	Inflation Rate*
	Simple	Weighted*					
Asia–Pacific	58.7	54.4	3,616,976,439	$6,361	7.6	6.3	5.0
Europe	66.8	63.1	799,629,184	$20,282	3.9	7.4	5.0
Americas	61.6	67.0	879,292,883	$20,568	3.0	6.9	4.5
Middle East/N. Africa	58.7	54.4	311,473,781	$7,508	4.6	13.4	7.7
Sub-Saharan Africa	54.5	55.5	633,132,970	$2,137	5.0	13.2	29.0
World	60.3	57.4	6,240,505,257	$9,775	6.1	7.5	7.5

* Weighted by population.

Sources: World Bank, World Development Indicators Online; Central Intelligence Agency, *The World Factbook 2005*; International Monetary Fund, World Economic Outlook database, April 2006; and Kim R. Holmes, Edwin J. Feulner, and Mary Anastasia O'Grady, *2008 Index of Economic Freedom* (Washington, D.C.: The Heritage Foundation and Dow Jones & Company, Inc., 2008), at *www.heritage.org/index*.

ASIA–PACIFIC

The Asia–Pacific region spans the world's largest surface area, stretching from Japan and New Zealand in the East to Azerbaijan in the West. With 3.6 billion inhabitants, this region contains over half of the world's population: one-third in China and nearly another third in India.

Despite having one of the world's poorest populations—the population-weighted average GDP per capita is $6,361—the Asia–Pacific region has far and away the fastest five-year per capita growth rate at 7.6 percent. It also has the lowest average unemployment rate (6.3 percent) and one of the lowest average inflation rates (5.0 percent).

Chart A1 compares the 1995–2008 time series of the average economic freedom score for the region to the world average. Chart A2 demonstrates the clear relationship between high levels of economic freedom and high GDP per capita.

In the 2008 *Index*, the scores of 18 countries in the region have improved, while those of 10 are worse. The scores for Laos and North Korea are unchanged. Mongolia is the region's most improved country. The performance of Tajikistan and Bangladesh registered the most deterioration in the region during the year. What sets Asia apart from other regions? It is the extraordinary disparity in levels of economic freedom. Four of the world's "Top 10" freest economies—Hong Kong, Singapore, Australia, and New Zealand—are in Asia. Regrettably, however, most countries in the region are ranked "mostly unfree." Countries such as Turkmenistan, Laos, Bangladesh, and Burma remain "repressed." North Korea remains the least free economy, both in the region and in the world, scoring poorly on every factor. It has nowhere to go but up—if its political leadership should ever choose to try.

Table A1 ranks the countries in the region from "most free" to "least free" based on their overall freedom scores. It also includes the change from last year's score, the country's world rank, and each country's 2008 scores for each of the 10 economic freedoms. Chart A3 shows the distribution of countries across five

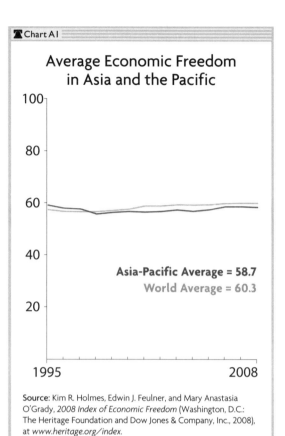

Chart A1

Average Economic Freedom in Asia and the Pacific

Asia-Pacific Average = 58.7
World Average = 60.3

Source: Kim R. Holmes, Edwin J. Feulner, and Mary Anastasia O'Grady, *2008 Index of Economic Freedom* (Washington, D.C.: The Heritage Foundation and Dow Jones & Company, Inc., 2008), at *www.heritage.org/index*.

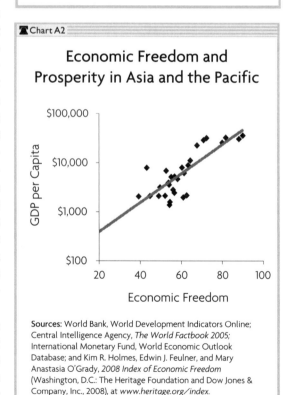

Chart A2

Economic Freedom and Prosperity in Asia and the Pacific

Sources: World Bank, World Development Indicators Online; Central Intelligence Agency, *The World Factbook 2005*; International Monetary Fund, World Economic Outlook Database; and Kim R. Holmes, Edwin J. Feulner, and Mary Anastasia O'Grady, *2008 Index of Economic Freedom* (Washington, D.C.: The Heritage Foundation and Dow Jones & Company, Inc., 2008), at *www.heritage.org/index*.

Economic Freedom Scores for Asia and the Pacific

2008 World Rank	2008 Regional Rank	Country	Economic Freedom 2008	Change from 2007	Business Freedom	Trade Freedom	Fiscal Freedom	Government Size	Monetary Freedom	Investment Freedom	Financial Freedom	Property Rights	Freedom from Corruption	Labor Freedom
1	1	Hong Kong	90.3	-0.3	88.2	95.0	92.8	93.1	87.2	90	90	90.0	83.0	93.3
2	2	Singapore	87.4	0.2	97.8	90.0	90.3	93.9	88.9	80	50	90.0	94.0	99.0
4	3	Australia	82.0	1.0	89.3	83.8	59.2	62.8	83.7	80	90	90.0	87.0	94.2
6	4	New Zealand	80.2	-0.8	99.9	80.8	60.5	56.0	83.7	70	80	90.0	96.0	85.5
17	5	Japan	72.5	0.3	88.1	80.0	70.3	56.2	94.3	60	50	70.0	76.0	79.8
25	6	Taiwan	71.0	0.8	70.7	86.7	75.9	87.8	83.3	70	50	70.0	59.0	56.9
41	7	Korea, South	67.9	0.7	84.0	66.4	71.1	77.3	80.1	70	60	70.0	51.0	49.0
51	8	Malaysia	64.5	0.1	69.0	76.2	82.2	80.8	78.6	40	40	50.0	50.0	78.7
54	9	Thailand	63.5	-1.3	72.1	75.2	74.7	90.7	66.7	30	50	50.0	36.0	89.6
62	10	Mongolia	62.8	3.0	71.1	81.4	85.0	71.7	78.2	60	60	30.0	28.0	62.4
69	11	Fiji	61.5	0.9	69.7	74.2	74.5	75.3	78.9	30	60	30.0	40.0	82.7
70	12	Kyrgyz Republic	61.1	0.8	60.4	81.4	93.9	76.1	75.6	50	50	30.0	22.0	72.0
76	13	Kazakhstan	60.5	1.4	56.5	86.2	80.1	84.7	71.9	30	60	30.0	26.0	80.0
90	14	Sri Lanka	58.3	-1.0	71.5	69.6	73.5	81.7	65.4	30	40	50.0	31.0	70.5
92	15	Philippines, The	56.9	-0.1	53.0	78.8	75.8	90.2	73.8	30	50	30.0	25.0	61.9
93	16	Pakistan	56.8	-1.7	70.8	65.2	79.1	90.1	72.2	40	30	30.0	22.0	69.1
100	17	Cambodia	56.2	0.1	43.0	52.2	91.4	94.2	80.9	50	50	30.0	21.0	49.1
107	18	Azerbaijan	55.3	0.5	61.6	78.4	80.3	82.9	76.5	30	30	30.0	24.0	59.2
112	19	Nepal	54.7	-0.4	60.0	61.4	86.5	92.0	78.5	30	30	30.0	25.0	53.4
114	20	Tajikistan	54.5	0.7	43.4	77.8	89.3	84.1	65.8	30	40	30.0	22.0	62.1
115	21	India	54.2	0.1	50.0	51.0	75.7	73.5	70.3	40	30	50.0	33.0	68.6
119	22	Indonesia	53.9	-0.1	48.8	73.0	77.5	89.7	68.2	30	40	30.0	24.0	57.5
126	23	China	52.8	1.0	50.0	70.2	66.4	89.7	76.5	30	30	20.0	33.0	62.4
130	24	Uzbekistan	52.3	0.3	67.8	68.4	88.0	68.3	57.5	30	20	30.0	21.0	72.1
135	25	Vietnam	49.8	0.4	60.0	62.8	74.3	78.0	67.4	30	30	10.0	26.0	59.5
137	26	Laos	49.2	-0.0	60.8	57.0	71.0	92.1	73.0	30	20	10.0	26.0	52.3
149	27	Bangladesh	44.9	-3.1	55.3	0.0	84.0	93.2	68.9	20	20	25.0	20.0	62.8
152	28	Turkmenistan	43.4	0.3	30.0	79.2	90.6	85.3	66.4	10	10	10.0	22.0	30.0
153	29	Burma (Myanmar)	39.5	-1.5	20.0	71.0	81.7	97.0	56.5	10	10	10.0	19.0	20.0
157	30	Korea, North	3.0	0.0	0.0	0.0	0.0	0.0	0.0	10	0	10.0	10.0	0.0

Sources: Kim R. Holmes, Edwin J. Feulner, and Mary Anastasia O'Grady, *2008 Index of Economic Freedom* (Washington, D.C.: The Heritage Foundation and Dow Jones & Company, Inc., 2008), at *www.heritage.org/index*.

different categories.

India and China are ranked 21st and 23rd, respectively, in the region, and both are categorized as "mostly unfree." Despite these seemingly low scores, however, there can be no denying that the winds of change are still blowing in Asia, particularly in these two economic leviathans. Notwithstanding very slow progress, it should be noted that economic freedom has been improving gradually in India and China over the years.

Asia–Pacific countries are significantly stronger than the world average in two of the 10 economic freedoms: government size and labor freedom. Lower government expenditures result in a government size score that is more than 10 percentage points better than the world average, whereas labor freedom is about 2 percentage points better.

However, the typical Asian country has notably lower scores in four factors: investment freedom, financial freedom, property rights, and freedom from corruption. This suggests that Asian countries could make the most progress by strengthening their banking and investment institutions, perhaps by enhancing transparency and corporate governance.

Hong Kong is clearly blazing a trail for others to follow. With the top scores in four of the 10 factors, Hong Kong once again becomes the "poster economy" for economic freedom around the world. Singapore is the top country in business freedom and labor freedom, meaning that it is easiest to start, operate, and close a firm there. Singapore also grants private firms the most flexibility in hiring and firing workers. New Zealand sets the standard for clean, corruption-free government, benefiting significantly from its transparent and straightforward business environment.

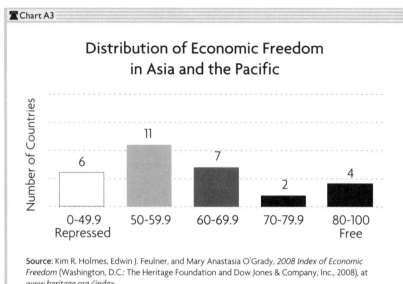

Chart A3

Distribution of Economic Freedom in Asia and the Pacific

Number of Countries:
- 0-49.9 Repressed: 6
- 50-59.9: 11
- 60-69.9: 7
- 70-79.9: 2
- 80-100 Free: 4

Source: Kim R. Holmes, Edwin J. Feulner, and Mary Anastasia O'Grady, *2008 Index of Economic Freedom* (Washington, D.C.: The Heritage Foundation and Dow Jones & Company, Inc., 2008), at *www.heritage.org/index.*

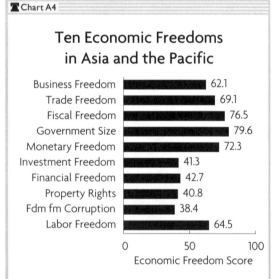

Chart A4

Ten Economic Freedoms in Asia and the Pacific

Economic Freedom Score	
Business Freedom	62.1
Trade Freedom	69.1
Fiscal Freedom	76.5
Government Size	79.6
Monetary Freedom	72.3
Investment Freedom	41.3
Financial Freedom	42.7
Property Rights	40.8
Fdm fm Corruption	38.4
Labor Freedom	64.5

Source: Kim R. Holmes, Edwin J. Feulner, and Mary Anastasia O'Grady, *2008 Index of Economic Freedom* (Washington, D.C.: The Heritage Foundation and Dow Jones & Company, Inc., 2008), at *www.heritage.org/index.*

EUROPE

Europe served as the testing ground for the two great economic philosophies of the past century and witnessed the collapse of one of them—Communism—which proved unable to generate standards of living even remotely approximating those of capitalist Western Europe. Now that the old Cold War contrast has been eclipsed by a new technology-driven globalization, many of the large economies in Europe that were built on a quasi-market welfare state model are looking for ways to improve their competitiveness as fast-growing small economies like Ireland and Estonia surpass them in economic performance.

Europe comprises 41 countries, the most of any region. Most people around the world equate Europe with prosperity because the people of most European countries enjoy incomes that average $20,282 per capita annually.

The European region enjoys moderate growth and inflation but has been plagued by higher unemployment rates than it should naturally endure because the welfare state economic model promoted by some as socially "superior" has failed to generate more employment opportunities year after year. Chart B1 illustrates the 1995–2008 time series of the average economic freedom score for the region, compared to the world average. Chart B2 confirms the clear relationship between high levels of economic freedom and high GDP per capita.

Taken as a whole, the economic picture depicts a region that enjoys prosperity and stability. However, the burdensome labor regulations that are in place to protect traditional sectors and occupations in Europe are plainly hindering both productivity growth and job creation. The lack of governmental freedom, added to distortionary subsidies in many parts of Europe, is also holding down the region's growth potential.

Table B1 ranks the countries in the region from most free to least free based on their overall freedom scores. Chart B3 shows the distribution of countries across five different categories.

Half of the world's 20 freest countries are in Europe, which is the only region to have a distribution of economies that is skewed toward

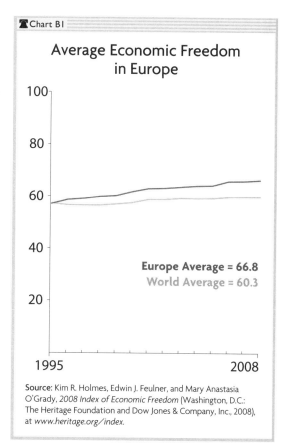

Chart B1

Average Economic Freedom in Europe

Europe Average = 66.8
World Average = 60.3

Source: Kim R. Holmes, Edwin J. Feulner, and Mary Anastasia O'Grady, *2008 Index of Economic Freedom* (Washington, D.C.: The Heritage Foundation and Dow Jones & Company, Inc., 2008), at *www.heritage.org/index*.

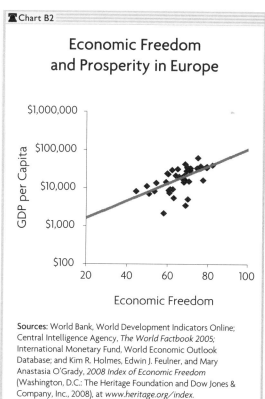

Chart B2

Economic Freedom and Prosperity in Europe

Sources: World Bank, World Development Indicators Online; Central Intelligence Agency, *The World Factbook 2005;* International Monetary Fund, World Economic Outlook Database; and Kim R. Holmes, Edwin J. Feulner, and Mary Anastasia O'Grady, *2008 Index of Economic Freedom* (Washington, D.C.: The Heritage Foundation and Dow Jones & Company, Inc., 2008), at *www.heritage.org/index*.

Economic Freedom Scores for Europe

2008 World Rank	2008 Regional Rank	Country	Economic Freedom 2008	Change from 2007	Business Freedom	Trade Freedom	Fiscal Freedom	Government Size	Monetary Freedom	Investment Freedom	Financial Freedom	Property Rights	Freedom from Corruption	Labor Freedom
3	1	Ireland	82.4	-0.2	92.2	86.0	71.5	64.5	84.9	90	90	90.0	74.0	80.4
9	2	Switzerland	79.7	1.6	83.9	87.2	68.0	61.6	83.6	70	80	90.0	91.0	82.0
10	3	United Kingdom	79.5	-0.5	90.8	86.0	61.2	40.1	80.7	90	90	90.0	86.0	80.7
11	4	Denmark	79.2	2.2	99.9	86.0	35.0	19.8	86.5	90	90	90.0	95.0	99.9
12	5	Estonia	77.8	-0.2	84.5	86.0	86.0	62.0	82.0	90	80	90.0	67.0	50.3
13	6	Netherlands, The	76.8	1.9	88.0	86.0	51.6	38.2	86.9	90	90	90.0	87.0	60.5
14	7	Iceland	76.5	-0.2	94.5	85.0	73.6	46.3	74.8	60	70	90.0	96.0	75.0
15	8	Luxembourg	75.2	-0.1	76.9	86.0	65.4	44.8	79.8	90	80	90.0	86.0	53.1
16	9	Finland	74.8	0.6	95.2	86.0	64.3	29.1	88.5	70	80	90.0	96.0	48.8
20	10	Belgium	71.5	-0.9	93.7	86.0	43.9	17.9	80.4	90	80	80.0	73.0	69.9
22	11	Cyprus	71.3	-0.4	70.0	81.0	78.2	43.0	85.0	70	70	90.0	56.0	70.0
23	12	Germany	71.2	-0.4	88.9	86.0	58.4	34.0	81.4	80	60	90.0	80.0	52.8
26	13	Lithuania	70.8	-0.7	83.2	86.0	86.3	68.3	78.5	70	80	50.0	48.0	57.6
27	14	Sweden	70.4	1.4	94.8	86.0	32.7	3.9	82.8	80	80	90.0	92.0	62.0
28	15	Armenia	70.3	1.0	81.3	85.0	89.0	86.4	84.6	70	70	35.0	29.0	73.1
30	16	Austria	70.0	-0.2	80.6	86.0	51.2	25.3	81.4	70	70	90.0	86.0	59.2
31	17	Spain	69.7	-0.2	77.5	86.0	54.5	56.2	78.1	70	80	70.0	68.0	56.7
32	18	Georgia	69.2	-0.1	85.0	71.0	90.7	81.2	71.4	70	60	35.0	28.0	99.9
34	19	Norway	69.0	0.6	89.1	86.2	50.3	46.3	76.1	60	50	90.0	88.0	53.9
35	20	Slovak Republic	68.7	0.3	69.3	86.0	89.4	53.9	76.9	70	80	50.0	47.0	64.9
37	21	Czech Republic	68.5	0.8	63.9	86.0	71.3	45.6	80.3	70	80	70.0	48.0	70.2
38	22	Latvia	68.3	0.1	74.3	86.0	83.4	59.2	73.8	70	70	55.0	47.0	64.6
43	23	Hungary	67.2	2.8	73.9	86.0	70.0	26.5	77.2	80	70	70.0	52.0	66.8
47	24	Malta	66.0	-0.1	70.0	86.0	61.3	29.1	79.8	50	70	90.0	64.0	60.0
48	25	France	65.4	2.5	87.1	81.0	53.2	13.2	81.2	60	70	70.0	74.0	63.8
53	26	Portugal	64.3	-0.2	79.6	86.0	61.3	32.6	79.4	70	50	70.0	66.0	48.0
56	27	Albania	63.3	0.9	55.6	75.8	90.3	76.0	80.4	70	70	30.0	26.0	59.3
59	28	Bulgaria	62.9	0.9	67.5	86.0	82.7	56.0	73.7	60	60	30.0	40.0	73.2
64	29	Italy	62.5	-0.2	76.8	81.0	54.3	29.4	80.6	70	60	50.0	49.0	73.5
68	30	Romania	61.5	0.3	74.1	86.0	85.6	70.8	72.5	60	50	30.0	31.0	55.3
71	31	Macedonia	61.1	0.5	65.1	83.4	88.1	61.6	85.5	50	60	30.0	27.0	60.7
74	32	Turkey	60.8	2.5	67.9	86.8	77.7	68.3	70.8	50	50	50.0	38.0	48.0
75	33	Slovenia	60.6	0.4	73.0	86.0	62.4	33.2	79.5	60	50	50.0	64.0	47.7
80	34	Greece	60.1	1.8	69.5	81.0	65.6	57.8	78.5	50	50	50.0	44.0	54.3
83	35	Poland	59.5	2.1	54.1	86.0	68.6	43.5	82.3	60	60	50.0	37.0	53.5
89	36	Moldova	58.4	-0.8	68.5	79.2	83.0	56.9	67.6	30	50	50.0	32.0	66.6
113	37	Croatia	54.6	0.7	58.1	87.6	68.8	28.0	78.8	50	60	30.0	34.0	50.5
121	38	Bosnia & Herzegovina	53.7	-0.6	56.1	79.8	73.7	48.3	76.6	50	60	10.0	29.0	53.7
133	39	Ukraine	51.1	-0.6	44.3	82.2	79.0	43.0	69.9	30	50	30.0	28.0	54.3
134	40	Russia	49.9	-2.5	52.8	44.2	79.2	69.5	64.4	30	40	30.0	25.0	64.2
150	41	Belarus	44.7	-1.8	58.6	52.2	81.0	55.5	66.2	20	10	20.0	21.0	62.0

Source: Kim R. Holmes, Edwin J. Feulner, and Mary Anastasia O'Grady, *2008 Index of Economic Freedom* (Washington, D.C.: The Heritage Foundation and Dow Jones & Company, Inc., 2008), at *www.heritage.org/index*.

freedom. Ireland is the highest-ranking European country in the 2008 *Index*. Ireland is ranked 3rd worldwide, followed by Switzerland at 9th, the United Kingdom at 10th, and Denmark at 11th. Scandinavian and Baltic countries, primarily, round out the top 20, along with Holland, Belgium, and Finland. Europe has definitely benefited from economic competition over the centuries, which

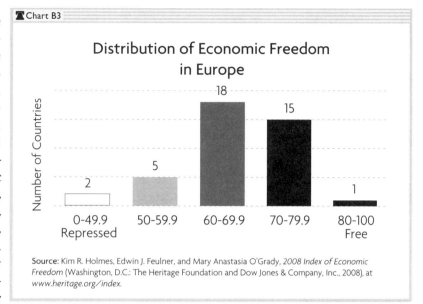

Chart B3

Distribution of Economic Freedom in Europe

Number of Countries

- 0-49.9 Repressed: 2
- 50-59.9: 5
- 60-69.9: 18
- 70-79.9: 15
- 80-100 Free: 1

Source: Kim R. Holmes, Edwin J. Feulner, and Mary Anastasia O'Grady, *2008 Index of Economic Freedom* (Washington, D.C.: The Heritage Foundation and Dow Jones & Company, Inc., 2008), at www.heritage.org/index.

may help to explain why economic repression is so rare in the West, but that competition has not generated enough reform in some of the Eastern European countries. Many post-Communist countries—such as Russia, Belarus, and Ukraine—take up the "less free" rear end of the distribution.

Extensive and long-established free-market institutions have generated higher-than-average scores for Europe in eight of the 10 economic freedoms. It is about 15 percentage points ahead in both investment freedom and financial freedom. The region's freedom from corruption and property rights both lead the world by slightly more than 15 percentage points. However, Europe suffers from the third-worst regional score in labor freedom and is last in fiscal freedom and government size—reflecting the price tag of welfare states that consume such a large percentage of GDP.

Ireland leads in financial freedom and property rights, reflecting Dublin's commitment to becoming a major European commercial and financial hub based on free-market principles. Impressively for a post-Communist state, Georgia leads in labor freedom and fiscal freedom because of a combination of low taxes and a highly flexible labor market, which is essential for a non–oil-producing economy.

In summary, Europe has continued to advance its economic freedom in the 2008

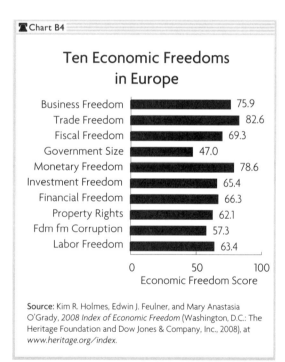

Chart B4

Ten Economic Freedoms in Europe

- Business Freedom: 75.9
- Trade Freedom: 82.6
- Fiscal Freedom: 69.3
- Government Size: 47.0
- Monetary Freedom: 78.6
- Investment Freedom: 65.4
- Financial Freedom: 66.3
- Property Rights: 62.1
- Fdm fm Corruption: 57.3
- Labor Freedom: 63.4

Economic Freedom Score

Source: Kim R. Holmes, Edwin J. Feulner, and Mary Anastasia O'Grady, *2008 Index of Economic Freedom* (Washington, D.C.: The Heritage Foundation and Dow Jones & Company, Inc., 2008), at www.heritage.org/index.

Index. Thanks to policy improvements such as tax cuts and other business-friendly reforms by many of the region's individual economies as they compete with one another to attract more investment, 21 countries have recorded overall score improvements.

THE AMERICAS

The countries of the Americas range from the prosperous United States and the developing economic colossus of Brazil to the small island economies of the Caribbean and poor nations of Central America. The average population per country is 30 million people, and the overall regional population is 871 million—second only to Asia on both counts. With the world's lowest average unemployment rate and years of economic reform efforts, the Americas would seem to be poised for broadly shared economic success. However, the region is one of the world's most economically diverse and presents a puzzle. The lack—and, in some cases, erosion—of economic freedom in the Americas reflects reversals of free-market policies and a failure by some governments to persevere in pursuing economic freedom.

Chart C1 displays the 1995–2008 time series of the average economic freedom score for the region, compared to the world average. The region has maintained a level of economic freedom higher than the global average during every year covered by the *Index* but has experienced noticeable deterioration in economic freedom in recent years. In the 2008 *Index*, on net, the scores for the Americas are worse for five economies, with scores for 17 countries having deteriorated and scores for 12 countries improved. Guyana, Venezuela, and Haiti have recorded the worst performances.

Across the region, the reality is that economies are stagnating. Among the five regions, the Americas has the slowest compound five-year growth rate. Population-weighted average income per capita is higher in the Americas than in any other region, even Europe. Ironically, however, the statistical evidence suggests that many nations in the Western Hemisphere are stuck in poverty traps with chronic income inequality.

Chart C2 denotes the vivid positive correlation between high levels of economic freedom and high GDP per capita, implying a large freedom gap. The recent rise of populists such as Venezuela's Hugo Chávez and Bolivia's Evo Morales threatens to widen the freedom gap in the Americas even more.

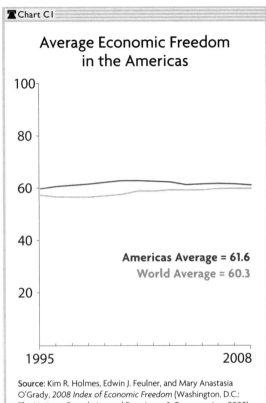

Chart C1

Average Economic Freedom in the Americas

Americas Average = 61.6
World Average = 60.3

Source: Kim R. Holmes, Edwin J. Feulner, and Mary Anastasia O'Grady, *2008 Index of Economic Freedom* (Washington, D.C.: The Heritage Foundation and Dow Jones & Company, Inc., 2008), at *www.heritage.org/index.*

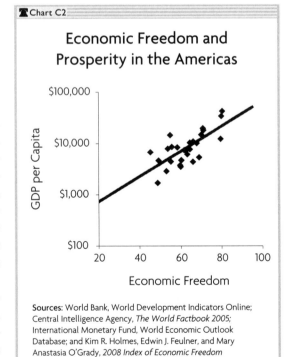

Chart C2

Economic Freedom and Prosperity in the Americas

Sources: World Bank, World Development Indicators Online; Central Intelligence Agency, *The World Factbook 2005*; International Monetary Fund, World Economic Outlook Database; and Kim R. Holmes, Edwin J. Feulner, and Mary Anastasia O'Grady, *2008 Index of Economic Freedom* (Washington, D.C.: The Heritage Foundation and Dow Jones & Company, Inc., 2008), at *www.heritage.org/index.*

Economic Freedom Scores for the Americas

2008 World Rank	2008 Regional Rank	Country	Economic Freedom 2008	Change from 2007	Business Freedom	Trade Freedom	Fiscal Freedom	Government Size	Monetary Freedom	Investment Freedom	Financial Freedom	Property Rights	Freedom from Corruption	Labor Freedom
5	1	United States	80.6	-0.3	91.7	86.8	68.3	59.8	83.7	80	80	90.0	73.0	92.3
7	2	Canada	80.2	2.1	96.7	87.0	75.5	53.7	81.0	70	80	90.0	85.0	82.9
8	3	Chile	79.8	0.8	67.5	82.2	78.1	88.2	78.8	80	70	90.0	73.0	90.0
21	4	Barbados	71.3	1.4	90.0	58.8	71.3	62.2	74.0	60	60	90.0	67.0	80.0
24	5	Bahamas, The	71.1	-0.9	80.0	32.0	96.2	86.4	76.3	40	70	80.0	70.0	80.0
29	6	Trinidad & Tobago	70.2	-1.1	64.1	79.0	81.1	81.7	72.6	70	70	65.0	32.0	86.9
33	7	El Salvador	69.2	-0.6	58.6	76.6	83.4	88.7	76.8	70	70	50.0	40.0	78.0
40	8	Uruguay	68.1	-0.7	59.8	83.0	85.9	76.6	74.2	60	30	70.0	64.0	77.3
44	9	Mexico	66.4	0.1	82.6	79.0	83.4	83.7	77.7	50	60	50.0	33.0	64.3
45	10	Jamaica	66.2	0.2	82.0	70.4	74.9	59.6	74.3	80	60	50.0	37.0	73.3
49	11	Costa Rica	64.8	0.2	59.7	81.8	82.9	87.4	67.9	70	40	50.0	41.0	66.8
50	12	Panama	64.7	0.1	72.8	76.2	83.0	89.1	80.2	70	70	30.0	31.0	44.4
55	13	Peru	63.5	1.0	64.5	73.4	80.2	91.8	85.9	60	60	40.0	33.0	45.8
61	14	Belize	62.8	-0.4	76.3	64.6	69.3	74.8	77.3	50	50	50.0	35.0	80.9
67	15	Colombia	61.9	2.3	72.5	70.8	72.8	71.2	71.4	60	60	40.0	39.0	61.4
77	16	Paraguay	60.5	1.6	57.6	78.4	96.6	90.8	76.6	50	60	35.0	26.0	34.2
78	17	Guatemala	60.5	-0.8	54.1	78.4	79.9	95.9	72.9	50	50	30.0	26.0	67.9
79	18	Honduras	60.2	-0.2	59.5	78.0	84.5	82.6	73.7	50	60	30.0	25.0	59.0
81	19	Nicaragua	60.0	-2.0	56.4	79.2	79.0	77.6	70.6	70	50	25.0	26.0	65.7
87	20	Dominican Republic	58.5	0.9	62.2	73.0	80.4	88.8	69.3	50	40	30.0	28.0	63.6
101	21	Brazil	55.9	-0.2	53.6	70.8	68.6	55.5	75.7	50	40	50.0	33.0	61.9
106	22	Ecuador	55.4	-0.2	58.1	67.6	86.4	82.3	74.1	40	50	30.0	23.0	42.4
108	23	Argentina	55.1	0.1	63.2	69.6	70.5	80.9	65.0	50	40	30.0	29.0	52.9
118	24	Suriname	53.9	-0.5	41.7	65.0	68.0	72.8	69.2	30	30	50.0	30.0	82.1
123	25	Bolivia	53.2	-1.1	58.6	79.0	87.8	68.1	76.5	20	60	25.0	27.0	30.5
136	26	Guyana	49.4	-5.0	56.4	65.8	67.3	16.1	73.9	40	40	40.0	25.0	69.1
138	27	Haiti	48.9	-2.4	35.7	67.0	77.8	93.2	65.3	30	30	10.0	18.0	62.4
148	28	Venezuela	45.0	-2.9	51.4	54.6	74.5	79.7	60.6	20	40	10.0	23.0	35.8
156	29	Cuba	27.5	-1.1	10.0	60.8	54.8	0.0	64.6	10	10	10.0	35.0	20.0

Source: Kim R. Holmes, Edwin J. Feulner, and Mary Anastasia O'Grady, *2008 Index of Economic Freedom* (Washington, D.C.: The Heritage Foundation and Dow Jones & Company, Inc., 2008), at *www.heritage.org/index*.

Table C1 ranks the countries in the region from "most free" to "least free" based on their overall freedom scores. It also includes the change from last year's score, the country's world rank, and each country's 2008 scores for each of the 10 economic freedoms. Chart C3 shows the distribution of countries across five different categories.

Three of the 29 countries in the Americas rank among the top 10 in the world: the United States (5), Canada (7) and Chile (8). Indeed, the region's countries are distributed in a more balanced fashion than are the countries of any other region, almost like a bell curve. All but six countries receive an economic freedom score between 50 percent and 80 percent, and roughly half fall in the middle category of "moderately free."

An examination of each of the specific economic freedoms demonstrates that the countries in the Americas perform better than the world average in eight of the 10 areas measured. Corruption and inflation are the major trouble areas, representing the long-standing problems of unstable money and weak rule of law.

The typical North, Central, or South American nation stands out positively in terms of limited government taxation and expenditures, as well as labor freedom. The other five freedoms are also slightly stronger in the Americas than they are elsewhere, with lighter trade, investment, financial, and regulatory burdens.

Table C1 reveals the regional freedom leaders. The United States and Canada are the leaders in most of the 10 categories. The U.S. is "most free" in investment freedom, financial freedom, property rights, and labor freedom. The result: a flexible, adaptive economy that remains one of the world's premier financial

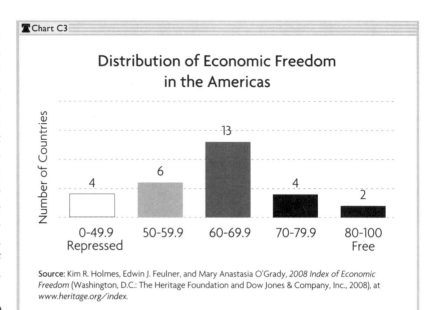

Chart C3

Distribution of Economic Freedom in the Americas

Number of Countries

- 0-49.9 Repressed: 4
- 50-59.9: 6
- 60-69.9: 13
- 70-79.9: 4
- 80-100 Free: 2

Source: Kim R. Holmes, Edwin J. Feulner, and Mary Anastasia O'Grady, *2008 Index of Economic Freedom* (Washington, D.C.: The Heritage Foundation and Dow Jones & Company, Inc., 2008), at www.heritage.org/index.

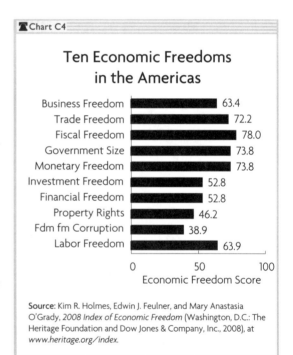

Chart C4

Ten Economic Freedoms in the Americas

Freedom	Economic Freedom Score
Business Freedom	63.4
Trade Freedom	72.2
Fiscal Freedom	78.0
Government Size	73.8
Monetary Freedom	73.8
Investment Freedom	52.8
Financial Freedom	52.8
Property Rights	46.2
Fdm fm Corruption	38.9
Labor Freedom	63.9

Source: Kim R. Holmes, Edwin J. Feulner, and Mary Anastasia O'Grady, *2008 Index of Economic Freedom* (Washington, D.C.: The Heritage Foundation and Dow Jones & Company, Inc., 2008), at www.heritage.org/index.

markets. Canada leads in freedom from corruption as well as trade freedom and business freedom. Guatemala (for its low government expenditures) and the Bahamas (for low taxes) round out the rest of the best.

MIDDLE EAST/NORTH AFRICA

Stretching from Morocco's Atlantic shores to Iran and Yemen's beaches on the Arabian Sea, the Middle East remains central to world affairs. The Middle East/North Africa region encompasses some of the world's most ancient civilizations. Today, however, most of the economies in this region are not free. Cursed in some ways by enormous natural oil resources, most of the local populations suffer from extreme concentrations of wealth and poverty.

The Middle East has a comparatively high GDP per capita because of its oil and gas resources. At $7,508 per person, the regional GDP remains at the world median point: lower than Europe and the Americas but higher than Asia and sub-Saharan Africa. Structural problems clearly abound, as the regional unemployment rate, which averages 13.6 percent, is the highest in the world and is most pronounced among the young and illiterate. Despite the outflow of crude oil, the actual trade flows of the region's countries remain very low, indicating a lack of economic dynamism.

Chart D1 displays the 1995–2008 time series of the simple average economic freedom score for the region, compared to the world average. Using a population-weighted average, the people of the Middle East/North Africa region have the lowest level of economic freedom found in the five regions surveyed in this year's *Index*. Egypt and Kuwait made the biggest leaps forward this year with 4.0 percentage point and 1.7 percentage point increases, respectively. Libya, Oman, Saudi Arabia, Bahrain, and Israel also improved their economic freedom scores, contributing to some improvement in overall economic freedom in the region.

The Middle East/North African region also demonstrates a correlation between economic freedom and prosperity. Chart D2 illustrates the positive relationship between high levels of economic freedom and high GDP per capita. The ongoing transformation of innovative states in Bahrain, Qatar, and the United Arab Emirates (UAE) may yet light the way for economic growth regionally.

Table D1 ranks the countries in the region from "most free" to "least free" based on their

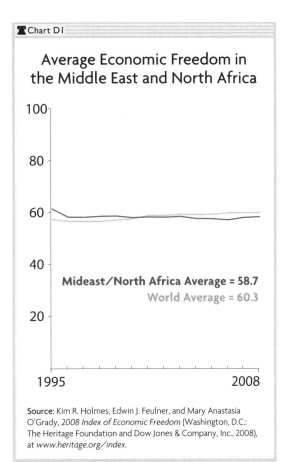

Chart D1

Average Economic Freedom in the Middle East and North Africa

Mideast/North Africa Average = 58.7
World Average = 60.3

1995 — 2008

Source: Kim R. Holmes, Edwin J. Feulner, and Mary Anastasia O'Grady, *2008 Index of Economic Freedom* (Washington, D.C.: The Heritage Foundation and Dow Jones & Company, Inc., 2008), at *www.heritage.org/index*.

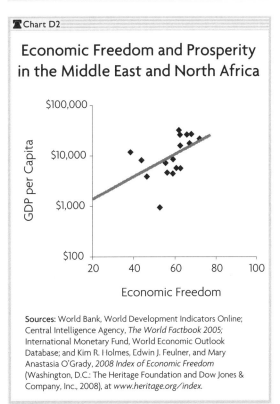

Chart D2

Economic Freedom and Prosperity in the Middle East and North Africa

GDP per Capita

Economic Freedom

Sources: World Bank, World Development Indicators Online; Central Intelligence Agency, *The World Factbook 2005*; International Monetary Fund, World Economic Outlook Database; and Kim R. Holmes, Edwin J. Feulner, and Mary Anastasia O'Grady, *2008 Index of Economic Freedom* (Washington, D.C.: The Heritage Foundation and Dow Jones & Company, Inc., 2008), at *www.heritage.org/index*.

Economic Freedom Scores
for the Middle East and North Africa

2008 World Rank	2008 Regional Rank	Country	Economic Freedom 2008	Change from 2007	Business Freedom	Trade Freedom	Fiscal Freedom	Government Size	Monetary Freedom	Investment Freedom	Financial Freedom	Property Rights	Freedom from Corruption	Labor Freedom
19	1	Bahrain	72.2	1.0	80.0	80.8	99.7	80.3	74.3	60	90	60.0	57.0	40.0
39	2	Kuwait	68.3	1.7	68.5	81.0	99.9	74.6	73.8	50	50	55.0	48.0	82.1
42	3	Oman	67.4	1.4	55.8	83.6	98.5	60.7	74.7	60	60	50.0	54.0	77.2
46	4	Israel	66.1	1.5	68.4	86.6	55.9	35.1	81.8	80	60	70.0	59.0	64.0
58	5	Jordan	63.0	-0.5	55.4	74.8	83.7	53.2	80.4	50	60	55.0	53.0	64.8
60	6	Saudi Arabia	62.8	1.2	72.5	76.8	99.7	69.1	76.7	30	40	50.0	33.0	80.6
63	7	United Arab Emirates	62.8	-0.1	47.9	80.4	99.9	80.2	70.9	30	40	40.0	62.0	76.2
66	8	Qatar	62.2	-0.7	60.0	70.8	99.8	72.1	69.4	30	50	50.0	60.0	60.0
73	9	Lebanon	60.9	-0.5	55.4	77.4	91.4	69.5	77.8	30	70	30.0	36.0	71.2
84	10	Tunisia	59.3	-0.2	79.2	71.8	76.4	77.1	77.6	30	30	50.0	46.0	55.3
85	11	Egypt	59.2	4.0	59.7	66.0	90.8	73.0	69.9	50	40	40.0	33.0	69.1
98	12	Morocco	56.4	-0.8	75.8	62.6	65.4	73.2	79.8	60	40	35.0	32.0	40.2
102	13	Algeria	55.7	0.6	72.7	68.8	77.0	74.6	80.2	40	30	30.0	31.0	52.3
125	14	Yemen	52.8	-0.4	53.7	66.4	83.2	58.5	62.9	50	30	30.0	26.0	67.7
144	15	Syria	46.6	-1.5	52.9	54.0	86.2	60.3	66.2	30	10	30.0	29.0	47.1
151	16	Iran	44.0	-0.1	55.0	57.4	81.1	84.5	61.3	10	10	10.0	27.0	43.8
154	17	Libya	38.7	1.6	20.0	39.6	81.7	63.5	74.9	30	20	10.0	27.0	20.0

Source: Kim R. Holmes, Edwin J. Feulner, and Mary Anastasia O'Grady, *2008 Index of Economic Freedom* (Washington, D.C.: The Heritage Foundation and Dow Jones & Company, Inc., 2008), at *www.heritage.org/index.*

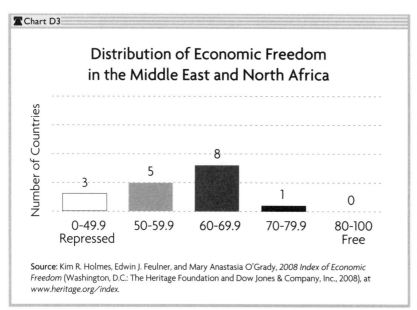

Distribution of Economic Freedom in the Middle East and North Africa

Number of Countries

0–49.9 Repressed	50–59.9	60–69.9	70–79.9	80–100 Free
3	5	8	1	0

Source: Kim R. Holmes, Edwin J. Feulner, and Mary Anastasia O'Grady, *2008 Index of Economic Freedom* (Washington, D.C.: The Heritage Foundation and Dow Jones & Company, Inc., 2008), at *www.heritage.org/index.*

overall freedom scores. It also includes the change from last year's score, the country's world rank, and each country's 2008 scores for each of the 10 economic freedoms. Bahrain, Kuwait, Oman, and Israel—nations that are dissimilar politically but united in their commitment to economic freedom—rank highest. The lowest ranking countries are Syria, Iran, and

Libya—a group of fairly disparate nations that are bonded together by their lack of economic or political liberalism. Chart D3 exhibits the distribution of countries across the five different categories.

Bahrain, ranked 19th globally with 72.2 percent economic freedom, is the only Middle Eastern country that places in the world's 20 most free economies. A small country in the Persian Gulf, Bahrain maintains a pro-business environment with low inflation, sound banking and finance systems, and low barriers to trade. Kuwait, globally ranked 39th, is the region's second freest economy, followed by Oman and Israel. The Middle East's stunted economic growth may be due to its overreliance on oil wealth. To determine whether this is so, we divided the region into two halves, categorizing 13 of the 17 countries as oil exporters and the other four as non-oil countries. The major oil-producing economies in the Middle East and North Africa include Qatar, Oman, Yemen, Algeria, Saudi Arabia, Kuwait, and the UAE. Our analysis reveals that the non-oil countries have about 10 percentage points more economic freedom, using a population-weighted average. They also have lower inflation and slightly better employment and income levels.

Oil revenue comes from the ground. In most Gulf States, even the process of extracting the oil is in the hands of foreigners. It requires very little investment in labor or human capital and only a marginal amount of investment in the land. People need different freedoms to be productive, but oil does not generate the incentives needed for societies to create those freedoms.

The Middle East is the absolute world leader in only one category: fiscal freedom. Fiscally, its 86.5 percent average score is well above the world average of 74.9 percent, a level reached because of the low income tax rates common to oil kingdoms. The region does score above the world average in other areas, however, such as government size and freedom from corruption—perhaps reflecting reform efforts that regional leaders are making to cut back on bribery and government malfeasance.

Chart D4

Ten Economic Freedoms in the Middle East and North Africa

Business Freedom	60.8
Trade Freedom	70.5
Fiscal Freedom	86.5
Government Size	68.2
Monetary Freedom	73.7
Investment Freedom	42.4
Financial Freedom	42.9
Property Rights	40.9
Fdm fm Corruption	41.9
Labor Freedom	59.5

Economic Freedom Score

Source: Kim R. Holmes, Edwin J. Feulner, and Mary Anastasia O'Grady, *2008 Index of Economic Freedom* (Washington, D.C.: The Heritage Foundation and Dow Jones & Company, Inc., 2008), at *www.heritage.org/index.*

SUB-SAHARAN AFRICA

Sub-Saharan Africa is well known as the world's poorest and most unstable region. Civil war flares sporadically from the Horn of Africa to the Atlantic Coast. HIV/AIDS is a continuing burden. Mass unemployment is common.

Average GDP per capita is only $2,137—the lowest of any region and barely one-tenth of the average incomes in Europe and the Americas. Unemployment hovers just above 13 percent, and the 29 percent average inflation rate, due mainly to Zimbabwe's hyperinflation, is twice as high as that of the next worst region. Unsurprisingly, with just a fraction of the population of Asia, sub-Saharan Africa receives more absolute foreign aid, both multilateral and bilateral, than any other region.

Chart E1 shows the 1995–2008 time series of the average economic freedom score for the region, compared with the world average. Africa's overall level of economic freedom is weaker than any other region's and has somewhat stagnated over the years. Nevertheless, there are some success stories, and they usually involve countries with greater freedom. Chart E2 confirms the strong relationship between high levels of economic freedom and high GDP per capita.

Mauritius, the second most improved economy in the 2008 *Index*, is the lone sub-Saharan Africa representative among the world's top 20 freest economies. With 72.3 percent economic freedom, the country is ranked 18th freest economy in the world and is the leader of economic freedom in the region. It scores 10 percentage points or more above the global average in six areas: investment freedom, property rights, business freedom, freedom from corruption, fiscal freedom, and government size. Mauritius has also demonstrated its strong commitment to enhancing economic freedom by accelerating major tax reforms. Botswana remains the second freest, followed by Uganda and South Africa.

Unlike regions that have a diverse range of free-market economies, in sub-Saharan Africa there are only distinctions among less free economies. A majority of nations are ranked "mostly unfree," with "moderately free" econ-

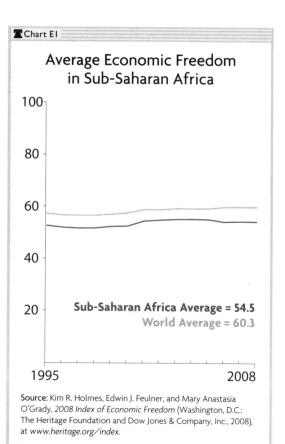

Chart E1

Average Economic Freedom in Sub-Saharan Africa

Sub-Saharan Africa Average = 54.5
World Average = 60.3

1995   2008

Source: Kim R. Holmes, Edwin J. Feulner, and Mary Anastasia O'Grady, *2008 Index of Economic Freedom* (Washington, D.C.: The Heritage Foundation and Dow Jones & Company, Inc., 2008), at *www.heritage.org/index*.

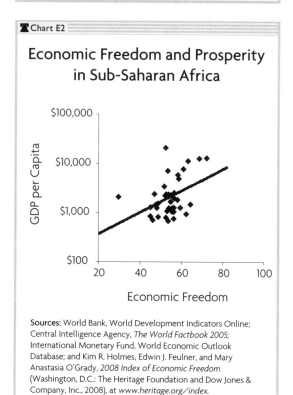

Chart E2

Economic Freedom and Prosperity in Sub-Saharan Africa

Sources: World Bank, World Development Indicators Online; Central Intelligence Agency, *The World Factbook 2005*; International Monetary Fund, World Economic Outlook Database; and Kim R. Holmes, Edwin J. Feulner, and Mary Anastasia O'Grady, *2008 Index of Economic Freedom* (Washington, D.C.: The Heritage Foundation and Dow Jones & Company, Inc., 2008), at *www.heritage.org/index*.

Economic Freedom Scores for Sub-Saharan Africa

2008 World Rank	2008 Regional Rank	Country	Economic Freedom 2008	Change from 2007	Business Freedom	Trade Freedom	Fiscal Freedom	Government Size	Monetary Freedom	Investment Freedom	Financial Freedom	Property Rights	Freedom from Corruption	Labor Freedom
18	1	Mauritius	72.3	3.1	81.6	80.6	92.1	81.4	75.7	70	60	60.0	51.0	70.6
36	2	Botswana	68.6	0.1	68.7	67.6	76.4	61.8	69.7	70	70	70.0	56.0	75.9
52	3	Uganda	64.4	0.7	56.3	72.0	80.5	86.0	78.5	50	70	30.0	27.0	93.9
57	4	South Africa	63.2	-0.2	71.2	74.2	69.5	76.8	77.2	50	60	50.0	46.0	57.5
65	5	Madagascar	62.4	1.3	56.0	79.6	80.9	86.4	72.2	70	50	50.0	31.0	47.9
72	6	Namibia	61.0	-2.1	73.8	87.4	67.9	71.0	76.8	30	50	30.0	41.0	82.4
82	7	Kenya	59.6	-0.4	65.3	75.0	78.2	84.8	72.2	50	50	35.0	22.0	63.2
86	8	Swaziland	58.9	-1.7	69.0	69.0	71.4	62.4	76.0	50	40	50.0	25.0	75.7
88	9	Cape Verde	58.4	1.3	55.1	41.2	66.2	60.5	78.7	60	50	70.0	40.0	62.3
91	10	Senegal	58.2	0.1	54.5	71.6	65.2	82.3	81.4	50	50	50.0	33.0	43.6
94	11	Ghana	56.7	-0.7	53.1	63.0	83.7	71.5	68.0	50	50	50.0	33.0	44.2
95	12	Gambia, The	56.6	-0.8	57.1	62.6	72.5	72.8	73.9	50	50	30.0	25.0	72.1
96	13	Mozambique	56.6	0.7	53.0	72.8	78.1	85.2	73.6	50	50	30.0	28.0	45.0
97	14	Tanzania	56.4	-0.4	47.9	73.2	80.5	79.9	75.4	50	50	30.0	29.0	48.1
99	15	Zambia	56.4	-0.8	62.4	71.2	72.6	80.3	62.9	50	50	40.0	26.0	48.2
103	16	Burkina Faso	55.6	0.6	49.8	66.6	77.5	85.9	78.8	40	50	30.0	32.0	45.7
104	17	Mali	55.5	0.8	41.9	68.6	69.3	81.5	79.9	50	40	30.0	28.0	66.0
105	18	Nigeria	55.5	-0.5	52.6	63.4	84.4	68.1	73.8	30	40	30.0	22.0	90.6
109	19	Mauritania	55.0	1.5	38.9	70.2	75.4	66.3	77.1	60	50	30.0	31.0	51.2
110	20	Benin	55.0	0.1	47.7	65.2	67.5	86.4	77.5	40	60	30.0	25.0	50.8
111	21	Ivory Coast	54.9	-1.0	47.0	59.8	52.3	88.1	80.7	40	60	30.0	21.0	70.5
116	22	Rwanda	54.1	1.7	51.8	70.6	76.9	75.6	73.3	40	40	30.0	25.0	58.2
117	23	Cameroon	54.0	-1.4	39.9	57.0	71.8	93.6	72.3	50	50	30.0	23.0	52.5
120	24	Malawi	53.8	-0.2	52.1	64.6	70.2	44.3	69.9	50	50	40.0	27.0	70.1
122	25	Gabon	53.6	-0.6	52.8	56.4	61.7	85.6	74.6	40	40	40.0	30.0	54.6
124	26	Ethiopia	53.2	-1.2	58.3	63.0	77.2	80.9	69.4	40	20	30.0	24.0	69.5
127	27	Guinea	52.8	-1.7	44.9	59.6	70.1	88.7	54.3	40	40	30.0	19.0	71.1
128	28	Niger	52.7	-0.4	36.0	64.4	66.4	89.3	86.0	50	40	30.0	23.0	42.2
129	29	Equatorial Guinea	52.5	-1.6	47.1	52.2	75.4	82.0	81.1	30	50	30.0	21.0	56.2
131	30	Djibouti	52.3	-1.2	37.5	28.2	80.8	57.8	78.3	50	60	30.0	30.0	70.6
132	31	Lesotho	51.9	-1.2	56.9	56.4	67.2	46.8	75.4	30	50	40.0	32.0	64.0
139	32	Sierra Leone	48.9	1.3	49.4	60.2	81.0	81.8	74.4	30	40	10.0	22.0	40.3
140	33	Togo	48.8	-0.9	36.1	69.2	53.9	88.8	78.2	30	30	30.0	24.0	48.2
141	34	Central African Rep.	48.2	-2.1	40.7	51.4	65.5	91.6	72.5	30	40	20.0	24.0	46.7
142	35	Chad	47.7	-2.3	34.6	60.0	49.9	94.9	73.6	40	40	20.0	20.0	44.2
143	36	Angola	47.1	1.9	36.5	73.0	85.2	72.8	57.8	20	40	20.0	22.0	44.1
145	37	Burundi	46.3	-0.7	35.5	50.2	72.1	59.4	74.7	30	30	30.0	24.0	57.4
146	38	Congo, Republic of	45.2	0.8	45.3	54.6	60.1	83.1	73.0	30	30	10.0	22.0	44.0
147	39	Guinea-Bissau	45.1	-1.7	24.8	56.8	88.4	56.5	75.7	30	30	20.0	10.0	58.5
155	40	Zimbabwe	29.8	-2.0	41.0	55.4	57.8	24.1	0.0	10	20	10.0	24.0	56.0

Source: Kim R. Holmes, Edwin J. Feulner, and Mary Anastasia O'Grady, *2008 Index of Economic Freedom* (Washington, D.C.: The Heritage Foundation and Dow Jones & Company, Inc., 2008), at *www.heritage.org/index*.

omies outnumbered by "repressed" economies. Nine of the 20 countries ranked "repressed" around the world are located in this region.

Table E1 ranks the countries in the region from "most free" to "least free" based on their overall freedom scores. It also includes the change from last year's score, the country's world rank, and each country's 2008 scores for each of the 10 economic freedoms. Chart E3 shows the distribution of countries across five different categories.

Sub-Saharan Africa is ranked last in eight of the 10 economic freedom categories and performs especially poorly in terms of property rights and freedom from corruption. Chart E4 illustrates regional scores in each of the 10 economic freedom categories. Some of the gaps between sub-Saharan Africa's score and the world average score are especially striking: over 10 percentage points for business freedom, 13 percentage points for freedom from corruption, and 12 percentage points for property rights. The single factor for which the region scores higher than the world average is government size. Ironically, however, it is worse than average in terms of taxation, which might indicate that tax revenues are being stolen rather than spent on government services. Labor freedom is restricted, reflecting in part the region's lack of progress toward a modern and efficient labor market. It appears that the countries of sub-Saharan Africa have been saddled with the worst policies of their former European colonizers but none of their prosperity.

The signs of government failure are overwhelming in the heart of Africa. In some cases, the situations are so severe that the next few years must inevitably be bleak. Zimbabwe remains in shambles. With political instability rampant in the region, it is hard to expect that

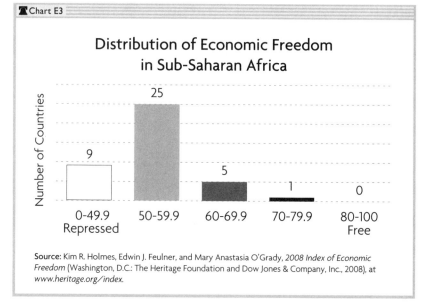

Chart E3

Distribution of Economic Freedom in Sub-Saharan Africa

Number of Countries

- 9 — 0–49.9 Repressed
- 25 — 50–59.9
- 5 — 60–69.9
- 1 — 70–79.9
- 0 — 80–100 Free

Source: Kim R. Holmes, Edwin J. Feulner, and Mary Anastasia O'Grady, *2008 Index of Economic Freedom* (Washington, D.C.: The Heritage Foundation and Dow Jones & Company, Inc., 2008), at www.heritage.org/index.

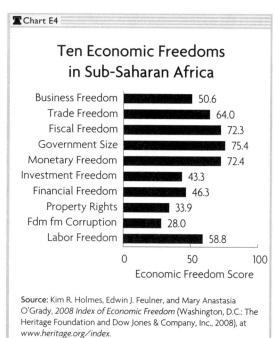

Chart E4

Ten Economic Freedoms in Sub-Saharan Africa

	Economic Freedom Score
Business Freedom	50.6
Trade Freedom	64.0
Fiscal Freedom	72.3
Government Size	75.4
Monetary Freedom	72.4
Investment Freedom	43.3
Financial Freedom	46.3
Property Rights	33.9
Fdm fm Corruption	28.0
Labor Freedom	58.8

Source: Kim R. Holmes, Edwin J. Feulner, and Mary Anastasia O'Grady, *2008 Index of Economic Freedom* (Washington, D.C.: The Heritage Foundation and Dow Jones & Company, Inc., 2008), at www.heritage.org/index.

even the liberalizing tendencies of Mauritius or Botswana can have a significant enough statistical impact to lift sub-Saharan Africa out of its last-place status.

Overall, economic freedom in sub-Saharan Africa has stagnated over the life of the *Index*, and the region has moved only marginally toward improved economic freedom in recent years. Sub-Saharan Africa and the Middle East/North Africa are the only two regions that possess but a single "mostly free" economy apiece.

Chapter 6

The Countries

This chapter is a compilation of the 162 countries covered in the *Index of Economic Freedom*. Only 157 countries receive total scores, because grading has been suspended for five countries (the Democratic Republic of Congo, Iraq, Montenegro, Sudan, and Serbia). Each graded country is given a percent score ranging from 0 to 100 for all 10 factors of overall economic freedom, and these scores are then averaged (using equal weights) to get the country's final *Index of Economic Freedom* score.

In addition to these factor and overall scores, each summary includes a brief introduction that describes the country's economic strengths and weaknesses, as well as its political and economic background, and provides a statistical profile with the country's main economic indicators. These statistics and their sources are outlined in detail below.

Two charts are included on each country page. The first shows a time series of the overall economic freedom score for the country for each year, from 1995 through 2008, compared

Chart 2

Albania's 2008 Economic Freedom Scores

ALBANIA'S TEN ECONOMIC FREEDOMS

Business Freedom	55.6 ▽	
Trade Freedom	75.8 ▲	
Fiscal Freedom	90.3 ▲	
Government Size	76.0 ▲	
Monetary Freedom	80.4 ▲	
Investment Freedom	70.0 ▲	
Financial Freedom	70.0 ▬	
Property Rights	30.0 ▬	
Fdm fm Corruption	26.0 ▲	
Labor Freedom	59.3 ▽	

0   50   100

100 = most free, | = world average

Source: Kim R. Holmes, Edwin J. Feulner, and Mary Anastasia O'Grady, *2008 Index of Economic Freedom* (Washington, D.C.: The Heritage Foundation and Dow Jones & Company, Inc., 2008), at *www.heritage.org/index*.

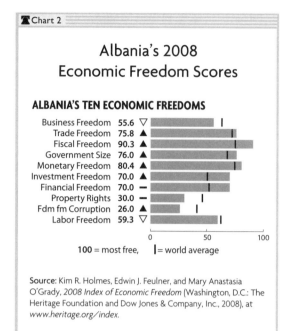

Albania's 2008 Economic Freedom Scores

ALBANIA'S TEN ECONOMIC FREEDOMS

Business Freedom	55.6 ▽	
Trade Freedom	75.8 ▲	
Fiscal Freedom	90.3 ▲	
Government Size	76.0 ▲	
Monetary Freedom	80.4 ▲	
Investment Freedom	70.0 ▲	
Financial Freedom	70.0 ▬	
Property Rights	30.0 ▬	
Fdm fm Corruption	26.0 ▲	
Labor Freedom	59.3 ▽	

0   50   100

100 = most free,   **❙** = world average

Source: Kim R. Holmes, Edwin J. Feulner, and Mary Anastasia O'Grady, *2008 Index of Economic Freedom* (Washington, D.C.: The Heritage Foundation and Dow Jones & Company, Inc., 2008), at *www.heritage.org/index.*

to the world average and regional average. In some cases, a country is not graded continuously for all 13 years, often because grading did not begin until 1996 and frequently because violence or natural disaster has resulted in a lack of reliable information. This year, five countries are not graded, so their respective charts show a line that stops in 2005 or earlier.

The second chart for each country graphs each of the 10 freedom scores for 2008 using horizontal bars. A hash mark is included to show the world average so that one can quickly identify the strengths and weaknesses of economic freedom in each country according to the 10 different component freedoms. Additionally, upward or downward arrow marks are placed to illustrate score changes for each freedom from the 2007 *Index* to the 2008 *Index*.

The charts for Albania presented here are examples of what the reader will see on each country page.

To assure consistency and reliability for each of the 10 factors on which the countries are graded, every effort has been made to use the same source consistently for each country; when data are unavailable from the primary source, secondary sources are used as explained in the chapter on methodology.

DEFINING THE "QUICK FACTS"

Each country page includes "Quick Facts" with 16 different categories of information: population size, macroeconomic data, official development assistance, and more. Unless otherwise indicated, the data in each country's profile are for 2005 (the year for which the most recent data are widely available) and in current 2005 U.S. dollars (also the most recent available). The few cases in which no reliable statistical data were available are indicated by "n/a." Definitions and sources for each category of information are as follows.

Population: 2005 data from World Bank, *World Development Indicators Online*. Another major source is U.S. Central Intelligence Agency, *The World Factbook 2007*. For some countries, another source is the country's statistical agency and/or central bank.

GDP: Gross domestic product—total production of goods and services—expressed as purchasing power parity (PPP). The primary source for GDP data is World Bank, *World Development Indicators Online*. Other sources include U.S. Central Intelligence Agency, *The World Factbook 2007*; the country's statistical agency; and the country's central bank.

GDP growth rate: Annual percentage growth rate of real GDP derived from constant national currency units, based on country-specific years. Annual percent changes are year-on-year. The primary source is International Monetary Fund, *World Economic Outlook Database April 2007*. Secondary sources include World Bank, *World Development Indicators Online*; Economist Intelligence Unit, *Country Reports*, 2006–2007, *Country Profiles*, 2006–2007; the country's statistical agency; and the country's central bank.

GDP five-year compound annual growth: The geometric average growth rate measured over a specified period of time. The compound annual growth rate is measured using data from 2001 to 2005, based on real GDP expressed in constant national currency units, based on country-specific years. It is calculated by taking the nth root of the total percentage growth rate, where n is the number of years in the period being considered. The primary source is International Monetary Fund, *World Economic Outlook Database*, April 2007.

GDP per capita: Gross domestic product expressed as PPP divided by total population. The sources for these data are World Bank, *World Development Indicators Online*; U.S. Central Intelligence Agency, *The World Factbook 2007*; and the country's statistical agency or central bank.

Unemployment rate: A measure of the portion of the workforce that is not employed but is actively seeking work. The primary sources are Economist Intelligence Unit, *Country Reports*, 2006–2007, and *Country Profiles*, 2005–2007; U.S. Central Intelligence Agency, *The World Factbook 2007*; and the country's statistical agency.

Inflation: The annual percent change in consumer prices as measured from 2004 to 2005. The primary source for 2005 data is International Monetary Fund, *World Economic Outlook Database*, April 2007. The secondary sources are Economist Intelligence Unit, *Country Reports*, 2006–2007, and *Country Profiles*, 2005–2007; U.S. Central Intelligence Agency, *The World Factbook 2007*; the country's statistical agency; and the country's central bank.

Foreign direct investment (FDI): This series indicates total annual flow of *net* FDI, which is the sum of FDI inflows less the sum of FDI outflows in 2005. Data are in current 2005 U.S. dollars. FDI flows are defined as investments that acquire a lasting management interest (10 percent or more of voting stock) in a local enterprise by an investor operating in another country. Such investment is the sum of equity capital, reinvestment of earnings, other long-term capital, and short-term capital as shown in the balance of payments and both short-term and long-term international loans. Data are from United Nations Conference on Trade and Development, *World Investment Report 2006*; World Bank, *World Development Indicators Online*; the country's statistical agency; and the country's central bank.

Official development assistance (ODA): Grants or loans to developing countries and territories, as defined by Part I of the Development Assistance Committee (DAC) list of aid recipients, that are undertaken either by the official sector, with promotion of economic development and welfare as the main objective, or on concessional financial terms (a loan that has a grant element of at least 25 percent). Aid includes technical cooperation as well as financial flows. Grants, loans, and credits for military purposes are excluded. Transfer payments to private individuals (e.g., pensions, reparations, or insurance payouts) are usually not counted. Data are listed in current 2005 U.S. dollars. The primary source is Organisation for Economic Co-operation and Development, *International Development Statistics Online*.

- **Multilateral:** In DAC statistics, this includes international institutions with governmental membership that conduct all or a significant part of their activities in favor of development and aid-recipient countries. They include multilateral development banks (e.g., the World Bank and regional development banks); United Nations agencies; and regional groupings. A contribution by a DAC member to such an agency is deemed multilateral if it is pooled with other contributions and disbursed at the discretion of the agency.
- **Bilateral:** Bilateral flows are provided directly by a donor country to an aid-recipient country.

External Debt: Debt owed to non-residents that is repayable in foreign currency, goods, or services. External debt is the sum of public, publicly guaranteed, and private non-guaranteed long-term debt, use of International Monetary Fund credit, and short-term debt. Short-term debt includes all debt having an original or extended maturity of one year or less and interest in arrears on long-term debt. Long-term debt is debt that has an original or extended maturity of more than one year. It has three components: public, publicly guaranteed, and private non-guaranteed debt. Public and publicly guaranteed debt comprises the long-term external obligations of public debtors, including the national government and political subdivisions (or an agency of either) and autonomous public bodies, as well as the external obligations of private debtors that are guaranteed for repayment by a public entity. Private non-guaranteed debt consists of the long-term external obligations of private debtors that are not guaranteed for repayment by a public entity. The data for 2005 are listed in current 2005 U.S. dollars, calculated on an exchange rate basis rather than in PPP terms. The primary source is World Bank, *World Development Indicators 2007*. The secondary source is U.S. Central Intelligence Agency, *The World Factbook 2007*.

Exports: The value of all goods and other market services, f.o.b. Included is the value of merchandise, freight, insurance, travel, and other non-factor services. Factor and property income, such as investment income, interest, and labor income, is excluded. Data are in current 2005 U.S. dollars. The primary source is World Bank, *World Development Indicators Online*. Other sources include Economist Intelligence Unit, *Country Reports*, 2006–2007, and *Country Profiles*, 2005–2007; U.S. Central Intelligence Agency, *The World Factbook 2007*; and the country's statistical agency.

Primary exports: The country's four to six principal export products. Data for major exports are from U.S. Central Intelligence Agency, *The World Factbook 2007*.

Imports: The value of all goods and other market services, f.o.b. Included is the value of merchandise, freight, insurance, travel, and other non-factor services. Factor and property income, such as investment income, interest, and labor income, is excluded. Data are in current 2005 U.S. dollars. The primary source is World Bank, *World Development Indicators Online*. Other sources include Economist Intelligence Unit, *Country Reports*, 2006–2007, and *Country Profiles*, 2005–2007; U.S. Central Intelli-

gence Agency, *The World Factbook 2007*; and the country's statistical agency.

Primary imports: The country's six to eight principal import products. Data for major imports are from U.S. Central Intelligence Agency, *The World Factbook 2007*.

COMMONLY USED ACRONYMS

CIS: Commonwealth of Independent States, consisting of Azerbaijan, Armenia, Belarus, Georgia, Kazakhstan, the Kyrgyz Republic, Moldova, Russia, Tajikistan, Turkmenistan, Ukraine, and Uzbekistan.

EU: European Union, consisting of Austria, Belgium, Bulgaria, Cyprus, the Czech Republic, Denmark, Estonia, Finland, France, Germany, Greece, Hungary, Ireland, Italy, Latvia, Lithuania, Luxembourg, Malta, the Netherlands, Poland, Portugal, Romania, Slovakia, Slovenia, Spain, Sweden, and the United Kingdom.

IMF: International Monetary Fund, established in 1945 to help stabilize countries during crises and now with 185 member countries.

MERCOSUR: Customs union that includes Argentina, Brazil, Paraguay, Uruguay, and Venezuela.

OECD: Organisation for Economic Co-operation and Development, an international organization of developed countries, founded in 1948, that now includes 30 member countries.

SACU: Southern African Customs Union, consisting of Botswana, Lesotho, Namibia, South Africa, and Swaziland.

VAT: Value-added tax.

WTO: World Trade Organization, founded in 1995 as the central organization dealing with the rules of trade between nations and based on signed agreements among 151 member countries.

ALBANIA

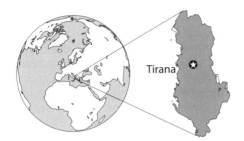

Tirana

Rank: 56

Regional Rank: 27 of 41

Albania's economy is 63.3 percent free, according to our 2008 assessment, which makes it the world's 56th freest economy. Its level of economic freedom increased by 0.9 percentage point during the past year, and it has improved in six of the 10 freedoms. Albania is ranked 27th freest among the 41 countries in the European region.

Comparatively, Albania's freedom level is on par with those of other developing Balkan states like Croatia and Macedonia but still higher than that of Greece, a member of the European Union. Fiscal freedom, investment freedom, and financial freedom all rate significantly higher than the typical country's. However, the overall score is reduced by Albania's poor performance in property rights and freedom from corruption. The unimpressive score in property rights is largely a result of political interference in the judiciary, leading to erratic enforcement of the laws.

Albania's economic freedom ranks above the world average, and its score has risen over the past few years, a noteworthy achievement in a region characterized by federal separatism and instability. If Albania maintains its impressively strong investment freedom while doing more to combat corruption, its score should continue to rise.

BACKGROUND: In 1992, Albania ended nearly 50 years of disastrous Communist rule. The 1990s were a period of transition. Economic growth and reform have advanced since then, but Albania remains one of Europe's poorest countries. In June 2006, Albania signed a Stabilization and Association Agreement with the European Union as the first step toward EU membership, as well as a free trade agreement giving Albanians duty-free access to key EU markets and opening the country to imports. The agricultural sector is the largest source of employment, but growth in service industries and construction has reinforced steady economic growth. In 2005, the OECD reported that informal activity may exceed 50 percent of the economy, and reform in critical areas such as property rights has been slow.

How Do We Measure Economic Freedom? See Chapter 4 (page 39) for an explanation of the methodology or visit the *Index* Web site at *heritage.org/index*.

The economy is 63.3% free

Europe Average = 66.8
World Average = 60.3

1995 — 2008

QUICK FACTS

Population: 3.1 million

GDP (PPP): $16.6 billion
5.5% growth in 2005
5.0% 5-yr. comp. ann. growth
$5,315 per capita

Unemployment: 14.2%

Inflation (CPI): 2.4%

FDI (net flow): $260.0 million

Official Development Assistance:
Multilateral: $135.3 million
Bilateral: $206 million (20.7% from the U.S.)

External Debt: $1.8 billion

Exports: $1.8 billion
Primarily textiles and footwear, asphalt, metals and metallic ores, crude oil, vegetables, fruits, tobacco

Imports: $3.7 billion
Primarily machinery and equipment, foodstuffs, textiles, chemicals

2005 data unless otherwise noted.

ALBANIA'S TEN ECONOMIC FREEDOMS

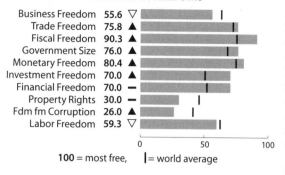

Business Freedom	55.6 ▽	
Trade Freedom	75.8 ▲	
Fiscal Freedom	90.3 ▲	
Government Size	76.0 ▲	
Monetary Freedom	80.4 ▲	
Investment Freedom	70.0 ▲	
Financial Freedom	70.0 —	
Property Rights	30.0 —	
Fdm fm Corruption	26.0 ▲	
Labor Freedom	59.3 ▽	

0   50   100

100 = most free, **|** = world average

BUSINESS FREEDOM — 55.6%

The overall freedom to start, operate, and close a business is constrained by Albania's national regulatory environment. Starting a business takes an average of 36 days, compared to the world average of 43 days. Obtaining a business license requires 24 procedures, compared to the world average of 19, and almost 100 more days than the world average of 234. Regulations are sometimes inconsistent, and businesses have difficulty getting copies of laws and regulations.

TRADE FREEDOM — 75.8%

Albania's weighted average tariff rate in 2005 was 7.1 percent. There are no official non-tariff barriers, but import taxes may be used to establish government-determined fair market prices for goods, and administrative bureaucracy can delay trade and increase costs. Consequently, 10 percentage points is deducted from Albania's trade freedom score.

FISCAL FREEDOM — 90.3%

Albania's low income tax rates enhance incentives for entrepreneurs and workers. In June 2007, the government approved a fiscal package that adopts a flat personal income tax and corporate tax of 10 percent. The new flat personal income tax rate went into effect on July 1, 2007. The current 20 percent corporate tax rate will be reduced to 10 percent in January 2008. Other taxes include a value-added tax (VAT), a property tax, and a vehicle tax. In the most recent year, overall tax revenue as a percentage of GDP was 21.7 percent.

GOVERNMENT SIZE — 76%

Total government expenditures, including consumption and transfer payments, are moderate. In the most recent year, government spending equaled 28.3 percent of GDP. Privatization of state-owned companies has been uneven and slow.

MONETARY FREEDOM — 80.4%

Inflation is relatively low, averaging 2.3 percent between 2004 and 2006. Relatively low and stable prices explain most of the monetary freedom score. Although privatization is slowly moving forward, the government continues to operate state-owned enterprises and oversee prices through regulatory agencies. An additional 10 percentage points is deducted from Albania's monetary freedom score to adjust for price control measures.

INVESTMENT FREEDOM — 70%

Foreign and domestic firms are treated equally under the law, and nearly all sectors of the economy are open to foreign investment. Foreigners are allowed to own 100 percent of Albanian companies, and monetary expatriation is legal. The International Monetary Fund reports that both residents and non-residents may hold foreign exchange accounts. Corruption and a thriving informal market discourage foreign investment, however, as does the absence of further major privatization of strategic sectors, such as oil, coal, and iron.

FINANCIAL FREEDOM — 70%

Albania's financial sector is small but growing rapidly in certain areas. Banking dominates the sector and is overseen by the central Bank of Albania. There are 17 banks, of which 15 are foreign-owned. In December 2005, the government sold its stake in the last partially state-owned bank. Government enforcement of financial regulations can be weak, but oversight of the non-bank financial sector was consolidated into one body in October 2006. The government has separated the Tirana Stock Exchange from the central bank, giving the country an independent stock exchange, but no shares are listed as yet.

PROPERTY RIGHTS — 30%

Albania's judicial system enforces the law weakly and is one of the country's most tainted institutions. Judges are often appointed strictly for political reasons and are sometimes corrupt. Organized crime is a significant obstacle to effective administration of justice. Judges are subject to intimidation, pressure, and bribery, and the pace of judicial reform remains very slow.

FREEDOM FROM CORRUPTION — 26%

Corruption is perceived as widespread. Albania ranks 111th out of 163 countries in Transparency International's Corruption Perceptions Index for 2006. This is something of an improvement over 2005, but the World Bank reports that businesses continue to complain that corruption is pervasive.

LABOR FREEDOM — 59.3%

The labor market operates under inflexible employment regulations that hinder overall productivity growth. The non-salary cost of employing a worker is very high, and dismissing a redundant employee is relatively costly. The high cost of laying off workers creates a serious risk aversion for companies that would otherwise hire more people and grow.

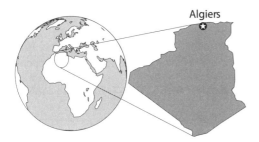

Algiers

ALGERIA

Rank: 102

Regional Rank: 13 of 17

Algeria's economy is 55.7 percent free, according to our 2008 assessment, which makes it the world's 102nd freest economy. Its overall score is 0.6 percentage point higher than last year, reflecting improvement in five of the 10 freedoms. Algeria is ranked 13th out of 17 countries in the Middle East/North Africa region.

Algeria scores moderately high in just a few of the 10 factors of economic freedom, notably business freedom. The income tax rate is high, but because of widespread poverty and substantial oil income, the government collects only a small proportion of GDP in taxes. Inflation is low.

In most areas, Algeria's economic freedoms are below the world average. Algeria has significant problems with overall size of government, banking restrictions, corruption, and political interference in the judiciary. The government and state-owned companies still dominate several critical industries, such as banking, which is why Algeria's financial freedom is 22 points below that of the average country.

BACKGROUND: Algeria gained its independence from France in 1962 and imposed a socialist economic model that stifled growth and wasted the country's huge oil and gas wealth. Algeria is the world's second-largest exporter of natural gas and has the world's seventh-largest natural gas reserves and 14th-largest oil reserves. In 1992, Islamic radicals launched a brutal civil war that claimed more than 100,000 lives. President Abdelaziz Bouteflika negotiated a fragile peace accord in 1999 and has delivered greater political stability. His government has made slow progress on liberalization, privatization, and attracting foreign investment, and the economy has benefited from high world energy prices.

How Do We Measure Economic Freedom? See Chapter 4 (page 39) for an explanation of the methodology or visit the *Index* Web site at *heritage.org/index*.

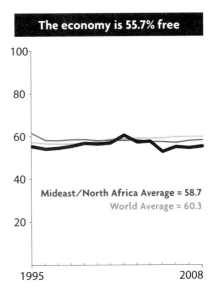

The economy is 55.7% free

Mideast/North Africa Average = 58.7
World Average = 60.3

QUICK FACTS

Population: 32.9 million

GDP (PPP): $232.0 billion
5.3% growth in 2005
5.5% 5-yr. comp. ann. growth
$7,062 per capita

Unemployment: 16.0%

Inflation (CPI): 1.6%

FDI (net flow): $1.1 billion

Official Development Assistance:
Multilateral: $83.9 million
Bilateral: $362.1 million (0.4% from the U.S.)

External Debt: $16.9 billion

Exports: $46.4 billion
Primarily petroleum, natural gas, petroleum products

Imports: $19.6 billion
Primarily capital goods, foodstuffs, consumer goods

2005 data unless otherwise noted.

ALGERIA'S TEN ECONOMIC FREEDOMS

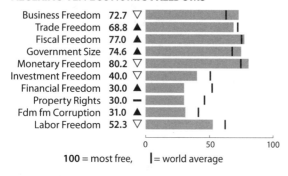

Business Freedom	72.7 ▽	
Trade Freedom	68.8 ▲	
Fiscal Freedom	77.0 ▲	
Government Size	74.6 ▲	
Monetary Freedom	80.2 ▽	
Investment Freedom	40.0 ▽	
Financial Freedom	30.0 ▲	
Property Rights	30.0 —	
Fdm fm Corruption	31.0 ▲	
Labor Freedom	52.3 ▽	

0   50   100

100 = most free, | = world average

BUSINESS FREEDOM — *72.7%*

The overall freedom to start, operate, and close a business is relatively well protected by Algeria's national regulatory environment. Starting a business takes an average of 24 days, compared to the world average of 43 days. However, obtaining a business license requires more than the global average of 19 procedures and 234 days. With more than 400 legislative and regulatory texts, business regulations can be complex and technical. Closing a business is relatively easy.

TRADE FREEDOM — *68.8%*

Algeria's weighted average tariff rate in 2005 was 10.6 percent. The government has made some progress in eliminating non-tariff barriers, but customs clearance procedures, some import and export controls, and restrictive labeling, sanitary, and phytosanitary regulations continue to delay trade and increase costs. Consequently, an additional 10 percentage points is deducted from Algeria's trade freedom score.

FISCAL FREEDOM — *77%*

Algeria has a high income tax rate and a moderate corporate tax rate. The top income tax rate is 40 percent, and the top corporate tax rate was lowered to 25 percent from 30 percent in 2006. Other taxes include a value-added tax (VAT), a capital gains tax, a tax on professional activity, and an apprenticeship tax. In the most recent year, overall tax revenue as a percentage of GDP was 8.4 percent.

GOVERNMENT SIZE — *74.6%*

The government has been trying to strengthen fiscal governance and modernize budget management. Total government expenditures, including consumption and transfer payments, are moderate. In the most recent year, government spending equaled 29.1 percent of GDP.

MONETARY FREEDOM — *80.2%*

Inflation is relatively low, averaging 2.4 percent between 2004 and 2006. Relatively stable prices explain most of the monetary freedom score. Government policies distort prices through subsidies and direct controls in some sectors, including water, energy, and agriculture. An additional 10 percentage points is deducted from Algeria's monetary freedom score to adjust for price-control measures.

INVESTMENT FREEDOM — *40%*

Foreign investors receive non-discriminatory treatment. Investors still face some burdensome procedures that, despite efforts to streamline them electronically, remain complex. Both residents and non-residents may hold foreign exchange accounts, subject to some restrictions. The government claims that 360 public enterprises were privatized in 2006, but none were in the strategic energy sector. The government reversed an earlier privatization law in July 2006 and now mandates 51 percent control in most hydrocarbon contracts for the state energy company, Sonatrach. Algeria's investment climate has been somewhat muted by persistent security concerns, but these are drawing down.

FINANCIAL FREEDOM — *30%*

The government exerts heavy influence on the financial sector, and the regulatory environment is weak. There were 15 private banks in 2004, but six state-owned banks accounted for over 86 percent of total assets in 2003. Fluctuating regulatory laws (like the minimum capital requirements) have also been difficult for private banks. Reform of the banking sector, ostensibly a goal since 1999, has been slow. The decision to privatize the state-owned CPA bank, along with the government's decision to allow its 51 percent share to be sold, is a promising step toward privatization. New regulations intended to streamline certain financial procedures were introduced by the central bank in 2006 but are not yet in widespread use. The insurance sector is small and dominated by six state-owned firms. The stock exchange is likewise undeveloped.

PROPERTY RIGHTS — *30%*

The constitution provides for an independent judiciary, but the legal system functions inefficiently. The judiciary is influenced by the executive branch and the Ministry of the Interior. Protection of intellectual property rights suffers from a lack of trained magistrates, although the government is taking some steps to improve enforcement.

FREEDOM FROM CORRUPTION — *31%*

Corruption is perceived as widespread, although a new law and several presidential decrees that took effect in 2006 are intended to bring Algeria into compliance with the U.N. Anti-Corruption Convention. Algeria ranks 84th out of 163 countries in Transparency International's Corruption Perceptions Index for 2006.

LABOR FREEDOM — *52.3%*

Algeria's labor market is shackled by restrictive employment regulations that hinder employment opportunity and productivity growth. The non-salary cost of employing a worker is high, but dismissing a redundant employee is relatively costless. Further flexibility in the labor market is needed to increase the private sector's competitiveness.

ANGOLA

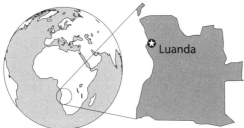
Luanda

Rank: 143
Regional Rank: 36 of 40

Angola's economy is 47.1 percent free, according to our 2008 assessment, which makes it the world's 143rd freest economy. Its overall score is 1.9 percentage points higher than last year. Angola is ranked 36th out of 40 countries in the sub-Saharan Africa region. Although data are spotty because of a protracted civil war, Angola has attained a moderate degree of economic freedom despite a devastated infrastructure and a fledgling government.

Angola scores relatively high in fiscal freedom because of relatively low taxes and a small government size, but it receives overwhelmingly negative scores for most of its policies. The income tax rate is low, and overall tax revenues are low as a percentage of GDP.

Angola is significantly below the world average in seven of the 10 freedoms. Inflation is high, regulation chokes business, investment is basically unwelcome, corruption is crippling, and political influence mars the judiciary. Commercial regulations are a severe hindrance to opening and closing a business, and inconsistent, confusing regulations make it hard to operate a successful company.

BACKGROUND: Despite extensive oil and gas resources, diamonds, hydroelectric potential, and rich agricultural land, Angola remains poor, and a third of the population relies on subsistence agriculture. Since 2002, when a 27-year civil war ended, the government has worked to repair and improve ravaged infrastructure and weakened political and social institutions. High international oil prices and rising oil production have led to strong economic growth in recent years, but corruption and public-sector mismanagement remain, particularly in the oil sector, which accounts for over 50 percent of GDP, over 90 percent of export revenue, and over 80 percent of government revenue. Long-delayed legislative elections are scheduled for mid-2008, and presidential elections are scheduled for 2009.

How Do We Measure Economic Freedom? See Chapter 4 (page 39) for an explanation of the methodology or visit the *Index* Web site at *heritage.org/index*.

The economy is 47.1% free

Sub-Saharan Africa Average = 54.7
World Average = 60.3

100

80

60

40

20

1995   2008

QUICK FACTS

Population: 15.9 million

GDP (PPP): $37.2 billion
20.6% growth in 2005
12.2% 5-yr. comp. ann. growth
$2,334 per capita

Unemployment: n/a

Inflation (CPI): 23.0%

FDI (net flow): −$53.0 billion

Official Development Assistance:
Multilateral: $188.5 million
Bilateral: $262.3 million (25.3% from the U.S.)

External Debt: $11.8 billion

Exports: $24 billion
Primarily crude oil, diamonds, refined petroleum products, gas, coffee, sisal, fish and fish products, timber, cotton

Imports: $15.1 billion
Primarily machinery and electrical equipment, vehicles and spare parts, medicines, food, textiles, military goods
2005 data unless otherwise noted.

ANGOLA'S TEN ECONOMIC FREEDOMS

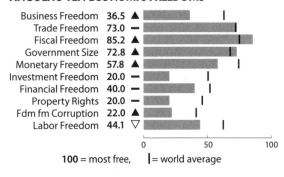

Business Freedom	36.5	▲
Trade Freedom	73.0	—
Fiscal Freedom	85.2	▲
Government Size	72.8	▲
Monetary Freedom	57.8	▲
Investment Freedom	20.0	—
Financial Freedom	40.0	—
Property Rights	20.0	—
Fdm fm Corruption	22.0	▲
Labor Freedom	44.1	▽

100 = most free, | = world average

BUSINESS FREEDOM — 36.5%

The overall freedom to start, operate, and close a business is very constrained by Angola's national regulatory environment. Starting a business takes an average of 119 days, compared to the world average of 43 days. Obtaining a business license requires more than the global average of 19 procedures and 234 days. Closing a business is also very difficult. The regulatory system is complicated and inconsistently enforced, making entrepreneurship far too difficult to enable a dynamic and vibrant economy.

TRADE FREEDOM — 73%

Angola's weighted average tariff rate was 6 percent in 2005. The government has made solid progress in reforming its trade regime, but such non-tariff barriers as subsidies, import restrictions, variable and high import taxes, inadequate customs capacity, prohibitive regulations and standards, non-transparent government procurement procedures, import substitution policies, and issues involving the enforcement and protection of intellectual property rights still add to the cost of trade. Consequently, an additional 15 percentage points is deducted from Angola's trade freedom score.

FISCAL FREEDOM — 85.2%

Angola has a low income tax rate but a high corporate tax rate. The top income tax rate is 15 percent, and the top corporate tax rate is 35 percent. Other taxes include a fuel tax and a consumption tax. In the most recent year, overall tax revenue as a percentage of GDP was 5.7 percent.

GOVERNMENT SIZE — 72.8%

Total government expenditures, including consumption and transfer payments, are high. In the most recent year, government spending equaled 30.1 percent of GDP. The transparency of the government's fiscal accounts needs to be strengthened.

MONETARY FREEDOM — 57.8%

Inflation is high, averaging 18.4 percent between 2004 and 2006. Relatively unstable prices explain most of the monetary freedom score. While privatization has progressed, key sectors remain government-owned, and price controls are pervasive in many sectors of the economy, including fuel and electricity. An additional 15 percentage points is deducted from Angola's monetary freedom score to adjust for the high economic cost of these price control measures.

INVESTMENT FREEDOM — 20%

Angola's Law on Private Investment (LPI) provides equal treatment to foreign investors, simplifies investment regulations, and lowers the required investment. However, the regulatory structure is insufficient to guarantee investment outside of hydrocarbons, and elements of the LPI (like capital repatriation) are vague. Smaller industries face more problems than larger, raw-resource companies. Capital and money market transactions and real estate sales are subject to strict controls. Foreign investment in defense, internal public order, state security, certain banking activities, and the administration of ports and airports is not explicitly prohibited but is somewhat off-limits. With few exceptions, the government is beginning to require foreign investors to hire Angolan nationals.

FINANCIAL FREEDOM — 40%

Angola's financial system is small and underdeveloped but growing. In 2006, the banking sector consisted of 15 commercial banks, of which three were foreign-owned. In December 2006, Angola inaugurated a new development bank aimed at infrastructure development and private-sector credits. The two state-owned banks are slated for privatization and control approximately 45 percent of banking assets. In February 2007, a group of eight Angolan banks announced their intention to float a loan in the largest Angolan syndicate financing project ever undertaken. The government has been liberalizing banking and insurance, but financial governance remains poor. The state remains heavily involved in the insurance sector. A formally constituted stock exchange has not yet begun to operate.

PROPERTY RIGHTS — 20%

The rule of law cannot be guaranteed by Angola's legal system, which suffers from political interference by vested interests and weak statutes. The judicial system does not handle commercial disputes efficiently. Legal fees are high, and most businesses avoid taking disputes to court.

FREEDOM FROM CORRUPTION — 22%

Corruption is perceived as pervasive, especially among government officials at all levels in this oil-rich nation, and it blights all other economic freedoms. Angola ranks 142nd out of 163 countries in Transparency International's Corruption Perceptions Index for 2006.

LABOR FREEDOM — 44.1%

Angola's labor market is shackled by restrictive employment regulations that hinder employment opportunity and productivity growth. The non-salary cost of employing a worker is low, but dismissing a redundant employee is relatively costly. The high cost of laying off workers creates a serious risk aversion for companies that would otherwise hire more people and grow. Angola's labor freedom is one of the 20 lowest in the world.

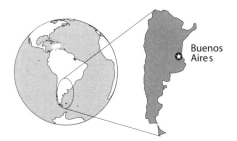

Buenos
Aires

ARGENTINA

Argentina's economy is 55.1 percent free, according to our 2008 assessment, which makes it the world's 108th freest economy. Its overall score is essentially unchanged from last year. Argentina is ranked 23rd out of 29 countries in the Americas, and its overall score is below the regional average.

Compared to the typical country, Argentina has only one economically favorable institution: relatively small government in terms of expenditures. Most advanced economies are cutting their corporate tax rates, but Argentina's top corporate and income tax rates are 35 percent. Yet tax revenue as a percentage of GDP is low, as is expenditure, as a result of tax avoidance and evasion.

Property rights, labor freedom, and freedom from corruption are low, but financial freedom is especially problematic. The foreign debt crisis remains unresolved, and local capital markets are not healthy. Political interference with an inefficient judiciary hinders foreign investment, and popular and official obstructions of due process make international courts preferable to Argentine courts.

BACKGROUND: The government of President Néstor Kirchner, whose term ended in December 2007, intervened heavily in the economy and in 2006 continued the trend by imposing price controls in many sectors as a means of slowing inflation. Mineral resources are abundant, and agriculture has always been important, but the principal industries are food processing and beverages, chemicals, petrochemicals, and automotive manufacturing. Tourism is growing. Economic growth in the past few years is largely attributable to high commodity prices and the predictable recovery process that follows a mega-devaluation and severe economic crisis. A debt moratorium and government borrowing from Venezuela have eased the government's fiscal pressures. Credit markets are not likely to return to normal until all unresolved international debts are paid.

How Do We Measure Economic Freedom? See Chapter 4 (page 39) for an explanation of the methodology or visit the *Index* Web site at *heritage.org/index*.

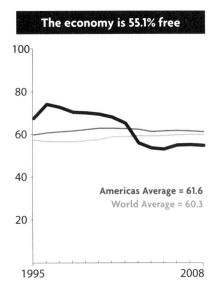

The economy is 55.1% free

Americas Average = 61.6
World Average = 60.3

1995 — 2008

QUICK FACTS

Population: 38.7 million

GDP (PPP): $553.3 billion
9.2% growth
3.7% 5-yr. comp. ann. growth
$14,279 per capita

Unemployment: 11.6%

Inflation (CPI): 9.6%

FDI (net flow): $3.5 billion

Official Development Assistance:
Multilateral: $29.7 million
Bilateral: $84.2 million (1.8% from the U.S.)

External Debt: $114.3 billion

Exports: $46.3 billion
Primarily edible oils, fuels and energy, cereals, feed, motor vehicles

Imports: $34.9 billion
Primarily machinery and equipment, motor vehicles, chemicals, metal manufactures, plastics

2005 data unless otherwise noted.

ARGENTINA'S TEN ECONOMIC FREEDOMS

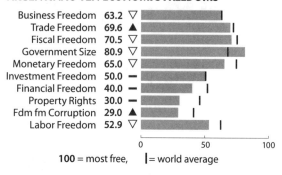

Business Freedom	63.2 ▽	
Trade Freedom	69.6 ▲	
Fiscal Freedom	70.5 ▽	
Government Size	80.9 ▽	
Monetary Freedom	65.0 ▽	
Investment Freedom	50.0 —	
Financial Freedom	40.0 —	
Property Rights	30.0 —	
Fdm fm Corruption	29.0 ▲	
Labor Freedom	52.9 ▽	

0   50   100

100 = most free, | = world average

BUSINESS FREEDOM — *63.2%*

The overall freedom to start, operate, and close a business is relatively well protected by Argentina's national regulatory environment, but inconsistency and lack of transparency persist. Starting a business takes an average of 31 days, compared to the world average of 43 days. Obtaining a business license requires more that the global average of 19 procedures and 234 days. Regulations are often applied inconsistently.

TRADE FREEDOM — *69.6%*

Argentina's weighted average tariff rate was 5.2 percent in 2005. Extensive non-tariff barriers designed to constrain trade, protect domestic industries, and maintain price controls for some goods include import and export controls, tariff escalation, import and export taxes, burdensome regulations, restrictive sanitary rules, subsidies, and issues involving the enforcement and protection of intellectual property rights. While the customs process has been improved, many delays continue. An additional 20 percentage points is deducted from Argentina's trade freedom score to account for non-tariff barriers.

FISCAL FREEDOM — *70.5%*

Argentina has high tax rates. Both the top income tax rate and the top corporate tax rate are 35 percent. Other taxes include a value-added tax (VAT) and a wealth tax. In the most recent year, overall tax revenue as a percentage of GDP was 22.4 percent.

GOVERNMENT SIZE — *80.9%*

Total government expenditures, including consumption and transfer payments, are moderate. In the most recent year, government spending equaled 25.2 percent of GDP. The state's role in the economy has grown in recent years, and structural budgetary weakness persists.

MONETARY FREEDOM — *65%*

Inflation is relatively high, averaging 10 percent between 2004 and 2006. Relatively unstable prices explain most of the monetary freedom score. The government regulates prices on numerous goods and services, including electricity, water, retail-level gas distribution, urban transport, and local telephone services. It also establishes price agreements with producers and sellers. An additional 15 percentage points is deducted from Argentina's monetary freedom score to adjust for measures that distort prices.

INVESTMENT FREEDOM — *50%*

Foreign and domestic investors have equal rights to establish and own businesses, and most local companies may be wholly owned by foreign investors. Foreign investment is prohibited in a few sectors, including shipbuilding, fishing, border-area real estate, and nuclear power generation, and is restricted in media and Internet companies. Foreign firms have been extensively involved in Argentina's large-scale privatization efforts. The most significant deterrent is legal uncertainty concerning creditor, contract, and property rights. The flow of capital is restricted, and repatriation is subject to some controls.

FINANCIAL FREEDOM — *40%*

There were 89 registered financial entities as of February 2006, including several foreign banks. The largest bank is state-owned and serves as the sole financial institution in parts of the country. The financial system is recovering from the devastating 2001–2002 debt default and banking crisis. The banking sector returned to profitability in 2006, mortgages and personal loans are increasing, and non-performing bank loans are down, although the government has not fully compensated banks for the conversion of dollar-denominated instruments to pesos. Argentina remains unable to gain full access to international capital markets because of its $21.8 billion of outstanding debt. Ever since the 2001 crisis, financial services have been subject to government regulation and supervision. The stock market is active, although market capitalization is dominated by a few firms.

PROPERTY RIGHTS — *30%*

The executive branch influences Argentina's judiciary, and independent surveys indicate that public confidence remains weak. Courts are notoriously slow, inefficient, secretive, and corrupt. Many foreign investors resort to international arbitration. An important violation of property rights is the "piquete," by which protestors take over private business, causing extensive losses with no effective punishment by the police or the government. Software piracy is increasing.

FREEDOM FROM CORRUPTION — *29%*

Corruption is perceived as widespread. Argentina ranks 93rd out of 163 countries in Transparency International's Corruption Perceptions Index for 2006. Foreign investors complain frequently about both government and private-sector corruption.

LABOR FREEDOM — *52.9%*

Argentina's labor market operates under restrictive employment regulations that hinder employment creation and productivity growth. The non-salary cost of employing a worker is high, and dismissing a redundant employee can be costly. Despite government efforts to reform labor regulations, barriers to increasing market flexibility still include severance costs, pension payments, mandatory contributions to a union-run health plan, and mandatory holidays.

Yerevan

ARMENIA

A rmenia's economy is 70.3 percent free, according to our 2008 assessment, which makes it the world's 28th freest economy. Its overall score is 1 percentage point higher than last year, reflecting some improvements in the investment regulations but an erosion of labor freedom. Armenia is ranked 15th freest among the 41 countries in the European region, and its score puts it above Europe's average—an impressive feat for an impoverished landlocked country.

Armenia rates significantly higher than the average country in eight of the 10 freedoms. Low tax rates, low government expenditure, and low revenue from state-owned businesses contribute to impressive fiscal and government freedom rankings. Inflation is low, and the banking sector is both wholly private and well regulated. Commercial regulations are flexible and relatively simple. Armenia's great strength is its investment climate, with few restrictions on foreign investment.

Armenia could still make some improvement in property rights and freedom from corruption. The judiciary is fairly weak and subject to political interference.

BACKGROUND: Since 1988, Armenia, a former Soviet republic, has been engaged in a prolonged conflict with neighboring Azerbaijan, occupying Azerbaijan's Nagorno–Karabakh region and adjacent lands. Its border with Turkey remains disputed. Successive coalition governments have been riven by fundamental policy differences. Despite these differences and high levels of corruption, the government has managed to achieve macroeconomic stabilization in recent years. Armenia's economy relies in nearly equal measure on manufacturing, services, remittances, and agriculture, including its famous cognac production. Modest economic growth contributes to larger household incomes, but weak rule of law and continued corruption remain obstacles to higher rates of growth.

How Do We Measure Economic Freedom? See Chapter 4 (page 39) for an explanation of the methodology or visit the *Index* Web site at *heritage.org/index*.

The economy is 70.3% free

100

80

60

40

20

Europe Average = 66.8
World Average = 60.3

1995   2008

QUICK FACTS

Population: 3.0 million

GDP (PPP): $14.9 billion
14.0% growth
12.9% 5-yr. comp. ann. growth
$4,945 per capita

Unemployment: 7.4%

Inflation (CPI): 0.6%

FDI (net flow): $212.0 million

Official Development Assistance:
Multilateral: $98.6 million
Bilateral: $150.8 million (36.7% from the U.S.)

External Debt: $1.9 billion

Exports: $1.3 billion
Primarily diamonds, mineral products, foodstuffs, energy

Imports: $2.0 billion
Primarily natural gas, petroleum, tobacco products, foodstuffs, diamonds

2005 data unless otherwise noted.

ARMENIA'S TEN ECONOMIC FREEDOMS

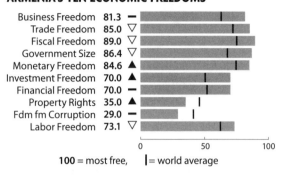

Business Freedom	81.3	—
Trade Freedom	85.0	▽
Fiscal Freedom	89.0	▽
Government Size	86.4	▽
Monetary Freedom	84.6	▲
Investment Freedom	70.0	▲
Financial Freedom	70.0	—
Property Rights	35.0	▲
Fdm fm Corruption	29.0	—
Labor Freedom	73.1	▽

0   50   100

100 = most free, | = world average

BUSINESS FREEDOM — 81.3%

The freedom to start, operate, and close a business is relatively well protected by Armenia's national regulatory environment. Starting a business takes an average of 18 days, compared to the world average of 43 days. Obtaining a business license requires about the world average of 19 procedures and about half of the world average of 234 days. Closing a business is easy. However, the business environment can be risky because of the poor implementation and application of business legislation.

TRADE FREEDOM — 85%

Armenia's weighted average tariff rate in 2001 was a relatively low 2.5 percent. Unpredictable customs valuation, improper implementation of the customs code, inefficient customs administration, and corruption in customs add to the cost of trade. An additional 10 percentage points is deducted from Armenia's trade freedom score to account for non-tariff barriers.

FISCAL FREEDOM — 89%

Armenia has low tax rates. Both the top income tax rate and the top corporate tax rate are 20 percent. Other taxes include a value-added tax (VAT) and a vehicle tax. In the most recent year, overall tax revenue as a percentage of GDP was 17.3 percent.

GOVERNMENT SIZE — 86.4%

Total government expenditures, including consumption and transfer payments, are low. In the most recent year, government spending equaled 21.3 percent of GDP. Despite some delays, privatization has accelerated over the past two years in sectors like mining and metals.

MONETARY FREEDOM — 84.6%

Inflation is relatively low, averaging 2.7 percent between 2003 and 2005. Relatively stable prices explain most of the monetary freedom score. Government subsidies and regulation policies distort prices in some sectors, such as public transportation, electricity, and gas. An additional 5 percentage points is deducted from Armenia's monetary freedom score to adjust for measures that distort domestic prices.

INVESTMENT FREEDOM — 70%

Officially, foreign investors and native Armenians have the same right to establish businesses in nearly all sectors of the economy. Armenia maintains a liberal trade regimen, receiving the highest classification from the International Monetary Fund. Non-residents may lease land but may not own it. The major impediments to foreign investors are weak implementation of business legislation and corruption in the bureaucracy. Privatization, though generally successful and legally open to all bidders, has not been transparent. Commercial arbitration laws passed in December 2006 allow a wider range of settlement procedures for parties contracted to the Republic of Armenia. The government maintains several incentives, such as tax holidays, for investors, but the regulation system is still not transparent. The IMF reports that there are no restrictions or controls on the holding of foreign exchange accounts, invisible transactions, or current transfers and no repatriation requirements.

FINANCIAL FREEDOM — 70%

Armenia's underdeveloped financial sector is dominated by banking. Following a banking crisis in the 1990s, the government embarked on a process of privatization and regulatory reform that included adopting International Accounting Standards. Under the revised rules and standards, many banks have closed or merged. In 2001, there were 31 banks; by the end if 2006, there were 21. The remaining banks are becoming more liquid and profitable. The state no longer has a stake in any bank, and all 21 are privately owned. However, banks remain hindered by difficulty in debt recovery. The central bank has intervened in the market to encourage dram transactions, but without much success. The Ministry of Finance and Economy regulates the small insurance industry. Foreign insurance companies and banks are permitted. In February 2006, the active stock exchange had a market capitalization of $18 million, with 190 countries listed.

PROPERTY RIGHTS — 35%

Armenian law provides substantial protection for intellectual property rights and is in compliance with the World Trade Organization's Trade Related Aspects of Intellectual Properties (TRIPS) Agreement. The government has increased enforcement of IPR laws. The judicial system is still recovering from underdevelopment and corruption—legacies of the Soviet era that substantially impede the enforcement of contracts. In November 2005, the constitution was amended to increase judicial independence, but it remains to be seen how this translates into practice.

FREEDOM FROM CORRUPTION — 29%

Corruption is perceived as widespread, although the government has introduced a number of reforms in the past few years. Petty corruption is pervades Armenian society. Armenia ranks 93rd out of 163 countries in Transparency International's Corruption Perceptions Index for 2006.

LABOR FREEDOM — 73.1%

Armenia's labor market operates under relatively flexible employment regulations that could be improved to enhance employment and productivity growth. The non-salary cost of employing a worker is moderate, and dismissing a redundant employee is relatively costless.

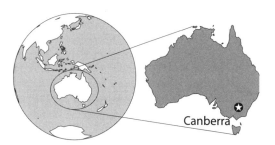

Canberra

AUSTRALIA

Rank: 4

Regional Rank: 3 of 30

A ustralia's economy is 82 percent free, according to our 2008 assessment, which makes it the world's 4th freest economy. Its overall score is 1 percentage point higher than last year, primarily because of an improved investment climate. Australia is ranked 3rd out of 30 countries in the Asia–Pacific region, and its overall score is well above the regional average.

Australia rates highly in virtually all areas but is most impressive in financial freedom, property rights, and freedom from corruption. Low inflation and low tariff rates buttress a globally competitive financial system based on market principles. A strong rule of law protects property rights and tolerates virtually no corruption. Foreign and domestic investors receive equal treatment, and both foreign and domestically owned businesses enjoy considerable flexibility in licensing, regulation, and employment practices.

The top income tax rate is high, as is government spending, with both scoring below the world average. The top income tax is especially oppressive. Yet, due to its deep freedoms generally, Australia's economy is a global competitor and a regional leader.

BACKGROUND: Australia, one of the Asia-Pacific region's richest democracies, has been governed by the conservative Liberal Party for 11 years. In the 1980s, the Labor Hawke and Keating governments deregulated financial and labor markets and reduced trade barriers. Although these changes transformed the country into an internationally competitive producer of services, technologies, and high-value-added manufactured goods, its export sector remains heavily dependent on mining and agriculture. Australia is in its 16th year of uninterrupted economic expansion, with unemployment at 32-year lows. The Howard government's policy agenda has been dominated in recent years by efforts to reform taxation, labor markets, and higher education.

How Do We Measure Economic Freedom? See Chapter 4 (page 39) for an explanation of the methodology or visit the *Index* Web site at *heritage.org/index*.

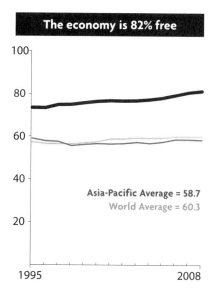

The economy is 82% free

Asia-Pacific Average = 58.7
World Average = 60.3

1995   2008

QUICK FACTS

Population: 20.7 million

GDP (PPP): $646.3 billion
2.8% growth in 2005
3.4% 5-yr. comp. ann. growth
$31,794 per capita

Unemployment: 5.2%

Inflation (CPI): 2.7%

FDI (net flow): −$6.4 billion

Official Development Assistance:
Multilateral: None
Bilateral: None

External Debt: $504.2 billion

Exports: $135.5 billion
Primarily coal, gold, meat, wool, alumina, iron ore, wheat, machinery and transport equipment

Imports: $149.7 billion
Primarily machinery and transport equipment, computers and office machines, telecommunication equipment and parts, crude oil and petroleum products
2005 data unless otherwise noted.

AUSTRALIA'S TEN ECONOMIC FREEDOMS

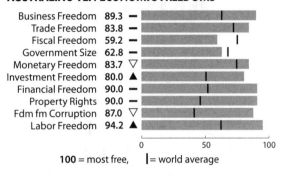

Business Freedom	89.3 —	
Trade Freedom	83.8 —	
Fiscal Freedom	59.2 —	
Government Size	62.8 —	
Monetary Freedom	83.7 ▽	
Investment Freedom	80.0 ▲	
Financial Freedom	90.0 —	
Property Rights	90.0 —	
Fdm fm Corruption	87.0 ▽	
Labor Freedom	94.2 ▲	

0   50   100

100 = most free, |= world average

BUSINESS FREEDOM — *89.3%*

The overall freedom to start, operate, and close a business is strongly protected by Australia's national regulatory environment. Starting a business takes an average of two days, compared to the world average of 43 days. Obtaining a business license requires less than the global average of 19 procedures and 234 days. Closing a business is very easy. In sectors dominated by small businesses, the government generally follows a hands-off approach.

TRADE FREEDOM — *83.8%*

Australia's weighted average tariff rate in 2005 was a relatively low 3.1 percent. A number of non-tariff barriers, including stringent sanitary measures, a burdensome quarantine regime, subsidies and other support programs for agriculture and manufacturing products, some barriers to trade in services, and state trading of wheat and other agriculture products, raise the cost of trade. Consequently, an additional 10 percentage points is deducted from Australia's trade freedom score.

FISCAL FREEDOM — *59.2%*

Australia has a high income tax rate and a moderate corporate tax rate. The top income tax rate is 47 percent, and the top corporate tax rate is 30 percent. Other taxes include a value-added tax (VAT), a tax on insurance contracts, and a fuel tax. In the most recent year, overall tax revenue as a percentage of GDP was 31.2 percent.

GOVERNMENT SIZE — *62.8%*

Total government expenditures, including consumption and transfer payments, are high. In the most recent year, government spending equaled 35.2 percent of GDP. The government has advanced its privatization agenda by selling its remaining share of Telstra, a telecommunications company, and other holdings.

MONETARY FREEDOM — *83.7%*

Inflation is moderate, averaging 3.2 percent between 2004 and 2006. Relatively stable prices explain most of the monetary freedom score. The government does not impose national price controls on goods, but states retain the power to impose their own controls, although the range of goods actually subject to control is diminishing as competition reforms are implemented. Retail gas and electricity prices are regulated. Consequently, an additional 5 percentage points is deducted from Australia's monetary freedom score.

INVESTMENT FREEDOM — *80%*

Foreign and domestic investors receive equal treatment. Proposals to start new businesses with an investment of A$10 million must be reported to the government, which accepts most of these proposals routinely but may reject those it deems inconsistent with the "national interest." In these cases, the legal burden is on the government, not the investor. Foreign investment in media, banking, airlines, airports, shipping, real estate, and telecommunications is subject to limitations. Australia offers investors several incentives, such as research and development tax breaks, streamlined immigration programs, and grants for early-stage commercialization projects. Residents and non-residents have access to foreign exchange and may conduct international payments and capital transactions. There are no controls on capital repatriation.

FINANCIAL FREEDOM — *90%*

Australia's highly developed, competitive financial system is the world's ninth-largest and includes advanced banking, insurance, and equity industries. The central bank has not set lending policies and interest rates since its 1980s financial market deregulation. Today, markets set interest rates. Government regulation of banks is minimal, and foreign banks, licensed as branches or subsidiaries, may offer a full range of banking operations. Australia subscribes to OECD codes on international investment, capital transfer, and invisible transactions. As of September 2006, there were 55 licensed financial institutions, of which 41 were foreign, and numerous other non-bank financial institutions. There are no government-owned banks, and banks are highly competitive. Foreign insurance companies are permitted, and regulation of the sector is focused on capital adequacy, solvency, and prudential behavior. The stock and futures markets are well developed and open to foreign listings.

PROPERTY RIGHTS — *90%*

Property rights are well protected. Protection of intellectual property rights meets or exceeds world standards. Contracts are secure, although subject to backlogs, and government expropriation is highly unusual. The rule of law is seen as fundamental to the functioning of government, and enforcement is even-handed.

FREEDOM FROM CORRUPTION — *87%*

Corruption is perceived as minimal. Australia ranks 9th out of 163 countries in Transparency International's Corruption Perceptions Index for 2006, ahead of the U.S., the U.K., and Canada, and the government actively promotes international efforts to curb the bribing of foreign officials.

LABOR FREEDOM — *94.2%*

Australia's labor market operates under highly flexible employment regulations that enhance employment creation and productivity growth. The non-salary cost of employing a worker can be moderate, and dismissing a redundant employee is costless. Australia's labor market flexibility is one of the 20 highest in the world.

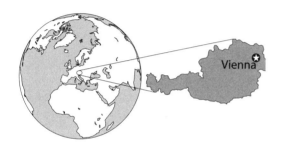

Vienna

AUSTRIA

A ustria's economy is 70 percent free, according to our 2008 assessment, which makes it the world's 30th freest economy. Its score remains essentially unchanged from last year. Austria is ranked 16th freest among the 41 countries in the European region, putting it well above the regional average.

Austria rates above the world average in seven freedoms but far below it in two. It has world-class property protections and clean government. As a member of the European Union, its tariff is standardized at a low rate, and inflation is relatively stable for the euro currency. Starting a business takes a relatively short time. Foreign investors are not subject to particularly stringent requirements.

Austria maintains very high personal income tax rates to support a significant welfare state. Its government size score is some 40 percentage points worse than the average. Commercial regulations have been reduced slightly, although labor laws remain rigid. Hiring and firing employees is difficult, as is true almost everywhere else in the EU, and labor market inflexibility hurts overall competitiveness.

BACKGROUND: Over the past decade, Austria's government has relinquished control of formerly nationalized oil, gas, steel, and engineering companies and has deregulated telecommunications and electricity. From 2000–2007, People's Party Chancellor Wolfgang Schüssel accelerated market reform and significantly limited government intervention in the economy. A major tax reform simplifying both wage and income taxes was enacted in May 2004. In 2005, corporate tax rates were reduced by nearly a third to 25 percent, giving Austria one of Western Europe's lowest corporate rates. Austria's primary trading partners are other EU member states, which account for more than 80 percent of imports and exports.

How Do We Measure Economic Freedom? See Chapter 4 (page 39) for an explanation of the methodology or visit the *Index* Web site at *heritage.org/index*.

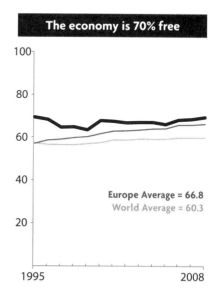

The economy is 70% free

Europe Average = 66.8
World Average = 60.3

1995 — 2008

QUICK FACTS

Population: 8.2 million

GDP (PPP): $277.5 billion
2.0% growth in 2005
1.6% 5-yr. comp. ann. growth
$33,699 per capita

Unemployment: 5.2%

Inflation (CPI): 2.1%

FDI (net flow): −$374.0 million

Official Development Assistance:
Multilateral: None
Bilateral: None

External Debt: $594.3 billion

Exports: $171.2 billion
Primarily machinery and equipment, motor vehicles and parts, paper and paperboard, metal goods, chemicals, iron and steel, textiles, foodstuffs

Imports: $162.9 billion
Primarily machinery and equipment, motor vehicles, chemicals, metal goods, oil and oil products, foodstuffs
2005 data unless otherwise noted.

AUSTRIA'S TEN ECONOMIC FREEDOMS

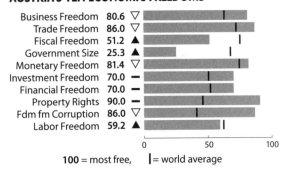

Business Freedom	80.6 ▽
Trade Freedom	86.0 ▽
Fiscal Freedom	51.2 ▲
Government Size	25.3 ▲
Monetary Freedom	81.4 ▽
Investment Freedom	70.0 —
Financial Freedom	70.0 —
Property Rights	90.0 —
Fdm fm Corruption	86.0 ▽
Labor Freedom	59.2 ▲

0   50   100

100 = most free, | = world average

BUSINESS FREEDOM — 80.6%

The overall freedom to start, operate, and close a business is relatively well protected by Austria's national regulatory environment. Starting a business takes an average of 28 days, compared to the world average of 43 days. Obtaining a business license involves less than the global average of 19 procedures, and closing a business is easy. The government has moved to streamline its complex and time-consuming regulatory environment.

TRADE FREEDOM — 86%

Austria's trade policy is the same as those of other members of the European Union. The common EU weighted average tariff rate was 2 percent in 2005. Non-tariff barriers reflected in EU and Austrian policy include agricultural and manufacturing subsidies, import restrictions for some goods and services, market access restrictions in some service sectors, non-transparent and restrictive regulations and standards, and inconsistent customs administration across EU members. Consequently, an additional 10 percentage points is deducted from Austria's trade freedom score.

FISCAL FREEDOM — 51.2%

Austria has a very high income tax rate and a low corporate tax rate. The top income tax rate is 50 percent, and the top corporate tax rate is 25 percent. Other taxes include a value-added tax (VAT), an advertising tax, and a tax on insurance contracts. In the most recent year, overall tax revenue as a percentage of GDP remained a very high 41.9 percent.

GOVERNMENT SIZE — 25.3%

Total government expenditures, including consumption and transfer payments, are very high. In 2004, government spending equaled 49.9 percent of GDP. With a limited deficit, Austria's government finances are better than those in some other euro zone economies.

MONETARY FREEDOM — 81.4%

Austria is a member of the euro zone. From 2004 to 2006, its weighted average annual rate of inflation was 1.8 percent. Relatively stable prices explain most of the monetary freedom score. As a participant in the EU's Common Agricultural Policy, the government subsidizes agricultural production, distorting the prices of agricultural products. It also subsidizes rail transportation and operates some state-owned firms, utilities, and services. An additional

10 percentage points is deducted from Austria's monetary freedom score to account for these policies.

INVESTMENT FREEDOM — 70%

There are no formal sectoral or geographic restrictions on foreign investment. The law grants foreign and domestic capital equal treatment. Foreign investment is forbidden in arms, explosives, and industries in which the state has a monopoly (such as casinos, printing of banknotes, and minting of coins). In 2006, the state partially privatized the postal service, following its earlier partial liberalization of telecommunications. Restrictions exist for non-residents in the auditing and legal professions, transportation, and electric power generation. Investment is subject to strict environmental restrictions. There are no controls or requirements on current transfers, access to foreign exchange, or repatriation of profits. Real estate transactions are subject to approval by local authorities.

FINANCIAL FREEDOM — 70%

Austria's financial system is subject to limited government intervention. An independent supervisory body oversees retirement funds, insurance, securities, and banking (where oversight is also performed by the central bank). Banks offer the full range of services, and the erosion of barriers has led to consolidation. Markets set interest rates, and foreign banks operate freely. The largest bank is a unit of Germany's Hypo-Vereinsbank. In March 2006, the government intervened to support Austria's fourth-largest bank, Bawag PSK, after it almost collapsed from a speculation debacle in a politically charged financial scandal. Tax incentives have been adopted to promote equity investment through pension funds. Financial regulations are transparent and consistent with international norms. The stock exchange, privatized in 1999 and modest in size, has performed consistently better than those of other industrialized countries in recent years. Additional capital is readily available from elsewhere in Europe.

PROPERTY RIGHTS — 90%

Private property is very secure. Contractual agreements are secure, and the protection of private property and intellectual property is well established and effective. There is a long-standing tradition of respect for the rule of law, and the judiciary is independent.

FREEDOM FROM CORRUPTION — 86%

Corruption is perceived as minimal. Austria ranks 11th out of 163 countries in Transparency International's Corruption Perceptions Index for 2006. Any person who bribes either an Austrian or foreign government official is subject to criminal penalties.

LABOR FREEDOM — 59.2%

The labor market operates under inflexible employment regulations that could hinder employment and productivity growth. The non-salary cost of employing a worker is high, and dismissing a redundant employee is costly. The cost of fringe benefits per employee still remains one of the highest in the EU.

AZERBAIJAN

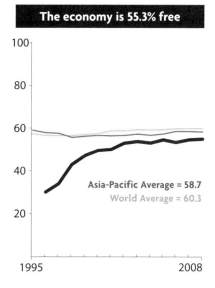

Baku

Rank: 107

Regional Rank: 18 of 30

Azerbaijan's economy is 55.3 percent free, according to our 2008 assessment, which makes it the world's 107th freest economy. Its overall score is 0.5 percentage point higher than last year. Azerbaijan is ranked 18th out of 30 countries in the Asia–Pacific region, and its overall score is below the world average.

Azerbaijan's relatively small government size is its one standout strength, helped by trade freedom and moderate taxes. A low corporate tax rate enhances Azerbaijan's score, although the government also imposes other taxes.

As a transforming economy, Azerbaijan still faces substantial challenges. Financial freedom, investment freedom, property rights, and corruption remain significantly worse than those of other countries, and an underdeveloped judicial system engenders a debilitating lack of property rights. Major hurdles, both formal and informal, hinder foreign investment, and wide sectors of the economy are off-limits to non-Azerbaijanis.

BACKGROUND: Azerbaijan gained its independence from the Soviet Union in 1991, but a long-running dispute with Armenia over the Nagorno–Karabakh region has cost Azerbaijan 16 percent of its territory. President Ilham Aliyev is likely to be reelected in the 2008 presidential election. Large inflows of foreign direct investment continue to support the hydrocarbons sector, resulting in unprecedented GDP growth. Surging exports of oil and gas are expected to raise GDP significantly in the years ahead. The main challenges will be assertive Russian foreign policy in the Caspian basin; economic diversification; development of the rule of law; corruption; the need to expand democratic institutions; and replacement of the old Soviet guard of senior politicians and bureaucrats with a more pro-Western, market-oriented younger generation.

How Do We Measure Economic Freedom? See Chapter 4 (page 39) for an explanation of the methodology or visit the *Index* Web site at *heritage.org/index.*

The economy is 55.3% free

Asia-Pacific Average = 58.7
World Average = 60.3

1995 — 2008

QUICK FACTS

Population: 8.4 million

GDP (PPP): $42.1 billion
24.3% growth
13.1% 5-yr. comp. ann. growth
$5,016 per capita

Unemployment: 1.1%

Inflation (CPI): 9.7%

FDI (net flow): $459.0 million

Official Development Assistance:
Multilateral: $110.1 million
Bilateral: $140.4 million (31.4% from the U.S.)

External Debt: $1.9 billion

Exports: $8.3 billion
Primarily oil and gas, machinery, cotton, foodstuffs

Imports: $7.0 billion
Primarily machinery and equipment, oil products, foodstuffs, metals, chemicals

2005 data unless otherwise noted.

AZERBAIJAN'S TEN ECONOMIC FREEDOMS

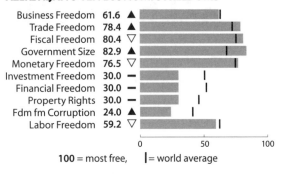

Business Freedom	61.6 ▲	
Trade Freedom	78.4 ▲	
Fiscal Freedom	80.4 ▽	
Government Size	82.9 ▲	
Monetary Freedom	76.5 ▽	
Investment Freedom	30.0 —	
Financial Freedom	30.0 —	
Property Rights	30.0 —	
Fdm fm Corruption	24.0 ▲	
Labor Freedom	59.2 ▽	

0   50   100

100 = most free, | = world average

BUSINESS FREEDOM — 61.6%

The overall freedom to start, operate, and close a business is limited by Azerbaijan's national regulatory environment. Starting a business takes an average of 30 days, compared to the world average of 43 days. Obtaining a business license involves more than the global average of 19 procedures, but closing a business is relatively easy. The lack of transparent regulations and inconsistent enforcement of existing laws remain impediments to investment and entrepreneurial activities.

TRADE FREEDOM — 78.4%

Azerbaijan's weighted average tariff rate was a relatively moderate 5.8 percent in 2005. A weak legal regime, arbitrary customs administration, conflicts of interest in regulatory matters, subsidies, export restrictions for some goods, and customs corruption add to the cost of trade. An additional 10 percentage points is deducted from Azerbaijan's trade freedom score to account for these non-tariff barriers.

FISCAL FREEDOM — 80.4%

Azerbaijan has a moderate income tax rate and a low corporate tax rate. The top income tax rate is 35 percent, and the top corporate tax rate is 22 percent. Other taxes include a value-added tax (VAT) and a property tax. In the most recent year, overall tax revenue as a percentage of GDP was 16 percent.

GOVERNMENT SIZE — 82.9%

Total government spending, including consumption and transfer payments, is low. In the most recent year, government spending equaled 23.9 percent of GDP. Privatization of small and medium-sized enterprises is almost complete, but privatization of large-scale enterprises has been limited.

MONETARY FREEDOM — 76.5%

Inflation is moderately high, averaging 8.6 percent between 2004 and 2006. Relatively unstable prices explain most of the monetary freedom score. The government continues to control prices on most energy products and operates a number of state-owned enterprises. An additional 5 percentage points is deducted from Azerbaijan's monetary freedom score to adjust for price-control policies.

INVESTMENT FREEDOM — 30%

Although the government has issued some formal decrees to improve the business environment, its regulatory agen-cies continue to act non-transparently and arbitrarily. Poor infrastructure also has a negative effect on foreign investment, as does the bureaucratic obstacles that companies face. The government prohibits investments in national security and defense sectors and restricts investment in government-controlled sectors like energy, mobile telephony, and oil and gas. Most investment is driven by the oil and gas sector, aside from which FDI is very low. Repatriation of profits is legal, as are certain guarantees against uncompensated nationalization and harmful legislation. The Azerbaijan National Bank regulates most foreign exchange transactions and most capital transactions. Direct investment abroad by residents, including real estate transactions, requires central bank approval.

FINANCIAL FREEDOM — 30%

Azerbaijan's financial system is underdeveloped but growing. The banking sector is weak and burdened by non-performing loans, but its capital is increasing rapidly. The central bank, independent since 1995, has overseen a process of closures, consolidation, and privatization under which the number of banks has fallen from 210 in 1994 to 43 in 2007. The banking sector is dominated by two major state-owned banks, which together account for about 60 percent of assets; provide financing for most government departments and many of the state-owned enterprises, often at below-market rates; and stunt the growth of private commercial banks. The central bank has raised minimum capital requirements, but many commercial banks are undercapitalized. Foreign banks have a minimal presence. The stock exchange, founded in 2000, is very small.

PROPERTY RIGHTS — 30%

The judiciary in Azerbaijan remains corrupt and inefficient and does not function independently of the executive. The poor quality, reliability, and transparency of governance, as well as abuse of the regulatory system and poor contract enforcement, significantly impede the ability of many companies to do business. Politically connected business interests benefit from their control of lucrative sectors of the economy.

FREEDOM FROM CORRUPTION — 24%

Corruption is perceived as widespread. Azerbaijan ranks 130th out of 163 countries in Transparency International's Corruption Perceptions Index for 2006. The country remains plagued by arbitrary tax and customs administration that creates opportunities for graft, regulatory regimes that favor monopolies, and corruption at all levels.

LABOR FREEDOM — 59.2%

Azerbaijan's labor market operates under restrictive employment regulations that hinder employment creation and productivity growth. The non-salary cost of employing a worker is high, and dismissing a redundant employee can be difficult. The high cost of laying off workers creates a risk aversion for companies that would otherwise hire more people and grow. The overly generous unemployment insurance program diminishes the incentive to work.

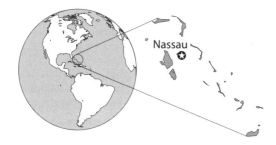

Nassau ✪

THE BAHAMAS

T he Bahamas' economy is 71.1 percent free, according to our 2008 assessment, which makes it the world's 24th freest economy. Its overall score is 0.9 percentage point lower than last year, primarily because of worsening trade freedom. The Bahamas is ranked 5th out of 29 countries in the Americas, and its overall score is higher than the regional average.

The Bahamas enjoys high scores in business freedom, government size, monetary freedom, fiscal freedom, property rights, and labor freedom. The government imposes no income or corporate tax. Regulations can be subject to official whim, but the environment remains generally business-friendly. The labor market is highly flexible. A focus on transparency represents the best traditions of English common law in protecting private property, which is nowhere more apparent than in the advanced financial system.

Despite a healthy respect for law and a relatively positive economic environment, very heavy tariffs are imposed on a wide array of trade goods, and non-tariff barriers further impede trade. Foreign investment is restricted and subject to numerous approvals by the civil service.

BACKGROUND: A tradition of political stability, relatively high per capita income, and a mostly favorable private investment climate have made the Bahamas one of the most prosperous nations in the Caribbean. Tourism generates about half of all jobs. Banking and international financial services also contribute heavily to the economy. The government is funded partly by high import tariffs, which serve as a mercantilist barrier to greater prosperity and to closer regional trade integration. Other problems include drug trafficking and an economy that is vulnerable to external shocks. Some offshore banks have left the country because of an aggressive effort against money laundering, and this has caused losses in the financial sector.

How Do We Measure Economic Freedom? See Chapter 4 (page 39) for an explanation of the methodology or visit the *Index* Web site at *heritage.org/index*.

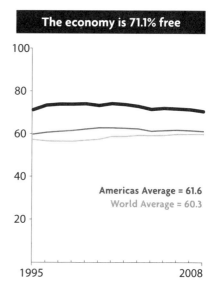

The economy is 71.1% free

Americas Average = 61.6
World Average = 60.3

1995 — 2008

QUICK FACTS

Population: 0.3 million

GDP (PPP): $6.3 billion
2.7% growth in 2005
2.0% 5-yr.comp. ann. growth
$19,390 per capita

Unemployment: 10.2.%

Inflation (CPI): 2.2%

FDI (net flow): $360.0 million

Official Development Assistance:
Multilateral: n/a
Bilateral: n/a

External Debt: $342.6 million (2004 estimate)

Exports: $3.0 billion
Primarily mineral products and salt, animal products, rum, chemicals, fruit and vegetables

Imports: $3.8 billion
Primarily machinery and transport equipment, manufactures, chemicals, mineral fuels, food and live animals
2005 data unless otherwise noted.

THE BAHAMAS' TEN ECONOMIC FREEDOMS

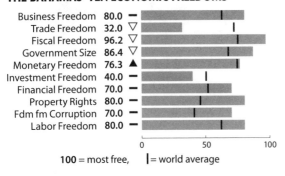

Business Freedom	80.0
Trade Freedom	32.0
Fiscal Freedom	96.2
Government Size	86.4
Monetary Freedom	76.3
Investment Freedom	40.0
Financial Freedom	70.0
Property Rights	80.0
Fdm fm Corruption	70.0
Labor Freedom	80.0

0   50   100

100 = most free, | = world average

BUSINESS FREEDOM — 80%

The overall freedom to start, operate, and close a business is relatively well protected by the Bahamas' national regulatory environment. The government generally follows a hands-off approach to business. However, dealing with licenses can be burdensome as the process may involve non-transparency caused by the existence of some discretionary issuances of business licenses.

TRADE FREEDOM — 32%

According to the World Bank, the Bahamas' weighted average tariff rate was a high 29 percent in 2005. The government imposes occasional import bans and implements import licensing procedures. Most imports are subject to a 7 percent "stamp tax," and higher stamp taxes are charged on some duty-free goods, including china, crystal, wristwatches, clocks, jewelry, table linens, leather goods, perfume, wine, and liquor. The government also uses import permits to restrict imports of some agricultural goods. An additional 10 percentage points is deducted from the Bahamas' trade freedom score to account for non-tariff barriers.

FISCAL FREEDOM — 96.2%

The Bahamas' tax burden is one of the lowest in the world. There is no income tax, no corporate income tax, no capital gains tax, no value-added tax (VAT), and no inheritance tax. In the most recent year, overall tax revenue (mainly from import tariffs) as a percentage of GDP was 19.6 percent.

GOVERNMENT SIZE — 86.4%

Total government spending, including consumption and transfer payments, is low. In the most recent year, government spending equaled 21.3 percent of GDP. Privatization of state-owned business has been slow, although the government has taken steps to revive the program in recent years.

MONETARY FREEDOM — 76.3%

Inflation is relatively low, averaging 1.9 percent between 2004 and 2006. Relatively stable prices explain most of the monetary freedom score. An additional 15 percentage points is deducted from the Bahamas' monetary freedom score to adjust for price-control measures that distort domestic prices for such "breadbasket" items as drugs, gasoline, diesel oil, and petroleum gas.

INVESTMENT FREEDOM — 40%

Foreign investment is restricted in many sectors, including (among others) real estate, newspapers, advertising, nightclubs and some restaurants, construction, cosmetics and beauty, and retail. The government maintains a monopoly on most of the telecommunications sector. All outward capital transfers and inward transfers by non-residents require exchange-control approval. Improvements in infrastructure, such as road and utility development, have continued. Foreign direct investment must be approved by the central bank. Environmental standards are more relaxed than those of the United States. To purchase real estate for commercial purposes or to purchase more than five acres, foreigners must obtain a permit from the Investments Board. Exchange controls exist but are not known to hamper repatriation of approved investment capital. Certain industries can be designated by the government with incentives for more investment.

FINANCIAL FREEDOM — 70%

The Bahamian financial sector is a developed international financial hub and is open to foreigners and to foreign scrutiny. As a result of pressure in the late 1990s, the government increased regulations on certain financial entities. The Bahamas was removed from a financial watch list in 2001 after also establishing a Financial Intelligence Unit and taking other steps. These changes impose acceptable regulatory costs on the financial sector, although stricter regulation and supervision did result in fewer licensed banks and companies, declining from 415 in 1999 to 256 as of June 2006. Nevertheless, the government has adopted incentives to encourage foreign financial business and remains involved in the financial sector. Growth of a captive insurance industry has been hurt by banking secrecy laws. The stock market, founded in 2000, is underdeveloped but has been somewhat revitalized by the inclusion of government debt securities and other initiatives.

PROPERTY RIGHTS — 80%

The Bahamas has an efficient legal system based on British common law. The judiciary is independent and conducts generally fair public trials. The judicial process tends to be very slow, however, and some investors complain of malfeasance by court officials.

FREEDOM FROM CORRUPTION — 70%

Piracy of software, music, and videos is a problem. Existing copyright laws are ignored. Illegal drug trafficking and money laundering are also significant.

LABOR FREEDOM — 80%

The labor market generally operates under flexible employment regulations that enhance overall productivity growth and job creation. Employment contracts, though not mandatory, are often prepared. Legal entitlement to notice of termination is not required, but one pay period is the custom.

BAHRAIN

Manama

B ahrain's economy is 72.2 percent free, according to our 2008 assessment, which makes it the world's 19th freest economy. Its overall score is 1 percentage point higher than last year, partially because of an improving investment climate. The negative changes have been caused by worsened scores in inflation and corruption. Bahrain is ranked 1st out of 17 countries in the Middle East/North Africa region, and its economy is ideal in several respects, such as tax and banking freedom.

Bahrain's economy is very free for the Middle East, with higher scores than the world average in eight of the 10 factors of economic freedom. Business freedom, fiscal freedom, monetary freedom, and especially financial freedom are high. The only weakness is labor freedom, which is 22 points below the world average, largely due to regulations mandating the hiring of Bahrainis. The absence of income or corporate taxes in all industries except oil gives Bahrain a competitive commercial advantage globally.

Bahrain's overall ranking is changed from last year's primarily because of a methodological refinement that provides for a better assessment of non-tariff barriers. The main area for improvement is labor freedom. The economy also would perform better if state-owned enterprises were not so dominant, generating three-quarters of government revenue.

BACKGROUND: Bahrain has become one of the Persian Gulf's most advanced economies and most progressive political systems since gaining its independence from Great Britain in 1971. Under a constitution promulgated by Sheikh Hamad bin Isa al-Khalifa, the country became a constitutional monarchy in 2002, and the government has sought to reduce dependence on declining oil reserves and encourage foreign investment by diversifying the economy. Because of its communications and transportation infrastructure, regulatory structure, and cosmopolitan outlook, Bahrain is home to many multinational firms that do business in the region. In 2005, the U.S. and Bahrain ratified a free trade agreement.

How Do We Measure Economic Freedom? See Chapter 4 (page 39) for an explanation of the methodology or visit the *Index* Web site at *heritage.org/index*.

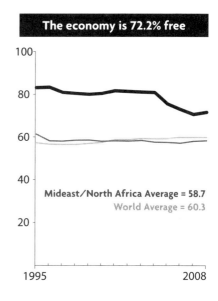

The economy is 72.2% free

Mideast/North Africa Average = 58.7
World Average = 60.3

1995 — 2008

QUICK FACTS

Population: 0.7 million

GDP (PPP): $15.6 billion
7.8% growth in 2005
6.4% 5-yr. comp. ann. growth
$21,482 per capita

Unemployment: 15.0%

Inflation (CPI): 2.6%

FDI (net flow): −$75.0 million

Official Development Assistance:
Multilateral: n/a
Bilateral: n/a

External Debt: $7.3 billion

Exports: $11.8 billion
Primarily petroleum and petroleum products, aluminum, textiles

Imports: $8.6 billion
Primarily crude oil, machinery, chemicals

2005 data unless otherwise noted.

BAHRAIN'S TEN ECONOMIC FREEDOMS

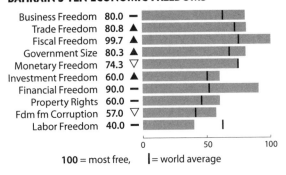

Business Freedom	80.0 ▬
Trade Freedom	80.8 ▲
Fiscal Freedom	99.7 ▲
Government Size	80.3 ▲
Monetary Freedom	74.3 ▽
Investment Freedom	60.0 ▲
Financial Freedom	90.0 ▬
Property Rights	60.0 ▬
Fdm fm Corruption	57.0 ▽
Labor Freedom	40.0 ▬

0   50   100

100 = most free, ▮ = world average

BUSINESS FREEDOM — 80%

Bahrain's commercial law system is relatively straightforward, but starting, operating, and closing a business can be slowed by an uncoordinated regulatory environment. Despite steps to streamline licensing and approval procedures, complicated bureaucratic procedures still make obtaining a business license difficult.

TRADE FREEDOM — 80.8%

Bahrain's simple average tariff rate was 4.6 percent in 2005. There are few non-tariff barriers, but a limited number of products are subject to import and export prohibitions and licenses, enforcement of intellectual property rights remains a concern, and the government uses price controls and subsidies to manage inflation and promote domestic supplies. An additional 10 percentage points is deducted from Bahrain's trade freedom score to account for non-tariff barriers.

FISCAL FREEDOM — 99.7%

Historically, Bahrain has imposed no taxes on personal income. However, in 2006, for the first time, the government announced that it would levy a 1 percent tax on Bahraini nationals' salaries to fund an unemployment scheme. Most companies are not subject to corporate tax, but a 46 percent corporate tax rate is levied on oil companies. In the most recent year, overall tax revenue as a percentage of GDP was 5.5 percent.

GOVERNMENT SIZE — 80.3%

Total government expenditures, including consumption and transfer payments, are moderate. In the most recent year, government spending equaled 25.6 percent of GDP. The government has focused on diversifying the economy from the oil sector and is also trying to reform itself by restructuring official bodies and privatizing a variety of state services, including power provision and port management.

MONETARY FREEDOM — 74.3%

Inflation is relatively low, averaging 2.8 percent between 2004 and 2006. Relatively stable prices explain most of the monetary freedom score. An additional 15 percentage points is deducted from Bahrain's monetary freedom score to adjust for extensive price controls and subsidies that distort domestic prices for many food products, electricity, water, and petroleum.

INVESTMENT FREEDOM — 60%

The government welcomes foreign investment, except in cases involving competition with established local enterprises or existing government-owned or parastatal companies. Bahrain has a comparatively advanced commercial code and is open to outside contract adjudication. Gulf Cooperation Council (GCC) nationals may own 100 percent of the shares of firms listed on the stock exchange, but non-GCC nationals are limited to 49 percent. Foreign-owned companies may now operate in some cases without a Bahraini partner. There are no restrictions on the repatriation of profits or capital, no exchange controls, and no restrictions on converting or transferring funds, whether associated with an investment or not. There have been reports of new restrictions on hiring expatriate workers. Local unrest and regional political situations, such as the Iraq war, can affect investment security.

FINANCIAL FREEDOM — 90%

Bahrain is a regional financial hub, and both foreign and local individuals and companies have access to credit on market terms. In August 2006, there were 25 commercial banks, but the financial sector is dominated by some 50 offshore banking units that use Bahrain as a base from which to conduct operations in other countries. Overall, there were 368 financial institutions in 2006. The central bank introduced new business classification rules in 2006, aiming to make the financial framework more flexible. The International Monetary Fund has praised Bahrain's financial supervision as effective and its regulation as modern and comprehensive. As of 2006, the stock exchange listed 52 companies, with GCC nationals allowed to invest freely and foreigners allowed to own up to 49 percent, and the growing insurance sector had 12 national and eight foreign insurance companies engaged in direct business.

PROPERTY RIGHTS — 60%

Property is secure, and expropriation is unlikely. The judiciary is not fully independent because the king has the right to appoint judges and amend the constitution. Nevertheless, the legal system is well regarded, and foreign firms can resolve disputes satisfactorily through the local courts. There are no prohibitions on the use of international arbitration to safeguard contracts.

FREEDOM FROM CORRUPTION — 57%

Corruption is perceived as present. Bahrain ranks 36th out of 163 countries in Transparency International's Corruption Perceptions Index for 2006.

LABOR FREEDOM — 40%

The labor market is still too inflexible to create overall productivity growth. Businesses are required by law to employ Bahrainis, and this hinders job creation as the government tries to micromanage decisions by private businesses. Rigid regulations about dismissing a worker still create a risk aversion for companies that would otherwise hire more people and grow.

BANGLADESH

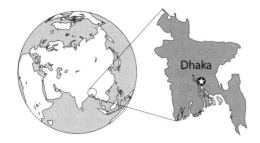

Dhaka

Bangladesh's economy is 44.9 percent free, according to our 2008 assessment, which makes it the world's 149th freest economy. Its overall score is 3.1 percentage points lower than last year—one of the biggest declines in the world, reflecting lower investment, business, and labor freedom. Bangladesh is ranked 27th out of 30 countries in the Asia–Pacific region.

Bangladesh's fiscal freedom and government size score relatively well, which probably reflects severe underdevelopment and black market activity more than genuine freedom. Restrictions on starting new businesses and obtaining commercial licenses are fairly loose. Closing a business, however, is not quite as simple.

Bangladesh's barriers to trade freedom are disastrous. Tariffs are prohibitively high. The country also suffers from weak investment freedom, property rights, and financial freedom. Corruption is common. Chaotic regulations and restricted market sectors impede greater foreign investment, as does a haphazard and politicized approach to the rule of law. The banking sector is plagued by similar problems.

BACKGROUND: The People's Republic of Bangladesh, formerly a parliamentary democracy, is now run by a military-backed regime that overthrew the elected government in January 2007. The generals have promised to hold elections by the end of this year. One of the world's poorest nations, Bangladesh had made progress in recent years with growth in its export sector, particularly in the garment industry. The formal financial system remains weak. The majority of Bangladeshis work in agriculture, though service industries now account for around half of GDP. Natural disasters and inadequate infrastructure hamper economic development.

How Do We Measure Economic Freedom? See Chapter 4 (page 39) for an explanation of the methodology or visit the *Index* Web site at *heritage.org/index*.

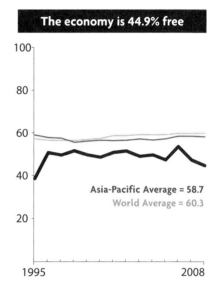

The economy is 44.9% free

Asia-Pacific Average = 58.7
World Average = 60.3

1995   2008

QUICK FACTS

Population: 141.8 million

GDP (PPP): $291.2 billion
6.3% growth in 2005
5.8% 5-yr. comp. ann. growth
$2,053.4 per capita

Unemployment: 2.5%

Inflation (CPI): 7.0%

FDI (net flow): $682.0 million

Official Development Assistance:
Multilateral: $1.0 billion
Bilateral: $756.6 million (11.1% from the U.S.)

External Debt: $18.9 billion

Exports: $10.4 billion
Primarily garments, jute and jute goods, leather, frozen fish and seafood

Imports: $14.5 billion
Primarily machinery and equipment, chemicals, iron and steel, textiles, foodstuffs, petroleum products, cement

2005 data unless otherwise noted.

BANGLADESH'S TEN ECONOMIC FREEDOMS

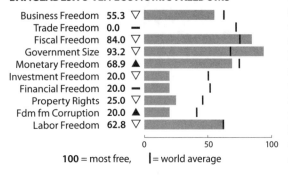

Business Freedom	55.3	▽
Trade Freedom	0.0	▬
Fiscal Freedom	84.0	▽
Government Size	93.2	▽
Monetary Freedom	68.9	▲
Investment Freedom	20.0	▽
Financial Freedom	20.0	▬
Property Rights	25.0	▽
Fdm fm Corruption	20.0	▲
Labor Freedom	62.8	▽

100 = most free, | = world average

BUSINESS FREEDOM — 55.3%

The overall freedom to start, operate, and close a business is limited by Bangladesh's national regulatory environment. Starting a business takes an average of 74 days, compared to the world average of 43 days. Obtaining a business license requires less than the world average of 19 procedures. However, commercial regulations can be unclear and inconsistent, and the lack of transparency raises start-up and operational costs. Closing a business is a lengthy process.

TRADE FREEDOM — 0%

Bangladesh's weighted average tariff rate was 55.8 percent in 2005. Import and export restrictions; numerous border taxes and fees; restrictive labeling requirements; burdensome import licensing rules; export subsidies and other support programs; government monopolies and state trading boards; complex, non-transparent government procurement; inefficient and corrupt customs administration; and weak enforcement of intellectual property rights also add to the cost of trade. An additional 20 percentage points is deducted from Bangladesh's trade freedom score to account for these non-tariff barriers.

FISCAL FREEDOM — 84%

Bangladesh has moderate tax rates. The top income tax rate is 25 percent, and the top corporate tax rate is 30 percent. Other taxes include a value-added tax (VAT), a property tax, and a tax on interest. In the most recent year, overall tax revenue as a percentage of GDP was 8.7 percent.

GOVERNMENT SIZE — 93.2%

Total government expenditures, including consumption and transfer payments, are low. In the most recent year, government spending equaled 15.1 percent of GDP. Privatization has been hindered by bureaucratic resistance and opposition from labor unions.

MONETARY FREEDOM — 68.9%

Inflation is moderate, averaging 6.5 percent between 2004 and 2006. Relatively unstable prices explain most of the monetary freedom score. An additional 15 percentage points is deducted from Bangladesh's monetary freedom score to adjust for price-control measures that distort domestic prices for goods produced in state-owned enterprises, some pharmaceuticals, and petroleum products.

INVESTMENT FREEDOM — 20%

Officially, foreign investment is generally welcomed, but utilities and other critical sectors are not open to the private sector, and potential investors face a host of challenges: bureaucratic procedures, unnecessary licenses, high levels of corruption, an unpredictable security situation, and uncertainty about contract and regulatory enforcement. Bangladesh is deeply in need of public administration reforms. Most capital transactions are controlled or prohibited. Non-resident companies are subject to a higher corporate tax rate (37.5 percent) than are publicly traded companies (30 percent).

FINANCIAL FREEDOM — 20%

Bangladesh's financial services sector is small and underdeveloped. Financial supervision is weak, and fraudulent transactions, mismanagement, and political influence in lending are common. The central bank is not independent. In 2006, the banking system consisted of four nationalized commercial banks, five development financial institutions, 30 private commercial banks, and 10 foreign banks. Foreign banks are generally restricted to offshore and foreign trade business. The nationalized commercial banks dominate the system, controlling over half of banking assets. An extensive microfinance presence is largely unsupervised. There are 30 private insurance companies, including a foreign-owned firm, but the major portion of insurance activity is controlled by two state-owned companies. Bangladesh has two stock exchanges, but market capitalization is low. In 2006, the government strengthened the criteria for the listing of firms on either stock market.

PROPERTY RIGHTS — 25%

Bangladesh has a civil court system based on the British model. Although the constitution provides for an independent judiciary, the lower courts are considered part of the executive branch and suffer from corruption. Contracts are weakly enforced, and dispute settlement is further hampered by shortcomings in accounting practices and real property registration.

FREEDOM FROM CORRUPTION — 20%

Corruption is perceived as pervasive. Bangladesh ranks 156th out of 163 countries in Transparency International's Corruption Perceptions Index for 2006. Given that corruption blights all other economic freedoms, this is a key area for improvement.

LABOR FREEDOM — 62.8%

Bangladesh's labor market is burdened by relatively inflexible employment regulations that hinder employment creation and productivity growth. The non-salary cost of employing a worker is low, but dismissing a redundant employee can be difficult. The difficulty of laying off workers creates a risk aversion for companies that would otherwise hire more people and grow.

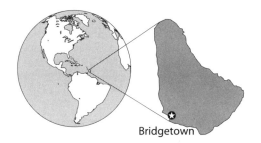
Bridgetown

BARBADOS

Barbados's economy is 71.3 percent free, according to our 2008 assessment, which makes it the world's 21st freest economy. Its overall score is 1.4 percentage points higher than last year, primarily because of improved investment freedoms. Barbados is ranked 4th out of 29 countries in the Americas, and its overall score is well above the regional average.

Barbados's business freedom, property rights, and labor freedom all rate highly, as does its freedom from corruption. Business regulations, clearly laid out in commercial laws and generally followed, are simple. The labor market is highly flexible and open. A focus on transparency levels the playing field for domestic and foreign businesses alike, despite certain restrictions on foreign investment and moderately high taxes. A strong legal system allows for the effective adjudication of business disputes and a relatively low level of corruption.

Despite a healthy respect for law and a relatively positive economic environment, Barbados does levy significant tariffs on non-CARICOM goods. Average tariff rates are similarly high, and non-tariff barriers are a hindrance to the more efficient flow of goods.

BACKGROUND: Barbados has a two-party parliamentary system, and the Barbados Labor Party, led by Owen Arthur, has been in power since 1994. Tourism is the most important economic sector, accounting for 11.3 percent of GDP. Barbados emphasizes economic and cultural cooperation within the Caribbean region and the development of a common trade policy within the Caribbean Community and Common Market (CARICOM) trade bloc. The heavily subsidized sugar industry, although diminishing in importance, remains an important employer and exporter. The offshore financial sector is smaller than others in the Caribbean, but it makes a significant contribution to the economy and is generally well regulated.

How Do We Measure Economic Freedom? See Chapter 4 (page 39) for an explanation of the methodology or visit the *Index* Web site at *heritage.org/index*.

The economy is 71.3% free

100

80

60

40

Americas Average = 61.6
World Average = 60.3

20

1995   2008

QUICK FACTS

Population: 0.3 million

GDP (PPP): $4.9 billion
4.1% growth in 2005
2.7% 5-yr. comp. ann. growth
$17,755 per capita

Unemployment: 9.1%

Inflation (CPI): 6.0%

FDI (net flow): $156.0 million

Official Development Assistance:
Multilateral: $1.5 million
Bilateral: $6.2 million (2.5% from the U.S.)

External Debt: $668.0 million (2003)

Exports: $1.8 billion
Primarily sugar and molasses, rum, other foods and beverages, chemicals, electrical components

Imports: $2.1 billion
Primarily consumer goods, machinery, foodstuffs, construction materials, chemicals, fuel, electrical components

2005 data unless otherwise noted.

BARBADOS'S TEN ECONOMIC FREEDOMS

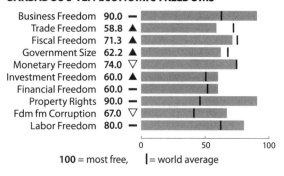

Business Freedom	90.0 —	
Trade Freedom	58.8 ▲	
Fiscal Freedom	71.3 ▲	
Government Size	62.2 ▲	
Monetary Freedom	74.0 ▽	
Investment Freedom	60.0 ▲	
Financial Freedom	60.0 —	
Property Rights	90.0 —	
Fdm fm Corruption	67.0 ▽	
Labor Freedom	80.0 —	

0   50   100

100 = most free, **❙** = world average

BUSINESS FREEDOM — *90%*

Starting, operating, and closing a business are straightforward and free from burdensome regulation. The Company Act ensures flexibility and simplicity for establishing and operating companies in Barbados. Transparent policies and effective laws enhance competition and establish clear rules for domestic and foreign investors alike.

TRADE FREEDOM — *58.8%*

Barbados's simple average tariff rate was 15.6 percent in 2003. The government requires permits, licenses, or permission prior to importation and maintains restrictive labeling, sanitary, and phytosanitary policies. An additional 10 percentage points is deducted from Barbados's trade freedom score to account for these non-tariff barriers.

FISCAL FREEDOM — *71.3%*

Barbados has a high income tax rate and a moderate corporate tax rate. The top income tax rate is 35 percent, and the top corporate income tax rate is 25 percent. Other taxes include a value-added tax (VAT) and a tax on interest. In the most recent year, overall tax revenue as a percentage of GDP was 31.9 percent.

GOVERNMENT SIZE — *62.2%*

Total government expenditures, including consumption and transfer payments, are high. In the most recent year, government spending equaled 35.5 percent of GDP. The government intends to privatize most state-owned enterprises, including seaports, airports, broadcasting, and oil companies, but this is not viewed as a pressing matter, and progress has been rather slow.

MONETARY FREEDOM — *74%*

Inflation is high, averaging 6.4 percent between 2004 and 2006. Relatively unstable prices explain most of the monetary freedom score. Although prices are generally set by the market, an additional 10 percentage points is deducted from Barbados's monetary freedom score to adjust for price-control measures that distort domestic prices for basic food items, transportation, and fuel.

INVESTMENT FREEDOM — *60%*

Foreign and domestic capital are equal under the law. Barbados permits 100 percent foreign ownership of enterprises and treats domestic and foreign firms equally, but

the government is more likely to approve projects that it believes will create jobs and increase exports. Barbados provides many incentives for investment, including tax breaks, subsidized industrial parks, and export bonuses. Foreign investors can be subject to performance requirements. There are no requirements to hire Bajan workers, and repatriation of capital is almost always allowed. Central bank approval is required for both residents and non-residents to hold foreign exchange accounts. Exchange control approval is required for direct investment and real estate purchases, and the central bank must approve all credit operations.

FINANCIAL FREEDOM — *60%*

Barbados has a smaller financial sector than other Caribbean financial hubs, with six commercial banks dominated by Caribbean Community and Common Market institutions. As of 2007, the offshore financial sector includes 4,932 international business companies, 426 exempt insurance companies, and 54 offshore banks. The government has intervened in the domestic credit market to influence interest rates, restrict the volumes of funds, and borrow funds. Compliance with international supervisory standards is high for both offshore and onshore banking institutions. Guidelines revised in 2006 further refined controls against money laundering. The insurance sector is vibrant but weakly regulated. The securities exchange is small, listing about two dozen local and foreign Caribbean companies in 2005. A two-tier listing regime allows smaller companies to list without having to meet the same requirements as more established companies.

PROPERTY RIGHTS — *90%*

Barbados has an efficient legal system based on British common law. Private property is well protected. The Caribbean Court of Justice is the court of final appeal for Barbados and other CARICOM member states. By regional standards, the police and court systems are efficient and unbiased, and the government operates in an essentially transparent manner.

FREEDOM FROM CORRUPTION — *67%*

Corruption is perceived as present. Barbados ranks 24th out of 163 countries in Transparency International's Corruption Perceptions Index for 2006.

LABOR FREEDOM — *80%*

The labor market generally operates under flexible employment regulations that enhance overall productivity growth. Employees are guaranteed a minimum of two weeks of annual leave and are covered by unemployment benefits and national insurance legislation. Under the Trade Union Act of 1964, employers have no legal obligation to recognize unions.

BELARUS

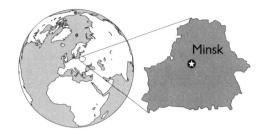

Minsk

Belarus's economy is 44.7 percent free, according to our 2008 assessment, which makes it the world's 150th freest economy. Its persistently low score has been blamed on the failure of post-Soviet reforms, and this year it experienced a further 1.8 percentage point decrease overall, primarily because of worsening trade freedom. Belarus is ranked last among the 41 countries in the European region.

Belarus is significantly worse than the world average in six freedoms but, because of moderate tax rates and tax revenues, does score above the average in fiscal freedom.

Belarus's economic institutions create major barriers to development. Its financial freedom, investment freedom, property rights, and freedom from corruption are 20–40 points below the world average. The government dominates the financial system and either owns or controls all but one of the 31 banks. Foreign investment in all sectors faces hurdles, from outright restrictions to bureaucratic incompetence. Weak rule of law allows for significant corruption and insecure property rights.

BACKGROUND: Belarus won its independence from the Soviet Union in 1991 but remains close to Russia economically and politically. President Alexander Lukashenko, in power since 1994, declared himself the winner of the disputed March 2006 elections and changed the constitution, effectively allowing himself to be elected for life. The economy has deteriorated since 1995, when Lukashenko vowed to guide his country toward a statist model of "market socialism." The government claims that the poverty rate dropped to 12.7 percent (less than one-third of the 1999 level) in 2005 and that real GDP growth reached 9.9 percent in 2006. In reality, Belarus's statist economy and policy of international isolation have discouraged foreign investment and development of the high-tech sector.

How Do We Measure Economic Freedom? See Chapter 4 (page 39) for an explanation of the methodology or visit the *Index* Web site at *heritage.org/index*.

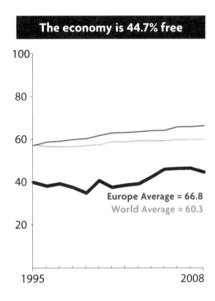

The economy is 44.7% free

Europe Average = 66.8
World Average = 60.3

1995   2008

QUICK FACTS

Population: 9.8 million

GDP (PPP): $77.4 billion
9.3% growth in 2005
8.2% 5-yr. comp. ann. growth
$7,918 per capita

Unemployment: 1.5%

Inflation (CPI): 10.3%

FDI (net flow): $303.0 million

Official Development Assistance:
Multilateral: $9.3 million
Bilateral: $48.1 million (11.1% from the U.S.)

External Debt: $4.7 billion

Exports: $18.1 billion
Primarily machinery and equipment, mineral products, chemicals, metals, textiles, foodstuffs

Imports: $18.0 billion
Primarily mineral products, machinery and equipment, chemicals, foodstuffs, metals

2005 data unless otherwise noted.

BELARUS'S TEN ECONOMIC FREEDOMS

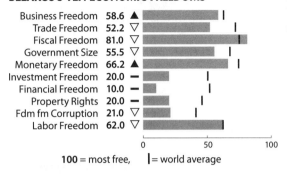

Business Freedom	58.6 ▲	
Trade Freedom	52.2 ▽	
Fiscal Freedom	81.0 ▽	
Government Size	55.5 ▽	
Monetary Freedom	66.2 ▲	
Investment Freedom	20.0 —	
Financial Freedom	10.0 —	
Property Rights	20.0 —	
Fdm fm Corruption	21.0 ▽	
Labor Freedom	62.0 ▽	

0   50   100

100 = most free, **|** = world average

BUSINESS FREEDOM —58.6%

The overall freedom to start, operate, and close a business is constrained by Belarus's national regulatory environment. Starting a business takes an average of 48 days, compared to the world average of 43 days. Obtaining a business license takes more than the global average of 234 days. Burdensome and non-transparent regulations lead small and medium-sized private companies to concentrate in retail and catering, where relatively low costs prevent excessively high losses. Closing a business is also difficult.

TRADE FREEDOM — 52.2%

Belarus's weighted average tariff rate was 16.4 percent in 2002. Extensive import restrictions and quotas, burdensome licensing requirements, and numerous government-provided subsidies add to the cost of trade. An additional 15 percentage points is deducted from Belarus's trade freedom score to account for non-tariff barriers.

FISCAL FREEDOM — 81%

Belarus has moderate tax rates. The top income tax rate is 30 percent, and the top corporate income tax rate is 24 percent. Other taxes include a value-added tax (VAT), an ecological tax, and a turnover tax. In the most recent year, overall tax revenue as a percentage of GDP was 20.6 percent.

GOVERNMENT SIZE — 55.5%

Total government expenditures, including consumption and transfer payments, are high. In the most recent year, government spending equaled 38.5 percent of GDP. Large state-owned enterprises still generate considerable output, and privatization continues to be resisted.

MONETARY FREEDOM — 66.2%

Inflation is relatively high, averaging 8.8 percent between 2004 and 2006. Relatively unstable prices explain most of the monetary freedom score. The government subsidizes many basic goods and services, sets prices of products made by state-owned enterprises, and regulates prices in the retail sector. An additional 15 percentage points is deducted from Belarus's monetary freedom score to adjust for measures that distort domestic prices.

INVESTMENT FREEDOM — 20%

There are significant restrictions on capital transactions. Foreign investment must be registered with the Minsk City

Executive Committee and is allowed only on a case-by-case basis. Narcotic products, national security industries, and some infrastructure are exclusively state-controlled. Profitable and strategic sectors are often under the *de facto* control of executive-allied firms or the government. Belarus has a skilled workforce, but inefficient bureaucracy, corruption, contradictory and often retroactively enforced legislation, enforced charities, and concerted resistance to the private sector all serve to hinder foreign investment. The government has begun to take control of certain businesses, irrespective of foreign ownership. Foreigners may not own land. Capital transactions, resident and non-resident accounts, invisibles, and current transfers are subject to strict controls.

FINANCIAL FREEDOM — 10%

Belarus's financial system is influenced very heavily by the government. All but one of the 31 banks are owned or controlled by the state. The financial sector is dominated by a handful of commercial banks, four of which are Soviet-era specialized banks that account for three-quarters of commercial banking's in-sector capital. Laws are applied inconsistently and often disregarded. The central bank is controlled by the state as a conduit for government economic policies. However, the banking system is more stable and developed than those in many other CIS countries. Foreign banks face major impediments, and barriers to credit are high. Businesses have access to various credit mechanisms, but long bureaucratic delays make the effort almost worthless for smaller companies. The non-bank financial sector is small and inhibited by state intervention and irregular regulatory enforcement. The stock market is small and largely dormant, and the insurance market has stagnated.

PROPERTY RIGHTS — 20%

The legal system does not fully protect private property, and the inefficient court system does not enforce contracts consistently. The judiciary is neither independent nor objective by international standards. The government has wide scope to interfere in commercial transactions. In 1997, independent lawyers were barred from practicing without a special license from the Ministry of Justice. Protection of intellectual property rights is weak.

FREEDOM FROM CORRUPTION — 21%

Corruption is perceived as pervasive. Belarus ranks 151st out of 163 countries in Transparency International's Corruption Perceptions Index for 2006. Owners of import–export businesses in particular complain that corruption exists at every point in a transaction.

LABOR FREEDOM — 62%

Belarus's labor market operates under relatively inflexible employment regulations that hinder employment creation and productivity growth. The non-salary cost of employing a worker is very high, but dismissing a redundant employee is relatively easy. The unemployment insurance system, funded almost entirely by employers with some government assistance, offers benefits that are approximately equivalent to 30 percent of an average worker's annual salary.

BELGIUM

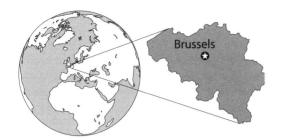

Brussels

Belgium's economy is 71.5 percent free, according to our 2008 assessment, which makes it the world's 20th freest economy. This is a 0.9 percentage point decrease from last year, primarily reflecting increased government spending. Belgium is ranked 10th freest among the 41 countries in the European region, and its overall score is above the regional average.

Belgium scores very high in investment freedom, property rights, monetary freedom, and business freedom and is above the world average in eight areas. A member of the European Union, it has a standardized monetary policy and relatively low inflation despite some government distortion in the agricultural sector. Its transparent rule of law protects property and encourages confidence among foreign investors.

Belgium's extensive welfare state is supported by exceptionally high government spending and income tax rates. Overall tax revenue is an uncommonly high percent of GDP, and Belgium's government size score is 50 percentage points worse than the world average.

BACKGROUND: Belgium is a federal state consisting of three economically different regions: Flanders, Wallonia, and the capital city of Brussels, which houses the headquarters of NATO and the EU and has been at the forefront in driving the supranationalization of power within the EU. After eight years, Guy Verhofstadt and his Liberal Party were ousted from power in 2007. His previous Socialist–Liberal coalition sought to ease the income tax burden and succeeded in balancing the budget, but growth remained sluggish. Christian Democratic leader Yves Leterme has since been invited to form a coalition government. Services account for around three-quarters of GDP. The leading exports are electrical equipment, vehicles, diamonds, and chemicals.

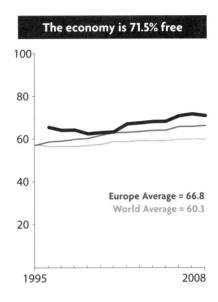

The economy is 71.5% free

Europe Average = 66.8
World Average = 60.3

1995 — 2008

QUICK FACTS

Population: 10.5 million

GDP (PPP): $336.6 billion
1.5% growth in 2004
1.7% 5-yr. comp. ann. growth
$32,119 per capita

Unemployment: 8.4%

Inflation (CPI): 2.5%

FDI (net flow): $766.0 million

Official Development Assistance:
Multilateral: None
Bilateral: None

External Debt: $1.1 trillion

Exports: $318.8 billion
Primarily machinery and equipment, chemicals, diamonds, metals and metal products, foodstuffs

Imports: $308.4 billion
Primarily machinery and equipment, chemicals, diamonds, pharmaceuticals, foodstuffs, transportation equipment, oil products

2005 data unless otherwise noted.

How Do We Measure Economic Freedom? See Chapter 4 (page 39) for an explanation of the methodology or visit the *Index* Web site at *heritage.org/index.*

BELGIUM'S TEN ECONOMIC FREEDOMS

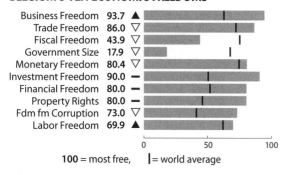

Business Freedom	93.7	▲
Trade Freedom	86.0	▽
Fiscal Freedom	43.9	▽
Government Size	17.9	▽
Monetary Freedom	80.4	▽
Investment Freedom	90.0	—
Financial Freedom	80.0	—
Property Rights	80.0	—
Fdm fm Corruption	73.0	▽
Labor Freedom	69.9	▲

0   50   100

100 = most free, | = world average

BUSINESS FREEDOM — *93.7%*

The overall freedom to start, operate, and close a business is strongly protected by Belgium's national regulatory environment. Starting a business takes an average of four days, compared to the world average of 43 days. Obtaining a business license requires less than the world average of 19 procedures and 234 days. Regulation is transparent, and the laws are enforced effectively. Closing a business is easy and straightforward.

TRADE FREEDOM — *86%*

Belgium's trade policy is the same as those of other members of the European Union. The common EU weighted average tariff rate was 2 percent in 2005. Non-tariff barriers reflected in EU policy include agricultural and manufacturing subsidies, import restrictions for some goods and services, market access restrictions in some service sectors, non-transparent and restrictive regulations and standards, and inconsistent customs administration across EU members. Enforcement of intellectual property rights remains problematic. Consequently, an additional 10 percentage points is deducted from Belgium's trade freedom score.

FISCAL FREEDOM — *43.9%*

Belgium's income tax rate is one of the world's highest, and its corporate tax rate is also high. The top income tax rate is 50 percent, and the top corporate tax rate is 34 percent (a 33 percent tax rate and 3 percent surcharge). Other taxes include a value-added tax (VAT), a transport tax, and a property tax. In the most recent year, overall tax revenue as a percentage of GDP was 44.9 percent.

GOVERNMENT SIZE — *17.9%*

Total government expenditures, including consumption and transfer payments, are very high. In the most recent year, government spending equaled 52.3 percent of GDP.

MONETARY FREEDOM — *80.4%*

Belgium is a member of the euro zone. Between 2004 and 2006, its weighted average annual rate of inflation was 2.3 percent. Relatively stable prices explain most of the monetary freedom score. As a participant in the EU's Common Agricultural Policy, the government subsidizes agricultural production, distorting the prices of agricultural products. Price-control policies affect water supply, waste handling, homes for the elderly, medicines and implantable medical devices, certain cars, compulsory insurance, fire insurance, petroleum products, cable television, and certain types of bread. An additional 10 percentage points is deducted from Belgium's monetary freedom score to account for these policies.

INVESTMENT FREEDOM — *90%*

Most restrictions on foreign investment also apply to domestic investment. Permits and licenses required for certain industries are not hard to obtain. Regional and national incentives are generally open to foreigners and Belgians, but taxes and certain employment criteria are federally controlled. Performance requirements, when present, are linked to job creation. EU regulations require some restrictions on non-EU investment in public works. There are no restrictions on the purchase of real estate, residents' and non-residents' accounts, repatriation of profit, or transfer of capital.

FINANCIAL FREEDOM — *80%*

Belgium has one of the world's most developed financial systems, with 104 banks, including over 70 foreign banks, and numerous financial service providers, but the five largest banks still hold 85 percent of deposits. An independent commission supervises the financial sector. Banks must provide a minimum set of services. Credit is allocated at market terms to both foreign and domestic investors. Belgian law differentiates between EU and non-EU banks, financial institutions, and insurance companies, although firms from European Economic Area or World Trade Organization countries may be treated equally. Regional authorities may subsidize medium- and long-term borrowing. The insurance sector is smaller and less robust than banking. The world's first stock market was organized in Antwerp, and Belgium's sound capital markets were recently integrated into Euronext, a broader European exchange.

PROPERTY RIGHTS — *80%*

Property is well protected, and contracts are secure. The laws are codified, and the judiciary and civil service, while often slow, are of high quality. Intellectual property rights are well protected, but implementation of relevant EU directives has been slow.

FREEDOM FROM CORRUPTION — *73%*

Corruption is perceived as minimal. Belgium ranks 20th out of 163 countries in Transparency International's Corruption Perceptions Index for 2006. Belgium outlaws both active bribery and "passive bribery," whereby an official requests or accepts a benefit for himself or somebody else in exchange for certain behavior.

LABOR FREEDOM — *69.9%*

Employment regulations are relatively flexible, but further reform is needed to foster employment creation and productivity growth. The non-salary cost of employing a worker can be very high, and dismissing a redundant employee is relatively costly. Belgium's high labor costs are sustainable for high-value-added processes, but market rigidities remain a considerable barrier to employing a worker.

BELIZE

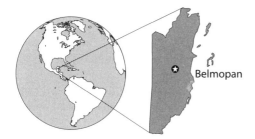
Belmopan

Belize's economy is 62.8 percent free, according to our 2008 assessment, which makes it the world's 61st freest economy. Its overall score is 0.4 percentage point lower than last year. Belize is ranked 14th out of 29 countries in the Americas.

Belize is similar to the rest of the world in nearly all economic freedoms, except for two that rate far above the rest: business freedom and labor freedom. Flexible labor regulations contribute to an elastic employment market with no major regulatory distortions, giving Belize a labor freedom score that is 19 points above average. Despite a high top income tax rate, corporate taxes are low, and government tax revenue is not particularly large as a percentage of GDP. Low inflation and stable prices contribute to the economic climate, but certain government price controls also exist.

Trade freedom and freedom from corruption are less strong. High tariffs are the main problem for trade freedom. Special licensing requirements discourage foreign investment in a wide array of sectors, and foreign exchange regulations are neither consistent nor transparent. The judicial system allows for some political interference in the courts, and corruption is too common.

BACKGROUND: Belize is a parliamentary democracy and a member of the British Commonwealth. Mismanagement of state-owned enterprises, a botched telecommunications privatization, and extensive social problems have undercut Prime Minister Said Musa's political influence. Tourism is a major contributor to the economy, as is agriculture. Sugar has been the principal export in recent years, but the government is fostering export diversification into other products including shrimp, citrus, bananas, papayas, and soybeans. Crime is a serious problem, and Belize has one of the highest murder rates in the Caribbean region. International relations are dominated by a territorial dispute with Guatemala.

How Do We Measure Economic Freedom? See Chapter 4 (page 39) for an explanation of the methodology or visit the *Index* Web site at *heritage.org/index*.

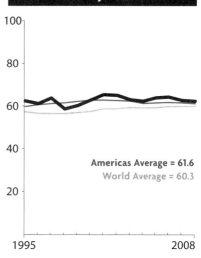

The economy is 62.8% free

Americas Average = 61.6
World Average = 60.3

QUICK FACTS

Population: 0.3 million

GDP (PPP): $2.1 billion
3.5% growth in 2005
5.6% 5-yr. comp. ann. growth
$7,109 per capita

Unemployment: 11.0%

Inflation (CPI): 3.7%

FDI (net flow): $106.0 million

Official Development Assistance:
Multilateral: $4.5 million
Bilateral: $10.1 million (18.2% from the U.S.)

External Debt: $1.2 billion

Exports: $614.8 million
Primarily sugar, bananas, citrus, clothing, fish products, molasses, wood

Imports: $713.9 million
Primarily machinery and transport equipment, manufactured goods, fuels, chemicals, pharmaceuticals, food, beverages, tobacco

2005 data unless otherwise noted.

BELIZE'S TEN ECONOMIC FREEDOMS

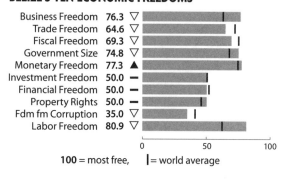

Business Freedom	76.3	▽
Trade Freedom	64.6	▽
Fiscal Freedom	69.3	▽
Government Size	74.8	▽
Monetary Freedom	77.3	▲
Investment Freedom	50.0	—
Financial Freedom	50.0	—
Property Rights	50.0	—
Fdm fm Corruption	35.0	▽
Labor Freedom	80.9	▽

0   50   100

100 = most free,   **▌= world average**

BUSINESS FREEDOM — *76.3%*

The overall freedom to start, operate, and close a business is relatively well protected by Belize's national regulatory environment. Starting a business takes an average of 44 days, compared to the world average of 43 days. Despite a lack of transparency in the administration of some laws and procedures, obtaining a business license takes less than the world average of 19 procedures and 234 days. The process for closing a business is relatively easy and straightforward.

TRADE FREEDOM — *64.6%*

Belize's weighted average tariff rate was 12.7 percent in 2003. Import restrictions, restrictive import and export licensing rules for some products, corruption in customs administration, and weak enforcement of intellectual property rights add to the cost of trade. An additional 10 percentage points is deducted from Belize's trade freedom score to account for these non-tariff barriers.

FISCAL FREEDOM — *69.3%*

Belize has a high income tax rate and a moderate corporate tax rate. The top income tax rate is 45 percent, and the top corporate tax rate is 25 percent. Other taxes include a goods and services tax (GST) and a stamp duty. In the most recent year, overall tax revenue as a percentage of GDP was 20.5 percent.

GOVERNMENT SIZE — *74.8%*

Total government expenditures, including consumption and transfer payments, are moderate. In the most recent year, government spending equaled 29 percent of GDP. The privatization process has been slow, and mismanagement of state-owned enterprises has put considerable pressure on the government's finances.

MONETARY FREEDOM — *77.3%*

Inflation is moderate, averaging 4 percent between 2004 and 2006. Relatively unstable prices explain most of the monetary freedom score. The government maintains the prices of some basic commodities, such as rice, flour, beans, sugar, bread, butane gas, and fuel, and controls the retail price of electricity. An additional 10 percentage points is deducted from Belize's monetary freedom score to adjust for measures that distort domestic prices.

INVESTMENT FREEDOM — *50%*

Belize generally is open to foreign investment but requires special licenses for commercial fishing within the barrier reef, merchandising, sugarcane farming, real estate and insurance, transportation, tourism activities, accounting and legal services, entertainment, beauty salons, and restaurants and bars. Full foreign ownership of businesses is legal, although the government encourages local partnerships. Laws and regulations do not seriously impede investment capital. Both residents and non-residents may hold foreign exchange accounts subject to government approval. The central bank controls some payments and requires that repatriation be made through an authorized dealer. All capital transactions must be approved by the central bank.

FINANCIAL FREEDOM — *50%*

Belize's small but growing financial system is dominated by the banking sector. There are five commercial banks, seven international banks, three quasi-government banks, and 14 credit unions. Subsidiaries of foreign banks are active and competitive, but approval is required to secure a foreign currency loan from outside Belize, and only authorized dealers are permitted to retain foreign currency. The government affects the allocation of credit through the quasi-government banks. A 2006 Senate investigation into financial practices found recklessness and negligence in the securitization of mortgages. The International Financial Services Act promotes offshore financial services, and the government offers extensive banking confidentiality.

PROPERTY RIGHTS — *50%*

Although the judiciary is independent under the terms of Belize's constitution, it is also subject to political influence. There is a severe lack of trained prosecutors, and police officers often assume that role in the magistrates' courts. The result is lengthy trial backlogs. Expropriation of personal property is possible but relatively rare. The government needs to strengthen its enforcement of laws protecting intellectual property rights.

FREEDOM FROM CORRUPTION — *35%*

Corruption is perceived as significant. Belize ranks 66th out of 163 countries in Transparency International's Corruption Perceptions Index for 2006. Money laundering, primarily related to narcotics trafficking and contraband smuggling, occurs through banks operating in Belize.

LABOR FREEDOM — *80.9%*

Belize's labor market operates under flexible employment regulations that can enhance employment and productivity growth. The non-salary cost of employing a worker is low, and dismissing a redundant employee can be costless. Labor regulations do not distort efficient business activities to any considerable degree. Belize's labor freedom is one of the 20 freest in the world.

BENIN

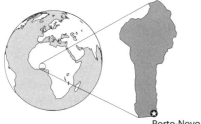

Porto-Novo

Benin's economy is 55 percent free, according to our 2008 assessment, which makes it the world's 110th freest economy. Its overall score is unchanged from last year, with three freedoms improving and five worsening slightly. Benin is ranked 20th out of 40 countries in the sub-Saharan African region, and its overall score is slightly higher than the regional average.

Benin scores well on government size and financial freedom. Though the banking system is imperfect, the provision of credit is robust and equitable. Relatively high tax rates on income and corporations dampen the fiscal score, but tax revenue is fairly low as a percentage of GDP. Government expenditures are moderate. Benin has pegged its currency to the euro, resulting in admirable price stability.

Economic development has been hampered, however, by a serious lack of liberalization in such areas as investment freedom, labor freedom, property rights, and business freedom. Bureaucratic inefficiency and corruption hamper virtually all areas of the economy. Foreign investment is subject to government approval and regulations that require the hiring of native Beninese. Court enforcement of intrusive labor regulations and of property rights is subject to pervasive political interference.

BACKGROUND: In 1990, dictator Mathieu Kérékou accepted the creation of a transitional government followed by elections, marking one of Africa's first peaceful transitions to elected government. Kérékou won the presidency in 1996 and 2001 but stepped down in 2006 in deference to constitutional limits on tenure. Boni Yayi, former president of the regional development bank, was elected president in 2006. Economic reform has encouraged growth, but Benin remains underdeveloped. Much of the population is engaged in agriculture. Cotton is the primary export and accounts for about 40 percent of GDP. Trade and transport with neighboring countries are extensive. Trade with Nigeria, which may account for up to a third of Benin's GDP, is mostly informal.

How Do We Measure Economic Freedom? See Chapter 4 (page 39) for an explanation of the methodology or visit the *Index* Web site at *heritage.org/index*.

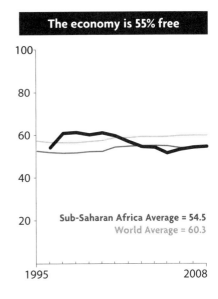

The economy is 55% free

Sub-Saharan Africa Average = 54.5
World Average = 60.3

1995　　　　　　　　　2008

QUICK FACTS

Population: 8.4 million

GDP (PPP): $9.6 billion
2.9% growth in 2005
3.6% 5-yr. comp. ann. growth
$1,141 per capita

Unemployment: n/a

Inflation (CPI): 5.4%

FDI (net flow): $21.0 million

Official Development Assistance:
Multilateral: $185.6 million
Bilateral: $219.4 million (10.8% from the U.S.)

External Debt: $1.9 billion

Exports: $784.2 million (2004)
Primarily cotton, cashews, shea butter, textiles, palm products, seafood

Imports: $1.1 billion (2004)
Primarily foodstuffs, capital goods, petroleum products

2005 data unless otherwise noted.

BENIN'S TEN ECONOMIC FREEDOMS

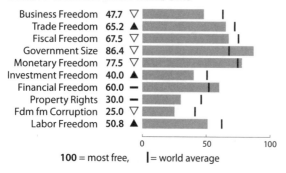

Business Freedom	47.7 ▽	
Trade Freedom	65.2 ▲	
Fiscal Freedom	67.5 ▽	
Government Size	86.4 ▽	
Monetary Freedom	77.5 ▽	
Investment Freedom	40.0 ▲	
Financial Freedom	60.0 —	
Property Rights	30.0 —	
Fdm fm Corruption	25.0 ▽	
Labor Freedom	50.8 ▲	

0   50   100

100 = most free, **❙ = world average**

BUSINESS FREEDOM — 47.7%

The overall freedom to start, operate, and close a business is significantly limited by Benin's national regulatory environment. Starting a business takes an average of 31 days, compared to the world average of 43 days. Obtaining a business license takes more than the world average of 234 days. Bureaucratic procedures are not streamlined and are often non-transparent. Closing a business can be burdensome.

TRADE FREEDOM — 65.2%

Benin's weighted average tariff rate was 12.4 percent in 2005. The customs process is inefficient and corrupt, and the government restricts some imports, applies selected import bans, and levies import taxes to protect "strategic products" such as rice and sugar against world price fluctuations. An additional 10 percentage points is deducted from Benin's trade freedom score to account for these non-tariff barriers.

FISCAL FREEDOM — 67.5%

Benin has high tax rates. The top income tax rate is 40 percent, and the top corporate tax rate is 38 percent. Other taxes include a value-added tax (VAT), a property tax, and a tax on insurance contracts. In the most recent year, overall tax revenue as a percentage of GDP was 14.5 percent.

GOVERNMENT SIZE — 86.4%

Total government expenditures, including consumption and transfer payments, are moderate. In the most recent year, government spending equaled 21.3 percent of GDP. Privatization of public enterprises has stalled.

MONETARY FREEDOM — 77.5%

As a member of the West African Economic and Monetary Union, Benin uses the CFA franc, which is pegged to the euro. Inflation is relatively low, averaging 3.9 percent between 2004 and 2006. Relatively low and stable prices explain most of the monetary freedom score. The government regulates prices in the state-owned water, telecommunications, and electricity sectors, and the parastatal cotton sector benefits from government subsidies and price supports. An additional 10 percentage points is deducted from Benin's monetary freedom score to adjust for measures that distort domestic prices.

INVESTMENT FREEDOM — 40%

Benin officially favors foreign investment. The bureaucracy, however, is inefficient and subject to corruption. Privatization, the largest incentive for foreign investment, is extremely slow-moving amid accusations of corruption and legal disputes, and the government requires part-Beninese ownership of any privatized company. Foreign exchange accounts must be authorized by the government and the Central Bank of West African States (BCEAO). Many capital transactions, including direct investment, are subject to reporting requirements and to government and BCEAO approval. There are no controls on the purchase of land by non-residents, except for investments in enterprises, branches, or corporations.

FINANCIAL FREEDOM — 60%

Benin's underdeveloped financial system is concentrated in banking. There were 12 licensed banks as of mid-2006, but 40 percent of market share is held by the largest bank. Enforcement of contracts, transparency in financial operations, and fraud prevention are somewhat weak. The Central Bank of West African States governs Benin's financial institutions, and regulatory oversight can be unwieldy. The banking sector is predominantly private, and foreign ownership in banking and insurance is prominent. Credit is allocated on market terms and is available without discrimination. Banks experience difficulty with non-performing loans and with recovering collateral on those loans. There are many microcredit and savings and loan institutions. The insurance sector accounts for less than 1 percent of GDP but is growing rapidly.

PROPERTY RIGHTS — 30%

Benin's legal system is weak and subject to corruption. There is no separate commercial court system, and backlogs of civil cases cause long delays. International donor assistance projects aim to improve the judiciary by training staff and expanding physical capacity.

FREEDOM FROM CORRUPTION — 25%

Corruption is perceived as widespread. Benin ranks 121st out of 163 countries in Transparency International's Corruption Perceptions Index for 2006. Endemic government corruption blights economic growth and is a significant disincentive to investment.

LABOR FREEDOM — 50.8%

Benin's labor market operates under restrictive employment regulations that hinder employment creation and productivity growth. Restrictions on increasing or contracting the number of working hours are rigid. The non-salary cost of employing a worker is high, but dismissing a redundant employee can be relatively costless.

BOLIVIA

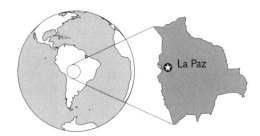

La Paz

Rank: 123

Regional Rank: 25 of 29

Bolivia's economy is 53.2 percent free, according to our 2008 assessment, which makes it the world's 123rd freest economy. Its overall score is 1.1 percentage points lower than last year, with a decline in seven of the 10 freedoms. Bolivia is ranked 25th out of 29 countries in the Americas, and its overall score is well below the regional average.

Bolivia rates highly in fiscal freedom, financial freedom, and trade freedom. Inflation is moderate, although the government imposes *de facto* price controls on most utilities.

Bolivia's investment freedom, property rights, labor freedom, and freedom from corruption scores are low. Pervasive corruption and significant regulation are major hurdles for foreign investment, as is possible nationalization of the energy sector. Rule of law is weak, and private property can be subject to bureaucratic interference, forced transactions, and expropriation. Restrictive labor laws further cloud the business climate.

BACKGROUND: Bolivia's history is punctuated by periods of military dictatorship interspersed with attempts at democratic self-rule. Since the 1980s, successive elected governments have had some success at economic and social reform. President Sanchez de Lozada (1993–1997) reduced the government's economic profile through partial privatization and lower taxes and tariffs. A 1999 economic downturn created fiscal pressures and social unrest. Mobs removed two presidents from office in 2003 and 2005, after which populist Evo Morales was elected as Bolivia's first indigenous president on an anti-globalization platform. Supported by Cuban dictator Fidel Castro and hard-left Venezuelan President Hugo Chavez, Morales has pushed expanded executive power, land reform, and state control of key natural resources and industries but has been constrained by an opposition-controlled Senate and powerful state governors.

How Do We Measure Economic Freedom? See Chapter 4 (page 39) for an explanation of the methodology or visit the *Index* Web site at *heritage.org/index*.

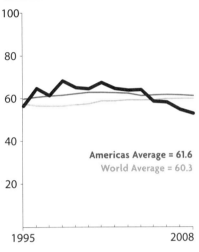

The economy is 53.2% free

Americas Average = 61.6
World Average = 60.3

1995 — 2008

QUICK FACTS

Population: 9.2 million

GDP (PPP): $25.9 billion
4.1% growth in 2005
3.3% 5-yr. comp. ann. growth
$2,819 per capita

Unemployment: 7.8%

Inflation (CPI): 5.4%

FDI (net flow): −$280.0 million

Official Development Assistance:
Multilateral: $265.7 million
Bilateral: $435.2 million (20.8% from the U.S.)

External Debt: $6.4 billion

Exports: $3.2 billion
Primarily natural gas, soybeans and soy products, crude petroleum, zinc ore, tin

Imports: $2.9 billion
Primarily petroleum products, plastics, paper, aircraft and aircraft parts, prepared foods, automobiles, insecticides, soybeans
2005 data unless otherwise noted.

BOLIVIA'S TEN ECONOMIC FREEDOMS

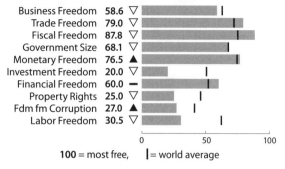

Business Freedom	58.6 ▽	
Trade Freedom	79.0 ▽	
Fiscal Freedom	87.8 ▽	
Government Size	68.1 ▽	
Monetary Freedom	76.5 ▲	
Investment Freedom	20.0 ▽	
Financial Freedom	60.0 ▬	
Property Rights	25.0 ▽	
Fdm fm Corruption	27.0 ▲	
Labor Freedom	30.5 ▽	

0   50   100

100 = most free, **❙ = world average**

BUSINESS FREEDOM — *58.6%*

The overall freedom to start, operate, and close a business is restricted by Bolivia's national regulatory environment. Starting a business takes an average of 50 days, compared to the world average of 43 days. Obtaining a business license requires about the world average of 19 procedures and slightly more than the world average of 234 days. Red tape and the lack of transparency still hinder entrepreneurial activities. Closing a business is relatively easy.

TRADE FREEDOM — *79%*

Bolivia's weighted average tariff rate was 5.5 percent in 2005. Lowering trade barriers and simplifying the trade regime have progressed, but import bans, restrictive sanitary and phytosanitary rules, some export subsidies, and issues related to the enforcement and protection of intellectual property rights add to the costs of trade. An additional 10 percentage points is deducted from Bolivia's trade freedom score to account for non-tariff barriers.

FISCAL FREEDOM— *87.8%*

Bolivia has low tax rates. The top income tax rate is 13 percent, and the corporate tax rate is 25 percent. Other taxes include a value-added tax (VAT), a transaction tax, and a property tax. In the most recent year, overall tax revenue as a percentage of GDP was 20.7 percent.

GOVERNMENT SIZE — *68.1%*

Total government expenditures, including consumption and transfer payments, are moderate. In the most recent year, government spending equaled 32.6 percent of GDP. In 2006, the government announced its nationalization of the hydrocarbon sector.

MONETARY FREEDOM — *76.5%*

Inflation is moderate, averaging 4.6 percent between 2004 and 2006. Relatively unstable prices explain most of the monetary freedom score. Regulations effectively control prices for hydrocarbons and most public utilities, and the prices of petroleum products, potable water, and garbage collection are controlled. An additional 10 percentage points is deducted from Bolivia's monetary freedom score to adjust for measures that distort domestic prices.

INVESTMENT FREEDOM — *20%*

Despite relatively simple laws, foreign investment is hin-

dered by social unrest, weak judicial security, arbitrary regulation, a cumbersome bureaucracy, rampant corruption, and a somewhat hostile populist government. Energy is heavily and increasingly regulated. In early 2006, the government nationalized the natural gas industry, ordering companies to relinquish control of fields or leave. Nationalization continued with the February 2007 seizure of a Swiss tin interest. Bolivia's property law was amended in November 2006 to certify that the state would seize "unproductive" private property. Both residents and non-residents may hold foreign exchange accounts. There are no restrictions or controls on payments, transactions, transfers, purchase of real estate, access to foreign exchange, or repatriation of profits.

FINANCIAL FREEDOM — *60%*

Bolivia's financial sector is concentrated in banking. The financial system in 2007 included 12 commercial banks, of which three were foreign-owned and others had some level of foreign ownership, and 45 non-bank institutions. Credit is allocated on market terms, but foreign borrowers may find it difficult to qualify for loans because such credit is issued against domestic collateral. Government-owned banks no longer exist. Financial-sector regulations and accounting standards are somewhat burdensome and do not fully conform to international standards. Greater exchange-rate and inflationary stability has generated a modest upturn in banking. Despite legal authorization, the development of a modern securities exchange has been hindered by political and social unrest. The insurance sector is small. Capital markets are focused on trading in government bonds, although corporate debt and mutual funds have grown in recent years.

PROPERTY RIGHTS — *25%*

Although statutes guarantee property rights, the judicial process is time-consuming and subject to political influence and pervasive corruption. The enforcement of intellectual property rights is erratic and largely ineffective. Competing claims to land titles and the absence of reliable dispute resolution make real property acquisition risky. Expropriation is a real possibility, as is illegal squatting on rural private property.

FREEDOM FROM CORRUPTION — *27%*

Corruption is perceived as widespread. Bolivia ranks 105th out of 163 countries in Transparency International's Corruption Perceptions Index for 2006. Corruption disproportionately affects lower-income groups. A government report rated the national police, customs, and justice system the most corrupt.

LABOR FREEDOM — *30.5%*

Bolivia's labor market operates under highly restrictive employment regulations that hinder employment creation and productivity growth. The government has established the minimum wage for the public and private sectors. The non-salary cost of employing a worker is moderate, but overall rigidity in hiring and firing is quite high. More than 60 percent of the workforce is employed by the informal economy. Bolivia's labor freedom is one of the 20 lowest in the world.

BOSNIA AND HERZEGOVINA

Sarajevo ✪

The economy of Bosnia and Herzegovina is 53.7 percent free, according to our 2008 assessment, which makes it the world's 121st freest economy. Its overall score is 0.6 percentage point lower than last year. Bosnia is ranked 38th freest among the 41 countries in the European region, and its overall score is well below the regional average.

Bosnia's score is exceptional for two reasons: Property rights are very weak, scoring 36 percentage points below average, and the size of government is very large, scoring 19 points below average. Only two freedoms stand out as relatively high: trade freedom and financial freedom. The tariff rate averages 5.1 percent, and non-tariff barriers are relatively low. Banking could improve even more but is remarkably well privatized.

Bosnia faces many challenges associated with recovering from a decade-long civil war. Government size, property rights, and freedom from corruption are problems, and complex and irregularly enforced regulations affect almost everything. Commercial courts do not exist, and trade disputes must be handled among the claimants or outside the country. Government expenditure is high but does not result in a more efficient or streamlined bureaucracy.

BACKGROUND: The 1995 Dayton Agreement finalized Bosnia–Herzegovina's secession from the former Yugoslavia. Within its loose central government, two separate governing entities exist along ethnic lines: Republika Srpska and the Bosnian–Croat Federation. The rule of law is weak, and local courts are subject to substantial political interference and lack the resources to prosecute complex crimes. The state's overly large role, characterized by an intrusive bureaucracy and costly registration procedures, reflects a history of central planning and has yet to be fully addressed. The economy still relies heavily on agriculture and requires strong market reforms in most areas. Integration into the international community, especially conclusion of the currently stalled Stabilization and Association Agreement talks with the European Union, is a priority.

How Do We Measure Economic Freedom? See Chapter 4 (page 39) for an explanation of the methodology or visit the *Index* Web site at *heritage.org/index*.

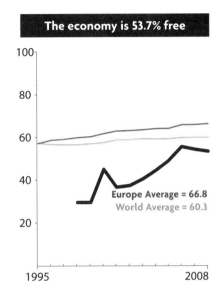

The economy is 53.7% free

Europe Average = 66.8
World Average = 60.3

1995 — 2008

QUICK FACTS

Population: 3.9 million

GDP (PPP): $31.1 billion
5.0% growth in 2005
5.0% 5-yr. comp. ann. growth
$7,928 per capita

Unemployment: 45.5% (2004)

Inflation (CPI): 1.9%

FDI (net flow): $295.0 million

Official Development Assistance:
Multilateral: $236.4 million
Bilateral: $310.2 million (15% from the U.S.)

External Debt: $5.6 billion

Exports: $3.6 billion
Primarily metals, clothing, wood products

Imports: $8.0 billion
Primarily machinery and equipment, chemicals, fuels, foodstuffs

2005 data unless otherwise noted.

BOSNIA & HERZEGOVINA'S TEN ECONOMIC FREEDOMS

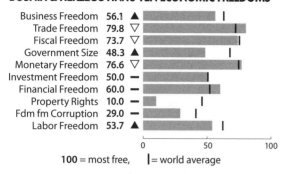

Business Freedom	56.1 ▲	
Trade Freedom	79.8 ▽	
Fiscal Freedom	73.7 ▽	
Government Size	48.3 ▲	
Monetary Freedom	76.6 ▽	
Investment Freedom	50.0 —	
Financial Freedom	60.0 —	
Property Rights	10.0 —	
Fdm fm Corruption	29.0 —	
Labor Freedom	53.7 ▲	

0   50   100

100 = most free, | = world average

BUSINESS FREEDOM — *56.1%*

The overall freedom to start, operate, and close a business is limited by Bosnia and Herzegovina's national regulatory environment. Starting a business takes an average of 54 days, compared to the world average of 43 days. Obtaining a business license takes almost twice as long as the world average of 234 days. Heavily bureaucratic and non-transparent systems remain a problem for investors and entrepreneurs. Closing a business can be relatively easy.

TRADE FREEDOM — *79.8%*

Bosnia and Herzegovina's weighted average tariff rate was 5.1 percent in 2001. Import and export restrictions, additional import duties on agriculture products, and numerous border fees add to the cost of trade. An additional 10 percentage points is deducted from Bosnia and Herzegovina's trade freedom score to account for these non-tariff barriers.

FISCAL FREEDOM — *73.7%*

Bosnia and Herzegovina is divided into three jurisdictions for purposes of taxation. The top income tax rate can be as high as 15 percent, and the top corporate income tax rate is 30 percent. Other taxes include a sales tax and a property tax. In the most recent year, overall tax revenue as a percentage of GDP was 38.8 percent.

GOVERNMENT SIZE — *48.3%*

Total government expenditures, including consumption and transfer payments, are high. In the most recent year, government spending equaled 41.5 percent of GDP. Bosnia and Herzegovina lags behind the rest of the European region in privatization.

MONETARY FREEDOM — *76.6%*

Inflation is moderate, averaging 4.5 percent between 2004 and 2006. Relatively unstable prices explain most of the monetary freedom score. Price controls apply to electricity, gas, and telecommunications services. An additional 10 percentage points is deducted from Bosnia and Herzegovina's monetary freedom score to adjust for measures that distort domestic prices.

INVESTMENT FREEDOM — *50%*

Foreign investment laws grant national treatment to foreign investors. Arms and media are the only sectors subject to restrictions. By the end of 2006, the Bosnian government was making major efforts to privatize telecommunications and energy, as well as selling off the country's oil distributor. This process moved much more quickly and attracted more greenfield investment in the Republika Srpska than in the Federation. The main obstacles to foreign investment elsewhere are a complex and non-transparent regulatory framework, weak judicial structures, and poor infrastructure. There are few restrictions on capital transactions and foreign exchange accounts.

FINANCIAL FREEDOM — *60%*

The country's two autonomous government entities operate functionally independent financial systems. The inherited banking system was dominated by large state-owned banks burdened with non-performing loans. Recently, however, the banking sector has expanded quickly, and consolidation has followed. By the end of 2006, there were 30 banks in Bosnia. The sector has come to be dominated by the six largest foreign bank branches, which control 65 percent of assets. Banking reform begun in 1997 led to consolidation and privatization. Most of Bosnia and Herzegovina's banks are now private, accounting for 86 percent of banking capital in 2004. Long-term lending is hindered by insufficient enforcement of contracts. The central bank is attempting to consolidate its financial oversight organs, but this regulatory federalization has stalled. International accounting standards are being adopted. Each region has an underdeveloped but growing non-bank financial sector and a small stock exchange.

PROPERTY RIGHTS — *10%*

Property registers are largely unreliable, leaving property transfers open to dispute. The judicial system does not cover commercial activities adequately. Court decisions are difficult to enforce. Contracts are almost unenforceable, and the government does not adequately enforce laws protecting intellectual property rights.

FREEDOM FROM CORRUPTION — *29%*

Corruption is perceived as widespread. Bosnia and Herzegovina ranks 93rd out of 163 countries in Transparency International's Corruption Perceptions Index for 2006. Judges typically request bribes and respond to pressure from public officials. The business registration and licensing process is particularly vulnerable to corruption.

LABOR FREEDOM — *53.7%*

The labor market operates under relatively inflexible employment regulations that hinder employment creation and productivity growth. The non-salary cost of employing a worker is moderate, but an inflexible wage determination system hinders job creation and worker mobility. Dismissing a redundant employee is relatively costless.

BOTSWANA

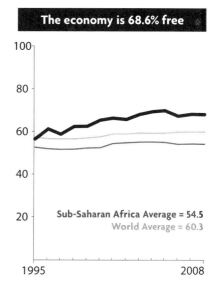

Gaborone

Rank: 36
Regional Rank: 2 of 40

Botswana's economy is 68.6 percent free, according to our 2008 assessment, which makes it the world's 36th freest economy. Its overall score is essentially unchanged from last year. Botswana is ranked 2nd out of 40 countries in the sub-Saharan Africa region, and its overall score is well above the regional average.

Botswana is an economic regional leader and scores above the world average on seven of 10 economic freedoms. It is very strong in property rights, investment freedom, financial freedom, freedom from corruption, and labor freedom. The financial sector is a regional leader with an independent central bank and little government intervention. The judiciary is independent, and the protection of intellectual property is strong.

The overall business climate is superior for Africa and a model for the world. Botswana could improve on its relatively weak scores in government size, trade freedom, and monetary freedom.

BACKGROUND: Botswana, a multi-party democracy since gaining its independence in 1966, has a market-oriented economy that encourages private enterprise and is ranked as Africa's least corrupt. It also had one of the world's highest average growth rates during the past four decades and possesses Africa's highest sovereign credit rating. However, sections of its population still suffer from high unemployment and poverty. Despite efforts to diversify the economy, diamonds accounted for 75 percent of exports, over 40 percent of GDP, and over 45 percent of government revenue in 2005. Botswana has one of the world's highest HIV/AIDS infection rates, and political turmoil in neighboring Zimbabwe is an ongoing concern.

How Do We Measure Economic Freedom? See Chapter 4 (page 39) for an explanation of the methodology or visit the *Index* Web site at *heritage.org/index*.

The economy is 68.6% free

Sub-Saharan Africa Average = 54.5
World Average = 60.3

1995 — 2008

QUICK FACTS

Population: 1.8 million

GDP (PPP): $21.9 billion
6.2% growth in 2005
6.0% 5-yr. comp. ann. growth
$12,388 per capita

Unemployment: 23.8% (2004)

Inflation (CPI): 8.6%

FDI (net flow): $289.0 million

Official Development Assistance:
Multilateral: $29.1 million
Bilateral: $61.1 million (66.7% from the U.S.)

External Debt: $473.0 million

Exports: $5.3 billion
Primarily diamonds, copper, nickel, soda ash, meat, textiles

Imports: $3.7 billion
Primarily foodstuffs, machinery, electrical goods, transport equipment, textiles, fuel and petroleum products, wood and paper products, metal and metal products
2005 data unless otherwise noted.

BOTSWANA'S TEN ECONOMIC FREEDOMS

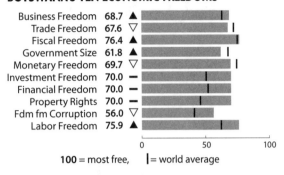

Business Freedom	68.7 ▲	
Trade Freedom	67.6 ▽	
Fiscal Freedom	76.4 ▲	
Government Size	61.8 ▲	
Monetary Freedom	69.7 ▽	
Investment Freedom	70.0 —	
Financial Freedom	70.0 —	
Property Rights	70.0 —	
Fdm fm Corruption	56.0 ▽	
Labor Freedom	75.9 ▲	

0   50   100

100 = most free, | = world average

BUSINESS FREEDOM — *68.7%*

The overall freedom to start, operate, and close a business is relatively well protected by Botswana's national regulatory environment. Starting a business takes an average of 108 days, compared to the world average of 43 days. Obtaining a business license takes less than the world average of 234 days. The government has established a one-stop shop for investors, and the process for closing a business is easy and straightforward.

TRADE FREEDOM — *67.6%*

Botswana's weighted average tariff rate was 11.2 percent in 2005. There are very few non-tariff barriers to trade, but the government maintains import bans on some products, import licensing requirements, a restrictive standards regime, domestic bias in government procurement, and weak enforcement of intellectual property rights. An additional 10 percentage points is deducted from Botswana's trade freedom score to account for these non-tariff barriers.

FISCAL FREEDOM — *76.4%*

Botswana's tax burden is one of the lowest in Southern Africa. Both the top income tax rate and the top corporate tax rate are 25 percent. Other taxes include a value-added tax (VAT), an additional company tax, and a fuel tax. Adjustments to the tax system in recent years include an increase in the income threshold that is exempt from taxation. In the most recent year, overall tax revenue as a percentage of GDP was 33.3 percent.

GOVERNMENT SIZE — *61.8%*

Total government expenditures, including consumption and transfer payments, are high. In the most recent year, government spending equaled 35.7 percent of GDP. Although Botswana has pursued privatization and other initiatives to improve the performance of its remaining public-sector enterprises, further reducing the size of government and its role in the economy remains a necessity.

MONETARY FREEDOM — *69.7%*

Inflation is high, averaging 10.2 percent between 2004 and 2006. Relatively unstable prices explain most of the monetary freedom score. Most prices are set by the market, but the government maintains price policies for some agricultural and livestock goods and is able to influence prices through numerous state-owned enterprises and service

providers. An additional 10 percentage points is deducted from Botswana's monetary freedom score to adjust for measures that distort domestic prices.

INVESTMENT FREEDOM — *70%*

Botswana's laws encourage foreign investment, particularly in the non-mining sector. The government has implemented reforms expediting the application process for business ventures. It also, however, restricts foreign investment in some areas reserved for Botswana citizens, including butchery and produce, gasoline filling stations, bars and liquor stores, supermarkets, and retail. The majority of investment capital has been directed toward the mining industry, followed by finance and wholesale and retail trade. Privatization has stalled with the intended sale of Air Botswana. There are no restrictions on capital transactions or foreign exchange accounts, residents' and non-residents' accounts, or international transfers.

FINANCIAL FREEDOM — *70%*

Botswana's banking system is competitive and one of Africa's most advanced. The central bank is independent. In 2007, there were seven commercial banks, mostly foreign-owned. The government is involved in the banking sector through state-owned financial institutions and a special financial incentives program that is aimed at increasing Botswana's status as a financial center. Credit is allocated on market terms, although the government provides subsidized loans. The insurance sector and pension funds are active, and Botswana boasts 12 insurance companies. The state owns the Botswana Motor Vehicle Insurance Fund, but private firms dominate the insurance sector. The small stock market is growing as the result of an extended bull market. The government has introduced bonds of varying maturities to stimulate the domestic capital market.

PROPERTY RIGHTS — *70%*

The constitution provides for an independent judiciary, and the government respects this in practice. The legal system is sufficient to conduct secure commercial dealings, although a serious and growing backlog of cases prevents timely trials. The protection of intellectual property rights has improved significantly.

FREEDOM FROM CORRUPTION — *56%*

Corruption is perceived as present. Botswana ranks 37th out of 163 countries in Transparency International's Corruption Perceptions Index for 2006 and is rated as Africa's least corrupt country. It is ahead of many European and Asian countries and has a proven record of good economic governance.

LABOR FREEDOM — *75.9%*

Botswana's labor market maintains relatively flexible employment regulations that could be improved to enhance employment and productivity growth. The non-salary cost of employing a worker is very low, and dismissing a redundant employee can be relatively costless. The employer is not required to make pension, health insurance, and unemployment insurance contributions.

BRAZIL

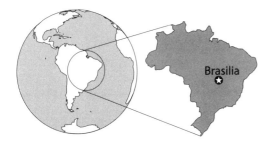

Brasilia

Brazil's economy is 55.9 percent free, according to our 2008 assessment, which makes it the world's 101st freest economy. Its overall score is 0.2 percentage point lower than last year, with lower scores in freedom from corruption and labor freedom. Brazil is ranked 21st out of 29 countries in the Americas, and its overall score is below the regional average.

Brazil is a regional economic power but is not notably strong in any of the 10 economic freedoms. The personal tax rate and the corporate tax rate are burdensome. Overall tax revenue is high as a percentage of GDP relative to other developing countries.

Brazil suffers from weak financial freedom and a large central government. Regulatory inflexibility makes starting a business take much longer than the world average. Significant restrictions on foreign capital exist in many areas, and the government remains heavily involved in banking and finance. The judicial system and other areas of the public sector are inefficient and subject to corruption.

BACKGROUND: The world's fifth-largest country, Brazil has abundant natural resources but has not realized its full economic potential. Real GDP growth was positive but relatively low over the past decade. High income inequality and the rapid growth of the urban poor population have fueled pressure for socialist policies. A convoluted tax system, inadequate transportation infrastructure, and barriers to foreign investment have also impeded growth. Other problems include government management of most of the oil and electricity sectors, an ineffective judiciary, weak public education, and excessive regulation. Agriculture and industry account for 10 percent and 40 percent, respectively, of GDP.

How Do We Measure Economic Freedom? See Chapter 4 (page 39) for an explanation of the methodology or visit the *Index* Web site at *heritage.org/index*.

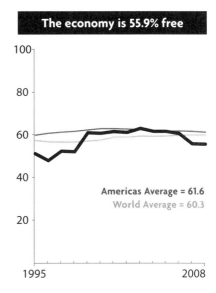

The economy is 55.9% free

Americas Average = 61.6
World Average = 60.3

QUICK FACTS

Population: 186.4 million

GDP (PPP): $1.57 trillion
2.9% growth in 2005
3.1% 5-yr. comp. ann. growth
$8,402 per capita

Unemployment: 9.8%

Inflation (CPI): 6.9%

FDI (net flow): $12.5 billion

Official Development Assistance:
Multilateral: $52.8 million
Bilateral: $361.8 million (6% from the U.S.)

External Debt: $188.0 billion

Exports: $134.4 billion
Primarily transport equipment, iron ore, soybeans, footwear, coffee, automobiles

Imports: $97.8 billion
Primarily machinery, electrical and transport equipment, chemical products, oil, automotive parts, electronics

2005 data unless otherwise noted.

BRAZIL'S TEN ECONOMIC FREEDOMS

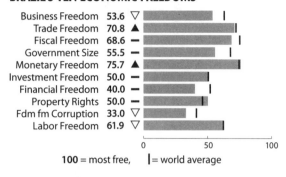

Business Freedom	53.6 ▽	
Trade Freedom	70.8 ▲	
Fiscal Freedom	68.6 —	
Government Size	55.5 —	
Monetary Freedom	75.7 ▲	
Investment Freedom	50.0 —	
Financial Freedom	40.0 —	
Property Rights	50.0 —	
Fdm fm Corruption	33.0 ▽	
Labor Freedom	61.9 ▽	

0   50   100

100 = most free, | = world average

BUSINESS FREEDOM — 53.6%

The overall freedom to start, operate, and close a business is limited by Brazil's national regulatory environment. Starting a business takes more than three times the world average of 43 days, and obtaining a business license takes more than the global average of 234 days. Despite reform efforts, regulation is complex, discretionary, and non-transparent. Closing a business is difficult.

TRADE FREEDOM — 70.8%

Brazil's weighted average tariff rate was 7.1 percent in 2005. Import and export quotas, bans and restrictions, market access barriers in services, prohibitive tariffs, border fees, restrictive regulatory and licensing rules, export support programs, non-transparent government procurement, and problematic protection of intellectual property rights persist. An additional 15 percentage points is deducted from Brazil's trade freedom score to account for these non-tariff barriers.

FISCAL FREEDOM — 68.6%

Brazil's top income tax rate is 27.5 percent. The standard corporate tax rate is 15 percent, but a surtax of 10 percent and a 9 percent social contribution on net profit bring the effective rate to 34 percent. Other taxes include a financial transactions tax and a tax on interest. In the most recent year, overall tax revenue as a percentage of GDP was 35 percent.

GOVERNMENT SIZE — 55.5%

Total government expenditures, including consumption and transfer payments, are relatively high. In the most recent year, government spending equaled 38.5 percent of GDP. Public debt is still around 50 percent of GDP. Besides debt service, government spending is focused mainly on pensions, transfers to local governments, and bureaucracy.

MONETARY FREEDOM — 75.7%

Inflation is relatively high, averaging 5.1 percent between 2004 and 2006. Relatively unstable prices explain most of the monetary freedom score. Although such public services as railways, telecommunications, and electricity have been privatized, the government oversees prices through regulatory agencies. The National Petroleum Agency fixes the wholesale price of fuel, and the government controls airfare prices. An additional 10 percentage points is deducted from Brazil's monetary freedom score to adjust for price controls.

INVESTMENT FREEDOM — 50%

Foreign capital enters freely and since 1995 has received national treatment. Foreign investment is restricted in nuclear energy, health services, media, rural and border property, fishing, mail and telegraph services, aviation, and aerospace. The government has carried out three major financial and energy privatizations since 2004 but has also established a more central role in setting energy prices and forecasting energy demand. Foreign exchange accounts are subject to limited restriction, and foreign participation in certain economic activities is prohibited. The central bank approves outward direct investment in some cases, including transfers and remittances, where it has broad administrative discretion.

FINANCIAL FREEDOM — 40%

Brazil's financial system is South America's largest and one of the largest among all emerging markets. Despite state involvement, banking and capital markets are diversified, dynamic, and competitive. Technically forbidden by the 1988 constitution, foreign investment in banking is nonetheless almost always approved. About 200 public and private commercial banks and many non-banking financial institutions conform to international best practices guidelines after a long period of consolidation. The top 10 banks hold 82.4 percent of total assets, and the sector is dominated by three publicly controlled banks. The growing insurance market remains fairly small. The stock market is not a major source of domestic corporate finance, but it is growing, and trading is active; there were 26 new IPOs in 2006.

PROPERTY RIGHTS — 50%

Contracts are generally considered secure, but Brazil's judiciary is inefficient, somewhat arbitrary, subject to political and economic influence, and lacking in resources and staff training. Decisions can take years, and decisions of the Supreme Federal Tribunal are not automatically binding on lower courts. Protection of intellectual property rights has improved, but piracy of copyrighted material persists.

FREEDOM FROM CORRUPTION — 33%

Corruption is perceived as significant. Brazil ranks 70th out of 163 countries in Transparency International's Corruption Perceptions Index for 2006. Businesses bidding on government procurement contracts at times encounter corruption, which is also a problem in the lower courts and can discourage investment.

LABOR FREEDOM — 61.9%

Brazil's inflexible employment regulations should be improved to enhance employment and productivity growth. The non-salary cost of employing a worker is high, and dismissing a redundant employee can be costly. Benefits mandated by rigid labor legislation amplify overall labor costs. The high cost of laying off a worker creates a risk aversion for companies that would otherwise hire more people and grow.

BULGARIA

Sofia

Rank: 59
Regional Rank: 28 of 41

Bulgaria's economy is 62.9 percent free, according to our 2008 assessment, which makes it the world's 59th freest economy. Its overall score is 0.9 percentage point higher than last year, primarily because of improved trade freedom. Bulgaria is ranked 28th freest among the 41 countries in the European region, and its overall score is slightly above the world average.

Bulgaria scores highly in six freedoms and significantly below average in two. Its strongest relative scores are in trade freedom, fiscal freedom, investment freedom, and financial freedom. A low corporate tax rate of 15 percent complements a top income tax rate of 24 percent. Licensing, opening, and closing a business are all relatively efficient.

Bulgaria still needs a more independent judicial system. Weak property rights, corruption, and inefficient bureaucracy affect other areas of economic freedom. The overall size of government spending is far worse than those of other countries and can crowd out private-sector activity.

BACKGROUND: In 1990, Bulgaria held its first multi-party election since World War II, ending nearly 50 years of Communist rule. Wide-ranging economic reforms initiated in the 1990s have stimulated capital flows, lowered inflation, and brought economic growth of more than 5 percent per year. Ongoing challenges include improving the investment climate and corporate governance and instituting more effective anti-corruption measures. The country joined the European Union in January 2007. Agriculture and tourism are strong. Natural resources such as coal, copper, and zinc play an important role, and the economy has benefited from significant economic policy reform since the fall of the socialist government in 1996.

How Do We Measure Economic Freedom? See Chapter 4 (page 39) for an explanation of the methodology or visit the *Index* Web site at *heritage.org/index*.

The economy is 62.9% free

Europe Average = 66.8
World Average = 60.3

1995   2008

QUICK FACTS

Population: 7.7 million

GDP (PPP): $69.9 billion
5.5% growth in 2005
5.2% 5-yr. comp. ann. growth
$9,032 per capita

Unemployment: 11.5%

Inflation (CPI): 5.0%

FDI (net flow): $1.9 billion

Official Development Assistance:
Multilateral: n/a
Bilateral: n/a

External Debt: $16.7 billion

Exports: $16.1 billion
Primarily clothing, footwear, iron and steel, machinery and equipment, fuels

Imports: $20.6 billion
Primarily machinery and equipment, metals and ores, chemicals and plastics, fuels, minerals, raw materials

2005 data unless otherwise noted.

BULGARIA'S TEN ECONOMIC FREEDOMS

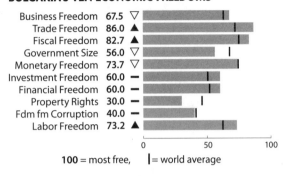

Business Freedom	67.5 ▽	
Trade Freedom	86.0 ▲	
Fiscal Freedom	82.7 ▲	
Government Size	56.0 ▽	
Monetary Freedom	73.7 ▽	
Investment Freedom	60.0 —	
Financial Freedom	60.0 —	
Property Rights	30.0 —	
Fdm fm Corruption	40.0 —	
Labor Freedom	73.2 ▲	

0   50   100

100 = most free, | = world average

BUSINESS FREEDOM — 67.5%

The overall freedom to start, operate, and close a business is relatively well protected by Bulgaria's national regulatory environment. Starting a business takes an average of 32 days, compared to the world average of 43 days. Obtaining a business license takes about half the world average of 234 days. However, regulations are interpreted and enforced arbitrarily. Closing a business is relatively easy.

TRADE FREEDOM — 86%

Bulgaria's trade policy is the same as those of other members of the European Union. The common EU weighted average tariff rate was 2 percent in 2005. Non-tariff barriers reflected in EU policy include agricultural and manufacturing subsidies, import restrictions for some goods and services, market access restrictions in some service sectors, non-transparent and restrictive regulations and standards, and inconsistent customs administration across EU members. Enforcement of intellectual property rights also remains problematic. Consequently, an additional 10 percentage points is deducted from Bulgaria's trade freedom score.

FISCAL FREEDOM — 82.7%

Bulgaria has low tax rates. The top income tax rate is 24 percent (a flat 10 percent as of January 2008), and the flat corporate tax rate was reduced to 10 percent from 15 percent as of January 1, 2007. Other taxes include a value-added tax (VAT), a road tax, and a vehicle tax. In the most recent year, overall tax revenue as a percentage of GDP was 32.4 percent.

GOVERNMENT SIZE — 56%

Total government expenditures, including consumption and transfer payments, are high. In the most recent year, government spending equaled 38.3 percent of GDP. About 60 percent of state enterprise assets had been sold by the end of November 2006.

MONETARY FREEDOM — 73.7%

Inflation is high, averaging 6.6 percent between 2004 and 2006. Relatively unstable prices explain most of the monetary freedom score. Privatization of state-owned firms has progressed, and the market determines most prices, but the regulatory regime affects the prices of electricity, water, natural gas, and pharmaceuticals. As a participant in the EU's Common Agricultural Policy, the government subsidizes agricultural production, distorting the prices of agricultural products. An additional 10 percentage points is deducted from Bulgaria's monetary freedom score to adjust for measures that distort domestic prices.

INVESTMENT FREEDOM — 60%

The law mandates equal treatment for foreign and domestic investors. The government requires approval for majority foreign ownership in some sectors. Many sub-federal authorities provide investment incentives beyond those offered by the national government, but bureaucracy, frequent changes in the legal framework, and corruption impede foreign investment. Residents may hold foreign exchange accounts subject to some restrictions; non-residents may hold them without restriction. The selling of state-owned film, aerospace, tobacco, and energy assets was completed in 2006. Prior registration with the central bank is required for a few capital transactions. Foreign ownership of land is permitted if the owners are from EU countries or countries with an international agreement permitting such purchases.

FINANCIAL FREEDOM — 60%

Bulgaria's financial system is dominated by banking. Since introduction of the currency board and stronger supervision and tighter prudential rules in 1997, the banking system has recovered from its 1996 crisis. With the possibility of bailouts eliminated, banks must focus on sound practices. EU accession has solidified external interest in banking. There are 33 commercial banks, with about 34 percent of assets concentrated in the three largest. Foreign banks hold 72 percent of the domestic credit market. The insurance market, with foreign insurers as strong participants, is now fully private and has expanded rapidly. The stock market is small, but because of new financial instruments and streamlining, market capitalization doubled in 2005 and rose further in 2006. More transparency and legal refinements are needed to ensure growth.

PROPERTY RIGHTS — 30%

Bulgaria's judicial system is ineffective in solving commercial disputes, registering businesses, and enforcing court judgments. The constitution provides for an independent judiciary, but ineffective rule of law limits investor confidence in the ability of the courts to enforce contracts, ownership and shareholders rights, and intellectual property rights.

FREEDOM FROM CORRUPTION — 40%

Corruption is perceived as significant. Bulgaria ranks 57th out of 163 countries in Transparency International's Corruption Perceptions Index for 2006. Bulgaria continues to suffer from substantial organized crime and high-level corruption in the government and the judiciary.

LABOR FREEDOM — 73.2%

Bulgaria's labor market is guided by relatively flexible employment regulations that could be further improved to enhance employment and productivity growth. The non-salary cost of employing a worker is high, but dismissing a redundant employee can be costless. Increasing labor market flexibilities is on the government's reform agenda.

BURKINA FASO

Ouagadougou

Rank: 103

Regional Rank: 16 of 40

Burkina Faso's economy is 55.6 percent free, according to our 2008 assessment, which makes it the world's 103rd freest economy. Its overall score is 0.6 percentage point higher than last year, almost entirely because of enhanced business freedom. Burkina Faso is ranked 16th out of 40 countries in the sub-Saharan Africa region, and its overall score is slightly higher than the regional average.

Burkina Faso scores relatively well in fiscal freedom, government size, and monetary freedom. The top income and corporate tax rates are comparable to those in the United States, but overall tax revenue is low.

Burkina Faso is exceptional because of its severe weakness in business freedom, labor freedom, property rights, investment freedom, and freedom from corruption. Extensive regulations prevent a flexible commercial environment, and licensing and bankruptcy procedures are costly. The lack of a universal, government-enforced judicial system means that property rights cannot be guaranteed or adjudicated effectively, and local villages often use traditional courts. As with most other nations in the region, Burkina Faso experiences significant corruption.

BACKGROUND: Blaise Compaore seized power in 1987, oversaw a transition to multi-party democracy, and won a third term as president in November 2005. (Under a constitutional amendment adopted in 2000, the president is limited to two terms starting in 2005.) Burkina Faso is a poor agrarian country beset by frequent drought, and over 80 percent of the population is engaged in subsistence agriculture. Many Burkinabé work abroad, and remittances are a substantial source of income. Rates of HIV/AIDS infection are high. Instability in the Ivory Coast and a policy in that country requiring foreigners to obtain a residence card disrupted trade and led many Burkina Faso émigrés to return home, but trade is recovering as stability returns to the Ivory Coast. Inadequate communications, poor infrastructure, high illiteracy, and a persistent policy of import substitution and trade protectionism have slowed development.

How Do We Measure Economic Freedom? See Chapter 4 (page 39) for an explanation of the methodology or visit the *Index* Web site at *heritage.org/index*.

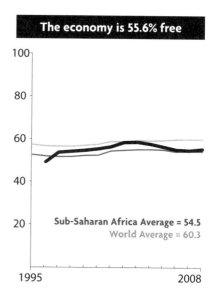

The economy is 55.6% free

100

80

60

40

20

Sub-Saharan Africa Average = 54.5
World Average = 60.3

1995   2008

QUICK FACTS

Population: 13.2 million

GDP (PPP): $16.0 billion
7.1% growth in 2005
6.1% 5-yr. comp. ann. growth
$1,213 per capita

Unemployment: n/a

Inflation (CPI): 6.4%

FDI (net flow): $23.0 million

Official Development Assistance:
Multilateral: $364.3 million
Bilateral: $355.0 million (5.6% from the U.S.)

External Debt: $2.0 billion

Exports: $543.5 million
Primarily cotton, livestock, gold

Imports: $1.016 billion
Primarily capital goods, foodstuffs, petroleum

2005 data unless otherwise noted.

119

BURKINA FASO'S TEN ECONOMIC FREEDOMS

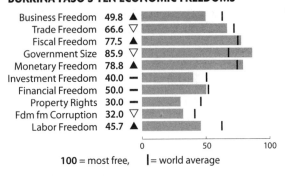

Business Freedom	49.8 ▲	
Trade Freedom	66.6 ▽	
Fiscal Freedom	77.5 ▲	
Government Size	85.9 ▽	
Monetary Freedom	78.8 ▲	
Investment Freedom	40.0 —	
Financial Freedom	50.0 —	
Property Rights	30.0 —	
Fdm fm Corruption	32.0 ▽	
Labor Freedom	45.7 ▲	

0   50   100

100 = most free, ❘ = world average

BUSINESS FREEDOM — *49.8%*

The overall freedom to start, operate, and close a business remains constrained by Burkina Faso's national regulatory environment. Starting a business can be costly. Despite the government's effort to implement a one-stop system for registering businesses in recent years, obtaining a business license requires more than the world average of 19 procedures. The process for closing a business can be lengthy.

TRADE FREEDOM — *66.6%*

Burkina Faso's weighted average tariff rate in 2005 was a relatively high 11.7 percent. The government imposes supplementary taxes on imports, targeted import bans, and restrictive licensing rules, and corruption is growing. An additional 10 percentage points is deducted from Burkina Faso's trade freedom score to account for these non-tariff barriers.

FISCAL FREEDOM — *77.5%*

Burkina Faso has a moderate tax rate and a high corporate tax rate. The top income tax rate is 30 percent, and the top corporate tax rate is 35 percent. Other taxes include a value-added tax (VAT) and a tax on insurance contracts. In the most recent year, overall tax revenue as a percentage of GDP was 11.1 percent.

GOVERNMENT SIZE — *85.9%*

Burkina Faso's total government expenditures, including consumption and transfer payments, are moderate. In the most recent year, government spending equaled 21.7 percent of GDP. Many state-owned companies have been privatized, but progress has been uneven and has slowed in recent years because of administrative delays.

MONETARY FREEDOM — *78.8%*

Inflation is moderate, averaging 3.1 percent between 2004 and 2006. Relatively unstable prices explain most of the monetary freedom score. The market determines most prices, but the government maintains price supports for the cotton sector and influences prices through the public sector. An additional 10 percentage points is deducted from Burkina Faso's monetary freedom score to adjust for measures that distort domestic prices.

INVESTMENT FREEDOM — *40%*

The investment code guarantees equal treatment of foreign and domestic investors, but the Ministry of Industry, Commerce, and Mines must approve new investment. The government is seeking investment in sectors other than mining, primarily hotels, textiles, agriculture, and communications. Poor infrastructure, a weak legal system, and corruption also deter investment. Residents may hold foreign exchange accounts with permission of the government and the Central Bank of West African States (BCEAO). Payments and transfers over a specified amount require supporting documents, and proceeds from non–West African Economic and Monetary Union countries must be surrendered to an authorized dealer. All capital investments abroad by residents require government approval, as do most commercial and financial credits.

FINANCIAL FREEDOM — *50%*

Burkina Faso's underdeveloped financial system is concentrated in banking. The BCEAO governs banking and other financial institutions. Banking reforms aimed at tightening supervision and improving credit access are ongoing. In 2004, the financial system was composed primarily of eight commercial banks, all of which had some foreign ownership, primarily French. The government has pursued banking privatization and restructuring since the 1990s and limits its participation to 25 percent. A network of microfinance institutions and credit unions has grown rapidly; by the end of 2005, 329 microfinance institutions were registered domestically. The insurance sector is small and dominated by three domestic providers. Burkina Faso participates in a regional stock exchange.

PROPERTY RIGHTS — *30%*

Burkina Faso's judicial system is weak. Villagers have their own customary or traditional courts. The executive has extensive appointment and other judicial powers. Systemic weaknesses include the arbitrary removal of judges, outdated legal codes, an insufficient number of courts, a lack of financial and human resources, and excessive legal costs.

FREEDOM FROM CORRUPTION — *32%*

Corruption is perceived as significant. Burkina Faso ranks 79th out of 163 countries in Transparency International's Corruption Perceptions Index for 2006. Public discontent over corruption among the active-duty and former military officers who wield most of the political power has led to recent outbreaks of violence.

LABOR FREEDOM — *45.7%*

Burkina Faso's labor market remains highly restrictive as burdensome employment regulations hinder employment and productivity growth. The non-salary cost of employing a worker is high, but dismissing a redundant employee is relatively costless. Night and weekend work are not allowed, and the minimum wage is about 77 percent of the average value-added worker. Burkina Faso's labor market flexibility is one of the 20 lowest in the world.

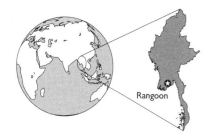

Rangoon

BURMA (MYANMAR)

Burma's economy is 39.5 percent free, according to our 2008 assessment, which makes it the world's 153rd freest economy. Its overall score is 1.5 percentage points lower than last year because of significantly worse monetary freedom. Burma is ranked 29th out of 30 countries in the Asia–Pacific region, and its overall score is much lower than the regional average.

Burma's economy is defined by severely low economic freedoms, with five of 10 areas at least 35 points below the world average. Only one area is notably positive: government size, which can be interpreted as a lack of effective government in certain areas. Burma will not develop effectively without serious economic reform.

Burma severely restricts many areas of its economy. Investment freedom, financial freedom, property rights, and freedom from corruption are weak. Business freedom is very low because it is hard to conduct formal private-sector activity with official approval. The almost complete lack of a judicial system forces domestic and foreign companies to negotiate directly with the government to resolve disputes. Foreign investment is adjudicated in each instance with no clear guidelines for investors.

BACKGROUND: Burma gained its independence from Britain in 1948 and has been ruled by a military junta since 1962. The ruling generals, through their State Peace and Development Council (SPDC), have publicized a "roadmap for democracy" and a national convention to rewrite the constitution as gestures of democratic reform, but there has been no real change. Despite significant natural resources, restrictive economic policies and international sanctions still impede economic development. Foreign aid plummeted during the 1990s in response to the government's harsh anti-democratic repression.

How Do We Measure Economic Freedom? See Chapter 4 (page 39) for an explanation of the methodology or visit the *Index* Web site at *heritage.org/index*.

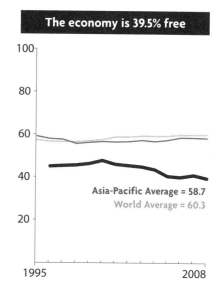

The economy is 39.5% free

Asia-Pacific Average = 58.7
World Average = 60.3

QUICK FACTS

Population: 47.4 million

GDP (PPP): $85.2 billion
5.2% growth in 2005
5-yr. comp. ann. growth n/a
$1,800 per capita

Unemployment: 10.2%

Inflation (CPI): 10.1%

FDI (net flow): $300.0 million

Official Development Assistance:
Multilateral: $60.9 million
Bilateral: $91.2 million (4.5% from the U.S.)

External Debt: $6.6 billion

Exports: $3.2 billion (2004)
Primarily gas, wood products, pulses, beans, fish, rice, clothing, jade and gems

Imports: $2.5 billion (2004)
Primarily fabric, petroleum products, fertilizer, plastics, machinery, transport equipment, cement, construction materials, crude oil, food products, edible oil
2005 data unless otherwise noted.

BURMA'S TEN ECONOMIC FREEDOMS

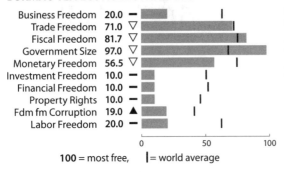

Business Freedom	20.0 ▬
Trade Freedom	71.0 ▽
Fiscal Freedom	81.7 ▽
Government Size	97.0 ▽
Monetary Freedom	56.5 ▽
Investment Freedom	10.0 ▬
Financial Freedom	10.0 ▬
Property Rights	10.0 ▬
Fdm fm Corruption	19.0 ▲
Labor Freedom	20.0 ▬

0   50   100

100 = most free, ▮ **= world average**

BUSINESS FREEDOM — 20%

The overall freedom to start, operate, and close a business is seriously impeded by Burma's lack of legal and regulatory transparency. Inconsistent enforcement of existing laws and bureaucratic red tape complicate the launching of entrepreneurial activities, and policy changes tend to be inconsistent and unpredictable.

TRADE FREEDOM — 71%

Burma's weighted average tariff rate was 4.5 percent in 2005. Restrictive trade policies protect "crony" companies and state-owned enterprises. Import and export bans and restrictions, high import and export taxes, restrictive import and export permit and licensing rules, arbitrary policy changes, non-transparent and outdated regulations and standards, foreign exchange controls, customs corruption, and an inefficient regulatory and customs bureaucracy further restrict trade. An additional 20 percentage points is deducted from Burma's trade freedom score to account for these non-tariff barriers.

FISCAL FREEDOM — 81.7%

Burma has moderate tax rates. Both the top income tax rate and the top corporate tax rate are 30 percent. In the most recent year, overall tax revenue as a percentage of GDP was 5.2 percent. The government's capacity to increase tax revenue is very limited because the huge informal economy is untaxed.

GOVERNMENT SIZE — 97%

Total government expenditures, including consumption and transfer payments, are low. In the most recent year, government spending equaled 10 percent of GDP. However, government intervention in the economy is pervasive, privatization has stalled, and the state sector's share of GDP has been about 20 percent of real GDP in recent years. The state controls such sectors as mining and power, and state-owned companies are prominent in transport, trade, and manufacturing.

MONETARY FREEDOM — 56.5%

Inflation is high, averaging 20.3 percent between 2004 and 2006. Relatively unstable prices explain most of the monetary freedom score. The state dominates some sectors, including mining and power, and state-owned firms are prominent in transport, trade, and manufacturing. The government relies

on controls and subsidies to keep a lid on price increases for such staples as gasoline, cooking oil, propane, and soap. The quantities of such products made available to customers are strictly rationed, so retailers often sell their stocks on the black market for a higher price. An additional 15 percentage points is deducted from Burma's monetary freedom score to adjust for measures that distort domestic prices.

INVESTMENT FREEDOM — 10%

Foreign investment is approved on a case-by-case basis. Once permission is granted, the foreign investor needs a business license to trade, but no licenses have been issued since 2002. U.S. law prohibits new investment in Burma but permits continuation of investments existing before 1997. The government restricts foreign exchange accounts and current transfers and controls all capital transactions. Multiple exchange rates make conversion and repatriation of foreign exchange very complex and ripe for corruption. Foreign firms may not own land, but it may be leased from the government.

FINANCIAL FREEDOM — 10%

Burma's financial sector is subject to very heavy government intervention, and forced loans to government projects have almost frozen new deposits and smaller loans. Opaque regulatory and legal institutions add to a fairly hostile investment climate. The private banking sector faced a depositor crisis in 2003 that persists today. As of 2007, there were five state-owned banks and a central bank. The government has made some efforts to halt money laundering. The state-owned insurer retains a near monopoly. The government began late in 2006 to develop a securities and exchange commission as a predecessor to a capital market.

PROPERTY RIGHTS — 10%

Private real property and intellectual property rights are not protected in Burma. Private and foreign companies are at a disadvantage in disputes with governmental and quasi-governmental organizations. The military regime controls the courts, so foreign investors who have had conflicts with the local government or whose businesses have been illegally expropriated have little success obtaining compensation.

FREEDOM FROM CORRUPTION — 19%

Corruption is perceived as rampant. Burma ranks 160th out of 163 countries in Transparency International's Corruption Perceptions Index for 2006. Burma is a major source of opium, and most Burmese view corruption as necessary for survival. Investors complain of official corruption in taxation, investment permission, import and export licenses, and land and real estate lease approvals.

LABOR FREEDOM — 20%

Burma's formal labor market is not fully developed and remains distorted by state intervention. Regulations regarding wage rates and maximum work hours are not uniformly observed. The government sets public-sector wages and influences wage setting in the private sector. The state uses forced labor to construct military buildings and commercial enterprises.

BURUNDI

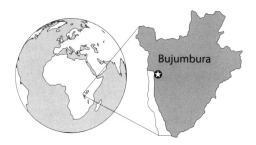

Bujumbura

Rank: 145

Regional Rank: 37 of 40

Burundi's economy is 46.3 percent free, according to our 2008 assessment, which makes it one of the world's least free economies. Yet its overall score is 0.7 percentage point lower than last year. Burundi is ranked 37th out of 40 countries in the sub-Saharan Africa region and scores worse than the world average in all but one of the 10 economic freedoms.

Burundi is significantly below the world average in six areas: business freedom, trade freedom, investment freedom, financial freedom, property rights, and freedom from corruption.

As a developing economy recovering from years of civil strife, Burundi faces significant economic challenges. The rule of law is highly politicized, inefficient, and subject to erratic control over much of the country. Virtually all aspects of business, from obtaining licenses to firing inefficient workers, are subject to intrusive regulation that inhibits business formation or survival. Investment regulations and trade barriers are so high that there is little potential for private foreign investment.

BACKGROUND: Burundi gained its independence in 1962. In 1993, the assassination of the country's first Hutu president, Melchior Ndadaye, by a faction of the Tutsi-dominated armed forces escalated historically high ethnic tensions and sparked a civil war. The subsequent violence and instability resulted in an estimated 300,000 deaths and 1.2 million refugees. In 2005, a transitional government adopted a new constitution and organized elections. Despite the government's announced commitment to fighting corruption, allegations of high-level corruption persist. Burundi remains very poor. A majority of the population is engaged in subsistence agriculture, and agriculture accounts for nearly 50 percent of GDP. The state remains heavily involved in the economy, and plans to privatize publicly held enterprises and liberalize the important coffee sector have stalled.

How Do We Measure Economic Freedom? See Chapter 4 (page 39) for an explanation of the methodology or visit the *Index* Web site at *heritage.org/index.*

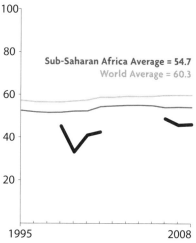

The economy is 46.3% free

Sub-Saharan Africa Average = 54.7
World Average = 60.3

1995   2008

QUICK FACTS

Population: 7.5 million

GDP (PPP): $5.3 billion
    0.9% growth in 2005
    2.2% 5-yr. comp. ann. growth
    $699 per capita

Unemployment: n/a

Inflation (CPI): 13.4%

FDI (net flow): −$1.0 million

Official Development Assistance:
Multilateral: $209.9 million
Bilateral: $188.8 million (29.0% from the U.S.)

External Debt: $1.3 billion

Exports: $91.6 million
Primarily coffee, tea, sugar, cotton, hides

Imports: $352.7 million
Primarily capital goods, petroleum products, foodstuffs

2005 data unless otherwise noted.

BURUNDI'S TEN ECONOMIC FREEDOMS

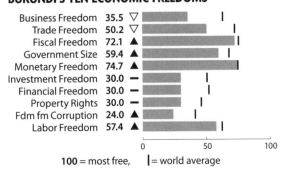

Business Freedom	35.5 ▽
Trade Freedom	50.2 ▽
Fiscal Freedom	72.1 ▲
Government Size	59.4 ▲
Monetary Freedom	74.7 ▲
Investment Freedom	30.0 —
Financial Freedom	30.0 —
Property Rights	30.0 —
Fdm fm Corruption	24.0 ▲
Labor Freedom	57.4 ▲

0   50   100

100 = most free, | = world average

BUSINESS FREEDOM — 35.5%

The overall freedom to start, operate, and close a business is seriously limited by Burundi's national regulatory environment. Starting a business takes about the world average of 43 days. Obtaining a business license requires more than the world average of 19 procedures and 234 days. Despite new regulations introduced in recent years, Burundi's continuing instability and massive, corrupt bureaucracy make it difficult to conduct entrepreneurial activities.

TRADE FREEDOM — 50.2%

Burundi's weighted average tariff rate was a high 19.9 percent in 2005. The government has removed most quantitative restrictions on imports but applies numerous fees and taxes. Inadequate administrative capacity and corruption in customs and excise administration also add to the cost of trade. An additional 10 percentage points is deducted from Burundi's trade freedom score to account for these non-tariff barriers.

FISCAL FREEDOM — 72.1%

Burundi has relatively high tax rates. Both the top income tax rate and the top corporate tax rate are 35 percent. Other taxes include a sales tax and a tax on interest. In the most recent year, overall tax revenue as a percentage of GDP was 20 percent.

GOVERNMENT SIZE — 59.4%

Total government expenditures in Burundi, including consumption and transfer payments, are high. In the most recent year, government spending equaled 36.8 percent of GDP. The government recently relaunched a privatization process that had been stalled, but progress has been slow.

MONETARY FREEDOM — 74.7%

Inflation is high, averaging 5.9 percent between 2004 and 2006. Relatively unstable prices explain most of the monetary freedom score. The government influences prices through state-owned enterprises, subsidies, and agriculture support programs. An additional 10 percentage points is deducted from Burundi's monetary freedom score to adjust for measures that distort domestic prices.

INVESTMENT FREEDOM — 30%

Foreign investment is officially welcome but hindered by political instability and poor infrastructure, particularly electricity and roads. The investment code reflects a policy of import substitution. Numerous investment incentives are offered, particularly for projects outside of the capital. Residents and non-residents may hold foreign exchange accounts and may withdraw funds up to a set limit upon presentation of documentation. Central bank approval is required for accounts held abroad. Most capital transactions, including credit operations, direct investment, and personal capital movements, are subject to restrictions or authorization requirements.

FINANCIAL FREEDOM — 30%

Burundi has a very small, undeveloped financial sector that is dominated by banking. Eight commercial banks, one development bank, and a housing promotion fund are supervised by the central bank; only three of the main commercial banks have access to private capital. The lack of domestic investment opportunity has hindered bank development, and the banking sector lags behind regional competitors technologically. Government participation in the banking sector is strong. The government retains stakes in several banks, and the many loans made to the government and to state-owned enterprises have resulted in a large number of non-performing loans. Regulation of banking is largely bureaucratic and arduous.

PROPERTY RIGHTS — 30%

Private property is subject to government expropriation and armed banditry. The constitution guarantees the independence of the judiciary, but judges are appointed by the executive branch and generally have proved to be strongly influenced by political pressure. Judicial personnel are predominantly Tutsi, however, and have shown increasing signs of independence in recent years under Hutu presidents.

FREEDOM FROM CORRUPTION — 24%

Corruption is perceived as pervasive. Burundi ranks 130th out of 163 countries in Transparency International's Corruption Perceptions Index for 2006. From senior government officials demanding large kickbacks on procurement tenders to low-level civil servants in ministries such as taxation or customs demanding petty bribes for services, licenses, or permits, corruption is present in every area of life.

LABOR FREEDOM — 57.4%

The labor market operates under restrictive employment regulations that hinder employment creation and productivity growth. The non-salary cost of employing a worker is low, but dismissing a redundant employee is relatively costly. The difficulty of laying off a worker creates a risk aversion for companies that would otherwise hire more people and grow. Restrictions on increasing or contracting the number of working hours are very rigid.

CAMBODIA

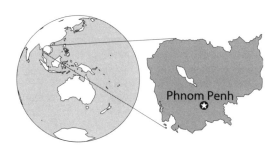

Phnom Penh

Rank: 100
Regional Rank: 17 of 30

Cambodia's economy is 56.2 percent free, according to our 2008 assessment, which makes it the world's 100th freest economy. Its overall score is essentially unchanged from last year. Cambodia is ranked 17th out of 30 countries in the Asia–Pacific region, and its overall score is slightly lower than the regional average.

Cambodia scores well in fiscal freedom and government size and moderately well in monetary freedom. Low income and corporate tax rates are complemented by a low level of government tax revenue, giving the country a high fiscal score despite some additional taxes. Government spending is also low.

Cambodia is still shaking off the legacy of a disastrous Communist history and could improve in several areas of economic freedom: Business freedom, trade freedom, property rights, and freedom from corruption all receive significantly low scores. A highly restrictive labor market makes it difficult for businesses to fill seasonal employment needs, and widespread corruption makes even simple regulations inconsistent. Weak rule of law in many areas leads to unreliable resolution of commercial disputes.

BACKGROUND: Cambodia is nominally a democracy, but Prime Minister Hun Sen has held either formal or *de facto* power since free elections in 1993. Since then, Cambodia has experienced solid economic growth without significant political liberalization. Even as the country has moved toward a market-based economic system, its international reputation has been hurt by the increasing centralization of power in the executive's hands and the government's repression of political opponents. A political environment that offered greater freedom and procedural transparency would support reform and attract the greater level of international investment that Cambodia needs.

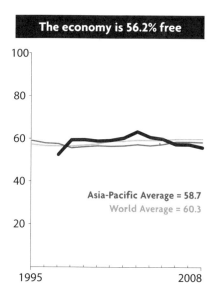

The economy is 56.2% free

100

80

60

40

Asia-Pacific Average = 58.7
World Average = 60.3

20

1995   2008

QUICK FACTS

Population: 14.1 million

GDP (PPP): $38.4 billion
13.4% growth in 2005
9.5% 5-yr. comp. ann. growth
$2,727 per capita

Unemployment: 2.5%

Inflation (CPI): 5.8%

FDI (net flow): $375.0 million

Official Development Assistance:
Multilateral: $190.1 million
Bilateral: $364.8 million (19% from the U.S.)

External Debt: $3.5 billion

Exports: $4.0 billion
Primarily clothing, timber, rubber, rice, fish, tobacco, footwear

Imports: $4.6 billion
Primarily petroleum products, cigarettes, gold, construction materials, machinery, motor vehicles, pharmaceutical products

2005 data unless otherwise noted.

How Do We Measure Economic Freedom? See Chapter 4 (page 39) for an explanation of the methodology or visit the *Index* Web site at *heritage.org/index*.

CAMBODIA'S TEN ECONOMIC FREEDOMS

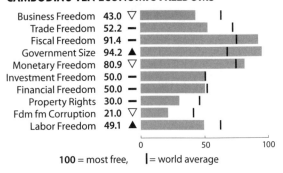

Business Freedom	43.0 ▽	
Trade Freedom	52.2 —	
Fiscal Freedom	91.4 —	
Government Size	94.2 ▲	
Monetary Freedom	80.9 ▽	
Investment Freedom	50.0 —	
Financial Freedom	50.0 —	
Property Rights	30.0 —	
Fdm fm Corruption	21.0 ▽	
Labor Freedom	49.1 ▲	

0   50   100

100 = most free, ▮**= world average**

BUSINESS FREEDOM — 43%

The overall freedom to start, operate, and close a business is considerably constrained by Cambodia's national regulatory environment. Starting a business takes twice the world average of 43 days. The process for obtaining a business license requires more than the world average of 19 procedures and 234 days. Regulatory transparency is very poor, and bureaucratic delays are common. Corruption also contributes to the high costs of entrepreneurial activities.

TRADE FREEDOM — 52.2%

Cambodia's weighted average tariff rate was a relatively high 16.4 percent in 2003. The government has eliminated most non-tariff barriers to trade. However, import bans and restrictions, non-automatic import licensing, non-transparent government procurement, export subsidies, and customs administration that can be discretionary and is both prone to delays and corrupt add to the cost of trade. An additional 10 percentage points is deducted from Cambodia's trade freedom score to account for these non-tariff barriers.

FISCAL FREEDOM — 91.4%

Cambodia has low tax rates. Both the top income tax rate and the top corporate tax rate are 20 percent. Other taxes include a value-added tax (VAT) and a tax on interest. In the most recent year, overall tax revenue as a percentage of GDP was 7.7 percent.

GOVERMENT SIZE — 94.2%

Total government expenditures, including consumption and transfer payments, are low. In the most recent year, government spending equaled 13.9 percent of GDP. The government has sold and leased state-owned enterprises and assets over the past two decades, and the role of state-owned companies is no longer substantial.

MONETARY FREEDOM — 80.9%

Inflation is moderate, averaging 5 percent between 2004 and 2006. Relatively moderate and unstable prices explain most of the monetary freedom score. The market determines most prices, but the government attempts to maintain stable retail prices for fuel through subsidies. An additional 5 percentage points is deducted from Cambodia's monetary freedom score to adjust for measures that distort domestic prices.

INVESTMENT FREEDOM — 50%

Foreign capital and domestic capital are treated equally in most sectors. The foreign investment regime is generally liberal, although certain sectors face restrictions, including gemstone exploitation, brick making, rice mills, wood and stone carving manufacture, and silk weaving. Private investment requires application to and approval by the appropriate government agency. The government allows 100 percent foreign-owned investment properties in most sectors and allows foreign workers to be imported in many cases. There are no restrictions or controls on the holding of foreign exchange accounts by residents or non-residents. Non-residents may not own land, and the government still must approve foreign direct investment.

FINANCIAL FREEDOM — 50%

Cambodia's financial system is small, underdeveloped, and subject to government influence, but it also has improved in recent years. The government has pursued privatization and consolidation since 2000. All 12 commercial banks are privately owned following the 46 percent sale of the Foreign Trade Bank of Cambodia to foreign investors, though the government still has a stake in specialized banking. The banking sector is strongly market-oriented, and banks are well capitalized. Much credit is in the informal sector. A state-owned firm dominates the insurance sector. There is no stock market. The National Bank of Cambodia, which used to operate as a commercial bank as well as the central bank, is now solely a regulatory and supervisory agency.

PROPERTY RIGHTS — 30%

Cambodia's legal system does not protect private property effectively, and there are many gaps in company law, bankruptcy, and arbitration. The executive branch usually dominates the legislature and the judiciary. Inconsistent judicial rulings and outright corruption are frequently encountered. The land titling system is not fully functional, and most property owners do not have documentation to prove their ownership.

FREEDOM FROM CORRUPTION — 21%

Corruption is perceived as pervasive. Cambodia ranks 151st out of 163 countries in Transparency International's Corruption Perceptions Index for 2006. Corruption hampers economic opportunity and competitiveness, and demands for petty bribes are common. In 2006, the World Bank froze payments for millions of dollars worth of projects said to involve corrupt schemes by government officials.

LABOR FREEDOM — 49.1%

The labor market operates under inflexible employment regulations that impede employment creation and productivity growth. The non-salary cost of employing a worker is low, but rigidity of work hours is relatively high. The formal labor market is not fully developed, and the rigidity of the labor market carries with it the risk of an arbitrary dual labor market.

CAMEROON

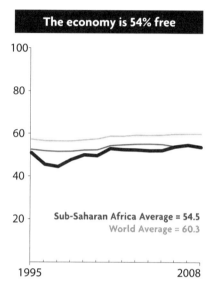

Yaoundé

Rank: 117

Regional Rank: 23 of 40

Cameroon's economy is 54 percent free, according to our 2008 assessment, which makes it the world's 117th freest economy. Its overall score is 1.4 percentage points lower than last year, primarily reflecting a lower financial freedom score. Cameroon is ranked 23rd out of 40 countries in the sub-Saharan Africa region, and its overall score is slightly lower than the regional average.

Cameroon scores extraordinarily well only in government size. Government expenditures are low, and total tax revenue is relatively small as a percentage of GDP, yet the top income and corporate tax rates are 35 percent and 38.5 percent. A simplified tax code with a lower rate would formalize much economic activity.

Cameroon faces challenges common to other developing African nations: inefficient bureaucracy, an unreliable legal system, and poor infrastructure. Employment regulations are costly and restrictive, and firing a worker is difficult. Business licenses are difficult to obtain.

BACKGROUND: Cameroon held its first multi-party legislative and presidential elections in 1992. Paul Biya has been president since 1982 and is scheduled to leave office in 2011. His party won a strong majority in the 2007 parliamentary election. Agriculture accounts for over 40 percent of GDP, and government intervention, including state ownership of utilities and industries and burdensome regulation, hinders foreign investment and economic growth. Rising oil prices have added to GDP growth and government revenues, and transparency of oil-related public finances has improved as Cameroon fulfills commitments made under an initiative sponsored by the United Kingdom. An anti-corruption campaign has led to several prominent arrests. Social unrest and protests are becoming more frequent.

How Do We Measure Economic Freedom? See Chapter 4 (page 39) for an explanation of the methodology or visit the *Index* Web site at *heritage.org/index*.

The economy is 54% free

Sub-Saharan Africa Average = 54.5
World Average = 60.3

1995   2008

QUICK FACTS

Population: 16.3 million

GDP (PPP): $37.5 billion
2.0% growth in 2005
3.4% 5-yr. comp. ann. growth
$2,299 per capita

Unemployment: 2.0%

Inflation: 30% (2001)

FDI (net flow): $18.0 million

Official Development Assistance:
Multilateral: $133.6 million
Bilateral: $518.4 million (2.6% from the U.S.)

External Debt: $7.2 billion

Exports: $4.3 billion
Primarily crude oil and petroleum products, lumber, cocoa beans, aluminum, coffee, cotton

Imports: $3.1 billion
Primarily machinery, electrical equipment, transport equipment, fuel, food

2005 data unless otherwise noted.

CAMEROON'S TEN ECONOMIC FREEDOMS

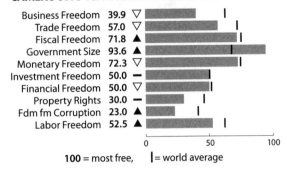

Business Freedom	39.9 ▽	
Trade Freedom	57.0 ▽	
Fiscal Freedom	71.8 ▲	
Government Size	93.6 ▲	
Monetary Freedom	72.3 ▽	
Investment Freedom	50.0 —	
Financial Freedom	50.0 ▽	
Property Rights	30.0 —	
Fdm fm Corruption	23.0 ▲	
Labor Freedom	52.5 ▲	

0   50   100

100 = most free, **|** **= world average**

BUSINESS FREEDOM — 39.9%

The overall freedom to start, operate, and close a business is seriously limited by Cameroon's national regulatory environment. Starting a business takes an average of 37 days, compared to the world average of 43 days. Obtaining a business license requires 15 procedures, compared to the global average of 19, but can take more than the world average of 234 days. Closing a business is difficult.

TRADE FREEDOM — 57%

Cameroon's weighted average tariff rate was 16.5 percent in 2005. Non-tariff barriers include surcharges and inappropriate customs valuation for certain imports, some import bans, issues involving the protection of intellectual property rights, customs fraud, and protracted negotiations with customs officers over the value of imported goods. An additional 10 percentage points is deducted from Cameroon's trade freedom score to account for these non-tariff barriers.

FISCAL FREEDOM — 71.8%

Cameroon has high tax rates. The top income tax rate is 35 percent, and the top corporate tax rate is 38.5 percent (35 percent plus an additional 10 percent council tax). The government also imposes a value-added tax (VAT), excise taxes, a property tax, and forestry taxation. In the most recent year, overall tax revenue as a percentage of GDP was 10.4 percent.

GOVERNMENT SIZE — 93.6%

Total government expenditures, including consumption and transfer payments, are low. In the most recent year, government spending equaled 14.6 percent of GDP. Despite efforts at fiscal control, government finances exhibit persistent structural weaknesses. Privatization has been sluggish. Major state companies still to be divested include the national water company and the Cameroon Development Cooperation.

MONETARY FREEDOM — 72.3%

Inflation is moderate, averaging 4 percent between 2004 and 2006. Relatively stable prices explain most of the monetary freedom score. The market determines most prices, but the government provides subsidies and controls prices for "strategic" goods and services, including rice, flour, consumer goods, agriculture inputs, electricity, water, petroleum products, telecommunications, cooking gas, pharmaceuticals, and cotton. An additional 15 percentage

points is deducted from Cameroon's monetary freedom score to adjust for measures that distort domestic prices.

INVESTMENT FREEDOM — 50%

A charter was passed in 2002 to improve the investment environment, but regulations will not be fully in place until the end of 2007. Recent privatization efforts have been mainly transparent, though the government retains sizeable stakes in privatized industries. Residents may open foreign exchange accounts with prior approval of the central bank and the Ministry of Finance and Budget. Many capital transactions, including foreign borrowing, foreign direct investment, liquidation, and foreign securities, are subject to controls and generally require the approval of or declaration to the government. Delay or corruption is encountered in resolving commercial disputes.

FINANCIAL FREEDOM — 50%

Cameroon is a member of the Central African Economic and Monetary Community, a group of six countries with a common central bank and a common currency pegged to the euro. The banking sector is private, consists of 10 commercial banks, and is highly concentrated, with three banks controlling two-thirds of all assets. Microfinance is growing, and there are about 700 microfinance institutions. The insurance sector is also concentrated, with four companies accounting for about 60 percent of the market. The largest is foreign-owned, but Cameroonian ownership is increasing. The first stock exchange was founded in 2003, but its first listing was not until 2006. Outdated bankruptcy laws discourage lending by favoring debtors.

PROPERTY RIGHTS — 30%

Corruption and an uncertain legal environment can lead to confiscation of private property. Administrative departments and courts frequently give domestic firms preferential treatment. Some foreign companies have alleged that unfavorable judgments were obtained through fraud or frivolous lawsuits. Trademarks and copyrights are routinely violated, and software piracy is widespread. Officials have only a rudimentary understanding of how to enforce laws to protect intellectual property rights.

FREEDOM FROM CORRUPTION — 23%

Corruption is perceived as pervasive. Cameroon ranks 138th out of 163 countries in Transparency International's Corruption Perceptions Index for 2006. Courts and government agencies have been accused of corrupt practices, but the government has undertaken several anti-corruption and good-governance initiatives since 2005.

LABOR FREEDOM — 52.5%

Relatively inflexible employment regulations hinder employment creation and productivity growth. The non-salary cost of employing a worker is moderate, and dismissing a redundant employee is relatively costless. Labor legislation mandates retraining or replacement before firing a worker. Despite an overall legal framework, an efficient labor market has not fully developed.

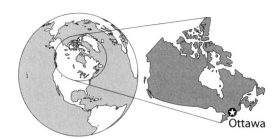
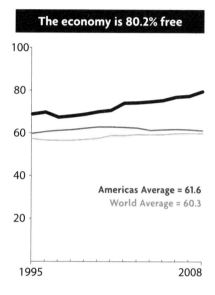

Ottawa

CANADA

Canada's economy is 80.2 percent free, according to our 2008 assessment, which makes it the world's 7th freest economy. Its overall score is 2.1 percentage points higher than last year, reflecting improvement in four freedoms. Canada is ranked 2nd out of 29 countries in the Americas, and its overall score is well above the regional average.

Canada scores very high in seven of the 10 economic freedoms, especially business freedom, property rights, and freedom from corruption. Opening or closing a business is not difficult. A strong rule of law ensures property rights, a low level of corruption, and transparent application of the commercial code. Financial freedom is strong because of a lightly regulated banking sector.

Canada trails the world average only in size and expense of government. As in many European democracies, government spending is high because of elaborate social programs and a welfare state.

BACKGROUND: One of the world's leading free-market democracies, Canada enjoys a large trade surplus, thanks to oil and mineral exports. Because of its bilateral trade relationship with the United States, its economy tends to track that of its larger southern neighbor. A protracted dispute with the United States over softwood lumber was settled in 2005. Despite one of the OECD's most restrictive foreign ownership policies in telecommunications, publishing, broadcasting, aviation, mining, and fishing, macroeconomic fundamentals remain strong, and unemployment is at a 30-year low.

How Do We Measure Economic Freedom? See Chapter 4 (page 39) for an explanation of the methodology or visit the *Index* Web site at *heritage.org/index*.

The economy is 80.2% free

Americas Average = 61.6
World Average = 60.3

1995   2008

QUICK FACTS

Population: 32.3 million

GDP (PPP): $1.1 trillion
    2.9% growth in 2005
    2.7% 5-yr. comp. ann. growth
    $33,375 per capita

Unemployment: 6.8%

Inflation (CPI): 2.2%

FDI (net flow): −$261.0 million

Official Development Assistance:
Multilateral: None
Bilateral: None

External Debt: $684.7 billion

Exports: $428.0 billion
Primarily motor vehicles and parts, industrial machinery, aircraft, telecommunications equipment, chemicals, plastics, fertilizers, wood pulp, timber, crude petroleum, natural gas, electricity, aluminum

Imports: $385.5 billion
Primarily machinery and equipment, vehicles and parts, crude oil, chemicals
2005 data unless otherwise noted.

CANADA'S TEN ECONOMIC FREEDOMS

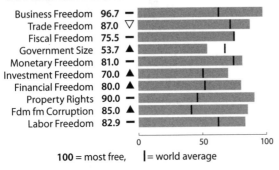

Business Freedom	96.7	—
Trade Freedom	87.0	▽
Fiscal Freedom	75.5	—
Government Size	53.7	▲
Monetary Freedom	81.0	—
Investment Freedom	70.0	▲
Financial Freedom	80.0	▲
Property Rights	90.0	—
Fdm fm Corruption	85.0	▲
Labor Freedom	82.9	—

100 = most free, | = world average

BUSINESS FREEDOM — 96.7%

The overall freedom to start, operate, and close a business is strongly protected by Canada's national regulatory environment. Starting a business takes an average of three days, compared to the world average of 43 days. Obtaining a business license requires less than the world average of 19 procedures and 234 days. Regulation is thorough but essentially transparent. Closing a business is easy.

TRADE FREEDOM — 87%

Canada's weighted average tariff rate was 1.5 percent in 2005. Some federal and provincial non-tariff barriers; restrictions on imports of domestic "supply managed" agricultural products; restricted access to telecommunications and media; export controls, import and export taxes, export support programs for industry and agriculture producers, and state trading boards for some agriculture products; and issues involving the protection of intellectual property rights add to the cost of trade. An additional 10 percentage points is deducted from Canada's trade freedom score to account for these non-tariff barriers.

FISCAL FREEDOM — 75.5%

Canada has moderate income tax rates. The top federal income tax rate is 29 percent, and provincial and local rates range from 4 percent to 24 percent. The general corporate tax rate of 22.1 percent will be reduced to 20.5 percent in 2008. Depending on the province, the effective tax rate ranges from 32 percent to 38 percent. Other taxes include a value-added tax (VAT), a tax on insurance contracts, and a property tax. In the most recent year, overall tax revenue as a percentage of GDP was 33.5 percent.

GOVERNMENT SIZE — 53.7%

Total government expenditures, including consumption and transfer payments, are high. In the most recent year, government spending equaled 39.3 percent of GDP. The government has sold many state-owned enterprises and encourages competition in sectors like telephone service and the distribution of natural gas and electricity that formerly were operated by government or privately owned monopolies.

MONETARY FREEDOM — 81%

Inflation is low, averaging 2 percent between 2004 and 2006. Relatively stable prices explain most of the monetary freedom score. The market determines most prices, but the government regulates the prices of some utilities, provides subsidies to industry and agriculture producers, controls prices for some agricultural products, and may also influence prices through state-owned enterprises. An additional 10 percentage points is deducted from Canada's monetary freedom score to adjust for measures that distort domestic prices.

INVESTMENT FREEDOM — 70%

Canada treats foreign and domestic capital equally in almost all situations. A federal agency, Investment Canada, must approve direct foreign investments, whether through a new venture or through an acquisition. Though investment is usually approved, Canada remains one of the few OECD countries to require approval. Restricted sectors include broadcasting and telecommunications, newspapers, energy monopolies, book publishing, filmmaking and distribution, retail banking and insurance, and air transport. There are no restrictions on current transfers, repatriation of profits, purchase of real estate, or access to foreign exchange.

FINANCIAL FREEDOM— 80%

Canada has a sound financial system. There are 18 domestic banks, and the six largest banks account for the largest portion of total assets. The 48 foreign banks operating in 2007 accounted for a very small portion of assets. The government owns the Business Development Bank, which makes loans to small and medium-size enterprises, and has loosened restrictions on financial institutions, giving them more freedom to offer financial services. Mergers between large banks are restricted, and large banks may not buy large insurance companies. The largest insurance companies are global and conduct more than half of their business overseas. Securities markets are well developed, and some competition has appeared with privatization of the two largest exchanges.

PROPERTY RIGHTS — 90%

Private property is well protected. The judiciary is independent, and judges and civil servants are generally honest. Foreign investors have full and fair access to the legal system, and private property rights are limited only by the rights of governments to establish monopolies and to expropriate for public purposes. Some companies have complained that intellectual property rights enforcement against counterfeiting and piracy is cumbersome and ineffective.

FREEDOM FROM CORRUPTION — 85%

Corruption is perceived as minimal. Canada ranks 14th out of 163 countries in Transparency International's Corruption Perceptions Index for 2006, ahead of the U.S., Germany, and Japan. Bribery and other forms of corruption are rare. Canada is a signatory to the U.N. Convention Against Corruption.

LABOR FREEDOM — 82.9%

Flexible employment regulations enhance employment and productivity growth. The non-salary cost of employing a worker is moderate, and dismissing a redundant employee is relatively costless. Rigidity of rules on expanding or contracting working hours is very low. Canada's labor freedom is one of the 20 highest in the world.

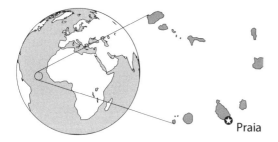

Praia

CAPE VERDE

Cape Verde's economy is 58.4 percent free, according to our 2008 assessment, which makes it the world's 88th freest economy. Its overall score is 1.3 percentage points higher than last year, mainly reflecting an enhanced investment climate and less corruption. Cape Verde is ranked 9th out of 40 countries in the sub-Saharan Africa region, and its overall score is slightly higher than the regional average.

Cape Verde scores well in monetary freedom, investment freedom, and especially property rights, with a score that is 24 percentage points higher than average. Inflation is low, although the government does subsidize some staples. Property rights are very well secured by the rule of law in comparison to the situation in neighboring countries.

Serious challenges, however, overwhelm Cape Verde's advantages. Trade freedom and the overall size of government taxation and expenditure are the main problems, and heavy business regulations are a barrier to investment and entrepreneurship. Trade is hindered by a high average tariff rate and significant non-tariff barriers.

BACKGROUND: The archipelago nation of Cape Verde, located off the west coast of Africa, is a stable multi-party parliamentary democracy in which power has changed hands peacefully since 1991. Cape Verde has few natural resources and is subject to frequent droughts and serious water shortages. The economy is dominated by services, but industry, agriculture, and fishing employ a majority of the workforce. Cape Verde has close economic and political ties to the European Union and is seeking EU associate status. Its currency is pegged to the euro. More Cape Verdeans live abroad than live on the islands, and it is estimated that remittances from this expatriate population contribute well over 10 percent to GDP. Economic growth through market liberalization, good governance, and judicious public investment has earned Cape Verde middle-income status.

How Do We Measure Economic Freedom? See Chapter 4 (page 39) for an explanation of the methodology or visit the *Index* Web site at *heritage.org/index*.

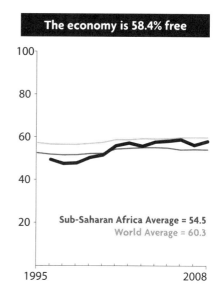

The economy is 58.4% free

Sub-Saharan Africa Average = 54.5
World Average = 60.3

1995   2008

QUICK FACTS

Population: 0.5 million

GDP (PPP): $2.9 billion
5.8% growth in 2005
5.0% 5-yr. comp. ann. growth
$5,802 per capita

Unemployment: 21.0% (2000 estimate)

Inflation (CPI): 0.4%

FDI (net flow): $19.0 million

Official Development Assistance:
Multilateral: $63.4 million
Bilateral: 113.3 million (10.7% from the U.S.)

External Debt: $325.0 million (2002 estimate)

Exports: $365.9 million
Primarily fuel, shoes, garments, fish, hides

Imports: $646.1 million
Primarily foodstuffs, industrial products, transport equipment, fuels

2005 data unless otherwise noted.

CAPE VERDE'S TEN ECONOMIC FREEDOMS

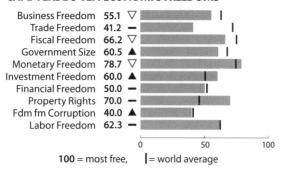

Business Freedom	55.1 ▽	
Trade Freedom	41.2 ▬	
Fiscal Freedom	66.2 ▽	
Government Size	60.5 ▲	
Monetary Freedom	78.7 ▽	
Investment Freedom	60.0 ▲	
Financial Freedom	50.0 ▬	
Property Rights	70.0 ▬	
Fdm fm Corruption	40.0 ▲	
Labor Freedom	62.3 ▬	

0   50   100

100 = most free, | = world average

BUSINESS FREEDOM — 55.1%

The overall freedom to start, operate, and close a business is restrained by Cape Verde's national regulatory environment. Starting a business takes an average of 52 days, compared to the world average of 43 days. In recent years, government has tried to streamline the cumbersome bureaucracy and increase transparency, but obtaining a business license still requires more than the world average of 19 procedures and 234 days. Closing a business is likewise difficult.

TRADE FREEDOM — 41.2%

Cape Verde's average tariff rate was a high 24.4 percent in 2003. Import restrictions, sanitary and phytosanitary regulations, and state trading of pharmaceuticals add to the cost of trade. An additional 10 percentage points is deducted from Cape Verde's trade freedom score to account for these non-tariff barriers.

FISCAL FREEDOM — 66.2%

Cape Verde has a high income tax rate and a moderate corporate tax rate. The top income tax rate is 45 percent, and the top corporate tax rate is 30 percent. Other taxes include a value-added tax (VAT) and a special consumption tax. In the most recent year, tax revenue as a percentage of GDP was 21.3 percent.

GOVERNMENT SIZE — 60.5%

Total government expenditures, including consumption and transfer payments, are moderate. In the most recent year, government spending equaled 36.3 percent of GDP. Sales to the private sector have significantly reduced the number of state-owned enterprises.

MONETARY FREEDOM — 78.7%

Inflation is moderate, averaging 3.2 percent between 2004 and 2006. Relatively stable prices explain most of the monetary freedom score. The market determines most prices, but the government controls the prices of water and electricity and regulates some other prices, including those for petroleum products and basic food items. An additional 10 percentage points is deducted from Cape Verde's monetary freedom score to adjust for measures that distort domestic prices.

INVESTMENT FREEDOM — 60%

The government encourages foreign investment, particu-

larly in tourism, fishing, light manufacturing, communications, and transportation, with a variety of incentives. It has simplified and expedited registration, opening most privatization to foreign investors. All sectors are now open, though real estate transactions require central bank approval. Both residents and non-residents may hold foreign exchange accounts, subject to government approval and regulations. Most payments and transfers are subject to controls. Most capital transactions are permitted, but most are also subject to advance approval by the central bank.

FINANCIAL FREEDOM — 50%

Cape Verde's small financial sector has five commercial banks and remains highly concentrated, with the two largest banks controlling 89 percent of total assets and deposits. Banking reform initiated in the 1990s led to privatization of these two banks, Comercial do Atlântico and Caixa Económica de Cabo Verde, although the government retains a large minority stake in the latter. The non-performing loan ratio has improved significantly. The financial sector has been strengthened by improved regulations and monetary policy autonomy. The government remains active in the banking sector through financial institutions that handle public investment and international aid. The insurance sector is small. The stock market, founded in 1999, has been largely inactive, but this is expected to change soon.

PROPERTY RIGHTS — 70%

Private property is fairly well protected. The constitution provides for an independent judiciary, and the government generally respects this provision. The right to an expeditious trial, however, is constrained by a seriously overburdened, understaffed, and inefficient judicial system. The case backlog routinely leads to trial delays of six months or more. Cape Verde recently signed several treaties that provide protection for intellectual property rights.

FREEDOM FROM CORRUPTION — 40%

In Africa, Cape Verde's record of good political and economic governance is generally regarded as second only to Botswana's. This contributes to a relatively low level of corruption. The economy is about 40 percent informal, which correlates with the still-significant poverty rate. Informal activities also correlate with corruption. The government has acknowledged the existence of corruption in the customs department and has adopted laws and regulations to combat corruption, which is criminally punishable.

LABOR FREEDOM — 62.3%

The labor market operates under relatively inflexible employment regulations that could be improved to enhance employment and productivity growth. The non-salary cost of employing a worker is moderate, and dismissing a redundant employee can be relatively costly. The cost of laying off a worker creates a risk aversion for companies that would otherwise hire more people and grow. The labor laws were revised recently to make labor contracts more flexible.

CENTRAL AFRICAN REPUBLIC

Bangui

The economy of the Central African Republic (CAR) is 48.2 percent free, according to our 2008 assessment, which makes it the world's 141st freest economy. Its overall score is 2.1 percentage points lower than last year, primarily because of worsening investment freedom and freedom from corruption. The CAR is ranked 34th out of 40 countries in the sub-Saharan Africa region, and its overall score is lower than the regional average.

The CAR scores better than the world average only in terms of government expenditures, which are low in formal terms, although this is likely a sign of government weakness, not efficiency. Tax revenue is not high as a percentage of GDP, but rates are high. Inflation is low, but government interference with market prices is extensive.

Business freedom, trade freedom, financial freedom, property rights, and freedom from corruption are weak. Regulation is burdensome, and business operations are significantly hampered by the government. Labor laws impose exceptionally high costs on employers. Banking and the rule of law are subject to political pressure. Property rights cannot be guaranteed, and corruption is rampant.

BACKGROUND: The Central African Republic gained its independence in 1960 and has been politically unstable or under strict authoritarian rule for much of its history. A civilian government established through multi-party elections in 1993 was overthrown in 2003 by General François Bozize. Despite pledging not to run, Bozize won the 2005 presidential election. He continues to face opposition from armed groups in the northern region. Instability has undermined economic activity and caused over 200,000 people to flee. Refugees from Sudan's Darfur region have fled to the northern CAR. Resources include timber, diamonds, gold, uranium, and possibly oil; but most of the population is engaged in subsistence farming, and agriculture comprises over half of GDP. Resources, aside from diamonds and timber, remain undeveloped. Infrastructure is poor, institutions are weak, and corruption is prevalent.

How Do We Measure Economic Freedom? See Chapter 4 (page 39) for an explanation of the methodology or visit the *Index* Web site at *heritage.org/index.*

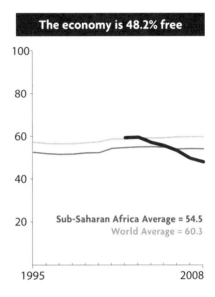

The economy is 48.2% free

Sub-Saharan Africa Average = 54.5
World Average = 60.3

1995   2008

QUICK FACTS

Population: 4.0 million

GDP (PPP): $4.9 billion
2.2% growth in 2005
−1.2% 5-yr. comp. ann. growth
$1,224 per capita

Unemployment: 8.0% (2001 estimate)

Inflation (CPI): 2.9%

FDI (net flow): $6.0 million

Official Development Assistance:
Multilateral: $38.2 million
Bilateral: $67.9 million (25.4% from the U.S.)

External Debt: $1.0 billion

Exports: $100.4 million (2004 estimate)
Primarily diamonds, timber, cotton, coffee, tobacco

Imports: $158.2 million (2004 estimate)
Primarily food, textiles, petroleum products, machinery, electrical equipment, motor vehicles, chemicals, pharmaceuticals
2005 data unless otherwise noted.

CENT. AFRICAN REP.'S TEN ECONOMIC FREEDOMS

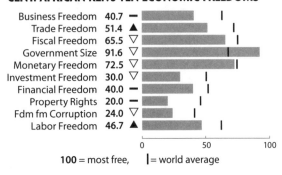

Business Freedom	40.7 —
Trade Freedom	51.4 ▲
Fiscal Freedom	65.5 ▽
Government Size	91.6 ▽
Monetary Freedom	72.5 ▽
Investment Freedom	30.0 ▽
Financial Freedom	40.0 —
Property Rights	20.0 —
Fdm fm Corruption	24.0 ▽
Labor Freedom	46.7 ▲

100 = most free, **|** = world average

BUSINESS FREEDOM — 40.7%

The overall freedom to start, operate, and close a business is impeded by the Central African Republic's national regulatory environment. Starting a business takes less than the world average of 43 days, but obtaining a business license requires more than the world average of 19 procedures and 234 days. Closing a business can be difficult.

TRADE FREEDOM — 51.4%

The Central African Republic's weighted average tariff rate was a high 16.8 percent in 2005. The government restricts imports of sugar and coffee, imposes import and export taxes, implements inappropriate customs valuation for certain imports, and subsidizes exports; other problems include inadequate infrastructure, weak regulatory and customs administration, and customs fraud and inefficiency. An additional 15 percentage points is deducted from the CAR's trade freedom score to account for these non-tariff barriers.

FISCAL FREEDOM — 65.5%

The Central African Republic has high tax rates. The top income tax rate is 50 percent, and the top corporate tax rate is 30 percent. Other taxes include a value-added tax (VAT) and a tax on check transactions. In the most recent year, overall tax revenue as a percentage of GDP was 7 percent.

GOVERNMENT SIZE — 91.6%

Total government expenditures, including consumption and transfer payments, are very low. In the most recent year, government spending equaled 16.7 percent of GDP. Poor public expenditure management has hurt economic growth.

MONETARY FREEDOM — 72.5%

Inflation is moderate, averaging 3.9 percent between 2004 and 2006. Relatively stable prices explain most of the monetary freedom score. The government influences most prices through the large public sector, subsidies, and price controls on 17 food staples, coffee, cotton, electricity, water, and petroleum. An additional 15 percentage points is deducted from the CAR's monetary freedom score to adjust for measures that distort domestic prices.

INVESTMENT FREEDOM — 30%

Banditry and extortion are major obstacles to foreign investment, which must be declared to the Ministry for the Economy, Finance, Planning and International Cooperation. Repeated insurrections and a coup in 2003 have virtually frozen foreign investment. Added to this are weak infrastructure, a limited domestic market, and landlocked status. Capital transfers and transactions are subject to exchange controls. Residents may hold foreign exchange accounts. All capital transactions, transfers, and payments to countries other than certain regional nations, France, and Monaco are subject to government approval and reporting requirements. Sale or issue of capital market securities and commercial credits likewise requires government approval.

FINANCIAL FREEDOM — 40%

The CAR's financial sector is underdeveloped. The regional Central African Economic and Monetary Community (CEMAC) countries share a common central bank and a common currency pegged to the euro. In addition to a branch of the regional central bank, there are three commercial banks, a microfinance institution, and two postal financial institutions. The two largest commercial banks, Banque Internationale pour le Centrafrique and Commercial Bank Centrafrique, have been privatized, but the Banque Populaire Maroco-Centrafricaine is still partly government-owned. The banking sector is used to finance government expenditures, and the accumulation of state debt and lack of promised credits have undermined the system. There are two insurance companies, also overseen by the CEMAC. There is no stock market.

PROPERTY RIGHTS — 20%

Protection of property rights is weak. The constitution has been suspended, allowing the president to rule by decree. Judges are appointed by the president, and the judiciary is subject to executive interference. The courts barely function because of inefficient administration, a shortage of trained personnel, growing salary arrears, and a lack of material resources.

FREEDOM FROM CORRUPTION — 24%

Corruption is perceived as pervasive. The Central African Republic ranks 130th out of 163 countries in Transparency International's Corruption Perceptions Index for 2006. Informal market activity and smuggling, especially in diamonds, are extensive. The formal sector has contracted significantly because of regulation and corruption. A significant part of the population works informally. The police and the judiciary are among the country's most corrupt institutions.

LABOR FREEDOM — 46.7%

Highly rigid employment regulations hinder employment and productivity growth. The non-salary cost of employing a worker is moderate, and dismissing a redundant employee is relatively difficult. Regulations on increasing or contracting the number of work hours are rigid. The Central African Republic's labor freedom is one of the 20 lowest in the world.

CHAD

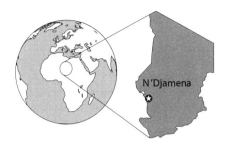

N'Djamena

Rank: 142

Regional Rank: 35 of 40

Chad's economy is 47.7 percent free, according to our 2008 assessment, which makes it the world's 142nd freest economy. Its overall score is 2.3 percentage points lower than last year. Chad is ranked 35th out of 40 countries in the sub-Saharan Africa region, and its overall score is lower than the regional average.

Chad scores better than the world average only in terms of government expenditures, which are low in formal terms, although this is likely a sign of government weakness, not efficiency. Inflation is low, but the government intervenes in the prices of certain goods.

Chad scores very low in business freedom, fiscal freedom, property rights, freedom from corruption, and labor freedom. Individual income tax rates are as high as 65 percent. Starting a business takes over two months, and both licensing and closing a business are time-consuming and costly. Chad has one of the world's most restrictive labor markets. Weak rule of law means that property rights and regulations are rarely observed, and corruption is endemic.

BACKGROUND: Chad is thinly populated, landlocked, politically unstable, and poor. Frequent coups and internal conflict preceded President Idriss Deby's seizure of power in 1991. Despite several coup attempts and fighting with rebel groups, Deby managed to stay in power with French military assistance and win elections in 1996, 2001, and 2006. Conflict and instability in eastern Chad near the border with Sudan have resulted in over 140,000 internally displaced persons. Eighty percent of the population is engaged in subsistence agriculture, herding, and fishing. Instability, corruption, poor infrastructure, and lack of administrative and judicial reform undermine the business climate. Oil exports have increased overall economic growth in recent years, and an agreement reached with the World Bank and the International Monetary Fund in 2006 eased donor concerns about how oil revenues will be allocated in the budget.

How Do We Measure Economic Freedom? See Chapter 4 (page 39) for an explanation of the methodology or visit the *Index* Web site at *heritage.org/index*.

The economy is 47.7% free

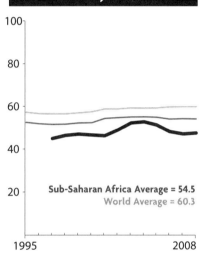

Sub-Saharan Africa Average = 54.5
World Average = 60.3

QUICK FACTS

Population: 9.7 million

GDP (PPP): $13.9 billion
8.6% growth in 2005
15.9% 5-yr. comp. ann. growth
$1,427 per capita

Unemployment: n/a

Inflation (CPI): 7.9%

FDI (net flow): $705.0 million

Official Development Assistance:
Multilateral: $252.6 million
Bilateral: $174.1 million (35.5% from the U.S.)

External Debt: $1.6 billion

Exports: $4.3 billion
Primarily cotton, cattle, gum arabic, oil

Imports: $823.1 million
Primarily machinery and transportation equipment, industrial goods, foodstuffs, textiles

2005 data unless otherwise noted.

CHAD'S TEN ECONOMIC FREEDOMS

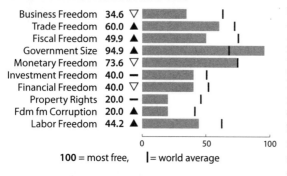

Business Freedom	34.6 ▽
Trade Freedom	60.0 ▲
Fiscal Freedom	49.9 ▲
Government Size	94.9 ▲
Monetary Freedom	73.6 ▽
Investment Freedom	40.0 —
Financial Freedom	40.0 ▽
Property Rights	20.0 —
Fdm fm Corruption	20.0 ▲
Labor Freedom	44.2 ▲

0   50   100

100 = most free, ❘ **= world average**

BUSINESS FREEDOM — *34.6%*

The overall freedom to start, operate, and close a business is seriously limited by Chad's national regulatory environment. Starting a business takes almost twice the world average of 43 days, but obtaining a business license has been easier in recent years, requiring less than the world average of 19 procedures and 234 days.

TRADE FREEDOM — *60%*

Chad's weighted average tariff rate was 12.5 percent in 2005. Burdensome export taxes, numerous import fees, inappropriate customs valuation for some products, a non-transparent customs code, weak enforcement of intellectual property rights, corruption, and inefficient customs administration add to the cost of trade. An additional 15 percentage points is deducted from Chad's trade freedom score to account for these non-tariff barriers.

FISCAL FREEDOM — *49.9%*

Chad has very high tax rates. The top income tax rate is 65 percent, and the top corporate tax rate is 40 percent. Other taxes include a value-added tax (VAT), a property tax, and an apprenticeship tax. In the most recent year, overall tax revenue as a percentage of GDP was 8.6 percent.

GOVERNMENT SIZE — *94.9%*

Total government expenditures, including consumption and transfer payments, are low. In the most recent year, government spending equaled 13 percent of GDP. Most state-owned enterprises have been privatized, but progress in such sectors as cotton, energy, and telecommunications has been slow.

MONETARY FREEDOM — *73.6%*

Inflation is relatively high, averaging 6.7 percent between 2004 and 2006. Relatively unstable prices explain most of the monetary freedom score. Most prices are determined in the market, but the government influences prices through state-owned enterprises and regulation of such important goods and services as cotton, telecommunications, water, road transportation, and energy. An additional 10 percentage points is deducted from Chad's monetary freedom score to adjust for measures that distort domestic prices.

INVESTMENT FREEDOM — *40%*

Chad does not limit foreign ownership and provides equal treatment to foreign investors, who must meet several bureaucratic requirements. Foreign investments in cotton, electricity, and telecommunications are restricted to protect state-owned enterprises. The main constraints are limited infrastructure, energy shortages, energy costs, the scarcity of skilled labor, burdensome taxes, and corruption. Many commercial disputes are settled privately, and the requirement that foreign businesses employ 98 percent Chad nationals in their Chad operations is often ignored because of labor constraints. Residents and non-residents may hold foreign exchange accounts with government approval. Capital transactions, payments, and transfers to certain countries are not subject to restrictions; when made to other countries, they are subject to controls.

FINANCIAL FREEDOM — *40%*

Chad's financial sector is small, underdeveloped, and hindered by political instability. Chad and the five other countries in the Central African Economic and Monetary Community share a common central bank and a common currency pegged to the euro. Significant banking privatization was completed in the 1990s. There are now five commercial banks. However, banking is weak, demand for retail banking is low, informal financial services are common, and supervision and regulation are insufficient. The government has encouraged lending to CotonTchad to finance restructuring of the cotton sector. The small insurance sector is dominated by the formerly state-owned Star Nationale. There is no capital or money market, and sophisticated financial instruments are unavailable.

PROPERTY RIGHTS — *20%*

Protection of private property is weak. It is widely felt that the courts should be avoided at all costs, and most disputes are settled privately. The constitution guarantees judicial independence, but most key judicial officials are named by the president and influenced by the executive branch. In mid-2006, several major international oil companies alleged that the government had violated its contractual obligations to them.

FREEDOM FROM CORRUPTION — *20%*

Corruption is perceived as rampant. Chad ranks 156th out of 163 countries in Transparency International's Corruption Perceptions Index for 2006. The ruling MPS party uses public administration and state enterprises to punish opponents and reward MPS members and allies. In early 2006, the World Bank froze $124 million in loans earmarked for Chad because of concerns that the government was misappropriating public resources generated from a new oil pipeline.

LABOR FREEDOM — *44.2%*

Burdensome employment regulations hinder employment creation and productivity growth. The non-salary cost of employing a worker is high, and dismissing a redundant employee is relatively costly. Restrictive labor laws and legal uncertainty discourage entrepreneurial activities. Chad's labor market flexibility is one of the 20 lowest in the world.

CHILE

Santiago

Chile's economy is 79.8 percent free, according to our 2008 assessment, which makes it the world's 8th freest economy. Its overall score is 0.8 percentage point higher than last year, mainly reflecting an improved investment climate. Chile is ranked 3rd out of 29 countries in the Americas and has been a regional leader for over a decade.

Chile is a regional economic power and scores higher than average in all 10 areas of economic freedom, especially investment freedom, property rights, and freedom from corruption. Foreign investment is a cornerstone of Chile's strong growth, and allowing easy repatriation is an attraction to inbound capital. Overall, the rule of law is remarkably transparent and impartial.

Chile's weakest scores relative to other economies are in business freedom, fiscal freedom, and monetary freedom. Bankruptcy procedures can be cumbersome, although regulatory licensing is easy. Income taxes on individuals are high, with a top rate of 40 percent.

BACKGROUND: Chile is the world's leading producer of copper. The export sector (e.g., minerals, wood, fruit, seafood, and wine) is the main engine of growth. Chile has pursued generally sound economic policies for nearly three decades. Higher energy prices and lagging consumer demand, however, slowed the economy in 2006. The coalition government of President Michele Bachelet, who is a Socialist, remains largely committed to Chile's successful free-market institutions, though her rhetoric emphasizes income equality over freedom. Chile is a member of the Asia–Pacific Economic Cooperation forum and seeks increased commercial ties with Asia. In addition to an important free trade agreement with the U.S., it has signed trade agreements with China, South Korea, New Zealand, Singapore, Brunei, India, and Japan. It is also negotiating agreements with Thailand, Malaysia, and Australia.

How Do We Measure Economic Freedom? See Chapter 4 (page 39) for an explanation of the methodology or visit the *Index* Web site at *heritage.org/index.*

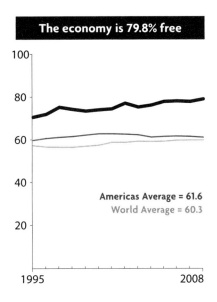

The economy is 79.8% free

Americas Average = 61.6
World Average = 60.3

1995   2008

QUICK FACTS

Population: 16.3 million

GDP (PPP): $196.0 billion
5.7% growth in 2005
4.5% 5-yr. comp. ann. growth
$12,026 per capita

Unemployment: 7.7%

Inflation (CPI): 3.1%

FDI (net flow): $4.5 billion

Official Development Assistance:
Multilateral: $77.1 million
Bilateral: $87.0 million (2.7% from the U.S.)

External Debt: $45.2 billion

Exports: $47.7 billion
Primarily copper, fruit, fish products, paper and pulp, chemicals, wine

Imports: $38.2 billion
Primarily petroleum and petroleum products, chemicals, electrical and telecommunications equipment, industrial machinery, vehicles, natural gas
2005 data unless otherwise noted.

CHILE'S TEN ECONOMIC FREEDOMS

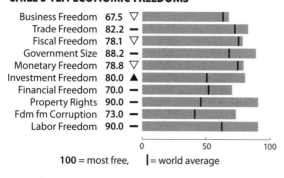

Business Freedom	67.5	▽
Trade Freedom	82.2	—
Fiscal Freedom	78.1	▽
Government Size	88.2	—
Monetary Freedom	78.8	▽
Investment Freedom	80.0	▲
Financial Freedom	70.0	—
Property Rights	90.0	—
Fdm fm Corruption	73.0	—
Labor Freedom	90.0	—

0   50   100

100 = most free, | = world average

BUSINESS FREEDOM — 67.5%

The overall freedom to start, operate, and close a business is relatively well protected by Chile's national regulatory environment. Starting a business takes an average of 27 days, compared to the world average of 43 days. Regulation is generally transparent and consistent. Obtaining a business license takes about the world average of 19 procedures and less than the world average of 234 days. Closing a business can be burdensome and lengthy.

TRADE FREEDOM — 82.2%

Chile's weighted average tariff rate was 3.9 percent in 2005. Imports of agricultural products and processed food require approval and face stringent sanitary and phytosanitary regulations, some imports are banned, exports are monitored, and the government provides some export subsidies. Issues related to the protection of intellectual property rights also add to the cost of trade. An additional 10 percentage points is deducted from Chile's trade freedom score to account for these non-tariff barriers.

FISCAL FREEDOM — 78.1%

Chile has a high income tax rate but a low corporate tax rate. The top income tax rate is 40 percent, and the top standard corporate tax rate is 17 percent. Other taxes include a value-added tax (VAT), a tax on check transactions, and a property tax. In the most recent year, overall tax revenue as a percentage of GDP was 17.3 percent.

GOVERNMENT SIZE — 88.2%

Total government expenditures, including consumption and transfer payments, are very moderate. The government has maintained its commitment to sound budget management. In the most recent year, government spending equaled 19.8 percent of GDP.

MONETARY FREEDOM — 78.8%

Inflation is moderate, averaging 3.1 percent between 2004 and 2006. Relatively unstable prices explain most of the monetary freedom score. Many prices are determined in the market, but the government maintains prices for utilities, including water, fixed-line telecommunications, and electricity, and prices for certain agricultural products are controlled within price bands. An additional 10 percentage points is deducted from Chile's monetary freedom score to adjust for measures that distort domestic prices.

INVESTMENT FREEDOM — 80%

Foreign and domestic investments receive equal treatment, and there are no restrictions on repatriation. Some additional authorizations are required for foreign ownership of local enterprises and joint ventures in the petroleum industry, uranium mining and other specialty mineral resources, communications and media, shipping, and fishing. All remaining exchange controls imposed in the late 1980s and early 1990s have been lifted, the minimum stay period on foreign investments has been eliminated, and procedures for placements in local capital markets have been eased. Residents and non-residents may hold foreign exchange accounts. There are no controls on current transfers and capital transactions, but some restrictions apply.

FINANCIAL FREEDOM — 70%

Chile's financial system is among the strongest and most developed among all emerging markets. The banking system is efficient and well supervised, with strict limits on lending to a single debtor or group of related companies. Twelve foreign banks compete on an equal footing with 14 domestic banks. Three large banks control 61 percent of assets. The state-owned Banco Estado is Chile's third largest, accounting for about 13 percent of assets. A series of reforms, including capitalization requirements and shareholder obligations, has increased competition and widened the range of operations for banks and other financial services. Credit is issued on market terms. Domestic and foreign banking and insurance companies receive equal treatment. The insurance sector is large and diverse, with 52 companies and a variety of services. Chile's liberal capital market is the largest in Latin America, with capitalization at 125 percent of GDP.

PROPERTY RIGHTS — 90%

Private property is well protected. Contracts are secure, and court administration is transparent and efficient. Expropriation is highly unlikely and receives compensation. Protection of intellectual property rights is inadequate for computer software and video recordings, and Chile lacks a clear and transparent system for protecting pharmaceutical patents and the proprietary clinical data related to innovative products.

FREEDOM FROM CORRUPTION — 73%

Corruption is perceived as minimal. Chile ranks 20th out of 163 countries in Transparency International's Corruption Perceptions Index for 2006, tied with the U.S. Chile has signed and ratified the Organization of American States Convention Against Corruption and the OECD Convention on Combating Bribery. Judicial corruption is rare.

LABOR FREEDOM — 90%

The non-salary cost of employing a worker is low, but dismissing a redundant employee is relatively costly and difficult. There are few restrictions on expanding or contracting the number of working hours.

CHINA, PEOPLE'S REPUBLIC OF

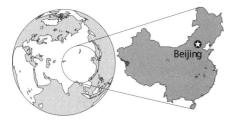

Beijing

China's economy is 52.8 percent free, according to our 2008 assessment, which makes it the world's 126th freest economy. Its overall score is 1 percentage point higher than last year. China is ranked 23rd out of 30 countries in the Asia–Pacific region, and its overall score is slightly lower than the regional average.

China scores well in government expenditures and equals the world average in trade freedom, monetary freedom, and labor freedom. Formal central government expenditures equal less than 20 percent of GDP, which is low compared to other major economies.

China severely restricts many areas of its economy and consequently scores lower than average in seven of the 10 economic freedoms. Investment freedom, financial freedom, and property rights are very weak. Foreign investment is highly controlled and regulated, and the judicial system is highly politicized. The state maintains tight control of the financial sector and directly or indirectly owns all banks.

BACKGROUND: China is a one-party state ruled by the Chinese Communist Party. Despite rhetoric about democratic development, the party maintains strict control of political expression, speech, assembly, and religion. Since opening up to foreign trade in the early 1980s, China's economy has expanded rapidly. It is now the world's second-largest economy in absolute terms, although per capita income remains low. Most workers are employed in the agricultural sector. The financial sector is largely opaque and state-controlled, raising concerns about lending practices. Since joining the World Trade Organization in 2002, China has liberalized many sectors of its economy, but it still suffers from the lack of a rule of law, poor protection of intellectual property rights, and corruption, among other hurdles.

How Do We Measure Economic Freedom? See Chapter 4 (page 39) for an explanation of the methodology or visit the *Index* Web site at *heritage.org/index*.

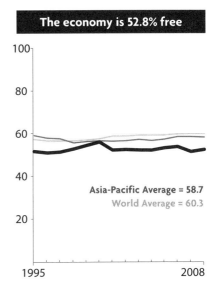

The economy is 52.8% free

Asia-Pacific Average = 58.7
World Average = 60.3

1995 — 2008

QUICK FACTS

Population: 1.3 billion

GDP (PPP): $8.8 trillion
10.4% growth in 2005
9.9% 5-yr. comp. ann. growth
$6,757 per capita

Unemployment: 9.0%

Inflation (CPI): 1.8%

FDI (net flow): $61.1 billion

Official Development Assistance:
Multilateral: $263.1 million
Bilateral: $2.8 billion (0.7% from the U.S.)

External Debt: $281.6 billion

Exports: $836.9 billion
Primarily machinery and equipment, plastics, optical and medical equipment, iron and steel

Imports: $712.1 billion
Primarily machinery and equipment, oil and mineral fuels, plastics, optical and medical equipment, organic chemicals, iron and steel
2005 data unless otherwise noted.

CHINA'S TEN ECONOMIC FREEDOMS

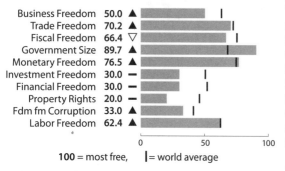

Business Freedom	50.0 ▲	
Trade Freedom	70.2 ▲	
Fiscal Freedom	66.4 ▽	
Government Size	89.7 ▲	
Monetary Freedom	76.5 ▲	
Investment Freedom	30.0 —	
Financial Freedom	30.0 —	
Property Rights	20.0 —	
Fdm fm Corruption	33.0 ▲	
Labor Freedom	62.4 ▲	

100 = most free, **|** = world average

BUSINESS FREEDOM — *50%*

The overall freedom to start, operate, and close a business is constrained by China's national regulatory environment. Starting a business takes an average of 35 days, compared to the world average of 43 days. Obtaining a business license requires more than the world average of 19 procedures and 234 days. China lacks legal and regulatory transparency.

TRADE FREEDOM — *70.2%*

China's weighted average tariff rate was 4.9 percent in 2005. The government has reduced its non-tariff barriers pursuant to WTO accession, but severe import bans and restrictions, inconsistent customs valuation, non-transparent tariff classification, inefficient and corruption-prone customs administration, and issues involving the protection of intellectual property rights add to the cost of trade. An additional 20 percentage points is deducted from China's trade freedom score to account for these non-tariff barriers.

FISCAL FREEDOM — *66.4%*

China has a high income tax rate and a moderate corporate tax rate. The top income tax rate is 45 percent, and the top corporate tax rate is 33 percent. Other taxes include a value-added tax (VAT) and a real estate tax. In the most recent year, overall tax revenue as a percentage of GDP was 15.8 percent.

GOVERNMENT SIZE — *89.7%*

Government expenditures, including consumption and transfer payments, are relatively low. In the most recent year, central government spending equaled 18.5 percent of GDP. Consolidated government spending (including local government spending and other expenditures on social security) is estimated to be more than 30 percent of GDP. The state still guides and directs much economic activity.

MONETARY FREEDOM — *76.5%*

Inflation is relatively low, averaging 1.8 percent between 2004 and 2006. Relatively stable prices explain most of the monetary freedom score. The market determines the prices of most traded products, but the government maintains prices for petroleum, electricity, pharmaceuticals, coal, agricultural products, and other "essential" goods. Subsidies allow state-owned enterprises to produce and sell goods to wholesalers and retailers at artificially low prices. An additional 15 percentage points is deducted from China's monetary freedom score to adjust for measures that distort domestic prices.

INVESTMENT FREEDOM — *30%*

Weak rule of law, lack of transparency, domestic favoritism, and a complex approval process remain major obstacles. Legally, foreign investment is allowed only in specific sectors. Government "encouragement" of foreign investment in certain geographic and high-value-added areas constitutes state action that could violate WTO rules. The central bank regulates foreign exchange, and the government controls investment in the stock market. There are extensive controls on foreign exchange, current transfers, and capital transactions.

FINANCIAL FREEDOM — *30%*

China's complex financial system is tightly controlled by the government. Roughly 35,000 financial institutions were operating in early 2006. The banking sector is the largest part of the system and is almost entirely state-owned. Four state-owned banks account for over 53 percent of assets. The state directs the allocation of credit, and the big four state-owned banks lend primarily to state-owned enterprises. Numerous foreign banks have opened branches but face burdensome regulations, though progress has accelerated since China joined the WTO. Foreign participation in capital markets is limited. A weak social security net has encouraged a competitive, market-driven insurance sector to emerge from a state-run monopoly.

PROPERTY RIGHTS — *20%*

China's judicial system is weak, and many companies resort to arbitration. Even when courts try to enforce decisions, local officials often ignore them with impunity. All land is state-owned, but individuals and firms, including foreigners, can own and transfer long-term leases for land use (subject to many restrictions), as well as structures and personal property. Under a new Property Law, residential property rights will be renewed automatically, and commercial and industrial grants should be renewed absent a conflicting public interest. Intellectual property rights are not enforced effectively. Copyrights, patents for inventions, brands and trademarks, and trade secrets are routinely stolen.

FREEDOM FROM CORRUPTION — *33%*

Corruption is perceived as significant. China ranks 70th out of 163 countries in Transparency International's Corruption Perceptions Index for 2006. Corruption limits foreign direct investment but affects banking, finance, government procurement, and construction most severely. China ratified the U.N. Anti-Corruption Convention in 2005 but still lacks independent investigative bodies and courts.

LABOR FREEDOM — *62.4%*

Restrictive employment regulations hinder employment and productivity growth. The non-salary cost of employing a worker is high. Dismissing a redundant employee can be relatively costly and may require prior consultation with the local labor bureau and labor union. In general, the capacity to end employment varies according to the location and size of the enterprise.

COLOMBIA

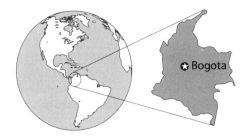

Rank: 67
Regional Rank: 15 of 29

Colombia's economy is 61.9 percent free, according to our 2008 assessment, which makes it the world's 67th freest economy. Its overall score is 2.3 percentage points higher than last year, reflecting improved scores in seven freedoms, including investment and monetary freedom. Colombia is ranked 15th out of 29 countries in the Americas, and its overall score is equal to the regional average.

Colombia scores moderately well in business freedom, investment freedom, and financial freedom but is average in most respects. That it maintains relatively robust institutions in spite of a violent subculture is a sign of promise for the future.

Labor freedom and property rights score more poorly. Despite nominal openness to foreign investment, regulations are complex and uncertain. Rule of law is uneven. Business contracts are generally respected, but judicial corruption makes legal transparency difficult.

BACKGROUND: Colombia is one of South America's oldest continuous democracies. In the 1980s, leftist insurgents and paramilitary vigilante groups took up drug trafficking, killing and marauding throughout much of the countryside. President Alvaro Uribe, re-elected by a landslide in May 2006, has ended years of fruitless appeasement and is enforcing the law against both rebels and paramilitaries. He has also moved to demobilize illegal rural armies. The lives of ordinary Colombians have improved dramatically, and a safer business environment has helped to cut unemployment by at least 5 percentage points in the past five years. Uribe's next challenge is to reduce the burden of government so that the economy can grow faster. Currently, it is heavily dependent on exports of petroleum, coffee, and cut flowers. A pending trade agreement with the U.S., if approved, should encourage economic diversification and stimulate growth.

How Do We Measure Economic Freedom? See Chapter 4 (page 39) for an explanation of the methodology or visit the *Index* Web site at *heritage.org/index*.

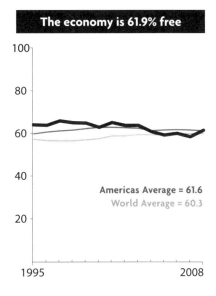

The economy is 61.9% free

Americas Average = 61.6
World Average = 60.3

QUICK FACTS

Population: 45.6 million

GDP (PPP): $333.1 billion
5.3% growth in 2005
4.0% 5-yr. comp. ann. growth
$7,304 per capita

Unemployment: 11.8%

Inflation (CPI): 5.0%

FDI (net flow): $5.6 billion

Official Development Assistance:
Multilateral: $79.5 million
Bilateral: $540.0 million (63.1% from the U.S.)

External Debt: $37.6 billion

Exports: $24.4 billion
Primarily petroleum, coffee, coal, nickel, emeralds, apparel, bananas, cut flowers

Imports: $24.9 billion
Primarily industrial equipment, transportation equipment, consumer goods, chemicals, paper products, fuels, electricity

2005 data unless otherwise noted.

141

COLOMBIA'S TEN ECONOMIC FREEDOMS

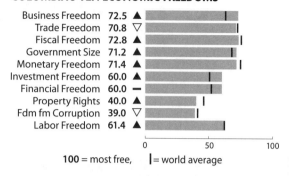

Business Freedom	72.5	▲
Trade Freedom	70.8	▽
Fiscal Freedom	72.8	▲
Government Size	71.2	▲
Monetary Freedom	71.4	▲
Investment Freedom	60.0	▲
Financial Freedom	60.0	—
Property Rights	40.0	▲
Fdm fm Corruption	39.0	▽
Labor Freedom	61.4	▲

0   50   100

100 = most free, | = world average

BUSINESS FREEDOM — 72.5%

The overall freedom to start, operate, and close a business is relatively well protected by Colombia's national regulatory environment. Starting a business takes an average of 42 days, compared to the world average of 43 days. Obtaining a business license requires less than the world average of 19 procedures and 234 days. Closing a business is relatively easy. Some bureaucratic procedures have been simplified.

TRADE FREEDOM — 70.8%

Colombia's weighted average tariff rate was 9.6 percent in 2005. Despite progress in dismantling non-tariff barriers, bureaucracy, non-transparent regulation, import bans and restrictions, restrictive import licensing, price bands, issues involving the protection of intellectual property rights, non-transparent customs administration and valuation, state export promotion programs, and corruption add to the cost of trade. Consequently, an additional 10 percentage points is deducted from Colombia's trade freedom score.

FISCAL FREEDOM — 72.8%

In December 2006, the top income tax rate and the top corporate tax rate were reduced to 34 percent from 35 percent. Other taxes include a value-added tax (VAT) and a financial transactions tax. In the most recent year, overall tax revenue as a percentage of GDP was 20.1 percent.

GOVERNMENT SIZE — 71.2%

Total government expenditures, including consumption and transfer payments, are low. In the most recent year, government spending equaled 31 percent of GDP. State ownership is now limited to a few utilities enterprises and some development banks.

MONETARY FREEDOM — 71.4%

Inflation is moderate, averaging 4.6 percent between 2004 and 2006. Relatively unstable prices explain most of the monetary freedom score. The government maintains prices for ground and air transport fares, some pharmaceutical products, petroleum derivatives, natural gas, some petrochemicals, public utility services, residential rents, schoolbooks, and school tuition, and the Agriculture Ministry may intervene temporarily to freeze prices of basic foodstuffs through agreements with regional wholesalers. An additional 15 percentage points is deducted from Colombia's monetary freedom score to adjust for measures that distort domestic prices.

INVESTMENT FREEDOM — 60%

Except for remittances abroad, foreign and domestic capital are treated equally. Most of the economy is open to foreign investment, except for activities related to national security and toxic waste disposal. A few areas like finance and energy development require authorization. Foreign investment in television networks and programming is capped at 40 percent, and reciprocal access to the investor's home country is required. The largest obstacles are regulation and constantly changing business rules, although consolidation has simplified compliance. In most sectors, 100 percent ownership is permitted. Portfolio foreign investment must remain in the country for one year. Residents who work in certain internationally related companies may hold foreign exchange accounts. All foreign investment must be registered with the central bank.

FINANCIAL FREEDOM — 60%

Colombia's financial sector is relatively large and sophisticated. Banking has undergone significant consolidation and privatization since the 1998–1999 financial crisis. The government has strengthened regulations and seized some banks for falling below solvency requirements. As of December 2006, there were 17 commercial banks: 11 domestically owned and six foreign-owned; one is state-owned. All financial institutions nationalized during the crisis were privatized or liquidated by mid-2006 except for the state-owned Granbanco-Bancafé. Foreign companies are prominent in the insurance sector, and competition has intensified since 2003. The informal credit market is extensive. Foreign investors face few restrictions in small equity markets, and renewed enthusiasm for investing in developing markets has stimulated foreign investment in Colombian equities.

PROPERTY RIGHTS — 40%

Contracts are generally respected. Arbitration is complex and dilatory, especially with regard to the enforcement of awards. The law guarantees indemnification in expropriation cases. Despite some progress, the enforcement of intellectual property rights is erratic. Infringements, especially the unauthorized use of trademarks, are common. In areas controlled by terrorist groups, property rights cannot be guaranteed.

FREEDOM FROM CORRUPTION — 39%

Corruption is perceived as significant. Colombia ranks 59th out of 163 countries in Transparency International's Corruption Perceptions Index for 2006. Despite significant advances in fighting corruption, criminal narcotics organizations influence the military and the lower levels of the judiciary and civil service.

LABOR FREEDOM — 61.4%

Restrictive employment regulations hinder employment and productivity growth. The non-salary cost of employing a worker is high, but dismissing a redundant employee can be relatively costless. Unemployment insurance consists of a mandatory individual severance account system. Regulations on modifying the number of working hours are relatively flexible.

CONGO, DEMOCRATIC REPUBLIC OF (FORMERLY ZAIRE)

Kinshasa

Rank: Not Ranked

Regional Rank: Not Ranked

The economic freedom of the Democratic Republic of Congo (DRC) cannot be graded because of the violence and chaos of recent years. The last time the DRC was graded was in 2000.

BACKGROUND: The Democratic Republic of Congo, despite abundant resources, is among the world's poorest countries, with most of the population engaged in subsistence agriculture. Aided by Rwandan and Ugandan troops, Laurent Kabila overthrew Mobutu Sese Seko in 1997. When those troops refused to leave and sought to oust Kabila, troops from Angola, Namibia, and Zimbabwe intervened, and the Rwandan and Ugandan forces retreated with their supporters to the eastern DRC. A 1999 accord established a cease-fire and paved the way for a U.N. peacekeeping force. The conflict and related consequences, such as starvation and inadequate access to health care, resulted in millions of deaths. After Kabila's 2001 assassination, his son assumed power. In July 2006, Joseph Kabila and his allies won Congo's first multi-party elections in 40 years. Instability continues, particularly in the eastern DRC; corruption and poor governance remain endemic; and infrastructure is virtually nonexistent in many areas.

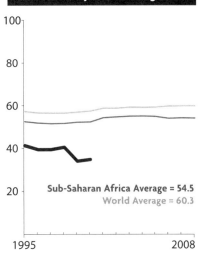

The economy cannot be graded

Sub-Saharan Africa Average = 54.5
World Average = 60.3

1995   2008

QUICK FACTS

Population: 57.5 million

GDP (PPP): $41.1 billion
6.5% growth in 2005
5.6% 5-yr. comp. ann. growth
$714 per capita

Unemployment: n/a

Inflation (CPI): 2.5%

FDI (net flow): $1.3 billion

Official Development Assistance:
Multilateral: $826.5 million
Bilateral: $1.1 billion (13.3% from the U.S.)

External Debt: $10.6 billion

Exports: $1.8 billion (2004 estimate)
Primarily petroleum, lumber, plywood, sugar, cocoa, coffee, diamonds

Imports: $2.1 billion (2004 estimate)
Primarily capital equipment, construction materials, foodstuffs

How Do We Measure Economic Freedom? See Chapter 4 (page 39) for an explanation of the methodology or visit the *Index* Web site at *heritage.org/index*.

2005 data unless otherwise noted.

BUSINESS FREEDOM — NOT GRADED

The overall freedom to start, operate, and close a business is restricted by the Democratic Republic of Congo's national regulatory environment. Starting a business takes an average of 155 days, compared to the world average of 43 days. Obtaining a business license takes about 322 days and involves 14 procedures, compared to the world average of 234 days and 19 procedures.

TRADE FREEDOM — NOT GRADED

The weighted average tariff rate was 13 percent in 2003. Most trade barriers result from complex regulations, a multiplicity of administrative agencies, corruption, and a frequent lack of professionalism and control by officials who are responsible for enforcement.

FISCAL FREEDOM — NOT GRADED

The Democratic Republic of Congo has high tax rates. The top income tax rate is 50 percent, and the top corporate tax rate is 40 percent. Other taxes include a sales tax and a tax on vehicles. In the most recent year, overall tax revenue as a percentage of GDP was 8.6 percent.

GOVERNMENT SIZE — NOT GRADED

Total government expenditures in the Democratic Republic of Congo, including consumption and transfer payments, are low. In the most recent year, government spending (which has been inrceasing over the past five years) equaled 19.5 percent of GDP.

MONETARY FREEDOM — NOT GRADED

Inflation is high, averaging 14.4 percent between 2004 and 2006. Relatively unstable prices explain most of the monetary freedom score. While important structural measures have recently been implemented, including the liberalization of most prices, some prices are still controlled to some degree through the public sector. Import price controls can be significant because nearly all manufactured goods and many food items sold in the DRC are imported.

INVESTMENT FREEDOM — NOT GRADED

War, economic and political instability, corruption, and anti-market policy decisions have deterred foreign investment. Hutu refugees and soldiers from Rwanda continue to be a destabilizing factor. The execution of routine transactions through official bodies is fraught with difficulty. Political interference and local cartels obstruct foreign investment. Nevertheless, foreign direct investment (for example, in telecommunications) has increased in the years since establishment of the transitional government, which has managed to make some progress in restoring peace. Reforms supervised by the International Monetary Fund have added some stability to the investment framework. There are no restrictions for residents or non-residents on foreign exchange accounts for the credit or debit of international transactions.

FINANCIAL FREEDOM — NOT GRADED

The banking system is unstable, and banks that function have been hurt by war, political instability, unpredictable monetary policy, and unrecoverable loans. In 2005, the International Monetary Fund noted that transparency, commercial bank liquidity, and an improved judicial framework were necessary for significant improvement. Most banks act as financial agents for the government or extend credit to international institutions operating in the country. As much as 70 percent of the currency is in U.S. dollars and therefore outside the banking system. Of the 12 commercial banks, five are being restructured. Another nine banks are being liquidated. Larger banks are mostly subsidiaries of foreign banks. Supervision is very poor, and most banks fail to meet basic prudential standards. Most credit is informal. There is no stock exchange.

PROPERTY RIGHTS — NOT GRADED

Private property is not secure. Local conflicts are common, and fighting, banditry, and abuses of human rights threaten property rights and deter economic activity. Courts suffer from widespread corruption, the public administration is unreliable, and expatriates and nationals are subject to selective application of a complex legal code. Although there is greater political stability now that five years of conflict have subsided with the help of international peacekeepers, the government faces challenges to its authority in some eastern areas where armed groups still hold sway.

FREEDOM FROM CORRUPTION — NOT GRADED

Corruption is perceived as rampant. The Democratic Republic of Congo ranks 156th out of 163 countries in Transparency International's Corruption Perceptions Index for 2006. Corruption and governmental policies have given rise to parallel economies. Law-abiding formal-sector citizens and businesses pay their taxes, causing operating expenses to rise. Because tax laws are enforced arbitrarily, many people and enterprises have moved to the informal sector, which accounts for more than 80 percent of economic activity and encourages more corruption.

LABOR FREEDOM — NOT GRADED

Formal-sector employment is negligible. The formal labor market operates under highly restrictive employment regulations that hinder employment and productivity growth. The non-salary cost of employing a worker is low, but dismissing a redundant employee is costly. Enforcement of existing laws is often inconsistent.

CONGO, REPUBLIC OF

Brazzaville

The Republic of Congo's economy is 45.2 percent free, according to our 2008 assessment, which makes it the world's 146th freest economy. Its overall score is 0.8 percentage point higher than last year, reflecting improved trade freedom and government size. Congo is ranked 38th out of 40 countries in the sub-Saharan Africa region, and its overall score is lower than the regional average.

Congo ranks strongly only in government expenditures, which are low in formal terms, although this is likely a sign of government weakness, not efficiency. The top income tax rate is 50 percent, and the top corporate tax rate is 38 percent, but overall tax revenue is relatively small as a percentage of GDP. Low inflation and stable prices help Congo's monetary freedom score, but the government interference with market prices is extensive.

Congo scores poorly in investment freedom, financial freedom, property rights, freedom from corruption, and labor freedom. Foreign investment restrictions, domestic regulations, and an inflexible labor market create a hostile business climate. The worst barrier to development is a profound lack of property rights.

BACKGROUND: Congo underwent a series of coups after gaining its independence in 1960. President Denis Sassou-Nguesso governed the country as a Marxist–Leninist state for two decades before moderating economic policy and making the transition to multi-party democracy in 1992. He was defeated in 1992 by Pascal Lissouba but seized power in 1997 and won a 2002 election. Since the 2003 peace accord between the government and most rebel groups, slow progress has been made toward a more market-oriented economy, but poor infrastructure, corruption, and onerous regulation discourage investment. The government has resisted World Bank pressure to improve transparency in the oil sector. Oil accounted for 44 percent of GDP, over 90 percent of exports, and over 85 percent of government revenue in 2005.

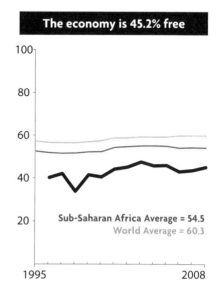

The economy is 45.2% free

Sub-Saharan Africa Average = 54.5
World Average = 60.3

QUICK FACTS

Population: 3.8 million

GDP (PPP): $5.0 billion
7.7% growth in 2005
4.2% 5-yr. comp. ann. growth
$1,262 per capita

Unemployment: n/a

Inflation (CPI): 2.5%

FDI (net flow): $402.0 million

Official Development Assistance:
Multilateral: $101.2 million
Bilateral: $1.5 billion (1.3% from the U.S.)

External Debt: $5.9 billion

Exports: $5.0 billion
Primarily diamonds, copper, crude oil, coffee, cobalt

Imports: $2.9 billion
Primarily foodstuffs, mining and other machinery, transport equipment, fuels

How Do We Measure Economic Freedom? See Chapter 4 (page 39) for an explanation of the methodology or visit the *Index* Web site at *heritage.org/index*.

2005 data unless otherwise noted.

REPUBLIC OF CONGO'S TEN ECONOMIC FREEDOMS

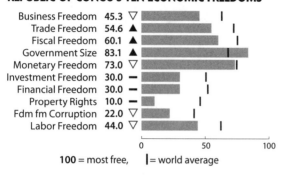

Business Freedom	45.3 ▽	
Trade Freedom	54.6 ▲	
Fiscal Freedom	60.1 ▲	
Government Size	83.1 ▲	
Monetary Freedom	73.0 ▽	
Investment Freedom	30.0 —	
Financial Freedom	30.0 —	
Property Rights	10.0 —	
Fdm fm Corruption	22.0 ▽	
Labor Freedom	44.0 ▽	

0   50   100

100 = most free,   ▌= world average

BUSINESS FREEDOM — 45.3%

The overall freedom to start, operate, and close a business is very limited by Congo's national regulatory environment. Starting a business takes an average of 37 days, compared to the world average of 43 days. The cost of launching a business is high, and legal and regulatory non-transparency impedes entrepreneurial activity. Obtaining a business license requires less than the world average of 19 procedures and 234 days. Closing a business is relatively easy but costly.

TRADE FREEDOM — 54.6%

Congo's weighted average tariff rate was 17.7 percent in 2005. Import and export quotas, restrictive import licensing rules, bureaucracy, government export promotion programs, an inefficient customs service, and corruption add to the cost of trade. An additional 10 percentage points is deducted from Congo's trade freedom score to adjust for these non-tariff barriers.

FISCAL FREEDOM — 60.1%

Congo has a very high income tax rate and a high corporate tax rate. The top income tax rate is 50 percent, and the top corporate tax rate is 38 percent. Other taxes include a value-added tax (VAT), a tax on rental values, and an apprenticeship tax. In the most recent year, overall tax revenue as a percentage of GDP was 6.7 percent.

GOVERNMENT SIZE — 83.1%

Total government expenditures, including consumption and transfer payments, are moderate. In the most recent year, government spending equaled 23.7 percent of GDP. Public-sector reform and privatization have made only marginal progress because of political turmoil.

MONETARY FREEDOM — 73%

Inflation is moderate, averaging 3.6 percent between 2004 and 2006. Relatively unstable prices explain most of the monetary freedom score. The prices of rail transport, telecommunications, electricity, water, and other goods and services are affected by government ownership and subsidization of the large public sector. An additional 15 percentage points is deducted from Congo's monetary freedom score to adjust for measures that distort domestic prices.

INVESTMENT FREEDOM — 30%

Congo's investment climate, particularly in the non-oil sector, is dismal. The administrative burden and corruption are major impediments. Energy prices have raised government revenues, and closer commercial links with non-traditional donors, especially China, make reform less likely. Investments of over CFAF 100 million require Ministry of Economy, Finance, and Budget approval within 30 days unless they involve creation of an enterprise with public–private ownership. Residents may not hold foreign exchange accounts, but companies may hold foreign exchange accounts with special approval. Non-residents may hold foreign exchange accounts subject to government approval. Payments and transfers to most countries are subject to documentation requirements.

FINANCIAL FREEDOM — 30%

Congo's financial sector is small, underdeveloped, and hurt by instability. Development of the banking sector has been stunted by war, poor management, bad loans, and political interference. Congo and the other five members of the Central African Economic and Monetary Community share a common central bank. In December 2004, the joint Commission bancaire de l'Afrique Centrale, which regulates Congo's commercial banks, considered two of Congo's four banks to be in good condition, the third to be fragile, and the fourth to be critical. The government took over the fourth bank but plans to reprivatize it after recapitalization. The state is still dealing with non-performing loans accumulated by state-owned banks before privatization because of poor management and political interference.

PROPERTY RIGHTS — 10%

The 1997–2003 civil war left the judiciary corrupt, overburdened, underfinanced, subject to political influence and bribery, and almost without judicial records. Security of contracts and the enforcement of justice cannot be guaranteed, and protection of intellectual property rights is virtually nonexistent. In rural areas, traditional courts handle many local disputes, especially those involving inheritance and property.

FREEDOM FROM CORRUPTION — 22%

Corruption is perceived as pervasive. The Republic of Congo ranks 142nd out of 163 countries in Transparency International's Corruption Perceptions Index for 2006. Corruption is seen as permeating the government. The World Bank and the International Monetary Fund note financial non-transparency, inadequate internal controls and accounting systems, and conflicts of interest in the state-owned oil company's marketing of oil. Low-level corruption by security personnel and customs and immigrations officials is said to be pervasive.

LABOR FREEDOM — 44%

Burdensome employment regulations hinder employment opportunities and productivity growth. The non-salary cost of employing a worker is high, but dismissing a redundant employee can be relatively costless. Restrictions on increasing or contracting the number of working hours are very rigid. Congo's labor flexibility is one of the world's lowest.

COSTA RICA

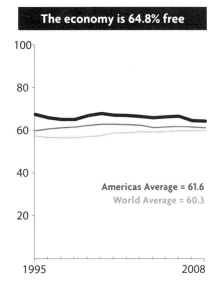

Costa Rica's economy is 64.8 percent free, according to our 2008 assessment, which makes it the world's 49th freest economy. Its overall score is 0.2 percentage point higher than last year. Costa Rica is ranked 11th out of 29 countries in the Americas, and its overall score is higher than the regional average.

Costa Rica scores well in investment freedom and government size. The economy ranks above average in six of 10 areas. Personal and corporate tax rates are moderate, and tax revenue is fairly low as a percentage of GDP. Other factors, including trade freedom, where it boasts a low average tariff rate, also score moderately well.

Costa Rica could improve its monetary freedom and financial freedom. State-owned banks dominate the financial sector. The court system, while transparent and not corrupt, is extremely time-consuming and complicated.

BACKGROUND: Costa Rica is a democracy but does not enjoy robust democratic capitalism. Since 1980, economic growth has been hurt by staggeringly high interest rates, heavy debt service requirements, 18 percent average annual inflation, and a bloated public sector. Former President Oscar Arias (1986–1990) was narrowly elected for a second time in February 2006 and pledged to break up state monopolies in telecommunications, utilities, petroleum, refining, banking, insurance, and social security pensions. His gradual and heavily regulated "openness" approach to privatization, however, has lacked momentum. Arias promises both to balance the budget and to ratify by referendum the already signed Central America–Dominican Republic–United States Free Trade Agreement in 2007. Costa Rica is the only CAFTA–DR partner for which the agreement is not yet in force. Hard-left Venezuelan President Hugo Chávez has supported opponents of the agreement.

How Do We Measure Economic Freedom? See Chapter 4 (page 39) for an explanation of the methodology or visit the *Index* Web site at *heritage.org/index*.

The economy is 64.8% free

Americas Average = 61.6
World Average = 60.3

1995   2008

QUICK FACTS

Population: 4.3 million

GDP (PPP): $44.1 billion
5.9% growth in 2005
4.9% 5-yr. comp. ann. growth
$10,180 per capita

Unemployment: 6.5%

Inflation (CPI): 13.8%

FDI (net flow): $696.0 million

Official Development Assistance:
Multilateral: $15.3 million
Bilateral: $57.3 million (5.5% from the U.S.)

External Debt: $6.2 billion

Exports: $9.7 billion
Primarily bananas, pineapples, coffee, melons, ornamental plants, sugar, textiles, electronic components, medical equipment

Imports: $10.7 billion
Primarily raw materials, consumer goods, capital equipment, petroleum
2005 data unless otherwise noted.

COSTA RICA'S TEN ECONOMIC FREEDOMS

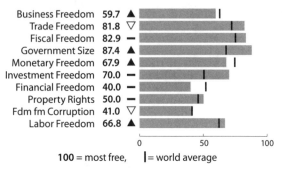

Business Freedom	59.7 ▲
Trade Freedom	81.8 ▽
Fiscal Freedom	82.9 ▲
Government Size	87.4 ▲
Monetary Freedom	67.9 ▲
Investment Freedom	70.0 —
Financial Freedom	40.0 —
Property Rights	50.0 —
Fdm fm Corruption	41.0 ▽
Labor Freedom	66.8 ▲

100 = most free, ❙ = world average

BUSINESS FREEDOM — *59.7%*

The overall freedom to start, operate, and close a business remains limited by Costa Rica's national regulatory environment. Starting a business takes an average of 77 days, compared to the world average of 43 days. Obtaining a business license requires less than the world average of 234 days. Bureaucratic procedures discourage entrepreneurial activities, and the process for closing a business is relatively lengthy.

TRADE FREEDOM — *81.8%*

Costa Rica's weighted average tariff rate was 4.1 percent in 2005. Despite an electronic one-stop import and export window and other improvements, customs processing procedures remain complex and bureaucratic. Sanitary and phytosanitary requirements, some export controls, service market access restrictions, peak tariffs, export promotion programs, and issues involving the protection of intellectual property rights add to the cost of trade. An additional 10 percentage points is deducted from Costa Rica's trade freedom score to account for these non-tariff barriers.

FISCAL FREEDOM — *82.9%*

Costa Rica has moderate tax rates. The top income tax rate is 25 percent, and the top corporate tax rate is 30 percent. Other taxes include a general sales tax and a tax on interest. In the most recent year, overall tax revenue as a percentage of GDP was 13.6 percent.

GOVERNMENT SIZE — *87.4%*

Total government expenditures, including consumption and transfer payments, are moderate. In the most recent year, government spending equaled 20.5 percent of GDP. A state-led economic development model has generated relative prosperity, but the complicated structure of state agencies is costly. Privatization is slow in the face of popular opposition.

MONETARY FREEDOM — *67.9%*

Inflation is relatively high, averaging 12.1 percent between 2004 and 2006. Relatively unstable prices explain most of the monetary freedom score. The government controls the prices of goods on a basic consumption list, including energy, petroleum, telecommunications, and water. An additional 10 percentage points is deducted from Costa Rica's monetary freedom score to adjust for measures that distort domestic prices.

INVESTMENT FREEDOM — *70%*

Costa Rica has one of Central America's better investment climates and treats foreign and domestic investors equally. A few sectors, such as insurance, telecommunications, hydrocarbons, and radioactive materials, are reserved for state companies; a few others, such as broadcasting and electrical power generation, require participation of a certain number of Costa Ricans. There are no restrictions on land purchases, although some expropriation of land owned by foreign investors has occurred. Political and economic stability and a skilled workforce are inducements, but litigation and dispute resolution can be protracted and costly. There are no controls on capital flows, but reporting requirements are mandatory for some transactions. There are no restrictions or controls on the holding of foreign exchange accounts, readily transferable and available at market clearing rates, by either residents or non-residents.

FINANCIAL FREEDOM — *40%*

The 15 private banks in Costa Rica's government-influenced financial system operate freely, but the three state-owned banks dominate the sector and account for 54 percent of assets. About half of the private banks are owned by foreign investors, and dollar-denominated lending is common. Nearly all Costa Rican banks have significant offshore banking operations. Credit is available on market terms, but the government retains considerable influence over lending, especially for projects deemed to be in the public interest. Accounting is transparent and compatible with international norms. The state-owned Instituto Nacional de Seguros monopolizes insurance, but other institutions may sell its underwritten policies. The pension system is partially privatized. Capital markets are small, and most trading involves government debt.

PROPERTY RIGHTS — *50%*

The judicial system can be slow and complicated. Contracts are generally upheld, and investments are secure, but it takes an average of more than 1.5 years to resolve a contract-related legal complaint. Resolution of squatter cases can be especially cumbersome; the system quickly recognizes rights acquired by squatters, especially when land is rural and not actively worked. Enforcement of laws protecting intellectual property rights is often ineffective.

FREEDOM FROM CORRUPTION — *41%*

Corruption is perceived as present. Costa Rica ranks 55th out of 163 countries in Transparency International's Corruption Perceptions Index for 2006. The government does not assign nearly enough resources to enforce anti-corruption laws, regulations, and penalties. Some foreign firms have complained of corruption in the administration of public tenders.

LABOR FREEDOM — *66.8%*

Relatively flexible employment regulations could be improved for further employment opportunities and productivity growth. The non-salary cost of employing a worker is high, but dismissing a redundant employee is relatively costless. Regulations on modifying working hours are flexible.

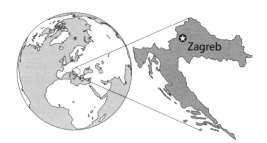
Zagreb

CROATIA

Rank: 113

Regional Rank: 37 of 41

Croatia's economy is 54.6 percent free, according to our 2008 assessment, which makes it the world's 113th freest economy. Its overall score is roughly 0.7 percentage point higher than last year, reflecting marginal improvements in business freedom and government size. Croatia is ranked 37th out of 41 countries in the European region, and its overall score is below the regional average.

Croatia scores slightly above average in trade freedom, financial freedom, and monetary freedom. Inflation is low, and prices are fairly stable, but Croatia's monetary freedom score is hurt by lingering government price manipulations.

Croatia's most glaring weakness in terms of economic freedom is its outsized government. This shows up in other areas, notably heavy regulations on business, labor, and even rights to property. The court system is prone to corruption, political interference, and inefficient bureaucracy, and some investors prefer international arbitration. Significant unofficial restrictions on foreign investment, such as highly politicized decision-making, exist for investors willing to brave the regulatory maze.

BACKGROUND: Croatia declared its independence from Yugoslavia in 1991 and after years of regional conflict has emerged as a strong candidate for full membership in both NATO and the European Union. However, key reforms have recently slowed, marking a decline in overall economic freedom and an increase in political corruption as noted by both the World Bank and the EU. The EU views the failure to carry out judicial reform as a central long-term obstacle to Croatia's possible membership, and additional economic reforms are also needed to complete the transition to a full market economy.

How Do We Measure Economic Freedom? See Chapter 4 (page 39) for an explanation of the methodology or visit the *Index* Web site at *heritage.org/index.*

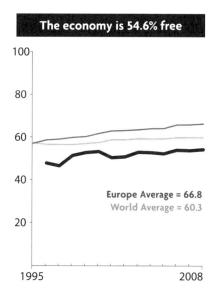

The economy is 54.6% free

Europe Average = 66.8
World Average = 60.3

1995   2008

QUICK FACTS

Population: 4.4 million

GDP (PPP): $57.9 billion
4.3% growth in 2005
4.7% 5-yr. comp. ann. growth
$13,041 per capita

Unemployment: 18.0%

Inflation (CPI): 3.3%

FDI (net flow): $1.5 billion

Official Development Assistance:
Multilateral: $60.8 million
Bilateral: $75.3 million (29.3% from the U.S.)

External Debt: $30.2 billion

Exports: $18.9 billion
Primarily transport equipment, textiles, chemicals, foodstuffs, fuels

Imports: $21.7 billion
Primarily machinery, transport and electrical equipment, chemicals, fuels and lubricants, foodstuffs

2005 data unless otherwise noted.

CROATIA'S TEN ECONOMIC FREEDOMS

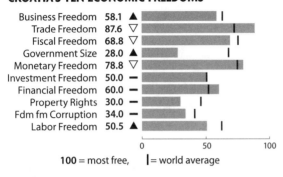

Business Freedom	58.1	▲
Trade Freedom	87.6	▽
Fiscal Freedom	68.8	▽
Government Size	28.0	▲
Monetary Freedom	78.8	▽
Investment Freedom	50.0	—
Financial Freedom	60.0	—
Property Rights	30.0	—
Fdm fm Corruption	34.0	—
Labor Freedom	50.5	▲

100 = most free, ▌ = world average

BUSINESS FREEDOM — 58.1%

The overall freedom to start, operate, and close a business is constrained by Croatia's national regulatory environment. Starting a business takes an average of 40 days, compared to the world average of 43 days. Obtaining a business license takes more than the world average of 19 procedures and 234 days. Burdensome and non-transparent administrative regulations, particularly at the local level, continue to challenge entrepreneurs. Closing a business is relatively simple.

TRADE FREEDOM — 87.6%

Croatia's weighted average tariff rate was 1.2 percent in 2005. Targeted restrictions on imported agriculture products, strict testing and certification requirements for some imports, and customs administration that can be inefficient and prone to corruption add to the cost of trade. An additional 10 percentage points is deducted from Croatia's trade freedom score to account for these non-tariff barriers.

FISCAL FREEDOM — 68.8%

Croatia has a high income tax rate but a low corporate tax rate. The top income tax rate is 45 percent, and the top corporate tax rate is 20 percent. The government also imposes a value-added tax (VAT). In the most recent year, overall tax revenue as a percentage of GDP was 26.4 percent.

GOVERNMENT SIZE — 28%

Total government expenditures, including consumption and transfer payments, are very high. In the most recent year, government spending equaled 49 percent of GDP. Government spending and wage bills and subsidies have contributed significantly to an increase in overall indebtedness that has reached over 80 percent of GDP in recent years. Privatization has progressed slowly.

MONETARY FREEDOM — 78.8%

Inflation is moderate, averaging 3.1 percent between 2004 and 2006. Relatively unstable prices explain most of the monetary freedom score. Many price supports and subsidies have been eliminated, but price changes on some 30 products, including milk and bread, must be submitted to the Ministry of Economy for approval. The government is also able to influence prices through state-owned enterprises. An additional 10 percentage points is deducted from Croatia's monetary freedom score to adjust for measures that distort domestic prices.

INVESTMENT FREEDOM — 50%

Foreigners may invest in nearly every sector of the economy, but because of a complex bureaucracy, very slow and opaque legal system, and subsidies to state-owned enterprises, personal and political loyalty can trump economic merit in establishing a competitive investment. Residents and non-residents may hold foreign exchange accounts, but there are numerous limitations, and government approval is required in certain instances. Though government expropriation for public purposes is legal, it has not occurred since Croatia became independent. The privatization fund has stakes in 1,012 companies, which are slowly being sold. Some capital transactions, such as inward portfolio investment, are subject to government conditions.

FINANCIAL FREEDOM — 60%

Croatia's financial system is stable and competitive. There were 34 commercial banks and five savings banks in 2006. Two national commercial banks are majority foreign-owned and control almost half of assets; overall, foreign banks own over 90 percent of banking system assets. Privatization and regulatory improvement have done much to reestablish confidence in the banking sector, which was shaken by a series of failure shocks in 1998. Many banking assets are foreign-owned, and newly adopted financial regulations harmonize with European Union standards. The small insurance sector is highly competitive, but the partially state-owned Croatia Osiguranje accounts for 47 percent of assets. The stock exchange has been growing rapidly, and securities markets are open to foreign investors.

PROPERTY RIGHTS — 30%

Observers view the judicial system as most affected by corruption. The court system is cumbersome and inefficient, and long case backlogs cause business disputes to drag on for years. Some investors insist that contract arbitration take place outside of Croatia. The government is committed to judicial reform, but much remains to be done. Croatia has intellectual property rights legislation but fails to protect IPR fully.

FREEDOM FROM CORRUPTION — 34%

Corruption is perceived as significant. Croatia ranks 69th out of 163 countries in Transparency International's Corruption Perceptions Index for 2006. The government has initiated a process to overhaul the principal sources of corruption: the judicial system, the health system, local governments, political party financing, public administration, and economic agencies.

LABOR FREEDOM — 50.5%

Croatia's labor market remains inflexible due to burdensome employment regulations that limit employment and productivity growth. The non-salary cost of employing a worker is high, and dismissing a redundant employee is relatively costly. The labor code mandates retraining or replacement before firing a worker. The cost of laying off a worker creates a risk aversion for companies that would otherwise hire more people and grow.

CUBA

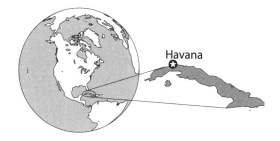

Havana

Cuba's economy is 27.5 percent free, according to our 2008 assessment, which makes it one of the world's most repressed economies, ahead of only North Korea. Its overall score is 1.1 percentage points lower than last year, mainly reflecting worsened government size and freedom from corruption. Cuba is ranked 29th out of 29 countries in the Americas, and its overall score is less than half of the regional average.

Cuba performs least egregiously in corruption, trade freedom, and monetary freedom. It has a moderate average tariff of 10 percent but very restrictive non-tariff barriers to trade. Inflation is moderate, but government efforts to control prices are pervasive.

Business freedom, investment freedom, financial freedom, property rights, freedom from corruption, and labor freedom are all weak. The Communist government dictates economic policy, all aspects of business are tightly controlled and government-dominated, and the private sector is very small. No courts are free of political interference, and private property (particularly land) is strictly regulated by the state.

BACKGROUND: A one-party Communist state with a command economy, Cuba depends heavily on external assistance and a captive labor force. Fidel Castro's government restricts basic human rights, such as freedom of expression and property ownership, and holds hundreds of political prisoners in harsh conditions. Little reliable, independent information is available, and official figures on per capita GDP may not reflect actual income. In July 2006, an ailing Castro handed over provisional authority to his younger brother Raul, who has signaled some moderation of Cuba's traditional Communist policies, but any significant increase in political or economic freedom appears unlikely at this time. Venezuelan oil has enabled Cuba to retreat on the limited reforms undertaken in the mid-1990s to recentralize the economy, throwing new obstacles into the path of foreign investors.

How Do We Measure Economic Freedom? See Chapter 4 (page 39) for an explanation of the methodology or visit the *Index* Web site at *heritage.org/index*.

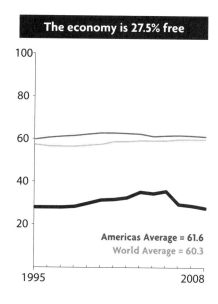

The economy is 27.5% free

Americas Average = 61.6
World Average = 60.3

1995 — 2008

QUICK FACTS

Population: 11.3 million

GDP (PPP): $45.5 billion
8.6 % growth in 2005
5-yr. comp. ann. growth n/a
$4,000 per capita

Unemployment: 1.9%

Inflation (CPI): 7.0 %

FDI (net flow): −$1.0 million

Official Development Assistance:
Multilateral: $18.9 million
Bilateral: $68.9 million (14.7% from the U.S.)

External Debt: $15.2 billion

Exports: $2.1 billion
Primarily sugar, nickel, tobacco, fish, medical products, citrus, coffee

Imports: $7.9 billion
Primarily petroleum, food, machinery and equipment, chemicals

2005 data unless otherwise noted.

CUBA'S TEN ECONOMIC FREEDOMS

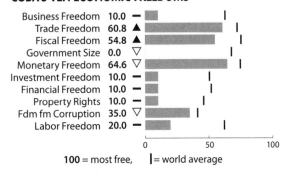

Business Freedom	10.0 —
Trade Freedom	60.8 ▲
Fiscal Freedom	54.8 ▲
Government Size	0.0 ▽
Monetary Freedom	64.6 ▽
Investment Freedom	10.0 —
Financial Freedom	10.0 —
Property Rights	10.0 —
Fdm fm Corruption	35.0 ▽
Labor Freedom	20.0 —

0   50   100

100 = most free, | = world average

BUSINESS FREEDOM — 10%

The overall freedom to start, operate, and close a business is seriously limited by Cuba's national regulatory environment. The government controls the economy, and only limited private entrepreneurship exists. Inconsistently and non-transparently applied regulations impede the creation of entrepreneurial activities.

TRADE FREEDOM — 60.8%

Cuba's weighted average tariff rate was 9.6 percent in 2005. Procedures for the allocation of hard currency and centralizing of imports have caused delays and bottlenecks, the trade regime remains largely non-transparent, and customs corruption is common. An additional 20 percentage points is deducted from Cuba's trade freedom score to account for these non-tariff barriers.

FISCAL FREEDOM — 54.8%

Cuba has a high income tax rate of 50 percent. The top corporate tax rate is 30 percent (levied at 35 percent for companies with entirely foreign capital). In the most recent year, overall tax revenue as a percentage of GDP equaled 33.4 percent.

GOVERNMENT SIZE — 0%

Total government expenditures, including consumption and transfer payments, are very high. In the most recent year, government spending equaled 71.6 percent of GDP. The state produces most economic output and accounts for about 75 percent of total employment. The industrial and services sectors are largely dominated by the state.

MONETARY FREEDOM — 64.6%

Inflation is moderate, averaging 6 percent between 2004 and 2006. Relatively moderate prices explain most of the monetary freedom score. The government determines prices for most goods and services and subsidizes much of the economy, although some private and black market retail activity is not government-controlled. An additional 20 percentage points is deducted from Cuba's monetary freedom score to adjust for measures that distort domestic prices.

INVESTMENT FREEDOM — 10%

The government maintains exchange controls. All investments must be approved by the government, and all businesses must be licensed. The government has backtracked on limited liberalization of foreign investment, citing a revised policy of "selectivity." New investment is expected to target certain sectors, such as energy, mining, and tourism. Other deterrents include delayed payments from Cuban enterprises and onerous regulations. By the end of 2005, 60 of 313 "international economic associations" had been shut down because of alleged failure to fulfill their objectives. Some restrictions have been loosened to permit investment commitments and credit lines from China and Venezuela.

FINANCIAL FREEDOM — 10%

Despite a decade of incremental changes in the financial sector, the government remains in control. The Cuban peso is the domestic currency, and a separate convertible peso is hard currency for foreign exchange and non-essential retail. Over a dozen foreign banks have opened offices but are not allowed to operate freely. New products, such as travel and medical insurance and personal pensions, are being introduced. The government established a central bank in 1997 and converted the Banco Nacional de Cuba into one of a new set of state banks. Central bank authority was enhanced in 2005 to allow closer control of the use of hard currency and convertible pesos. Foreign-currency bonds were first listed on the London Stock Exchange in 2006. Credit and insurance markets are heavily controlled by the central government.

PROPERTY RIGHTS — 10%

Cuban citizens may enjoy private ownership of land and productive capital for farming and self-employment. The constitution subordinates the courts to the National Assembly of People's Power (NAPP) and the Council of State, headed by Fidel Castro. The NAPP and its lower-level counterparts choose all judges. The law and trial practices do not meet international standards for fair public trials. The Castro regime has retreated from earlier market reforms and is seeking tighter state control of the economy.

FREEDOM FROM CORRUPTION — 35%

Corruption is perceived as significant. Cuba ranks 66th out of 163 countries in Transparency International's Corruption Perceptions Index for 2006. Independent and official press sources have reported incidents of government corruption. For example, customs officials have requested unauthorized fees illegally or have confiscated the belongings of citizens legally residing overseas who were returning to Cuba after visiting relatives, and senior officials in large state-run tourism organizations have been jailed for corruption.

LABOR FREEDOM — 20%

Rigid employment regulations hinder employment and productivity growth. The formal labor market is not fully developed, and the rigid government-controlled labor market has helped to create a large informal economy. A labor code drafted in 2006, which enhances the efficiency of entrepreneurial activities and contains strict penalties for the use of work time for personal benefit, took effect in April 2007.

CYPRUS (GREEK)

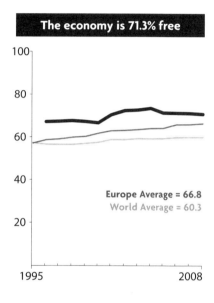

The economy is 71.3% free

Europe Average = 66.8
World Average = 60.3

1995 — 2008

Cyprus's economy is 71.3 percent free, according to our 2008 assessment, which makes it the world's 22nd freest economy. Its overall score is 0.4 percentage point lower than last year, reflecting slightly lower scores in four of 10 economic freedoms. Cyprus is ranked 11th out of 41 countries in the European region, and its overall score is higher than the regional average.

Cyprus scores above average in nine categories. The economy enjoys world-class property rights and solid investment, monetary, trade, labor, business, and financial freedom. The judiciary is independent. The labor market is relatively flexible, with moderate severance packages and unemployment benefits. Inflation and average tariff rates are low, although monetary and trade freedom are muted by adherence to the standard EU subsidies of agriculture. The financial market is sound and open to foreign competition.

High government expenditures are the primary weakness. Total government expenditures amount to more than two-fifths of GDP.

BACKGROUND: Cyprus is divided between the Greek Cypriot Republic of Cyprus and the Turkish Republic of Northern Cyprus. The Republic of Cyprus acts as the internationally recognized administration of Cyprus, and hostility between the two sides is deep. The Greek Cypriot economy is dominated by services, especially tourism and financial services, and restrictions have been lifted for foreign investors. Economic liberalization was enhanced in 2004 with membership in the European Union, although privatization has yet to occur in such key sectors as telecommunications and utilities. Fiscal policy has been focused on consolidating the budget to prepare for entry into the Economic and Monetary Union on January 1, 2008.

How Do We Measure Economic Freedom? See Chapter 4 (page 39) for an explanation of the methodology or visit the *Index* Web site at *heritage.org/index.*

QUICK FACTS

Population: 0.8 million

GDP (PPP): $21 billion
3.9% growth in 2005
3.0% 5-yr. comp. ann. growth
$27,765 per capita

Unemployment: 5.3%

Inflation (CPI): 2.6%

FDI (net flow): $734.0 million

Official Development Assistance:
Multilateral: n/a
Bilateral: n/a

External Debt: $12.6 billion

Exports: $8.0 billion
Primarily citrus, potatoes, pharmaceuticals, cement, clothing, cigarettes

Imports: $8.5 billion
Primarily consumer goods, petroleum and lubricants, intermediate goods, machinery, transport equipment

2005 data unless otherwise noted.

CYPRUS'S TEN ECONOMIC FREEDOMS

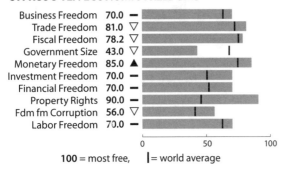

Business Freedom	70.0 —
Trade Freedom	81.0 ▽
Fiscal Freedom	78.2 ▽
Government Size	43.0 ▽
Monetary Freedom	85.0 ▲
Investment Freedom	70.0 —
Financial Freedom	70.0 —
Property Rights	90.0 —
Fdm fm Corruption	56.0 ▽
Labor Freedom	70.0 —

0   50   100

100 = most free,   ▮ = world average

BUSINESS FREEDOM — 70%

The overall freedom to start, operate, and close a business is relatively well protected by the national regulatory environment. Establishing a business is relatively easy. Regulations have been streamlined, administrative procedures have been simplified, and regulations affecting business are transparent and consistently applied. Cyprus has been pursuing policies designed to support a favorable business environment and private initiative.

TRADE FREEDOM — 81%

Cyprus's trade policy is the same as those of other members of the European Union. The common EU weighted average tariff rate was 2 percent in 2005. Non-tariff barriers reflected in EU policy include agricultural and manufacturing subsidies, import restrictions for some goods and services, market access restrictions in some service sectors, non-transparent and restrictive regulations and standards, and inconsistent customs administration across EU members. Enforcement of intellectual property rights remains problematic, and there is a growing dichotomy between the trade regimes of Greek-controlled and Turkish-controlled Cyprus. Consequently, an additional 15 percentage points is deducted from Cyprus's trade freedom score.

FISCAL FREEDOM — 78.2%

Cyprus has a moderate income tax rate and a very low corporate tax rate. The top income tax rate is 30 percent, and the top corporate tax rate is 10 percent. Other taxes include a value-added tax (VAT) and a real estate tax. In the most recent year, tax revenue as a percentage of GDP was 34.4 percent.

GOVERNMENT SIZE — 43%

Total government expenditures, including consumption and transfer payments, are high. In the most recent year, government spending equaled 43.6 percent of GDP. For two decades, budget deficits have tended to be around 5 percent of GDP, although fiscal consolidation has lowered the deficit more recently.

MONETARY FREEDOM — 85%

Inflation is relatively low, averaging 2.5 percent between 2004 and 2006. Relatively stable prices explain most of the monetary freedom score. As a participant in the EU's Common Agricultural Policy, the government subsidizes agricultural production, distorting the prices of agricultural products. An additional 5 percentage points is deducted from Cyprus's monetary freedom score to adjust for this policy.

INVESTMENT FREEDOM — 70%

The government grants national treatment to foreign investors. Cyprus has a stable macroeconomic environment, skilled English-speaking workforce, excellent telecommunications, and a modern legal and regulatory framework. Non-EU investors may invest directly or indirectly in most sectors. Remaining exceptions involve the acquisition of property and investments in tertiary education, banking (for Cypriots and non-Cypriots), and mass media. Accession to the EU has further reduced barriers to investment, though some have been replaced by EU-wide barriers. EU residents may own 100 percent of local companies and any company listed on the stock exchange. Some payments, current transfers, and capital transactions are subject to central bank approval or restriction.

FINANCIAL FREEDOM — 70%

Cyprus's financial sector is diverse and relatively sound. In compliance with EU requirements, the central bank is fully independent. As of January 2007, there were 11 domestic banks, two foreign bank branches, and 27 international banking units. Two largely government-owned specialty banks are minor parts of the system. The government lifted exchange controls and abolished the interest rate ceiling in 2001. The insurance sector is recovering from an equity market downturn in the early 2000s. The stock exchange still suffers from a lack of trust caused by a speculative bubble that was encouraged by ineffective regulation.

PROPERTY RIGHTS — 90%

Contracts and property rights are enforced effectively. The civil judiciary, including the Supreme Court (which carries out the functions of a constitutional court, a high court of appeal, and an administrative court), is independent constitutionally but not always in practice. Intellectual property rights are not adequately protected in the area administered by Turkish Cypriots. Real property remains one of the key contested issues on the divided island.

FREEDOM FROM CORRUPTION — 56%

Corruption is perceived as present. Cyprus ranks 37th out of 163 countries in Transparency International's Corruption Perceptions Index for 2006. Some foreign companies have complained of a lack of transparency and possible bias in government consideration of competing bids.

LABOR FREEDOM — 70%

Relatively flexible employment regulations could be improved to enhance employment and productivity growth. Government intervention in labor relations is limited to setting minimum standards for the terms and conditions of employment. Unemployment benefits last for six months. A mandatory earnings-related social security scheme applies to both employed and self-employed individuals. The government mandates a minimum wage.

CZECH REPUBLIC

Prague

The Czech Republic's economy is 68.5 percent free, according to our 2008 assessment, which makes it the world's 37th freest economy. Its overall score is 0.8 percentage point higher than last year. The Czech Republic is ranked 21st out of 41 countries in the European region, and its overall score is higher than the regional average.

The Czech Republic scores above average in eight economic freedoms, especially finance, investment, and property rights. Trade freedom is also relatively strong. Inflation is very low, though the government maintains some price supports. The extensive banking sector includes significant foreign ownership, and financial services are highly developed. Labor flexibility is fairly high, though hiring and firing workers can be costly.

A recently approved flat personal income tax of 15 percent, effective in early January 2008, could significantly enhance the Czech Republic's future economic freedom score. Very large government expenditures make its government size score 22 percentage points below the world average.

BACKGROUND: The Czech Republic separated from Slovakia and became an independent nation in 1993. Since 2006, no party has won a clear mandate, and close elections have resulted in political deadlock, slowing the pace of economic reform. Economic growth over the past five years has relied heavily on exports to the European Union. Traditionally, the Czech Republic has had a strong manufacturing sector, but tourism also plays a central role in the economy. Real GDP growth has continued to rise around 5.5 percent to 6 percent annually since the initiation of significant financial and enterprise reforms in 2000. GDP growth has been sustained primarily by high domestic demand.

How Do We Measure Economic Freedom? See Chapter 4 (page 39) for an explanation of the methodology or visit the *Index* Web site at *heritage.org/index*.

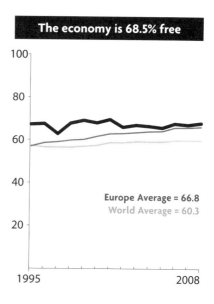

The economy is 68.5% free

Europe Average = 66.8
World Average = 60.3

1995 — 2008

QUICK FACTS

Population: 10.2 million

GDP (PPP): $210.2 billion
6.1% growth in 2005
3.9% 5-yr. comp. ann. growth
$20,538 per capita

Unemployment: 8.9%

Inflation (CPI): 1.8%

FDI (net flow): $10.1 billion

Official Development Assistance:
Multilateral: n/a
Bilateral: n/a

External Debt: $50.2 billion

Exports: $89.0 billion
Primarily machinery and transport equipment, chemicals, raw materials and fuels

Imports: $86.5 billion
Primarily machinery and transport equipment, raw materials and fuels, chemicals

2005 data unless otherwise noted.

CZECH REPUBLIC'S TEN ECONOMIC FREEDOMS

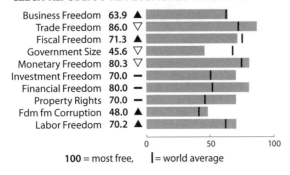

Business Freedom	63.9	▲
Trade Freedom	86.0	▽
Fiscal Freedom	71.3	▲
Government Size	45.6	▽
Monetary Freedom	80.3	▽
Investment Freedom	70.0	—
Financial Freedom	80.0	—
Property Rights	70.0	—
Fdm fm Corruption	48.0	▲
Labor Freedom	70.2	▲

0   50   100

100 = most free, ▌= world average

BUSINESS FREEDOM — 63.9%

The overall freedom to start, operate, and close a business is somewhat constrained by the Czech Republic's national regulatory environment. Starting a business takes an average of 17 days, compared to the world average of 43 days. Despite bureaucracy and red tape, regulation is generally consistent with a market economy. Obtaining a business license requires twice the world average of 19 procedures. Closing a business is burdensome. A bankruptcy law was passed in 2007.

TRADE FREEDOM — 86%

The Czech Republic's trade policy is the same as those of other members of the European Union. The common EU weighted average tariff rate was 2 percent in 2005. Non-transparency in pharmaceuticals regulation and government procurement exceeds general EU policy, and the enforcement of intellectual property rights remains problematic. Consequently, an additional 10 percentage points is deducted from the Czech Republic's trade freedom score.

FISCAL FREEDOM — 71.3%

The Czech Republic has a moderate income tax rate and a low corporate tax rate. The top income tax rate is 32 percent, and the top corporate tax rate is 24 percent. Other taxes include a value-added tax (VAT), a property transfer tax, and a tax on dividends. A major tax reform unveiled in April 2007 includes a flat 15 percent personal income tax (effective January 2008), a significantly reduced corporate income tax, and changes in the VAT. In the most recent year, overall tax revenue as a percentage of GDP was 35.6 percent.

GOVERNMENT SIZE — 45.6%

Total government expenditures, including consumption and transfer payments, are high. In the most recent year, government spending equaled 42.6 percent of GDP. The private sector's share of GDP is above 85 percent. The government has sold its remaining stakes in leading utilities, including a telecommunications company and a petrochemicals refiner.

MONETARY FREEDOM — 80.3%

Inflation is low, averaging 2.4 percent between 2004 and 2006. As a participant in the EU's Common Agricultural Policy, the government subsidizes agricultural production, distorting the prices of agricultural products. The Ministry of Finance can fix prices, set minimum or maximum commercial transaction prices, and establish periods when pric-

es may not change. Energy, some raw materials, domestic rents, and rail and bus transport are subject to controls. Maximum prices apply to mail and telecommunications tariffs. An additional 10 percentage points is deducted from the Czech Republic's monetary freedom score to adjust for these policies.

INVESTMENT FREEDOM — 70%

The law treats foreign and domestic capital equally. Foreign investors can establish joint ventures and participate in existing enterprises, with 100 percent foreign ownership allowed in both cases. Upon accession to the EU in 2004, the Czechs harmonized their investment climate with the EU standard. Foreign persons may not purchase land, but branches or offices of foreign companies may buy local real estate, except for farmland or woodland. Licensing is required for a few sectors, such as insurance, media, and energy, where the state is a partner. There are no restrictions on payments or current transfers, and residents and non-residents may hold foreign exchange accounts. Non-transparent procurement is an obstacle to foreign tenders for government contracts.

FINANCIAL FREEDOM — 80%

The Czech Republic's financial sector is one of Central and Eastern Europe's most advanced. Direct government involvement in banking has been minimal since the 1990s decline and subsequent privatization. There were 37 licensed commercial banks in June 2006; foreign-controlled banks accounted for over 90 percent of assets in 2007 and are treated the same as domestic banks. Three Communist-era banks still control 62 percent of total assets. Insurance companies and pension funds are numerous and competitive, with significant foreign and EU participation. Capital markets are small and lack transparency, but regulatory bodies have been merged to streamline oversight.

PROPERTY RIGHTS — 70%

Private property is well protected, and contracts are generally secure. The judiciary is independent, although decisions may vary from court to court. Commercial disputes can take years to resolve. Registration of companies is in the hands of the courts and can be slow and complicated. The law protects all forms of intellectual property rights.

FREEDOM FROM CORRUPTION — 48%

Corruption is perceived as significant. The Czech Republic ranks 46th out of 163 countries in Transparency International's Corruption Perceptions Index for 2006. Giving and receiving bribes carry long prison terms. The Czech Republic ratified the OECD's anti-bribery convention in January 2000. The government signed the U.N. Convention Against Corruption in 2005 but has not ratified it.

LABOR FREEDOM — 70.2%

Employment regulations are relatively flexible, but greater flexibility would create more employment opportunities and productivity growth. The non-salary cost of employing a worker can be high, but dismissing a redundant employee is relatively costless.

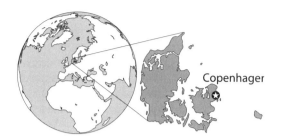

Copenhagen

DENMARK

Denmark's economy is 79.2 percent free, according to our 2008 assessment, which makes it the world's 11th freest economy. Its overall score is 2.2 percentage points higher than last year, one of the largest increases in the world, reflecting improved scores in four freedoms. Denmark is now ranked 4th freest among the 41 countries in the European region, and its overall score is well above the regional average.

Denmark scores highly in eight of the 10 freedoms and is among the world's freest economies in six categories. Its perfect score in labor freedom is a 25-point increase from its 2007 score. Financial markets are transparent, highly developed, and open to foreign capital. As a modern Western democracy, Denmark has an efficient, independent judiciary that protects property rights effectively, and the level of corruption is extraordinarily low.

Denmark has two significant weaknesses that are typical of large European welfare states. The top personal income tax rate is very high, and tax revenue collected is correspondingly high. Although there are few state-owned industries, government spending equals over 50 percent of GDP. As a result, scores in these two freedoms are over 40 percentage points below average.

BACKGROUND: Denmark's economy is fundamentally strong. It depends heavily on foreign trade, and the private sector is characterized by many small and medium-sized companies. A large welfare state provides public education, lifelong health care coverage, and subsidized care for children and the elderly; about 25 percent of working-age Danes rely on some kind of government transfer payment. A brief boycott of Danish products in some parts of the Muslim world followed the controversy over caricatures of the Prophet Muhammad printed in a Danish newspaper in September 2005, but its economic effects were not significant. Danes are currently debating how best to reform their costly social welfare system, which will be further burdened as the population ages.

How Do We Measure Economic Freedom? See Chapter 4 (page 39) for an explanation of the methodology or visit the *Index* Web site at *heritage.org/index*.

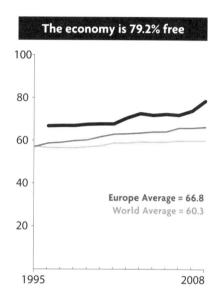

The economy is 79.2% free

Europe Average = 66.8
World Average = 60.3

1995 — 2008

QUICK FACTS

Population: 5.4 million

GDP (PPP): $184.0 billion
3.1% growth in 2005
1.5% 5-yr. comp. ann. growth
$33,972 per capita

Unemployment: 4.8%

Inflation (CPI): 1.8%

FDI (net flow): –$4.0 billion

Official Development Assistance:
Multilateral: None
Bilateral: None

External Debt: $405.0 billion

Exports: $125.0 billion
Primarily machinery and instruments, meat and meat products, dairy products, fish, pharmaceuticals, furniture, windmills

Imports: $112.5 billion
Primarily machinery and equipment, raw materials and semi-manufactures for industry, chemicals, grain and foodstuffs, consumer goods

2005 data unless otherwise noted.

DENMARK'S TEN ECONOMIC FREEDOMS

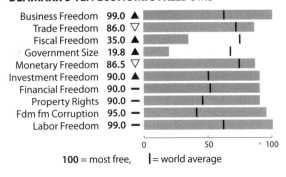

Business Freedom	99.0 ▲
Trade Freedom	86.0 ▽
Fiscal Freedom	35.0 ▲
Government Size	19.8 ▲
Monetary Freedom	86.5 ▽
Investment Freedom	90.0 ▲
Financial Freedom	90.0 —
Property Rights	90.0 —
Fdm fm Corruption	95.0 —
Labor Freedom	99.0 —

0   50   100

100 = most free, | = world average

BUSINESS FREEDOM — 99%

The overall freedom to start, operate, and close a business is strongly protected by Denmark's regulatory environment. Starting a business takes an average of six days, compared to the world average of 43 days. Obtaining a business license requires much less than the world average of 19 procedures and 234 days. Transparent regulations are applied evenly and efficiently in most cases. Closing a business is easy and not costly.

TRADE FREEDOM — 86%

Denmark's trade policy is the same as those of other members of the European Union. The common EU weighted average tariff rate was 2 percent in 2005. Non-tariff barriers reflected in EU policy include agricultural and manufacturing subsidies, import restrictions for some goods and services, market access restrictions in some service sectors, non-transparent and restrictive regulations and standards, and inconsistent customs administration across EU members. The lack of transparency in pharmaceuticals regulation and government procurement exceeds that found in EU policy. Consequently, an additional 10 percentage points is deducted from Denmark's trade freedom score.

FISCAL FREEDOM — 35%

Denmark has a very high income tax rate and a moderate corporate tax rate. The top income tax rate is 59 percent, and the top corporate tax rate was cut to 25 percent from 28 percent in 2007. Other taxes include a value-added tax (VAT) and an excise tax. In the most recent year, overall tax revenue as a percentage of GDP was 50.4 percent.

GOVERNMENT SIZE — 19.8%

Total government expenditures, including consumption and transfer payments, are very high. Government spending has been marginally decreasing and in the most recent year equaled 51.7 percent of GDP. Most industry and business is now in private hands.

MONETARY FREEDOM — 86.5%

Inflation is low, averaging 1.8 percent between 2004 and 2006. As a participant in the EU's Common Agricultural Policy, the government subsidizes agricultural production, distorting the prices of agricultural products. Medication is heavily subsidized, but measures have been taken to limit such subsidies. An additional 5 percentage points is deducted from Denmark's monetary freedom score to account for these distortionary policies.

INVESTMENT FREEDOM — 90%

Foreign and domestic investors are subject to the same laws. In 2006, according to the Economist Intelligence Unit, Denmark was the world's best nation for foreign investment because of such factors as its macroeconomic stability, pro-business climate, and infrastructure. As a rule, foreign direct investment is not subject to restrictions or pre-screening. Incentive financing, often targeted to preserve the environment, is available to foreign and domestic businesses. Ownership restrictions apply to a few sectors, such as real estate, where there is usually a five-year residency requirement for non-residents. There are no restrictions on capital transfers.

FINANCIAL FREEDOM — 90%

Denmark's well-developed financial system is open to foreign competition. The banking system is sound, and the two largest banks account for about 75 percent of assets. There are 187 domestic and foreign commercial and savings banks, nine subsidiaries and 26 branches of foreign banks, and four Faroese banks. The national payment system is jointly owned by Danish banks. Foreign banks have access to Danish markets, but only Nordic institutions have attracted a sizeable market share. Intense competition encourages technological advancements and a wide array of services. Supervision and regulation are based on EU legislation, and there is a single regulator. There are over 200 insurance companies and 30 multi-employer pension funds. The securities market is highly developed and efficient. The bond market is one of the world's largest.

PROPERTY RIGHTS — 90%

The judiciary is independent and generally fair and efficient. The legal system is independent and based on a centuries-old tradition. Commercial and bankruptcy laws are consistently applied, and secured interests in property are recognized and enforced. Denmark adheres to key international conventions and treaties on the protection of intellectual property rights.

FREEDOM FROM CORRUPTION — 95%

Corruption is perceived as almost nonexistent. Denmark ranks 4th out of 163 countries in Transparency International's Corruption Perceptions Index for 2006. Denmark has signed the OECD Anti-Bribery Convention. A new "Business Anti-corruption Portal" shows that the fight against corruption is an integral part of Danish development assistance.

LABOR FREEDOM — 99.9%

Highly flexible employment regulations enhance employment opportunities and productivity growth. The non-salary cost of employing a worker is low, and dismissing a redundant employee is relatively costless.

DJIBOUTI

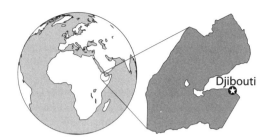

Djibouti

Rank: 131
Regional Rank: 30 of 40

Djibouti's economy is 52.3 percent free, according to our 2008 assessment, which makes it the world's 131st freest economy. Its overall score is 1.2 percentage points lower than last year, mainly reflecting a lower trade freedom score. Djibouti is ranked 30th out of 40 countries in the sub-Saharan Africa region, and its overall score is slightly lower than the regional average.

Djibouti has relatively high levels of fiscal freedom, financial freedom, labor freedom, and monetary freedom. The top income taxes on individuals and corporations are moderate. Employment restrictions are moderate, resulting in a flexible labor market. Inflation is low, but the government does try to control some consumer prices.

Economic development has been hurt by very weak business freedom and trade freedom. High tariffs averaging more than 30 percent inhibit trade and create a disincentive for foreign direct investment. Bureaucratic inefficiency and corruption hamper virtually all areas of the economy. Court enforcement of intrusive labor regulations and of property rights is clouded by political interference and rampant corruption.

BACKGROUND: President Ismael Omar Guelleh was elected in 1999 and re-elected in 2005, and his party controls all levels of government. Three-quarters of the population is urban, and most of those who live outside the capital city depend on nomadic subsistence. Djibouti has few natural resources. Its climate is arid, and most of its territory is desert and pasture. Djibouti is located along the shipping route between the Mediterranean Sea and the Indian Ocean, and over half of the world's commercial ships travel through its waters. Its service-based economy centers around port facilities, the railway, and foreign military bases. War between Ethiopia and Eritrea led Ethiopia to divert its trade from Eritrea to Djibouti, and Ethiopia is responsible for over half of the trade moving through Djibouti's port.

How Do We Measure Economic Freedom? See Chapter 4 (page 39) for an explanation of the methodology or visit the *Index* Web site at *heritage.org/index.*

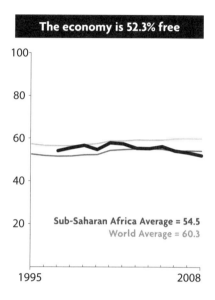

The economy is 52.3% free

Sub-Saharan Africa Average = 54.5
World Average = 60.3

1995 — 2008

QUICK FACTS

Population: 0.8 million

GDP (PPP): $1.7 billion
3.2% growth in 2005
3.0% 5-yr. comp. ann. growth
$2,177 per capita

Unemployment: 50% (2004 estimate)

Inflation (CPI): 3.1%

FDI (net flow): $23.0 million

Official Development Assistance:
Multilateral: $26.7 million
Bilateral: $56.4 million (13.2% from the U.S.)

External Debt: $394.0 million (2004 estimate)

Exports: $250.0 million (2004 estimate)
Primarily re-exports, hides and skins, coffee (in transit)

Imports: $987 million (2004 estimate)
Primarily foods, beverages, transport equipment, chemicals, petroleum products

2005 data unless otherwise noted.

159

DJIBOUTI'S TEN ECONOMIC FREEDOMS

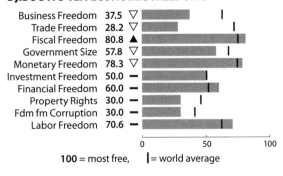

Business Freedom	37.5	▽
Trade Freedom	28.2	▽
Fiscal Freedom	80.8	▲
Government Size	57.8	▽
Monetary Freedom	78.3	▽
Investment Freedom	50.0	—
Financial Freedom	60.0	—
Property Rights	30.0	—
Fdm fm Corruption	30.0	—
Labor Freedom	70.6	—

0   50   100

100 = most free, ▌**= world average**

BUSINESS FREEDOM — 37.5%

The overall freedom to start, operate, and close a business is seriously limited by Djibouti's regulatory environment. Starting a business takes an average of 37 days, compared to the world average of 43 days. Obtaining a business license requires less than the world average of 19 procedures and 234 days. However, the entry cost of launching a business and the licensing cost are high. A lack of transparency and the inconsistent application of the commercial code discourage entrepreneurial activities. Closing a business can be lengthy and burdensome.

TRADE FREEDOM — 28.2%

Djibouti's average tariff rate was 30.9 percent in 2002. Much trade with neighboring countries is informal. Import and export bans, variable and sometimes high import taxes and fees, import licensing requirements, non-transparent and inefficient customs, and market access restrictions in the services sector add to the cost of trade. An additional 10 percentage points is deducted from Djibouti's trade freedom score to account for non-tariff barriers.

FISCAL FREEDOM — 80.8%

Djibouti has moderate tax rates. The top income tax rate is 30 percent, and the top corporate tax rate is 25 percent. Other taxes include a property tax and an excise tax. In the most recent year, overall tax revenue as a percentage of GDP was 20 percent.

GOVERNMENT SIZE — 57.8%

Total government expenditures, including consumption and transfer payments, are high. In the most recent year, government spending equaled 37.5 percent of GDP. Privatization of state-owned enterprises, including pharmaceutical factories and dairy plants, has been discussed, but progress has been slow.

MONETARY FREEDOM — 78.3%

Inflation is moderate, averaging 3.4 percent between 2004 and 2006. Relatively stable prices explain most of the monetary freedom score. Goods and services such as medicines, "common bread," water, electricity, telecommunications, postal services, and urban transport are subject to price controls. The government also influences prices through regulation of state-owned enterprises. An additional 10 percentage points is deducted from Djibouti's monetary freedom score to account for measures that distort domestic prices.

INVESTMENT FREEDOM — 50%

No major laws discourage incoming foreign investment, and there is no screening. Certain sectors, such as public utilities, are state-owned and not open to investors. Bureaucratic procedures are complicated; for example, the Finance Ministry will issue a license only if an investor possesses an approved investor visa, and the Interior Ministry will issue an investor visa only to a licensed business. Privatization has progressed, particularly in ports and railways. The legal system, derived from French civil law, is complex, opaque, and slow. Corruption is also a deterrent, and prohibitory laws are rarely enforced. Residents and non-residents may hold foreign exchange accounts, and there are no restrictions on payments or transfers.

FINANCIAL FREEDOM — 60%

Djibouti's financial sector consists primarily of a small banking system dominated by foreign banks. One majority-owned and one fully-owned French bank together account for 95 percent of deposits and 85 percent of credit. The government has a 49 percent minority stake in Banque pour le Commerce et l'Industrie-Mer Rouge. An Ethiopian bank focuses on international transactions for Ethiopian customers. Commercial banks generally provide only short-term financing and lending. A law against money laundering was adopted in 2002. There are no capital markets, and little formal economic activity occurs outside of the capital city.

PROPERTY RIGHTS — 30%

Protection of private property is weak. The courts are frequently overburdened, and the enforcement of contracts can be time-consuming. Trials and judicial proceedings are subject to corruption. Political manipulation undermines the judicial system's credibility. Commercial and bankruptcy laws are not applied consistently. The government does not enforce laws protecting intellectual property rights. Pirated trademarks are sold openly in the informal markets.

FREEDOM FROM CORRUPTION — 30%

Most economic activity still occurs informally. It is estimated that more than 80 percent of enterprises are within the informal and semi-informal sectors, including informal microenterprises that play a key role in the economy. Anti-corruption laws are rarely enforced. Administrative delays, demands for petty bribes, and a non-transparent judicial system are barriers to foreign direct investment.

LABOR FREEDOM — 70.6%

Relatively inflexible employment regulations hinder employment and productivity growth. The non-salary cost of employing a worker is moderate, but dismissing a redundant employee can be relatively costly. Regulations on the number of work hours can be rigid. A more flexible labor code adopted in December 2005 is not fully enforced.

DOMINICAN REPUBLIC

Santo
Domingo

The Dominican Republic's economy is 58.5 percent free, according to our 2008 assessment, which makes it the world's 87th freest economy. Its overall score is 0.9 percentage point higher than last year, partially reflecting improved business freedom, labor freedom, and monetary freedom. The Dominican Republic is ranked 20th out of 29 countries in the Americas, and its overall score is slightly lower than the regional average.

The Dominican Republic is generally below average in half of the 10 economic freedoms. However, it does stand out in one area: government size, where its score is 21 percentage points above the world average because of relatively limited government expenditures. In addition, personal and corporate tax rates are moderate, and overall tax revenue is not particularly high as a percentage of GDP.

The Dominican Republic scores poorly in financial freedom, property rights, and freedom from corruption. Failure to recover from scandals in the financial sector reflects the rudimentary level of banking operations. The weak application of commercial law means that private property is subject to adjudication based on political interference and corruption.

BACKGROUND: The Dominican Republic has held regular competitive elections since 1996. An economic boom in the 1990s, led by tourism and *maquiladora* manufacturing, slowed to negative growth by 2003. Elected in 2004, President Leonel Fernandez promised to reduce inflation, stabilize the exchange rate, and restore investor confidence. In 2007, the country ratified the Central America–Dominican Republic–United States Free Trade Agreement (CAFTA–DR), which the government hopes will revive sagging textile exports. The country's infrastructure has deteriorated, and its weak judicial system, starved of resources and personnel, lacks the ability to confront widespread corruption. Additionally the electricity sector is plagued by corruption, theft, seasonal drought, high oil prices, and frequent outages.

How Do We Measure Economic Freedom? See Chapter 4 (page 39) for an explanation of the methodology or visit the *Index* Web site at *heritage.org/index.*

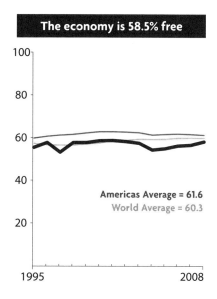

The economy is 58.5% free

100
80
60
40
20

Americas Average = 61.6
World Average = 60.3

1995   2008

QUICK FACTS

Population: 8.9 million

GDP (PPP): $73.1 billion
9.3% growth in 2005
3.4% 5-yr. comp. ann. growth
$8,217 per capita

Unemployment: 17.9%

Inflation (CPI): 4.2%

FDI (net flow): $899.0 million

Official Development Assistance:
Multilateral: $53.2 million
Bilateral: $94.0 million (27.9% from the U.S.)

External Debt: $7.4 billion

Exports: $10.1 billion
Primarily ferronickel, sugar, gold, silver, coffee, cocoa, tobacco, meats, consumer goods

Imports: $11.3 billion
Primarily foodstuffs, petroleum, cotton and fabrics, chemicals and pharmaceuticals
2005 data unless otherwise noted.

DOMINICAN REPUBLIC'S TEN ECONOMIC FREEDOMS

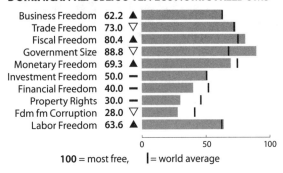

Business Freedom	62.2	▲
Trade Freedom	73.0	▽
Fiscal Freedom	80.4	▲
Government Size	88.8	▽
Monetary Freedom	69.3	▲
Investment Freedom	50.0	—
Financial Freedom	40.0	—
Property Rights	30.0	—
Fdm fm Corruption	28.0	▽
Labor Freedom	63.6	▲

0   50   100

100 = most free, | = world average

BUSINESS FREEDOM — 62.2%

The overall freedom to start, operate, and close a business is limited by the Dominican Republic's national regulatory environment. Starting a business takes an average of 22 days, compared to the world average of 43 days. Obtaining a business license requires less than the world average of 19 procedures and 234 days. Despite some improvement in the transparency and enforcement of commercial laws, regulations are burdensome, and interpretation of the commercial code is often arbitrary. Closing a business can be difficult.

TRADE FREEDOM — 73%

The Dominican Republic's weighted average tariff rate was 8.5 percent in 2005. Customs valuation that is subject to reference pricing for many products, cumbersome and restrictive standards, frequent delays in clearing customs, corruption and a lack of transparency in most of the trade process, and problems involving the protection of intellectual property rights add to the cost of trade. An additional 10 percentage points is deducted from the Dominican Republic's trade freedom score to account for non-tariff barriers.

FISCAL FREEDOM — 80.4%

The Dominican Republic has moderate tax rates. Both the top income tax rate and the top corporate tax rate were reduced to 29 percent from 30 percent, effective in 2007. Other taxes include a value-added tax (VAT) and a tax on dividends. In the most recent year, overall tax revenue as a percentage of GDP was 16.8 percent.

GOVERNMENT SIZE — 88.8%

Total government expenditures, including consumption and transfer payments, are low. In the most recent year, government spending equaled 19.3 percent of GDP. The government has been reviewing the system of transfers to local governments to ensure that the transfer of resources is consistent with expenditure responsibility.

MONETARY FREEDOM — 69.3%

Inflation is high, averaging 10.7 percent between 2004 and 2006. Relatively unstable prices explain most of the monetary freedom score. The government applies price controls to electricity and fuel and subsidizes some agricultural products and electricity generation. An additional 10 percentage points is deducted from the Dominican Republic's monetary freedom score to account for policies that distort domestic prices.

INVESTMENT FREEDOM — 50%

Foreign investment is generally welcomed, but some laws discriminate between domestic and foreign investments. Investments must be registered with the Central Bank of the Dominican Republic. Foreign direct investment is not permitted in sectors involving the treatment of hazardous waste, public health, and national security. A weak legal and enforcement system, lack of contract sanctity, disregard of official rulings, and corruption deter investment. The law mandates that 80 percent of a company's non-management labor force must be Dominican. Residents and non-residents may hold foreign exchange accounts. Payments and transfers are subject to documentation requirements. Some capital transactions are subject to approval, documentation, or reporting requirements.

FINANCIAL FREEDOM — 40%

The small financial sector is poorly supervised and regulated. Confidence has been shaky since the crisis spurred by the 2003 collapse of Banco Intercontinental (Baninter), the country's second-largest bank. An attempt to create a new financial regulatory network was circumvented by a government bailout of several banks later in 2003. Skepticism was fueled by a 2005 revelation that the head of the fifth-largest bank's board of directors had misappropriated funds. Structural reforms suggested by the International Monetary Fund have been met with postponements of official reviews, though the IMF recognized Dominican financial policy as sound in 2006. Financial-sector assets are largely controlled by the 13 multiple service banks, including three foreign-owned banks, and five state-owned banks. Offshore banking is growing. Capital markets are small and underdeveloped.

PROPERTY RIGHTS — 30%

The court system is inefficient, and red tape is common. The government can expropriate property arbitrarily. Most confiscated property has been used for infrastructure or commercial development. Although the government has slowly improved its patent and trademark laws, the enforcement of intellectual property rights remains poor.

FREEDOM FROM CORRUPTION — 28%

Corruption is perceived as significant. The Dominican Republic ranks 99th out of 163 countries in Transparency International's Corruption Perceptions Index for 2006. Official corruption is pervasive. Despite recent reforms, Dominican and foreign business leaders complain that judicial and administrative corruption affects the settlement of business disputes.

LABOR FREEDOM — 63.6%

Relatively flexible employment regulations could be improved to enhance employment opportunities and productivity growth. The non-salary cost of employing a worker is moderate, but dismissing a redundant employee can be costly. Restrictions on working hours remain relatively rigid.

ECUADOR

Ecuador's economy is 55.4 percent free, according to our 2008 assessment, which makes it the world's 106th freest economy. Its overall score is 0.2 percentage point lower than last year, with very few changes. Ecuador is ranked 22nd out of 29 countries in the Americas, and its overall score is much lower than the regional average.

Ecuador receives relatively high scores for fiscal freedom and government size but is lower than the world average in eight of 10 economic freedoms. Personal and corporate tax rates are moderate (although there are other taxes), and overall tax revenue is not excessively high as a percentage of GDP. Government expenditures are less than 25 percent of GDP.

Ecuador's scores in property rights, labor freedom, and freedom from corruption are especially low. Heavy regulation hurts business and labor flexibility. The rule of law is politically influenced and inefficient, and outright expropriation of private property is a constant concern. The judiciary often rules erratically and is subject to corruption.

BACKGROUND: Ecuador is the world's largest banana exporter and has ample petroleum reserves. Mismanagement and corruption plague the government-run oil industry, and production is dwindling. Feuding factions in the national legislature have fueled political and institutional instability. There is a lack of respect for the rule of law. In November 2006, U.S.-trained economist Rafael Correa was elected president on a platform of tighter government control of banking and oil production, default on debt owed to international lenders, and opposition to a free trade agreement with the United States. As a result, capital flight has soared and foreign direct investment has fallen. Correa, who is an ally of Venezuela's hard-left President Hugo Chávez, has also begun the process of rewriting Ecuador's constitution and has impinged on press freedom.

How Do We Measure Economic Freedom? See Chapter 4 (page 39) for an explanation of the methodology or visit the *Index* Web site at *heritage.org/index*.

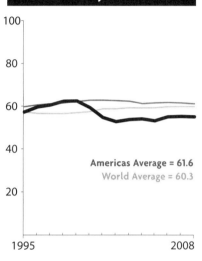

The economy is 55.4% free

Americas Average = 61.6
World Average = 60.3

1995   2008

QUICK FACTS

Population: 13.2 million

GDP (PPP): $57.4 billion
4.7% growth in 2005
5.1% 5-yr. comp. ann. growth
$4,340 per capita

Unemployment: 10.7%

Inflation (CPI): 2.1%

FDI (net flow): $1.9 billion

Official Development Assistance:
Multilateral: $66.4 million
Bilateral: $267.3 million (21.7% from the U.S.)

External Debt: $17.1 billion

Exports: $11.4 billion
Primarily petroleum, bananas, cut flowers, shrimp

Imports: $11.8 billion
Primarily vehicles, medicinal products, telecommunications equipment, electricity

2005 data unless otherwise noted.

163

ECUADOR'S TEN ECONOMIC FREEDOMS

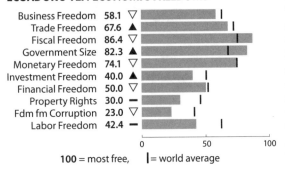

Business Freedom	58.1 ▽	
Trade Freedom	67.6 ▲	
Fiscal Freedom	86.4 ▽	
Government Size	82.3 ▲	
Monetary Freedom	74.1 ▽	
Investment Freedom	40.0 ▲	
Financial Freedom	50.0 ▽	
Property Rights	30.0 —	
Fdm fm Corruption	23.0 ▽	
Labor Freedom	42.4 —	

0   50   100

100 = most free, l = world average

BUSINESS FREEDOM — 58.1%

The overall freedom to start, operate, and close a business is restricted by Ecuador's national regulatory environment. Starting a business takes an average of 65 days, compared to the world average of 43 days. Obtaining a business license takes about half of the world average of 234 days. Bureaucratic rules are complex, and commercial laws are applied inconsistently. Closing a business is lengthy.

TRADE FREEDOM — 67.6%

Ecuador's weighted average tariff rate was 8.7 percent in 2005. Restrictive import licensing, mandatory government authorization before importing agriculture products, import bans, inefficient administration of tariff rate quotas, issues involving the protection of intellectual property rights, burdensome and non-transparent government procurement, and arbitrary and cumbersome customs procedures add to the cost of trade. An additional 15 percentage points is deducted from Ecuador's trade freedom score to account for non-tariff barriers.

FISCAL FREEDOM — 86.4%

Ecuador has moderate tax rates. Both the top income tax rate and the top corporate tax rate are 25 percent. Other taxes include a value-added tax (VAT) and a capital gains tax. In the most recent year, overall tax revenue as a percentage of GDP was 10.7 percent.

GOVERNMENT SIZE — 82.3%

Total government expenditures, including consumption and transfer payments, are low. In the most recent year, government spending equaled 24.3 percent of GDP. Despite some progress in reducing public debt, inefficiencies in state-owned enterprises in electricity and telecommunications hinder effective management of fiscal resources.

MONETARY FREEDOM — 74.1%

Inflation is relatively low, averaging 3 percent between 2004 and 2006, which explains most of the monetary freedom score. The government applies price bands for agricultural products; controls the prices of electricity, telecommunications services, and pharmaceuticals; and subsidizes public transportation and cooking gas. An additional 15 percentage points is deducted from Ecuador's monetary freedom score to adjust for measures that distort domestic prices.

INVESTMENT FREEDOM — 40%

The law grants foreign firms national treatment, but investment is hindered by cumbersome labor laws and a lack of contract enforcement. Regulatory enforcement can lead to bribery. Tax breaks are granted for investments in targeted areas, such as hydroelectric generation. Prior government approval is required for investment in petroleum exploration and development, mining, domestic fishing, electricity, telecommunications, broadcast media, coastal and border real estate, and national security. Profit repatriation and foreign access to Ecuador's credit market are allowed. There are no restrictions on foreign exchange accounts, direct investment, or current transfers.

FINANCIAL FREEDOM — 50%

Regulation of Ecuador's financial system, which is still recovering from a late 1990s banking crisis that spurred government default on foreign bonds and the takeover of many banks, has increased. Because the U.S. dollar is the official currency, the central bank is no longer the lender of last resort. Banks say that this reduces their lending potential, leading to a disparity between deposits and loans. In 2007, there were 25 commercial banks (one of them state-run), down from 48 in 1998. The four largest banks control 65 percent of total deposits. The state controlled 10.9 percent of bank assets at the end of 2006. There also were 11 finance companies, 36 co-operatives, and five mutual finance companies. The two stock markets are undeveloped, and little equity has been traded since the financial crisis. Foreign takeovers of limited-partnership banks and insurance companies are restricted.

PROPERTY RIGHTS — 30%

Weak rule of law and non-enforcement of intellectual property rights are major problems. Processing delays are significant, judgments are unpredictable, rulings are inconsistent, and the courts are subject to corruption. Expropriation is possible. Many foreign and local investors have experienced agricultural land seizures by squatters.

FREEDOM FROM CORRUPTION — 23%

Corruption is perceived as pervasive. Ecuador ranks 138th out of 163 countries in Transparency International's Corruption Perceptions Index for 2006. Corruption is blamed for a decade of steady decline in state oil production. The government has not enforced the anti-corruption statutes. Demands for petty bribes and theft of public property are common among officials.

LABOR FREEDOM — 42.4%

Burdensome employment regulations still hinder employment opportunities and productivity growth. The non-salary cost of employing a worker is moderate, but dismissing a redundant employee can be very costly. Job-tenure regulations create a risk aversion for companies that would otherwise hire more people and grow. Many employers resort to short-term outsourcing contracts. Ecuador's labor market flexibility is one of the lowest in the world.

EGYPT

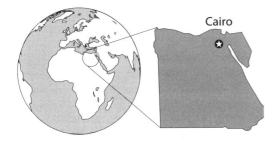

Cairo

Egypt's economy is 59.2 percent free, according to our 2008 assessment, which makes it the world's 85th freest economy. Its overall score is 4 percentage points higher than last year, the largest improvement of any country. Improvements in business, financial, and trade freedom were significant. Egypt is ranked 11th out of 17 countries in the Middle East/North Africa region, and its overall score is above the regional average.

Despite recent reforms, Egypt remains weak in most of the 10 economic freedoms, scoring above average only in fiscal freedom, government size, and labor freedom. The top income and corporate tax rates are very low, and government tax revenue relative to GDP is not high. Total government expenditures are moderately low.

Egypt could improve in several areas, but nowhere is it extremely below average. Its lowest relative score is in financial freedom, which is 12 points below average. Corruption and weak property rights are also serious problems; corruption is common, and the fair adjudication of property rights cannot be guaranteed.

BACKGROUND: Egypt is the most populous Arab country and a major force in Middle Eastern affairs. Although President Hosni Mubarak's government has undertaken incremental reforms to liberalize the socialist economic system that has hampered economic growth since the 1950s, the government continues to maintain heavy subsidies on food, energy, and other key commodities. Economic reform has become a higher priority under Prime Minister Ahmed Nazif, a technocrat who took office in 2004 and has placed liberal reformers in key positions. In 2005, the government reduced personal and corporate tax rates, cut energy subsidies, and privatized several enterprises.

How Do We Measure Economic Freedom? See Chapter 4 (page 39) for an explanation of the methodology or visit the *Index* Web site at *heritage.org/index.*

The economy is 59.2% free

Mideast/North Africa Average = 58.7
World Average = 60.3

1995 — 2008

QUICK FACTS

Population: 74.0 million

GDP (PPP): $321.1 billion
4.5% growth in 2005
3.7% 5-yr. comp. ann. growth
$4,337 per capita

Unemployment: 9.5%

Inflation (CPI): 8.8%

FDI (net flow): $5.3 billion

Official Development Assistance:
Multilateral: $328.5 million
Bilateral: $1.2 billion (51.4% from the U.S.)

External Debt: $34.1 billion

Exports: $30.7 billion
Primarily crude oil and petroleum products, cotton, textiles, metal products, chemicals

Imports: $34.3 billion
Primarily machinery and equipment, foodstuffs, chemicals, wood products, fuels

2005 data unless otherwise noted.

EGYPT'S TEN ECONOMIC FREEDOMS

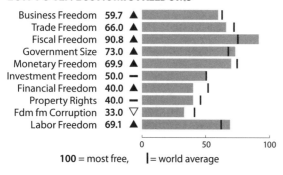

Business Freedom	59.7 ▲	
Trade Freedom	66.0 ▲	
Fiscal Freedom	90.8 ▲	
Government Size	73.0 ▲	
Monetary Freedom	69.9 ▲	
Investment Freedom	50.0 —	
Financial Freedom	40.0 ▲	
Property Rights	40.0 ▲	
Fdm fm Corruption	33.0 ▽	
Labor Freedom	69.1 ▲	

0   50   100

100 = most free, | = world average

BUSINESS FREEDOM — *59.7%*

The overall freedom to start, operate, and close a business has benefited from efforts to improve the business climate. Starting a business takes an average of nine days, compared to the world average of 43 days. Obtaining a business license requires more than the world average of 19 procedures and 234 days. The government has established a "one-stop-shop" for investment and has moved to revamp regulation. Closing a business can be burdensome.

TRADE FREEDOM — *66%*

Egypt's weighted average tariff rate was 12 percent in 2005. Reform continues slowly, and import restrictions, service market access restrictions, some high tariffs, burdensome and non-transparent sanitary and phytosanitary measures, cumbersome bureaucracy and non-transparent regulations, weak enforcement of intellectual property rights, and non-transparent customs administration add to the cost of trade. An additional 10 percentage points is deducted from Egypt's trade freedom score to account for non-tariff barriers.

FISCAL FREEDOM — *90.8%*

Egypt has low personal income and corporate tax rates. Both the top income tax rate and the top corporate tax rate are 20 percent. Other taxes include a value-added tax (VAT) and a property tax. In the most recent year, overall tax revenue as a percentage of GDP was 10.8 percent.

GOVERNMENT SIZE — *73%*

Total government expenditures, including consumption and transfer payments, are moderate, but subsidy spending has caused significant fiscal deficits. In the most recent year, government spending equaled 30 percent of GDP. Despite setbacks, privatization is proceeding.

MONETARY FREEDOM — *69.9%*

Inflation is relatively high, averaging 5.7 percent between 2004 and 2006. Relatively unstable prices explain most of the monetary freedom score. The government controls prices for some basic foods, energy (including fuel), transport, and medicine and subsidizes basic food items, sugar and pharmaceuticals, and public transportation. An additional 15 percentage points is deducted from Egypt's monetary freedom score to adjust for measures that distort domestic prices.

INVESTMENT FREEDOM — *50%*

All investment projects must be reviewed to gain legal status and qualify for incentives. Investment in certain sectors, such as tourism, mining, and oil, falls under Law 8, and approval is nearly automatic. Foreigners may own 100 percent of Law 8 investment projects and may repatriate capital. Foreign investment in Sinai, military products, and tobacco requires approval from the relevant ministries; foreign ownership of the main agricultural land is almost always prohibited. Residents and non-residents may hold foreign exchange accounts. There are no restrictions on payments and transfers. Bond issues require the Capital Market Authority's approval.

FINANCIAL FREEDOM — *40%*

There were 43 licensed banks in 2006, including 36 local financial institutions and seven foreign banks, and the four large state-owned banks controlled about 50 percent of assets. The smallest state bank was approved for sale in 2006, and the government has sold its shares in some private banks. Non-performing loans are significant, and new banks face constraints. Bankers are reluctant to lend privately because of loan scandals and the lack of an institution capable of judging credit-worthiness. In 2004, Egypt was removed from a blacklist of countries that were insufficiently combating money laundering. There were 21 insurance companies in 2006, including four dominant state-owned firms and another state-owned reinsurance company. Capital markets are large for the region, and the stock exchange has been the world's best-performing emerging-market exchange for two years.

PROPERTY RIGHTS — *40%*

The government sometimes circumvents the judiciary by using fast-track military courts. On average, it takes six years to decide commercial cases, and appeal procedures can extend court cases beyond 15 years. Local contractual arrangements are generally secure. Islamic law is officially the main inspiration for legislation, but the Napoleonic Code exerts a significant influence. Judicial procedures tend to be protracted, costly, and subject to political pressure. The enforcement of intellectual property rights is seriously deficient.

FREEDOM FROM CORRUPTION — *33%*

Corruption is perceived as significant. Egypt ranks 70th out of 163 countries in Transparency International's Corruption Perceptions Index for 2006. Bribery of low-level civil servants seems to be a part of daily life, and there are allegations of significant corruption among high-level officials.

LABOR FREEDOM — *69.1%*

The government has adopted a new labor code in recent years. Relatively flexible employment regulations could be improved to enhance employment opportunities and productivity growth. The non-salary cost of employing a worker can be high, but restrictions on working hours are relatively flexible.

EL SALVADOR

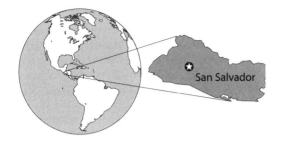

San Salvador

Rank: 33

Regional Rank: 7 of 29

El Salvador's economy is 69.2 percent free, according to our 2008 assessment, which makes it the world's 33rd freest economy. Its overall score is 0.6 percentage point lower than last year. El Salvador is ranked 7th out of 29 countries in the Americas, and its overall score is notably higher than the regional average.

El Salvador receives high scores for investment freedom, financial freedom, government size, and labor freedom. Government expenditures are less than 15 percent of GDP, and regulation of the free market is generally light, efficient, and transparent. The labor market is fairly flexible and one of the economy's most attractive features, although firing an employee can be costly.

In terms of the other economic freedoms, El Salvador is average, with no scores significantly below the world average. Inflation is low thanks to a currency pegged to the U.S. dollar, but government price controls do distort prices on certain staples.

BACKGROUND: Since the 1992 peace accord, El Salvador's political parties have cooperated on political and economic reforms. Steady economic growth and reduced poverty are due in part to the free-market policies of the center-right National Republican Alliance (ARENA) party. Coffee exports remain significant, but much growth has come from *maquila* industries (e.g., textiles) and the services sector. Annual emigrants' remittances of roughly $3 billion are vital to the economy. Elected to a five-year term in 2004, President Elias "Tony" Saca of ARENA continues to support free-market policies, albeit with less purpose. El Salvador's participation in the Central America–Dominican Republic–United States Free Trade Agreement (CAFTA–DR) should encourage further reform, but the country still suffers from a weak justice system, a poor education system, and rising gang violence.

How Do We Measure Economic Freedom? See Chapter 4 (page 39) for an explanation of the methodology or visit the *Index* Web site at *heritage.org/index*.

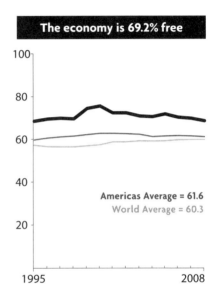

The economy is 69.2% free

Americas Average = 61.6
World Average = 60.3

1995   2008

QUICK FACTS

Population: 6.9 million

GDP (PPP): $36.2 billion
2.8% growth in 2005
2.3% 5-yr. comp. ann. growth
$5,254 per capita

Unemployment: 6.5%

Inflation (CPI): 3.7%

FDI (net flow): $300.0 million

Official Development Assistance:
Multilateral: $63.9 million
Bilateral: $193.1 million (30.1% from the U.S.)

External Debt: $7.1 billion

Exports: $4.6 billion
Primarily offshore assembly exports, coffee, sugar, shrimp, textiles, chemicals, electricity

Imports: $7.7 billion
Primarily raw materials, consumer goods, capital goods, fuels, foodstuffs, petroleum, electricity

2005 data unless otherwise noted.

EL SALVADOR'S TEN ECONOMIC FREEDOMS

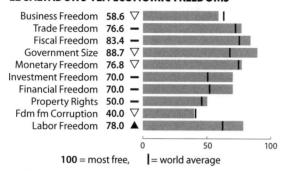

Business Freedom	58.6 ▽	
Trade Freedom	76.6 —	
Fiscal Freedom	83.4 —	
Government Size	88.7 ▽	
Monetary Freedom	76.8 ▽	
Investment Freedom	70.0 —	
Financial Freedom	70.0 —	
Property Rights	50.0 —	
Fdm fm Corruption	40.0 ▽	
Labor Freedom	78.0 ▲	

0   50   100

100 = most free, | = world average

BUSINESS FREEDOM — 58.6%

The overall freedom to start, operate, and close a business is restricted by El Salvador's national regulatory environment. Starting a business takes about the half of the world average of 43 days. Despite significant progress in reducing onerous regulations, obtaining a business license requires more than the world average of 19 procedures and 234 days. Bankruptcy is somewhat lengthy but not costly.

TRADE FREEDOM — 76.6%

El Salvador's weighted average tariff rate was 6.7 percent in 2005. Import restrictions and bans, service market access barriers, restrictive sanitary and phytosanitary regulations, export subsidies, and a few other discriminatory applications of standards add to the cost of trade. An additional 10 percent is deducted from El Salvador's trade freedom score to account for non-tariff barriers.

FISCAL FREEDOM — 83.4%

El Salvador has a moderate personal income tax rate and a low corporate tax rate. The top personal income tax rate is 30 percent, and the top corporate tax rate is 25 percent. Other taxes include a value-added tax (VAT), which is the largest source of government revenue, and a tax on insurance contracts. In the most recent year, overall tax revenue as a percentage of GDP was 11.6 percent.

GOVERNMENT SIZE — 88.7%

Total government expenditures, including consumption and transfer payments, are low. In the most recent year, government spending equaled 18.6 percent of GDP. The share of state-owned enterprises in the economy has been diminishing with privatization.

MONETARY FREEDOM — 76.8%

Inflation is moderate, averaging 4.4 percent between 2004 and 2006, partly because of the fixed exchange rate with the dollar. Relatively unstable prices explain most of the monetary freedom score. The government controls the prices of some goods, including electricity, and subsidizes diesel, petroleum, and liquid propane gas. An additional 10 percent is deducted from El Salvador's monetary freedom score to adjust for measures that distort domestic prices.

INVESTMENT FREEDOM — 70%

Foreign investors receive equal treatment and may obtain credit in the local financial market under the same conditions as local investors. The government limits foreign direct investment in commerce, industry, certain services, and fishing. Investments in railroads, piers, and canals require government approval, and there are some restrictions on land ownership. El Salvador's priority of encouraging foreign investment is marred slightly by an inefficient commercial legal system. Privatization has helped to attract foreign capital, particularly in electricity generation, telecommunications, and pension funds. There are no controls or requirements on current transfers, access to foreign exchange, or most capital transactions.

FINANCIAL FREEDOM — 70%

The financial sector has experienced significant liberalization since the 1990s. In 2006, there were 13 banks: nine private commercial banks, two state-owned banks, and two foreign branches. Four of El Salvador's private banks are included in the six largest Central American establishments. Banks offer a wide range of financial services. Interest rates are set by the market. Banking regulations are open and transparent. Non-bank financial institutions are limited due to the lack of personal savings and low disposable income. There were 18 insurance companies in 2006, three of which were foreign-dominated. Foreign banks and insurance companies receive national treatment. Most of the stock market's transactions are in the form of public-sector securities. The exchange participates in a regional association of stock exchanges.

PROPERTY RIGHTS — 50%

Property rights are moderately well protected. Lawsuits move very slowly and can be costly and unproductive. The legal system is subject to manipulation by private interests, and final rulings may not be enforced. Judicial inefficiency and crime are cited as among the main constraints on doing business. Studies done after the 12-year civil war identified weaknesses in the judiciary and recommended that all incompetent judges be replaced, but this goal has not been fully realized.

FREEDOM FROM CORRUPTION — 40%

Corruption is perceived as significant. El Salvador ranks 57th out of 163 countries in Transparency International's Corruption Perceptions Index for 2006. It is against the law to solicit, offer, or accept a bribe. Most governmental corruption occurs at the lower levels of the bureaucracy.

LABOR FREEDOM — 78%

Relatively flexible employment regulations could be further improved to enhance employment opportunities and productivity growth. The non-salary cost of employing a worker is low, but dismissing a redundant employee is somewhat difficult. Restrictions on the number of working hours can be flexible.

EQUATORIAL GUINEA

Malabo

E quatorial Guinea's economy is 52.5 percent free, according to our 2008 assessment, which makes it the world's 129th freest economy. Its overall score is 1.6 percentage points lower than last year, with four freedoms improving and four declining. Equatorial Guinea is ranked 29th out of 40 countries in the sub-Saharan Africa region, and its overall score is equal to the regional average.

Equatorial Guinea does not rank strongly in any category and is significantly below average in five of the 10 economic freedoms. Although tax revenue is not large as a percentage of GDP, the top income and corporate tax rates are a high 35 percent. Relatively low government expenditures are one bright spot. Inflation is also mild because the currency is pegged to the euro.

Equatorial Guinea is beset by serious self-imposed economic barriers. Business freedom, trade freedom, and investment freedom are very weak. Regulations are burdensome, and business operations are significantly hampered by red tape. The average tariff rate is high, and the inefficient and corrupt bureaucracy makes the customs process difficult. Property rights are not secured by an independent judiciary, and corruption is rampant.

BACKGROUND: Teodoro Obiang Nguema Mbasogo, who seized power in 1979, was elected president in 1982 and re-elected to a fourth seven-year term in 2002. Despite the end of one-party rule in 1991, opposition parties have won few victories. Obiang maintains tight control of the military and the government. Oil and gas reportedly accounted for 93 percent of GDP, 94 percent of government revenue, and 99 percent of exports in 2005. Per capita income has risen sharply since the discovery of oil, but most people engage in subsistence farming, hunting, and fishing. Government management of oil wealth is not transparent. Despite an open investment and trade regime, investment is discouraged by a dysfunctional judiciary, poor infrastructure, regulatory complexity, and corruption.

How Do We Measure Economic Freedom? See Chapter 4 (page 39) for an explanation of the methodology or visit the *Index* Web site at *heritage.org/index*.

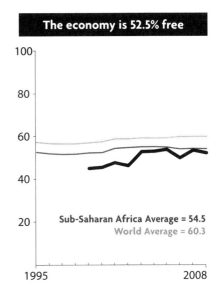

The economy is 52.5% free

Sub-Saharan Africa Average = 54.5
World Average = 60.3

1995   2008

QUICK FACTS

Population: 0.5 million

GDP (PPP): $26.6 billion
6.5% growth in 2005
18.9% 5-yr. comp. ann. growth
$22,042 per capita

Unemployment: 30% (1998 estimate)

Inflation (CPI): 5.7%

FDI (net flow): $1.9 billion

Official Development Assistance:
Multilateral: $11.5 million
Bilateral: $31.6 million

External Debt: $289.0 million

Exports: $8.96 billion
Primarily petroleum, methanol, timber, cocoa

Imports: $2.54 billion
Primarily petroleum-sector equipment, other equipment

2005 data unless otherwise noted.

EQUATORIAL GUINEA'S TEN ECONOMIC FREEDOMS

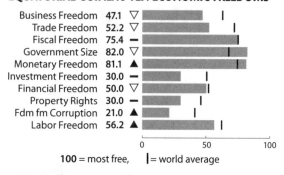

Business Freedom	47.1 ▽	
Trade Freedom	52.2 ▽	
Fiscal Freedom	75.4 —	
Government Size	82.0 ▽	
Monetary Freedom	81.1 ▲	
Investment Freedom	30.0 —	
Financial Freedom	50.0 ▽	
Property Rights	30.0 —	
Fdm fm Corruption	21.0 ▲	
Labor Freedom	56.2 ▲	

0   50   100

100 = most free, | = world average

BUSINESS FREEDOM — 47.1%

The overall freedom to start, operate, and close a business is considerably restricted by Equatorial Guinea's national regulatory environment. Starting a business takes more than three times the world average of 43 days. Obtaining a business license requires less than the world average of 19 procedures and 234 days. Lack of transparency and uneven application of commercial regulations are still major problems. Modern bankruptcy procedures have not been developed.

TRADE FREEDOM — 52.2%

Equatorial Guinea's weighted average tariff rate was 18.9 percent in 2005. A burdensome and corrupt customs process remains an important barrier to trade, and the government subsidizes cocoa exports. An additional 10 percentage points is deducted from Equatorial Guinea's trade freedom score to account for non-tariff barriers.

FISCAL FREEDOM — 75.4%

Equatorial Guinea has high tax rates. Both the top income tax rate and the top corporate tax rate are 35 percent. In the most recent year, overall tax revenue as a percentage of GDP was 2.3 percent. The oil sector accounts for more than 90 percent of total government revenue.

GOVERNMENT SIZE — 82%

Total government expenditures, including consumption and transfer payments, are moderate. In the most recent year, government spending equaled 24.5 percent of GDP. Increasing oil production and high oil prices have allowed the government to adopt an expansionary fiscal policy in recent years, particularly investment in public infrastructure.

MONETARY FREEDOM — 81.1%

Inflation is relatively high, averaging 4.8 percent between 2004 and 2006. Relatively unstable prices explain most of the monetary freedom score. The government sets the price of electricity and subsidizes both electricity and cocoa production. An additional 5 percentage points is deducted from Equatorial Guinea's monetary freedom score to adjust for measures that distort domestic prices.

INVESTMENT FREEDOM — 30%

The government welcomes foreign investment, particularly in the non-energy sector, but excessive bureaucracy, corruption, and lax enforcement of investment law are serious impediments to investment, although the commercial law code is under revision. Foreign investors are required to obtain a local partner. Residents and non-residents may hold foreign exchange accounts, subject to some approval processes. Efforts to increase national transparency for investment and financial purposes have met with some success; the International Monetary Fund has praised the country for its sound fiscal laws. Capital transactions, payments, and transfers to countries other than France, Monaco, and regional partners are subject to restrictions.

FINANCIAL FREEDOM — 50%

Equatorial Guinea's financial system is small and underdeveloped. After near-total collapse in the 1970s, Equatorial Guinea joined the CFA Franc Zone in 1985, and the Commission Bancaire de L'Afrique Centrale has acted as the central bank ever since. The banking sector consists of five main banks, all primarily foreign-owned and currently benefiting from a recent oil boom. The government maintains minority ownership in two banks. Compliance with banking regulations is mixed, and the number of non-performing loans has increased in recent years. Financial supervision is adequate. The insurance sector is very small, consisting of three insurance companies and one reinsurance company. Equatorial Guinea has no stock exchange or securities market.

PROPERTY RIGHTS — 30%

Senior government officials sometimes extort money from foreign companies, threatening to take away concessions. The judicial system is open to political influence. Equatorial Guinea is a member of OHADA (Organisation pour l'Harmonisation en Afrique du Droit des Affaires), a regional organization that trains judges and lawyers in commercial law to help reform the enforcement of contracts. Enforcement of intellectual property rights is weak.

FREEDOM FROM CORRUPTION — 21%

Corruption is perceived as rampant. Equatorial Guinea ranks 151st out of 163 countries in Transparency International's Corruption Perceptions Index for 2006. Due in large part to the "curse of oil," corruption among officials is pervasive, and many business deals are concluded under non-transparent circumstances. *Forbes* estimates President Obiang's net worth at $600 million.

LABOR FREEDOM — 56.2%

Restrictive employment regulations hinder employment opportunities and productivity growth. The non-salary cost of employing a worker is high, and dismissing a redundant employee is costly. The cost of laying off a worker creates a risk aversion for companies that would otherwise hire more people and grow. Restrictions on increasing and contracting the number of work hours can be rigid.

ESTONIA

Estonia's economy is 77.8 percent free, according to our 2008 assessment, which makes it the world's 12th freest economy. Its overall score is slightly lower than last year, reflecting improvement in five freedoms and declines in three others. Estonia is ranked 5th out of 41 countries in the European region, and its overall score is much higher than the regional average.

Estonia scores highly in investment freedom, financial freedom, property rights, business freedom, and freedom from corruption. Major reforms after independence from the Soviet Union in the early 1990s have proven to be successful and are a model for all of Europe. The top income and corporate tax rates are low, and business regulation is efficient. Investment is easy but subject to government licensing in some areas of the economy. Estonia's financial sector is the most developed among the Baltic States. The judiciary, independent of politics and free of corruption, protects property rights effectively.

Estonia could do slightly better in government size and labor freedom. Total government spending is high, although in line with other EU economies, and the labor market is unnecessarily rigid.

BACKGROUND: Since the fall of the Soviet Union, Estonia, the smallest Baltic state, has been one of the most radical economic reformers among the former Soviet nations and has transformed itself into one of the world's most dynamic and modern economies. High GDP growth upwards of 9 percent per annum over the past two decades has helped to repair the country's economy. Estonia has strong trade ties to Finland, Sweden, and Germany, and its services and manufacturing sectors are thriving. The country aims to join the European Economic and Monetary Union in January 2010.

How Do We Measure Economic Freedom? See Chapter 4 (page 39) for an explanation of the methodology or visit the *Index* Web site at *heritage.org/index.*

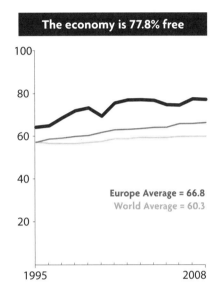

The economy is 77.8% free

Europe Average = 66.8
World Average = 60.3

1995 — 2008

QUICK FACTS

Population: 1.3 million

GDP (PPP): $20.8 billion
10.5% growth in 2005
8.4% 5-yr. comp. ann. growth
$15,477 per capita

Unemployment: 7.9%

Inflation (CPI): 4.1%

FDI (net flow): $2.3 billion

Official Development Assistance:
Multilateral: $130.7 million (2004)
Bilateral: $32.6 million (20.5% from the U.S.) (2004)

External Debt: $11.3 billion

Exports: $10.9 billion
Primarily machinery and equipment, mineral products, wood and paper textiles

Imports: $11.8 billion
Primarily machinery and mechanical appliances, mineral products, transportation equipment
2005 data unless otherwise noted.

171

ESTONIA'S TEN ECONOMIC FREEDOMS

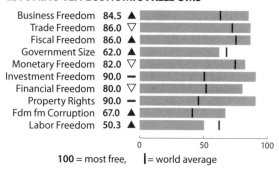

Business Freedom	84.5 ▲	
Trade Freedom	86.0 ▽	
Fiscal Freedom	86.0 ▲	
Government Size	62.0 ▲	
Monetary Freedom	82.0 ▽	
Investment Freedom	90.0 —	
Financial Freedom	80.0 ▽	
Property Rights	90.0 —	
Fdm fm Corruption	67.0 ▲	
Labor Freedom	50.3 ▲	

0   50   100

100 = most free, | = world average

BUSINESS FREEDOM — 84.5%

The overall freedom to start, operate, and close a business is relatively well protected by Estonia's national regulatory environment. Starting a business takes an average of seven days, compared to the world average of 43 days. Obtaining a business license requires less than the world average of 19 procedures and 234 days. Regulations are transparent and evenly applied. Closing a business is relatively easy and not costly.

TRADE FREEDOM — 86%

Estonia's trade policy is the same as those of other members of the European Union. The common EU weighted average tariff rate was 2 percent in 2005. Non-tariff barriers reflected in EU policy include agricultural and manufacturing subsidies, import restrictions for some goods and services, market access restrictions in some service sectors, non-transparent and restrictive regulations and standards, and inconsistent customs administration across EU members. Consequently, an additional 10 percentage points is deducted from Estonia's trade freedom score.

FISCAL FREEDOM — 86%

Estonia has low tax rates. The personal income tax rate is a flat 22 percent, scheduled to be reduced to 20 percent by 2009. Distributed profits are subject to the 22 percent corporate tax rate; undistributed profits are not subject to taxation whether invested or merely retained. Other taxes include a value-added tax (VAT) and an excise tax. In the most recent year, overall tax revenue as a percentage of GDP was 30.3 percent.

GOVERNMENT SIZE — 62%

Total government expenditures, including consumption and transfer payments, are high. In the most recent year, government spending equaled 35.6 percent of GDP. Privatization is nearly complete, and the private sector generates more than 80 percent of GDP. Public finance management is generally sound, and the government runs a budget surplus.

MONETARY FREEDOM — 82%

Inflation is relatively high, averaging 4.2 percent between 2004 and 2006. Relatively unstable prices explain most of the monetary freedom score. As a participant in the EU's Common Agricultural Policy, the government subsidizes agricultural production, distorting the prices of agricultural products. The government also subsidizes fuel and rent. An additional 5 percentage points is deducted from Estonia's monetary freedom score to account for policies that distort domestic prices.

INVESTMENT FREEDOM — 90%

The foreign investment code is transparent, and foreign and domestic capital are legally equivalent. Foreigners may invest in all sectors and own real estate. Licenses required for investment in banking, mining, gas and water supply or related structures, railroads and transport, energy, and communications networks are reviewed in a non-discriminatory manner. Residents and non-residents may hold foreign exchange accounts, and payments, transfers, and most capital transactions are not subject to controls. Only the main port, power plants, and the lottery are still state-owned. FDI rules on sectors like aviation and real estate are harmonized with the EU standard.

FINANCIAL FREEDOM — 80%

Before its accession to the EU, Estonia dramatically reformed its financial system through a series of consolidations and mergers. In September 2006, there were seven licensed credit institutions and seven branches of foreign institutions. Applications for new banks (particularly EU companies) abound, but the top four banks still control 95 percent of assets. The central bank may not lend to the public but allows all services to be offered by financial institutions. Foreign financial institutions are welcome, and insurance is dominated by foreign firms. Credit is allocated on market terms, and foreign investors may obtain credit freely. The small but active stock exchange is part of a network of Scandinavian and Baltic exchanges.

PROPERTY RIGHTS — 90%

Estonia's judiciary is independent and insulated from government influence. Property rights and contracts are enforced, and the commercial code is applied consistently. Estonian law is in compliance with EU directives protecting intellectual property rights.

FREEDOM FROM CORRUPTION — 67%

Corruption is perceived as somewhat present. Estonia ranks 24th out of 163 countries in Transparency International's Corruption Perceptions Index for 2006. Estonia has laws, regulations, and penalties to combat corruption, and the corruption that does exist is generally not targeted at foreign investors.

LABOR FREEDOM — 50.3%

Rigid employment regulations are barriers to enhanced employment opportunities and productivity growth. The non-salary cost of employing a worker can be high, and dismissing a redundant employee is relatively difficult and costly. The difficulty of laying off a worker creates a risk aversion for companies that would otherwise hire more people and grow. Restrictions on the number of work hours remain rigid.

ETHIOPIA

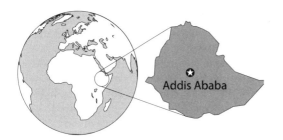

Addis Ababa

Ethiopia's economy is 53.2 percent free, according to our 2008 assessment, which makes it the world's 124th freest economy. Its overall score is 1.2 percentage points lower than last year, partly reflecting declines in five areas. Ethiopia is ranked 26th out of 40 countries in the sub-Saharan Africa region, and its overall score is slightly worse than the regional average.

Ethiopia does not rank strongly in any category but does score moderately well in fiscal freedom, government size, and labor freedom. The top income and corporate tax rates are moderate, and overall tax revenue is not large as a percentage of GDP. Government expenditures are not high, and labor markets, unlike those in most of Europe and the rest of Africa, are lightly regulated.

A developing nation, Ethiopia does not score well in trade freedom, investment freedom, financial freedom, property rights, and freedom from corruption. The banking system is weak and subject to strong political pressure, as is the rule of law. Property rights cannot be guaranteed.

BACKGROUND: Ethiopia is one of sub-Saharan Africa's poorest countries. A military council, the Derg, deposed and killed Emperor Haile Selassie in 1974 and established a repressive socialist regime under Mengistu Haile Mariam. The Derg was overthrown in 1991. While Ethiopia is moving toward multi-party democracy, obstacles to progress are abundant, as demonstrated by the 2005 post-election crackdown on protestors. Agriculture contributes over 45 percent of GDP, accounts for over 80 percent of exports, and employs over 80 percent of the population. The government remains involved in key economic sectors and reserves others for Ethiopians. Since its war with Eritrea, Ethiopia has depended heavily on Djibouti for access to foreign goods. The border remains heavily armed, and conflict could be renewed. Ethiopia invaded Somalia in support of Somalia's transitional federal government in December 2006.

How Do We Measure Economic Freedom? See Chapter 4 (page 39) for an explanation of the methodology or visit the *Index* Web site at *heritage.org/index*.

The economy is 53.2% free

```
100
 80
 60
 40
 20
```

Sub-Saharan Africa Average = 54.5
World Average = 60.3

1995   2008

QUICK FACTS

Population: 71.3 million

GDP (PPP): $75.1 billion
10.3% growth in 2005
5.1% 5-yr. comp. ann. growth
$1,055 per capita

Unemployment: n/a

Inflation (CPI): 6.8%

FDI (net flow): $205.0 million

Official Development Assistance:
Multilateral: $777.9 million
Bilateral: $1.3 billion (53.2% from the U.S.)

External Debt: $6.3 billion

Exports: $1.9 billion
Primarily coffee, gold, leather products, live animals, oilseeds

Imports: $4.9 billion
Primarily food and live animals, petroleum and petroleum products, chemicals, machinery, motor vehicles, cereals, textiles

2005 data unless otherwise noted.

ETHIOPIA'S TEN ECONOMIC FREEDOMS

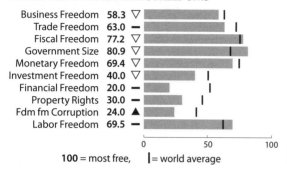

Business Freedom	58.3 ▽
Trade Freedom	63.0 —
Fiscal Freedom	77.2 ▽
Government Size	80.9 ▽
Monetary Freedom	69.4 ▽
Investment Freedom	40.0 ▽
Financial Freedom	20.0 —
Property Rights	30.0 —
Fdm fm Corruption	24.0 ▲
Labor Freedom	69.5 —

0   50   100

100 = most free, **I** = world average

BUSINESS FREEDOM — *58.3%*

The overall freedom to start, operate, and close a business is restricted by Ethiopia's national regulatory environment. Starting a business takes an average of 16 days, compared to the world average of 43 days. Although the cost is high, obtaining a business license requires less than the world average of 19 procedures and 234 days. Regulation is generally regarded as fair but not always transparent. Bureaucracy is cumbersome, but closing a business is relatively easy.

TRADE FREEDOM — *63%*

Ethiopia's weighted average tariff rate was 13.5 percent in 2002. Restrictive foreign exchange controls, burdensome trade-related regulations and bureaucracy, import restrictions, and inadequate infrastructure add to the cost of trade. An additional 10 percentage points is deducted from Ethiopia's trade freedom score to account for these non-tariff barriers.

FISCAL FREEDOM — *77.2%*

Ethiopia has burdensome tax rates. The top income tax rate is 35 percent, and the top corporate tax rate is 30 percent. Other taxes include a value-added tax (VAT) and a capital gains tax. In the most recent year, overall tax revenue as a percentage of GDP was 12.6 percent.

GOVERNMENT SIZE — *80.9%*

Total government expenditures, including consumption and transfer payments, are low. In the most recent year, government spending equaled 25.2 percent of GDP. Despite a decade of privatization, state ownership and management still guide many sectors of the economy.

MONETARY FREEDOM — *69.4%*

Inflation is relatively high, averaging 10.6 percent between 2004 and 2006. Relatively unstable prices explain most of the monetary freedom score. The government influences prices through its regulation of state-owned enterprises and utilities, subsidizes and controls the prices of petroleum products, and controls the prices of pharmaceuticals and fertilizers. An additional 10 percentage points is deducted from Ethiopia's monetary freedom score to adjust for measures that distort domestic prices.

INVESTMENT FREEDOM — *40%*

Despite efforts to liberalize foreign investment laws and streamline registration, official and unofficial barriers persist. Sectarian and ethnic violence (particularly on the Somali border) continues. Certain sectors remain off-limits. The Ethiopian Investment Commission provides a one-stop service that significantly cuts the cost of obtaining licenses. An investment promotion authority has been established to lure foreign capital into certain sectors like textiles. Foreign exchange accounts, payments, and current transfers are subject to controls and restrictions, as are capital transactions. All investments must be approved and certified by the government.

FINANCIAL FREEDOM — *20%*

Ethiopia's financial sector is small and significantly government-influenced. The central bank is not independent, and the government strongly influences lending, controls interest rates, and owns the largest bank (Commercial Bank of Ethiopia), which accounts for two-thirds of outstanding credit. Six local private banks have appeared since the mid-1990s and have increased their share of total deposits, loans, and credit, but foreign banks remain barred. The state-run bank faced collapse several years ago, but its over 50 percent of non-performing loans has since been reduced to just over 25 percent. Foreign firms may not invest in banking or insurance. One of the insurance sector's nine companies is state-owned. There is no stock market, but the private sale of equity is common.

PROPERTY RIGHTS — *30%*

Enforcement of property rights is weak. The judicial system is underdeveloped, poorly staffed, and inexperienced despite efforts to strengthen its capacity. Property and contractual rights are recognized, but judges lack an understanding of commercial issues. An international arbitration body's decision may not be fully accepted and implemented by Ethiopian authorities. A highly restrictive land-tenure policy makes it very difficult to register property. Private ownership of land is prohibited; land must be leased from the state.

FREEDOM FROM CORRUPTION — *24%*

Corruption is perceived as widespread. Ethiopia ranks 130th out of 163 countries in Transparency International's Corruption Perceptions Index for 2006. Despite legal restrictions on corruption, officials have been accused of manipulating the privatization process, and state-owned and party-owned businesses receive preferential access to land leases and credit.

LABOR FREEDOM — *69.5%*

Burdensome employment regulations hinder employment opportunities and productivity growth. The non-salary cost of employing a worker is very low, but dismissing a redundant employee is relatively costly. The difficulty of laying off a worker creates a risk aversion for companies that would otherwise hire more people and grow. Restrictions on the number of work hours are rigid.

FIJI

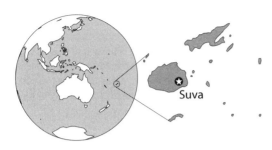

Suva

Fiji's economy is 61.5 percent free, according to our 2008 assessment, which makes it the world's 69th freest economy. Its overall score is 0.9 percentage point higher than last year, partly reflecting improvements in monetary freedom. Fiji is ranked 11th out of 30 countries in the Asia–Pacific region, and its overall score is slightly above the regional average.

Fiji scores higher than the world average in six of 10 economic freedoms but is very strong in only one area: labor freedom. The labor market operates under highly flexible conditions that make hiring and firing workers very easy. Government expenditures are relatively low. Inflation is also fairly low, but Fiji's monetary freedom score is hurt by government price controls.

Fiji is weak in investment freedom and property rights. Foreign investment is highly controlled and regulated, and the judicial system's enforcement of these regulations is both erratic and clogged by a significant backlog of cases.

BACKGROUND: Fiji, a Pacific island nation, has suffered a number of military coups in recent years that have stunted its crucial tourism industry and the economy more generally. A developing country, Fiji relies heavily on its agriculture, clothing, and fishing industries for employment. Tourism expanded rapidly for two decades and is now a major source of foreign exchange earnings. The government has tried to diversify the economy and make Fiji an easier place to do business, but with little success. Political uncertainty and weak protection of property rights remain major risk factors.

The economy is 61.5% free

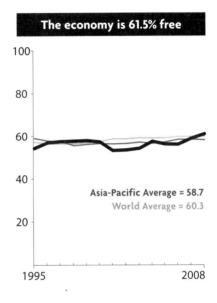

Asia-Pacific Average = 58.7
World Average = 60.3

1995　　　　　　　2008

QUICK FACTS

Population: 0.8 million

GDP (PPP): $5.1 billion
0.7% growth in 2005
3.3% 5-yr. comp. ann. growth
$6,049 per capita

Unemployment: 12.1% (2000)

Inflation (CPI): 2.4%

FDI (net flow): −$14 million

Official Development Assistance:
Multilateral: $24.8 million
Bilateral: $40.4 million (2.3% from the U.S.)

External Debt: $127.0 million (2004 estimate)

Exports: $719.6 million
Primarily sugar, garments, gold, timber, fish, molasses, coconut oil

Imports: $1.5 billion
Primarily manufactured goods, machinery and transport equipment, petroleum products, food, chemicals
2005 data unless otherwise noted.

How Do We Measure Economic Freedom? See Chapter 4 (page 39) for an explanation of the methodology or visit the *Index* Web site at *heritage.org/index.*

FIJI'S TEN ECONOMIC FREEDOMS

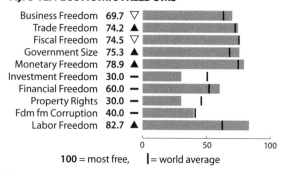

Business Freedom	69.7 ▽	
Trade Freedom	74.2 ▲	
Fiscal Freedom	74.5 ▽	
Government Size	75.3 ▲	
Monetary Freedom	78.9 ▲	
Investment Freedom	30.0 —	
Financial Freedom	60.0 —	
Property Rights	30.0 —	
Fdm fm Corruption	40.0 —	
Labor Freedom	82.7 ▲	

0   50   100

100 = most free,   ▌= world average

BUSINESS FREEDOM — *69.7%*

The overall freedom to start, operate, and close a business is relatively well protected by Fiji's national regulatory environment. Starting a business takes an average of 46 days, compared to the world average of 43 days. Obtaining a business license requires less than the world average of 19 procedures and 234 days. Bankruptcy proceedings are generally straightforward. However, the lack of transparency impedes entrepreneurial activities.

TRADE FREEDOM — *74.2%*

Fiji's average tariff rate was 7.9 percent in 2005. Import licensing restrictions, variable import taxes, and tax concessions for exporters add to the cost of trade. An additional 10 percentage points is deducted from Fiji's trade freedom score to account for non-tariff barriers.

FISCAL FREEDOM — *74.5%*

Fiji has moderate tax rates. Both the top income tax rate and the top corporate tax rate are 31 percent. Other taxes include a value-added tax (VAT) and a property tax. In the most recent year, overall tax revenue as a percentage of GDP was 25 percent.

GOVERNMENT SIZE — *75.3%*

Total government expenditures, including consumption and transfer payments, are moderate. In the most recent year, government spending equaled 28.7 percent of GDP. The monopoly position of state-owned enterprises adds growing costs to the economy.

MONETARY FREEDOM — *78.9%*

Inflation is moderate, averaging 3.1 percent between 2004 and 2006. Relatively stable prices explain most of the monetary freedom score. The government influences prices through state-owned utilities and controls the prices of various products, including food. An additional 10 percentage points is deducted from Fiji's monetary freedom score to adjust for measures that distort domestic prices.

INVESTMENT FREEDOM — *30%*

Fiji restricts foreign investment but also offers tax incentives to investors in preferred activities. The government requires foreign investors to undergo several bureaucratic procedures to register and must approve all investments, often in a non-transparent manner. Fiji's large sugar industry depends on high prices paid by the EU; as this system is being phased out in 2008, the government is attempting to diversify foreign investment. Foreign acquisition of local enterprises is discouraged. Foreign real estate ownership is permitted but complex. Residents may hold foreign exchange accounts subject to approval by the government; non-residents face certain restrictions as well. Most payments and transfers (including capital) are subject to government approval and limitations on amounts.

FINANCIAL FREEDOM — *60%*

Fiji's financial system is relatively well developed and is characterized by a significant degree of foreign participation. The banking system accounts for 35 percent of financial system assets and is largely private, though the state-owned Fiji Development Bank provides business development loans and offers some commercial banking services. The government sold its minority stake in the National Bank in January 2006, withdrawing from the pure commercial banking sector. The two largest banks are Australian and account for 80 percent of the banking market; three other foreign banks operate freely. The insurance sector consists of 10 companies and is dominated by foreign firms. Fiji's small but developing stock exchange listed 16 companies in 2006.

PROPERTY RIGHTS — *30%*

Protection of property is highly uncertain. The backlog of cases in the courts is significant, and processing is slowed by a shortage of prosecutors. Purported abrogations of the constitution and other events, including abolition of the Supreme Court, have undermined the independence of the judiciary. The many difficulties involved in obtaining land titles are serious obstacles to investment and growth. Foreign investors are discouraged from acquiring controlling interest in, or taking over established, locally owned enterprises.

FREEDOM FROM CORRUPTION — *40%*

Corruption is perceived as significant. Fiji was ranked 55th out of 158 countries in Transparency International's Corruption Perceptions Index for 2005. It was not ranked by TI in 2006. Because Fiji has a small population and a limited number of persons in positions of power, personal relationships can be a significant factor in business and government decisions.

LABOR FREEDOM — *82.7%*

The labor market operates under flexible employment regulations that could enhance employment opportunities and productivity growth. The non-salary cost of employing a worker is low, and dismissing a redundant employee is costless. Restrictions on increasing or contracting the number of working hours have become more flexible. Fiji's labor freedom is one of the highest in the world.

FINLAND

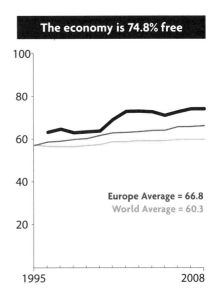

Helsinki

Rank: 16

Regional Rank: 9 of 41

Finland's economy is 74.8 percent free, according to our 2008 assessment, which makes it the world's 16th freest economy. Its overall score is 0.6 percentage point higher than last year. Finland is ranked 9th out of 41 countries in the European region, and its overall score is well above the regional average.

Finland is a world leader in four of 10 economic freedoms: financial freedom, monetary freedom, freedom from corruption, and business freedom. A business-friendly environment with minimal regulation is enabling the rapid growth of private enterprise. Property is protected by a transparent rule of law, and foreign investors enjoy excellent market access. There is virtually no corruption, and business operations are not hampered by government bureaucracy. As a member of the euro zone, Finland has a standardized monetary policy that yields low inflation despite some government distortion in the agricultural sector.

Finland could improve its labor freedom and reduce its government size. As in many other European social democracies, high government spending supports an extensive welfare state: Government spending equals half of Finland's GDP. The labor market operates under fairly restrictive regulations, such as a limited number of working hours allowed per week and very high unemployment benefits.

BACKGROUND: Finland joined the European Union in 1995 and has one its the best-performing economies. It also joined the single European currency in January 1999 and has been a strong supporter of further European integration. Finland boasts a modern, competitive, transparent economy with vibrant information and communications technology sectors, but labor market rigidities still hamper job creation, and unemployment remains relatively high. Finland is a member of NATO's Partnership for Peace program but has not pursued full membership because of its neutral military status.

How Do We Measure Economic Freedom? See Chapter 4 (page 39) for an explanation of the methodology or visit the *Index* Web site at *heritage.org/index*.

The economy is 74.8% free

Europe Average = 66.8
World Average = 60.3

1995 — 2008

QUICK FACTS

Population: 5.2 million

GDP (PPP): $168.7 billion
2.9% growth in 2005
2.5% 5-yr. comp. ann. growth
$32,152 per capita

Unemployment: 8.4%

Inflation (CPI): 0.8%

FDI (net flow): $1.9 billion

Official Development Assistance:
Multilateral: None
Bilateral: None

External Debt: $251.9 billion

Exports: $82.5 billion
Primarily machinery and equipment, chemicals, metals, timber, paper, pulp

Imports: $71.1 billion
Primarily foodstuffs, petroleum and petroleum products, chemicals, transport equipment, iron and steel, machinery, textile yarn and fabrics, grains

2005 data unless otherwise noted.

FINLAND'S TEN ECONOMIC FREEDOMS

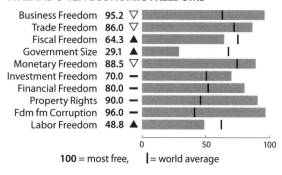

Business Freedom	95.2	▽
Trade Freedom	86.0	▽
Fiscal Freedom	64.3	▲
Government Size	29.1	▲
Monetary Freedom	88.5	▽
Investment Freedom	70.0	—
Financial Freedom	80.0	—
Property Rights	90.0	—
Fdm fm Corruption	96.0	—
Labor Freedom	48.8	▲

0   50   100

100 = most free, ▌= world average

BUSINESS FREEDOM — 95.2%

The overall freedom to start, operate, and close a business is strongly protected by Finland's national regulatory environment. Starting a business takes an average of 14 days, compared to the world average of 43 days. Obtaining a business license requires less than the world average of 19 procedures and 234 days. Bankruptcy proceedings are straightforward and not costly.

TRADE FREEDOM — 86%

Finland's trade policy is the same as those of other members of the European Union. The common EU weighted average tariff rate was 2 percent in 2005. Non-tariff barriers reflected in EU policy include agricultural and manufacturing subsidies, import restrictions for some goods and services, market access restrictions in some service sectors, non-transparent and restrictive regulations and standards, and inconsistent customs administration across EU members. Consequently, an additional 10 percentage points is deducted from Finland's trade freedom score.

FISCAL FREEDOM — 64.3%

Finland has moderate tax rates. The top income tax rate is 32 percent, and the top corporate tax rate is 26 percent. Other taxes include a value-added tax (VAT) and a real estate tax. In the most recent year, overall tax revenue as a percentage of GDP was 43.3 percent.

GOVERNMENT SIZE — 29.1%

Total government expenditures, including consumption and transfer payments, are very high. In the most recent year, government spending equaled 48.6 percent of GDP. State ownership remains considerable, and the government still holds major stakes in over 50 companies.

MONETARY FREEDOM — 88.5%

Finland uses the euro as its currency. Between 2004 and 2006, Finland's weighted average annual rate of inflation was 1.1 percent. Stable prices explain most of the monetary freedom score. As a participant in the EU's Common Agricultural Policy, the government subsidizes agricultural production, distorting the prices of agricultural products. It also imposes artificially low prices on pharmaceutical products. An additional 5 percentage points is deducted from Finland's monetary freedom score to account for these policies.

INVESTMENT FREEDOM — 70%

Finland welcomes foreign investment and imposes few restrictions. The main incentives are its highly educated workforce, stable policies, and excellent infrastructure. Foreign acquisitions of large Finnish companies may require follow-up clearance from the Ministry of Trade and Industry. Non–European Economic Area investors must apply for a license to invest in many sectors, including security, electrical contracting, alcohol, telecommunications, aviation, and restaurants. The state invests actively in promising high-tech companies, holding shares in over 50 companies. Restrictions on the purchase of land apply only to non-residents purchasing land in the Aaland Islands. Some residency restrictions apply to foreign investment to ensure jurisdiction of the court system. There are no exchange controls and no restrictions on current transfers or repatriation of profits, and residents and non-residents may hold foreign exchange accounts.

FINANCIAL FREEDOM — 80%

The use of information technology in Finland's modern and sophisticated banking system is extensive, and almost 90 percent of transactions are electronic. Deregulation in the 1980s and a banking and financial crisis in the 1990s led to consolidation, international mergers, and links to insurance companies in the banking sector. There were 345 domestic banks at the end of 2005, but the banking system is dominated by three major bank groups (Nordea, OP Bank Group, and the Sampo group), which together account for over 80 percent of the market. The government owns about 14 percent of the Sampo Group. Banking is open to foreign competition. Capital markets determine interest rates, and credit is available to nationals and foreigners equally. The stock exchange is part of OMX Exchanges, an integrated network of Baltic and Nordic exchanges, and has strong high-tech equity representation.

PROPERTY RIGHTS — 90%

Property rights are well protected, and contractual agreements are strictly honored. The quality of the judiciary and civil service is generally high. Expropriation is unlikely. Finland adheres to numerous international agreements concerning intellectual property.

FREEDOM FROM CORRUPTION — 96%

Corruption is perceived as almost nonexistent. Finland ranks 1st out of 163 countries in Transparency International's Corruption Perceptions Index for 2006. Finland is a signatory to the OECD Anti-Bribery Convention, and it is a criminal act to give or accept a bribe.

LABOR FREEDOM — 48.8%

Burdensome employment regulations hamper employment opportunities and productivity growth. The non-salary cost of employing a worker is high, and dismissing a redundant employee is relatively costly. Restrictions on the number of work hours remain rigid.

FRANCE

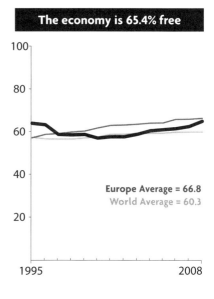
Paris

Rank: 48

Regional Rank: 25 of 41

France's economy is 65.4 percent free, according to our 2008 assessment, which makes it the world's 48th freest economy. Its overall score is 2.5 percentage points higher than last year. France is ranked 25th out of 41 countries in the European region, and its overall score is lower than the regional average.

France scores above the world average in eight of 10 economic freedoms and especially strongly in business freedom, property rights, and freedom from corruption. As a member of the European Union, it has a standardized monetary policy that yields relatively low inflation, despite agricultural distortions. Property is protected by transparent rule of law.

However, France's fiscal freedom and government size scores are extraordinarily weak. As in many other European social democracies, government spending and tax rates are exceptionally high to support an extensive welfare state. Government expenditures are more than half the size of the nation's GDP.

BACKGROUND: In the wake of the government's failure to enact serious market reforms in the 1990s, France's economy has suffered significantly in comparison to the economies of its Western neighbors. Faced with chronic unemployment, lack of growth, and escalating social disorder, France elected conservative reformer Nicolas Sarkozy to the presidency in 2007. Immediate challenges will be to introduce new labor legislation and reform the tax code to make work pay. France continues to be both a driving force for further European integration and a major recipient of enormously distorting agricultural subsidies under the European Union's Common Agricultural Policy. Protectionist policies toward politically sensitive industries such as wine, cheese, and mustard are likely to continue under Sarkozy, as is state intervention to protect French jobs from the perceived pressures of globalization.

How Do We Measure Economic Freedom? See Chapter 4 (page 39) for an explanation of the methodology or visit the *Index* Web site at *heritage.org/index*.

The economy is 65.4% free

Europe Average = 66.8
World Average = 60.3

1995 — 2008

QUICK FACTS

Population: 60.9 million

GDP (PPP): $1.8 trillion
1.2% growth in 2005
1.4% 5-yr. comp. ann. growth
$30,385 per capita

Unemployment: 9.5%

Inflation (CPI): 1.9%

FDI (net flow): −$52.1 billion

Official Development Assistance:
Multilateral: None
Bilateral: None

External Debt: $3.5 trillion

Exports: $555.2 billion
Primarily machinery and transportation equipment, aircraft, plastics, chemicals, pharmaceutical products, iron and steel, beverages

Imports: $577.5 billion
Primarily machinery and equipment, vehicles, crude oil, aircraft, plastics, chemicals

2005 data unless otherwise noted.

FRANCE'S TEN ECONOMIC FREEDOMS

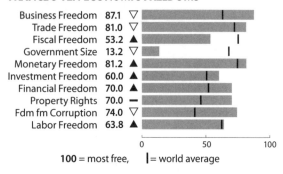

Business Freedom	87.1	▽
Trade Freedom	81.0	▽
Fiscal Freedom	53.2	▲
Government Size	13.2	▽
Monetary Freedom	81.2	▲
Investment Freedom	60.0	▲
Financial Freedom	70.0	▲
Property Rights	70.0	—
Fdm fm Corruption	74.0	▽
Labor Freedom	63.8	▲

0   50   100

100 = most free, I = world average

BUSINESS FREEDOM — 87.1%
The overall freedom to start, operate, and close a business is well protected by France's regulatory environment. Starting a business takes an average of seven days, compared to the world average of 43 days. Obtaining a business license requires less than the world average of 19 procedures and 234 days. Closing a business is relatively easy.

TRADE FREEDOM — 81%
France's trade policy is the same as those of other members of the European Union. The common EU weighted average tariff rate was 2 percent in 2005. Non-tariff barriers reflected in EU policy include agricultural and manufacturing subsidies, import restrictions for some goods and services, market access restrictions in some service sectors, non-transparent and restrictive regulations and standards, and inconsistent customs administration across EU members. Lack of transparency in standards and regulations, barriers to service market access, and pharmaceutical restrictions exceed EU policy benchmarks. Consequently, an additional 15 percentage points is deducted from France's trade freedom score.

FISCAL FREEDOM — 53.2%
Beginning with the 2006 tax year, the top personal income tax rate is 40 percent, down from 48.1 percent. The top corporate tax rate is 33.8 percent (33.3 percent plus a 1.5 percent surcharge). Other taxes include a value-added tax (VAT) and a business tax. In the most recent year, overall tax revenue as a percentage of GDP was 44 percent.

GOVERNMENT SIZE — 13.2%
Total government expenditures, including consumption and transfer payments, are very high. In the most recent year, government spending equaled 53.8 percent of GDP. State-owned or state-controlled enterprises dominate such industries as postal services, electricity, and rail. Semi-public companies in which the state holds shares employ almost 4 percent of the labor force.

MONETARY FREEDOM — 81.2%
France is a member of the euro zone. Between 2004 and 2006, France's weighted average annual rate of inflation was 1.9 percent. Relatively low and stable prices explain most of the monetary freedom score. As a participant in the EU's Common Agricultural Policy, the government subsidizes agricultural production, distorting the prices of agricul-

tural products. Prices of pharmaceuticals, books, electricity, gas, and rail transportation are regulated. Consequently, an additional 10 percentage points is deducted from France's monetary policy score.

INVESTMENT FREEDOM — 60%
Regulations are fairly simple, and many incentives are available. Foreign companies complain of high payroll and income taxes, pervasive regulation of labor and products markets, and negative attitudes toward foreign investors. Prior approval is necessary for investment in strategic sectors like public health, defense, or casinos. In late 2006, the European Commission challenged the EU legality of France's investment regulation law. Foreign investment is restricted in sectors like agriculture, aircraft production, air transport, audiovisual, insurance, and maritime transport. Residents and non-residents may hold foreign exchange accounts. There are no restrictions or controls on payments, transfers, or repatriation of profits, and non-residents may purchase real estate.

FINANCIAL FREEDOM — 70%
France's financial, legal, regulatory, and accounting systems are somewhat burdensome but consistent with international norms. There is no distinction between commercial and investment banks. Most loans are provided at market terms. The government has sold its majority stake in most financial institutions but still owns the Caisse des Depots et Consignations and holds minority stakes elsewhere. At the end of 2005, 161 foreign banks, including 57 non-EU banks, accounted for about 10 percent of total assets. France is the world's fourth-largest insurance market, and foreign companies held 21.5 percent of the market in 2004. The government owns stakes in several insurance companies. Capital markets are well developed, and foreign investors participate freely.

PROPERTY RIGHTS — 70%
Contractual agreements are secure, and the judiciary and civil service are professional, though bureaucratic entanglements are common. Any company defined as a national public service or natural monopoly must pass into state ownership. Protection of intellectual property rights is strong.

FREEDOM FROM CORRUPTION — 74%
Corruption is perceived as minimal. France ranks 18th out of 163 countries in Transparency International's Corruption Perceptions Index for 2006. France enforces the OECD Anti-Bribery Convention domestically through amendments to its criminal code.

LABOR FREEDOM — 63.8%
Employment rules could be further improved to enhance employment opportunities and productivity growth. The non-salary cost of employing a worker is very high, and dismissing a redundant employee can be relatively costly. Restrictions on the number of work hours remain inflexible.

GABON

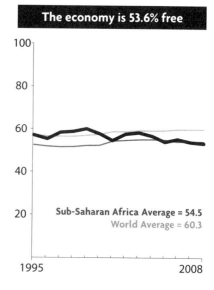

Rank: 122

Regional Rank: 25 of 40

Gabon's economy is 53.6 percent free, according to our 2008 assessment, which makes it the world's 122nd freest economy. Its overall score is 0.6 percentage point lower than last year, partly reflecting lower monetary freedom. Gabon is ranked 25th out of 40 countries in the sub-Saharan Africa region, and its overall score is almost equal to the regional average.

Gabon is above the world average only in government size, which is a measure of how large government expenditures are relative to GDP. Though tax rates are high, overall revenue is relatively small, which may be a sign of tax avoidance and a weak state. Inflation is exceptionally low, but the government distorts market prices through price controls on certain goods.

Gabon scores lowest in fiscal freedom, trade freedom, investment freedom, financial freedom, property rights, and freedom from corruption. The average tariff rate is extremely high and supplemented by non-tariff barriers. The government agreed with the International Monetary Fund in 2005 to liberalize foreign investment, but little has been done. Civil service corruption is present, but not as extensively as in other developing countries in the region.

BACKGROUND: President Omar Bongo Ondimba has ruled since the death of President Leon M'Ba in 1967. In 1968, Bongo established a one-party state that continued until 1990, when domestic unrest led him to introduce political reforms, including a transformation to multi-party democracy and freedom of assembly and the press. The economy is driven by oil, forestry, and minerals. In 2006, oil accounted for over 60 percent of GDP, over 65 percent of government revenues, and over 85 percent of exports. Declining oil production poses a great challenge unless Gabon can diversify its economy. Despite the rising price of oil, economic growth has been disappointing in recent years. Ongoing problems include mismanagement, a lack of transparency in government finances, corruption, and outdated infrastructure.

How Do We Measure Economic Freedom? See Chapter 4 (page 39) for an explanation of the methodology or visit the *Index* Web site at *heritage.org/index*.

The economy is 53.6% free

Sub-Saharan Africa Average = 54.5
World Average = 60.3

1995 — 2008

QUICK FACTS

Population: 1.4 million

GDP (PPP): $9.6 billion
3.0% growth in 2005
1.6% 5-yr. comp. ann. growth
$6,954 per capita

Unemployment: 21.0%

Inflation (CPI): 0.0%

FDI (net flow): $328.0 million

Official Development Assistance:
Multilateral: $30.9 million
Bilateral: $77.7 million (2.3% from the U.S.)

External Debt: $3.9 billion

Exports: $6.7 billion
Primarily crude oil, timber, manganese, uranium

Imports: $1.6 billion
Primarily machinery and equipment, foodstuffs, chemicals, construction materials

2005 data unless otherwise noted.

GABON'S TEN ECONOMIC FREEDOMS

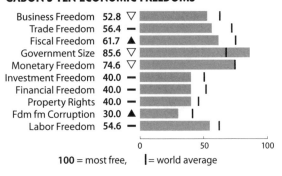

Business Freedom	52.8 ▽	
Trade Freedom	56.4 —	
Fiscal Freedom	61.7 ▲	
Government Size	85.6 ▽	
Monetary Freedom	74.6 ▽	
Investment Freedom	40.0 —	
Financial Freedom	40.0 —	
Property Rights	40.0 —	
Fdm fm Corruption	30.0 ▲	
Labor Freedom	54.6 —	

0   50   100

100 = most free, **|** = world average

BUSINESS FREEDOM — 52.8%

The overall freedom to start, operate, and close a business is restricted by Gabon's regulatory environment. Starting a business takes an average of 58 days, compared to the world average of 43 days. Obtaining a business license requires less than the world average of 19 procedures and 234 days. Closing a business can be lengthy and costly.

TRADE FREEDOM — 56.4%

Gabon's weighted average tariff rate was 16.8 percent in 2005. Import bans, high import taxes, inappropriate customs valuation, and export subsidies add to the cost of trade. An additional 10 percentage points is deducted from Gabon's trade freedom score to account for non-tariff barriers.

FISCAL FREEDOM — 61.7%

Gabon has high tax rates. The top income tax rate is 50 percent, and the top corporate tax rate is 35 percent. The government also imposes a value-added tax (VAT). In the most recent year, overall tax revenue as a percentage of GDP was 10.3 percent.

GOVERNMENT SIZE — 85.6%

Total government expenditures, including consumption and transfer payments, are moderate. In the most recent year, government spending equaled 21.9 percent of GDP. Privatization has progressed somewhat. Around 30 state-owned enterprises have been divested, and the state post office, which has consumed substantial public funding since 2003, is being reorganized.

MONETARY FREEDOM — 74.6%

Inflation is low, averaging 2.7 percent between 2004 and 2006. Stable prices explain most of the monetary freedom score. The government influences prices through subsidies to state-owned enterprises and controls the prices of various products, including fuel, pharmaceuticals, and medical equipment. An additional 15 percentage points is deducted from Gabon's monetary freedom score to adjust for measures that distort domestic prices.

INVESTMENT FREEDOM — 40%

Foreign investment and domestic capital are legally equal under a 1998 regional investment code. An agreement signed with the IMF in 2005 commits Gabon to economic liberalization, but little has been done. An unpredictable legal system, political influence and corruption, and high production costs impede investment. Certain economic sectors have their own business code, separate from the 1998 agreement. Residents may hold foreign exchange accounts subject to some restrictions. Non-residents may hold foreign exchange accounts but must report them to the government. Transfers and payments to most countries must be officially approved. Capital transactions are subject to reporting requirements, controls, and official authorization. All real estate transactions must be reported.

FINANCIAL FREEDOM — 40%

Gabon's small financial system is extensively government-influenced. Government-ownership shares account for about 25 percent of total financial-sector assets. Gabon shares certain financial institutions, such as a common central bank and a common currency, with other West African countries. The banking sector is composed of five commercial banks and is open to foreign competition. Three banks are affiliated with French banks, and another is entirely foreign-owned. Most banks are at least partly state-owned. The two largest banks control 70 percent of deposits and accounts. Domestic credit is limited and expensive, though available without discrimination to foreign investors with prior authorization. There are four major insurance companies, the largest two of which dominate the market. Trading on a small regional stock exchange headquartered in Gabon is set to begin by 2008.

PROPERTY RIGHTS — 40%

Private property is moderately well protected. The president influences the judiciary and both chambers of parliament, and other countries doing business in Gabon do not always treat giving or accepting a bribe as a criminal act. Expropriation is unlikely. As a member of the Central African Economic and Monetary Community and the Economic Community of Central African States, Gabon adheres to the laws of the African Intellectual Property Office.

FREEDOM FROM CORRUPTION — 30%

Corruption is perceived as widespread. Gabon ranks 90th out of 163 countries in Transparency International's Corruption Perceptions Index for 2006. Foreign firms reportedly are asked by government officials for campaign contributions to support ruling party candidates. Weak financial management and corruption have contributed to significant arrears in domestic and external debt payments.

LABOR FREEDOM — 54.6%

Employment regulations hinder employment opportunities and productivity growth. The non-salary cost of employing a worker is high, and dismissing a redundant employee is relatively costly. The difficulty of laying off a worker creates a risk aversion for companies that would otherwise hire more people and grow. Regulations related to the number of work hours are very rigid.

THE GAMBIA

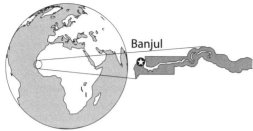

Banjul

Rank: 95

Regional Rank: 12 of 40

The Gambia's economy is 56.6 percent free, according to our 2008 assessment, which makes it the world's 95th freest economy. Its overall score is 0.8 percentage point lower than last year. The Gambia is ranked 12th out of 40 countries in the sub-Saharan Africa region, and its overall score is slightly higher than the regional average.

The Gambia scores highly in only two freedoms but is also significantly below the world average in only two others. Its positives are relatively small government size and strong labor freedom. The labor market is highly flexible, and dismissing a redundant employee is easy.

As a developing nation, The Gambia faces significant challenges. Both property rights and freedom from corruption score 16 percentage points below the world average. An inefficient and corrupt bureaucracy has a negative impact on most aspects of commercial life. Property rights are not secured by an independent judiciary, and the courts are subject to political interference. In addition, the average tariff rate is high, inhibiting both trade and investment opportunities.

BACKGROUND: The Gambia achieved independence in 1965. President Sir Dawda Kairaba Jawara led the country for almost 30 years until 1994, when he was ousted by a military coup led by Lieutenant Yahya A.J.J. Jammeh. Jammeh won the presidential election in 1996, was re-elected in 2001, and won a third term in 2006. Most of the population is rural and engaged in subsistence agriculture. Agriculture accounts for over 30 percent of GDP and employs over 75 percent of the labor force. Corruption is widespread, and many parts of the government are poorly managed, lacking in transparency, and inefficient. Privatization has been slow, and most major companies are government-controlled. The infrastructure is improving but still inadequate, with frequent power shortages and poor roads.

How Do We Measure Economic Freedom? See Chapter 4 (page 39) for an explanation of the methodology or visit the *Index* Web site at *heritage.org/index*.

The economy is 56.6% free

Sub-Saharan Africa Average = 54.5
World Average = 60.3

1995 — 2008

QUICK FACTS

Population: 1.5 million

GDP (PPP): $2.9 billion
5.1% growth in 2005
3.8% 5-yr. comp. ann. growth
$1,921 per capita

Unemployment: n/a

Inflation (CPI): 3.2%

FDI (net flow): $11.0 million

Official Development Assistance:
Multilateral: $53.6 million
Bilateral: $16.3 million (12.0% from the U.S.)

External Debt: $672.0 million

Exports: $180.5 million
Primarily peanut products, fish, cotton lint, palm kernels, re-exports

Imports: $260.9 million
Primarily foodstuffs, manufactures, fuel, machinery and transport equipment

2005 data unless otherwise noted.

THE GAMBIA'S TEN ECONOMIC FREEDOMS

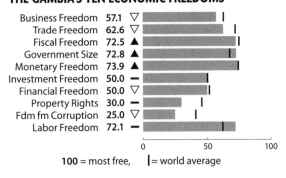

Business Freedom	57.1 ▽	
Trade Freedom	62.6 ▽	
Fiscal Freedom	72.5 ▲	
Government Size	72.8 ▲	
Monetary Freedom	73.9 ▲	
Investment Freedom	50.0 —	
Financial Freedom	50.0 ▽	
Property Rights	30.0 —	
Fdm fm Corruption	25.0 ▽	
Labor Freedom	72.1 —	

0   50   100

100 = most free, | = world average

BUSINESS FREEDOM — *57.1%*

The overall freedom to start, operate, and close a business is restricted by The Gambia's regulatory environment. Starting a business takes an average of 32 days, compared to the world average of 43 days. Obtaining a business license requires less than the world average of 19 procedures and 234 days. Closing a business can be burdensome and relatively costly. Bureaucratic inefficiency and lack of transparency persist.

TRADE FREEDOM — *62.6%*

The Gambia's simple average tariff rate was 13.7 percent in 2003. Inefficient and sometimes corrupt regulatory administration, restrictive licensing arrangements, sanitary and phytosanitary prohibitions on a few products, and a large informal trade sector add to the cost of trade. An additional 10 percentage points is deducted from The Gambia's trade freedom score to account for non-tariff barriers.

FISCAL FREEDOM — *72.5%*

The Gambia has moderately high tax rates. Both the top income tax rate and the top corporate tax rate are 35 percent. Other taxes include a capital gains tax, a sales tax, and a road tax. In the most recent year, overall tax revenue as a percentage of GDP was 17.2 percent.

GOVERNMENT SIZE — *72.8%*

Total government expenditures, including consumption and transfer payments, are moderate. In the most recent year, government spending equaled 30.1 percent of GDP. A consistently high fiscal deficit makes sound public finance management increasingly critical to economic growth. Most leading companies are still government-controlled, and privatization has been limited.

MONETARY FREEDOM — *73.9%*

Inflation is moderate, averaging 3.1 percent between 2004 and 2006. Relatively unstable prices explain most of the monetary freedom score. The government influences prices through a large public sector, and most leading companies, including those in agriculture, water, electricity, maritime services, public transportation, and telecommunications, remain in government hands. An additional 15 percentage points is deducted from The Gambia's monetary freedom score to adjust for measures that distort domestic prices.

INVESTMENT FREEDOM — *50%*

Foreign and domestic investment receive equal treatment. There are no limits on foreign ownership or control of businesses, except in television broadcasting and defense-related activities. Investment in fishing, agriculture, manufacturing, and tourism is especially encouraged. Repatriation of profits is permitted, and foreign investors may invest without a local partner, though joint ventures are encouraged. Investment flows have recovered from the political violence and alleged human rights violations from 2000–2003. Addressing regulatory barriers, including the absence of a transparent competition law, would attract the foreign capital needed to jump-start sustainable growth. Residents and non-residents may hold foreign exchange accounts. There are no restrictions on payments and transfers. Some capital transactions are controlled.

FINANCIAL FREEDOM — *50%*

The Gambia's financial system is small and dominated by banking. The Gambia is a member of the Economic Community of West African States, which promotes regional trade and economic integration. The largest commercial bank is a locally incorporated subsidiary of the U.K.-based Standard Chartered and is 25 percent Gambian-owned. There are four other commercial banks and a development bank. Rules on bank reporting requirements and money laundering are being tightened. A new supervisory authority has been established, though institutional power remains weak in practice. The insurance sector and the stock market remain small. Supervision and regulation of the financial system remain deficient because of weak institutional capacity, and the central bank is subject to government influence.

PROPERTY RIGHTS — *30%*

The judiciary, especially at the lower levels, is subject to pressure from the executive branch. Intimidation of lawyers, a lack of independence, and a lack of technical support severely undermine the administration of justice. Lack of judicial security is one of the main deterrents to doing business. The Supreme Court has not functioned since 2003. Gambian law provides adequate protection for intellectual property, patents, copyrights, and trademarks.

FREEDOM FROM CORRUPTION — *25%*

Corruption is perceived as widespread. The Gambia ranks 121st out of 163 countries in Transparency International's Corruption Perceptions Index for 2006. Official corruption remains serious. Corruption has been reported in government procurement and taxation.

LABOR FREEDOM — *72.1%*

Relatively flexible employment regulations could be further improved to enhance employment opportunities and productivity growth. The non-salary cost of employing a worker is moderate, and dismissing a redundant employee is relatively costless. Restrictions on the number of work hours are relatively flexible.

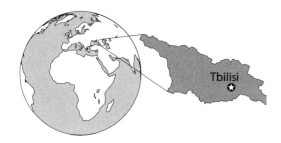

Tbilisi

GEORGIA

Rank: 32

Regional Rank: 18 of 41

Georgia's economy is 69.2 percent free, according to our 2008 assessment, which makes it the world's 32nd freest economy. Its overall score is 0.1 percentage point lower than last year. Georgia is ranked 18th out of 41 countries in the European region, and its overall score is equal to the regional average.

Georgia scores extraordinarily well in business freedom, fiscal freedom, government size, investment freedom, and labor freedom. Business operations are simple and not hampered by red tape. A very low top income tax rate complements the low corporate tax rate, and tax revenue is fairly low as a percentage of GDP. The strongest national institution is the labor market, which is highly flexible and far freer than those of most advanced economies.

As a transforming post-Communist economy, Georgia had much to improve a decade ago. Currently, only two categories remain significantly below the world average: property rights and freedom from corruption. Property rights cannot be guaranteed by the courts because of inefficiency and persistent corruption.

BACKGROUND: Georgia is one of the oldest countries in the Caucasus region and has deep roots in Eastern Christianity. It became independent with the collapse of the Soviet Union in 1991, but its survival was later threatened by civil wars and secessionist movements. Reformer and President Mikheil Saakashvili has been politically dominant since February 2005. Since 2006, Russia has subjected Georgia to economic sanctions, but GDP growth remains high at around 8.8 percent. The government has undertaken several privatizations and structural reforms, such as streamlining trade tariffs and taxes. Corruption remains one of the country's most difficult problems despite efforts to control it. Georgia has benefited from completion of the Baku–Tbilisi–Ceyhan oil pipeline from Azerbaijan to Turkey, which provides oil transit revenue.

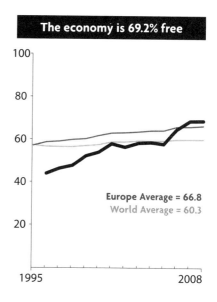

The economy is 69.2% free

100

80

60

40

20

Europe Average = 66.8
World Average = 60.3

1995 — 2008

QUICK FACTS

Population: 4.5 million

GDP (PPP): $15.1 billion
9.6% growth in 2005
8.0% 5-yr. comp. ann. growth
$3,365 per capita

Unemployment: 13.6%

Inflation (CPI): 8.3%

FDI (net flow): $539.0 million

Official Development Assistance:
Multilateral: $155.2 million
Bilateral: $210.2 million (34.9% from the U.S.)

External Debt: $2.0 billion

Exports: $2.2 billion
Primarily scrap metal, machinery, chemicals, fuel re-exports, citrus fruits, tea, wine

Imports: $3.3 billion
Primarily fuels, machinery and parts, transport equipment, grain and other foods, pharmaceuticals

2005 data unless otherwise noted.

How Do We Measure Economic Freedom? See Chapter 4 (page 39) for an explanation of the methodology or visit the *Index* Web site at *heritage.org/index*.

GEORGIA'S TEN ECONOMIC FREEDOMS

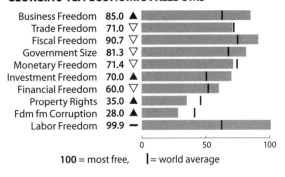

Business Freedom	85.0 ▲
Trade Freedom	71.0 ▽
Fiscal Freedom	90.7 ▽
Government Size	81.3 ▽
Monetary Freedom	71.4 ▽
Investment Freedom	70.0 ▲
Financial Freedom	60.0 ▽
Property Rights	35.0 ▲
Fdm fm Corruption	28.0 ▲
Labor Freedom	99.9 —

100 = most free, | = world average

BUSINESS FREEDOM — 85%

The overall freedom to start, operate, and close a business is relatively well protected by Georgia's national regulatory environment. Starting a business takes an average of 11 days, compared to the world average of 46 days. Obtaining a business license requires less than the world average of 19 procedures and 234 days. Closing a business is relatively simple.

TRADE FREEDOM — 71%

Georgia's weighted average tariff rate was 9.5 percent in 2004. Georgia has made significant progress toward liberalizing its trade regime, but agriculture subsidies, an inefficient customs process, and other barriers continue to add to the cost of trade. Some border trade goes unreported. An additional 10 percentage points is deducted from Georgia's trade freedom score to account for non-tariff barriers.

FISCAL FREEDOM — 90.7%

Georgia has low tax rates. The top income tax rate is a flat 12 percent, and the top corporate tax rate is 20 percent. Other taxes include a value-added tax (VAT), a tax on interest, and a tax on dividends. In the most recent year, overall tax revenue as a percentage of GDP was 19.7 percent.

GOVERNMENT SIZE — 81.3%

Total government expenditures, including consumption and transfer payments, are moderate, but spending has been increasing. In the most recent year, government spending equaled 25 percent of GDP. Progress in privatizing state-owned enterprises has been substantial.

MONETARY FREEDOM — 71.4%

Inflation is relatively high, averaging 8.7 percent between 2004 and 2006. Relatively unstable prices explain most of the monetary freedom score. Prices are generally set in the market, but the government may impose controls through state-owned enterprises. The government also provides subsidies for agricultural products and energy. An additional 10 percentage points is deducted from Georgia's monetary freedom score to adjust for measures that distort domestic prices.

INVESTMENT FREEDOM — 70%

Foreign investment receives equal treatment. In 2007, the World Bank recognized Georgia as the world's most rap-idly reforming economy. Corruption and legal reform are also proceeding rapidly. There are no restrictions on ownership of domestic companies, stocks, bonds, or other property, and local participation in businesses or investments is not required. Simple commercial registration and some licensing requirements do apply, however. Foreign firms may participate freely in privatizations, though transparency has been an issue. Residents and non-residents may hold foreign exchange accounts. There are limits and tests for payments and current transfers; capital transactions are not restricted but must (like investment) be registered.

FINANCIAL FREEDOM — 60%

Georgia's small financial sector has undergone substantial liberalization. Beginning in the 1990s, the central bank assumed a supervisory role and imposed stringent reporting and capital requirements that led to the closure or merging of a number of banks. There were 21 banks at the end of 2005, down from 247 in 1995. The eight largest banks account for about 90 percent of assets. Foreign bank branches are welcome, and foreign investors are majority owners of several banks. The government does not have a stake in any bank. Non-performing loans are a problem for some banks, which are generally risk-averse and prefer to issue most credit-financing trade. Significant informal transactions contribute to the weakness of the banking sector. The insurance sector includes significant foreign participation. The stock exchange is small and underdeveloped. The government issued its first bond in 2000.

PROPERTY RIGHTS — 35%

Judicial corruption is still a problem despite substantial improvement in trying to raise the level of efficiency and fairness in the courts. Both foreigners and Georgians continue to doubt the judicial system's ability to protect private property and contracts. Enforcement of laws protecting intellectual property rights is weak.

FREEDOM FROM CORRUPTION — 28%

Corruption is perceived as significant. Georgia now ranks 99th out of 163 countries in Transparency International's Corruption Perceptions Index for 2006. The government still faces a persistent challenge in controlling corruption. It has fired thousands of civil servants and police, and several high-level officials have been prosecuted for corruption-related offenses.

LABOR FREEDOM — 99.9%

Highly flexible employment regulations enhance employment opportunities and productivity growth. The non-salary cost of employing a worker can be moderate, and dismissing a redundant employee is costless. Rules on the number of work hours are very flexible. Georgia leads the world in labor market freedom.

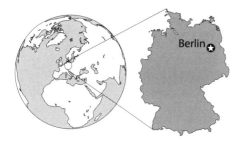

Berlin

GERMANY

G ermany's economy is 71.2 percent free, according to our 2008 assessment, which makes it the world's 23rd freest economy. Its overall score is 0.4 percentage point lower than last year. Germany is ranked 12th out of 41 countries in the European region, and its overall score is higher than the regional average.

Germany is strongest in its defense of property rights, backed by world-class freedom from corruption. The economy also enjoys strong business freedom and investment freedom. Business regulations are clear and efficient, enforced by the rule of law, and free of political interference. The government imposes few restrictions on foreign capital, which is subject to the same regulations as domestic investment.

Germany scores below the world average in terms of government size, fiscal freedom, and labor freedom. As in many other European social democracies, government spending and tax rates are exceptionally high in order to support an extensive welfare state. The labor market operates under restrictive conditions, although Germany has made a serious effort to lower its labor protectionism.

BACKGROUND: Germany, the European Union's largest economy, is home to many world-class companies and has an enormous export industry. Yet the economy has performed poorly in recent years, with structural unemployment, weak growth, and a fiscal budget deficit violating the EU's Stability and Growth Pact. The election of conservative reformer Angela Merkel to the chancellorship in 2006 led to some economic reforms, and initial signs point to a strong recovery for the economy. However, the inclusion of the Social Democrats in a grand coalition has reduced the likelihood that the more radical reforms needed to deal with Germany's structural challenges and ensure sustainable economic development will be implemented. Labor market reforms, deregulation, and reform of the government education system, for example, are urgently needed.

How Do We Measure Economic Freedom? See Chapter 4 (page 39) for an explanation of the methodology or visit the *Index* Web site at *heritage.org/index.*

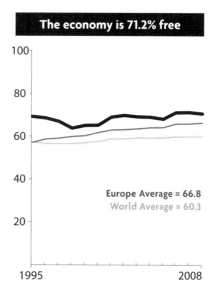

The economy is 71.2% free

Europe Average = 66.8
World Average = 60.3

QUICK FACTS

Population: 82.5 million

GDP (PPP): $2.4 trillion
0.9% growth in 2005
0.5% 5-yr. comp. ann. growth
$29,461 per capita

Unemployment: 11.7%

Inflation (CPI): 1.9%

FDI (net inflow): −$13.0 billion

Official Development Assistance:
Multilateral: None
Bilateral: None

External Debt: $3.9 trillion

Exports: $1.1 trillion
Primarily machinery, vehicles, chemicals, metals and manufactures, foodstuffs, textiles

Imports: $985.7 billion
Primarily machinery, vehicles, chemicals, foodstuffs, textiles, metals

2005 data unless otherwise noted.

GERMANY'S TEN ECONOMIC FREEDOMS

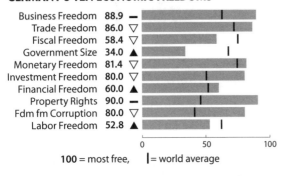

Business Freedom	88.9	—
Trade Freedom	86.0	▽
Fiscal Freedom	58.4	▽
Government Size	34.0	▲
Monetary Freedom	81.4	▽
Investment Freedom	80.0	▽
Financial Freedom	60.0	▲
Property Rights	90.0	—
Fdm fm Corruption	80.0	▽
Labor Freedom	52.8	▲

100 = most free, **l** = world average

BUSINESS FREEDOM — *88.9%*

The overall freedom to start, operate, and close a business is protected by Germany's regulatory environment. Starting a business takes an average of 18 days, compared to the world average of 43 days. Obtaining a business license requires less than the world average of 19 procedures and 234 days. Closing a business is easy.

TRADE FREEDOM — *86%*

Germany's trade policy is the same as those of other members of the European Union. The common EU weighted average tariff rate was 2 percent in 2005. Non-tariff barriers reflected in EU policy include agricultural and manufacturing subsidies, import restrictions for some goods and services, market access restrictions in some service sectors, non-transparent and restrictive regulations and standards, and inconsistent customs administration across EU members. The burden of regulations and standards exceeds EU policy, and the enforcement of intellectual property rights is problematic. Consequently, an additional 10 percentage points is deducted from Germany's trade freedom score.

FISCAL FREEDOM — *58.4%*

Germany has a high income tax rate and a burdensome corporate income tax rate. The top income tax rate is 47.5 percent (45 percent plus a 5.5 percent solidarity surcharge). The federal corporate tax rate is 25 percent (raised to 26.4 percent by a 5.5 percent solidarity tax), but the effective rate can be almost 39 percent. Other taxes include a value-added tax (VAT) and a trade tax that varies from 13 percent to 20 percent. In the most recent year, overall tax revenue as a percentage of GDP was 34.7 percent.

GOVERNMENT SIZE — *34%*

Total government expenditures, including consumption and transfer payments, are very high. In the most recent year, government spending equaled 46.9 percent of GDP. Social welfare programs remain large and expensive.

MONETARY FREEDOM — *81.4%*

Germany is a member of the euro zone. Between 2004 and 2006, Germany's weighted average annual rate of inflation was 1.8 percent. Relatively stable prices explain most of the monetary freedom score. As a participant in the EU's Common Agricultural Policy, the government subsidizes agricultural production, distorting the prices of agricul-

tural products. It also regulates prices for pharmaceuticals, electricity, telecommunications, and other public services. An additional 10 percentage points is deducted from Germany's monetary freedom score to adjust for measures that distort domestic prices.

INVESTMENT FREEDOM — *80%*

Foreign and domestic investors are treated equally in accordance with EU standards. There are no restrictions on capital transactions or current transfers, real estate purchases, repatriation of profits, or access to foreign exchange. There are no serious limitations on new projects, except that sale of defense companies to foreign investors requires permission, and no permanent currency controls on foreign investments. In a blow to financial privatization, the European Commission ruled in mid-2006 that public bank protection was legal. Some businesses, including certain financial institutions, passenger transport businesses, and real estate agencies, require licenses.

FINANCIAL FREEDOM — *60%*

Germany's financial system is open and modern. Regulations are generally transparent and consistent with international norms. Banking is dominated by public-sector institutions. Most of the roughly 2,000 banks are local savings banks and cooperative institutions. Private banks account for less than 30 percent of the market, and government-linked publicly owned banks account for nearly 50 percent. Government bank guarantees that made it easier for public banks to access financing were eliminated by EU competitiveness mandates in mid-2005. Interest rates are market-determined, and foreign investors may access credit freely. Non-European banks need a license to open branches or subsidiaries. The insurance sector and capital markets are open to foreign participation.

PROPERTY RIGHTS — *90%*

All property, including intellectual property, is well protected. Contracts are secure, and the judiciary and civil service are highly professional. Separate supreme courts deal with commercial, tax, labor, and constitutional cases.

FREEDOM FROM CORRUPTION — *80%*

Corruption is perceived as minimal. Germany ranks 16th out of 163 countries in Transparency International's Corruption Perceptions Index for 2006. Strict anti-corruption laws are enforced, and Germany has ratified the OECD Anti-Bribery Convention.

LABOR FREEDOM — *52.8%*

Restrictive employment regulations hinder employment and productivity growth. The non-salary cost of employing a worker is high, and dismissing a redundant employee is costly. The difficulty of laying off a worker creates a risk aversion for companies that would otherwise hire more people and grow. Wages and fringe benefits remain among the world's highest.

GHANA

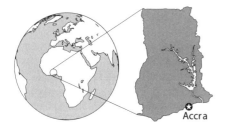

Accra

Ghana's economy is 56.7 percent free, according to our 2008 assessment, which makes it the world's 94th freest economy. Its overall score is 0.7 percentage point lower than last year due to declines in four of 10 economic freedoms. Ghana is ranked 11th out of 40 countries in the sub-Saharan Africa region, and its overall score is slightly higher than the regional average.

Ghana scores relatively well in fiscal freedom, government size, and property rights. The top income and corporate tax rates are fairly low, and overall tax revenue is not excessive as a percentage of GDP. However, none of the freedoms is more than 10 percentage points higher than average.

Ghana could make significant progress in several other areas such as investment freedom, financial freedom, labor freedom, and freedom from corruption. Commercial regulations are extensive, and labor market laws are especially inflexible. Ghana restricts foreign investment in several sectors, and the weak rule of law undermines consistent judicial adjudication. This inconsistency is due more to an inefficient public sector than to outright corruption.

BACKGROUND: In 1957, Ghana became the first colony in sub-Saharan Africa to gain independence. It experienced a series of coups and steady economic decline during the next few decades; but in the years since a ban on party politics was lifted in 1992 and multi-party elections were held, it has been a stable democracy. Political discourse is deepening with the development of private radio and mobile telephony. In 2005, agriculture accounted for over half of employment, 36 percent of GDP, and 40 percent of exports (predominantly cocoa and timber). Significant oil reserves were reportedly discovered in 2007. The government has generally followed through on economic reform and has privatized over 300 of approximately 350 state-owned enterprises. Regulatory barriers can be onerous, and corruption, while lower than in other African countries, remains a problem.

> How Do We Measure Economic Freedom? See Chapter 4 (page 39) for an explanation of the methodology or visit the *Index* Web site at *heritage.org/index*.

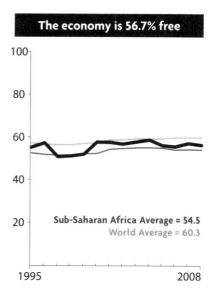

The economy is 56.7% free

Sub-Saharan Africa Average = 54.5
World Average = 60.3

1995   2008

QUICK FACTS

Population: 22.1 million

GDP (PPP): $54.8 billion
5.9% growth in 2005
5.3% 5-yr. comp. ann. growth
$2,479 per capita

Unemployment: 20.0%

Inflation (CPI): 15.1%

FDI (net flow): $155.0 million

Official Development Assistance:
Multilateral: $649.4 million
Bilateral: $969.6 million (6.9% from the U.S.)

External Debt: $6.7 billion

Exports: $3.8 billion
Primarily gold, cocoa, timber, tuna, bauxite, aluminum, manganese ore, diamonds

Imports: $6.6 billion
Primarily capital equipment, petroleum, foodstuffs

2005 data unless otherwise noted.

189

GHANA'S TEN ECONOMIC FREEDOMS

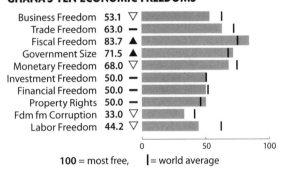

Business Freedom	53.1 ▽
Trade Freedom	63.0
Fiscal Freedom	83.7 ▲
Government Size	71.5 ▲
Monetary Freedom	68.0 ▽
Investment Freedom	50.0 ▬
Financial Freedom	50.0 ▬
Property Rights	50.0 ▬
Fdm fm Corruption	33.0 ▽
Labor Freedom	44.2 ▽

0   50   100

100 = most free, | = world average

BUSINESS FREEDOM — 53.1%

The overall freedom to start, operate, and close a business is limited by Ghana's regulatory environment. The government has been streamlining regulations, but bureaucratic processes remain slow. Starting a business takes an average of 42 days, compared to the world average of 43 days. Obtaining a business license requires about the same as the world average of 19 procedures and 234 days, and fees are costly.

TRADE FREEDOM — 63%

Ghana's weighted average tariff rate was 11 percent in 2004. Special import fees and taxes, import bans and restrictions, cumbersome and non-transparent standards and regulations, weak enforcement of intellectual property rights, non-transparent government procurement, and customs that can be complex and prone to corruption add to the cost of trade. The government supports domestic private enterprise with financial incentives and tax holidays as part of its export-promotion policies. An additional 15 percentage points is deducted from Ghana's trade freedom score to account for non-tariff barriers.

FISCAL FREEDOM — 83.7%

Ghana has moderate tax rates. Both the top income tax rate and the top corporate tax rate are 25 percent. Other taxes include a value-added tax (VAT) and a capital gains tax. In the most recent year, overall tax revenue as a percentage of GDP was 19.4 percent.

GOVERNMENT SIZE — 71.5%

Total government expenditures, including consumption and transfer payments, are moderate. In the most recent year, government spending equaled 30.8 percent of GDP. There have been efforts to revitalize privatization in recent years.

MONETARY FREEDOM — 68%

Inflation is relatively high, averaging 12.1 percent between 2004 and 2006. Relatively unstable prices explain most of the monetary freedom score. The government influences prices through its regulation of state-owned utilities and controls prices for petroleum products. An additional 10 percentage points is deducted from Ghana's trade freedom score to adjust for measures that distort domestic prices.

INVESTMENT FREEDOM — 50%

The foreign investment code eliminates screening of foreign investment, guarantees capital repatriation, and does not discriminate against foreign investors. Foreign capital is restricted in banking, securities, fishing, and real estate. Privatization has been extremely successful; 351 firms had been sold off by the end of 2005, and only a few remain government-controlled. Residents may hold foreign exchange accounts, and non-residents may hold them subject to restrictions. Payments and current transfers are subject to restrictions. The government does not generally intervene in commercial law cases. The Bank of Ghana must approve most capital transactions, and foreign direct investment faces a minimum capital requirement.

FINANCIAL FREEDOM — 50%

Ghana's financial system is small and dominated by banking. Ghana is a member of the Economic Community of West African States, which promotes regional trade and economic integration. In 2006, there were 10 commercial banks (five of them foreign-owned), five merchant banks, and three development banks. The government owns over 34 percent of the Ghana Commercial Bank (the largest domestic bank, which dominates the banking sector) and owns two other banks. Much lending is directed to public enterprise initiatives. The relatively developed insurance sector is dominated by two state-owned companies. The stock exchange is small, and foreign investors face some restrictions. A 2005 downturn in which the market lost 30 percent of its market capitalization reflected investor reliance on capital gains.

PROPERTY RIGHTS — 50%

Ghana's judicial system suffers from corruption, albeit less than the systems in some other African countries, and is subject to political influence. The courts are slow to dispose of cases and at times face challenges in enforcing decisions, largely because of resource constraints and institutional inefficiencies. The are laws to protect intellectual property rights, but very few cases have been filed.

FREEDOM FROM CORRUPTION — 33%

Corruption is perceived as significant. Ghana ranks 70th out of 163 countries in Transparency International's Corruption Perceptions Index for 2006, a deterioration since 2005. Recent reports indicate a growing perception that government-related corruption is on the rise.

LABOR FREEDOM — 44.2%

Highly restrictive employment regulations hinder employment and productivity growth. The non-salary cost of employing a worker is moderate, but dismissing a redundant employee is costly and difficult. The difficulty of laying off a worker creates a risk aversion for companies that would otherwise hire more people and grow. Ghana's labor freedom is one of the lowest in the world.

GREECE

reece's economy is 60.1 percent free, according to our 2008 assessment, which makes it the world's 80th freest economy. Its overall score is 1.8 percentage points higher than last year, reflecting gains in six of the 10 economic freedoms. Greece is ranked 34th out of 41 countries in the European region, and its overall score is much lower than the regional average.

As a developed nation, Greece scores highly in surprisingly few areas but is above average in half of the freedoms measured. Trade freedom and business freedom are the strongest parts of the economy. The average tariff rate is low, but trade suffers from numerous non-tariff barriers. As a member of the European Union, Greece has a standardized monetary policy that yields relatively low inflation, but government distortions in the agricultural sector persist.

Government size, fiscal freedom, and labor freedom are most in need of improvement. As in many other European welfare states, government spending is exceptionally high. A highly restrictive labor market is another problem, as firing employees is difficult and keeping them on the payroll is costly.

BACKGROUND: Since the abolition of the monarchy in 1974, Greece has been governed by a parliamentary democracy. Despite membership in the single European currency in 2001 and an increase in tourism and infrastructure upgrades as a result of the Athens Olympics in 2004, the Greek economy is still relatively weak, with an excessive fiscal deficit and high levels of debt. Unemployment is high, especially among the young, and Greece continues to rely heavily on aid from the European Union. Structural reform should be a priority for the government, especially in pensions, the privatizing of state enterprises, and the revamping of an inefficient bureaucracy that continues to deter foreign investment.

How Do We Measure Economic Freedom? See Chapter 4 (page 39) for an explanation of the methodology or visit the *Index* Web site at *heritage.org/index*.

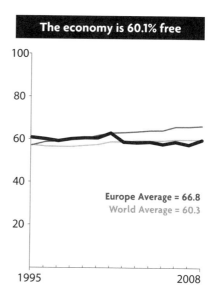

The economy is 60.1% free

Europe Average = 66.8
World Average = 60.3

QUICK FACTS

Population: 11.1 million

GDP (PPP): $259.6 billion
3.7% growth in 2005
4.3% 5-yr. comp. ann. growth
$23,380 per capita

Unemployment: 9.9%

Inflation (CPI): 3.5%

FDI (net flow): −$844 million

Official Development Assistance:
Multilateral: None
Bilateral: None

External Debt: $301.9 billion

Exports: $51.8 billion
Primarily food and beverages, manufactured goods, petroleum products, chemicals, textiles

Imports: $66.6 billion
Primarily machinery, transport equipment, fuels, chemicals

2005 data unless otherwise noted.

GREECE'S TEN ECONOMIC FREEDOMS

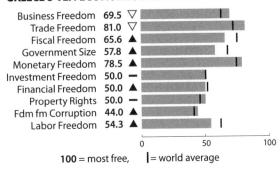

Business Freedom	69.5 ▽	
Trade Freedom	81.0 ▽	
Fiscal Freedom	65.6 ▲	
Government Size	57.8 ▲	
Monetary Freedom	78.5 ▲	
Investment Freedom	50.0 —	
Financial Freedom	50.0 ▲	
Property Rights	50.0 —	
Fdm fm Corruption	44.0 ▲	
Labor Freedom	54.3 ▲	

0   50   100

100 = most free, | = world average

BUSINESS FREEDOM — 69.5%

The overall freedom to start, operate, and close a business is relatively well protected by Greece's regulatory environment. Starting a business takes an average of 38 days, compared to the world average of 43 days. Obtaining a business license requires less than the world average of 19 procedures and 234 days. Closing a business is relatively easy.

TRADE FREEDOM — 81%

Greece's trade policy is the same as those of other members of the European Union. The common EU weighted average tariff rate was 2 percent in 2005. Non-tariff barriers reflected in EU policy include agricultural and manufacturing subsidies, import restrictions for some goods and services, market access restrictions in some service sectors, non-transparent and restrictive regulations and standards, and inconsistent customs administration across EU members. The burden of subsidies, regulations, and standards exceeds EU policy, and the enforcement of intellectual property rights is problematic. Consequently, an additional 15 percentage points is deducted from Greece's trade freedom score.

FISCAL FREEDOM — 65.6%

Greece has a high income tax rate and a low corporate tax rate. The top income tax rate is 40 percent, and the top corporate tax rate is 25 percent. Other taxes include a value-added tax (VAT) and a tax on interest. In the most recent year, overall tax revenue as a percentage of GDP was 34.9 percent.

GOVERNMENT SIZE — 57.8%

Total government expenditures, including consumption and transfer payments, are very high. In the most recent year, government spending equaled 37.5 percent of GDP. Progress has been made in reforming and privatizing state-owned enterprises.

MONETARY FREEDOM — 78.5%

Greece is a member of the euro zone. Between 2004 and 2006, Greece's weighted average annual rate of inflation was 3.3 percent. Relatively moderate prices explain most of the monetary freedom score. As a participant in the EU's Common Agricultural Policy, the government subsidizes agricultural production, distorting the prices of agricultural products. It also can set a ceiling on retail prices if it

determines that increases might adversely affect the economy; regulates prices for pharmaceuticals, transportation, and energy; and sets margins for wholesalers and retailers. An additional 10 percentage points is deducted from Greece's monetary freedom score to account for policies that distort domestic prices.

INVESTMENT FREEDOM — 50%

While Greece officially welcomes foreign investment, it restricts investment in utilities, and non-EU investors receive less advantageous treatment in banking, mining, broadcasting, maritime, and air transport. Despite inefficient bureaucracy and confusing commercial laws, improved infrastructure and liberalized energy and telecommunications have spurred investment. Investment is screened when the relevant party wants to claim an incentive bonus. Residents and non-residents may hold foreign exchange accounts. There are no restrictions or controls on payments, real estate transactions, transfers, or repatriation of profits. Investment in border regions is restricted to EU residents.

FINANCIAL FREEDOM — 50%

At the end of 2005, there were 21 domestic banks, 23 foreign commercial banks, 16 cooperative banks, and two specialty institutions. The government dominated banking in the 1990s, but privatization and mergers have reduced its influence. Five large commercial groups that operate as private universal banks now dominate the system. The state still directly controls one bank and indirectly controls two others. The insurance sector is small, and capital markets are well established, with 347 listings in mid-2006 and several tiers of capitalization.

PROPERTY RIGHTS — 50%

Court enforcement of property and contractual rights is time-consuming and often problematic. The judiciary is nominally nonpartisan but tends to reflect the government's political sensibilities. Seeking legal advice and assistance before entering into a lawsuit is critical. Expropriation of property is unlikely. The enforcement of intellectual property rights remains lax.

FREEDOM FROM CORRUPTION — 44%

Corruption is perceived as significant. Greece ranks 54th out of 163 countries in Transparency International's Corruption Perceptions Index for 2006. Ties to long-time suppliers and subtle political pressures are widely believed to play a significant role in official evaluations of procurement tenders.

LABOR FREEDOM — 54.3%

Restrictive employment regulations hinder employment opportunities and productivity growth. The non-salary cost of employing a worker is high, but dismissing a redundant employee can be relatively costless. Labor codes limit working hours and part-time employment, although a labor law passed in 2005 gives employers greater flexibility. Regulations on the number of work hours remain rigid.

GUATEMALA

Guatemala City

Guatemala's economy is 60.5 percent free, according to our 2008 assessment, which makes it the world's 78th freest economy. Its overall score is 0.8 percentage point lower than last year. Guatemala is ranked 17th out of 29 countries in the Americas, and its overall score is slightly lower than the regional average.

Guatemala receives high scores in trade freedom, in labor freedom, and especially in government size, where its score is 28 percentage points above the world average. Personal and corporate tax rates are moderate, and overall tax revenue is relatively low as a percentage of GDP. Government expenditures are very low at almost 10 percent of GDP. The labor market is fairly flexible, although firing an employee can be costly.

Guatemala scores poorly in business freedom, property rights, and freedom from corruption. Closing a business is difficult, and licensing procedures are burdensome. The judiciary is not an effective arbiter of cases, and corruption is extensive.

BACKGROUND: About 80 percent of Guatemalans live below the poverty line, less than half of all age-appropriate youth are enrolled in secondary schools, and nearly half of the labor force works in agriculture. The country's most advanced and competitive sector is telecommunications, which was fully deregulated under a spectrum allocation system in 1996. The government of Oscar Berger (2004–2008) partially privatized some energy utilities, and the Central America–Dominican Republic–United States Free Trade Agreement (CAFTA–DR), ratified in 2005, is expected to boost trade and employment. Leading exports include such agricultural products as coffee, sugar, bananas, winter vegetables, and cut flowers, as well as *maquila* textiles. A new president elected at the end of 2007 will have to face ongoing problems that include high crime rates, rising youth gang membership, and a judiciary that is both weak and corrupt.

How Do We Measure Economic Freedom? See Chapter 4 (page 39) for an explanation of the methodology or visit the *Index* Web site at *heritage.org/index*.

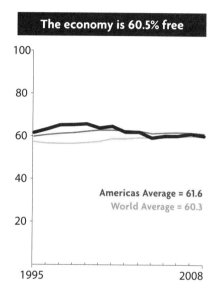

The economy is 60.5% free

Americas Average = 61.6
World Average = 60.3

1995 — 2008

QUICK FACTS

Population: 12.6 million

GDP (PPP): $57.6 billion
3.2% growth in 2005
2.6% 5-yr. comp. ann. growth
$4,568 per capita

Unemployment: 6.5%

Inflation (CPI): 9.1%

FDI (net flow): $208 million

Official Development Assistance:
Multilateral: $55.4 million
Bilateral: $254.7 million (24.6% from the U.S.)

External Debt: $5.3 billion

Exports: $4.9 billion
Primarily coffee, sugar, petroleum, apparel, bananas, fruits and vegetables, cardamom

Imports: $9.5 billion
Primarily fuels, machinery and transport equipment, construction materials, grain, fertilizers, electricity

2005 data unless otherwise noted.

GUATEMALA'S TEN ECONOMIC FREEDOMS

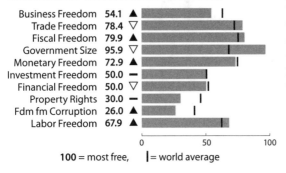

Business Freedom	54.1	▲
Trade Freedom	78.4	▽
Fiscal Freedom	79.9	▲
Government Size	95.9	▽
Monetary Freedom	72.9	▲
Investment Freedom	50.0	—
Financial Freedom	50.0	▽
Property Rights	30.0	—
Fdm fm Corruption	26.0	▲
Labor Freedom	67.9	▲

0   50   100

100 = most free, | = world average

BUSINESS FREEDOM — 54.1%

The overall freedom to start, operate, and close a business is restricted by Guatemala's regulatory environment. Starting a business takes an average of 26 days, compared to the world average of 43 days. Obtaining a business license requires more than the world average of 19 procedures and 234 days. Closing a business can be difficult. Bureaucratic impediments persist.

TRADE FREEDOM — 78.4%

Guatemala's weighted average tariff rate was 5.8 percent in 2005. Non-transparent and restrictive regulations, limitations on market access in the services sector, some high tariffs, occasional inconsistencies in customs valuation and administration, and customs corruption add to the cost of trade. An additional 10 percentage points is deducted from Guatemala's trade freedom score to account for non-tariff barriers.

FISCAL FREEDOM — 79.9%

Guatemala has moderate tax rates. Both the top income tax rate and the top corporate tax rate are 31 percent. Other taxes include a value-added tax (VAT), a capital gains tax, and a tax on interest. In the most recent year, overall tax revenue as a percentage of GDP was 9.6 percent.

GOVERNMENT SIZE — 95.9%

Total government expenditures, including consumption and transfer payments, are low. In the most recent year, government spending equaled 11.7 percent of GDP. Guatemala's public debt to GDP ratio is one of the lowest in the region.

MONETARY FREEDOM — 72.9%

Inflation is relatively high, averaging 7.3 percent between 2004 and 2006. Relatively unstable prices explain most of the monetary freedom score. The government maintains few price controls but subsidizes numerous economic activities and products, such as fuel and housing construction. An additional 10 percentage points is deducted from Guatemala's monetary freedom score to adjust for measures that distort domestic prices.

INVESTMENT FREEDOM — 50%

Guatemala grants foreign investors national treatment and allows full repatriation of profits. The investment climate has continued to improve as the result of President Oscar Berger's election in 2004. Several major investment projects were initiated in 2006 and 2007, including Aero Union, an air-transport company, and Banco Azteca Centroamerica, a banking and retail firm. Licenses to foreign investors to provide professional services are restricted, as is foreign ownership of domestic airlines, newspapers, commercial radio stations, mining and forestry, petroleum operations, and real estate. Time-consuming administrative procedures, an arbitrary and opaque bureaucratic process, a high crime rate, and corruption continue to impede investment. Residents and non-residents may hold foreign exchange accounts. There are no restrictions or controls on payments, transactions, and transfers.

FINANCIAL FREEDOM — 50%

Guatemala's small financial system is dominated by bank-centered financial conglomerates. At the end of 2006, there were 25 banks, one of them foreign. The top four banks together account for over 60 percent of assets. One of these, Banco de Café, was suspended in 2006 for failure to meet capital requirements and will likely be liquidated. The third- and tenth-largest banks are partially or fully government-owned and together account for about 14 percent of assets. Foreign borrowers can secure domestic credit. Bank supervision and transparency have been strengthened under a legal and regulatory framework adopted in 2002, as well as legislation passed in 2005 and 2006, which also makes government intervention easier. There are 18 insurance companies. Capital markets are small and involved primarily in trading government debt.

PROPERTY RIGHTS — 30%

Judicial resolution of disputes is time-consuming and often unreliable. Civil cases can take as long as a decade. Judicial corruption is not uncommon. Land invasions by squatters are increasingly common in rural areas, and evicting squatters can be difficult. Successful prosecution of intellectual property rights violators is rare.

FREEDOM FROM CORRUPTION — 26%

Corruption is perceived as widespread. Guatemala ranks 111th out of 163 countries in Transparency International's Corruption Perceptions Index for 2006. Corruption is a serious problem at many levels of government. Guatemala signed the U.N. Convention Against Corruption in December 2003 but has not ratified it.

LABOR FREEDOM — 67.9%

Relatively flexible employment regulations could be further improved to enhance employment and productivity growth. The non-salary cost of employing a worker is moderate, but dismissing a redundant employee is relatively costly. The cost of laying off a worker creates a risk aversion for companies that would otherwise hire more people and grow. Restrictions on the number of work hours are relatively flexible.

GUINEA

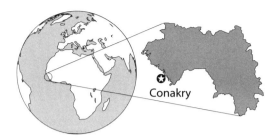

Conakry

Rank: 127

Regional Rank: 27 of 40

Guinea's economy is 52.8 percent free, according to our 2008 assessment, which makes it the world's 127th freest economy. Its overall score is 1.7 percentage points lower than last year, reflecting declines in five of the 10 economic freedoms. Guinea is ranked 27th out of 40 countries in the sub-Saharan Africa region, sharply down from last year, and its overall score is now below the regional average.

Guinea scores well only in government size and labor freedom. The labor market is highly flexible, although the non-salary cost of employing a worker is high. Guinea's labor freedom score is 9 percentage points higher than the world average.

Guinea scores below average on eight of the 10 economic freedoms. A developing country, it faces severe challenges in business freedom, monetary freedom, property rights, and freedom from corruption. Bureaucratic inefficiency and corruption affect virtually all areas of the economy, and the lack of basic infrastructure merely exacerbates this inefficiency and corruption. The judiciary is subject to pervasive political interference and corruption at all levels despite nominal government efforts to improve.

BACKGROUND: After gaining its independence in 1958, Guinea was dominated by a repressive one-party dictatorship under Ahmed Sékou Touré that pursued socialist economic policies. Lansana Conté, who seized power when Touré died in 1984, won his first election in 1993 and a third term in 2003. The government is corrupt, and there is a lack of transparency. Labor strikes to protest economic decline and corruption forced Conté to appoint Lansana Kouyaté as prime minister in 2007 with enhanced authority. Instability in the Ivory Coast, Sierra Leone, and Liberia has affected Guinea's social, political, and economic situation. Infrastructure is poor, electricity and water shortages are common, and much of the population is engaged in subsistence agriculture. Guinea possesses rich mineral resources, including iron, gold, diamonds, and perhaps half of the world's bauxite reserves.

How Do We Measure Economic Freedom? See Chapter 4 (page 39) for an explanation of the methodology or visit the *Index* Web site at *heritage.org/index.*

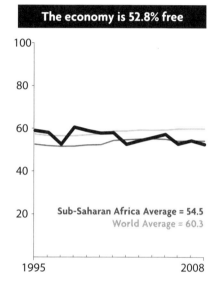

The economy is 52.8% free

Sub-Saharan Africa Average = 54.5
World Average = 60.3

1995　　　　　　　　　　　　　2008

QUICK FACTS

Population: 9.4 million

GDP (PPP): $21.8 billion
3.3% growth in 2005
2.9% 5-yr. comp. ann. growth
$2,316 per capita

Unemployment: n/a

Inflation (CPI): 31.4%

FDI (net flow): $102 million

Official Development Assistance:
Multilateral: $115.6 million
Bilateral: $144.7 million (31.8% from the U.S.)

External Debt: $3.2 billion

Exports: $810.9 million (2004)
Primarily bauxite, alumina, gold, diamonds, coffee, fish, agricultural products

Imports: $963.6 million (2004)
Primarily petroleum products, metals, machinery, transport equipment, textiles, grain and other foodstuffs

2005 data unless otherwise noted.

GUINEA'S TEN ECONOMIC FREEDOMS

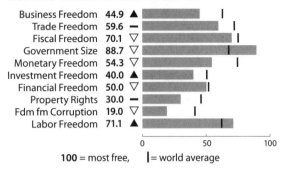

Business Freedom	44.9 ▲	
Trade Freedom	59.6 —	
Fiscal Freedom	70.1 ▽	
Government Size	88.7 ▽	
Monetary Freedom	54.3 ▽	
Investment Freedom	40.0 ▲	
Financial Freedom	50.0 ▽	
Property Rights	30.0 —	
Fdm fm Corruption	19.0 ▽	
Labor Freedom	71.1 ▲	

0   50   100

100 = most free, | = world average

BUSINESS FREEDOM — 44.9%

The overall freedom to start, operate, and close a business is very restricted by Guinea's regulatory environment. The application of commercial law is non-transparent and inconsistent. Starting a business takes an average of 41 days, compared to the world average of 43 days. Obtaining a business license requires more than the world average of 19 procedures and 234 days. Closing a business is relatively lengthy but not costly.

TRADE FREEDOM — 59.6%

Guinea's average tariff rate was 12.7 percent in 2005. A lack of foreign currency for transacting formal trade, numerous import taxes, state-owned import and export monopolies, pre-import and export authorization requirements, subsidies, inadequate infrastructure, and customs corruption add to the cost of trade. An additional 15 percentage points is deducted from Guinea's trade freedom score to account for non-tariff barriers.

FISCAL FREEDOM — 70.1%

Guinea has high tax rates. The top income tax rate is 40 percent, and the top corporate tax rate is 35 percent. Other taxes include a value-added tax (VAT), a tax on insurance contracts, and an apprenticeship tax. In the most recent year, overall tax revenue as a percentage of GDP was 12.7 percent.

GOVERNMENT SIZE — 88.7%

Total government expenditures, including consumption and transfer payments, are low. In the most recent year, government spending equaled 19.4 percent of GDP. Poor spending management and excessive reliance on the mining sector have contributed to fiscal deficit. Privatization of state-owned enterprises has progressed only marginally.

MONETARY FREEDOM — 54.3%

Inflation is high, averaging 31.8 percent between 2004 and 2006. Unstable prices explain most of the monetary freedom score. The government influences prices through the regulation of state-owned enterprises and administrative price controls for cement, petroleum products, water, and electricity. It also subsidizes rice importers. An additional 10 percentage points is deducted from Guinea's monetary freedom score to adjust for measures that distort domestic prices.

INVESTMENT FREEDOM — 40%

Investment is deterred by bureaucratic inefficiency, lack of basic services infrastructure, and opaque application procedures that allow for significant corruption. Foreign majority ownership in radio, television, and newspapers is restricted. Liberalization of telecommunications in the 1990s led to higher investment in cellular telephone services in 2006. Foreigners are allowed 100 percent ownership in the commercial, industrial, mining, agricultural, and services sectors. Residents (with some restrictions) and non-residents may hold foreign exchange accounts. Payments and transfers are subject to government approval in some cases, and repatriation is controlled. All capital transfers through the official exchange market and many capital transactions must be authorized by the central bank.

FINANCIAL FREEDOM — 50%

Guinea's small financial system is dominated by banking. Guinea is a member of the Economic Community of West African States, which promotes regional trade and economic integration. Regulation can be burdensome, and supervision is weak. The financial sector consists of six deposit-taking banks, four insurance companies, a social security institution, two cooperative banks, and several foreign exchange bureaus and microfinance institutions. There are few restrictions on banks, and foreign banks dominate the sector. The rise of demand deposits as a proportion of the money supply reflects growing confidence in the sector. Increased investment in mining has been accompanied by increased medium-term lending. Overall, however, the banking system remains fairly fragile, risk-averse, and unable to meet private-sector development needs. There is no stock market.

PROPERTY RIGHTS — 30%

Property is weakly protected. Poorly trained magistrates, high levels of corruption, and nepotism reportedly plague the administration of justice. The government intends to reform the judiciary with the help of international donor agencies, but there are few cases to demonstrate that the system provides effective protection of real or intellectual property rights.

FREEDOM FROM CORRUPTION — 19%

Corruption is perceived as rampant. Guinea ranks 160th out of 163 countries in Transparency International's Corruption Perceptions Index for 2006. Corruption, encouraged by the business and political cultures, low salaries for most civil servants, and a very large informal economy, is perhaps the single biggest obstacle to foreign investment. Payment of bribes in order to conduct business is the rule.

LABOR FREEDOM — 71.1%

Relatively flexible employment regulations could be further improved to enhance employment opportunities and productivity growth. The non-salary cost of employing a worker is high, but dismissing a redundant employee is costless. Regulations on the number of work hours remain rigid.

GUINEA-BISSAU

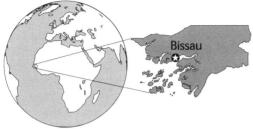

Guinea–Bissau's economy is 45.1 percent free, according to our 2008 assessment, which makes it the world's 147th freest economy. Its overall score is 1.7 percentage points lower than last year, reflecting improvements in three areas and declines in five others. Guinea–Bissau is ranked 39th out of 40 countries in the sub-Saharan Africa region, and its overall score is one of the lowest in Africa and in the world.

Guinea–Bissau scores well only in fiscal freedom. The top income tax is a relatively low 20 percent, and tax revenues are not excessive as a percentage of GDP.

Guinea–Bissau scores very poorly in business freedom, investment freedom, financial freedom, property rights, and freedom from corruption. Normal business operations are intensely difficult. Significant restrictions on foreign investment combine with domestic regulations to create a business-hostile climate. As a partial consequence, Guinea–Bissau has the West African Economic and Monetary Union's weakest financial system. Weak rule of law jeopardizes the protection of property rights. Corruption is so rampant that the informal market (mainly in diamonds) dwarfs the legitimate market.

BACKGROUND: After a series of coups in the 1980s, Guinea–Bissau held its first multi-party elections in 1994. An army uprising triggered civil war in 1998, and President Joao Bernardo Vieira was deposed in 1999. Opposition party leader Kumba Yala assumed power after elections under a transitional government but was forced out by the military in 2003. The military appointed a civilian transitional government, and legislative elections were held in March 2004. Former President Vieira again won the presidency in 2005 but has struggled to maintain control. Agriculture accounts for 60 percent of GDP, employs over 80 percent of the labor force, and comprises over 90 percent of exports. Cashew nuts are the primary export. Instability hinders economic growth, infrastructure is dilapidated, and corruption is substantial.

How Do We Measure Economic Freedom? See Chapter 4 (page 39) for an explanation of the methodology or visit the *Index* Web site at *heritage.org/index.*

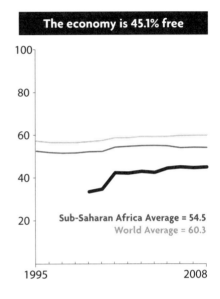

The economy is 45.1% free

Sub-Saharan Africa Average = 54.5
World Average = 60.3

1995 — 2008

QUICK FACTS

Population: 1.6 million

GDP (PPP): $1.3 billion
3.2% growth in 2005
−0.7% 5-yr. comp. ann. growth
$827 per capita

Unemployment: n/a

Inflation (CPI): 3.4%

FDI (net flow): $14.0 million

Official Development Assistance:
Multilateral: $50.9 million
Bilateral: $39.6 million (3.5% from the U.S.)

External Debt: $693 million

Exports: $83.5 million (2004)
Primarily cashew nuts, shrimp, peanuts, palm kernels, sawn lumber

Imports: $127.2 million (2004)
Primarily foodstuffs, machinery and transport equipment, petroleum products
2005 data unless otherwise noted.

GUINEA-BISSAU'S TEN ECONOMIC FREEDOMS

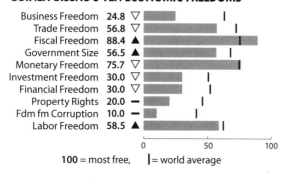

Business Freedom	24.8	▽
Trade Freedom	56.8	▽
Fiscal Freedom	88.4	▲
Government Size	56.5	▲
Monetary Freedom	75.7	▽
Investment Freedom	30.0	▽
Financial Freedom	30.0	▽
Property Rights	20.0	—
Fdm fm Corruption	10.0	—
Labor Freedom	58.5	▲

0   50   100

100 = most free,   ▌ = world average

BUSINESS FREEDOM — *24.8%*

The overall freedom to start, operate, and close a business is severely limited by Guinea–Bissau's national regulatory environment. Starting a business takes more that five times the world average of 43 days. The government has tried to streamline registration and reduce bureaucracy, and obtaining a business license requires less than the world average of 19 procedures and 234 days.

TRADE FREEDOM — *56.8%*

Guinea–Bissau's weighted average tariff rate was 14.1 percent in 2005. Abuses in customs, including irregularities in the valuation of imports and difficulty tracking and monitoring goods, add to the cost of trade. The government intervenes in the export of cashews, the principal export. An additional 15 percentage points is deducted from Guinea–Bissau's trade freedom score to account for non-tariff barriers.

FISCAL FREEDOM — *88.4%*

Guinea–Bissau has a low income tax rate but a moderate corporate tax rate. The top income tax rate is 20 percent, and the top corporate tax rate is 25 percent. In the most recent year, overall tax revenue as a percentage of GDP was 11.5 percent.

GOVERNMENT SIZE — *56.5%*

Total government expenditures, including consumption and transfer payments, are high. In the most recent year, government spending equaled 38.1 percent of GDP. Structural reform has focused on reducing direct state participation in the economy, but progress has been slow.

MONETARY FREEDOM — *75.7%*

Inflation is relatively low, averaging 2.2 percent between 2004 and 2006. Relatively stable prices explain most of the monetary freedom score. The government influences prices through the regulation of state-owned utilities and controls prices for cashew nuts, the primary export and source of roughly 30 percent of GDP. An additional 15 percentage points is deducted from Guinea–Bissau's monetary freedom score to adjust for measures that distort domestic prices.

INVESTMENT FREEDOM — *30%*

Political and economic instability, weak infrastructure, and an unskilled workforce discourage foreign investment. The new investment code drafted in 2006 provides for incentives and guarantees against nationalization and expropriation. Investors were seriously hurt by the 1998–1999 civil war. Non-residents may hold foreign exchange accounts with permission of the Central Bank of West African States (BCEAO), and residents may hold them with permission of the Ministry of Finance and the BCEAO. France and the EU have undertaken a US$10.9 million program to rebuild Guinea–Bissau's roads as one of several initiatives meant to strengthen the investment climate and economy. Capital transfers to most foreign countries are restricted. The government must approve most personal capital movements between residents and non-residents.

FINANCIAL FREEDOM — *30%*

Guinea–Bissau has the least developed financial sector among the eight members of the West African Economic and Monetary Union. The BCEAO governs banking and other financial institutions, and the eight BCEAO countries use the CFA franc, pegged to the euro. Three banks were operating in the first half of 2006, and the government, regional government institutions, and foreign investors participate in the banking sector. The first microfinance institution opened at the end of 2005 as a subsidiary of a regional development bank that, along with a regional stock exchange, is based in the Ivory Coast. A fourth (foreign) bank is expected to open an office in 2007.

PROPERTY RIGHTS — *20%*

Protection of property is extremely weak. The judiciary is subject to executive influence and control. Judges are poorly trained, poorly paid, and subject to corruption. Traditional practices prevail in most rural areas, and persons who live in urban areas often bring judicial disputes to traditional counselors to avoid the costs and bureaucratic impediments of the official system. The police often resolve disputes without recourse to the courts.

FREEDOM FROM CORRUPTION — *10%*

Guinea–Bissau's informal sector eclipses the formal economy. Trade in smuggled diamonds, food, and fishing products is very large. Corruption and lack of transparency pervade all levels of government. Customs officers frequently accept bribes for not collecting import taxes.

LABOR FREEDOM — *58.5%*

Burdensome employment regulations hinder employment opportunities and productivity growth. The non-salary cost of employing a worker is high, and dismissing a redundant employee is relatively costly. The difficulty of laying off a worker creates a risk aversion for companies that would otherwise hire more people and grow. Restrictions on the number of work hours are not flexible.

GUYANA

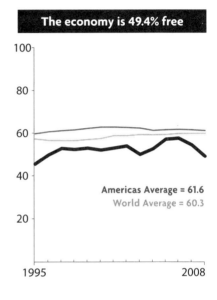

Georgetown

Rank: 136

Regional Rank: 26 of 29

G uyana's economy is 49.4 percent free, according to our 2008 assessment, which makes it the world's 136th freest economy. Its overall score is 5 percentage points lower than last year, the most severe decline among all countries. Guyana is now ranked 26th out of 29 countries in the Americas, and its overall score is much lower than the regional average.

Guyana does not rank strongly in any category and is above the world average only in labor freedom, where it is up by 7 percentage points. Guyana benefits from a highly flexible labor market. Firing a worker can be difficult, but employing labor is relatively easy. Its monetary freedom equals the world average because of moderate inflation.

As a developing nation, Guyana faces substantial economic challenges. The biggest barrier to development is Guyana's oversized government, with expenditures exceeding half of GDP. Investment freedom, business freedom, property rights, and freedom from corruption all score poorly. Significant restrictions on foreign investment are slowly being addressed, and these restrictions, combined with an inefficient bureaucracy, substantially limit Guyana's economic freedom. The substandard rule of law means that property rights are protected only erratically, and corruption is a problem in all areas of government.

BACKGROUND: Colonized by the Dutch and later by the British, Guyana gained its independence in 1966. Support for the two major political parties is highly polarized along ethnic and racial lines, and any attempts at reform have been made only under framework agreements with international organizations. Guyana's economy depends mainly on agriculture and mining. Parliamentary and presidential elections were held in late August 2006, although they were delayed because of problems with voter registration. Recent high-profile killings—for example, the April 2006 assassination of Agriculture Minister Satyadeo Sawh—have highlighted a growing crime problem and threaten public order.

How Do We Measure Economic Freedom? See Chapter 4 (page 39) for an explanation of the methodology or visit the *Index* Web site at *heritage.org/index.*

The economy is 49.4% free

Americas Average = 61.6
World Average = 60.3

1995   2008

QUICK FACTS

Population: 0.8 million

GDP (PPP): $3.4 billion
−1.9% growth in 2005
0.02% 5-yr. comp. ann. growth
$4,508.3 per capita

Unemployment: 9.1% (2000)

Inflation (CPI): 6.9%

FDI (net flow): $77.0 million

Official Development Assistance:
Multilateral: $117.6 million
Bilateral: $70.7 million (68.1% from the U.S.)

External Debt: $1.2 billion (2002)

Exports: $692.7 million
Primarily sugar, gold, bauxite, alumina, rice, shrimp, molasses, rum, timber

Imports: $916.5 million
Primarily manufactures, machinery, petroleum, food

2005 data unless otherwise noted.

GUYANA'S TEN ECONOMIC FREEDOMS

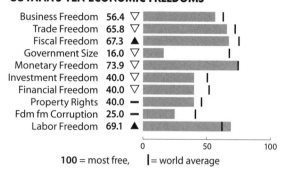

Business Freedom	56.4	▽
Trade Freedom	65.8	▽
Fiscal Freedom	67.3	▲
Government Size	16.0	▽
Monetary Freedom	73.9	▽
Investment Freedom	40.0	▽
Financial Freedom	40.0	▽
Property Rights	40.0	—
Fdm fm Corruption	25.0	—
Labor Freedom	69.1	▲

100 = most free, ▌= world average

BUSINESS FREEDOM — 56.4%

The overall freedom to start, operate, and close a business is restricted by Guyana's regulatory environment. Starting a business takes an average of 44 days, roughly equal to the world average of 43 days. Obtaining a business license requires less than the world average of 19 procedures and 234 days. Closing a business can be lengthy and costly. Bureaucratic procedures are burdensome and time-consuming.

TRADE FREEDOM — 65.8%

Guyana's weighted average tariff rate was 12.1 percent in 2003. Import-licensing requirements for a relatively large number of products, delays, customs corruption, import taxes, import restrictions, and burdensome standards and regulations add to the cost of trade. An additional 20 percentage points is deducted from Guyana's trade freedom score to account for non-tariff barriers.

FISCAL FREEDOM — 67.3%

Guyana has high tax rates. The top income tax rate is 33.3 percent, and the top corporate tax rate is 35 percent. Other taxes include a fuel tax and a sales tax. A value-added tax (VAT) was implemented in January 2007. In the most recent year, overall tax revenue as a percentage of GDP was 30.6 percent.

GOVERNMENT SIZE — 16%

Total government expenditures, including consumption and transfer payments, are high. In recent years, government spending has grown because of increases in transfer payments, wages, and the salaries of public servants. In the most recent year, government spending equaled 52.9 percent of GDP. Privatization of state-owned enterprises has achieved mixed results.

MONETARY FREEDOM — 73.9%

Inflation is relatively high, averaging 6.5 percent between 2004 and 2006. Relatively unstable prices explain most of the monetary freedom score. Guyana has made progress in removing most price controls and privatizing the large public sector, but the government still influences prices through the regulation of state-owned utilities and enterprises. An additional 10 percentage points is deducted from Guyana's monetary freedom score to adjust for measures that distort domestic prices.

INVESTMENT FREEDOM — 40%

Guyana has been moving toward a more welcoming environment for foreign investors, although the government remains cautious about approving new investment. The approval process can be bureaucratic and non-transparent. A new commercial court was established in June 2006 to alleviate the backlog of commercial cases. The government still screens most investment, and the relevant ministries carry significant power in issuing licenses and approval. Residents (with restrictions) and non-residents are allowed to hold foreign exchange accounts. Payments and transfers are not restricted. Most capital transactions are unrestricted, but all credit operations are controlled. The constitution guarantees the right of foreigners to own property or land.

FINANCIAL FREEDOM — 40%

Guyana's financial system is small, underdeveloped, and dominated by banking. Legislation implemented in 1997 introduced more effective regulation and supervision, but weaknesses (including many non-performing loans) remain. Non-performing loans are relatively high at 14 percent, down from 25 percent during the mid-1990s. There are six commercial banks, the two largest of which—the Bank of Nova Scotia and Republic Bank (Guyana)—are foreign-owned. The last state-owned bank, the Guyana National Co-Operative Bank, was sold in 2003. Though money-laundering legislation was introduced in 2000, effective application has been slow. There are some restrictions on financial activities with non-residents. Guyana also has six insurance companies and a small stock exchange, which lists 11 companies.

PROPERTY RIGHTS — 40%

Guyana's judicial system is often slow and inefficient. It is also subject to corruption. Law enforcement officials and prominent lawyers question the independence of the judiciary and accuse the government of intervening in some cases. A shortage of trained court personnel and magistrates, poor resources, and persistent bribery prolong the resolution of court cases unreasonably. There is no enforcement mechanism to protect intellectual property rights.

FREEDOM FROM CORRUPTION — 25%

Corruption is perceived as widespread. Guyana ranks 121st out of 163 countries in Transparency International's Corruption Perceptions Index for 2006. There is extensive corruption at every level of law enforcement and government. Widespread corruption undermines poverty-reduction efforts by international aid donors and discourages potential foreign investors.

LABOR FREEDOM — 69.1%

Relatively flexible employment regulations could be improved to enhance employment and productivity growth. The non-salary cost of employing a worker is low, but dismissing a redundant employee is relatively costly. The difficulty of laying off a worker creates a risk aversion for companies that would otherwise hire more people and grow.

HAITI

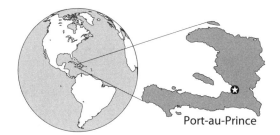

Port-au-Prince

Rank: 138
Regional Rank: 27 of 29

Haiti's economy is 48.9 percent free, according to our 2008 assessment, which makes it the world's 138th freest economy. Its overall score is 2.4 percentage points lower than last year and one of the five largest declines this year. Haiti is ranked 27th out of 29 countries in the Americas, and its overall score is much lower than the regional average.

Haiti scores better than the world average in terms of government expenditures, which are low in formal terms, but this is likely a sign of government weakness. Its fiscal freedom is just barely above the world average.

Haiti ranks 20 or more percentage points below the world average in business freedom, investment freedom, financial freedom, property rights, and freedom from corruption. Starting a business takes four times longer than the world average, and regulation is intrusive. There are significant restrictions on foreign capital, and investment is subject to an arbitrary bureaucracy. Rule of law is weak because of prolonged political instability.

BACKGROUND: Haiti, the Western Hemisphere's poorest country and one of the world's least-developed nations, is plagued by corruption, gang violence, drug trafficking, and organized crime. The 30-year Duvalier dictatorship ended with the adoption of a democratic constitution in 1986, but President Jean-Bertrand Aristide (elected in 1991 and again in 2001) did not respect democratic norms, and his regime collapsed in February 2004. René Préval won a U.N.-supervised election in 2006. Haiti is 95 percent deforested, its infrastructure is deplorable, and unemployment is very high. Many in rural areas have fled to the cities; 80 percent of the economy is informal. Emigrants' remittances are key to survival for some. Only 20 percent of age-appropriate children have access to secondary education. Despite a claimed commitment to democracy, market reforms, and fiscal restraint, Préval has close ties Cuba's Fidel Castro and Venezuela's Hugo Chávez.

How Do We Measure Economic Freedom? See Chapter 4 (page 39) for an explanation of the methodology or visit the *Index* Web site at *heritage.org/index*.

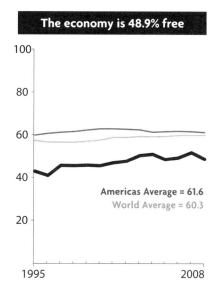

The economy is 48.9% free

Americas Average = 61.6
World Average = 60.3

1995   2008

QUICK FACTS

Population: 8.5 million

GDP (PPP): $14.2 billion
0.4% growth in 2005
−0.6% 5-yr. comp. ann. growth
$1,663 per capita

Unemployment: n/a

Inflation (CPI): 15.8%

FDI (net flow): $10.0 million

Official Development Assistance:
Multilateral: $193.7 million
Bilateral: $355.7 million (43.5% from the U.S.)

External Debt: $1.3 billion

Exports: $592.9 million
Primarily manufactures, coffee, oils, cocoa, mangoes

Imports: $1.8 billion
Primarily food, manufactured goods, machinery and transport equipment, fuels, raw materials

2005 data unless otherwise noted.

HAITI'S TEN ECONOMIC FREEDOMS

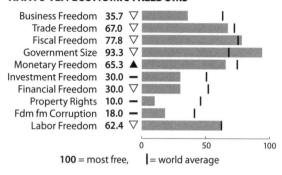

Business Freedom	35.7 ▽	
Trade Freedom	67.0 ▽	
Fiscal Freedom	77.8 ▽	
Government Size	93.3 ▽	
Monetary Freedom	65.3 ▲	
Investment Freedom	30.0 —	
Financial Freedom	30.0 ▽	
Property Rights	10.0 —	
Fdm fm Corruption	18.0 —	
Labor Freedom	62.4 ▽	

0   50   100

100 = most free, | = world average

BUSINESS FREEDOM — *35.7%*

The overall freedom to start, operate, and close a business is severely impeded by Haiti's regulatory environment. Starting a business takes an average of 202 days, compared to the world average of 43 days. Obtaining a business license takes about five times longer than the world average of 234 days. Commercial laws are applied inconsistently and non-transparently. Closing a business is lengthy and costly.

TRADE FREEDOM — *67%*

Haiti's simple average tariff rate was 9 percent in 2003. The high cost of shipping goods through inefficient state-owned international seaports, customs corruption, some import controls, import quotas on some food products, and import licensing requirements for agricultural products, chemicals, and pharmaceuticals add to the cost of trade. An additional 15 percentage points is deducted from Haiti's trade freedom score to account for non-tariff barriers.

FISCAL FREEDOM — *77.8%*

Haiti has a moderate income tax rate and a high corporate tax rate. The top income tax rate is 30 percent, and the top corporate tax rate is 35 percent. Other taxes include a value-added tax (VAT) and a capital gains tax. In the most recent year, overall tax revenue as a percentage of GDP was 9.7 percent.

GOVERNMENT SIZE — *93.3%*

Total government expenditures, including consumption and transfer payments, are low. In the most recent year, government spending equaled 15 percent of GDP. Political instability has made government economic and financial management weak and inconsistent. The restructuring of inefficient state enterprises is an important objective, but progress has been very limited.

MONETARY FREEDOM — *65.3%*

Inflation is high, averaging 15.2 percent between 2004 and 2006. Unstable prices explain most of the monetary freedom score. Prices are generally determined by the market, but the government restricts mark-ups of some products (retailers, for example, may not mark up pharmaceutical products by more than 40 percent) and strictly controls the prices of petroleum products. An additional 10 percentage points is deducted from Haiti's monetary freedom score to adjust for measures that distort domestic prices.

INVESTMENT FREEDOM — *30%*

Authorization is required for some foreign investments, particularly in electricity, water, public health, and telecommunications. The government has expressed interest in liberalizing aspects of the investment regime, such as telecommunications and energy, but there has been little progress. Foreign ownership of land is restricted. Judicial inadequacies, corruption, bureaucratic inefficiency, and political instability also deter investment. Residents may hold foreign exchange accounts for specified purposes, and non-residents may hold them without restriction. There are no restrictions on payments, transfers, or capital transactions.

FINANCIAL FREEDOM — *30%*

Haiti's financial sector is very small and prone to crisis. Supervision and regulation of the financial system is poor and does not comply with international norms. The banking sector consists of 11 banks and remains undeveloped. The two state-owned banks accounted for slightly less than 10 percent of assets in 2006. Two foreign-owned banks accounted for around 7 percent of assets. Credit is available on market terms, foreigners have access to domestic credit, and banks may offer a full range of banking services. There is no stock or bond market.

PROPERTY RIGHTS — *10%*

Protection of investors is severely compromised by weak enforcement, a paucity of updated laws to handle modern commercial practices, and a dysfunctional, resource-poor legal system. Litigants are often frustrated with the legal process, and most commercial disputes are settled out of court if at all. Widespread corruption allows disputing parties to purchase favorable outcomes. Despite statutes protecting both real and intellectual property, the weak judiciary and a lack of political will hinder enforcement.

FREEDOM FROM CORRUPTION — *18%*

Corruption is perceived as rampant. Haiti ranks 163rd out of 163 countries in Transparency International's Corruption Perceptions Index for 2006. Haiti's reputation as one of the world's most corrupt countries is a major impediment to doing business. Customs officers often demand bribes to clear shipments. Smuggling is a major problem, and contraband accounts for a large percentage of the manufactured consumables market.

LABOR FREEDOM — *62.4%*

Restrictive employment regulations hinder employment opportunities and productivity growth. The non-salary cost of employing a worker is moderate, but dismissing a redundant employee is relatively costly. The difficulty of laying off a worker creates a risk aversion for companies that would otherwise hire more people and grow. Restrictions on the number of work hours can be rigid.

HONDURAS

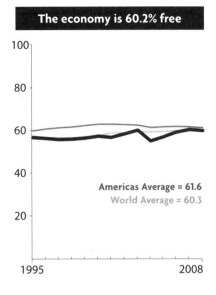

Tegucigalpa

Rank: 79

Regional Rank: 18 of 29

The economy of Honduras is 60.2 percent free, according to our 2008 assessment, which makes it the world's 79th freest economy. Its overall score is 0.2 percentage point lower than last year. Honduras is ranked 18th out of 29 countries in the Americas, and its overall score is slightly lower than the regional average.

Honduras receives high scores for trade freedom, fiscal freedom, government size, and financial freedom. Personal and corporate income tax rates are fairly low, and overall tax revenue is just 17 percent of GDP. Government expenditures are similarly moderate. Honduran financial freedom is enhanced by the developing banking sector, which has been instituting stronger rules and better, more transparent oversight.

The two lowest-ranking scores for Honduras are property rights and freedom from corruption. Public administration is inefficient and widely corrupt. The rule of law is undermined by weak basic security.

BACKGROUND: Two-thirds of Hondurans live below the poverty line. The economy has diversified beyond its traditional exports of coffee and bananas to include shrimp, melons, tourism, and *maquila* textiles. More than one-third of the labor force works in agriculture. Unemployment remains high at about 28 percent. Honduras is one of Central America's poorest countries, and the government hopes that the Central America–Dominican Republic–United States Free Trade Agreement (CAFTA–DR) will expand trade and investment. Narrowly elected in November 2005, President Jose Manuel "Mel" Zelaya Rosales has vowed to increase governmental transparency and fight economic inequality. The government has met targeted macroeconomic objectives and is reducing debt under World Bank and International Monetary Fund initiatives. Ongoing problems include drug trafficking, violent crime, and the proliferation of street-youth gangs known as *maras*.

How Do We Measure Economic Freedom? See Chapter 4 (page 39) for an explanation of the methodology or visit the *Index* Web site at *heritage.org/index*.

The economy is 60.2% free

Americas Average = 61.6
World Average = 60.3

1995   2008

QUICK FACTS

Population: 7.2 million

GDP (PPP): $24.7 billion
4.1% growth in 2005
3.8% 5-yr. comp. ann. growth
$3,430 per capita

Unemployment: 28.0%

Inflation (CPI): 8.8%

FDI (net flow): $243.0 million

Official Development Assistance:
Multilateral: $290.8 million
Bilateral: $1.0 billion (8.5% from the U.S.)

External Debt: $5.2 billion

Exports: $3.4 billion
Primarily coffee, shrimp, bananas, gold, palm oil, fruit, lobster, lumber

Imports: $5.0 billion
Primarily machinery and transport equipment, industrial raw materials, chemical products, fuels, foodstuffs

2005 data unless otherwise noted.

HONDURAS'S TEN ECONOMIC FREEDOMS

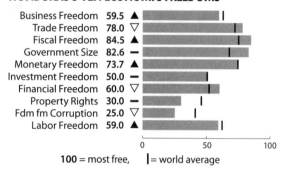

Business Freedom	59.5	▲
Trade Freedom	78.0	▽
Fiscal Freedom	84.5	▲
Government Size	82.6	—
Monetary Freedom	73.7	▲
Investment Freedom	50.0	—
Financial Freedom	60.0	▽
Property Rights	30.0	—
Fdm fm Corruption	25.0	▽
Labor Freedom	59.0	▲

0   50   100

100 = most free, | = world average

BUSINESS FREEDOM — 59.5%

The overall freedom to start, operate, and close a business is limited by Honduras's regulatory environment. Starting a business takes about the half the world average of 43 days. Obtaining a business license requires less than the world average of 19 procedures and 234 days. However, the government does not always publish regulations before they enter into force, and obtaining approval for investment activities involves procedural red tape. Closing a business can be difficult.

TRADE FREEDOM — 78%

Honduras's weighted average tariff rate was 6 percent in 2005. Differential import taxes, customs corruption, limitations on market access in the services sector, subsidies, coffee export fees, and restrictive sanitary and phytosanitary rules add to the cost of trade. An additional 10 percentage points is deducted from Honduras's trade freedom score to account for non-tariff barriers.

FISCAL FREEDOM — 84.5%

Honduras has moderate tax rates. Both the top income tax rate and the top corporate tax rate are 25 percent. Other taxes include a value-added tax (VAT) and a capital gains tax. In the most recent year, overall tax revenue as a percentage of GDP was 17.4 percent.

GOVERNMENT SIZE — 82.6%

Total government expenditures, including consumption and transfer payments, are low. In the most recent year, government spending equaled 24.1 percent of GDP. Privatization of state-owned enterprises has languished for years.

MONETARY FREEDOM — 73.7%

Inflation is relatively high, averaging 6.6 percent between 2004 and 2006. Relatively high and unstable prices explain most of the monetary freedom score. The government regulates the price of petroleum products, steel, pharmaceuticals, and services from state-owned utilities and can impose price controls across other goods and services as needed. An additional 10 percentage points is deducted from Honduras's monetary freedom score to adjust for measures that distort domestic prices.

INVESTMENT FREEDOM — 50%

Foreign investment is generally accorded the same rights as domestic investment. Screening is minimal. Investment is hurt by high levels of crime, a weak judicial system, and significant corruption. Some foreign investment has moved to nearby countries because of lower labor and power costs. Government authorization is required for foreign investment in sectors like basic health services, telecommunications, air transport, fishing and hunting, exploration and exploitation of minerals, forestry, and private education. The government is trying to promote investment in tourism with incentive packages. Foreign ownership of coast or border land is often prohibited. Residents and non-residents may hold foreign exchange accounts. Payments and transfers are not restricted, and few capital transactions require approval.

FINANCIAL FREEDOM — 60%

The Honduran financial sector is developing. Banking has undergone consolidation through mergers and closures since the 1998–2001 banking crisis. The collapse of several banks has led to stronger capital-adequacy rules, clarification of the central bank's role, and greater oversight. Regulation and the stability of government monetary policy have improved. There were 16 private commercial banks (several with foreign ownership), two state-owned banks, and about a dozen other small financial institutions in 2006. Foreign investors face few formal restrictions on accessing domestic credit, but informal constraints can be significant. Foreign banks have a small client base, often comprised of foreign companies. The insurance sector consisted of nine domestic and two foreign insurance companies as of November 2006. There is only one stock exchange, the second one having closed in April 2004.

PROPERTY RIGHTS — 30%

Protection of property is weak. The lack of judicial security, a deteriorating security environment, and endemic corruption make business disputes difficult to resolve. Expropriation of property is possible, but compensation, when awarded, is in 20-year government bonds. Foreigners seeking to buy real estate should be especially cautious in light of confusing laws and problems with land titles.

FREEDOM FROM CORRUPTION — 25%

Corruption is perceived as widespread. Honduras ranks 121st out of 163 countries in Transparency International's Corruption Perceptions Index for 2006. Decades of cronyism, nepotism, secrecy, and prevarication have removed the stigma that once attached to corruption, making its eradication all the more difficult.

LABOR FREEDOM — 59%

Restrictive employment regulations impede employment and productivity growth. The non-salary cost of employing a worker can be low, but dismissing a redundant employee is costly. The difficulty of laying off a worker creates a risk aversion for companies that would otherwise hire more people and grow. Restrictions on the number of work hours can be rigid.

2008 Index of Economic Freedom

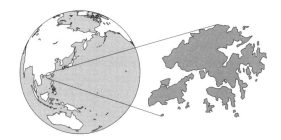

HONG KONG

Hong Kong's economy is 90.3 percent free, according to our 2008 assessment, which makes it the world's freest economy. Its overall score is 0.3 percentage point lower than last year, mainly reflecting a lower monetary freedom score. Hong Kong is ranked 1st out of 30 countries in the Asia–Pacific region, and its overall score is well above the regional average.

Hong Kong scores exceptionally well in almost all areas. Income and corporate tax rates are very competitive, and overall taxation is relatively small as a percentage of GDP. Business regulation is simple, and the labor market is highly flexible. Investment is strongly encouraged, and there are virtually no restrictions on foreign capital. The island is one of the world's leading financial centers, and regulation of banking and financial services is non-intrusive and transparent. Property rights are protected by an independent and virtually corruption-free judiciary.

Hong Kong could do slightly better in trade freedom. Although the average tariff rate is zero percent, enforcement of intellectual property rights is a problem. The weakest score is in monetary freedom, which is still 13 percentage points higher than the world average and would be higher if Hong Kong ended its remaining price controls.

BACKGROUND: The Special Administrative Region (SAR) of Hong Kong is part of the People's Republic of China but retains a separate political governance structure and economic system. Chief Executive Donald Tsang has pledged to advance universal suffrage, a promise made in the territory's mini-constitution, the Basic Law. A British colony for more than 150 years until the 1997 transfer of sovereignty to China, Hong Kong retains its rule of law, simple procedures for enterprises, free entry of foreign capital, repatriation of earnings, and financial transparency. It is a major gateway for business with China. Major industries include financial services, shipping, and other services. Manufacturing has largely migrated to mainland China.

How Do We Measure Economic Freedom? See Chapter 4 (page 39) for an explanation of the methodology or visit the *Index* Web site at *heritage.org/index*.

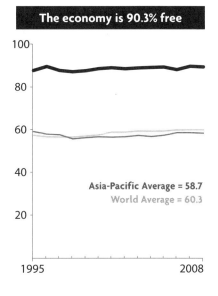

The economy is 90.3% free

Asia-Pacific Average = 58.7
World Average = 60.3

1995 — 2008

QUICK FACTS

Population: 6.9 million

GDP (PPP): $241.9 billion
7.5% growth in 2005
5.2% 5-yr. comp. ann. growth
$34,833 per capita

Unemployment: 5.2%

Inflation (CPI): 0.9%

FDI (net flow): $3.3 billion

Official Development Assistance:
Multilateral: None
Bilateral: $6.9 million (2.7% from the U.S.)

External Debt: $472.9 billion

Exports: $351.8 billion
Primarily financial services, tourism, transportation services, electrical machinery and appliances, textiles

Imports: $329.6 billion
Primarily travel and transportation services, raw materials and semi-manufactures, consumer goods, capital goods, fuel (mostly re-exported)
2005 data unless otherwise noted.

HONG KONG'S TEN ECONOMIC FREEDOMS

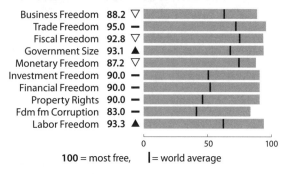

Business Freedom	88.2	▽
Trade Freedom	95.0	—
Fiscal Freedom	92.8	▽
Government Size	93.1	▲
Monetary Freedom	87.2	▽
Investment Freedom	90.0	—
Financial Freedom	90.0	—
Property Rights	90.0	—
Fdm fm Corruption	83.0	—
Labor Freedom	93.3	▲

0   50   100

100 = most free,   **▌= world average**

BUSINESS FREEDOM — 88.2%

The overall freedom to start, operate, and close a business is protected by Hong Kong's regulatory environment. Starting a business takes less than the half the world average of 43 days, and obtaining a business license takes less than the world average of 234 days. Bankruptcy proceedings are very easy and relatively costless.

TRADE FREEDOM — 95%

Hong Kong's weighted average tariff rate was zero percent in 2005. Except for liquor, tobacco, hydrocarbon oil, and methyl alcohol, trade is essentially duty-free. Restrictive pharmaceuticals regulation, market access restrictions for legal services, limited import licensing, and issues involving intellectual property rights add to the cost of trade. An additional 5 percentage points is deducted from Hong Kong's trade freedom score to account for non-tariff barriers.

FISCAL FREEDOM — 92.8%

Hong Kong's tax rates are among the world's lowest. Individuals are taxed either progressively, between 2 percent and 17 percent, on income adjusted for deductions and allowances or at a flat rate of 16 percent on gross income, depending on which liability is lower. The top corporate income tax rate is 17.5 percent. In the most recent year, overall tax revenue as a percentage of GDP was 12.7 percent.

GOVERNMENT SIZE — 93.1%

Total government expenditures, including consumption and transfer payments, are fairly low. In the most recent year, government spending equaled 15.2 percent of GDP. The government has made efforts to maintain a balanced budget.

MONETARY FREEDOM — 87.2%

Inflation is low, averaging 1.5 percent between 2004 and 2006. Stable prices explain most of the monetary freedom score. The government regulates the prices of public transport and electricity and some residential rents. An additional 5 percentage points is deducted from Hong Kong's monetary freedom score to adjust for measures that distort domestic prices.

INVESTMENT FREEDOM — 90%

Foreign capital receives domestic treatment, and foreign investment is strongly encouraged. There are no limits on foreign ownership and no screening or special approval procedures to set up a foreign firm, except in broadcasting, where foreign entities may own no more than 49 percent of the local stations, and specific legal services. The government owns all land and treats foreign and domestic lessors equally. The Hong Kong dollar is freely convertible. There are no controls or requirements on current transfers, purchase of real estate, access to foreign exchange, or repatriation of profits.

FINANCIAL FREEDOM — 90%

Hong Kong is a global financial center. Its regulatory and legal environment is focused on prudent minimum standards and transparency. At the end of 2006, there were 137 licensed banks, 31 restricted license banks, and 33 "deposit-taking companies." Banks are overseen by the independent Hong Kong Monetary Authority. Credit is allocated on market terms. There are no restrictions on foreign banks, which are treated the same as domestic institutions. The stock exchange ranks eighth in the world in terms of capitalization, but its regulation and transparency have been criticized in the past. The government intervened in the stock market in 1998 by purchasing $15.2 billion in private stocks but has since divested itself of all but $410 million of these holdings.

PROPERTY RIGHTS — 90%

Contracts are strongly protected. Hong Kong's legal system is transparent and based on common law, and its constitution strongly supports private property and freedom of exchange. Despite government public awareness campaigns to protect intellectual property rights, pirated and counterfeit products such as CDs, DVDs, software, and designer apparel are sold openly. The government controls all land and, through public auctions, grants renewable leases that are valid up to 2047 for all land in the SAR.

FREEDOM FROM CORRUPTION — 83%

Corruption is perceived as minimal. Hong Kong ranks 15th out of 163 countries in Transparency International's Corruption Perceptions Index for 2006, and foreign firms do not see corruption as an obstacle to investment. Giving or accepting a bribe, whether by foreign officials or by private citizens and government employees, is a criminal act.

LABOR FREEDOM — 93.3%

Highly flexible employment regulations enhance employment opportunities and productivity growth. The labor code is strictly enforced but not burdensome. The non-salary cost of employing a worker is low, but dismissing a redundant employee can be relatively costly. Regulations on expanding or contracting the number of working hours are very flexible. Hong Kong's labor freedom is one of the highest in the world.

HUNGARY

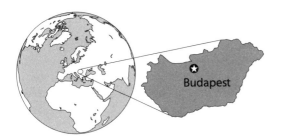

Budapest

Rank: 43

Regional Rank: 23 of 41

Hungary's economy is 67.2 percent free, according to our 2008 assessment, which makes it the world's 43rd freest economy. Its overall score is 2.8 percentage points higher than last year, reflecting improved scores in seven of the 10 economic freedoms. Hungary is ranked 23rd out of 41 countries in the European region, and its overall score is slightly lower than the regional average.

Hungary enjoys strong trade freedom, business freedom, property rights, investment freedom, financial freedom, and freedom from corruption. Investing in Hungary is easy, although it is subject to government licensing in security-sensitive areas. Foreign capital enjoys virtually the same protections and privileges as domestic capital. The rule of law is strong, a professional judiciary protects property rights, and the level of corruption is low.

The size of government is Hungary's biggest weakness, with a score in that category that is fully 41 percentage points below the world average. High tax rates and tax revenues also cause its score for fiscal freedom to fall below average.

BACKGROUND: Hungary held its first multi-party elections in 1990 following nearly 50 years of Communist rule and has succeeded in transforming its centrally planned economy into a market economy. Both foreign ownership of and foreign investment in Hungarian firms are widespread. The governing coalition, comprising the Hungarian Socialist Party and the liberal Alliance of Free Democrats, prevailed in the April 2006 general election. Hungary needs to reduce the size of its government budget relative to the economy and complete further economic reform in order to meet the deadlines for accession to the euro zone.

How Do We Measure Economic Freedom? See Chapter 4 (page 39) for an explanation of the methodology or visit the *Index* Web site at *heritage.org/index*.

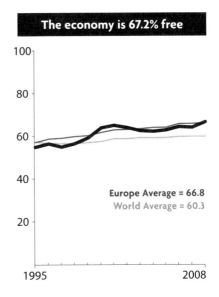

The economy is 67.2% free

Europe Average = 66.8
World Average = 60.3

QUICK FACTS

Population: 10.1 million

GDP (PPP): $180.4 billion
4.2% growth in 2005
4.4% 5-yr. comp. ann. growth
$17,887 per capita

Unemployment: 7.2%

Inflation (CPI): 3.6%

FDI (net inflow): $5.4 billion

Official Development Assistance:
Multilateral: $241.0 million (2004)
Bilateral: $63.0 million (2% from the U.S.) (2004)

External Debt: $66.1 billion

Exports: $74.2 billion
Primarily machinery and equipment, other manufactures, food products, raw materials, fuels and electricity

Imports: $75.6 billion
Primarily machinery and equipment, other manufactures, fuels and electricity, food products, raw materials
2005 data unless otherwise noted.

HUNGARY'S TEN ECONOMIC FREEDOMS

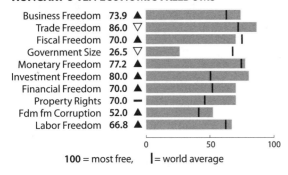

Business Freedom	73.9 ▲
Trade Freedom	86.0 ▽
Fiscal Freedom	70.0 ▲
Government Size	26.5 ▽
Monetary Freedom	77.2 ▲
Investment Freedom	80.0 ▲
Financial Freedom	70.0 ▲
Property Rights	70.0 —
Fdm fm Corruption	52.0 ▲
Labor Freedom	66.8 ▲

0   50   100

100 = most free, | = world average

BUSINESS FREEDOM — 73.9%

The overall freedom to start, operate, and close a business is relatively well protected by Hungary's regulatory environment. Starting a business takes less than half of the world average of 43 days, but obtaining a business license requires more than the world average of 19 procedures. Closing a business is relatively easy and costless.

TRADE FREEDOM — 86%

Hungary's trade policy is the same as those of other members of the European Union. The common EU weighted average tariff rate was 2 percent in 2005. Non-tariff barriers reflected in EU policy include agricultural and manufacturing subsidies, import restrictions for some goods and services, market access restrictions in some service sectors, non-transparent and restrictive regulations and standards, and inconsistent customs administration across EU members. Food and feed products are subject to restrictive biotechnology regulations. Consequently, an additional 10 percentage points is deducted from Hungary's trade freedom score.

FISCAL FREEDOM — 70%

Hungary has a high income tax rate but a low corporate tax rate. The top income tax rate is 36 percent, and the top corporate tax rate is 16 percent. Other taxes include a value-added tax (VAT), a property tax, and a community tax. In the most recent year, overall tax revenue as a percentage of GDP was 38 percent.

GOVERNMENT SIZE — 26.5%

Total government expenditures, including consumption and transfer payments, are extremely high. In the most recent year, government spending equaled 49.5 percent of GDP. The private sector has grown substantially, but the government remains directly involved in such sectors as agriculture and electric power.

MONETARY FREEDOM — 77.2%

Inflation is moderate, averaging 4.1 percent between 2004 and 2006. Relatively unstable prices explain most of the monetary freedom score. As a participant in the EU's Common Agricultural Policy, the government subsidizes agricultural production, distorting the prices of agricultural products. It also regulates prices for energy, telecommunications services, and subsidized pharmaceutical prod-

ucts, among others. An additional 10 percentage points is deducted from Hungary's monetary freedom score to account for policies that distort domestic prices.

INVESTMENT FREEDOM — 80%

Foreign capital receives domestic legal treatment, and foreign companies account for a large share of manufacturing, telecommunications, and energy activity. The government allows 100 percent foreign ownership with the exception of some defense-related industries, some types of land, airlines, and broadcasting. Residents and non-residents may hold foreign exchange accounts. Commercial law is fairly well developed, though the corporate code could be improved. Cost controls on pharmaceuticals, energy, and a few other items are expected to be phased out. There are no restrictions or controls on payments for invisible transactions, current transfers, or repatriation of profits and no restrictions on issues or sales of capital market instruments, although there are some reporting requirements.

FINANCIAL FREEDOM — 70%

To prepare for accession to the EU, Hungary undertook to reform financial system regulation, privatization, and recapitalization. Financial institutions still may not offer a full range of services, but banking is increasingly competitive. As of 2007, 32 banks were registered domestically. Foreign investors account for over 80 percent of banking capital. Partial state ownership of two major banks and the FHB Land Credit and Mortgage Bank is expected to change. There were 28 insurance companies and 34 insurance co-operatives in 2007, and the top three insurers were foreign companies. Capital markets are well developed, and foreign investors participate freely.

PROPERTY RIGHTS — 70%

The judiciary is constitutionally independent, and the government respects this in practice. The threat of expropriation is low. The courts are slow and severely overburdened, and a final ruling on a contract dispute can take more than a year. Protection of intellectual property rights has improved, but more needs to be done.

FREEDOM FROM CORRUPTION — 52%

Corruption is perceived as present. Hungary ranks 41st out of 163 countries in Transparency International's Corruption Perceptions Index for 2006. Despite anti-corruption laws, non-transparency leads to persistent rumors of corruption in government procurement.

LABOR FREEDOM — 66.8%

Relatively flexible employment regulations could be further improved to enhance employment opportunities and productivity growth. The non-salary cost of employing a worker can be high, and dismissing a redundant employee is relatively costly. The difficulty of laying off a worker creates a risk aversion for companies that would otherwise hire more people and grow. Regulations on the number of work hours are not flexible.

ICELAND

Reykjavik

Rank: 14

Regional Rank: 7 of 41

Iceland's economy is 76.5 percent free, according to our 2008 assessment, which makes it the world's 14th freest economy. Its overall score is 0.2 percentage point lower than last year, reflecting moderately better scores in three of the 10 economic freedoms. Iceland is ranked 7th out of 41 countries in the European region, and its overall score is higher than the regional average.

Iceland enjoys some of the strongest economic freedoms among all countries and has the second-highest score in terms of freedom from corruption, which is 55 percentage points above the world average. It also has exceptionally high scores for business freedom, investment freedom, trade freedom, financial freedom, property rights, and labor freedom. The average tariff rate is low, and business regulation is efficient. Virtually all commercial operations are simple and transparent. Foreign investment is permitted without government approval, although capital is subject to restrictions in some areas of the economy. Iceland's financial sector is very modern. The judiciary, independent of politics and free of corruption, has an exemplary ability to protect property rights.

Iceland is relatively weaker in terms of fiscal freedom, monetary freedom, and especially government size. Total government spending equals roughly half of GDP.

BACKGROUND: The Republic of Iceland is a wealthy, centuries-old democracy with very low unemployment and a dynamic and diversified economy that continues to grow steadily. It also has high levels of literacy, longevity, and income by world standards. Iceland is not a member of the European Union, largely because of its huge fishing industry, which would be subsumed by the Common Fisheries Policy in the event of EU membership. It is, however, a member of the European Free Trade Association and the European Economic Area, which allows for free cross-border movement of capital, labor, goods, and services with the EU.

How Do We Measure Economic Freedom? See Chapter 4 (page 39) for an explanation of the methodology or visit the *Index* Web site at *heritage.org/index*.

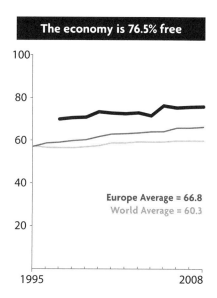

The economy is 76.5% free

Europe Average = 66.8
World Average = 60.3

1995 — 2008

QUICK FACTS

Population: 0.3 million

GDP (PPP): $10.8 billion
7.5% growth in 2005
4.3% 5-yr. comp. ann. growth
$36,510 per capita

Unemployment: 2.1%

Inflation (CPI): 4%

FDI (net flow): −$4.4 billion

Official Development Assistance:
Multilateral: None
Bilateral: None

External Debt: $3.1 billion (2002 estimate)

Exports: $5.1 billion
Primarily fish and fish products, aluminum, animal products, ferrosilicon, diatomite

Imports: $7.1 billion
Primarily machinery and equipment, petroleum products, foodstuffs, textiles

2005 data unless otherwise noted.

ICELAND'S TEN ECONOMIC FREEDOMS

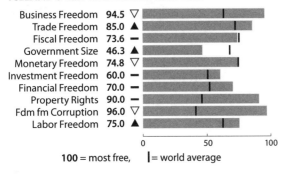

Business Freedom	94.5	▽
Trade Freedom	85.0	▲
Fiscal Freedom	73.6	—
Government Size	46.3	▲
Monetary Freedom	74.8	▽
Investment Freedom	60.0	—
Financial Freedom	70.0	—
Property Rights	90.0	—
Fdm fm Corruption	96.0	▽
Labor Freedom	75.0	▲

0   50   100

100 = most free, ▌= world average

BUSINESS FREEDOM — *94.5%*

The overall freedom to start, operate, and close a business is strongly protected by Iceland's regulatory environment. Starting a business takes an average of five days, compared to the world average of 43 days. Obtaining a business license requires less than the world average of 19 procedures and 234 days. Bankruptcy proceedings are straightforward and not costly.

TRADE FREEDOM — *85%*

Iceland's weighted average tariff rate was 2.5 percent in 2005. Strict phytosanitary regulations, import taxes, import bans and restrictions on agriculture products, prohibitively high agriculture tariffs, and an agricultural policy that includes export subsidies and a price equalization mechanism to support agricultural exports add to the cost of trade. An additional 10 percentage points is deducted from Iceland's trade freedom score to account for non-tariff barriers.

FISCAL FREEDOM — *73.6%*

Iceland has a competitive flat tax system. The main income tax rate is a flat 22.75 percent (which, combined with the local government rate, can rise to 35.72 percent). The corporate tax rate is a flat 18 percent. Other taxes include a value-added tax (VAT) and a net wealth tax. In the most recent year, overall tax revenue as a percentage of GDP was 42.4 percent.

GOVERNMENT SIZE — *46.3%*

Total government expenditures, including consumption and transfer payments, are high. In the most recent year, government spending equaled 42.3 percent of GDP. Privatization of state-owned enterprises progressed over the past 10 years. The government recently concluded the long-waited privatization of the state-owned telephone company, Iceland Telecom.

MONETARY FREEDOM — *74.8%*

Inflation is high, averaging 5.8 percent between 2004 and 2006. Relatively unstable prices explain most of the monetary freedom score. The government subsidizes agricultural production; milk is subject to production-linked direct payments, production quotas, and administered prices; and sheep farmers receive direct payments based on support targets and quality-dependent payments. An

additional 10 percentage points is deducted from Iceland's monetary freedom score to account for policies that distort domestic prices.

INVESTMENT FREEDOM — *60%*

Foreign capital receives domestic legal treatment. Iceland generally welcomes foreign investment, although the government maintains restrictions in some key areas. Foreign ownership in the fishing industry, a major portion of the economy, is limited to 25 percent. Airlines and real estate are likewise restricted; individuals must live in Iceland to purchase real estate. The legal system is transparent and modern, and there have been no major investment disputes for many years. Residents and non-residents may own declared foreign exchange accounts. There are no controls or requirements on payments or current transfers, access to foreign exchange, or repatriation of profits.

FINANCIAL FREEDOM — *70%*

Iceland's financial sector is modern. Since joining the European Economic Area, Iceland has liberalized and deregulated its financial markets, allowing Icelandic financial institutions to operate on a cross-border basis in the EEA and vice versa. There are four commercial banks, three of which offer a full set of banking services. The government sold its stakes in two partially state-owned banks in 2003 and no longer has a presence in the commercial banking sector. Iceland's financial health was in question early in 2006 as a result of severe macro imbalances and bank soundness that led to upheaval in the securities markets. There were 13 domestic insurance companies and a number of foreign insurance companies operating in June 2005. The stock market has expanded rapidly and is part of a regional integrated network of exchanges in Nordic and some Baltic countries.

PROPERTY RIGHTS — *90%*

Private property is well protected. The constitution provides for an independent judiciary, and the government generally respects this in practice. Trials are generally public and conducted fairly, with no official intimidation. Iceland is one of the few countries with efficient, property rights–based fisheries management.

FREEDOM FROM CORRUPTION — *96%*

Corruption is perceived as almost nonexistent. Iceland ranks 1st out of 163 countries in Transparency International's Corruption Perceptions Index for 2006. Its thousand-year history of parliamentary government has encouraged the institutionalization of such principles as accountability and transparency.

LABOR FREEDOM — *75%*

Relatively flexible employment regulations could be further improved to enhance employment opportunities and productivity growth. The non-salary cost of employing a worker is moderate, but dismissing a redundant employee can be difficult and costly. Regulations on the number of work hours are rigid.

INDIA

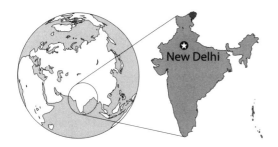

New Delhi

India's economy is 54.2 percent free, according to our 2008 assessment, which makes it the world's 115th freest economy. Its overall score is 0.1 percentage point higher than last year, partly reflecting improved labor freedom. India is ranked 21st out of 30 countries in the Asia–Pacific region, and its overall score is lower than the regional average.

India has no notably strong economic institutions, and the few areas that score better than the world average are limited government size, labor freedom, and property rights. Government expenditure is relatively low.

India could improve in several areas, including business freedom, trade freedom, financial freedom, investment freedom, and freedom from corruption. The average tariff rate is high, and the government imposes severe non-tariff barriers. Foreign investment is overly regulated, and the judicial system is erratic and clogged by a significant backlog of cases. Though the country has a large financial sector, the government interferes extensively with foreign capital.

BACKGROUND: India is the world's most populous democracy and one of Asia's fastest-growing economies. The current Congress Party coalition government is politically dependent on left-leaning parties, crippling its ability to enact desperately needed economic reforms—and leaving state governments to push forward liberalization. Nevertheless, the economy continues to grow strongly on the back of a vibrant services sector and an expanding manufacturing sector. India's economic challenges include heavy regulatory burdens, high trade barriers, and an outdated and heavily protected agricultural sector, which employs the majority of the country's workers.

How Do We Measure Economic Freedom? See Chapter 4 (page 39) for an explanation of the methodology or visit the *Index* Web site at *heritage.org/index*.

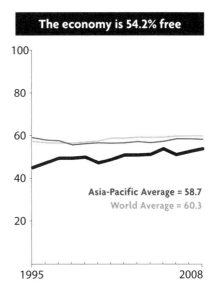

The economy is 54.2% free

Asia-Pacific Average = 58.7
World Average = 60.3

1995 — 2008

QUICK FACTS

Population: 1.1 billion

GDP (PPP): $3.8 trillion
9.2% growth in 2005
7.1% 5-yr. comp. ann. growth
$3,452 per capita

Unemployment: 8.9%

Inflation (CPI): 4.2%

FDI (net flow): $5.2 billion

Official Development Assistance:
Multilateral: $1.5 billion
Bilateral: $1.8 billion (9.0% from the U.S.)

External Debt: $123.1 billion

Exports: $112.0 billion
Primarily textile goods, gems and jewelry, engineering goods, chemicals, leather manufactures

Imports: $187.9 billion
Primarily crude oil, machinery, gems, fertilizer, chemicals

2005 data unless otherwise noted.

211

INDIA'S TEN ECONOMIC FREEDOMS

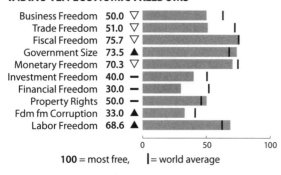

Business Freedom	50.0 ▽
Trade Freedom	51.0 ▽
Fiscal Freedom	75.7 ▽
Government Size	73.5 ▲
Monetary Freedom	70.3 ▽
Investment Freedom	40.0 —
Financial Freedom	30.0 —
Property Rights	50.0 —
Fdm fm Corruption	33.0 ▲
Labor Freedom	68.6 ▲

0   50   100

100 = most free, | = world average

BUSINESS FREEDOM — 50%

The overall freedom to start, operate, and close a business is considerably restricted by India's regulatory environment. Starting a business takes an average of 33 days, compared to the world average of 43 days. Obtaining a business license requires 20 procedures and 224 days. Bankruptcy proceedings are onerous and lengthy.

TRADE FREEDOM — 51%

India's weighted average tariff rate was 14.5 percent in 2005. Export restrictions, a negative import list, service market access restrictions, high tariffs, import taxes and fees, a complex and non-transparent trade regime, onerous standards and certifications, discriminatory sanitary and phytosanitary measures, problematic enforcement of intellectual property rights, restrictive licensing, domestic bias in government procurement, export subsidies, inadequate infrastructure, counter-trade policies, and complex and non-transparent customs add to the cost of trade. An additional 20 percentage points is deducted from India's trade freedom score to account for non-tariff barriers.

FISCAL FREEDOM — 75.7%

India's tax rates are moderate. Both the top income tax rate and the top corporate tax rate are 33 percent (30 percent plus a 10 percent surcharge). Other taxes include a dividend tax, a property tax, and a tax on insurance contracts. In the most recent year, overall tax revenue as a percentage of GDP was 15.8 percent.

GOVERNMENT SIZE — 73.5%

Total government expenditures, including consumption and transfer payments, are low. In the most recent year, government spending equaled 29.7 percent of GDP. The state still plays a major role in over 200 public-sector enterprises.

MONETARY FREEDOM — 70.3%

Inflation is moderate, averaging 5.4 percent between 2004 and 2006. Relatively unstable prices explain most of the monetary freedom score. The government subsidizes agricultural, gas, and kerosene production; applies factory, wholesale, and retail-level price controls on "essential" commodities, 25 crops, services, electricity, water, some petroleum products, and certain types of coal; and controls the prices of 74 bulk drugs that cover 40 percent of the market, with another 354 to be brought under con-

trols by a new pharmaceutical policy. Domestic price and marketing arrangements apply to commodities like sugar and certain cereals. An additional 15 percentage points is deducted from India's monetary freedom score to account for policies that distort domestic prices.

INVESTMENT FREEDOM — 40%

Highly complex rules and laws limit foreign direct investment. Rules established in 2005 maintain restrictions on most existing joint ventures but allow some new negotiations. Foreign investment is prohibited in most real estate, retailing, legal services, agriculture, security services, and railways. Foreign investors may bid for privatization contracts, but privatization has stalled. Residents need central bank approval to open foreign currency accounts domestically or abroad. Non-residents may hold conditional foreign exchange and domestic currency accounts. Capital transactions and some credit operations are subject to restrictions and requirements.

FINANCIAL FREEDOM — 30%

India's 28 state-owned banks control about 75 percent of loans and deposits, and 29 private banks and 31 foreign banks make up the rest. The government owns nearly all of the approximately 600 rural and cooperative banks and most other financial institutions. Banks must lend to "priority" borrowers. Foreign ownership of banks and insurance companies is restricted. The insurance sector is partially liberalized, but five state-owned insurers dominate the growing market. Capital markets are widespread, and the stock market is one of Asia's largest, but foreign participation is restricted.

PROPERTY RIGHTS — 50%

Because of large backlogs, it takes several years for the courts to reach decisions, and foreign corporations often resort to international arbitration. Protection of property for local investors is weak, and protection of intellectual property rights is problematic. Proprietary test results and other data about patented products submitted to the government by foreign pharmaceutical companies have been used by domestic companies without any legal penalties.

FREEDOM FROM CORRUPTION — 33%

Corruption is perceived as significant. India ranks 70th out of 163 countries in Transparency International's Corruption Perceptions Index for 2006. Corruption continues to be a major concern, especially in government procurement of telecommunications, power, and defense contracts.

LABOR FREEDOM — 68.6%

Relatively flexible employment regulations could be improved to enhance employment opportunities and productivity growth. The informal economy employs about 90 percent of workers. The non-salary cost of employing a worker is moderate, but dismissing a redundant employee is costly. The difficulty of laying off a worker creates a risk aversion for companies that would otherwise hire more people and grow.

INDONESIA

Jakarta

Rank: 119

Regional Rank: 22 of 30

Indonesia's economy is 53.9 percent free, according to our 2008 assessment, which makes it the world's 119th freest economy. Its overall score is 0.1 percentage point lower than last year, mainly reflecting lower scores in monetary freedom. Indonesia is ranked 22nd out of 30 countries in the Asia–Pacific region, and its overall score is lower than the regional average.

Indonesia has no strong economic institutions and scores better than the world average except in terms of government expenditures, which are low in formal terms. However, this is likely a sign of government weakness, not efficiency. Tax revenue is low as a percentage of GDP, but tax rates are high. Likewise, inflation is low, but the government interferes extensively with market prices.

Indonesia is weak in business freedom, investment freedom, financial freedom, property rights, and freedom from corruption. Starting a business takes more than twice as long as the world average, and regulations are onerous. Foreign investment is restricted, and judicial enforcement is both erratic and non-transparent with respect to the treatment of foreigners. Because corruption is rampant, impartial adjudication of cases is not guaranteed.

BACKGROUND: Indonesia is the world's largest Muslim majority country and third-largest democracy. Since his election in 2004, President Susilo Bambang Yudhoyono has pursued a program to improve the business climate through changes in investment laws and regulations, tax reform, customs reform, and infrastructure financing. Many of the government's goals, such as labor reform, simplifying regulatory burdens, and rooting out corruption, have run into obstacles. As a result, despite competent macroeconomic stewardship, the government has been hard-pressed to deliver on its promises to boost employment.

The economy is 53.9% free

100

80

60

40

Asia-Pacific Average = 58.7
World Average = 60.3

20

1995   2008

QUICK FACTS

Population: 220.6 million

GDP (PPP): $847.6 billion
5.7% growth in 2005
5.0% 5-yr. comp. ann. growth
$3,843 per capita

Unemployment: 6.8%

Inflation (CPI): 10.5%

FDI (net flow): $2.2 billion

Official Development Assistance:
Multilateral: $284.3 million
Bilateral: $2.6 billion (6.4% from the U.S.)

External Debt: $138.3 billion

Exports: $99.1 billion
Primarily oil and gas, electrical appliances, plywood, textiles, rubber

Imports: $87.6 billion
Primarily machinery and equipment, chemicals, fuels, foodstuffs

How Do We Measure Economic Freedom? See Chapter 4 (page 39) for an explanation of the methodology or visit the *Index* Web site at *heritage.org/index*.

2005 data unless otherwise noted.

INDONESIA'S TEN ECONOMIC FREEDOMS

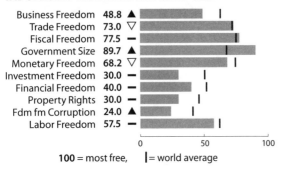

Business Freedom	48.8 ▲	
Trade Freedom	73.0 ▽	
Fiscal Freedom	77.5 —	
Government Size	89.7 —	
Monetary Freedom	68.2 ▽	
Investment Freedom	30.0 —	
Financial Freedom	40.0 —	
Property Rights	30.0 —	
Fdm fm Corruption	24.0 ▲	
Labor Freedom	57.5 —	

0   50   100

100 = most free,   ▐ = world average

BUSINESS FREEDOM — 48.8 %

The overall freedom to start, operate, and close a business is significantly restricted by Indonesia's regulatory environment. Starting a business takes an average of 105 days, compared to the world average of 43 days. Obtaining a business license requires about the world average of 19 procedures. Closing a business is difficult.

TRADE FREEDOM — 73%

Indonesia's weighted average tariff rate was 6 percent in 2005. Import and export bans and restrictions, service market access barriers, high and complex tariffs, non-transparent and arbitrary regulations, import and export licensing requirements, restrictive sanitary and phytosanitary regulations, weak enforcement of intellectual property rights, and customs valuation that can be inconsistent and prone to corruption add to the cost of trade. An additional 15 percentage points is deducted from Indonesia's trade freedom score to account for non-tariff barriers.

FISCAL FREEDOM — 77.5%

Indonesia has a high income tax rate and a moderate corporate tax rate. The top individual income tax rate is 35 percent, and the top corporate tax rate is 30 percent. Implementation of a tax reform package has been slow. Other taxes include a value-added tax (VAT) and a tax on interest. In the most recent year, overall tax revenue as a percentage of GDP was 11.4 percent.

GOVERNMENT SIZE — 89.7%

Total government expenditures, including consumption and transfer payments, are low. In the most recent year, government spending equaled 18.5 percent of GDP. State-owned enterprises are estimated to account for almost 40 percent of GDP. Privatization is very slow.

MONETARY FREEDOM — 68.2%

Inflation is relatively high, averaging 11.8 percent between 2004 and 2006. Relatively high and unstable prices explain most of the monetary freedom score. Fuel, housing, and health care are subsidized, and gasoline, electricity, liquefied petroleum gas, rice, cigarettes, cement, hospital services, potable/piped water, city transport, air transport, telephone charges, trains, salt, toll-road tariffs, and postage are under "administered prices." An additional 10 percent-

age points is deducted from Indonesia's monetary freedom score to account for policies that distort domestic prices.

INVESTMENT FREEDOM — 30%

Corruption, contradictory regulations, and taxation and labor issues make negotiating and enforcing contracts difficult and the treatment of foreign investors unequal. The voiding of a major issue of corporate bonds late in 2006 shook investor confidence. Foreigners may not invest in forests, logging, taxi and bus services, sailing, films, and trading. Subject to restrictions, residents and non-residents may hold foreign exchange accounts. Most capital transactions are restricted. Non-residents may not purchase real estate. Several investments require domestic partners, and foreign workers must contribute to a training fund for Indonesians.

FINANCIAL FREEDOM — 40%

After the 1997–1998 Asian financial crisis, the number of banks fell from 238 in 1997 to 130 at the end of 2006. Consolidation is encouraged, with certain restrictions on acquisitions and capital requirements. Almost all banks taken over in the wake of the crisis have been privatized, but the state still owns several banks. Provincial governments own and operate development banks. At the end of 2005, 41 of the 130 banks were foreign-owned or foreign-controlled and accounted for over 45 percent of assets. Supervision is insufficient, regulation is somewhat burdensome, and privatization has stalled. Several insurers and foreign insurers rank among the top 10 companies. Capital markets are developing, and two small stock exchanges were operating in 2006.

PROPERTY RIGHTS — 30%

Court rulings can be arbitrary and inconsistent, and corruption is substantial. Judges have been known to rule against foreigners in commercial disputes, ignoring contracts between the parties. It is difficult to get the courts to enforce international arbitration awards. Lack of clear land titles and the inability to own land in "fee simple" are also problems. Enforcement of intellectual property rights is weak.

FREEDOM FROM CORRUPTION — 24%

Corruption is perceived as pervasive. Indonesia ranks 130th out of 163 countries in Transparency International's Corruption Perceptions Index for 2006. Companies cite demands for irregular fees to obtain required permits or licenses as well as the award of government contracts and concessions based on personal relationships.

LABOR FREEDOM — 57.5%

Restrictive employment regulations impede employment opportunities and productivity growth. The non-salary cost of employing a worker is moderate, but dismissing a redundant employee can be costly. The difficulty of laying off a worker creates a risk aversion for companies that would otherwise hire more people and grow.

IRAN

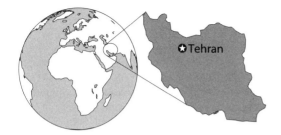

○Tehran

Iran's economy is 44 percent free, according to our 2008 assessment, which makes it the world's 151st freest economy. Its overall score is 0.1 percentage point lower than last year, mainly reflecting a worsened score in freedom from corruption. Iran is ranked 16th out of 17 countries in the Middle East/North Africa region, and its overall score is extremely low—almost one-third below the regional average.

Iran has no strong economic institutions and scores better than the world average only in terms of government expenditures, which are low in formal terms, although this is likely a sign of government weakness, not efficiency. Examples of self-defeating statism include protectionism and price controls that have led to double-digit tariffs and double-digit inflation.

Iran's economy is unfree in many ways. Trade freedom, monetary freedom, investment freedom, financial freedom, property rights, and freedom from corruption are all weak. Business licensing and closing are regulated heavily by an intrusive and highly inefficient bureaucracy. High tariff rates and non-tariff barriers impede trade and foreign investment alike. Corruption is rampant, and the fair adjudication of property rights in a court of law cannot be guaranteed.

BACKGROUND: Iran's economy, once one of the most advanced in the Middle East, was crippled by the 1979 Islamic revolution and the Iran–Iraq war and still suffers from long-standing economic mismanagement. Mahmoud Ahmadinejad became president in 2005 and halted tentative efforts to reform the state-dominated economy. Ahmadinejad has promised the poor a greater share of Iran's oil wealth, greater subsidies, and greater state control. High world oil prices have raised export revenues and helped to service Iran's large foreign debt, but the economy remains burdened by high unemployment, inflation, corruption, costly subsidies, and a public sector that is both bloated and inefficient.

How Do We Measure Economic Freedom? See Chapter 4 (page 39) for an explanation of the methodology or visit the *Index* Web site at *heritage.org/index*.

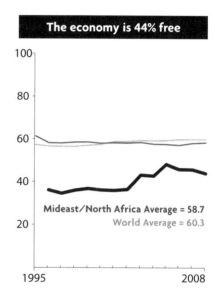

The economy is 44% free

Mideast/North Africa Average = 58.7
World Average = 60.3

1995 — 2008

QUICK FACTS

Population: 68.3 million

GDP (PPP): $543.8 billion
4.4% growth in 2005
6.0% 5-yr. comp. ann. growth
$7,968 per capita

Unemployment: 11.6%

Inflation (CPI): 12.1%

FDI (net flow): −$46.0 million

Official Development Assistance:
Multilateral: $21.0 million
Bilateral: $101.9 million (3.7% from the U.S.)

External Debt: $21.3 billion

Exports: $18.2 billion (2004 estimate)
Primarily petroleum, chemical and petrochemical products, fruits and nuts, carpets

Imports: $14.9 billion (2004 estimate)
Primarily industrial raw materials and intermediate goods, capital goods, foodstuffs and other consumer goods, technical services, military supplies

2005 data unless otherwise noted.

IRAN'S TEN ECONOMIC FREEDOMS

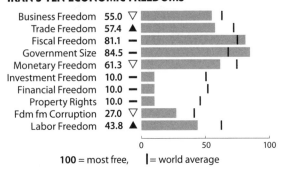

Business Freedom	55.0 ▽	
Trade Freedom	57.4 ▲	
Fiscal Freedom	81.1 —	
Government Size	84.5 —	
Monetary Freedom	61.3 ▽	
Investment Freedom	10.0 —	
Financial Freedom	10.0 —	
Property Rights	10.0 —	
Fdm fm Corruption	27.0 ▽	
Labor Freedom	43.8 ▲	

0   50   100

100 = most free,   I = world average

BUSINESS FREEDOM — 55%

The overall freedom to start, operate, and close a business is restricted by Iran's regulatory environment. Starting a business takes an average of 47 days, compared to the world average of 43 days. Obtaining a business license takes 670 days, compared to the world average of 234 days. Closing a business is difficult.

TRADE FREEDOM — 57.4%

Iran's weighted average tariff rate was 13.8 percent in 2004. Import bans and restrictions, high tariffs and import taxes, export licensing requirements, restrictive sanitary and phytosanitary regulations, burdensome customs procedures, government control of imports, tariff and tax schedules that change frequently, and weak enforcement of intellectual property rights add to the cost of trade. An additional 15 percentage points is deducted from Iran's trade freedom score to account for non-tariff barriers.

FISCAL FREEDOM — 81.1%

Iran has a high income tax rate and a moderate corporate tax rate. The top income tax rate is 35 percent, and the top corporate tax rate is 25 percent. Other taxes include a tax on check transactions and a tax of property transfers. In the most recent year, overall tax revenue as a percentage of GDP was 6 percent.

GOVERNMENT SIZE — 84.5%

Total government expenditures, including consumption and transfer payments, are moderate. In the most recent year, government spending equaled 22.7 percent of GDP. More than 500 companies are state-owned, and around 1,000 are semi-public.

MONETARY FREEDOM — 61.3%

Inflation is high, averaging 14 percent between 2004 and 2006. Relatively unstable prices explain most of the monetary freedom score. The government controls the prices of petroleum products, electricity, water, and wheat for the production of bread; provides economic subsidies; and influences prices through regulation of Iran's many state-owned enterprises. An additional 15 percentage points is deducted from Iran's monetary freedom score to adjust for measures that distort domestic prices.

INVESTMENT FREEDOM — 10%

Foreign investment is restricted in banking, telecommunications, transport, and border control and banned in defense, oil, and gas. The government allows the sale of 65 percent of the shares of state-owned enterprises, except for defense and security-related industries and the National Iranian Oil Company. President Ahmadinejad has fired several public and private banking leaders who supported privatization. Political unrest and uncertainty over international sanctions further deter investment. The parliament can veto projects in which foreign investors have a majority stake and has blocked two proposed investments. Most payments, transfers, credit operations, and capital transactions are subject to limitations, quantitative limits, or approval requirements.

FINANCIAL FREEDOM — 10%

All banks were nationalized following the 1979 revolution and reopened under the principles of Islamic law, which prohibits functions like interest. There are six state-owned commercial banks and three state-owned specialized institutions. State banks account for 98 percent of banking assets. Six small private banks operate under strict restrictions regarding *de facto* interest rates and capital requirements. Credit is often supplied by traditional money lenders in the bazaar, which encourages Iranians to invest in cash-based businesses. Foreign banks are legally permitted to operate in free trade zones. The government directs credit allocation. All insurance companies were nationalized during the revolution, and the sector remains dominated by five state-owned companies. The stock exchange is very small.

PROPERTY RIGHTS — 10%

Resort to the courts is often counterproductive, and finding an influential local business partner with substantial political patronage is a more effective way to protect contracts. Few laws protect intellectual property, computer software piracy is extensive, and infringement of industrial designs, trademarks, and copyrights is widespread.

FREEDOM FROM CORRUPTION — 27%

Corruption is perceived as widespread. Iran ranks 105th out of 163 countries in Transparency International's Corruption Perceptions Index for 2006. Graft is extensive and viewed as growing worse by the day. The anti-corruption agency has less than 1,000 inspectors to monitor the 2.3 million full-time civil servants and numerous government contractors who control most of Iran's economy.

LABOR FREEDOM — 43.8%

Restrictive employment regulations hinder employment opportunities and productivity growth. The non-salary cost of employing a worker is high, and firing a worker requires approval of the Islamic Labor Council or the Labor Discretionary Board. The difficulty of laying off a worker creates a risk aversion for companies that would otherwise hire more people and grow. Regulations on the number of work hours are very rigid.

IRAQ

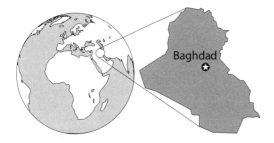

Baghdad

Rank: Not ranked

Regional Rank: Not ranked

The level of economic freedom in Iraq cannot be scored in our 2008 assessment because sufficient reliable data for the country are not available. In the years since the invasion by U.S. military forces in 2003, the Iraqi economy has slowly recovered. However, the country is still unstable and faces continuing violence among different ethnic and religious factions. Iraq was last graded in 2002, when it received an overall score of 15.6 percent.

The Iraqi economy should benefit from many excellent reforms and institutions that have been put in place since 2003, including tax policies, simple and low tariffs, new investment laws, and a significantly liberalized and modernized banking system; but these reforms and institutions cannot be fully effective as long as they have to depend on a foundation of weak physical security and persistent corruption.

BACKGROUND: Iraq gained its independence from Britain in 1932 and was a constitutional monarchy until a 1958 military coup led to a series of dictatorships. Saddam Hussein's regime was ousted in 2003, and an elected government led by Prime Minister Nuri al-Maliki took office in May 2006. Iraq's oil industry provides more than 90 percent of hard-currency earnings but has been hurt by pipeline sabotage, electricity outages, and years of neglect and postponed maintenance. Economic recovery, though helped by high oil prices and economic aid from the United States and other foreign donors, is hampered by continued insurgency and instability.

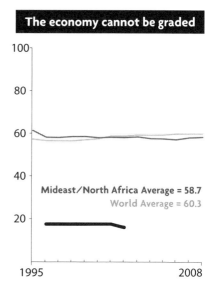

The economy cannot be graded

Mideast/North Africa Average = 58.7
World Average = 60.3

1995 — 2008

QUICK FACTS

Population: 27.5 million

GDP (PPP): $87.9 billion
3.7% growth in 2005
5-yr. comp. ann. growth n/a
$1,900 per capita

Unemployment: 25%–30%

Inflation (CPI): 31.6%

FDI (net flow): $300.0 million

Official Development Assistance:
Multilateral: $53.2 million
Bilateral: $21.6 billion (50.1% from the U.S.)

External Debt: $81.5 billion

Exports: $32.2 billion
Primarily crude oil, crude materials excluding fuels, food and live animals

Imports: $20.8 billion
Primarily food, medicine, manufactures

How Do We Measure Economic Freedom? See Chapter 4 (page 39) for an explanation of the methodology or visit the *Index* Web site at *heritage.org/index*.

2005 data unless otherwise noted.

BUSINESS FREEDOM — NOT GRADED

Despite some progress in establishing an investment-friendly business environment, significant problems remain to be addressed as Iraq tries to deal with challenges to its security and stability.

TRADE FREEDOM — NOT GRADED

Iraq is in the process of rebuilding its economy. According to the U.S. Department of Commerce, Iraq applied a flat tariff rate of 5 percent in 2004. Non-tariff barriers include significant delays in trade through customs as well as some import and export bans.

FISCAL FREEDOM — NOT GRADED

The suspension of individual and corporate income taxes was lifted in 2004. Currently, both individual and corporate income tax rates are capped at 15 percent. Despite slow progress, some structural reforms, including steps to reduce subsidies and modernize government financial management, have been made. Maintaining fiscal sustainability remains one of the policy priorities. Further modernization of the tax system and introduction of a sales tax are under consideration.

GOVERNMENT SIZE — NOT GRADED

Total government expenditures in Iraq, including consumption and transfer payments, are very high. It is estimated that government spending equals about 90 percent of GDP. The oil sector accounts for over 95 percent of exports and government revenue.

MONETARY FREEDOM — NOT GRADED

Inflation in Iraq is high, averaging 46 percent between 2004 and 2006. Such unstable prices are harmful to savings and therefore to investment. Iraq's very high inflation was mainly due to shortages of key commodities (particularly fuel), caused in part by the ongoing insurgency. The government maintains a large public sector, provides a number of subsidies, and imposes a number of price controls.

INVESTMENT FREEDOM — NOT GRADED

The elected Iraqi government created a new investment law in October 2006, opening Iraq to foreign capital. Inflation and sluggish growth, combined with a deleterious security situation and rampant corruption, are major hindrances to investment. Iraq does not subscribe to international arbitration agreements, although it does have a domestic arbitration framework. The regulatory system is confusing, since most of the laws are new, having been established by the 2006 investment law, and thus fairly ambiguous for investors. Capital and profits can be transferred out of Iraq. Speculation in the new Iraqi dinar is illegal because of central bank efforts to reduce inflation. Laws concerning state expropriation are not fully formed, though the constitution reserves the power for national interest situations.

FINANCIAL FREEDOM — NOT GRADED

The Coalition Provisional Authority and the new Iraqi government have introduced many changes into Iraq's financial system. A March 2004 banking law significantly liberalized and modernized the banking system, allowing credit to be allocated on market terms and making the central bank independent. Although there were 17 private banks in 2006, the two largest state-owned banks—Rafidain and Rasheed—accounted for 85 percent of banking-sector assets. In addition, there were four specialized state-owned banks serving the agricultural, industrial, real estate, and social sectors. Heavy dollarization of the economy is destabilizing to the financial system, although the government claims that use of the dinar is rising. Three foreign banks have been granted licenses, two from the United Kingdom (HSBC and Standard Chartered) and one from Kuwait (NBK). Operations have yet to begin, however, because of security concerns. Both the insurance sector and the new stock exchange are very small.

PROPERTY RIGHTS — NOT GRADED

There is no protection of property in Iraq. Ongoing wartime conditions and a high degree of personal insecurity discourage investment. The absence of an enforceable legal system means that foreigners are further disadvantaged in terms of dispute resolution, although this affects local investors to a large degree as well. U.S. forces, working with Iraqi military and police units, are trying to improve conditions but still face daunting challenges.

FREEDOM FROM CORRUPTION — NOT GRADED

Corruption is perceived as rampant. Iraq ranks 160th out of 163 countries in Transparency International's Corruption Perceptions Index for 2006. Under the regime of Saddam Hussein, corruption was a fact of life for every Iraqi and touched on every economic transaction. This legacy of corruption remains a significant obstacle to Iraq's development.

LABOR FREEDOM — NOT GRADED

Iraq's formal labor market is not yet fully developed. Most jobs in the private sector are informal. It is estimated that unemployment and underemployment combined are around 50 percent.

IRELAND

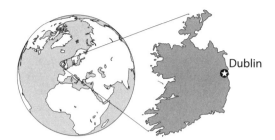

Dublin

Rank: 3

Regional Rank: 1 of 41

Ireland's economy is 82.4 percent free, according to our 2008 assessment, which makes it the world's 3rd freest economy. Its overall score is slightly lower than last year. Ireland is ranked 1st out of 41 countries in the European region, and its overall score is much higher than the regional average.

Ireland has high levels of business freedom, investment freedom, financial freedom, property rights, and freedom from corruption. Government regulation is light. Inflation is low, but Ireland's monetary score suffers somewhat from distortionary EU agricultural subsidies. Foreign investment is restricted only in a few sectors. Financial markets are transparent and open to foreign competition. Property rights are well protected by an efficient, independent judiciary.

Ireland's economy is significantly free, with only two categories slightly below the average world score. Fiscal freedom and government size both score 3 percentage points below average. Government spending as a proportion of GDP is just over one-third, and the top individual income tax rate is a high 42 percent.

BACKGROUND: Ireland's modern, highly industrialized economy performed well throughout the 1990s and has enjoyed sustained growth, earning Ireland a reputation as the "Celtic Tiger." The country has one of the world's most business-friendly environments, especially for investment, and enjoys the European Union's second-highest GDP per capita. In January 2003, the government lowered the corporate tax rate to 12.5 percent—far below the EU average. Because of its pro-business government policies, Ireland receives a substantial portion of U.S. investment directed at the EU. However, it also is struggling with an underperforming health sector, and the provision of decent public services remains a major topic of political debate.

How Do We Measure Economic Freedom? See Chapter 4 (page 39) for an explanation of the methodology or visit the *Index* Web site at *heritage.org/index*.

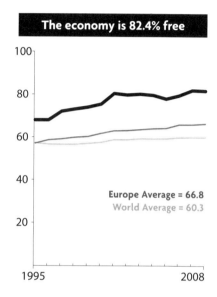

The economy is 82.4% free

Europe Average = 66.8
World Average = 60.3

1995   2008

QUICK FACTS

Population: 4.2 million

GDP (PPP): $160.1 billion
5.5% growth in 2005
5.0% 5-yr. comp. ann. growth
$38,504 per capita

Unemployment: 4.3%

Inflation (CPI): 2.2%

FDI (net flow): −$22.8 billion

Official Development Assistance:
Multilateral: None
Bilateral: None

External Debt: $1.4 trillion

Exports: $161.4 billion
Primarily machinery and equipment, chemicals, pharmaceuticals, computer and technology, travel services

Imports: $137.1 billion
Primarily data processing equipment, other machinery and equipment, chemicals, petroleum, financial services

2005 data unless otherwise noted.

IRELAND'S TEN ECONOMIC FREEDOMS

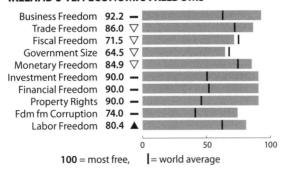

Business Freedom	92.2	—
Trade Freedom	86.0	▽
Fiscal Freedom	71.5	▽
Government Size	64.5	▽
Monetary Freedom	84.9	▽
Investment Freedom	90.0	—
Financial Freedom	90.0	—
Property Rights	90.0	—
Fdm fm Corruption	74.0	—
Labor Freedom	80.4	▲

0   50   100

100 = most free, | = world average

BUSINESS FREEDOM — 92.2%

The overall freedom to start, operate, and close a business is strongly protected by Ireland's regulatory environment. Starting a business takes an average of 13 days, compared to the world average of 43 days. Obtaining a business license requires less than the world average of 19 procedures and 234 days. Bankruptcy procedures are simple and straightforward.

TRADE FREEDOM — 86%

Ireland's trade policy is the same as those of other members of the European Union. The common EU weighted average tariff rate was 2 percent in 2005. Non-tariff barriers reflected in EU policy include agricultural and manufacturing subsidies, import restrictions for some goods and services, market access restrictions in some service sectors, non-transparent and restrictive regulations and standards, and inconsistent customs administration across EU members. Government procurement rules are restrictive. An additional 10 percentage points is deducted from Ireland's trade freedom score to account for non-tariff barriers.

FISCAL FREEDOM — 71.5%

Ireland has a high income tax rate but a low corporate tax rate. The top income tax rate is 42 percent, and the top corporate tax rate is 12.5 percent. Other taxes include a value-added tax (VAT) and a tax on interest. In the most recent year, overall tax revenue as a percentage of GDP was 30.5 percent.

GOVERNMENT SIZE — 64.5%

Total government expenditures, including consumption and transfer payments, are high. In the most recent year, government spending equaled 34.4 percent of GDP. Despite considerable progress in privatization, the government maintains some controls over several key sectors of the economy.

MONETARY FREEDOM — 84.9%

Ireland is a member of the euro zone. Inflation is relatively low, averaging 2.5 percent between 2004 and 2006. Relatively low and stable prices explain most of the monetary freedom score. As a participant in the EU's Common Agricultural Policy, the government subsidizes agricultural production, distorting the prices of agricultural products. It also influences prices through state-owned enterprises. An

additional 5 percentage points is deducted from Ireland's monetary freedom score to account for policies that distort domestic prices.

INVESTMENT FREEDOM — 90%

Ireland welcomes foreign investment, especially high-technology ventures. Domestic and foreign firms incorporated in Ireland receive equal treatment. Restrictions apply to airlines owned by non-EU residents and the purchase of agricultural lands. Stock in certain state-owned companies (like the national airline) continues to be sold, and foreigners may participate. There is no approval process for foreign investment or capital inflows unless the company is applying for incentives. Investment dispute arbitration is available. The judicial system upholds commercial contracts involving foreign investment. There are no restrictions or barriers with respect to current transfers, repatriation of profits, or access to foreign exchange. Most land purchases are legal for residents and non-residents.

FINANCIAL FREEDOM — 90%

Some 115 banks and other credit institutions, a majority of them foreign, were authorized to conduct business in 2004. Domestic banking is dominated by two Irish banks that together account for about 75 percent of deposits. Credit is allocated on market terms. The government sold its shares in the last state-owned financial institution in 2002. As an EU member, Ireland is a member of the European System of Central Banks. Increasingly an international hub for insurance, fund management, and venture capital, Ireland has about 190 insurance companies and subsidiaries. The stock exchange is small and independent, trades mostly in Irish equities and government bonds, and has recovered from a downturn in 2002. An exchange opened in 2005 under the aegis of the main index caters to small companies with less market capitalization.

PROPERTY RIGHTS — 90%

Expropriation is highly unlikely. The courts protect property, and contracts are secure. Ireland has one of Europe's most comprehensive legal frameworks for the protection of intellectual property rights.

FREEDOM FROM CORRUPTION — 74%

Corruption is perceived as minimal. Ireland ranks 18th out of 163 countries in Transparency International's Corruption Perceptions Index for 2006. It is illegal for public servants to accept bribes, and the police investigate allegations of corruption. Ireland has ratified the OECD Anti-Bribery Convention and is a member of the OECD Working Group on Bribery and the Group of States Against Corruption.

LABOR FREEDOM — 80.4%

Flexible employment regulations enhance employment opportunities and productivity growth. The non-salary cost of employing a worker is low, and dismissing a redundant employee is relatively costless. Restrictions on the number of working hours are flexible.

ISRAEL

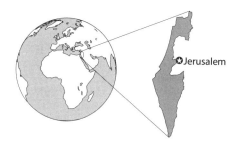
Jerusalem

Israel's economy is 66.1 percent free, according to our 2008 assessment, which makes it the world's 46th freest economy. Its overall score is 1.5 percentage points higher than last year, reflecting improved scores in investment freedom and financial freedom. Israel is ranked 4th out of 17 countries in the Middle East/North Africa region, and its overall score is much higher than the regional average.

Israel enjoys high levels of trade freedom, investment freedom, property rights, and freedom from corruption. The economy is open to foreign investment in almost all sectors except defense. Tariff rates are low. Inflation is low, although the government interferes with the market by subsidizing certain basic goods.

Israel is weak in two areas: government size and fiscal freedom. Government spending is high, constituting almost half of GDP. Income tax rates on individuals and corporations are also relatively high, as is total tax revenue. Although relatively advanced for the region, Israel's financial sector is still subject to government intervention and control.

BACKGROUND: Israel gained its independence from Britain in 1948 and fought a series of wars against its Arab neighbors that imposed a high defense burden on the state-dominated economy. Despite few natural resources, Israel has developed a modern market economy with a thriving technology sector. The collapse of the 1993 Oslo peace agreement with the Palestinians and the onset of the Intifada in September 2000 depressed tourism, discouraged foreign investment, and contributed to economic recession. A recovery in 2003 and 2004 was due to increased tourism, foreign investment, and greater demand for Israeli exports, especially high-technology goods and services, but Israel's overall economic prospects may be adversely affected by persistent conflict with radical Palestinian, Lebanese, and Islamic terrorist groups.

How Do We Measure Economic Freedom? See Chapter 4 (page 39) for an explanation of the methodology or visit the *Index* Web site at *heritage.org/index*.

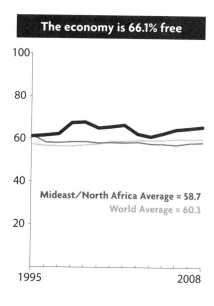

The economy is 66.1% free

Mideast/North Africa Average = 58.7
World Average = 60.3

QUICK FACTS

Population: 6.9 million

GDP (PPP): $179.1 billion
5.2% growth in 2005
2.6% 5-yr. comp. ann. growth
$25,864 per capita

Unemployment: 9.0%

Inflation (CPI): 1.3%

FDI (net flow): $3.1 billion

Official Development Assistance:
Multilateral: $2.0 million (2004)
Bilateral: $588.0 million (93% from the U.S.) (2004)

External Debt: $82.0 billion

Exports: $57.9 billion
Primarily machinery and equipment, software, cut diamonds, agricultural products, chemicals, textiles and apparel

Imports: $57.6 billion
Primarily raw materials, military equipment, investment goods, rough diamonds, fuels, grain, consumer goods
2005 data unless otherwise noted.

ISRAEL'S TEN ECONOMIC FREEDOMS

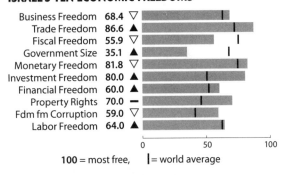

Business Freedom	68.4 ▽	
Trade Freedom	86.6 ▲	
Fiscal Freedom	55.9 ▽	
Government Size	35.1 ▲	
Monetary Freedom	81.8 ▽	
Investment Freedom	80.0 ▲	
Financial Freedom	60.0 ▲	
Property Rights	70.0 —	
Fdm fm Corruption	59.0 ▽	
Labor Freedom	64.0 ▲	

0   50   100

100 = most free,   I = world average

BUSINESS FREEDOM — 68.4%

The overall freedom to start, operate, and close a business is relatively well protected by Israel's regulatory environment. Starting a business takes an average of 34 days, compared to the world average of 43 days. Obtaining a business license requires slightly more than the world average of 19 procedures and 234 days. Bankruptcy procedures can be lengthy and costly. Despite moves toward deregulation, bureaucracy still impedes investment.

TRADE FREEDOM — 86.6%

Israel's weighted average tariff rate was 1.7 percent in 2005. Import bans and restrictions, high agriculture tariffs, import fees and taxes, a complex and non-transparent tariff rate quota system, kosher certification procedures, restrictive labeling requirements, import licensing, non-transparent technical standards and government procurement, and export subsidies add to the cost of trade. The enforcement of intellectual property rights remains problematic. An additional 10 percentage points is deducted from Israel's trade freedom score to account for non-tariff barriers.

FISCAL FREEDOM — 55.9%

The top income tax rate is 47 percent (to be reduced to 44 percent by 2010), and the top corporate tax rate is 29 percent (to be reduced to 25 percent by 2010). Other taxes include a value-added tax (VAT) and a capital gains tax. In the most recent year, overall tax revenue as a percentage of GDP was 36.9 percent.

GOVERNMENT SIZE — 35.1%

Total government expenditures, including consumption and transfer payments, are high. In the most recent year, government spending equaled 46.5 percent of GDP. Privatization has accelerated in recent years.

MONETARY FREEDOM — 81.8%

Inflation is low, averaging less than 1.7 percent between 2004 and 2006. Stable prices explain most of the monetary freedom score. The government influences prices through the public sector and provides some subsidies, especially for agriculture production. The energy sector remains largely state-owned and heavily regulated, and the government can impose price controls on vital goods and services. An additional 10 percentage points is deducted from

Israel's monetary freedom score to account for policies that distort domestic prices.

INVESTMENT FREEDOM — 80%

Foreign investment is restricted in a few sectors, such as defense, but is not screened, and regulations on acquisitions, mergers, and takeovers apply to both foreign and domestic investors. Investments in regulated industries, such as banking, require prior government approval, as does the receipt of investment incentive benefits. Commercial law is consistent and standardized, and international arbitration is binding in dispute settlements with the state. Bureaucracy can be difficult, and labor, health, and safety laws can be complex. Residents and non-residents may hold foreign exchange accounts, and there are no controls or restrictions on current transfers, repatriation of profits, or other transactions.

FINANCIAL FREEDOM — 60%

Credit is available on market terms, and financial institutions offer a wide array of credit instruments. Supervision is prudent, and regulations conform to international norms. At the end of 2006, 29 companies were licensed, including five foreign banks with a small share of the market. Only three foreign banks are active; BNP Paribas entered the market in 2006. Five main banking groups hold more than 95 percent of assets. Privatization was nearly complete by 2006. Bank ownership of insurance companies is restricted. The 2005 Bachar Reform bars commercial banks from owning holdings in mutual funds, and a second reform is being debated. Foreign investments in banking and insurance require prior government approval. Israel has one medium-sized securities exchange.

PROPERTY RIGHTS — 70%

Contractual arrangements are generally secure. Commercial law is clear and consistently applied. Expropriation reportedly occurs only if the property is linked to a terrorist threat and expropriation is deemed to be in the interest of national security. Jurisdiction for intellectual property rights enforcement is problematic, especially since responsibility in the West Bank and Gaza rests with the Palestinian Authority.

FREEDOM FROM CORRUPTION — 59%

Corruption is perceived as present. Israel ranks 34th out of 163 countries in Transparency International's Corruption Perceptions Index for 2006. There is concern that the civil service is becoming more politicized.

LABOR FREEDOM — 64%

Relatively flexible employment regulations could be improved to enhance employment and productivity growth. The non-salary cost of employing a worker is low, but dismissing a redundant employee is relatively costly. The difficulty of laying off a worker creates a risk aversion for companies that would otherwise hire more people and grow. Restrictions on the number of work hours are not flexible.

ITALY

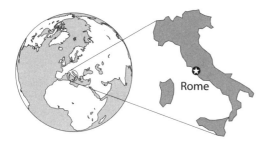

Rome

Rank: 64

Regional Rank: 29 of 41

Italy's economy is 62.5 percent free, according to our 2008 assessment, which makes it the world's 64th freest economy. Its overall score is 0.2 percentage point lower than last year. Italy is ranked 29th out of 41 countries in the European region, and its overall score is not improving as quickly as it might because of deeper reforms implemented in neighboring countries.

Italy scores highly in business freedom, trade freedom, investment freedom, and labor freedom when compared to the world average. Starting a business takes about 13 days, which is far below the world average. The tariff rate is low, although an inefficient bureaucracy implements some non-tariff barriers that also deter foreign investment. As a member of the EU, Italy has a standardized monetary policy that yields relatively low inflation despite government distortion in the agricultural sector.

Property rights and freedom from corruption are relatively weak compared to other European states. Italy scores below the world average and is exceptionally weak in fiscal freedom and government size because of having to support an extensive welfare state. Tax revenues equal 40 percent of GDP, and government expenditures equal nearly half of GDP.

BACKGROUND: Italy has been a central force in European integration ever since the end of World War II. It also is a member of NATO and the G-8. Despite having one of the world's largest economies, Italy faces serious economic challenges, including a high tax burden, large pension liabilities, and labor market rigidities. However, the center-left government of Romano Prodi continues to face tough opposition to structural reform from labor unions. Despite strong international competition from emerging Asian economies, small and medium-sized enterprises continue to thrive in manufacturing and high design, particularly in the country's northern regions. Tourism and services are among the most important sectors.

How Do We Measure Economic Freedom? See Chapter 4 (page 39) for an explanation of the methodology or visit the *Index* Web site at *heritage.org/index*.

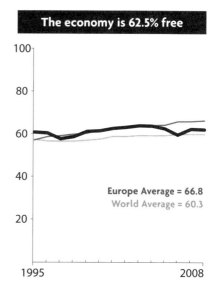

The economy is 62.5% free

Europe Average = 66.8
World Average = 60.3

QUICK FACTS

Population: 58.6 million

GDP (PPP): $1.7 trillion
0.1% growth in 2005
0.4% 5-yr. comp. ann. growth
$28,529 per capita

Unemployment: 7.9%

Inflation (CPI): 2.2%

FDI (net inflow): −$19.7 billion

Official Development Assistance:
Multilateral: None
Bilateral: None

External Debt: $2.0 trillion

Exports: $462.7 billion
Primarily engineering products, textiles and clothing, production machinery, motor vehicles, transport equipment

Imports: $463.3 billion
Primarily engineering products, chemicals, transport equipment, energy products, minerals and nonferrous metals, textiles and clothing, food, beverages, tobacco
2005 data unless otherwise noted.

ITALY'S TEN ECONOMIC FREEDOMS

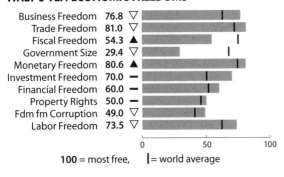

Business Freedom	76.8 ▽	
Trade Freedom	81.0 ▽	
Fiscal Freedom	54.3 ▲	
Government Size	29.4 ▽	
Monetary Freedom	80.6 ▲	
Investment Freedom	70.0 —	
Financial Freedom	60.0 —	
Property Rights	50.0 —	
Fdm fm Corruption	49.0 ▽	
Labor Freedom	73.5 ▽	

0   50   100

100 = most free, | = world average

BUSINESS FREEDOM — 76.8%

The overall freedom to start, operate, and close a business is relatively well protected by Italy's regulatory environment. The government has streamlined bureaucratic procedures. Starting a business takes an average of 13 days, compared to the world average of 43 days. Obtaining a business license requires less than the world average of 19 procedures and slightly more than the world average of 234 days. Closing a business is relatively easy.

TRADE FREEDOM — 81%

Italy's trade policy is the same as those of other members of the European Union. The common EU weighted average tariff rate was 2 percent in 2005. Non-tariff barriers reflected in EU policy include multiple restrictions. Pharmaceutical and biotechnology regulations are restrictive, government procurement is non-transparent and prone to corruption, service market access barriers can exceed the EU norm, and enforcement of intellectual property is weak. An additional 15 percentage points is deducted from Italy's trade freedom score to account for non-tariff barriers.

FISCAL FREEDOM — 54.3%

Italy has high tax rates. The top income tax rate is 43 percent, and the top corporate tax rate is 33 percent. Other taxes include a value-added tax (VAT), a tax on interest, and an advertising tax. In the most recent year, overall tax revenue as a percentage of GDP was 40.4 percent.

GOVERNMENT SIZE — 29.4%

Total government expenditures, including consumption and transfer payments, are very high. In the most recent year, government spending equaled 48.5 percent of GDP. Reducing the budget deficit and public debt (still equivalent to over 100 percent of GDP) is a priority, but progress has been sluggish.

MONETARY FREEDOM — 80.6%

Italy is a member of the euro zone. Inflation is relatively low, averaging 2.2 percent between 2004 and 2006. Relatively stable prices explain most of the monetary freedom score. As a participant in the EU's Common Agricultural Policy, the government subsidizes agricultural production, distorting agricultural prices. It also can introduce price controls. Items subject to rate setting at the national level include drinking water, electricity, gas, highway tolls, pre-

scription drugs reimbursed by the national health service, telecommunications, and domestic travel. An additional 10 percentage points is deducted from Italy's monetary freedom score to account for policies that distort domestic prices.

INVESTMENT FREEDOM — 70%

Italy welcomes foreign investment, but the government can veto acquisitions involving foreign investors. Since the election of Romano Prodi in 2006, certain investments in large Italian companies have been blocked. Foreign investment is closely regulated in defense, aircraft manufacturing, petroleum exploration and development, domestic airlines, and shipping. The Sviluppo Italia agency is trying to attract investment with incentive packages. Bureaucracy, inadequate infrastructure, legislative complexity, and a rigid labor market are major disincentives. Foreigners may not buy land along the border. There are no barriers to repatriation of profits, transfers, payments, or current transfers.

FINANCIAL FREEDOM — 60%

Credit is allocated on market terms, and foreign participation is welcome. Only three major financial institutions (Cassa Depositi e Prestiti, Bancoposta, and the sports bank Instituto per il Credito Sportivo) remain state-controlled. There were 784 banks at the end of 2005, down from over 1,150 in the early 1990s. The six largest banks account for over 54.6 percent of assets, though the market is less concentrated than elsewhere in Europe. Regulations and prohibitions can be burdensome, and approval is needed to gain control of a financial institution. Legislation to improve the regulatory environment was passed in late 2005. Italy has the EU's fourth-largest insurance market. The government is taking steps to reform underdeveloped capital markets.

PROPERTY RIGHTS — 50%

Property rights and contracts are secure, but judicial procedures are is extremely slow, and many companies choose to settle out of court. Many judges are politically oriented. Enforcement of intellectual property rights falls below the standards of other developed Western European countries.

FREEDOM FROM CORRUPTION — 49%

Corruption is perceived as present. Italy ranks 45th out of 163 countries in Transparency International's Corruption Perceptions Index for 2006. Corruption is more common than in other European countries. Italians regard investment-related sectors as corrupt.

LABOR FREEDOM — 73.5%

Relatively flexible employment regulations could be further improved to enhance employment opportunities and productivity growth. The non-salary cost of employing a worker is very high, but dismissing a redundant employee can be costless. Rules on the number of work hours are relatively rigid.

IVORY COAST

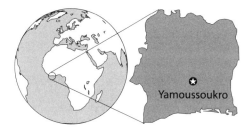

Yamoussoukro

I vory Coast's economy is 54.9 percent free, according to our 2008 assessment, which makes it the world's 111th freest economy. Its overall score is 1 percentage point lower than last year, reflecting improved scores in five of the 10 freedoms.

Ivory Coast has relatively high scores in four areas: government size, monetary freedom, financial freedom, and labor freedom. Government expenditures are low, and the level of income from state-owned businesses is relatively low. Inflation is also low, but the government subsidizes basic goods like petroleum.

Business freedom, trade freedom, fiscal freedom, investment freedom, property rights, and freedom from corruption all score poorly. Commercial regulation and bureaucratic red tape are burdensome. The average tariff rate is high, and imports are subject to substantial nontariff barriers. The political atmosphere makes it difficult to invest in Ivory Coast even though the state nominally welcomes capital. Property rights are not secured by an independent judiciary, and corruption is debilitating.

BACKGROUND: General Robert Guei seized power in 1999 and, after his claim of victory in the 2000 presidential election sparked a popular uprising, was replaced as president by his opponent, Laurent Gbagbo. Civil war erupted in 2002 after a failed coup. A tenuous peace was reached in 2003, but the country remained divided, with the former rebels controlling the north and the government controlling the south. A United Nations peacekeeping force has helped to monitor the peace since 2004. Under the Ouagadougou Accord, reached in March 2007, the country has been reunified, and new elections are to be held in 2008. The economy relies on cash crops, and the agricultural sector employs more than 60 percent of the population. Corruption remains a problem. Much economic activity, including regional trade, has moved to the informal sector, and most businesses operate far below capacity.

How Do We Measure Economic Freedom? See Chapter 4 (page 39) for an explanation of the methodology or visit the *Index* Web site at *heritage.org/index*.

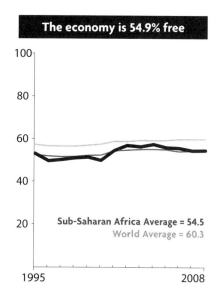

The economy is 54.9% free

Sub-Saharan Africa Average = 54.5
World Average = 60.3

1995 — 2008

QUICK FACTS

Population: 18.2 million

GDP (PPP): $33.0 billion
1.5% growth in 2005
−0.1% 5-yr. comp. ann. growth
$1,760 per capita

Unemployment: 4.9% (2000)

Inflation (CPI): 3.9%

FDI (net flow): $196.0 million

Official Development Assistance:
Multilateral: $63.0 million
Bilateral: $196.6 million (16.6% from the U.S.)

External Debt: $10.7 billion

Exports: $8.3 billion
Primarily cocoa, coffee, timber, petroleum, cotton, bananas, pineapples, palm oil, fish

Imports: $7.2 billion
Primarily fuel, capital equipment, foodstuffs

2005 data unless otherwise noted.

IVORY COAST'S TEN ECONOMIC FREEDOMS

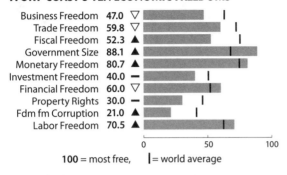

Business Freedom	47.0 ▽	
Trade Freedom	59.8 ▽	
Fiscal Freedom	52.3 ▲	
Government Size	88.1 ▲	
Monetary Freedom	80.7 ▲	
Investment Freedom	40.0 —	
Financial Freedom	60.0 ▽	
Property Rights	30.0 —	
Fdm fm Corruption	21.0 ▲	
Labor Freedom	70.5 ▲	

0   50   100

100 = most free, | = world average

BUSINESS FREEDOM — 47%

The overall freedom to start, operate, and close a business is considerably impeded by Ivory Coast's regulatory environment. Despite efforts to increase transparency, red tape and bureaucracy persist. Starting a business takes an average of 40 days, compared to the world average of 43 days. Obtaining a business license requires more than the world average of 19 procedures and 234 days. Closing a business can be costly and prolonged.

TRADE FREEDOM — 59.8%

Ivory Coast's weighted average tariff rate was 12.6 percent in 2005. Import fees and taxes, import price floors, import prohibitions and restrictions, customs and government procurement corruption, weak protection of intellectual property rights, and import authorization requirements for various goods including petroleum products, animal products, live plants, seeds, plastic bags, distilling equipment, and saccharin add to the cost of trade. An additional 15 percentage points is deducted from Ivory Coast's trade freedom score to account for non-tariff barriers.

FISCAL FREEDOM — 52.3%

Ivory Coast has high tax rates. The top income tax rate is 60 percent, and the top corporate tax rate is 35 percent. Other taxes include a value-added tax (VAT) and a tax on interest. In the most recent year, overall tax revenue as a percentage of GDP was 14.5 percent.

GOVERNMENT SIZE — 88.1%

Total government expenditures, including consumption and transfer payments, are low. In the most recent year, government spending equaled 19.9 percent of GDP. Social and political instability has prevented meaningful progress in privatization.

MONETARY FREEDOM — 80.7%

Inflation is moderate, averaging 2.2 percent between 2004 and 2006. Relatively moderate and unstable prices explain most of the monetary freedom score. The government regulates the prices of pharmaceuticals, petroleum products, and public-sector goods and services, and cocoa and coffee prices and quotas are part of a price stabilization program. An additional 10 percentage points is deducted from Ivory Coast's monetary freedom score to account for policies that distort domestic prices.

INVESTMENT FREEDOM — 40%

Foreign and domestic capital are treated equally. The government welcomes foreign investment, but the political crisis and corruption are significant disincentives. There is no screening, and investment incentives are offered in various areas. Residents may hold foreign exchange accounts with the approval of the government and the Central Bank of West African States (BCEAO), and non-residents may hold them with BCEAO approval. Transfers to countries other than France, Monaco, and certain regional countries require government approval. Other transfers are subject to requirements, controls, and authorization, depending on the transaction. Many capital transactions are subject to government authorization.

FINANCIAL FREEDOM — 60%

The political crisis has shut 50 bank branches in the affected zones. The regional BCEAO governs banking and other financial institutions. Banking accounts for 80 percent of financial-sector assets. There were 20 commercial banks and three other financial institutions in 2007. The largest banks include foreign ownership and are more reliable in the unstable climate. The financial system remains functional, but commercial banks in rebel-controlled areas remain closed; cash needs are handled through foreign wire transfers and government-area bank visits. The government has sold its shares in smaller banks and has only minority holdings in several larger institutions. The insurance sector consists of about 30 companies and is part of a larger regional system involving 14 countries. Trading on the Ivorian-based regional stock market is minimal despite 45 company listings.

PROPERTY RIGHTS — 30%

The judiciary is constitutionally independent but slow, inefficient, and subject to executive branch, military, and other outside influence. Judges serve at the discretion of the executive, and it is common for judges who are open to bribery to distort the merits of a case.

FREEDOM FROM CORRUPTION — 21%

Corruption is perceived as pervasive. Ivory Coast ranks 151st out of 163 countries in Transparency International's Corruption Perceptions Index for 2006. Government corruption and lack of transparency affect judicial proceedings, contract awards, customs and tax issues, and the accountability of the security forces.

LABOR FREEDOM — 70.5%

Relatively flexible employment regulations can enhance employment opportunities and productivity growth. The non-salary cost of employing a worker is relatively low, but dismissing a redundant employee is costly. The difficulty of laying off a worker creates a risk aversion for companies that would otherwise hire more people and grow. Regulations on the number of work hours remain rigid.

JAMAICA

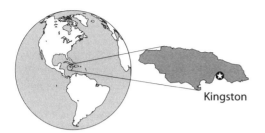

Kingston

Jamaica's economy is 66.2 percent free, according to our 2008 assessment, which makes it the world's 45th freest economy. Its overall score is 0.2 percentage point higher than last year, reflecting slightly improved monetary freedom. Jamaica is ranked 10th out of 29 countries in the Americas, and its overall score is higher than the regional average.

Jamaica scores very well in investment freedom and business freedom and above the world average in four other areas. Starting and closing a business are easy despite bureaucratic inefficiency. The labor market is flexible and open. Foreign investment is welcome in almost all areas, including the purchase of privatized state enterprises.

Jamaica is weakest in government size and freedom from corruption. Despite a positive economic environment, average tariff rates are high. The court system is rooted in English common law, but it suffers from a significant backlog and some corruption, and the police force is understaffed. Government expenditure is high as a percentage of GDP and up to the level of some EU social welfare states.

BACKGROUND: Once a major sugar producer, Jamaica is now a net sugar importer. Most foreign exchange comes from remittances, tourism, and bauxite. The economy is diverse, but industries lack investment and modernization. Growing competition from Mexico, Central America, and Asia has led to factory closures, more than 12 percent unemployment, and high underemployment. For years, GDP growth has been relatively flat, and the debt-to-GDP ratio has mounted. Almost 60 percent of government revenue goes to debt service and recurrent expenditures, making it difficult to channel funds into social and physical infrastructure. The growing use of ethanol blends in gasoline could lead to a revival of Jamaica's sugar industry. Prime Minister Portia Simpson-Miller took office in March 2006. Crime, corruption, money laundering, and drug-related violence increasingly threaten public security.

How Do We Measure Economic Freedom? See Chapter 4 (page 39) for an explanation of the methodology or visit the *Index* Web site at *heritage.org/index*.

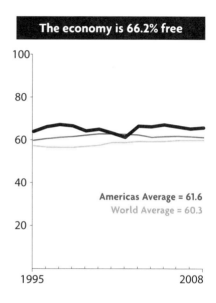

The economy is 66.2% free

Americas Average = 61.6
World Average = 60.3

1995   2008

QUICK FACTS

Population: 2.7 million

GDP (PPP): $11.4 billion
1.4% growth in 2005
1.4% 5-yr. comp. ann. growth
$4,291 per capita

Unemployment: 11.3%

Inflation (CPI): 15.3%

FDI (net flow): $507.0 million

Official Development Assistance:
Multilateral: $44.1 million
Bilateral: $103.4 million (52.7% from the U.S.)

External Debt: $6.5 billion

Exports: $4.0 billion
Primarily alumina, bauxite, sugar, bananas, rum, coffee, yams, beverages, chemicals, wearing apparel, mineral fuels

Imports: $6.0 billion
Primarily food, other consumer goods, industrial supplies, fuel, capital goods parts and accessories, machinery
2005 data unless otherwise noted.

JAMAICA'S TEN ECONOMIC FREEDOMS

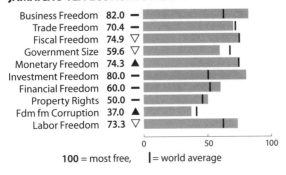

Business Freedom	82.0 ▬	
Trade Freedom	70.4 ▬	
Fiscal Freedom	74.9 ▽	
Government Size	59.6 ▽	
Monetary Freedom	74.3 ▲	
Investment Freedom	80.0 ▬	
Financial Freedom	60.0 ▬	
Property Rights	50.0 ▬	
Fdm fm Corruption	37.0 ▲	
Labor Freedom	73.3 ▽	

0   50   100

100 = most free, ▐ = world average

BUSINESS FREEDOM — 82%

The overall freedom to start, operate, and close a business is relatively well protected by Jamaica's regulatory environment. Starting a business takes an average of eight days, compared to the world average of 43 days. Obtaining a business license requires 10 procedures and takes about the world average of 234 days. Bankruptcy proceedings are relatively easy and straightforward.

TRADE FREEDOM — 70.4%

Jamaica's weighted average tariff rate was 9.8 percent in 2003. Non-tariff barriers remain fairly low, but restrictive import and export licensing rules, import fees and taxes, import and export bans and restrictions, and export subsidies add to the cost of trade. An additional 10 percentage points is deducted from Jamaica's trade freedom score to account for non-tariff barriers.

FISCAL FREEDOM — 74.9%

Jamaica has moderate tax rates. The top income tax rate is 25 percent, and the top corporate tax rate is 33.3 percent. Other taxes include a value-added tax (VAT) and a property transfer tax. In the most recent year, overall tax revenue as a percentage of GDP was 27.8 percent.

GOVERNMENT SIZE — 59.6%

Total government expenditures, including consumption and transfer payments, are moderate. In the most recent year, government spending equaled 36.7 percent of GDP. Public debt stands at around 130 percent of GDP, and almost 50 percent of government spending goes to interest payments on the debt.

MONETARY FREEDOM — 74.3%

Inflation is high, averaging 10.7 percent between 2004 and 2006. Unstable prices explain most of the monetary freedom score. Most prices are set in the market, but the government regulates utility services, including electricity, water, and bus fares. There are no official policies on price regulation or control, but the government monitors the pricing of consumer items. An additional 5 percentage points is deducted from Jamaica's monetary freedom score to account for policies that distort domestic prices.

INVESTMENT FREEDOM — 80%

Jamaica encourages foreign investment in all sectors. Foreign investors and domestic interests receive equal treatment, and foreign investors can acquire privatized state-owned enterprises. There is no screening, but projects that affect national security, have a negative impact on the environment, or involve sectors such as life insurance, media, or mining are subject to some restrictions. Applications for incentives require approval, which is usually straightforward and non-discriminatory. There are no limits on foreign control of companies. The legal system upholds the sanctity of contracts. The government is trying to improve bureaucratic efficiency and transparency. Residents and non-residents may hold foreign exchange accounts. There are no restrictions on transactions, transfers, or repatriation of funds, and non-residents may purchase real estate.

FINANCIAL FREEDOM — 60%

Jamaica's underdeveloped financial markets are recovering from a mid-1990s financial crisis. While strengthening supervision and regulation of banking and insurance, the government acquired control of the seven largest commercial banks, which were reprivatized in 2001 and 2002. After restructuring and consolidation, six commercial banks, five merchant banks, four building societies, and several credit unions were operational in 2007. The three largest commercial banks account for 85 percent of commercial bank assets, and five commercial banks are foreign-owned. Financial regulation is now in line with international standards. There were 21 insurance companies in 2004. Capital markets are small and centered on the stock exchange. There are no specific restrictions on foreign participation in capital markets.

PROPERTY RIGHTS — 50%

Jamaica's legal system is based on English common-law principles, but the judiciary lacks adequate resources, and trials can be delayed for years. Bureaucracy can cause significant delays in securing land titles. An inadequate police force weakens the security of property rights, and crime threatens foreign investment. Jamaica's patent law is not WTO/TRIPS-compliant.

FREEDOM FROM CORRUPTION — 37%

Corruption is perceived as significant. Jamaica ranks 61st out of 163 countries in Transparency International's Corruption Perceptions Index for 2006. The executive and legislative branches of government, as well as the Jamaica Constabulary Force, are widely regarded as subject to corruption.

LABOR FREEDOM — 73.3%

Relatively flexible employment regulations could be further improved to enhance employment opportunities and productivity growth. The non-salary cost of employing a worker is moderate, but dismissing a redundant employee is costly. The difficulty of laying off a worker creates a risk aversion for companies that would otherwise hire more people and grow. Regulations on the number of work hours are flexible.

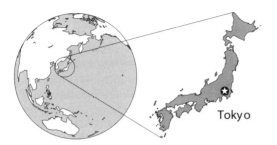

Tokyo

JAPAN

Japan's economy is 72.5 percent free, according to our 2008 assessment, which makes it the world's 17th freest economy. Its overall score is 0.3 percentage point higher than last year. Japan is ranked 5th out of 30 countries in the Asia–Pacific region, and its overall score is much higher than the regional average.

Japan enjoys very high levels of business freedom, monetary freedom, property rights, freedom from corruption, and labor freedom. Business regulation is efficient. Virtually all commercial operations are simple and transparent. Contracts are often imprecise, and this can impede smooth judicial handling of commercial disputes. Despite the confusion, contract agreements are highly respected by the judiciary. There is almost no corruption in the civil service.

Japan has relatively weak scores in government size and financial freedom. Total government spending equals more than a third of GDP. The financial sector is wholly modern and developed, but it is also subject to strong government influence and host to a variety of legal restrictions on capital. Taxes are fairly high, and overall tax revenue is moderate as a percentage of GDP.

BACKGROUND: Japan, a democratic nation, is the world's second-largest economy. After World War II, it achieved rapid economic growth by pursuing an aggressive export-oriented economic policy. In the 1990s, a banking crisis sent the economy into a decade-long recession from which it has only recently recovered. Former Prime Minister Junichiro Koizumi is credited with reform of banking and the financial sector, privatization of the postal system, and political reform of the dominant Liberal Democratic Party. It is unclear whether his successors will continue to reduce trade barriers, increase economic liberalization, and make Japan an easier place in which to do business.

How Do We Measure Economic Freedom? See Chapter 4 (page 39) for an explanation of the methodology or visit the *Index* Web site at *heritage.org/index*.

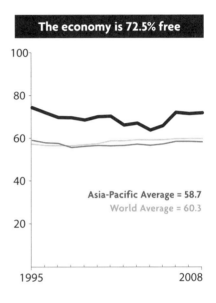

The economy is 72.5% free

Asia-Pacific Average = 58.7
World Average = 60.3

1995   2008

QUICK FACTS

Population: 127.8 million

GDP (PPP): $4.0 trillion
1.9% growth in 2005
1.6% 5-yr. comp. ann. growth
$31,267 per capita

Unemployment: 4.4%

Inflation (CPI): −0.6%

FDI (net flow): −$43.0 billion

Official Development Assistance:
Multilateral: None
Bilateral: None

External Debt: $1.5 trillion

Exports: $677.8 billion
Primarily transport equipment, motor vehicles, semiconductors, electrical machinery, chemicals

Imports: $607.9 billion
Primarily machinery and equipment, fuels, foodstuffs, chemicals, textiles, raw materials

2005 data unless otherwise noted.

JAPAN'S TEN ECONOMIC FREEDOMS

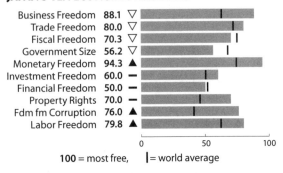

Business Freedom	88.1 ▽	
Trade Freedom	80.0 ▽	
Fiscal Freedom	70.3 ▽	
Government Size	56.2 ▽	
Monetary Freedom	94.3 ▲	
Investment Freedom	60.0 —	
Financial Freedom	50.0 —	
Property Rights	70.0 —	
Fdm fm Corruption	76.0 ▲	
Labor Freedom	79.8 ▲	

0   50   100

100 = most free, ▮ = world average

BUSINESS FREEDOM — 88.1%

The overall freedom to start, operate, and close a business is strongly protected by Japan's regulatory environment. Starting a business takes about the half the world average of 43 days. Obtaining a business license takes less than the world average of 19 procedures and 234 days. Bankruptcy proceedings are easy and straightforward.

TRADE FREEDOM — 80%

Japan's weighted average tariff rate was 2.5 percent in 2005. Import and export bans and restrictions, import quotas, service market access barriers, non-transparent regulations and standards, restrictive sanitary and phytosanitary rules, state trade in primary goods, agricultural and other subsidies, and customs inefficiency add to the cost of trade. An additional 15 percentage points is deducted from Japan's trade freedom score to account for non-tariff barriers.

FISCAL FREEDOM — 70.3%

Japan has a high income tax rate and a burdensome corporate tax rate. The top income tax rate is 37 percent, which local taxes can raise to almost 50 percent. The standard corporate tax rate is 30 percent, which local taxes can raise to around 41 percent. Other taxes include a value-added tax (VAT), a tax on interest, and an inhabitants' tax. In the most recent year, overall tax revenue as a percentage of GDP was 26.4 percent.

GOVERNMENT SIZE — 56.2%

Total government expenditures, including consumption and transfer payments, are high. In the most recent year, government spending equaled 38.2 percent of GDP. Efforts to reinvigorate the economy and the rising cost of social welfare for the aging have put government spending on an upward trend.

MONETARY FREEDOM — 94.3%

Inflation is low, averaging 0.01 percent between 2004 and 2006. Stable prices explain most of the monetary freedom score. Formal price controls apply to rice, but major producers, backed by regulators, are able to dictate retail and wholesale prices. An additional 5 percentage points is deducted from Japan's monetary freedom score to account for policies that distort domestic prices.

INVESTMENT FREEDOM — 60%

Foreign investment is officially welcomed, and inward direct investment is subject to few restrictions, but foreign acquisition of Japanese firms is inhibited by insufficient financial disclosure and cross-holding of shares among companies in the same business grouping (*keiretsu*). Public resistance to foreign acquisitions, private business networks, and the high cost of operations are further deterrents. Foreign investors need government approval for investments in agriculture, forestry, petroleum, electricity, gas, water, aerospace, telecommunications, and leather manufacturing. There are no controls on the holding of foreign exchange accounts or on transactions, current transfers, repatriation of profits, or real estate transactions by residents or non-residents.

FINANCIAL FREEDOM — 50%

Japan's financial system is subject to considerable government influence. Transparency is insufficient. Deregulation and competition have led to consolidation in an effort to create banks large enough to be major players abroad. Japanese corporations and banks maintain tight relationships, and banks often hold shares in companies with which they conduct business, giving them access to cheap credit and lessening accountability. At the end of 2006, there were six city banks, 31 trust banks, 64 first-tier regional banks, 46 second-tier regional banks, 66 foreign banks, 287 credit associations, and 168 cooperatives. Credit is available at market rates. State-run institutions affect the supply of credit. The government-owned postal savings system is the world's largest single pool of savings and accounts for a third of deposits. The insurance industry, a quarter of which is foreign-owned, is the world's second-largest. Capital markets are well developed.

PROPERTY RIGHTS — 70%

Real and intellectual property rights are generally secure, but obtaining and protecting patent and trademark rights can be time-consuming and costly. The courts do not discriminate against foreign investors but are not well suited to litigation of investment and business disputes. Businesses tend to write their contracts in general terms, but contracts are highly respected.

FREEDOM FROM CORRUPTION — 76%

Corruption is perceived as minimal. Japan ranks 17th out of 163 countries in Transparency International's Corruption Perceptions Index for 2006. Foreign investors cite the close relationships among companies, politicians, government organizations, and universities that foster an inwardly cooperative business climate within a tight circle.

LABOR FREEDOM — 79.8%

Relatively flexible employment regulations could be further improved to enhance employment opportunities and productivity growth. The non-salary cost of employing a worker is moderate, and dismissing a redundant employee is not costly. Regulations on the number of work hours remain rigid.

JORDAN

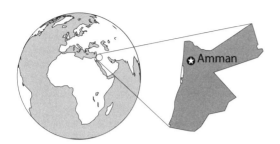
★ Amman

Jordan's economy is 63 percent free, according to our 2008 assessment, which makes it the world's 58th freest economy. Its overall score is 0.5 percentage point lower than last year, reflecting worsened freedom from corruption and monetary freedom. Jordan is ranked 5th out of 17 countries in the Middle East/North Africa region, and its overall score is higher than the regional average.

Jordan has no exceptional economic weaknesses or strengths, but it does have relative strengths in terms of very low corruption, strong property rights, and low tax rates on individual and corporate income. Overall tax revenue represents about one-fifth of GDP. Inflation is low, and the government has succeeded in phasing out direct subsidies of goods. Developed and increasingly modern, Jordan's financial sector is making serious efforts to meet international standards. Corruption is extremely low, particularly for the Middle East.

Jordan is weaker in terms of trade freedom, but especially because of large government size overall. The government maintains regulatory obstacles to trade and an opaque bureaucracy. A variety of restrictions have limited the opportunities for foreign investment in Jordan.

BACKGROUND: Jordan gained its independence from Britain in 1946 and is a constitutional monarchy with relatively few natural resources and an economy that is supported by foreign loans, international aid, and remittances from expatriate workers, many of whom work in the Persian Gulf oil kingdoms. King Abdullah II has undertaken political, economic, and regulatory reforms since coming to power in 1999. Jordan joined the World Trade Organization in 2000, signed a free trade agreement with the United States in 2000, and signed an association agreement with the European Union in 2001. The country suffers from high unemployment, heavy debt, and the high cost of oil imports.

How Do We Measure Economic Freedom? See Chapter 4 (page 39) for an explanation of the methodology or visit the *Index* Web site at *heritage.org/index.*

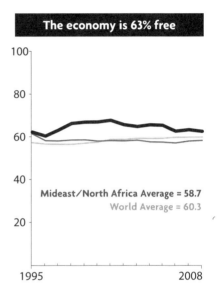

The economy is 63% free

Mideast/North Africa Average = 58.7
World Average = 60.3

1995　　　　　　　　　2008

QUICK FACTS

Population: 5.5 million

GDP (PPP): $30.3 billion
7.2% growth in 2005
6.4% 5-yr. comp. ann. growth
$5,530 per capita

Unemployment: 15.4%

Inflation (CPI): 3.5%

FDI (net flow): $1.5 billion

Official Development Assistance:
Multilateral: $163.5 million
Bilateral: $564.8 million (63.4% from the U.S.)

External Debt: $7.7 billion

Exports: $6.6 billion
Primarily clothing, pharmaceuticals, potash, phosphates, fertilizers, vegetables, manufactures

Imports: $11.9 billion
Primarily crude oil, textile fabrics, machinery, transport equipment, manufactured goods
2005 data unless otherwise noted.

JORDAN'S TEN ECONOMIC FREEDOMS

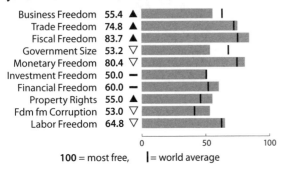

Business Freedom	55.4	▲
Trade Freedom	74.8	▲
Fiscal Freedom	83.7	▲
Government Size	53.2	▽
Monetary Freedom	80.4	▽
Investment Freedom	50.0	—
Financial Freedom	60.0	—
Property Rights	55.0	▲
Fdm fm Corruption	53.0	▽
Labor Freedom	64.8	▽

0   50   100

100 = most free, | = world average

BUSINESS FREEDOM — 55.4%

The overall freedom to start, operate, and close a business is restricted by Jordan's regulatory environment. Starting a business takes an average of 14 days, compared to the world average of 43 days. Obtaining a business license requires less than the world average of 19 procedures and 234 days. Closing a business is difficult. Despite efforts at reform, bureaucratic obstacles and delays persist.

TRADE FREEDOM — 74.8%

Jordan's weighted average tariff rate was 7.6 percent in 2005. Import bans and restrictions, import taxes and fees, import licensing requirements, sanitary and phytosanitary regulations, customs red tape and delays, export subsidies, and weak enforcement of intellectual property rights add to the cost of trade despite progress in liberalization. An additional 10 percentage points is deducted from Jordan's trade freedom score to account for non-tariff barriers.

FISCAL FREEDOM — 83.7%

Jordan has low tax rates. Both the top income tax rate and the top corporate tax rate are 25 percent. Other taxes include a value-added tax (VAT), a tax on interest, and a property transfer tax. In the most recent year, overall tax revenue as a percentage of GDP was 19.6 percent.

GOVERNMENT SIZE — 53.2%

Total government expenditures, including consumption and transfer payments, are high. In the most recent year, government spending equaled 39.5 percent of GDP. Sound public finance management and privatization are part of the structural reform agenda.

MONETARY FREEDOM — 80.4%

Inflation is relatively high, averaging 5.4 percent between 2004 and 2006. Relatively unstable prices explain most of the monetary freedom score. Most controls and subsidies have been eliminated, but the government influences the prices of fuel products through subsidies and sets prices for electricity, telecommunications, and water. An additional 5 percentage points is deducted from Jordan's monetary freedom score to account for policies that distort domestic prices.

INVESTMENT FREEDOM — 50%

Foreign and domestic investment receive equal treatment. There is no formal screening, but there are minimum capi-

tal requirements. Jordan offers incentives in several areas as well as special duty-free industrial zones. In 2006, the government sold five companies in one month. Residents and non-residents may hold foreign exchange accounts. There are no restrictions or controls on payments, transactions, transfers, or repatriation of profits. Real estate purchases require approval. Foreign investments may not exceed 50 percent in sectors like construction, wholesale and retail trade, transport, import and export services, and advertising. Foreigners may not invest in investigative and security services, sports clubs, stone quarrying, custom clearance services, and land transportation.

FINANCIAL FREEDOM — 60%

Jordan's financial sector is dominated by banking and fairly well developed. The government is trying to bring supervision and regulation into line with international standards. As of June 2006, there were nine domestic commercial banks, two Islamic banks, five investment banks, and eight foreign banks. Three major Middle Eastern banks entered the market in 2004, offering more variety of financial services. The Arab Bank dominates the sector, accounting for about 60 percent of total assets. Government-encouraged consolidation among smaller banks has been resisted because of their traditional corporate structures. The government owns no commercial banks but does own five specialized credit institutions focused on agricultural credit, housing, rural and urban development, and industry. The insurance sector is small but open to foreign competition. Capital markets are small but fairly robust by regional standards.

PROPERTY RIGHTS — 55%

The judiciary is generally independent, but the king is the ultimate authority. Despite a law passed in 2001 to limit its influence, the Ministry of Justice significantly influences judges' careers. Expropriation is unlikely. Jordan's record in protecting intellectual property rights has improved, but further refinements are needed.

FREEDOM FROM CORRUPTION — 53%

Corruption is perceived as present. Jordan ranks 40th out of 163 countries in Transparency International's Corruption Perceptions Index for 2006. Use of personal ties to gain an advantage is pervasive. There are allegations of non-transparency and influence peddling in dispute settlement and government procurement.

LABOR FREEDOM — 64.8%

Relatively flexible employment regulations could be further improved to enhance employment opportunities and productivity growth. The non-salary cost of employing a worker is moderate, but dismissing a redundant employee is not easy. The difficulty of laying off a worker creates a risk aversion for companies that would otherwise hire more people and grow. Regulations on the number of work hours are not rigid.

KAZAKHSTAN

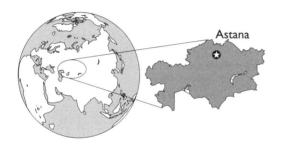

Astana

Kazakhstan's economy is 60.5 percent free, according to our 2008 assessment, which makes it the world's 76th freest economy. Its overall score is 1.4 percentage points higher than last year, mainly reflecting a significant improvement in trade freedom. Kazakhstan is ranked 13th out of 30 countries in the Asia–Pacific region, and its overall score is above the regional average.

Kazakhstan scores highly in trade freedom, government size, and labor freedom. Government expenditure is somewhat high, although the government has gradually been privatizing businesses. Kazakhstan has a highly flexible labor system.

Kazakhstan's economy has significant shortcomings in three areas: investment freedom, property rights, and freedom from corruption. Foreign investment in virtually all sectors is restricted by exclusive barriers and bureaucratic incompetence. Government policy actively favors domestic businesses, and the weak rule of law allows for significant corruption and insecure property rights.

BACKGROUND: Kazakhstan became independent in 1991 following the collapse of the Soviet Union. Nursultan Nazarbayev prevailed in the December 2005 presidential election with 91 percent of the vote under serious clouds of fraud and even the murder of opposition leader Altynbek Sarsenbayev. In 2007, the parliament approved constitutional reforms that increase its role in governing the country and abolish term limits for the president. The energy sector has driven economic growth, thanks to a boom that began in 2000. China has invested billions in oil companies and pipelines to access Kazakhstan's hydrocarbon resources, and output is projected to grow from 1.2 million barrels a day in 2006 to 3.5 million barrels a day in 2020. Russia maintains a special relationship with the country.

How Do We Measure Economic Freedom? See Chapter 4 (page 39) for an explanation of the methodology or visit the *Index* Web site at *heritage.org/index*.

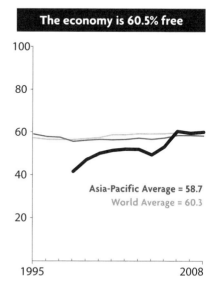

The economy is 60.5% free

Asia-Pacific Average = 58.7
World Average = 60.3

1995 — 2008

QUICK FACTS

Population: 15.1 million

GDP (PPP): $119.0 billion
9.7% growth in 2005
9.6% 5-yr. comp. ann. growth
$7,856.7 per capita

Unemployment: 8.0%

Inflation (CPI): 7.6%

FDI (net flow): $1.7 billion

Official Development Assistance:
Multilateral: $21.9 million
Bilateral: $211.3 million (27% from the U.S.)

External Debt: $43.4 billion

Exports: $30.5 billion
Primarily oil and oil products, ferrous metals, chemicals, machinery, grain, wool, meat, coal

Imports: $25.5 billion
Primarily machinery and equipment, metal products, foodstuffs

2005 data unless otherwise noted.

KAZAKHSTAN'S TEN ECONOMIC FREEDOMS

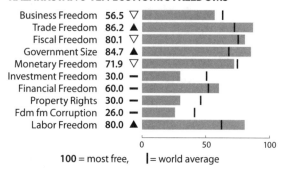

Business Freedom	56.5 ▽	
Trade Freedom	86.2 ▲	
Fiscal Freedom	80.1 ▽	
Government Size	84.7 ▲	
Monetary Freedom	71.9 ▽	
Investment Freedom	30.0 —	
Financial Freedom	60.0 —	
Property Rights	30.0 —	
Fdm fm Corruption	26.0 —	
Labor Freedom	80.0 ▲	

0   50   100

100 = most free, | = world average

BUSINESS FREEDOM — *56.5%*

The overall freedom to start, operate, and close a business is restricted by Kazakhstan's regulatory environment. Starting a business takes an average of 21 days, compared to the world average of 43 days. Obtaining a business license requires more than the world average of 19 procedures, and fees are high. Bankruptcy proceedings can be burdensome and lengthy.

TRADE FREEDOM — *86.2%*

Kazakhstan's average tariff rate was 1.9 percent in 2004. Liberalization has progressed, but non-transparent regulations and standards, service market access barriers, import licensing requirements, opaque government procurement, weak enforcement of intellectual property rights, and customs inefficiency and complexity still add to the cost of trade. An additional 10 percentage points is deducted from Kazakhstan's trade freedom score to account for non-tariff barriers.

FISCAL FREEDOM — *80.1%*

Kazakhstan has a low income tax rate and a moderate corporate tax rate. The top income tax rate is 20 percent, and the top corporate tax rate is 30 percent. Other taxes include a value-added tax (VAT) and a vehicle tax. In the most recent year, overall tax revenue as a percentage of GDP was 26.3 percent.

GOVERNMENT SIZE — *84.7%*

Total government expenditures, including consumption and transfer payments, are low. In the most recent year, government spending equaled 22.6 percent of GDP. Privatization has been gradual but successful, and much of the economy is now in private hands.

MONETARY FREEDOM — *71.9%*

Inflation is relatively high, averaging 8.2 percent between 2004 and 2006. Relatively unstable prices explain most of the monetary freedom score. The market sets most prices, but the government retains the right to control prices, influences them through state-owned enterprises and manufacturing subsidies, and has made little progress in promoting competition in agriculture. An additional 10 percentage points is deducted from Kazakhstan's monetary freedom score to account for policies that distort domestic prices.

INVESTMENT FREEDOM — *30%*

Despite a high rate of foreign investment, foreign companies increasingly must use local firms in commercial operations. Market economy status was granted by the EU in 2000 and the U.S. in 2002. No sector is closed, but there is a 25 percent cap on foreign capital in banking and a 20 percent ceiling on foreign ownership in media companies. Screening of foreign investment proposals is often non-transparent, arbitrary, and slow. An unclear legal code, legislative favoritism toward Kazakh companies, and government interference in commercial operations further deter investment. Subject to restrictions, foreign exchange accounts may be held by residents and non-residents. Most capital transactions, payments, and transfers are subject to government approval, quantitative limits, and strict documentary requirements.

FINANCIAL FREEDOM — *60%*

Kazakhstan's banking system is Central Asia's most developed. All banks must meet international standards, including a risk-weighted 8 percent capital-adequacy ratio. The number of banks has fallen from 130 at the end of 1995 to 34 with licenses in January 2006. The central bank imposed more capital requirements on commercial banks in mid-2006. Kazkommertsbank, Turan-Alem Bank, and the state-owned Halyk Bank dominate the market. Foreign banks may not have branches but may establish subsidiaries, joint ventures, and representative offices. There are three state-owned banks (a development bank, an export–import bank, and a housing finance bank), two development funds, and a number of microfinance institutions. The insurance sector is small, and foreign companies are limited to joint ventures with local companies. Capital markets are underdeveloped, though the bond market has grown.

PROPERTY RIGHTS — *30%*

Most legal disputes arise from breaches of contract or non-payment by the government. Corruption is widespread, and the judiciary views itself more as an arm of the executive than as an enforcer of contracts or guardian of property rights. Some foreign investors have encountered serious problems short of expropriation. Piracy of copyrighted products is widespread. Enforcement of intellectual property rights is weak.

FREEDOM FROM CORRUPTION — *26%*

Corruption is perceived as widespread. Kazakhstan ranks 111th out of 163 countries in Transparency International's Corruption Perceptions Index for 2006. Foreign firms cite corruption as a significant obstacle to investment, and law enforcement agencies occasionally pressure foreign investors to cooperate with government demands.

LABOR FREEDOM — *80%*

Flexible employment regulations generally enhance employment opportunities and productivity growth. The non-salary cost of employing a worker is moderate, and dismissing a redundant employee is not costly. Regulations on the number of work hours can be rigid.

KENYA

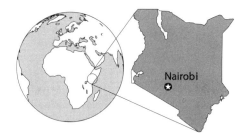

Kenya's economy is 59.6 percent free, according to our 2008 assessment, which makes it the world's 82nd freest economy. Its overall score is 0.4 percentage point lower than last year. Kenya is ranked 7th out of 40 countries in the sub-Saharan Africa region, and its overall score is higher than the regional average.

Kenya receives average scores for most of the 10 economic freedoms, which makes it one of the leaders in terms of economic freedom on the African continent. The one area where it scores exceptionally well is in terms of government expenditures, which are relatively low at one-fourth of GDP.

Property rights and freedom from corruption are Kenya's weakest scores. Corruption is extremely high, giving Kenya one of the world's lowest freedom from corruption scores. Non-transparent trade regulations and customs inefficiency hurt trade. Kenya has a well-developed financial sector, particularly for the region, but it is vulnerable to government influence. As in many other sub-Saharan African nations, Kenya's judiciary is underdeveloped and subject to the political whims of the executive.

BACKGROUND: Kenya is the transportation, communication, and financial hub of East Africa. Independent since 1963, it operated as a one-party state until its first multiparty elections in 1992. Daniel arap Moi, who first became president in 1978, won the 1992 and 1997 elections, and Mwai Kibaki won in 2002, supported by a coalition of opposition parties. Government mismanagement, counterproductive economic policies, and corruption hindered economic growth for decades. Despite some steps under Kibaki to combat corruption, several government officials have been implicated in scandals. Limited progress has been made on economic reform, and growth has improved. Civil service reform has been slow, and the government employs about one-third of the formal labor force. Agriculture accounts for about 24 percent of GDP and employs a majority of the population.

How Do We Measure Economic Freedom? See Chapter 4 (page 39) for an explanation of the methodology or visit the *Index* Web site at *heritage.org/index.*

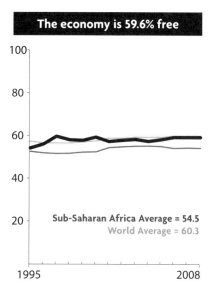

The economy is 59.6% free

Sub-Saharan Africa Average = 54.5
World Average = 60.3

1995 — 2008

QUICK FACTS

Population: 34.3 million

GDP (PPP): $42.5 billion
5.8% growth in 2005
3.3% 5-yr. comp. ann. growth
$1,240 per capita

Unemployment: 40% (2001)

Inflation (CPI): 10.3%

FDI (net flow): $12.0 million

Official Development Assistance:
Multilateral: $350.7 million
Bilateral: $566.8 million (24.3% from the U.S.)

External Debt: $6.2 billion

Exports: $5.1 billion
Primarily tea, horticultural products, coffee, petroleum products, fish, cement

Imports: $6.5 billion
Primarily machinery and transportation equipment, petroleum products, motor vehicles, iron and steel, resins and plastics

2005 data unless otherwise noted.

KENYA'S TEN ECONOMIC FREEDOMS

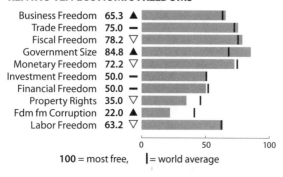

Business Freedom	65.3 ▲
Trade Freedom	75.0 —
Fiscal Freedom	78.2 ▽
Government Size	84.8 ▲
Monetary Freedom	72.2 ▽
Investment Freedom	50.0 —
Financial Freedom	50.0 —
Property Rights	35.0 ▽
Fdm fm Corruption	22.0 ▲
Labor Freedom	63.2 ▽

100 = most free, **|** = world average

BUSINESS FREEDOM — *65.3%*

The overall freedom to start, operate, and close a business is relatively well protected by Kenya's regulatory environment. Starting a business takes an average of 44 days, compared to the world average of 43 days. Obtaining a business license requires less than the world average of 19 procedures and 234 days. Closing a business is lengthy and costly.

TRADE FREEDOM — *75%*

Kenya's weighted average tariff rate was 7.5 percent in 2005. Import bans and restrictions, import and export taxes, manipulation of import taxes to protect strategic sectors, import and export licensing requirments, non-transparent and restrictive regulations, burdensome sanitary and phytosanitary rules and standards, opaque government procurement, export promotion programs, weak enforcement of intellectual property rights, and customs corruption add to the cost of trade. An additional 10 percentage points is deducted from Kenya's trade freedom score to account for non-tariff barriers.

FISCAL FREEDOM — *78.2%*

Kenya has moderate income and corporate tax rates. Both the top income tax and top corporate tax rates are 30 percent. Other taxes include a value-added tax (VAT) and an apprentice tax. In the most recent year, overall tax revenue as a percentage of GDP was 19.4 percent.

GOVERNMENT SIZE — *84.8%*

Total government expenditures, including consumption and transfer payments, are low. In the most recent year, government spending equaled 22.5 percent of GDP. After some delays and sluggish progress, privatization of state-owned enterprises has gathered new momentum with passage of a new privatization law.

MONETARY FREEDOM — *72.2%*

Inflation is relatively high, averaging 12.9 percent between 2004 and 2006. Relatively unstable prices explain most of the monetary freedom score. Price controls were officially dismantled in 1994, but the government reserves the right to set maximum prices in certain cases and influences prices through agricultural marketing boards and state-owned utilities and enterprises. An additional 5 percentage points is deducted from Kenya's monetary freedom score to account for policies that distort domestic prices.

INVESTMENT FREEDOM — *50%*

The government has relaxed its screening standards and has replaced the Investment Promotion Center with the Kenya Investment Authority to approve investments. Investment-enhancement laws passed in 2004 have had limited effect. Work permits are required for all foreigners and are hard to obtain. Foreigners may not own more than 70 percent of a telecommunications company, 67 percent of an insurance company, or 40 percent of an Internet service provider. Real estate purchases by non-residents are subject to government approval. Residents and non-residents may hold foreign exchange accounts. There are no controls or requirements on payments and transfers. Most capital transactions are permitted, but government approval is required for the sale or issue of most capital and money market instruments.

FINANCIAL FREEDOM — *50%*

Kenya's financial system, one of sub-Saharan Africa's most developed, is subject to considerable government influence and inadequate supervision. By late 2006, there were 41 commercial banks, one non-bank financial institution, two mortgage finance companies, two building societies, and 95 foreign-exchange offices. The five largest banks, including two majority state-owned banks and two foreign banks, control just over 50 percent of assets. The government also owns or owns shares in several other domestic financial institutions and influences the allocation of credit. Non-performing loans, particularly from state-owned banks to state-owned enterprises, encourage reluctance to accept loan risk. Capital markets are relatively small but growing and are subject to weak regulation. Foreign investors may acquire shares in the stock market, subject to specified limits.

PROPERTY RIGHTS — *35%*

Kenya's judicial system is modeled after the British system. Commercial courts deal with commercial cases. Property and contractual rights are enforceable but subject to long delays. The process for acquiring land titles is often non-transparent and cumbersome. Courts generally do not permit sales of land by mortgage lenders to collect debts. Protection of intellectual property rights is weak.

FREEDOM FROM CORRUPTION — *22%*

Corruption is perceived as pervasive. Kenya ranks 142nd out of 163 countries in Transparency International's Corruption Perceptions Index for 2006. Widespread corruption has led to disinvestment by foreigners. There have been several scandals involving large public and military procurement programs. The government has taken some halting steps to address judicial corruption.

LABOR FREEDOM — *63.2%*

Relatively flexible employment regulations could be further improved to enhance employment and productivity growth. The non-salary cost of employing a worker is low, but dismissing a redundant employee can be costly.

KOREA, DEMOCRATIC PEOPLE'S REPUBLIC OF (NORTH KOREA)

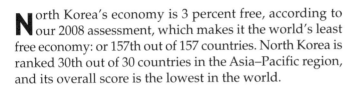

Rank: 157

Regional Rank: 30 of 30

North Korea's economy is 3 percent free, according to our 2008 assessment, which makes it the world's least free economy: or 157th out of 157 countries. North Korea is ranked 30th out of 30 countries in the Asia–Pacific region, and its overall score is the lowest in the world.

North Korea does not score well in a single area of economic freedom, although it does score 10 percent in investment freedom and property rights. The opening of the Kaesong industrial venture in cooperation with South Korea has been a start in foreign investment.

Business freedom, investment freedom, trade freedom, financial freedom, freedom from corruption, and labor freedom are nonexistent. All aspects of business operations are controlled and dominated by the government. Normal foreign trade is almost zero. No courts are independent of political interference, and private property (particularly land) is strictly regulated by the state. Corruption is virtually immeasurable and, in the case of North Korea, hard to distinguish from necessity. Much of North Korea's economy cannot be measured, and world bodies like the International Monetary Fund and World Bank are not permitted to gather information. Our policy is to give countries low marks for specific freedoms when it is country policy to restrict measurement of those freedoms.

BACKGROUND: Ruled by dictator Kim Jong Il, the Democratic People's Republic of Korea has maintained a Communist system since its founding in 1948. With the fall of the Soviet Union, North Korea lost an important source of economic support. In the 1990s, floods and droughts exacerbated systemic shortcomings and led to severe famine and thousands of civilian deaths. Today, North Korea's economy is supported by South Korea and China. North Korea itself earns money through the counterfeiting of foreign currency, arms sales, and other illicit activities.

How Do We Measure Economic Freedom? See Chapter 4 (page 39) for an explanation of the methodology or visit the *Index* Web site at *heritage.org/index*.

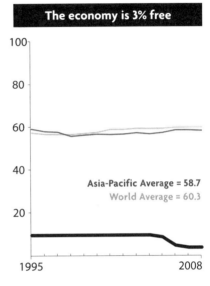

The economy is 3% free

Asia-Pacific Average = 58.7
World Average = 60.3

1995 — 2008

QUICK FACTS

Population: 22.5 million

GDP (PPP): n/a
n/a
n/a
n/a

Unemployment: n/a

Inflation (CPI): n/a

FDI (net flow): $113.0 million

Official Development Assistance:
Multilateral: $42.4 million
Bilateral: $40.4 million (19.6% from U.S.)

External Debt: $12.0 billion (1996 estimate)

Exports: n/a
Primarily minerals, metallurgical products, manufactures (including armaments), textiles, agricultural and fishery products

Imports: n/a
Primarily petroleum, coking coal, machinery and equipment, textiles, grain
2005 data unless otherwise noted.

NORTH KOREA'S TEN ECONOMIC FREEDOMS

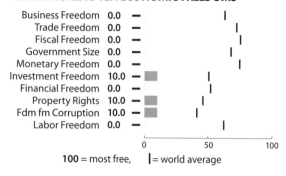

Business Freedom	0.0	
Trade Freedom	0.0	
Fiscal Freedom	0.0	
Government Size	0.0	
Monetary Freedom	0.0	
Investment Freedom	10.0	
Financial Freedom	0.0	
Property Rights	10.0	
Fdm fm Corruption	10.0	
Labor Freedom	0.0	

0   50   100

100 = most free,   **I** = world average

BUSINESS FREEDOM — *0%*

The overall freedom to start, operate, and close a business is extremely restricted by the national regulatory environment. The state regulates the economy heavily through central planning. Economic reforms implemented in 2002 allegedly brought some changes at the enterprise and industrial level, but any entrepreneurial activity is virtually impossible.

TRADE FREEDOM — *0%*

The government controls all imports and exports, and formal trade is minimal. Data on North Korean trade are limited and compiled from trading partners' statistics. Most trade is *de facto* aid, mainly from North Korea's two main trading partners, China and South Korea. Non-tariff barriers are significant. Inter-Korean trade remains constrained by North Korea's difficulties in implementing needed reform. Given the lack of necessary tariff data, a score of zero is assigned.

FISCAL FREEDOM — *0%*

No data on income or corporate tax rates are available because no effective tax system is in place. The government plans and manages almost every part of the economy. Given the absence of published official macroeconomic data, such figures as are available with respect to North Korea's government expenditures are suspect and outdated.

GOVERNMENT SIZE — *0%*

The government owns virtually all property and sets production levels for most products, and state-owned industries account for nearly all GDP. The state directs all significant economic activity. Large military spending further drains scarce resources.

MONETARY FREEDOM — *0%*

Price and wage reforms introduced in July 2002 consisted of reducing government subsidies and telling producers to charge prices that more closely reflect costs. Without matching supply-side measures to boost output, the result has been rampant inflation for many staple goods. With the ongoing crisis in agriculture, the government has banned sales of grain at markets and returned to rationing. Given the lack of necessary inflation data, a score of zero is assigned.

INVESTMENT FREEDOM — *10%*

North Korea does not welcome foreign investment. Numerous countries employ sanctions against North Korea, and the ongoing concern over Pyongyang's nuclear program and resulting political disruptions make investment extremely hazardous. Internal laws do not allow for international dispute arbitration. One attempt to open the economy to foreigners was North Korea's first special economic zone, located at the remote Rajin-Sonbong site in the northeast. Wage rates in the special zone are unrealistically high because the state controls the labor supply and insists on taking its share. More recent special zones at Mt. Kumgang and Kaesong are more enticing. Aside from these few economic zones where investment is approved on a case-by-case basis, foreign investment is prohibited.

FINANCIAL FREEDOM — *0%*

North Korea is a Communist command economy and has no private financial sector. The central bank also serves as a commercial bank and had 227 local branches in mid-2007. The government provides most funding for industries and takes a percentage from enterprises. Foreign aid agencies have set up microcredit schemes to lend to farmers and small businesses. A rumored overhaul of the financial system to permit firms to borrow from banks rather than receive state-directed capital has not materialized. There is a significant unofficial economy in dollars, which were technically banned in 2002 in favor of the euro. Because of debts dating back to the 1970s, most foreign banks will not enter North Korea. A South Korean bank has opened a branch in the Kaesong zone. The state holds a monopoly on insurance, and there are no equity markets.

PROPERTY RIGHTS — *10%*

Property rights are not guaranteed. Almost all property, including nearly all real property, belongs to the state, and the judiciary is not independent. The government even controls all chattel property (domestically produced goods as well as all imports and exports).

FREEDOM FROM CORRUPTION — *10%*

After the mid-1990s economic collapse and subsequent famines, North Korea developed an immense informal market, especially in agricultural goods. Informal trading with China in currency and goods is active. There are many indicators of corruption in the government and security forces. Military and government officials reportedly divert food aid from international donors and demand bribes before distributing it.

LABOR FREEDOM — *0%*

As the main source of employment, the government determines all wages. Since the 2002 economic reforms, factory managers have had more autonomy to set wages and offer incentives, but highly restrictive government regulations hinder employment opportunities and productivity growth.

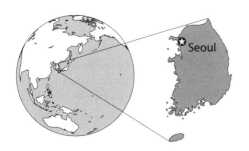

KOREA, REPUBLIC OF (SOUTH KOREA)

South Korea's economy is 67.9 percent free, according to our 2008 assessment, which makes it the world's 41st freest economy. Its overall score is 0.7 percentage point higher than last year, reflecting improvement in four of the 10 freedoms. South Korea is ranked 7th out of 30 countries in the Asia–Pacific region, and its overall score is higher than the regional average.

South Korea has high levels of business freedom, investment freedom, and property rights. Both total government expenditures relative to GDP and inflation are fairly low as well, but South Korea's monetary score is hurt by government subsidies of several sectors. Investment in South Korea is exceptionally easy because the government has made several efforts over the past decade to open the economy to foreign capital. The rule of law is strong, and property rights are protected in a transparent manner.

South Korea's trade freedom, fiscal freedom, and labor freedom are relatively weak. Non-tariff barriers are common. The labor market remains rigid despite the government's efforts to enhance market flexibility in recent years.

BACKGROUND: South Korea is one of Asia's most vibrant democracies and the world's 10th-largest economy. Unlike other Asian countries hit hard by the Asian financial crisis, South Korea liberalized its financial and economic sectors in the aftermath of the crisis. Yet its economy remains dominated by the *chaebols* (large conglomerates), and foreign investors remain wary of lingering protectionism. South Korea's greatest challenge is managing its increasing interaction with North Korea in light of ongoing tensions resulting from North Korea's nuclear programs.

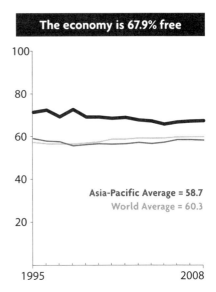

The economy is 67.9% free

Asia-Pacific Average = 58.7
World Average = 60.3

QUICK FACTS

Population: 48.3 million

GDP (PPP): $1.1 trillion
4.2% growth in 2005
4.7% 5-yr. comp. ann. growth
$22,029 per capita

Unemployment: 3.7%

Inflation (CPI): 2.8%

FDI (net flow): $2.9 billion

Official Development Assistance:
Multilateral: $0.5 million (2004)
Bilateral: $108.6 million (0% from the U.S.) (2004)

External Debt: $249.4 billion

Exports: $334.4 billion
Primarily semiconductors, wireless telecommunications equipment, motor vehicles, computers, steel, ships

Imports: $314.0 billion
Primarily machinery, electronics and electronic equipment, oil, steel, transport equipment, organic chemicals
2005 data unless otherwise noted.

How Do We Measure Economic Freedom? See Chapter 4 (page 39) for an explanation of the methodology or visit the *Index* Web site at *heritage.org/index*.

SOUTH KOREA'S TEN ECONOMIC FREEDOMS

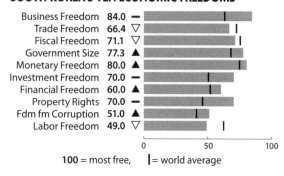

Business Freedom	84.0	—
Trade Freedom	66.4	▽
Fiscal Freedom	71.1	▽
Government Size	77.3	▲
Monetary Freedom	80.0	▲
Investment Freedom	70.0	—
Financial Freedom	60.0	▲
Property Rights	70.0	—
Fdm fm Corruption	51.0	▲
Labor Freedom	49.0	▽

0   50   100

100 = most free,   ▮ = world average

BUSINESS FREEDOM — 84%

The overall freedom to start, operate, and close a business is well protected by South Korea's regulatory environment. Starting a business takes an average of 17 days, compared to the world average of 43 days. Obtaining a business license requires less than the world average of 19 procedures and 234 days. Closing a business is easy.

TRADE FREEDOM — 66.4%

South Korea's weighted average tariff rate was 9.3 percent in 2004. Import restrictions, quantitative restrictions, service market access barriers, import taxes, prohibitive tariffs, use of "adjustment" tariffs and taxes to increase import costs, non-transparent standards and regulations, non-transparent labeling requirements, weak enforcement of intellectual property rights, and export subsidies add to the cost of trade. An additional 15 percentage points is deducted from South Korea's trade freedom score to account for non-tariff barriers.

FISCAL FREEDOM — 71.1%

South Korea has a high income tax rate but a moderate corporate tax rate. The top income tax rate is 38.5 percent (35 percent plus a 10 percent resident surcharge), and the top corporate tax rate is 27.5 percent (25 percent plus a 10 percent resident surcharge). Other taxes include a value-added tax (VAT), a special excise tax, and a property tax. In the most recent year, overall tax revenue as a percentage of GDP was 25.6 percent.

GOVERNMENT SIZE — 77.3%

Total government expenditures, including consumption and transfer payments, are modest. In the most recent year, government spending equaled 27.5 percent of GDP. There were 32 state-owned enterprises as of December 2006. No privatizations took place in 2006.

MONETARY FREEDOM — 80%

Inflation is low, averaging 2.5 percent between 2004 and 2006. Relatively stable prices explain most of the monetary freedom score. The government can control prices on several products by emergency decree; can cap prices on key raw materials; and regulates or controls prices in certain sectors, including agriculture, telecommunications, other utilities, pharmaceuticals and medical services, and some energy products. An additional 10 percentage points is deducted from South Korea's monetary freedom score to account for policies that distort domestic prices.

INVESTMENT FREEDOM — 70%

The investment climate is increasingly open, but media, electric power, newspapers, fishing, power generation, airline transport, certain agricultural sectors, and a few other sectors remain restricted. Restrictions on foreign investors that acquire companies through mergers and acquisitions have been removed. The government offers incentives such as cash grants and zero-corporate tax zones; has a one-stop-shop for foreign investments; and assigns an official to facilitate each project. Residents and non-residents may hold foreign exchange accounts. Payments, transactions, transfers, or repatriation of profits are subject to reporting requirements or restrictions on amounts permitted for specified periods.

FINANCIAL FREEDOM — 60%

At the end of September 2006, there were 13 commercial banks, 36 foreign operating branches, five specialized banks, two merchant banking corporations, 54 securities firms, 51 insurers, 50 asset-management companies, 20 leasing companies, and six credit-card suppliers. Foreign banks own majority stakes in four of the eight major commercial banks and account for roughly one-third of banking assets, though foreign ownership remains restricted. The government has been selling its shares in private banks but retains some ownership positions, including a majority of the second-largest domestic bank. Supervision and transparency remain insufficient. The insurance sector is well developed, and foreign insurers are prominent among the 51 participants. Capital markets are deep and sophisticated.

PROPERTY RIGHTS — 70%

Private property is secure, and expropriation is highly unlikely, but the justice system can be inefficient and slow. Contracts are often considered a matter of consensus. The protection of intellectual property rights needs to be improved, and piracy of copyrighted material is significant.

FREEDOM FROM CORRUPTION — 51%

Corruption is perceived as present. South Korea ranks 42nd out of 163 countries in Transparency International's Corruption Perceptions Index for 2006. Some foreign investors say that corruption is encouraged by non-transparent rule-making and law formulation; inwardly cooperative societal, political, and business structures; and insufficient institutional checks and balances.

LABOR FREEDOM — 49%

Burdensome employment regulations hinder employment opportunities and productivity growth. The non-salary cost of employing a worker is low, but dismissing a redundant employee is costly. The high cost of laying off a worker creates a risk aversion for companies that would otherwise hire more people and grow. Regulations related to the number of work hours are not flexible.

KUWAIT

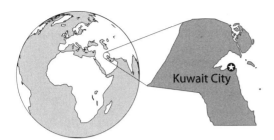

Kuwait City

Kuwait's economy is 68.3 percent free, according to our 2008 assessment, which makes it the world's 39th freest economy. Its overall score is 1.7 percentage points higher than last year, reflecting improved scores in four of the 10 economic freedoms. Kuwait is ranked 2nd out of 17 countries in the Middle East/North Africa region, and its overall score is much higher than the regional average.

Kuwait scores highly many areas and is significantly higher than the world average in fiscal freedom and labor freedom. There is no income tax, but corporate tax rates on foreign businesses can be high. Kuwait is a major energy producer, and overall tax revenue relative to GDP is not high. The labor market is exceptionally flexible.

There are no areas in which Kuwait scores poorly, although it is slightly below average in terms of monetary freedom, investment freedom, and financial freedom.

BACKGROUND: Kuwait, an Arab constitutional monarchy that gained its independence from Britain in 1961, is endowed with 96 billion barrels of oil reserves—roughly 10 percent of the world's oil supply. Oil accounts for nearly 50 percent of GDP and 95 percent of export revenues. The Al-Sabah dynasty has used state-owned oil revenues to build a modern infrastructure and cradle-to-grave welfare system for Kuwait's small population. Former Prime Minister Sabah al-Ahmad al-Jabr al-Sabah was chosen as amir in January 2006 and remains committed to cautious economic reforms, but he faces opposition from Islamic fundamentalists and populist members of parliament.

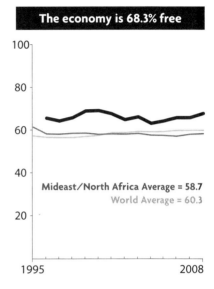

The economy is 68.3% free

Mideast/North Africa Average = 58.7
World Average = 60.3

1995   2008

QUICK FACTS

Population: 2.5 million

GDP (PPP): $66.7 billion
10.0% growth in 2005
9.9% 5-yr. comp. ann. growth
$26,321 per capita

Unemployment: 2.2% (2004 estimate)

Inflation (CPI): 4.1%

FDI (net flow): −$4.5 billion

Official Development Assistance:
Multilateral: $0.4 million (2004)
Bilateral: $2.0 million (0% from the U.S.)
(2004)

External Debt: $19.7 billion

Exports: $51.6 billion
Primarily oil and refined products, fertilizers

Imports: $24.5 billion
Primarily food, construction materials, vehicles and parts, clothing

How Do We Measure Economic Freedom? See Chapter 4 (page 39) for an explanation of the methodology or visit the *Index* Web site at *heritage.org/index*.

2005 data unless otherwise noted.

KUWAIT'S TEN ECONOMIC FREEDOMS

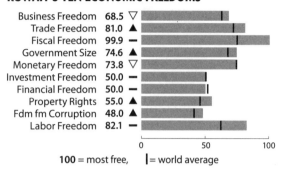

Business Freedom	68.5 ▽	
Trade Freedom	81.0 ▲	
Fiscal Freedom	99.9 —	
Government Size	74.6 ▲	
Monetary Freedom	73.8 ▽	
Investment Freedom	50.0 —	
Financial Freedom	50.0 —	
Property Rights	55.0 ▲	
Fdm fm Corruption	48.0 ▲	
Labor Freedom	82.1 —	

0   50   100

100 = most free,   ▌= world average

BUSINESS FREEDOM — *68.5%*

The overall freedom to start, operate, and close a business is relatively well protected by Kuwait's regulatory environment. Starting a business takes an average of 35 days, compared to the world average of 43 days. Obtaining a business license requires less than the world average of 19 procedures and 234 days.

TRADE FREEDOM — *81%*

Kuwait's weighted average tariff rate was 4.5 percent in 2005. Prohibitive tariffs, import bans, import licensing requirements, non-transparent customs implementation, restrictive burdensome regulations and standards, service market access barriers, and weak enforcement of intellectual property rights add to the cost of trade. An additional 10 percentage points is deducted from Kuwait's trade freedom score to account for non-tariff barriers.

FISCAL FREEDOM — *99.9%*

Kuwait does not tax individual income or domestic business income. Foreign-owned firms and joint ventures are the only businesses subject to corporate income tax, which can be as high as 55 percent. In the most recent year, overall tax revenue (mainly from duties on international trade and tractions) was 1 percent of GDP.

GOVERNMENT SIZE— *74.6%*

Total government expenditures, including consumption and transfer payments, are high. In the most recent year, government spending equaled 29.1 percent of GDP. Private-sector participation in state-dominated sectors such as telecommunications, airlines, and infrastructure development has increased. A draft privatization law approved by a parliamentary committee in May 2006 is awaiting final approval by the parliament.

MONETARY FREEDOM — *73.8%*

Inflation is moderate, averaging 3.1 percent between 2004 and 2006. Relatively moderate prices explain most of the monetary freedom score. The government provides numerous subsidies and controls prices through state-owned utilities and enterprises, including telecommunications, ports, and transportation. An additional 15 percentage points is deducted from Kuwait's monetary freedom score to account for policies that distort domestic prices.

INVESTMENT FREEDOM — *50%*

Kuwait is open to some types of foreign investment, but restrictions are significant. Foreign investors may own 100 percent of investments in such areas as water, power, waste water treatment, or communications; investment and exchange companies; air, land, and sea freight; tourism, hotels, and entertainment; and housing projects and urban development. Foreign investment in the upstream petroleum and downstream gas and petroleum sectors remains restricted. Incentives, such as land grants and tax holidays, are tied to the number of Kuwaitis employed. Privatization of assets acquired during the late 1970s and early 1980s is ongoing. Residents and non-residents may hold foreign exchange accounts, and there are no restrictions or controls on payments, transactions, transfers, or repatriation of profits.

FINANCIAL FREEDOM — *50%*

Kuwait's financial system is well developed by regional standards. The seven commercial banks, including one based on Islamic banking principles, operating in 2005 are mostly privately owned and together have 140 branches. The government retains stakes in a number of these banks, acquired after the 1982 stock market crash, but intends to privatize them. In 2004, Kuwait increased its regulatory power to intervene more directly in banks that violate the law. Three government-owned specialized banks provide medium- and long-term financing. Foreign investors may own 100 percent of Kuwaiti banks, subject to central bank approval. Foreign banks may open branches, subject to strict restrictions, and are more active in investment banking than in commercial banking. Capital markets are relatively well developed, and stock market trading is vigorous, with foreigners allowed to trade on the exchange.

PROPERTY RIGHTS — *55%*

The constitution provides for an independent judiciary, but the amir appoints all judges. The majority are non-citizens, and renewal of their appointments is subject to government approval. Foreign residents involved in legal disputes with citizens frequently claim that the courts favor Kuwaitis. Trials are lengthy. In 2006, the government formed an intellectual property rights committee and announced plans for an IPR court.

FREEDOM FROM CORRUPTION — *48%*

Corruption is perceived as significant. Kuwait ranks 46th out of 163 countries in Transparency International's Corruption Perceptions Index for 2006. The executive, legislative, and (to a lesser extent) judicial branches are widely perceived as subject to corruption.

LABOR FREEDOM — *82.1%*

Flexible employment regulations can enhance employment and productivity growth. The non-salary cost of employing a worker is low, but dismissing a redundant employee can be costly. There is no private-sector minimum wage. Restrictions on the number of work hours can be rigid. Kuwait's labor freedom is one of the highest in the world.

KYRGYZ REPUBLIC

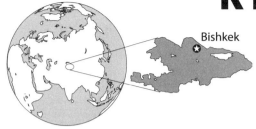

Bishkek

The Kyrgyz Republic's economy is 61.1 percent free, according to our 2008 assessment, which makes it the world's 70th freest economy. Its overall score is 0.8 percentage point higher than last year, mainly reflecting an improved investment climate. The Kyrgyz Republic is ranked 12th out of 30 countries in the Asia–Pacific region, and its overall score is higher than the regional average.

The Kyrgyz Republic scores highly in trade freedom, fiscal freedom, labor freedom, and government size. The labor system is very flexible; despite some remaining restrictions, the implementation of a new labor code has helped to tailor employment to free-market conditions. The top income and corporate tax rates are low, although the government imposes other taxes as well. Government expenditure is also moderate.

The Kyrgyz Republic's property rights and freedom from corruption are weak. The weak rule of law allows for significant corruption and insecure property rights.

BACKGROUND: The Kyrgyz Republic (formerly the Kyrgyz Soviet Socialist Republic) is located in the heart of Eurasia between China, Kazakhstan, and Uzbekistan. Autocratic President Askar Akayev ruled the nation from 1990 to 2005, when violent protests over fraudulent parliamentary elections brought President Kurmanbek Bakiyev to power. The government has made significant progress in market reforms, including privatization and trade liberalization, but political turmoil continues. The country is landlocked, with underdeveloped agricultural and industrial sectors, and has had difficulty attracting significant foreign investment. GDP growth in the past two years has been strong, but the Kyrgyz Republic remains saddled with a large external debt and heavy dependence on foreign aid.

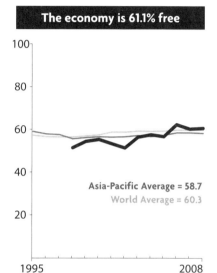

The economy is 61.1% free

Asia-Pacific Average = 58.7
World Average = 60.3

1995 — 2008

QUICK FACTS

Population: 5.1 million

GDP (PPP): $9.9 billion
−0.2% growth in 2005
3.4% 5-yr. comp. ann. growth
$1,927 per capita

Unemployment: 18.0% (2004 estimate)

Inflation (CPI): 4.3%

FDI (net flow): $47.0 million

Official Development Assistance:
Multilateral: $119.9 million
Bilateral: $185.3 million (22.3% from the U.S.)

External Debt: $2.0 billion

Exports: $942.4 million
Primarily cotton, wool, meat, tobacco, gold, mercury, uranium, natural gas, hydropower, machinery, shoes

Imports: $1.4 billion
Primarily oil and gas, machinery and equipment, chemicals, foodstuffs

2005 data unless otherwise noted.

How Do We Measure Economic Freedom? See Chapter 4 (page 39) for an explanation of the methodology or visit the *Index* Web site at *heritage.org/index*.

KYRGYZ REPUBLIC'S TEN ECONOMIC FREEDOMS

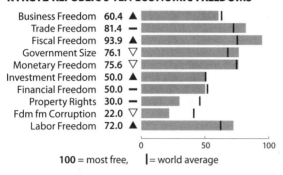

Business Freedom	60.4	▲
Trade Freedom	81.4	—
Fiscal Freedom	93.9	▲
Government Size	76.1	▽
Monetary Freedom	75.6	▽
Investment Freedom	50.0	▲
Financial Freedom	50.0	—
Property Rights	30.0	—
Fdm fm Corruption	22.0	▽
Labor Freedom	72.0	▲

0   50   100

100 = most free, | **= world average**

BUSINESS FREEDOM — 60.4%

The overall freedom to start, operate, and close a business is partially protected by the Kyrgyz Republic's regulatory environment. Starting a business takes an average of 21 days, compared to the world average of 43 days. Obtaining a business license requires slightly more than the world average of 19 procedures and 234 days. Closing a business can be difficult and lengthy.

TRADE FREEDOM — 81.4%

The Kyrgyz Republic's weighted average tariff rate was 4.3 percent in 2003. Import bans and restrictions, import fees, export and import licensing requirements, complex regulations and standards, restrictive sanitary and phyto-sanitary rules, weak enforcement of intellectual property rights, and customs inefficiency and corruption add to the cost of trade despite progress in dismantling barriers. An additional 10 percentage points is deducted from the Kyrgyz Republic's trade freedom score to account for non-tariff barriers.

FISCAL FREEDOM — 93.9%

The Kyrgyz Republic implemented a flat tax in January 2006. Both the income tax rate and the corporate tax rate are a flat 10 percent, down from 20 percent. Other taxes include a value-added tax (VAT) and a land tax. In the most recent year, overall tax revenue as a percentage of GDP was 20.2 percent.

GOVERNMENT SIZE — 76.1%

Total government expenditures, including consumption and transfer payments, are moderate. In the most recent year, government spending equaled 28.2 percent of GDP. The government has used expenditure controls to reduce the deficit. Progress in selling state-owned assets is marginal.

MONETARY FREEDOM — 75.6%

Inflation is high, averaging 5.1 percent between 2004 and 2006. Relatively unstable prices explain most of the monetary freedom score. Many price controls and subsidies have been eliminated, but the government regulates or influences prices through state-owned industries, including electricity, agriculture, telecommunications, water, and energy. Consequently, an additional 10 percentage points is deducted from the Kyrgyz Republic's monetary freedom score.

INVESTMENT FREEDOM — 50%

Most of the economy is open to foreign investment, there are guarantees against expropriation or nationalization, and investors may bid on privatized firms. However, rules and regulations are not always applied consistently. In 2006, the government participated in the seizure of a foreign investment. Incentives such as tax holidays have been replaced in accordance with WTO entry preferences. Foreign corporations may not purchase land. Residents and non-residents may hold foreign exchange accounts. There are no restrictions on payments and transfers, but most capital transactions must be registered with the relevant government authority or are subject to controls.

FINANCIAL FREEDOM — 50%

The financial system is underdeveloped but improving, with 20 commercial banks and a settlement-saving company, all but three of them private, and a large number of credit unions, but the banking sector remains generally undercapitalized. Government officials may not own or control over 5 percent of any bank. There are no limits on foreign ownership of banks and microcredit institutions. Eight banks are foreign-owned, and foreign-controlled banks account for about half of assets. Political unrest in 2005 caused transactions and deposits in foreign currency to increase. The central bank has improved supervision and established minimum capital requirements, but it is subject to executive and legislative interference. The state dominates the insurance sector, although several companies provide private services. Capital markets are limited and centered on the small stock exchange, with 14 countries listed as of December 2006.

PROPERTY RIGHTS — 30%

The legal system does not protect property sufficiently. There are disputes over licensing, registration, and enforcement of contracts. Property registration improved in 2006, but the country has not recovered from the looting and redistribution that occurred in 2005 when Askar Akayev's regime was ousted.

FREEDOM FROM CORRUPTION — 22%

Corruption is perceived as pervasive. The Kyrgyz Republic ranks 142nd out of 163 countries in Transparency International's Corruption Perceptions Index for 2006. Tax and customs agencies, law enforcement bodies, courts, and agencies controlling construction and the issuance of business licenses are notably corrupt. Thousands of cases of suspected official bribe-taking, negligence, fraud, embezzlement, and malfeasance have reportedly led to hundreds of arrests but no convictions.

LABOR FREEDOM — 72%

Relatively flexible employment regulations could be further improved to enhance employment and productivity growth. The non-salary cost of employing a worker is high, and dismissing a redundant employee can be difficult. Restrictions on the number of work hours remain rigid. The government has implemented a new labor code.

LAOS

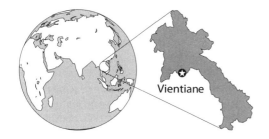

The Laotian economy is 49.2 percent free, according to our 2008 assessment, which makes it the world's 137th freest economy. Its overall score is unchanged from last year, reflecting worsened scores in three of the 10 economic freedoms, especially freedom from corruption. Laos is ranked 26th out of 30 countries in the Asia–Pacific region, and its overall score is much lower than the regional average.

Laos scores better than the world average only in terms of government expenditures, which are low in formal terms, although this is likely a sign of government weakness, not efficiency. For example, Laos has top tax rates of 40 percent, but official revenue is under 10 percent of GDP.

As an avowedly Communist nation, Laos could improve in most areas of economic freedom. Financial freedom and property rights stand out as the weakest areas relative to other countries. Trade freedom, investment freedom, and freedom from corruption also receive low scores. Business regulations hinder entrepreneurship, and enforcement is in the hands of an opaque bureaucracy. The rule of law does not operate independently of political influence, and corruption is rampant. The average tariff rate is high, and there are substantial non-tariff barriers.

BACKGROUND: Laos, one of the world's few remaining Communist regimes, is also one of Asia's poorest nations. The current government came to power in 1975 and immediately imposed a rigid socialist economic program. Change began in 1986 with the loosening of restrictions on private enterprise. Since then, Laos has enjoyed high economic growth, despite poor national infrastructure and a dominant, inefficient agriculture sector. It is also heavily reliant on international assistance programs. In 1998, Laos began formal negotiations with the World Trade Organization with an eye to joining the WTO by 2010.

How Do We Measure Economic Freedom? See Chapter 4 (page 39) for an explanation of the methodology or visit the *Index* Web site at *heritage.org/index.*

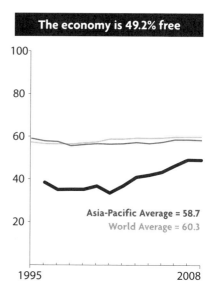

The economy is 49.2% free

Asia-Pacific Average = 58.7
World Average = 60.3

1995   2008

QUICK FACTS

Population: 5.9 million

GDP (PPP): $12.1 billion
7.1% growth in 2005
6.4% 5-yr. comp. ann. growth
$2,039 per capita

Unemployment: 2.4%

Inflation (CPI): 7.2%

FDI (net flow): $28.0 million

Official Development Assistance:
Multilateral: $155.3 million
Bilateral: $173.6 million (4.2% from the U.S.)

External Debt: $2.7 billion

Exports: $982.2 million
Primarily garments, wood products, coffee, electricity, tin

Imports: $1.4 billion
Primarily machinery and equipment, vehicles, fuel, consumer goods

2005 data unless otherwise noted.

LAOS'S TEN ECONOMIC FREEDOMS

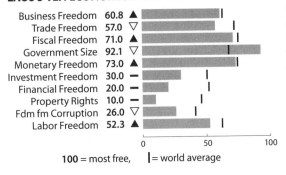

Business Freedom	60.8	▲
Trade Freedom	57.0	▽
Fiscal Freedom	71.0	▲
Government Size	92.1	▽
Monetary Freedom	73.0	▲
Investment Freedom	30.0	—
Financial Freedom	20.0	—
Property Rights	10.0	—
Fdm fm Corruption	26.0	▽
Labor Freedom	52.3	▲

0   50   100

100 = most free, | = world average

BUSINESS FREEDOM — 60.8%

The overall freedom to start, operate, and close a business is restricted by Laos's regulatory environment. Starting a business takes an average of 103 days, compared to the world average of 43 days. Obtaining a business license requires more than the world average of 19 procedures but takes less than the world average of 234 days. Modern bankruptcy proceedings have not been fully developed.

TRADE FREEDOM — 57%

Laos's weighted average tariff rate was 14 percent in 2005. There has been some progress in liberalization, but customs corruption and inefficiency, weak border control, prohibitive tariffs, import bans and restrictions, discriminatory import taxes, preauthorization and planning restrictions, import licensing requirements, and weak enforcement of intellectual property rights still add to the cost of trade. An additional 15 percentage points is deducted from Laos's trade freedom score to account for non-tariff barriers.

FISCAL FREEDOM — 71%

Laos has high tax rates. The top income tax rate is 40 percent, and the top corporate tax rate is 35 percent. Other taxes include a vehicle tax and a tax on insurance contracts. In the most recent year, overall tax revenue as a percentage of GDP was 8.8 percent.

GOVERNMENT SIZE — 92.1%

Total government expenditures, including consumption and transfer payments, are low. In the most recent year, government spending equaled 16.2 percent of GDP. Spending management has improved, and the restructuring of state-owned enterprises progresses slowly.

MONETARY FREEDOM — 73%

Inflation is high, averaging 7.2 percent between 2004 and 2006. Relatively unstable prices explain most of the monetary freedom score. The government influences many prices through state-owned enterprises and utilities and sets the price of fuel products. An additional 10 percentage points is deducted from Laos's monetary freedom score to account for policies that distort domestic prices.

INVESTMENT FREEDOM — 30%

Foreign investors are legally guaranteed that their investments will be protected, their property will not be con-

fiscated without compensation, and their operations will be free from government interference. A series of liberalizations and privatizations during the early 1990s partially opened the economy, but investment is threatened by macroeconomic instability, inconsistent application of the investment law, and the potential for deterioration in security. Foreign investment is screened, and capital in excess of US$20 million must be approved by the prime minister's office. Commercial dispute resolution is not independent, but the government allows international arbitration. Residents and non-residents may hold foreign exchange accounts subject to restrictions and government approval. Some payments and transfers face quantitative restrictions.

FINANCIAL FREEDOM — 20%

The financial system is small and subject to heavy government involvement. Supervision and regulation are weak. Three state-owned banks dominate banking, and one bank accounts for almost 50 percent of assets. Activities of the 10 private and foreign banks are limited. A new banking law was passed in late 2006 to encourage foreign participation. The government directs credit, and the central bank is not independent. The banking sector is hindered by non-performing loans, predominantly from state-owned banks to state-owned enterprises. Microfinance has a small presence. Capital markets are primitive; in 2006, the government announced its intention to open Laos's first stock market.

PROPERTY RIGHTS — 10%

The judiciary is not independent, and judges can be bribed. Foreign investors are generally advised to seek arbitration outside of Laos, since the domestic arbitration authority cannot enforce its decisions. Foreign investors may not own land but may lease it with government permission. There is no copyright system. An intellectual property law drafted in 1996 with help from the World Intellectual Property Organization is still pending.

FREEDOM FROM CORRUPTION — 26%

Corruption is perceived as widespread. Laos ranks 111th out of 163 countries in Transparency International's Corruption Perceptions Index for 2006. Corruption is getting worse. It is assumed that low-level officials must be bribed to expedite business licenses, import permits, etc., and anecdotal evidence indicates that many higher-level officials within the executive and judicial branches are corrupt.

LABOR FREEDOM — 52.3%

Employment regulations hinder employment opportunities and productivity growth. The non-salary cost of employing a worker is low, but dismissing a redundant employee can be both costly and difficult. The difficulty of laying off a worker creates a risk aversion for companies that would otherwise hire more people and grow. Modifying the number of work hours can be difficult.

LATVIA

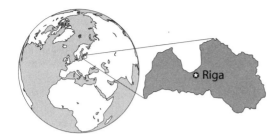

○ Riga

Latvia's economy is 68.3 percent free, according to our 2008 assessment, which makes it the world's 38th freest economy. Its overall score is 0.1 percentage point higher than last year, reflecting improved scores in property rights and freedom from corruption. Latvia is ranked 22nd out of 41 countries in the European region, and its overall score is higher than the regional average.

Latvia scores well in most areas of economic freedom, including business freedom, trade freedom, fiscal freedom, investment freedom, and financial freedom. The top income and corporate tax rates are low, and business regulation is relatively light. In accordance with the European Union standard, the average tariff is low. Investment in Latvia is welcome, with a few restrictions. The financial sector is modern and subject to few intrusive regulations.

Latvia's weakest relative scores are in government size and monetary freedom. Total government spending is high, although not as high as in other EU states.

BACKGROUND: Latvia regained its independence when the Soviet Union collapsed in 1991. In 2004 it joined the European Union. Its political system has remained stable despite almost annual changes of ruling coalitions and prime ministers. The economy, including financial and transportation services, banking, electronic manufacturing, and dairy, is developing quickly, and GDP has grown rapidly as a result. Foreign investment flows and the country's currency are strong. Latvia's May 2005 admission to the European Exchange Rate Mechanism has further aligned its economy with that of the euro zone, and the country plans to adopt the euro between 2010 and 2012.

How Do We Measure Economic Freedom? See Chapter 4 (page 39) for an explanation of the methodology or visit the *Index* Web site at *heritage.org/index*.

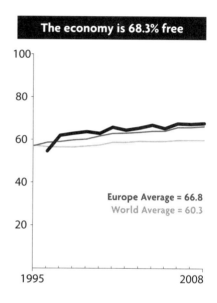

The economy is 68.3% free

Europe Average = 66.8
World Average = 60.3

1995   2008

QUICK FACTS

Population: 2.3 million

GDP (PPP): $31.4 billion
10.2% growth in 2005
8.1% 5-yr. comp. ann. growth
$13,646 per capita

Unemployment: 8.9%

Inflation (CPI): 6.7%

FDI (net flow): $497.0 million

Official Development Assistance:
Multilateral: $135.0 million (2004)
Bilateral: $29.0 million (11% from the U.S.) (2004)

External Debt: $14.3 billion

Exports: $7.5 billion
Primarily wood and wood products, machinery and equipment, metals, textiles, foodstuffs

Imports: $9.9 billion
Primarily machinery and equipment, chemicals, fuels, vehicles

2005 data unless otherwise noted.

LATVIA'S TEN ECONOMIC FREEDOMS

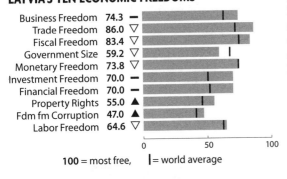

Business Freedom	74.3	—
Trade Freedom	86.0	▽
Fiscal Freedom	83.4	▽
Government Size	59.2	▽
Monetary Freedom	73.8	▽
Investment Freedom	70.0	—
Financial Freedom	70.0	—
Property Rights	55.0	▲
Fdm fm Corruption	47.0	▲
Labor Freedom	64.6	▽

0   50   100

100 = most free, | **= world average**

BUSINESS FREEDOM — 74.3%

The overall freedom to start, operate, and close a business is relatively well protected by Latvia's regulatory environment. Starting a business takes about half the world average of 43 days. Obtaining a business license takes less than the world average of 234 days. Closing a business is relatively straightforward.

TRADE FREEDOM — 86%

Latvia's trade policy is the same as those of other members of the European Union. The common EU weighted average tariff rate was 2 percent in 2005. Non-tariff barriers reflected in EU policy include agricultural and manufacturing subsidies, import restrictions for some goods and services, market access restrictions in some service sectors, non-transparent and restrictive regulations and standards, and inconsistent customs administration across EU members. An additional 10 percentage points is deducted from Latvia's trade freedom score to account for non-tariff barriers.

FISCAL FREEDOM — 83.4%

Latvia has a moderate income tax rate and a low corporate tax rate. The income tax rate is a flat 25 percent, and the corporate tax rate is 15 percent. Other taxes include a value-added tax (VAT) and a real estate tax. In the most recent year, overall tax revenue as a percentage of GDP was 28.5 percent.

GOVERNMENT SIZE — 59.2%

Total government expenditures, including consumption and transfer payments, are high. The budget deficit has been moderate. In the most recent year, government spending equaled 36.9 percent of GDP. Privatization of remaining state-owned enterprises has been sluggish.

MONETARY FREEDOM — 73.8%

Inflation is relatively high, averaging 6.5 percent between 2004 and 2006. Relatively unstable prices explain most of the monetary freedom score. As a participant in the EU's Common Agricultural Policy, the government subsidizes agricultural production, distorting the prices of agricultural products. It also regulates rents, utility rates, transportation, and energy prices and influences prices through state-owned enterprises. An additional 10 percentage points is deducted from Latvia's monetary freedom score to account for policies that distort domestic prices.

INVESTMENT FREEDOM — 70%

Foreigners receive equal treatment consistent with EU and WTO standards. Investment is not screened, but procedural information is not readily available, and many civil servants lack professionalism. Foreign investors may not hold controlling shares in companies involved in security services, air transport, or gambling but may own land for agricultural or forestry purposes, subject to prerequisites like reciprocal access. There are no restrictions on repatriation of profits. Adjudication of commercial disputes is slightly hampered by a slow legal process. Residents and non-residents may hold foreign exchange accounts. There are no restrictions or controls on payments, transactions, transfers, or repatriation of profits.

FINANCIAL FREEDOM — 70%

Latvia's modern financial sector includes substantial foreign participation. Regulations are transparent, meet EU standards, and focus on minimum accounting and financial standards, minimum capital requirements, restrictions on exposure, and open foreign exchange. Credit is allocated at market rates. There were 23 commercial banks in 2004, with the top 10 banks accounting for about 80 percent of assets and foreign-owned banks controlling approximately 50 percent of assets. Foreign banks receive domestic treatment, and bank formation faces few barriers. The one government-owned bank accounts for over 4 percent of assets. Efforts to combat money laundering have increased since a warning from the U.S. in 2005. There were about 20 insurance companies in 2004. The largest insurer is majority foreign-owned. Capital markets are small, and the stock exchange is part of a regional network of exchanges that includes Nordic and most Baltic countries.

PROPERTY RIGHTS — 55%

The judiciary is constitutionally independent, but inefficient court hearings and enforcement of decisions are subject to long delays, and some judges are not well trained. The constitution guarantees the right to own private property, and there is a land title registration system. In 2006, Latvia improved its protection of intellectual property rights.

FREEDOM FROM CORRUPTION — 47%

Corruption is perceived as significant. Latvia ranks 49th out of 163 countries in Transparency International's Corruption Perceptions Index for 2006. In 2006, the government overhauled bankruptcy procedures and initiated an electronic tax filing system, but more is needed to reduce corruption and strengthen the rule of law.

LABOR FREEDOM — 64.6%

Relatively flexible employment regulations could be further improved to enhance employment and productivity growth. The non-salary cost of employing a worker is high, and dismissing a redundant employee can be difficult. Restrictions on the number of work hours remain rigid.

LEBANON

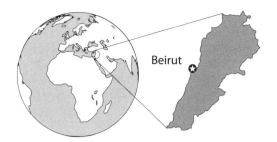

Beirut

Rank: 73

Regional Rank: 9 of 17

Lebanon's economy is 60.9 percent free, according to our 2008 assessment, which makes it the world's 73rd freest economy. Its overall score is 0.5 percentage point lower than last year, mainly reflecting a lower monetary freedom score. Lebanon is ranked 9th out of 17 countries in the Middle East/North Africa region, and its overall score is slightly higher than the regional average.

Lebanon's economy is a mixture of very strong economic institutions and weak economic institutions. Its strongest scores are in fiscal freedom, financial freedom, and labor freedom. The top income and corporate tax rates are low. The financial sector is well developed for the region, with an array of private banks and services. The labor market is highly flexible.

Business freedom, investment freedom, property rights, and freedom from corruption are all areas in which Lebanon could improve. Intrusive bureaucracy makes closing a business difficult, and the generally chaotic regulatory regime deters foreign capital. Corruption is rampant, and fair adjudication of property rights cannot be guaranteed because the courts are subject to significant influence from the security services and the police.

BACKGROUND: Lebanon gained its independence from France in 1943 and developed one of the Middle East's most advanced economies. As a trading and international banking center, it was known as "the Switzerland of the Middle East" until its disastrous 1975–1990 civil war. Syria intervened with a stranglehold on Lebanese politics that continued until it was forced to withdraw in 2005 after being implicated in the February assassination of former Lebanese Prime Minister Rafiq Hariri. Prime Minister Fuad Siniora has pledged to carry out economic reforms, but the Hezbollah-instigated conflict with Israel in 2006 will undoubtedly haunt the economy for years to come. Lebanon's huge $26 billion foreign debt will pose another obstacle to reconstruction.

How Do We Measure Economic Freedom? See Chapter 4 (page 39) for an explanation of the methodology or visit the *Index* Web site at *heritage.org/index*.

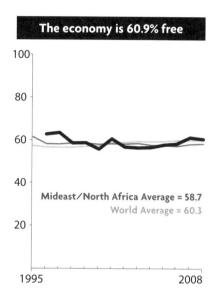

The economy is 60.9% free

Mideast/North Africa Average = 58.7
World Average = 60.3

1995 — 2008

QUICK FACTS

Population: 3.6 million

GDP (PPP): $20.0 billion
1% growth in 2005
3.8% 5-yr. comp. ann. growth
$5,584 per capita

Unemployment: 20.0%

Inflation (CPI): −0.7%

FDI (net flow): $1.9 billion

Official Development Assistance:
Multilateral: $118.8 million
Bilateral: $140.7 million (27.3% from the U.S.)

External Debt: $22.4 billion

Exports: $13.0 billion
Primarily jewelry, inorganic chemicals, consumer goods, fruit, tobacco, construction minerals, electric power machinery and switchgear, textile fibers

Imports: $16.2 billion
Primarily petroleum products, cars, medicinal products, clothing, meat and live animals, consumer goods, paper
2005 data unless otherwise noted.

LEBANON'S TEN ECONOMIC FREEDOMS

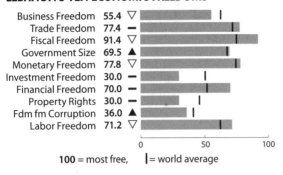

Business Freedom	55.4	▽
Trade Freedom	77.4	—
Fiscal Freedom	91.4	▽
Government Size	69.5	▲
Monetary Freedom	77.8	▽
Investment Freedom	30.0	—
Financial Freedom	70.0	—
Property Rights	30.0	—
Fdm fm Corruption	36.0	▲
Labor Freedom	71.2	▽

0   50   100

100 = most free,   I = world average

BUSINESS FREEDOM — 55.4%

The overall freedom to start, operate, and close a business is restricted by Lebanon's regulatory environment. Starting a business takes an average of 46 days, compared to the world average of 43 days. Obtaining a business license takes about the same as the world average of 19 procedures and 234 days. Closing a business is lengthy and costly.

TRADE FREEDOM — 77.4%

Lebanon's weighted average tariff rate was 6.3 percent in 2005. Import bans, restrictive licensing rules, quotas, subsidies, burdensome sanitary and phytosanitary regulations, and corruption add to the cost of trade. An additional 10 percentage points is deducted from Lebanon's trade freedom score to account for non-tariff barriers.

FISCAL FREEDOM — 91.4%

Lebanon has low tax rates. The top income tax rate is 20 percent, and the top corporate tax rate is 15 percent. Other taxes include a value-added tax (VAT) and a capital gains tax. In the most recent year, tax revenue as a percentage of GDP was 15.2 percent.

GOVERNMENT SIZE — 69.5%

Total government expenditures, including consumption and transfer payments, are moderate. In the most recent year, government spending equaled 31.9 percent of GDP. Privatization has been slow, but the government sold the mobile phone network in early 2007.

MONETARY FREEDOM — 77.8%

Inflation is moderate, averaging 3.7 percent between 2004 and 2006. Relatively unstable prices explain most of the monetary freedom score. The government influences prices through state-owned enterprises and subsidies and controls the prices of bread, petroleum derivatives, pharmaceuticals, and electricity. An additional 10 percentage points is deducted from Lebanon's monetary freedom score to account for policies that distort domestic prices.

INVESTMENT FREEDOM — 30%

Foreign and domestic capital are legally equal, except in real estate. Lebanon welcomes foreign investment, with some restrictions in land, insurance, media, and banking. The passage of several laws to promote investment has led to some success, but red tape and corruption, arbitrary licensing decisions, archaic legislation, and an ineffectual judicial system are serious impediments, as are ongoing violence and the threat of war. Implementation of commercial laws can be inconsistent. Privatization has progressed somewhat in the telecommunications and power industries. Residents and non-residents may hold foreign exchange accounts, money market instruments, and derivatives. Some credit operations are prohibited. There are no restrictions on payments and transfers.

FINANCIAL FREEDOM — 70%

Lebanon's financial sector, one of the region's most sophisticated, offers a wide range of services. There are few restrictions on domestic bank formation and few barriers to foreign banks. Regulations are fairly transparent, and credit is allocated on market terms. As of mid-2005, there were 54 commercial banks, 10 investment banks, and 15 foreign bank representatives: in all, 825 bank branches. After limited government success in promoting consolidation because of the number of smaller private banks, two of the largest banks merged in 2004. The insurance sector is moderate, and regulations have been passed to tighten supervision and establish minimum capital requirements because of small, undercapitalized firms that charge low premiums but rarely pay claims. After some anemic years in the early 2000s, the stock market grew strongly in 2005 before slumping during the 2006 Israel–Lebanon war.

PROPERTY RIGHTS — 30%

The judiciary is significantly influenced by the security services and the police. The government-appointed prosecuting magistrate exerts considerable influence over judges by, for example, recommending verdicts and sentences. Trials, particularly commercial cases, drag on for years. Although Lebanese law provides for some protection of intellectual property rights, enforcement is weak.

FREEDOM FROM CORRUPTION — 36%

Corruption is perceived as significant. Lebanon ranks 63rd out of 163 countries in Transparency International's Corruption Perceptions Index for 2006. The public sector remains corrupt, especially in procurement, public works, taxation, and real estate registration. Although Lebanon's score has improved, the data used were gathered before the 2006 conflict with Israel. Lebanon is again engaged in major reconstruction, which is particularly vulnerable to corruption.

LABOR FREEDOM — 71.2%

Relatively flexible employment regulations could be further improved to enhance employment opportunities and productivity growth. The non-salary cost of employing a worker can be high, and dismissing a redundant employee is relatively costly. The difficulty of laying off a worker creates a risk aversion for companies that would otherwise hire more people and grow. Restrictions on the number of work hours are flexible.

LESOTHO

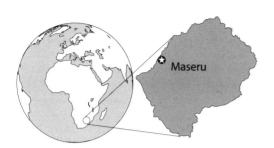

Maseru

Rank: 132
Regional Rank: 31 of 40

Lesotho's economy is 51.9 percent free, according to our 2008 assessment, which makes it the world's 132nd freest economy. Its overall score is 1.2 percentage points lower than last year, mainly reflecting worsened scores in four of the 10 economic freedoms. Lesotho is ranked 31st out of 40 countries in the sub-Saharan Africa region, and its overall score is lower than the regional average.

Lesotho does not rank strongly in any category and equals the world average in monetary freedom. Inflation is moderate, although the government intervenes in the price structure of certain goods.

Lesotho's substantial economic challenges include a large central government, which is not the norm among African nations. Its trade freedom, investment freedom, property rights, and freedom from corruption are weak. The average tariff rate is high, and non-tariff barriers to trade are significant. Regulation is oppressive, and business operations are significantly impeded by red tape. Government spending is also far too high. Property rights are not secured by an independent judiciary, and corruption is a problem.

BACKGROUND: Lesotho became independent in 1966. Instability in the 1990s led to military intervention by South Africa and Botswana. An interim authority overhauled the government and oversaw elections in 2002. Lesotho has a constitutional monarchy with King Letsie III as the ceremonial head of state. Prime Minister Pakalitha Mosisili is the head of government and holds executive authority. Lesotho is surrounded by and economically integrated with South Africa. It sells water and electricity to South Africa, and a number of households depend on work as migrant miners in South Africa. Half of the population earns income from agriculture, and over half of GDP comes from the agricultural sector. The government is working toward privatization and an improved business environment. Lesotho's HIV/AIDS rate is one of the world's highest.

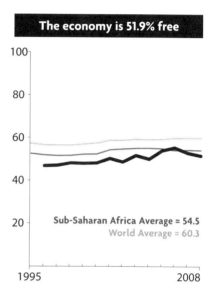

The economy is 51.9% free

Sub-Saharan Africa Average = 54.5
World Average = 60.3

1995   2008

QUICK FACTS

Population: 1.8 million

GDP (PPP): $6.0 billion
   3.7% growth in 2005
   3.3% 5-yr. comp. ann. growth
   $3,335 per capita

Unemployment: 45.0% (2002 estimate)

Inflation (CPI): 3.4%

FDI (net flow): $47.0 million

Official Development Assistance:
Multilateral: $41.1 million
Bilateral: $41.0 million (4.7 % from the U.S.)

External Debt: $690.0 million

Exports: $705.4 million
Primarily manufactures, clothing, footwear, road vehicles, wool and mohair, food and live animals

Imports: $1.4 billion
Primarily food, building materials, vehicles, machinery, medicines, petroleum products
2005 data unless otherwise noted.

How Do We Measure Economic Freedom? See Chapter 4 (page 39) for an explanation of the methodology or visit the *Index* Web site at *heritage.org/index.*

LESOTHO'S TEN ECONOMIC FREEDOMS

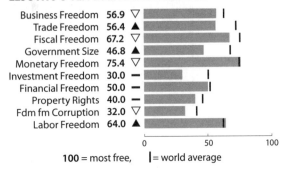

Business Freedom	56.9 ▽
Trade Freedom	56.4 ▲
Fiscal Freedom	67.2 ▽
Government Size	46.8 ▲
Monetary Freedom	75.4 ▽
Investment Freedom	30.0 ▬
Financial Freedom	50.0 ▬
Property Rights	40.0 ▬
Fdm fm Corruption	32.0 ▽
Labor Freedom	64.0 ▲

0   50   100

100 = most free,   ▮ = world average

BUSINESS FREEDOM — 56.9%

The overall freedom to start, operate, and close a business is impeded by Lesotho's regulatory environment. Starting a business takes an average of 73 days, compared to the world average of 43 days. Obtaining a business license requires more than the world average of 234 days, and fees are high. Closing a business is relatively simple.

TRADE FREEDOM — 56.4%

Lesotho's weighted average tariff rate was 16.8 percent in 2005. Non-transparent and arbitrary import licensing, import bans and restrictions, and corruption add to the cost of trade. An additional 10 percentage points is deducted from Lesotho's trade freedom score to account for non-tariff barriers.

FISCAL FREEDOM — 67.2%

Lesotho has burdensome tax rates. The top income tax rate is 35 percent, and the top corporate tax rate for all companies other than manufacturing is 25 percent (a 10 percent rate applies to all manufacturing companies). Other taxes include a value-added tax (VAT) and a tax on dividends. In the most recent year, overall tax revenue as a percentage of GDP was 37.8 percent.

GOVERNMENT SIZE — 46.8%

Total government expenditures, including consumption and transfer payments, are high. Mounting pressures from different social programs make it difficult to control public spending. In the most recent year, government spending equaled 42.1 percent of GDP. Privatization is slow but progressing better than in other countries in the region.

MONETARY FREEDOM — 75.4%

Inflation is high, averaging 5.3 percent between 2004 and 2006. Relatively unstable prices explain most of the monetary freedom score. Although many prices are freely determined in the market, the government influences prices through state-owned enterprises and utilities, especially in agriculture. A tradition of direct government involvement limits private-sector development, and privatization of agricultural parastatals has made little headway. An additional 10 percentage points is deducted from Lesotho's monetary freedom score to account for policies that distort domestic prices.

INVESTMENT FREEDOM — 30%

The government recognizes that it needs to do more to attract foreign investment, but political instability and a lack of transparency are deterrents. Enforcement of commercial legislation often is untimely, and local unrest often leads to the destruction of property owned by foreign businesses. Foreign investors have participated in privatization without discrimination. Residents and non-residents may hold foreign exchange accounts, but quantitative restrictions apply. Some payments and transfers are subject to prior government approval and limitations. Many capital transactions face restrictions or quantitative limits, and real estate purchases abroad require government approval.

FINANCIAL FREEDOM — 50%

Lesotho's small, underdeveloped financial system is closely tied to South Africa through the Common Monetary Area that also includes Namibia and Swaziland. Much of the population lacks adequate access to banking services. There are four commercial banks, three of which are owned by South Africa. The central bank has promoted competition with some success. It also established a Rural Credit Guarantee Fund in 2003 to encourage rural lending and opened the Lesotho PostBank in 2005 to provide similarly targeted services. The historically high non-performing loan rate has been significantly reduced. Financial supervision remains insufficient. The insurance sector has significant South African participation and one state-dominated company. Capital markets are rudimentary.

PROPERTY RIGHTS — 40%

Private property is guaranteed, and expropriation is unlikely. The judiciary is independent and has generally carried out its role effectively, even during the years of military rule, but draconian internal security legislation gives considerable power to the police and restricts the right of assembly and some forms of industrial action. The government received international praise in 2006 for enacting a law to ensure the access of married women to property rights.

FREEDOM FROM CORRUPTION — 32%

Corruption is perceived as significant. Lesotho ranks 79th out of 163 countries in Transparency International's Corruption Perceptions Index for 2006. Corruption and lack of transparency remain major problems. Fallout continues from a scandal that began in the early 1990s and involved corrupt government officials and bribe-paying corporations engaged in constructing the multimillion-dollar, World Bank-funded Lesotho Highlands Water Scheme to transport water to South Africa.

LABOR FREEDOM — 64%

Relatively flexible employment regulations could be further improved to enhance employment opportunities and productivity growth. The non-salary cost of employing a worker is low, and dismissing a redundant employee is relatively costless. Restrictions on the number of work hours remain somewhat inflexible.

LIBYA

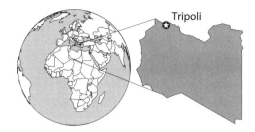

Tripoli

Rank: 154

Regional Rank: 17 of 17

Libya's economy is 38.7 percent free, according to our 2008 assessment, which makes it the world's 154th freest economy. Its overall score is 1.6 percentage points higher than last year, mainly reflecting an improved score in government size. Libya is ranked 17th out of 17 countries in the Middle East/North Africa region, and its overall score is much lower than the regional average.

Most of Libya's economic institutions are unfree. The country's one relative advantage is a moderately high level of fiscal freedom. The top income and corporate tax rates are moderate, but surtaxes can be extremely high. Government tax revenue relative to GDP is low, perhaps because of oil revenues. Inflation is also moderate, although price controls distort the market.

Libya scores poorly in business freedom, trade freedom, government size, investment freedom, financial freedom, property rights, labor freedom, and freedom from corruption. Oil dominates the economy, and the government dominates the oil sector. Forming, operating, or closing a business is heavily regulated by an avowedly socialist state that also manages the labor market inflexibly. Fairly high tariff rates and non-tariff barriers impede trade and foreign investment. Corruption is widespread, and fair adjudication of property rights is unlikely.

BACKGROUND: Oil revenues generate almost all export earnings in Libya's state-dominated economy. Despite having one of Africa's highest per capita incomes, Libya has suffered from more than 30 years of socialist economic policies and from international sanctions imposed as a result of its role in the 1989 Lockerbie bombing. The United Nations lifted its sanctions in 2003 after Libya agreed to pay compensation to victims' families, and the U.S. lifted most of its sanctions in 2004 after Libyan leader Muammar Qadhafi abandoned his efforts to build weapons of mass destruction. The Department of State removed Libya from its list of state sponsors of terrorism in 2006.

How Do We Measure Economic Freedom? See Chapter 4 (page 39) for an explanation of the methodology or visit the *Index* Web site at *heritage.org/index*.

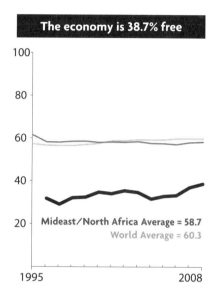

The economy is 38.7% free

Mideast/North Africa Average = 58.7

World Average = 60.3

1995 — 2008

QUICK FACTS

Population: 5.9 million

GDP (PPP): $77.7 billion
6.3% growth in 2005
4.6% 5-yr. comp. ann. growth
$12,768 per capita

Unemployment: 30.0% (2004 estimate)

Inflation (CPI): 2.0%

FDI (net flow): $123.0 million

Official Development Assistance:
Multilateral: $3.6 million
Bilateral: $20.8 million (0.6% from the U.S.)

External Debt: $4.5 billion

Exports: $29.4 billion
Primarily crude oil, refined petroleum products, natural gas, chemicals

Imports: $13.5 billion
Primarily machinery, semi-finished goods, food, transport equipment, consumer products

2005 data unless otherwise noted.

LIBYA'S TEN ECONOMIC FREEDOMS

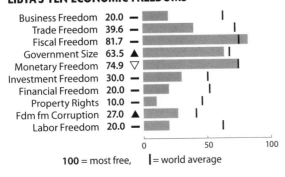

Business Freedom	20.0 —
Trade Freedom	39.6 —
Fiscal Freedom	81.7 —
Government Size	63.5 ▲
Monetary Freedom	74.9 ▽
Investment Freedom	30.0 —
Financial Freedom	20.0 —
Property Rights	10.0 —
Fdm fm Corruption	27.0 ▲
Labor Freedom	20.0 —

0   50   100

100 = most free, ❙ = world average

BUSINESS FREEDOM — 20%

The overall freedom to start, operate, and close a business is significantly restricted by Libya's regulatory environment. Despite modest improvements in the business and investment climate, Libya's bureaucracy is one of the region's most burdensome.

TRADE FREEDOM — 39.6%

Libya's weighted average tariff rate was 25.2 percent in 2002. Import bans and restrictions, import fees, non-transparent and discretionary regulation, state trade in petroleum products, subsidies, and customs corruption add to the cost of trade. An additional 10 percentage points is deducted from Libya's trade freedom score to account for non-tariff barriers.

FISCAL FREEDOM — 81.7%

The top tax rate on individual income from labor and any service or function, permanent or temporary, is 15 percent. A jihad tax is also applied to all taxable income. For incomes over 200,000 Libyan dinars, other taxes (such as those on commercial and industrial profits) may raise the top rate to 90 percent. The top corporate tax rate is 40 percent. Oil companies are subject to special provisions. Libya has no value-added tax (VAT) or inheritance tax. In the most recent year, overall tax revenue as a percentage of GDP was 2.8 percent.

GOVERNMENT SIZE — 63.5%

Total government expenditures, including consumption and transfer payments, are very high. In the most recent year, government spending equaled 34.9 percent of GDP. Despite some steps toward privatization, the economy remains highly centralized and dominated by the energy sector.

MONETARY FREEDOM — 74.9%

Inflation is low, averaging 2.6 percent between 2004 and 2006. Stable prices explain most of the monetary freedom score. The government determines most prices through price controls and state-owned enterprises and utilities. An additional 15 percentage points is deducted from Libya's monetary freedom score to account for policies that distort domestic prices.

INVESTMENT FREEDOM — 30%

Almost all foreign direct investment is in hydrocarbons.

The government screens investment. Despite partially liberalized rules in sectors like agriculture, industry, tourism, services, and health, the regulatory and bureaucratic environment remains complex. Libya's actions to alleviate concern over its nuclear program have led to the lowering of many international sanctions; its 2007 release of six foreigners held on murder charges should reinforce this momentum. The government privatized 360 state companies in 2004 in a process favoring Libyans. Residents and non-residents may hold foreign currency accounts with prior approval. Repatriation and most capital transactions, including transactions involving capital, credit operations, and direct investment, are subject to controls, including approval requirements. Foreigners may not own land in most cases.

FINANCIAL FREEDOM — 20%

Libya's financial system is primitive and highly centralized. The government nationalized all banks in 1970 and maintains tight control. Private ownership of financial institutions was permitted in 1993, and the government announced in 2007 that it was seeking bids for a stake in one of the public banks, Sahara Bank. The 10 primary financial institutions include a central bank that owns shares in a Bahrain-based foreign banking company and, through its own overseas arm, controls all international banking operations domestically. There is no coherent plan to privatize state banks, although the government has said this is a goal. Legislation passed in 2005 permits foreign banks to open branches, and 14 foreign banks had representative offices as of mid-2007. Regulation is bureaucratic and antiquated, and central bank transparency is weak. There is no capital market, although the government adopted a law to establish a stock market in June 2006.

PROPERTY RIGHTS — 10%

The judiciary is not independent, the private practice of law is illegal, and all lawyers must be members of the Secretariat of Justice. There is little land ownership, and the government may renationalize the little private property that is granted, especially to foreign companies. The government has a history of expropriation. Trademark violations are widespread.

FREEDOM FROM CORRUPTION — 27%

Corruption is perceived as widespread. Libya ranks 105th out of 163 countries in Transparency International's Corruption Perceptions Index for 2006. Government efficiency is impeded by favoritism based on personal and family connections. The Qadhafi clan exercises near total control of major government decisions.

LABOR FREEDOM — 20%

Highly restrictive employment regulations hinder employment opportunities and productivity growth. The labor law specifies minimum wage, working hours, night shift, and dismissal regulations. Unemployment remains high, and the growing number of job seekers makes job creation a major challenge.

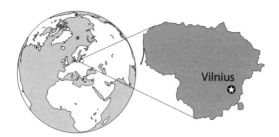

LITHUANIA

Lithuania's economy is 70.8 percent free, according to our 2008 assessment, which makes it the world's 26th freest economy. Its overall score is 0.7 percentage point lower than last year, reflecting slightly worsened scores in six of the 10 economic freedoms. Lithuania is ranked 13th out of 41 countries in the European region, and its overall score is higher than the regional average.

Lithuania scores above average or average in many areas of economic freedom. Its strongest scores are in business freedom, trade freedom, investment freedom, and financial freedom. Business regulation is simple. Investment is welcome, and foreign capital is subject to the same rules as domestic capital. The financial sector is advanced, regionally integrated, and subject to few intrusive regulations. In addition, the top income and corporate tax rates are low, giving Lithuania a strong fiscal freedom score.

BACKGROUND: Lithuania is the largest of the Baltic states and has historic ties to Poland. In 1993, Russian troops withdrew, and the country achieved its independence. Lithuania is a member of the European Union and NATO. Despite frequent political change, the country remains stable. With more than 80 percent of its enterprises now privatized, Lithuania continues to navigate the transition from a command economy to a market economy successfully. Economic growth, driven by domestic demand, has averaged 7.5 percent since 2001, making Lithuania's economy one of the fastest growing among former Soviet Union states and in the European Union. The strongest sectors are construction, financial services, and retail. Reducing inflation will remain a top priority.

How Do We Measure Economic Freedom? See Chapter 4 (page 39) for an explanation of the methodology or visit the *Index* Web site at *heritage.org/index*.

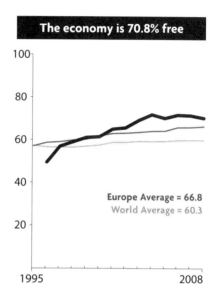

The economy is 70.8% free

Europe Average = 66.8
World Average = 60.3

1995 — 2008

QUICK FACTS

Population: 3.4 million

GDP (PPP): $49.5 billion
7.6% growth in 2005
8.0% 5-yr. comp. ann. growth
$14,494 per capita

Unemployment: 4.8%

Inflation (CPI): 2.7%

FDI (net flow): $680.0 million

Official Development Assistance:
Multilateral: $219.0 million (2004)
Bilateral: $43.0 million (12% from the U.S.) (2004)

External Debt: $11.2 billion

Exports: $14.9 billion
Primarily mineral products, textiles and clothing, machinery and equipment, chemicals, wood and wood products

Imports: $16.7 billion
Primarily mineral products, machinery and equipment, transport equipment, chemicals, textiles and clothing, metals
2005 data unless otherwise noted.

LITHUANIA'S TEN ECONOMIC FREEDOMS

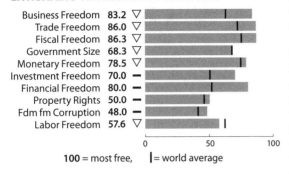

Business Freedom	83.2 ▽	
Trade Freedom	86.0 ▽	
Fiscal Freedom	86.3 ▽	
Government Size	68.3 ▽	
Monetary Freedom	78.5 ▽	
Investment Freedom	70.0 —	
Financial Freedom	80.0 —	
Property Rights	50.0 —	
Fdm fm Corruption	48.0 —	
Labor Freedom	57.6 ▽	

0   50   100

100 = most free,   ▌= world average

BUSINESS FREEDOM — 83.2%

The overall freedom to start, operate, and close a business is protected by Lithuania's regulatory environment. Starting a business takes an average of 26 days, compared to the world average of 43 days. Obtaining a business license requires less than the world average of 19 procedures and 234 days. Closing a business is easy and straightforward.

TRADE FREEDOM — 86%

Lithuania's trade policy is the same as those of other members of the European Union. The common EU weighted average tariff rate was 2 percent in 2005. Non-tariff barriers reflected in EU policy include agricultural and manufacturing subsidies, import restrictions for some goods and services, market access restrictions in some service sectors, non-transparent and restrictive regulations and standards, and inconsistent customs administration across EU members. Procurement is non-transparent and burdensome, and enforcement of intellectual property rights is weak. Consequently, an additional 10 percentage points is deducted from Lithuania's trade freedom score.

FISCAL FREEDOM — 86.3%

Lithuania has a moderate income tax rate and a low corporate tax rate. The income tax rate is a flat 27 percent (to be reduced to 24 percent effective January 2008), and the corporate tax rate is 15 percent. Other taxes include a value-added tax (VAT), a land tax, and a road tax. In the most recent year, overall tax revenue as a percentage of GDP was 20.3 percent.

GOVERNMENT SIZE — 68.3%

Total government expenditures, including consumption and transfer payments, are moderate. In the most recent year, government spending equaled 32.5 percent of GDP. Privatization of state-owned enterprises continues, and the private sector now accounts for about 80 percent of GDP.

MONETARY FREEDOM — 78.5%

Inflation is moderate, averaging 3.3 percent between 2004 and 2006. Relatively stable prices explain most of the monetary freedom score. As a participant in the EU's Common Agricultural Policy, the government subsidizes agricultural production, distorting the prices of agricultural products. The government also regulates rents, electricity rates, and some energy prices and influences prices through state-

owned enterprises. An additional 10 percentage points is deducted from Lithuania's monetary freedom score to account for these policies.

INVESTMENT FREEDOM — 70%

Foreign and domestic capital are treated equally. The only closed sectors are security and defense. Activities involving increased danger to human life, health, environment, manufacturing, or trade in weapons require permission. The prohibition on foreign ownership of land for agriculture or logging is due to be phased out in 2011 in accordance with EU regulations. Lithuania offers a diversified economy, EU-friendly investment laws, a highly developed (for the region) infrastructure, a skilled workforce, and political stability, but regulations and procedures are complex. Residents may hold foreign exchange accounts. There are no controls or restrictions on repatriation of profits, current transfers, or payments. Some capital transactions must be registered with the central bank, and there are limits on open foreign exchange positions by banks.

FINANCIAL FREEDOM — 80%

The banking system is stable and regulated according to EU standards. Non-EU banks must be approved by the central bank. Credit is allocated on market terms. There were nine commercial banks in 2007. The three largest banks account for 69 percent of assets. Most commercial banks are foreign-owned, and foreign-owned banks accounted for 86 percent of capital at the end of 2005. Banks may now offer investment funds to a wider array of clients. Foreign firms dominate the insurance sector. Capital markets are well developed but small; the stock exchange is part of a Baltic and Nordic network of exchanges.

PROPERTY RIGHTS — 50%

Accession to the EU has encouraged judicial reform, including strengthened independence and streamlined proceedings to clear the backlog of criminal cases. Investors cite weak enforcement of contracts. Lithuania remains a transshipment point for pirated optical media products from the East.

FREEDOM FROM CORRUPTION — 48%

Corruption is perceived as significant. Lithuania ranks 46th out of 163 countries in Transparency International's Corruption Perceptions Index for 2006. Domestic firms report the need for bribes, but large foreign investors report that senior government officials help them solve problems. With more than 50 governmental institutions regulating commerce, there are many opportunities for corruption.

LABOR FREEDOM — 57.6%

Restrictive employment regulations hinder employment opportunities and productivity growth. The non-salary cost of employing a worker can be very high, but dismissing a redundant employee is relatively costless. Restrictions on the number of work hours are rigid.

LUXEMBOURG

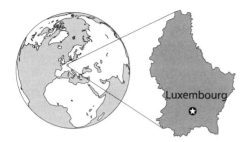

Luxembourg

Luxembourg's economy is 75.2 percent free, according to our 2008 assessment, which makes it the world's 15th freest economy. Its overall score is 0.1 percentage point lower than last year, reflecting worsened scores in three of the 10 economic freedoms. Luxembourg is ranked 8th out of 41 countries in the European region, and its overall score is much higher than the regional average.

Luxembourg has high levels of investment freedom, trade freedom, financial freedom, property rights, and business freedom. The average tariff rate is low (though non-tariff barriers include EU subsidies), and business regulation is efficient. Virtually all commercial operations are simple and transparent. The government has streamlined registration for all new businesses. Foreign investment is welcome but subject to government licensing in some sectors. The financial sector is highly developed and is regarded as a global financial hub that maintains depositor secrecy. The judiciary, independent of politics and free of corruption, has an exemplary ability to protect property rights.

Luxembourg scores below the world average in three areas: fiscal freedom, labor freedom, and government size. Total government spending, although still lower than that of some other EU member countries, equals more than two-fifths of GDP.

BACKGROUND: The Grand Duchy of Luxembourg is a small, stable, and wealthy country. A founding member of the European Union, it continues to be a primary driver of further European integration. Luxembourg maintains one of the world's highest income levels, and Luxembourgers enjoy a high standard of living. During the 20th century, Luxembourg evolved from an industrial economy into a manufacturing and services economy. With a financial services industry that accounts for about one-third of GDP, Luxembourg is Europe's principal center for mutual funds and a major force in the banking and insurance industries. It possesses a skilled workforce and a well-developed infrastructure.

How Do We Measure Economic Freedom? See Chapter 4 (page 39) for an explanation of the methodology or visit the *Index* Web site at *heritage.org/index*.

The economy is 75.2% free

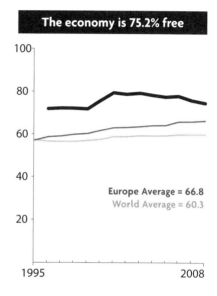

Europe Average = 66.8
World Average = 60.3

1995 — 2008

QUICK FACTS

Population: 0.5 million

GDP (PPP): $27.5 billion
4% growth in 2005
3.2% 5-yr. comp. ann. growth
$60,228 per capita

Unemployment: 4.8%

Inflation (CPI): 2.5%

FDI (net flow): $750.0 million

Official Development Assistance:
Multilateral: None
Bilateral: None

External Debt: n/a

Exports: $55.0 billion
Primarily machinery and equipment, steel products, chemicals, rubber products, glass

Imports: $43.5 billion
Primarily minerals, metals, foodstuffs, quality consumer goods

2005 data unless otherwise noted.

LUXEMBOURG'S TEN ECONOMIC FREEDOMS

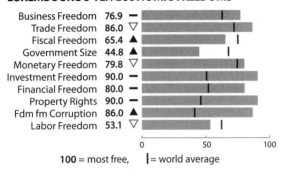

Business Freedom	76.9	—
Trade Freedom	86.0	▽
Fiscal Freedom	65.4	▲
Government Size	44.8	▲
Monetary Freedom	79.8	▽
Investment Freedom	90.0	—
Financial Freedom	80.0	—
Property Rights	90.0	—
Fdm fm Corruption	86.0	▲
Labor Freedom	53.1	▽

0   50   100

100 = most free, | = world average

BUSINESS FREEDOM — 76.9%

The overall freedom to start, operate, and close a business is relatively well protected by Luxembourg's regulatory environment. Starting a business takes about half the world average of 43 days. Obtaining a business license requires less than the world average of 19 procedures and 234 days.

TRADE FREEDOM — 86%

Luxembourg's trade policy is the same as those of other members of the European Union. The common EU weighted average tariff rate was 2 percent in 2005. Non-tariff barriers reflected in EU policy include agricultural and manufacturing subsidies, import restrictions for some goods and services, market access restrictions in some service sectors, non-transparent and restrictive regulations and standards, and inconsistent customs administration across EU members. Some biotechnology bans and service market access barriers exceed the EU norm. An additional 10 percentage points is deducted from Luxembourg's trade freedom score to account for non-tariff barriers.

FISCAL FREEDOM — 65.4%

Luxembourg has a high income tax rate but a low corporate tax rate. The top income tax rate is 38.95 percent (38 percent plus a 2.5 percent surcharge). The top corporate tax rate is 22.9 percent (including a 4 percent employment fund contribution), but municipal business taxes can raise the effective rate to as high as 29.6 percent. Other taxes include a value-added tax (VAT) and a wealth tax. In the most recent year, overall tax revenue as a percentage of GDP was 37.6 percent.

GOVERNMENT SIZE — 44.8%

Total government expenditures, including consumption and transfer payments, are high. In the most recent year, government spending equaled 42.9 percent of GDP. The highly specialized economy is mainly in private hands. The welfare system is Europe's most generous, and the government has undertaken gradual reform to increase sustainability.

MONETARY FREEDOM — 79.8%

Luxembourg is a member of the euro zone. Inflation is low, averaging 2.6 percent between 2004 and 2006. Relatively stable prices explain most of the monetary freedom score. As a participant in the EU's Common Agricultural Policy,

the government subsidizes agricultural production, distorting the prices of agricultural products. The government also regulates electricity rates and some fuel prices and influences prices through state-owned enterprises. An additional 10 percentage points is deducted from Luxembourg's monetary freedom score to account for these policies.

INVESTMENT FREEDOM — 90%

Foreign and domestic businesses receive equal treatment. Branches or subsidiaries of non–European Economic Area banks must be licensed. Investments that directly affect national security are restricted. State-owned companies dominate telecommunications, electric power, and cable television, but foreigners may compete. Incentives are offered in light, medium, and high technology. The courts uphold contracts. Foreign companies may bid on privatization tenders. Residents and non-residents may hold foreign exchange accounts. There are no restrictions or barriers with respect to capital transactions, current transfers, repatriation of profits, purchase of real estate, or access to foreign exchange.

FINANCIAL FREEDOM — 80%

Luxembourg is a global financial hub, and banking is very competitive. Of the world's 50 leading banks, 30 have subsidiaries in Luxembourg. Financial regulations are transparent and effective. Banking secrecy is legally enforced, and EU efforts to attract savings back to citizens' home countries have been limited; there is a withholding tax on interest from accounts held by non-residents. At the end of January 2007, there were 156 banks from over 20 countries; the overall number is down as a result of mergers. Banks offer an unrestricted range of services. The one state-owned bank offers medium- and long-term financing of investments by Luxembourg-based companies. The investment fund industry has been expanding rapidly. Credit is allocated on market terms. Insurance is less developed than banking.

PROPERTY RIGHTS — 90%

Private property is well protected. Contracts are secure. Luxembourg adheres to key international agreements on intellectual property rights and protects patents, copyrights, trademarks, and trade secrets.

FREEDOM FROM CORRUPTION — 86%

Corruption is perceived as minimal. Luxembourg ranks 11th out of 163 countries in Transparency International's Corruption Perceptions Index for 2006. Giving or accepting a bribe is subject to criminal penalty. Anti-corruption laws, regulations, and penalties are enforced impartially, and efforts against money laundering and the financing of terrorism are a priority.

LABOR FREEDOM — 53.1%

Inflexible employment regulations hamper employment opportunities and productivity growth. Unemployment benefits are almost twice as high as those in neighboring countries. Restrictions on the number of work hours are rigid.

MACEDONIA

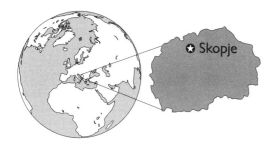

Skopje

Rank: 71

Regional Rank: 31 of 41

Macedonia's economy is 61.1 percent free, according to our 2008 assessment, which makes it the world's 71st freest economy. Its overall score is 0.5 percentage point higher than last year, reflecting improved scores in four of the 10 economic freedoms. Macedonia is ranked 31st out of 41 countries in the European region, and its overall score is lower than the regional average.

Macedonia scores above the world average in five areas: business freedom, trade freedom, fiscal freedom, financial freedom, and monetary freedom. Personal and corporate income tax rates are very low, although total tax revenue is somewhat high as a percentage of GDP. Inflation is moderate but has risen recently.

Macedonia has relatively low scores in three areas: government size, property rights, and freedom from corruption. Government expenditures are high. Property rights are not secure, especially in contrast with other states in Europe, largely because the court system is prone to corruption, political interference, and inefficiency, partially as a result of political turmoil.

BACKGROUND: Since gaining its independence from the former Yugoslavia in 1991, the Republic of Macedonia has been undergoing a troubled political and economic transition. Following civil strife in 2001, the Ohrid Agreement prevented an all-out civil war by giving greater recognition to the Albanian minority within a unitary state. Macedonia still has one of the lowest per capita GDPs in Europe, extremely high unemployment, and worrisome levels of corruption. The high level of informal economic activity also remains a concern. Nikola Gruevski became prime minister in August 2006 and has promised solid economic reforms. Government policy is oriented toward Euro-Atlantic membership, particularly membership in the European Union and NATO.

How Do We Measure Economic Freedom? See Chapter 4 (page 39) for an explanation of the methodology or visit the *Index* Web site at *heritage.org/index*.

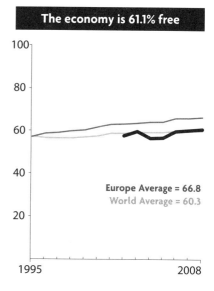

The economy is 61.1% free

Europe Average = 66.8
World Average = 60.3

1995   2008

QUICK FACTS

Population: 2.0 million

GDP (PPP): $14.6 billion
3.8% growth in 2005
2.9% 5-yr. comp. ann. growth
$7,200 per capita

Unemployment: 36.0%

Inflation (CPI): 0.5%

FDI (net flow): $97.0 million

Official Development Assistance:
Multilateral: $72.2 million
Bilateral: $178.0 million (25.7% from the U.S.)

External Debt: $2.2 billion

Exports: $2.5 billion
Primarily food, beverages, tobacco, textiles, miscellaneous manufactures, iron and steel

Imports: $3.6 billion
Primarily machinery and equipment, automobiles, chemicals, fuels, food products
2005 data unless otherwise noted.

MACEDONIA'S TEN ECONOMIC FREEDOMS

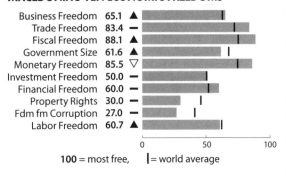

Business Freedom	65.1 ▲	
Trade Freedom	83.4 —	
Fiscal Freedom	88.1 ▲	
Government Size	61.6 ▲	
Monetary Freedom	85.5 ▽	
Investment Freedom	50.0 —	
Financial Freedom	60.0 —	
Property Rights	30.0 —	
Fdm fm Corruption	27.0 —	
Labor Freedom	60.7 ▲	

0   50   100

100 = most free, | = world average

BUSINESS FREEDOM — 65.1%
The overall freedom to start, operate, and close a business is somewhat limited by Macedonia's regulatory environment. Starting a business takes an average of 15 days, compared to the world average of 43 days. Obtaining a business license takes less than the world average of 234 days. Bankruptcy proceedings can be lengthy and burdensome.

TRADE FREEDOM — 83.4%
Macedonia's weighted average tariff rate was 3.3 percent in 2005. Import taxes, import and export quotas, some import licensing, non-transparent regulations and standards, and customs corruption add to the cost of trade. An additional 10 percentage points is deducted from Macedonia's trade freedom score to account for non-tariff barriers.

FISCAL FREEDOM — 88.1%
Effective January 2007, both the individual income tax rate and the corporate tax rate are a flat 12 percent. Other taxes include a value-added tax (VAT) and a property transfer tax. In the most recent year, overall tax revenue as a percentage of GDP was 30 percent.

GOVERNMENT SIZE — 61.6%
Total government expenditures, including consumption and transfer payments, are high. In the most recent year, government spending equaled 35.8 percent of GDP. The privatization of small and medium-sized enterprises is almost complete but has not led to sound corporate governance.

MONETARY FREEDOM — 85.5%
Inflation is low, averaging 2.3 percent between 2004 and 2006. Stable prices explain most of the monetary freedom score. Most prices are determined in the market, but the government subsidizes agriculture and influences certain prices through state-owned enterprises and utilities, such as electricity. An additional 5 percentage points is deducted from Macedonia's monetary freedom score to account for policies that distort domestic prices.

INVESTMENT FREEDOM — 50%
Foreign and domestic investors receive equal treatment, and non-residents may invest in domestic firms, except in arms manufacturing and narcotics production. Investment in financial services involves licensing. Privatization is nearly complete, and foreign investors may bid on assets. Despite steps to guarantee foreign investments, political instability and an occasionally politicized legal system weaken the business environment. Residents and non-residents may hold foreign exchange accounts subject to some approvals and restrictions. Payments and transfers face few controls and restrictions. Most capital and money market activities require government consent or registration. The currency is not convertible on international markets. Residents generally may not buy real estate abroad.

FINANCIAL FREEDOM — 60%
Despite efforts to strengthen the financial sector, it remains relatively weak. Supervision and regulation are insufficient. As of mid-2006, there were 20 banks and one state-owned bank, with foreign capital present in 16 out of the 20; 15 savings banks offer restricted services. The private sector controls about 90 percent of banking assets. Regional adoption of the euro in 2002 led many Macedonians to change non-banking savings into the new currency, raising deposit rates. Foreign-owned banks may establish branches or representative offices and controlled over half of assets as of mid-2006. Banking concentration has been accentuated by cancellation of Communist-era links between banks and major companies; three banks account for about 75 percent of all deposits and 70 percent of loans. The insurance industry and stock exchange are small; the securities sector is underdeveloped, and local businesses acquire financing mainly from cash flow.

PROPERTY RIGHTS — 30%
Protection of property is weak. The judiciary is subject to executive influence. The lack of an effective rule of law and the uncertainty of property rights, especially registering real property and obtaining land titles, undermine investment and development. The government has taken some action to combat piracy of items like CDs, DVDs, and software, but many such pirated items remain for sale.

FREEDOM FROM CORRUPTION — 27%
Corruption is perceived as widespread. Macedonia ranks 105th out of 163 countries in Transparency International's Corruption Perceptions Index for 2006. Corruption is found in all branches of government, especially the police and judicial system. Enforcement of laws against offenses like drug abuse, money laundering, and corrupt practices has been lackluster.

LABOR FREEDOM — 60.7%
Burdensome employment regulations hinder employment opportunities and productivity growth. The non-salary cost of employing a worker is very high, and the difficulty of laying off a worker creates a risk aversion for companies that would otherwise hire more people and grow. Regulations related to the number of work hours remain rigid. The parliament has passed new legislation on labor relations.

MADAGASCAR

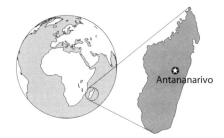

Antananarivo

Rank: 65
Regional Rank: 5 of 40

Madagascar's economy is 62.4 percent free, according to our 2008 assessment, which makes it the world's 65th freest economy. Its overall score is 1.3 percentage points higher than last year, with minor improvements across six of the 10 economic freedoms. Madagascar is ranked 5th out of 40 countries in the sub-Saharan Africa region, and its overall score is well above the regional average.

Madagascar scores well in fiscal freedom, government size, trade freedom, property rights, and investment freedom. Personal income and corporate income tax rates are moderate, and overall tax revenue is fairly low as a percentage of GDP. Foreign investment is welcome, and foreigners, despite some regulatory burdens, may own 100 percent of many businesses. Government expenditures are moderate, and state-owned businesses account for virtually no tax revenue.

Economic development is hurt by a lack of freedom in business and labor regulations. Freedom from corruption is also weak. As in many other sub-Saharan African nations, Madagascar's judiciary is underdeveloped and subject to the political whims of the executive.

BACKGROUND: Madagascar has been independent since 1960. President Didier Ratsiraka, who came to power following a provisional military directorate, pursued socialism with a centralized state and limited tolerance for opposition. Restrictions on the press and political opposition were eased in the late 1980s. Ratsiraka and opposition candidate Marc Ravalomanana both claimed victory in the 2001 presidential elections, and the resulting violence and economic disruption ended when Ratsiraka fled to exile in France. Ravalomanana won re-election in 2006 and has pursued a program that includes combating corruption, reforming land-ownership laws to clarify land rights and register titles, privatization, and removing restrictions on investment. Economic growth has increased in the wake of these reforms. Poor weather threatens the livelihood of the three-quarters of the population engaged in agriculture. Corruption, poor infrastructure, and onerous bureaucracy remain problems.

How Do We Measure Economic Freedom? See Chapter 4 (page 39) for an explanation of the methodology or visit the *Index* Web site at *heritage.org/index*.

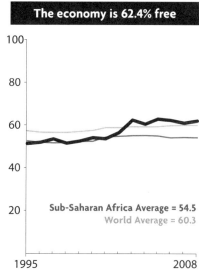

The economy is 62.4% free

Sub-Saharan Africa Average = 54.5
World Average = 60.3

1995 — 2008

QUICK FACTS

Population: 18.6 million

GDP (PPP): $17.2 billion
4.6% growth in 2005
1.4% 5-yr. comp. ann. growth
$923 per capita

Unemployment: n/a

Inflation (CPI): 18.4%

FDI (net flow): $48.0 million

Official Development Assistance:
Multilateral: $483.3 million
Bilateral: $699.1 million (11.5% from the U.S.)

External Debt: $3.5 billion

Exports: $450.2 billion
Primarily coffee, vanilla, shellfish, sugar, cotton cloth, chromite, petroleum products

Imports: $691.3 billion
Primarily capital goods, petroleum, consumer goods, food

2005 data unless otherwise noted.

261

MADAGASCAR'S TEN ECONOMIC FREEDOMS

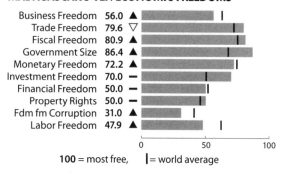

Business Freedom	56.0 ▲	
Trade Freedom	79.6 ▽	
Fiscal Freedom	80.9 ▲	
Government Size	86.4 ▲	
Monetary Freedom	72.2 ▲	
Investment Freedom	70.0 —	
Financial Freedom	50.0 —	
Property Rights	50.0 —	
Fdm fm Corruption	31.0 ▲	
Labor Freedom	47.9 ▲	

0   50   100

100 = most free,   ❘ = world average

BUSINESS FREEDOM — 56%

The overall freedom to start, operate, and close a business is restricted by Madagascar's regulatory environment. Starting a business takes an average of seven days, compared to the world average of 43 days. Despite efforts to streamline the regulatory process, red tape and lack of transparency persist. Obtaining a business license requires more than the world average of 234 days, and fees are costly. Madagascar lacks modern and efficient bankruptcy procedures.

TRADE FREEDOM — 79.6%

Madagascar's weighted average tariff rate was 5.2 percent in 2005. Import restrictions, import bans, sanitary and phytosanitary regulations, inadequate infrastructure to support trade, and a customs process that is susceptible to corruption add to the cost of trade. An additional 10 percentage points is deducted from Madagascar's trade freedom score to account for non-tariff barriers.

FISCAL FREEDOM — 80.9%

Madagascar has moderate tax rates. Both the top income tax rate and the top corporate tax rate are 30 percent. Other taxes include a value-added tax (VAT) and a capital gains tax. In the most recent year, overall tax revenue as a percentage of GDP was 10.4 percent.

GOVERNMENT SIZE — 86.4%

Total government expenditures, including consumption and transfer payments, are low. In the most recent year, government spending equaled 21.3 percent of GDP. Privatization has progressed significantly. All major banks are now in private hands, and key steps have been taken in cotton, sugar, telecommunications, and other sectors.

MONETARY FREEDOM — 72.2%

Inflation is high, averaging 12.9 percent between 2004 and 2006. Relatively unstable prices explain most of the monetary freedom score. Most prices are determined in the market, but the government influences certain prices through state-owned enterprises and utilities, such as electricity, although this influence is diminishing as privatization advances. An additional 5 percentage points is deducted from Madagascar's monetary freedom score to account for policies that distort domestic prices.

INVESTMENT FREEDOM — 70%

Foreign investors face a heavy bureaucratic burden, but the government has taken measures to improve the investment climate, such as a one-stop shop for approvals. A new foreign investment plan released in November 2006 streamlined and liberalized procedures. Foreigners may now own land, and most sectors of the economy are open to 100 percent foreign ownership. Hindrances to investment are poor infrastructure, a slow commercial legal system, and limited financing mechanisms. Residents and non-residents may open foreign exchange accounts, subject to certain restrictions and government approval. There are no restrictions on payments or transfers. Most international capital movements require government authorization.

FINANCIAL FREEDOM — 50%

Madagascar's small financial system is dominated by the banking sector. The government has been pursuing banking reform, and all the major banks are now partially privatized, often with French capital. There are five major commercial banks, and the central bank controls over a third of financial-sector assets. Credit is allocated at market rates. An extensive network of savings and loan associations extends deposit functions more broadly. Non-performing loans remain a problem. Eight insurance companies, including two state-owned and several foreign-owned companies, were operating in 2007 following liberalization of the sector in late 2005. Capital markets are insignificant, and there is no stock market.

PROPERTY RIGHTS — 50%

The judiciary is influenced by the executive and subject to corruption. Investors face a legal and judicial environment in which neither the security of private property nor the enforcement of contracts can be guaranteed. The land titling process is very bureaucratic. Pirated copies of VHS movie tapes, music CDs, DVDs, and software are sold openly. Foreign and domestic private entities may establish and own businesses, and foreigners may now own land.

FREEDOM FROM CORRUPTION — 31%

Corruption is perceived as significant. Madagascar ranks 84th out of 158 countries in Transparency International's Corruption Perceptions Index for 2006. Complicated administrative procedures create opportunities for corruption. The government has been pursuing an anti-corruption plan since 2004, and Madagascar's improved score reflects some positive results. The Independent Anti-Corruption Bureau initially targeted 10 key sectors including justice, customs, and the police. The next sectors are tourism, mining, and industry.

LABOR FREEDOM — 47.9%

Highly restrictive employment regulations hinder employment opportunities and productivity growth. The non-salary cost of employing a worker is high, and dismissing a redundant employee is not easy. Regulations on the number of work hours remain rigid.

MALAWI

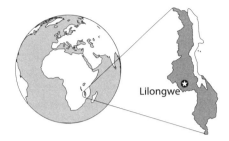

Lilongwe

Malawi's economy is 53.8 percent free, according to our 2008 assessment, which makes it the world's 120th freest economy. Its overall score is 0.2 percentage point lower than last year, reflecting worsened scores in four of the 10 economic freedoms. Malawi is ranked 24th out of 40 countries in the sub-Saharan African region, and its overall score is slightly lower than the regional average.

Malawi has a high level of labor freedom and average levels of investment freedom and financial freedom. The labor market is surprisingly flexible, and employment regulation does not impede job creation.

Malawi's substantial economic problems are characteristic of the region. Monetary freedom, freedom from corruption, government size, and property rights are weak. Inflation is very high, although government subsidies are not widespread. Government spending is over two-fifths of GDP. A weak rule of law jeopardizes the protection of property rights, and corruption is widespread. Although overall tax revenue is not large as a percentage of GDP, the top income tax and corporate tax rates are fairly high.

BACKGROUND: Malawi became fully independent in 1964 and shortly thereafter became a one-party state ruled by Dr. Hastings Kamuzu Banda. Growing domestic unrest and pressure from abroad led the government in 1993 to permit a referendum to allow multi-party democracy, which passed easily. Multi-party elections were held in 1994, and the 2004 election saw a transition between democratically elected presidents. Malawi is one of the continent's most densely populated countries. Over 85 percent of the population is engaged in agriculture, which accounts for over 35 percent of GDP and over 90 percent of exports. Tobacco, tea, cotton, coffee, and sugar are the primary exports. Drought can have severe economic consequences. Malawi's economy is hindered by bureaucracy, burdensome regulation, corruption, inadequate infrastructure, and state-owned enterprises and utilities.

How Do We Measure Economic Freedom? See Chapter 4 (page 39) for an explanation of the methodology or visit the *Index* Web site at *heritage.org/index*.

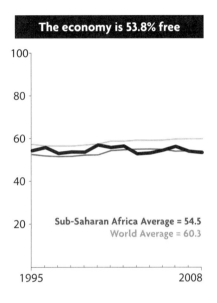

The economy is 53.8% free

Sub-Saharan Africa Average = 54.5
World Average = 60.3

1995 — 2008

QUICK FACTS

Population: 12.9 million

GDP (PPP): $8.6 billion
2.1% growth in 2005
3.3% 5-yr. comp. ann. growth
$667 per capita

Unemployment: n/a

Inflation (CPI): 12.3%

FDI (net flow): $3.0 million

Official Development Assistance:
Multilateral: $311.0 million
Bilateral: $345.2 million (15.4% from the U.S.)

External Debt: $3.2 billion

Exports: $513.1 million
Primarily tobacco, tea, sugar, cotton, coffee, peanuts, wood products, apparel

Imports: $768 million
Primarily food, petroleum products, semi-manufactures, consumer goods, transportation equipment

2005 data unless otherwise noted.

MALAWI'S TEN ECONOMIC FREEDOMS

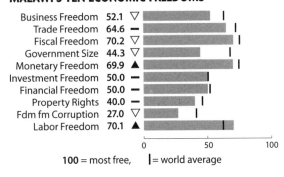

Business Freedom	52.1 ▽
Trade Freedom	64.6 ▬
Fiscal Freedom	70.2 ▽
Government Size	44.3 ▽
Monetary Freedom	69.9 ▲
Investment Freedom	50.0 ▬
Financial Freedom	50.0 ▬
Property Rights	40.0 ▬
Fdm fm Corruption	27.0 ▽
Labor Freedom	70.1 ▲

0   50   100

100 = most free, | = world average

BUSINESS FREEDOM — 52.1%

The overall freedom to start, operate, and close a business is restricted by Malawi's regulatory environment. Starting a business takes an average of 37 days, compared to the world average of 43 days. Obtaining a business license requires more than the world average of 19 procedures and 234 days. Closing a business is relatively straightforward but costly.

TRADE FREEDOM — 64.6%

Malawi's weighted average tariff rate was 10.2 percent in 2001. Subsidies, import controls, export controls on maize, import and export licensing requirements, import taxes, burdensome regulations, and a customs process that can be non-transparent and corrupt still add to the cost of trade. An additional 15 percentage points is deducted from Malawi's trade freedom score to account for non-tariff barriers.

FISCAL FREEDOM — 70.2%

Malawi has high tax rates. The top income tax rate is 40 percent, and the top corporate tax rate is 30 percent. Other taxes include a value-added tax (VAT) and a property tax. In the most recent year, overall tax revenue as a percentage of GDP was 22 percent.

GOVERNMENT SIZE — 44.3%

Total government expenditures, including consumption and transfer payments, are high. In the most recent year, government spending equaled 43.1 percent of GDP. Progress with privatization has been very sluggish.

MONETARY FREEDOM — 69.9%

Inflation is high, averaging 10 percent between 2004 and 2006. Unstable prices explain most of the monetary freedom score. Although most prices are determined in the market, the government influences certain prices through state-owned enterprises and utilities, such as electricity, transportation, water, and telecommunications; controls the prices of petroleum products and sugar; and uses subsidies to stabilize maize and fertilizer prices. An additional 10 percentage points is deducted from Malawi's monetary freedom score to account for policies that distort domestic prices.

INVESTMENT FREEDOM — 50%

There is no screening of foreign investment. A short list of products requires a license for both domestic and foreign investors, and public-interest restrictions affect investment in weapons, explosives, and manufacturing that involves hazardous waste or radioactive material. A secretariat was established in 2006 to monitor acquisitions that might pose a threat as monopolies. Privatization is more than 50 percent complete, and foreign investment in any portfolio is limited to 49 percent. The legal system is slow, and contract enforcement can be uncertain. Residents may not hold foreign exchange accounts abroad. Non-residents may hold foreign exchange accounts, subject to restrictions and government approval in some cases. Some payments and transfers face quantitative limits. Most capital transactions by residents require approval.

FINANCIAL FREEDOM — 50%

Malawi's developing financial sector remains dominated by banking. Financial institutions offer a variety of services, generally allocated on market terms. Much lending goes to the government or subsidiaries, though a decline in state borrowing has led to greater competition for private-sector lending. There were nine full-service commercial banks in 2007. The two largest banks are the domestic National Bank of Malawi, half owned by the government, and Stanbic, a subsidiary of a South African bank. A state-owned development bank services industry. Small investment is dominated by the government and foreigners and is subject to regulatory problems. Capital markets are very small, and foreign investors participate actively in the stock market.

PROPERTY RIGHTS — 40%

All rights to property, including real and intellectual property, are legally protected. There are reports of government intervention in some cases and frequent allegations of bribery in civil and criminal cases. Court administration is weak, and due process can be very slow. Malawi has laws protecting intellectual property rights and adheres to international IPR treaties and agreements.

FREEDOM FROM CORRUPTION — 27%

Corruption is perceived as widespread. Malawi ranks 105th out of 163 countries in Transparency International's Corruption Perceptions Index for 2006. There have been allegations of serious corruption in agencies handling customs, taxes, and procurement. Cases are still pending against several senior ruling party officials and three former cabinet ministers who were indicted on corruption offenses.

LABOR FREEDOM — 70.1%

Relatively flexible employment regulations could be further improved to enhance employment opportunities and productivity growth. The non-salary cost of employing a worker is very low, but the cost of laying off a worker creates a risk aversion for companies that would otherwise hire more people and grow. Regulations on the number of work hours are flexible.

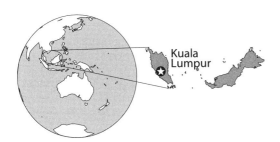

Kuala
Lumpur

MALAYSIA

Malaysia's economy is 64.5 percent free, according to our 2008 assessment, which makes it the world's 51st freest economy. Its overall score is essentially unchanged from last year, reflecting worsened scores in three of the 10 economic freedoms. Malaysia is ranked 8th freest out of 30 countries in the Asia–Pacific region, and its overall score is higher than the regional average.

Malaysia scores above average in eight of the 10 areas measured and scores highest in government size, freedom from corruption, and labor freedom. The labor sector is highly flexible, with simple employment procedures and no minimum wage. The top income and corporate tax rates are moderate, and overall tax revenue is relatively low as a percentage of GDP. Inflation is minor, and direct subsidies do not widely distort market prices. The tariff rate is fairly low, and the government has been working to eliminate some non-tariff barriers.

Malaysia suffers from weak investment freedom and financial freedom. Despite efforts to liberalize procedures, impediments include limited voting shares in companies, enforced hiring of ethnic Malays, and case-by-case government pre-investment approval. The financial sector is fairly well developed but subject to government interference and some restrictions on foreign involvement.

BACKGROUND: Malaysia is a constitutional monarchy, and politics is dominated by the ruling United Malays National Organization. Prime Minister Abdullah Ahmad Badawi has pledged to achieve developed-nation status by 2020. A leading exporter of electronics and information technology products, Malaysia has industries that range from agricultural goods to automobiles. Government ownership in certain key sectors, such as banking and airlines, remains high. The government recently relaxed capital controls and foreign investment restrictions in a bid to attract foreign capital. It also indicated a willingness to ease politically formidable affirmative action policies that have discouraged foreign investment and economic development.

How Do We Measure Economic Freedom? See Chapter 4 (page 39) for an explanation of the methodology or visit the *Index* Web site at *heritage.org/index.*

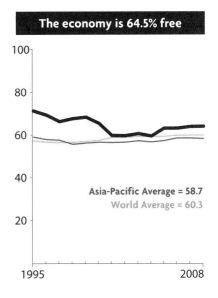

The economy is 64.5% free

Asia-Pacific Average = 58.7
World Average = 60.3

1995 — 2008

QUICK FACTS

Population: 25.3 million

GDP (PPP): $275.8 billion
5.2% growth in 2005
5.6% 5-yr. comp. ann. growth
$10,882 per capita

Unemployment: 3.6%

Inflation (CPI): 3%

FDI (net flow): $996.0 million

Official Development Assistance:
Multilateral: $7.4 million
Bilateral: $219.3 million (1.5% from the U.S.)

External Debt: $51.0 billion

Exports: $161.4 billion
Primarily electronic equipment, petroleum and liquefied natural gas, wood and wood products, palm oil, rubber

Imports: $130.6 billion
Primarily electronics, machinery, petroleum products, plastics, vehicles, iron and steel products, chemicals
2005 data unless otherwise noted.

MALAYSIA'S TEN ECONOMIC FREEDOMS

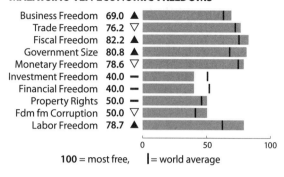

Business Freedom	69.0 ▲	
Trade Freedom	76.2 ▽	
Fiscal Freedom	82.2 ▲	
Government Size	80.8 ▲	
Monetary Freedom	78.6 ▽	
Investment Freedom	40.0 —	
Financial Freedom	40.0 —	
Property Rights	50.0 —	
Fdm fm Corruption	50.0 ▽	
Labor Freedom	78.7 ▲	

0   50   100

100 = most free, | = world average

BUSINESS FREEDOM — *69%*

The overall freedom to start, operate, and close a business is somewhat limited by Malaysia's regulatory environment. Starting a business takes an average of 24 days, compared to the world average of 43 days. Obtaining a business licenses takes more than the world average of 19 procedures and 234 days. Bankruptcy proceedings are relatively straightforward.

TRADE FREEDOM — *76.2%*

Malaysia's weighted average tariff rate was 4.4 percent in 2005. Liberalization has progressed, but import restrictions, high service market access barriers, high tariffs, import and export taxes, non-automatic import licensing for import-sensitive industries, non-transparent regulations and standards, non-transparent government procurement, export subsidies, and weak protection of intellectual property rights still add to the cost of trade. An additional 15 percentage points is deducted from Malaysia's trade freedom score to account for non-tariff barriers.

FISCAL FREEDOM — *82.2%*

Malaysia has moderate tax rates. The top individual income tax rate is 28 percent, and the corporate tax rate has been reduced to 27 percent in 2007 and 26 percent in 2008. Other taxes include a capital gains tax and a vehicle tax. The real property gains tax has been abolished. In the most recent year, overall tax revenue as a percentage of GDP was 16.3 percent.

GOVERNMENT SIZE — *80.8%*

Total government expenditures, including consumption and transfer payments, are moderate. In the most recent year, government spending equaled 25.3 percent of GDP. The retains considerable industrial and commercial holdings.

MONETARY FREEDOM — *78.6%*

Inflation is moderate, averaging 3.3 percent between 2004 and 2006. Relatively unstable prices explain most of the monetary freedom score. Most prices are determined in the market, but the government influences certain prices through state-owned enterprises; controls the prices of petroleum products, steel, cement, wheat flour, sugar, milk, bread, and chicken meat; and usually sets ceiling prices for a list of essential foods during major holidays. An addi-

tional 10 percentage points is deducted from Malaysia's monetary freedom score to account for policies that distort domestic prices.

INVESTMENT FREEDOM — *40%*

Rules have been eased, but foreign investors still face such restrictions as limited voting shares, prior approval, and mandatory hiring of ethnic Malays. Investment is banned in the news media, lotteries, or security paper. Foreigners may own 100 percent of certain kinds of new companies, but most existing corporate equity requires that a 30 percent stake be Malay-owned, and foreign ownership is capped in most sectors. Certain kinds of investment are screened, though commercial operations can begin before approval. Residents and non-residents may hold foreign exchange accounts, subject in many cases to government approval. Nearly all capital transactions are prohibited, are subject to restrictions, or require government approval.

FINANCIAL FREEDOM — *40%*

Nine of the 32 commercial banks as of September 2006 were domestically owned, and 13 were foreign-owned. Ten Islamic banks account for over 10 percent of assets. The government owns a majority of the two largest local commercial banks and is active in creating larger "anchor banks" to compete internationally. Banks must lend to certain groups like low-cost housing projects. There are several offshore banks, insurance companies, and other financial institutions. Non-performing loans remain a problem. The 41 insurance companies are subject to (among other limits) restrictions on expatriate employment and foreign equity. Foreigners may trade in securities and derivatives, but participation in stock brokering and trust management is restricted.

PROPERTY RIGHTS — *50%*

Private property is protected, but the judiciary is subject to political influence. Corporate lawsuits take over a year to file, and many contracts include a mandatory arbitration clause. The International Intellectual Property Association estimates piracy-related 2004 industry losses in Malaysia at $188 million. The manufacture and sale of counterfeit products and medicines have led to serious losses for producers of consumer products and pharmaceuticals.

FREEDOM FROM CORRUPTION — *50%*

Corruption is perceived as present. Malaysia ranks 44th out of 163 countries in Transparency International's Corruption Perceptions Index for 2006. Bribery is a criminal act, but perceptions of widespread corruption and "crony capitalism" persist.

LABOR FREEDOM — *78.7%*

Relatively flexible employment regulations could be further improved to enhance employment opportunities and productivity growth. The non-salary cost of employing a worker is low, but dismissing a redundant employee can be difficult and costly. There is no national minimum wage, and restrictions on the number of work hours are flexible.

MALI

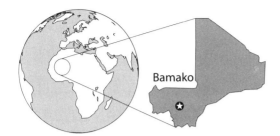

Bamako

Mali's economy is 55.5 percent free, according to our 2008 assessment, which makes it the world's 104th freest economy. Its overall score is 0.8 percentage point higher than last year, reflecting improved scores in five of the 10 economic freedoms. Mali is ranked 17th out of 40 countries in the sub-Saharan Africa region, and its overall score is higher than the regional average.

Mali scores relatively high in just one area: government size. It also scores well in terms of monetary freedom and labor freedom. Government expenditures are moderately low. The state controls prices on some staples, such as fuel, but on the whole does not significantly influence prices, and inflation is fairly low.

Mali has very weak business freedom and has other low scores in financial freedom, property rights, and freedom from corruption. Business operations are difficult and inconsistently regulated, and the country's inefficient and corrupt bureaucracy negatively affects most aspects of commercial life. Property rights are not secured by the judiciary, which is subject to political interference. The labor market is highly inflexible.

BACKGROUND: Mali quickly became a one-party socialist state after becoming independent in 1960. A 1968 military coup brought Moussa Traore to power. President Traore was arrested in 1991 by military officers who yielded power to a transitional civilian government, and multi-party elections were held in 1992. Retired General Amadou Toumani Toure, who headed the government immediately following Traore's arrest, won the 2002 election and was re-elected in 2007. Most people in drought-prone Mali work in agriculture and herding. The government has pursued economic liberalization, and while Mali remains one of the world's poorest countries, economic growth over the past decade has been strong. Mining is a growing industry, but mineral resources are generally underexploited. Inadequate infrastructure, an inefficient judiciary, and corruption hurt the economy.

How Do We Measure Economic Freedom? See Chapter 4 (page 39) for an explanation of the methodology or visit the *Index* Web site at *heritage.org/index*.

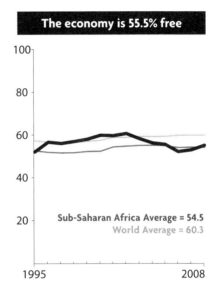

The economy is 55.5% free

Sub-Saharan Africa Average = 54.5
World Average = 60.3

1995   2008

QUICK FACTS

Population: 13.5 million

GDP (PPP): $14.0 billion
6.1% growth in 2005
5.0% 5-yr. comp. ann. growth
$1,033 per capita

Unemployment: 14.6% (2001 estimate)

Inflation (CPI): 6.4%

FDI (net flow): $157.0 million

Official Development Assistance:
Multilateral: $376.8 million
Bilateral: $403.3 million (14.4% from the U.S.)

External Debt: $3.0 billion

Exports: $1.2 billion (2004)
Primarily cotton, gold, livestock

Imports: $1.6 billion (2004)
Primarily petroleum, machinery and equipment, construction materials, foodstuffs, textiles

2005 data unless otherwise noted.

MALI'S TEN ECONOMIC FREEDOMS

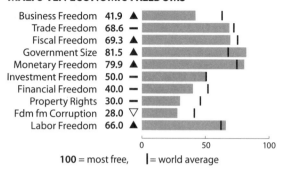

Business Freedom	41.9 ▲	
Trade Freedom	68.6 ▬	
Fiscal Freedom	69.3 ▲	
Government Size	81.5 ▲	
Monetary Freedom	79.9 ▲	
Investment Freedom	50.0 ▬	
Financial Freedom	40.0 ▬	
Property Rights	30.0 ▬	
Fdm fm Corruption	28.0 ▽	
Labor Freedom	66.0 ▲	

0   50   100

100 = most free,   ▐ = world average

BUSINESS FREEDOM — *41.9%*

The overall freedom to start, operate, and close a business is significantly restricted by Mali's regulatory environment. Starting a business takes an average of 26 days, compared to the world average of 43 days. Obtaining a business license requires less than the world average of 19 procedures and 234 days, but fees are high.

TRADE FREEDOM — *68.6%*

Mali's weighted average tariff rate was 10.7 percent in 2005. Import restrictions, export controls, inefficient customs implementation, import licensing restrictions, and import taxes add to the cost of trade. An additional 10 percentage points is deducted from Mali's trade freedom score to account for non-tariff barriers.

FISCAL FREEDOM — *69.3%*

Mali has high tax rates. The top income tax rate is 40 percent, and the top corporate tax rate is 35 percent. Other taxes include a value-added tax (VAT) and an insurance tax. In the most recent year, overall tax revenue as a percentage of GDP was 15.5 percent.

GOVERNMENT SIZE — *81.5%*

Total government expenditures, including consumption and transfer payments, are low. In the most recent year, government spending equaled 24.8 percent of GDP. The results of privatization have been mixed.

MONETARY FREEDOM — *79.9%*

Inflation is relatively low, averaging 2.6 percent between 2004 and 2006. Relatively stable prices explain most of the monetary freedom score. Although most prices are determined in the market, the government influences certain prices through state-owned enterprises and utilities, such as telecommunications, and controls the price of fuel and cotton, which is one of the most important sectors of the economy. An additional 10 percentage points is deducted from Mali's monetary freedom score to account for policies that distort domestic prices.

INVESTMENT FREEDOM — *50%*

The government allows 100 percent foreign ownership of any new business. Real estate purchases require special authorization. Inconsistent law enforcement, corruption in the commercial bureaucracy, uneven legal reliability, and poor infrastructure are deterrents. Mali is the third West African nation (after Ivory Coast and Senegal) to create a one-stop-shop for investment. Residents and non-residents must obtain permission to hold foreign exchange accounts. Payments and transfers to some countries require government approval. Credit and loan operations and issues and purchases of securities, derivatives, and other instruments are subject to requirements, controls, and authorization depending on the transaction.

FINANCIAL FREEDOM — *40%*

Mali's participates in an economic union with several other West African francophone countries, along with seven other countries, and a regional central bank governs banking and other financial institutions. There were over 10 commercial banks late in 2006, including a development bank, an agricultural bank, and a housing bank. Only three commercial banks are fully private. Significant government ownership has hindered banking growth and limited the range of services offered. The government has a minority stake in the three main banks and a majority share in Banque Internationale du Mali, which is being privatized. A microfinance industry with over 400 institutions primarily serves rural areas. The insurance market is very small. A relatively small regional stock exchange is based in the Ivory Coast.

PROPERTY RIGHTS — *30%*

In theory, property rights are protected and the judiciary is constitutionally independent, but Mali's judicial system is described as notoriously inefficient and corrupt, with frequent bribery and influence-peddling in the courts. The government is a signatory to the WTO's Trade-Related Aspects of Intellectual Property Rights (TRIPS) agreement and a member of the African Property Rights Organization (OAPI).

FREEDOM FROM CORRUPTION — *28%*

Corruption is perceived as widespread. Mali ranks 99th out of 163 countries in Transparency International's Corruption Perceptions Index for 2006. Corruption appears to be most prevalent in government procurement and dispute settlement; it is not uncommon for government procurement agents to be paid a commission of 5 percent to 10 percent. Critics allege that senior government officials and major private and parastatal companies have engaged in widespread tax evasion and customs duty fraud.

LABOR FREEDOM — *66%*

Relatively flexible employment regulations could be further improved to enhance employment opportunities and productivity growth. The non-salary cost of employing a worker is high, and the difficulty of laying off a worker creates a risk aversion for companies that would otherwise hire more people and grow. Regulations on the number of work hours are not flexible.

MALTA

Valletta

Malta's economy is 66 percent free, according to our 2008 assessment, which makes it the world's 47th freest economy. Its overall score is 0.1 percentage point lower than last year, reflecting worsened scores in three of the 10 economic freedoms. Malta is ranked 24th out of 41 countries in the European region, and its overall score is slightly lower than the regional average.

Malta scores highly in property rights, trade freedom, monetary freedom, business freedom, and financial freedom. The judiciary is independent and not politically influenced. In accordance with European Union standards, the average tariff rate is low, although Malta's trade freedom score is hurt by the standard EU subsidies of agricultural and other goods. All aspects of business formation are relatively efficient and straightforward, providing a flexible commercial environment. The financial market is small but sound and open to foreign competition.

Fiscal freedom, government size, and labor freedom are relatively weak. Total government expenditures remain high, equaling nearly half of GDP. The labor market is inflexible, with rigid employment regulations that hamper employment opportunities. Foreign investment is deterred somewhat by government scrutiny, as decisions on foreign capital are made individually to judge the likely impact on domestic businesses.

BACKGROUND: The economy of Malta, which gained its independence from Great Britain in 1964, depends on tourism, foreign trade, and manufacturing. The country's well-trained workers, low labor costs, and proximity to the European Union attract foreign companies, but the government also maintains a sprawling socialist bureaucracy, with the majority of spending allocated to housing, education, and health care. As a member of the EU, Malta has made some moves toward liberalizing its economy, and its membership in the single European currency is on schedule for adoption on January 1, 2008. Fiscal consolidation and job creation remain significant economic challenges.

How Do We Measure Economic Freedom? See Chapter 4 (page 39) for an explanation of the methodology or visit the *Index* Web site at *heritage.org/index*.

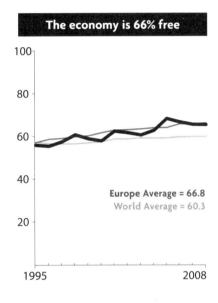

The economy is 66% free

Europe Average = 66.8
World Average = 60.3

1995 — 2008

QUICK FACTS

Population: 0.4 million

GDP (PPP): $7.7 billion
2.2% growth in 2005
0.6% 5-yr. comp. ann. growth
$19,189 per capita

Unemployment: 11.7%

Inflation (CPI): 2.5%

FDI (net inflow): $588.0 million

Official Development Assistance:
Multilateral: $7 million (2004)
Bilateral: $2.0 million (29% from the U.S.) (2004)

External Debt: $188.8 million

Exports: $4.1 billion
Primarily machinery and transport equipment, manufactures

Imports: $4.6 billion
Primarily machinery and transport equipment, manufactured and semi-manufactured goods, food, drink, tobacco

2005 data unless otherwise noted.

MALTA'S TEN ECONOMIC FREEDOMS

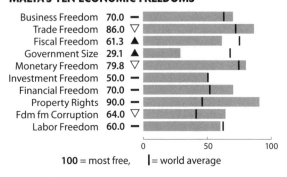

Business Freedom	70.0	—
Trade Freedom	86.0	▽
Fiscal Freedom	61.3	▲
Government Size	29.1	▲
Monetary Freedom	79.8	▽
Investment Freedom	50.0	—
Financial Freedom	70.0	—
Property Rights	90.0	—
Fdm fm Corruption	64.0	▽
Labor Freedom	60.0	—

0   50   100

100 = most free, | = world average

BUSINESS FREEDOM — *70%*

The overall freedom to start, operate, and close a business is relatively well protected by Malta's regulatory environment. Malta has adopted transparent and effective policies and regulations to foster competition and is striving to eliminate unnecessary bureaucratic procedure. Although they can be burdensome, existing regulations are relatively straightforward and applied uniformly most of the time.

TRADE FREEDOM — *86%*

Malta's trade policy is the same as those of other members of the European Union. The common EU weighted average tariff rate was 2 percent in 2005. Non-tariff barriers reflected in EU policy include agricultural and manufacturing subsidies, import restrictions for some goods and services, market access restrictions in some service sectors, non-transparent and restrictive regulations and standards, and inconsistent customs administration across EU members. Consequently, an additional 10 percentage points is deducted from Malta's trade freedom score.

FISCAL FREEDOM — *61.3%*

Malta has burdensome tax rates. Both the top income tax rate and the top corporate tax rate are 35 percent. Other taxes include a value-added tax (VAT) and a capital gains tax. In the most recent year, overall tax revenue as a percentage of GDP was 37.7 percent.

GOVERNMENT SIZE — *29.1%*

Total government expenditures, including consumption and transfer payments, are very high. In the most recent year, government spending equaled 48.6 percent of GDP. Privatization has progressed in telecommunications and the international airport.

MONETARY FREEDOM — *79.8%*

Inflation is relatively low, averaging 2.6 percent between 2004 and 2006. Relatively stable prices explain most of the monetary freedom score. As a participant in the EU's Common Agricultural Policy, the government subsidizes agricultural production, distorting the prices of agricultural products. The government also influences prices through state-owned enterprises, controls the prices of bread and milk, and heavily subsidizes energy. An additional 10 percentage points is deducted from Malta's monetary freedom score to account for these policies.

INVESTMENT FREEDOM — *50%*

Malta welcomes foreign investment, except in real estate, wholesale retail trade, and public utilities, and restricts foreign ownership in information technology. Manufacturing is open as long as investors intend to export their products from Malta. The government examines all investments and carefully screens foreign proposals that are in direct competition with local business. In accordance with EU requirements, state-dominated sectors like electricity generation and fuel distribution are being liberalized. Residents and non-residents may hold foreign exchange accounts, subject to certain restrictions and maximums. Some capital transactions, including selected capital and money market transactions and real estate purchases by non-residents, require government approval.

FINANCIAL FREEDOM — *70%*

Malta's financial sector is small but competitive. Supervision and regulation of the financial system are transparent and consistent with international norms. Malta is scheduled to adopt the euro on January 1, 2008. Under liberalizing legislation passed in 2000, the formerly state-owned banks are now largely privatized, and foreign banks have a significant presence. HSBC (Malta) Ltd., and the Bank of Valletta dominate the banking market. The government continues to hold a 25 percent stake in the Bank of Valletta but intends to sell its remaining interest. The insurance sector is concentrated and dominated by a group of companies linked to the Bank of Valletta. There were over 30 licensed insurers in mid-2006, including a number of foreign insurers. The stock exchange is small but active, and regulation is conducted by the securities supervisory board rather than the central bank.

PROPERTY RIGHTS — *90%*

Malta's judiciary is independent, both constitutionally and in practice. Property rights are protected, and expropriation is unlikely. Foreigners can never have full rights to buy property in Malta unless they obtain Maltese nationality. Malta has implemented the pertinent provisions of EU and WTO Trade-Related Aspects of Intellectual Property Rights (TRIPS) rules.

FREEDOM FROM CORRUPTION — *64%*

Corruption is perceived as present. Malta ranks 28th out of 163 countries in Transparency International's Corruption Perceptions Index for 2006. Malta still lacks both a comprehensive anti-corruption strategy and appropriate coordination for implementing and monitoring such a strategy in the public sector and specific areas of law.

LABOR FREEDOM — *60%*

Restrictive employment regulations could be improved to enhance employment and productivity growth. Labor relationships can be confrontational, and outdated and inefficient practices are persistent problems. The government mandates a minimum wage.

2008 Index of Economic Freedom

MAURITANIA

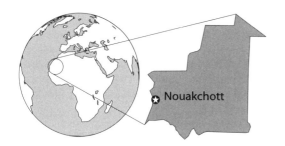

Nouakchott

Rank: 109

Regional Rank: 19 of 40

Mauritania's economy is 55 percent free, according to our 2008 assessment, which makes it the world's 109th freest economy. Its overall score is 1.5 percentage points higher than last year, reflecting improvements in labor market flexibility and the business climate. Mauritania is ranked 19th out of 40 countries in the sub-Saharan Africa region, and its overall score is higher than the regional average.

Mauritania scores well in monetary freedom and investment freedom. Inflation is relatively high, but the government does not intervene actively in market prices. Foreign investment is welcome in almost all sectors. Relatively high tax rates on income are balanced by low corporate tax rates, and overall tax revenue is fairly low as a percentage of GDP, leading to a fiscal freedom score equal to the world average.

Economic development is hampered by serious weakness in business freedom, labor freedom, freedom from corruption, and property rights. Opening a business and related licensing and operational procedures are grueling. Bureaucratic inefficiency and corruption burden the entire economy. Court enforcement of property rights and labor regulations is subject to pervasive political interference.

BACKGROUND: Mauritania gained its independence in 1960. Moktar Ould Daddah served as its first president until being ousted in a 1978 coup. A military junta ruled until 1992, when the first multi-party elections were held. President Maaouiya Ould Sid'Ahmed Taya, who first became chief of state through a 1984 coup, won elections in 1992, 1997, and 2003. A 2005 coup ousted Taya and appointed a transitional government. Sidi Ould Cheikh Abdellahi was elected president in 2007. Mauritania is predominantly desert and beset by drought, poor harvests, and unemployment. Mining and fishing dominate the economy. Oil production from offshore fields began in 2006. The government has announced plans to cut subsidies to public enterprises, reform taxes, and enhance transparency in public finances.

How Do We Measure Economic Freedom? See Chapter 4 (page 39) for an explanation of the methodology or visit the *Index* Web site at *heritage.org/index*.

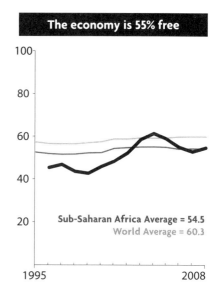

The economy is 55% free

Sub-Saharan Africa Average = 54.5
World Average = 60.3

1995   2008

QUICK FACTS

Population: 3.1 million

GDP (PPP): $6.9 billion
5.4% growth in 2005
4.3% 5-yr. comp. ann. growth
$2,235 per capita

Unemployment: 20% (2004 estimate)

Inflation (CPI): 12.1%

FDI (net flow): $115.0 million

Official Development Assistance:
Multilateral: $100.8 million
Bilateral: $133.4 million (16.1% from the U.S.)

External Debt: $2.3 billion

Exports: $784.0 million (2004 estimate)
Primarily iron ore, fish and fish products, gold

Imports: $1.1 billion (2004 estimate)
Primarily machinery and equipment, petroleum products, capital goods, foodstuffs, consumer goods

2005 data unless otherwise noted.

MAURITANIA'S TEN ECONOMIC FREEDOMS

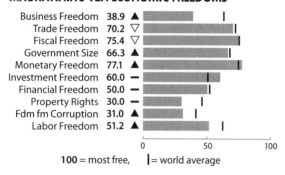

Business Freedom	38.9	▲
Trade Freedom	70.2	▽
Fiscal Freedom	75.4	▽
Government Size	66.3	▲
Monetary Freedom	77.1	▲
Investment Freedom	60.0	—
Financial Freedom	50.0	—
Property Rights	30.0	—
Fdm fm Corruption	31.0	▲
Labor Freedom	51.2	▲

0   50   100

100 = most free, | = world average

BUSINESS FREEDOM — 38.9%

The overall freedom to start, operate, and close a business is considerably restricted by Mauritania's regulatory environment. Starting a business takes an average of 65 days, compared to the world average of 43 days. Obtaining a business license requires more than the world average of 19 procedures, and fees are costly. Despite an effort to streamline the regulatory environment, bureaucratic obstacles and delays persist.

TRADE FREEDOM — 70.2%

Mauritania's weighted average tariff rate was 9.9 percent in 2001. Import restrictions, import taxes, weak enforcement of intellectual property rights, inadequate infrastructure to support trade, and customs complexity and non-transparency add to the cost of trade. An additional 10 percentage points is deducted from Mauritania's trade freedom score to account for non-tariff barriers.

FISCAL FREEDOM — 75.4%

Mauritania has a high income tax rate and a low corporate tax rate. The top income tax rate is 40 percent, and the top corporate tax rate is 25 percent. Other taxes include a value-added tax (VAT) and a tax on insurance contracts. In the most recent year, overall tax revenue as a percentage of GDP was 15.3 percent.

GOVERNMENT SIZE — 66.3%

Total government expenditures, including consumption and transfer payments, are high. In the most recent year, government spending equaled 33.5 percent of GDP. Privatization and deregulation of the public sector have reduced the government's role in the economy, but progress has been sluggish.

MONETARY FREEDOM — 77.1%

Inflation is relatively high, averaging 8 percent between 2004 and 2006. Relatively unstable prices explain most of the monetary freedom score. Most prices are determined in the market, but the government influences certain prices through state-owned enterprises and utilities, such as electricity. An additional 5 percentage points is deducted from Mauritania's monetary freedom score to account for policies that distort domestic prices.

INVESTMENT FREEDOM — 60%

Almost all sectors welcome foreign investment, except for fishing boats. The 2002 investment code encourages foreign investors with privatization and liberalization, guarantees freedom to transfer most capital and wages abroad, and makes foreign and domestic investment legally equal. Certain financial activity, mining and hydrocarbons, telecommunications, and certain utilities are subject to additional restrictions. Foreign investment is screened. Investment is hurt by bureaucratic corruption. Residents and non-residents may hold foreign exchange accounts, but non-resident accounts are subject to some restrictions. Payments and transfers are subject to quantitative limits, *bona fide* tests, and prior approval in some cases.

FINANCIAL FREEDOM — 50%

Mauritania's financial sector is small, underdeveloped, concentrated in urban areas, and dominated by banking. Supervision and enforcement of regulation are insufficient. There are 10 commercial banks, one of which is half-owned by the government. Two French bank subsidiaries opened in 2006 and 2007: the first foreign banks to set up operations. The banking sector has been undermined by non-performing loans. The insufficiency of financial regulation in several areas is exemplified by a corruption scandal at the Central Bank in 2006. The financial sector also includes a government-owned development bank and a growing number of microfinance institutions, but microfinance companies are not well developed, leaving many rural areas without credit access. Capital markets are virtually nonexistent, and there is no stock market.

PROPERTY RIGHTS — 30%

Mauritania's judicial system is chaotic and corrupt. The judiciary is subject to influence from the executive. Poorly trained judges are intimidated by social, financial, tribal, and personal pressures. Mauritania signed and ratified the WTO's Trade-Related Aspects of Intellectual Property Rights (TRIPS) agreement in 1994 but has yet to implement it.

FREEDOM FROM CORRUPTION — 31%

Corruption is perceived as widespread. Mauritania ranks 84th out of 163 countries in Transparency International's Corruption Perceptions Index for 2006. All levels of government and society are affected by corrupt practices. Affluent business groups and senior government officials reportedly receive favorable treatment with regard to taxes, special grants of land, and government procurement. Tax laws are routinely flouted. Widespread corruption weakens government's ability to provide needed services.

LABOR FREEDOM — 51.2%

Restrictive employment regulations hinder employment opportunities and productivity growth. The non-salary cost of employing a worker is moderate, but the difficulty of laying off a worker creates a risk aversion for companies that would otherwise hire more people and grow. Restrictions on the number of work hours remain rigid.

MAURITIUS

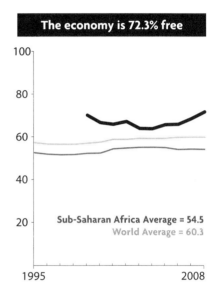

The economy of Mauritius is 72.3 percent free, according to our 2008 assessment, which makes it the world's 18th freest economy. Its overall score is 3.1 percentage points higher than last year, one of the year's biggest increases, reflecting improved scores in six of the 10 economic freedoms. Mauritius is ranked 1st out of 40 countries in the sub-Saharan Africa region, and its overall score is well above the regional average. Mauritius is the second most improved economy in the 2008 *Index*.

Mauritius scores above the world average in each of the 10 areas measured. It also scores 10 percentage points or more above the world average in six areas: investment freedom, property rights, business freedom, freedom from corruption, fiscal freedom, and government size. The environment is business-friendly, and licensing procedures are simple. Virtually all commercial operations are efficient and transparent. Foreign investment is actively promoted, although land ownership is restricted to arbitration on a case-by-case basis. The top income and corporate tax rates are moderate, and government expenditures are moderate as a percentage of GDP. The judiciary, independent of politics and relatively free of corruption, is able to protect property rights exceptionally well.

BACKGROUND: With a well-developed legal and commercial infrastructure and a long tradition of entrepreneurship and representative government, Mauritius has one of Africa's strongest economies. Sugar and textiles, the traditional economic mainstays, are facing stronger international competition and the erosion of trade preferences, which has undermined growth in recent years and led to increased unemployment. The government is addressing this problem through business-friendly policies, training, and attempting to diversify the economy by promoting information and communication technology, financial and business services, seafood processing and exports, and free trade zones.

How Do We Measure Economic Freedom? See Chapter 4 (page 39) for an explanation of the methodology or visit the *Index* Web site at *heritage.org/index*.

The economy is 72.3% free

Sub-Saharan Africa Average = 54.5
World Average = 60.3

1995 — 2008

QUICK FACTS

Population: 1.2 million

GDP (PPP): $15.8 billion
3.0% growth in 2005
3.2% 5-yr. comp. ann. growth
$12,714 per capita

Unemployment: 9.6%

Inflation (CPI): 5.6%

FDI (net flow): −$24.0 million

Official Development Assistance:
Multilateral: $21.5 million
Bilateral: $44.3 million (2.6% from the U.S.)

External Debt: $2.2 billion

Exports: $3.8 billion
Primarily clothing and textiles, sugar, cut flowers, molasses

Imports: $4.2 billion
Primarily manufactured goods, capital equipment, foodstuffs, petroleum products, chemicals

2005 data unless otherwise noted.

MAURITIUS'S TEN ECONOMIC FREEDOMS

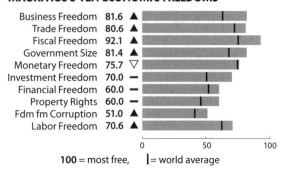

Business Freedom	81.6 ▲
Trade Freedom	80.6 ▲
Fiscal Freedom	92.1 ▲
Government Size	81.4 ▲
Monetary Freedom	75.7 ▽
Investment Freedom	70.0 —
Financial Freedom	60.0 —
Property Rights	60.0 —
Fdm fm Corruption	51.0 ▲
Labor Freedom	70.6 ▲

0   50   100

100 = most free, ▌= world average

BUSINESS FREEDOM — *81.6%*

The overall freedom to start, operate, and close a business is relatively well protected by Mauritius's regulatory environment. Starting a business takes an average of seven days, compared to the world average of 43 days. Obtaining a business license requires less than the world average of 19 procedures and 234 days. Closing a business is easy.

TRADE FREEDOM — *80.6%*

Mauritius's weighted average tariff rate was 4.7 percent in 2005. The government has made progress in liberalizing the trade regime, but subsidies, some quotas, import restrictions, weak enforcement of intellectual property rights, and controls on imports and exports of certain goods by means of special permit requirements add to the cost of trade. The government also controls imports of rice, flour, petroleum products, and cement. An additional 10 percentage points is deducted from Mauritius's trade freedom score to account for non-tariff barriers.

FISCAL FREEDOM — *92.1%*

Mauritius has a very competitive tax regime. In June 2007, both the income tax rate and the corporate tax rate were reduced to a flat 15 percent. Other taxes include a value-added tax (VAT) and a transfer tax. In the most recent year, overall tax revenue as a percentage of GDP was 18.5 percent.

GOVERNMENT SIZE — *81.4%*

Total government expenditures, including consumption and transfer payments, are moderate. In the most recent year, government spending equaled 24.9 percent of GDP. The government has made slow progress toward sound fiscal consolidation and public spending management.

MONETARY FREEDOM — *75.7%*

Inflation is moderate, averaging 5.1 percent between 2004 and 2006. Relatively unstable prices explain most of the monetary freedom score. The government controls prices for a number of goods, including flour, sugar, milk, bread, rice, petroleum products, steel, cement, fertilizers, and pharmaceuticals; influences prices through state-owned enterprises and utilities; and subsidizes some agriculture and industry. An additional 10 percentage points is deducted from Mauritius's monetary freedom score to account for policies that distort domestic prices.

INVESTMENT FREEDOM — *70%*

Foreign and domestic capital are treated equally. A transparent and well-defined foreign investment code makes Mauritius one of the best places in Africa for foreign investment. In its 2006–2007 budget statement, the government redoubled its efforts to diversify and liberalize the economy. Foreigners may control 100 percent of Mauritian companies. The only restrictions on foreign business ownership apply to casinos, public utilities, and real estate. Residents and non-residents may hold foreign exchange accounts. There are no controls on payments or transfers and few controls on capital transactions.

FINANCIAL FREEDOM — *60%*

Mauritius has an open, efficient, and competitive financial system. The 2004 Banking Act eliminated distinctions between onshore and offshore banks. There were 19 banks as of 2006. The two largest domestic banks (the Mauritius Commercial Bank and the minority state-owned State Bank of Mauritius) control 71 percent of assets. The government also wholly owns the Development Bank of Mauritius Ltd. and the Mauritius Post and Cooperative Bank Ltd. and owns a majority of First City Bank. Financial regulation is relatively solid and is being improved. The three largest insurance firms account for approximately 75 percent of the market. Capital markets are growing, and the Stock Exchange of Mauritius, with links to regional exchange networks in Africa and Asia, had a market capitalization of about US$4 billion at the end of 2006.

PROPERTY RIGHTS — *60%*

The judiciary is independent, and trials are fair. The legal system is generally non-discriminatory and transparent. The highest court of appeal is the judicial committee of the Privy Council of England. Corruption is much lower than elsewhere in Africa. Expropriation is unlikely. Trademark and patent laws comply with the WTO's Trade-Related Aspects of Intellectual Property Rights (TRIPS) agreement.

FREEDOM FROM CORRUPTION — *51%*

Mauritius ranks 42nd out of 163 countries in Transparency International's Corruption Perceptions Index for 2006. Mauritius is one of Africa's least corrupt countries, and corruption is not seen as an obstacle to foreign direct investment.

LABOR FREEDOM — *70.6%*

Relatively flexible employment regulations could be further improved to enhance employment opportunities and productivity growth. The non-salary cost of employing a worker is low, but dismissing a redundant employee can be relatively costly and difficult. Restrictions on the number of work hours have become more flexible in recent years.

MEXICO

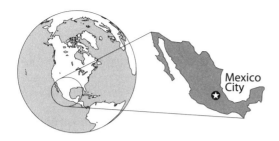

Mexico City

Mexico's economy is 66.4 percent free, according to our 2008 assessment, which makes it the world's 44th freest economy. Its overall score is 0.1 percentage point higher than last year. Mexico is ranked 9th out of 29 countries in the Americas, and its overall score is higher than the regional average.

Mexico scores relatively well in business freedom, fiscal freedom, trade freedom, government size, property rights, and financial freedom. Commercial operations are becoming more streamlined, and business formation is efficient. Income and corporate tax rates are moderate, and overall tax revenue is low as a percentage of GDP. Government expenditures are fairly low.

Freedom from corruption is the only factor that is worse than the world average. Foreign investment in many sectors is deterred by special licensing requirements, although the government is working to make commercial regulations more investment-friendly. A weak judicial system produces slow resolution of cases and is subject to fairly significant corruption.

BACKGROUND: Mexico is a member of the North American Free Trade Agreement with Canada and the United States. The economy depends heavily on commercial relations with, and more than $20 billion in remittances from migrant workers in, the U.S. Under center-right National Action Party (PAN) President Vicente Fox (2000–2006), a divided Congress adopted some needed reforms after 71 years of rule by the center-left Institutional Revolutionary Party. The PAN's Felipe Calderon, who succeeded Fox in December 2006, promised further economic liberalization but has spent most of his political capital fighting organized crime networks that traffic in illegal drugs. Mexicans are still waiting to see whether his government will challenge *de facto* monopolies in energy, telecommunications, and transportation that have undermined competitiveness and job creation. Mexico also needs to dismantle the corporatist system of price supports, subsidies, and special-interest tax exemptions.

How Do We Measure Economic Freedom? See Chapter 4 (page 39) for an explanation of the methodology or visit the *Index* Web site at *heritage.org/index*.

The economy is 66.4% free

100

80

60

40

Americas Average = 61.6
World Average = 60.3

20

1995   2008

QUICK FACTS

Population: 103.1 million

GDP (PPP): $1.1 trillion
2.8% growth in 2005
2.3% 5-yr. comp. ann. growth
$10,751 per capita

Unemployment: 3.6%

Inflation (CPI): 4.0%

FDI (net flow): $11.9 billion

Official Development Assistance:
Multilateral: $30.9 million
Bilateral: $264.5 million (48.6% from the U.S.)

External Debt: $167.2 billion

Exports: $230.4 billion
Primarily manufactured goods, oil and oil products, silver, fruits, vegetables

Imports: $243.3 billion
Primarily metalworking machines, steel mill products, agricultural machinery, electrical equipment, car parts for assembly, repair parts for motor vehicles, aircraft
2005 data unless otherwise noted.

MEXICO'S TEN ECONOMIC FREEDOMS

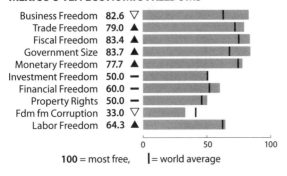

Business Freedom	82.6	▽
Trade Freedom	79.0	▲
Fiscal Freedom	83.4	▲
Government Size	83.7	▲
Monetary Freedom	77.7	▲
Investment Freedom	50.0	—
Financial Freedom	60.0	—
Property Rights	50.0	—
Fdm fm Corruption	33.0	▽
Labor Freedom	64.3	▲

0   50   100

100 = most free, ▌ **= world average**

BUSINESS FREEDOM — 82.6%

The overall freedom to start, operate, and close a business is protected by Mexico's regulatory environment. Starting a business takes an average of 27 days, compared to the world average of 43 days. Obtaining a business license requires less than the world average of 19 procedures and 234 days. Bankruptcy proceedings are relatively easy.

TRADE FREEDOM — 79%

Mexico's weighted average tariff rate was 3 percent in 2005. Import restrictions, service market access barriers, import licensing for sensitive products, import taxes, restrictive standards and labeling rules, burdensome sanitary and phytosanitary regulations, non-transparent and inconsistent customs administration and valuation, customs corruption, and weak enforcement of intellectual property rights add to the cost of trade. An additional 15 percentage points is deducted from Mexico's trade freedom score to account for non-tariff barriers.

FISCAL FREEDOM — 83.4%

Mexico has moderate tax rates. Both the top income tax rate and the top corporate tax rate were cut to 28 percent effective January 2007. Other taxes include a value-added tax (VAT), a property tax, and a vehicle tax. In the most recent year, overall tax revenue as a percentage of GDP was 9.7 percent.

GOVERNMENT SIZE — 83.7%

Total government expenditures, including consumption and transfer payments, are low. In the most recent year, government spending equaled 23.3 percent of GDP. Privatization has progressed, but the energy and electricity industries remain government-controlled.

MONETARY FREEDOM — 77.7%

Inflation is moderate, averaging 3.8 percent between 2004 and 2006. Relatively unstable prices explain most of the monetary freedom score. Although most prices are determined in the market, the government maintains suggested retail prices for medicines and influences prices through state-owned enterprises and utilities, including electricity and energy. An additional 10 percentage points is deducted from Mexico's monetary freedom score to account for policies that distort domestic prices.

INVESTMENT FREEDOM — 50%

Foreign and domestic capital may not be treated equally. Foreign investors are barred from important sectors, such as petroleum and electricity, and restricted in others like telecommunications. Foreign investment in real estate is somewhat restricted. Recent improvements include less legal and administrative red tape, higher foreign equity ceilings, fewer local content requirements, better intellectual property legislation, and elimination of most import license requirements. About 95 percent of foreign investment does not require official approval. Residents and non-residents may hold foreign exchange accounts. Most payments, transactions, and transfers are allowed. Some capital transactions are subject to government permission and controls.

FINANCIAL FREEDOM — 60%

Mexico's increasingly competitive financial sector has recovered from the 1994 currency devaluation. Government holdings in commercial banking are significantly reduced, and foreign participation has grown rapidly since liberalization in 1998. Of 30 commercial banks in 2006, 29 were foreign-owned and constituted more than 80 percent of the banking sector. Banks offer a wide range of services. Six government-owned development banks provide financing to specific areas of the economy and influence credit. The government has adopted U.S. accounting standards. The insurance sector is well developed, with five firms (three foreign-owned) accounting for nearly 59 percent of policies. Although most large Mexican companies are traded on U.S. exchanges, Mexico has the largest stock market in Latin America after Brazil.

PROPERTY RIGHTS — 50%

The threat of expropriation is low. Contracts are generally upheld, but the courts are slow to resolve disputes and are allegedly subject to corruption. Despite a legal framework for the enforcement of intellectual property rights, the enforcement and prosecution of infringement cases is ineffective. Foreign real estate investors have found it difficult to secure enforcement of their property interests in state-level courts.

FREEDOM FROM CORRUPTION — 33%

Corruption is perceived as significant. Mexico ranks 70th out of 163 countries in Transparency International's Corruption Perceptions Index for 2006. Corruption has been pervasive for many years, but since enactment of a 2002 law providing for public access to government information, transparency in federal public administration has improved noticeably. Local civil society organizations focused on fighting corruption are still developing.

LABOR FREEDOM — 64.3%

Somewhat inflexible employment regulations hamper employment opportunities and productivity growth. The non-salary cost of employing a worker can be high, and the difficulty of laying off a worker creates a risk aversion for companies that would otherwise hire more people and grow. Labor reform remains stalled.

MOLDOVA

Chişinău

Rank: 89
Regional Rank: 36 of 41

Moldova's economy is 58.4 percent free, according to our 2008 assessment, which makes it the world's 89th freest economy. Its overall score is 0.8 percentage point lower than last year, reflecting deteriorated scores in five of the 10 economic freedoms. Moldova is ranked 36th out of 41 countries in the European region, and its overall score is lower than the regional average.

Moldova scores slightly above the world average in trade freedom, business freedom, labor freedom, and fiscal freedom, and property rights. The average tariff rate is low, but non-tariff barriers include burdensome regulations and restrictive customs.

As the poorest country in Europe, Moldova has an economy with significant shortcomings. Monetary freedom, investment freedom, and freedom from corruption are weak. Inflation is high, although the government has been phasing out price supports on certain goods. Foreign investment in virtually all sectors faces hurdles from bureaucratic inefficiency to outright restriction. There is significant corruption in most areas of the bureaucracy, and although the government has been reforming the judiciary, public institutions are weak overall.

BACKGROUND: Moldova, a small landlocked country located between Romania and Ukraine, has struggled since gaining its independence after the collapse of the Soviet Union in 1991. It also has had to deal with problems created by a secessionist, pro-Russian enclave in Transnistria. The Communist Party of Moldova, which enjoys a parliamentary majority, supports European integration and has not reversed market reforms instituted in the early 1990s. Agriculture remains central to the economy, and foodstuffs, wine, and animal and vegetable products are the main exports. In 2006, Russia lifted its ban on Moldovan wine imports. However, Russian bureaucrats have been slow to allow wine imports to pass through customs, and sales of Moldovan wines remain sluggish as a result.

How Do We Measure Economic Freedom? See Chapter 4 (page 39) for an explanation of the methodology or visit the *Index* Web site at *heritage.org/index*.

The economy is 58.4% free

Europe Average = 66.8
World Average = 60.3

1995 — 2008

QUICK FACTS

Population: 4.2 million

GDP (PPP): $8.8 billion
7.5% growth in 2005
7.3% 5-yr. comp. ann. growth
$2,099.8 per capita

Unemployment: 8.8%

Inflation (CPI): 11.9%

FDI (net flow): $225.0 million

Official Development Assistance:
Multilateral: $77.4 million
Bilateral: $114.3 million (26.7% from the U.S.)

External Debt: $2.1 billion

Exports: $1.5 billion
Primarily foodstuffs, textiles, machinery

Imports: $2.7 billion
Primarily mineral products and fuel, machinery and equipment, chemicals, textiles

2005 data unless otherwise noted.

277

MOLDOVA'S TEN ECONOMIC FREEDOMS

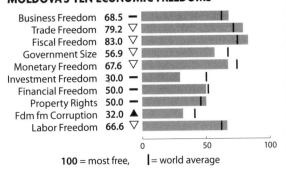

Business Freedom	68.5
Trade Freedom	79.2
Fiscal Freedom	83.0
Government Size	56.9
Monetary Freedom	67.6
Investment Freedom	30.0
Financial Freedom	50.0
Property Rights	50.0
Fdm fm Corruption	32.0
Labor Freedom	66.6

0   50   100

100 = most free, | = world average

BUSINESS FREEDOM — 68.5%

The overall freedom to start, operate, and close a business is relatively well protected by Moldova's regulatory environment. Starting a business takes an average of 23 days, compared to the world average of 43 days. Obtaining a business license requires more than the world average of 19 procedures and 234 days. Closing a business is relatively simple and straightforward.

TRADE FREEDOM — 79.2%

Moldova's weighted average tariff rate was 2.9 percent in 2001. Import and export restrictions, import taxes and fees, burdensome regulations, and an inefficient and non-transparent customs process that is prone to corruption add to the cost of trade. An additional 15 percentage points is deducted from Moldova's trade freedom score to account for non-tariff barriers.

FISCAL FREEDOM — 83%

Moldova's tax rates have been gradually reduced over the years. The top income tax rate is 20 percent, and the top corporate tax rate is 15 percent. Other taxes include a value-added tax (VAT), an advertising tax, and a vehicle tax. In the most recent year, overall tax revenue as a percentage of GDP was 32.8 percent.

GOVERNMENT SIZE — 56.9%

Total government expenditures, including consumption and transfer payments, are moderate. In the most recent year, government spending equaled 37.9 percent of GDP. Privatization has become sluggish. The government retains considerable ownership in companies like MoldTelecom and electricity generators. The privatization law expired early in 2007, and a new law has not been enacted.

MONETARY FREEDOM — 67.6%

Inflation is relatively high, averaging 12.5 percent between 2004 and 2006. Relatively high and unstable prices explain most of the monetary freedom score. The government has phased out most price controls and many subsidies but still influences prices through numerous state-owned enterprises and utilities, including electricity and energy. An additional 10 percentage points is deducted from Moldova's monetary freedom score to account for policies that distort domestic prices.

INVESTMENT FREEDOM — 30%

Foreign and domestic capital are legally equal. Foreign investment that does not conflict with national security interests, anti-monopoly legislation, environmental protection norms, public health, and public order is welcome. Non-Moldovans may not buy agricultural and forestry land. There is no screening of investment. Progress is being made toward a more transparent and less regulatory investment climate, and a national development plan scheduled to take effect in 2008 is aimed at further improving FDI conditions and ensuring macroeconomic stability. Residents and non-residents may hold foreign exchange accounts, subject to certain approvals. Some payments and transfers require National Bank of Moldova approval. Nearly all capital transactions require approval by or registration with the National Bank of Moldova.

FINANCIAL FREEDOM — 50%

Moldova's small financial system, wholly state-controlled as recently as the 1990s, has been undergoing restructuring and consolidation. Banking supervision and regulation meet most international standards, and new regulation of the non-banking financial sectors is being implemented. There are 15 commercial banks, including two foreign bank branches. The top five banks control 66 percent of assets. The government holds shares in two banks and has announced its intention to sell its majority stake in Banca de Economii, one of the largest banks. Foreign capital in banking has been increasing steadily. The insurance market was opened to foreign competition in mid-1999 and consisted of 33 insurance operators by the end of 2006. Two companies (one foreign) control more than 45 percent of premiums. Capital markets are immature, and the stock market is very small.

PROPERTY RIGHTS — 50%

The judiciary has been improved but is still subject to executive influence. Delays in salary payments make it difficult for judges to remain independent from outside influence and free from corruption. Moldova adheres to key international agreements on intellectual property rights, although enforcement of IPR laws is sometimes weak.

FREEDOM FROM CORRUPTION — 32%

Corruption is perceived as widespread. Moldova ranks 79th out of 163 countries in Transparency International's Corruption Perceptions Index for 2006. Moldova is trying to adopt European anti-corruption and anti-crime standards and to participate in international cooperation and evaluation mechanisms.

LABOR FREEDOM — 66.6%

Relatively flexible employment regulations can hamper rather than enhance employment opportunities and productivity growth. The non-salary cost of employing a worker is high, and dismissing a redundant employee is not easy. Restrictions on the number of work hours can be rigid.

MONGOLIA

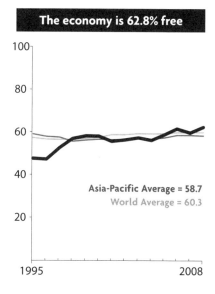

Mongolia's economy is 62.8 percent free, according to our 2008 assessment, which makes it the world's 62nd freest economy. Its overall score is 3 percentage points higher than last year, mainly reflecting improved scores in four of the 10 economic freedoms. Mongolia is ranked 10th out of 30 countries in the Asia–Pacific region, and its overall score is slightly higher than the regional average.

Mongolia enjoys high levels of fiscal freedom, financial freedom, business freedom, investment freedom, and trade freedom. The top income and corporate tax rates are moderate. The average tariff rate is also moderate, although non-tariff barriers (such as customs corruption) have undermined the government's policy of liberalization. Although commercial registration and licensing are efficient, closing a business takes longer than it should. Inflation is fairly high, but the government has eliminated almost all of its price supports and market distortions.

Mongolia has very weak property rights and freedom from corruption. The judicial protection of property rights is still weak, and judges often do not validate previously agreed contracts. The judiciary is further hampered by corruption.

BACKGROUND: Democratic Mongolia achieved its independence from the former Soviet Union in 1990. Since then, political liberalization and economic reform have progressed gradually if unevenly. Wedged between Russia and China, Mongolia is a primary transportation conduit for trade between its two giant neighbors, which account for 40 percent of its foreign direct investment. Livestock herding employs a majority of the population, but the mining industry attracts the bulk of foreign direct investment.

How Do We Measure Economic Freedom? See Chapter 4 (page 39) for an explanation of the methodology or visit the *Index* Web site at *heritage.org/index*.

The economy is 62.8% free

Asia-Pacific Average = 58.7
World Average = 60.3

1995 — 2008

QUICK FACTS

Population: 2.6 million

GDP (PPP): $5.4 billion
6.6% growth in 2005
6.9% 5-yr. comp. ann. growth
$2,107 per capita

Unemployment: 3.3%

Inflation (CPI): 12.1%

FDI (net flow): $182.0 million

Official Development Assistance:
Multilateral: $66.2 million
Bilateral: $167.9 million (10.8% from the U.S.)

External Debt: $1.3 billion

Exports: $1.5 billion
Primarily copper, apparel, livestock, animal products, cashmere, wool, hides, fluorspar, other nonferrous metals

Imports: $1.6 billion
Primarily machinery and equipment, fuel, cars, food products, industrial consumer goods, chemicals, building materials
2005 data unless otherwise noted.

MONGOLIA'S TEN ECONOMIC FREEDOMS

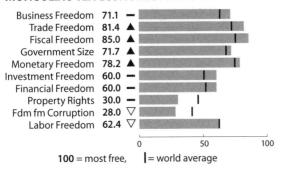

Business Freedom	71.1	—
Trade Freedom	81.4	▲
Fiscal Freedom	85.0	▲
Government Size	71.7	▲
Monetary Freedom	78.2	▲
Investment Freedom	60.0	—
Financial Freedom	60.0	—
Property Rights	30.0	—
Fdm fm Corruption	28.0	▽
Labor Freedom	62.4	▽

100 = most free, | = world average

BUSINESS FREEDOM — *71.1%*

The overall freedom to start, operate, and close a business is relatively well protected by Mongolia's regulatory environment. Starting a business takes an average of 20 days, compared to the world average of 43 days. Obtaining a business license takes less than the world average of 234 days and is not costly. Bankruptcy proceedings can be lengthy.

TRADE FREEDOM — *81.4%*

Mongolia's average tariff rate was 4.3 percent in 2005. Liberalization is progressing, but import and export restrictions, import and export taxes, and non-transparent, inefficient, and corrupt customs implementation add to the cost of trade. An additional 10 percentage points is deducted from Mongolia's trade freedom score to account for non-tariff barriers.

FISCAL FREEDOM— *85%*

Under a comprehensive tax reform implemented in 2006, the individual income tax rate is a flat 10 percent, and the top corporate tax rate is 25 percent, down from 30 percent. Other taxes include a value-added tax (VAT), a property tax, and a dividend tax. In the most recent year, overall tax revenue as a percentage of GDP was 27.8 percent.

GOVERNMENT SIZE — *71.7%*

Total government expenditures, including consumption and transfer payments, are moderate. Government spending has been reduced considerably and in the most recent year equaled 30.7 percent of GDP. The government sold 14 state-owned enterprises in 2006.

MONETARY FREEDOM — *78.2%*

Inflation is relatively high, averaging 7 percent between 2004 and 2006. Relatively unstable prices explain most of the monetary freedom score. Although most price controls and many subsidies have been phased out, the government influences prices through the public sector or through regulation, sometimes intervenes in the market to stabilize commodity prices, and still controls air fares and fuel prices. An additional 5 percentage points is deducted from Mongolia's monetary freedom score to account for policies that distort domestic prices.

INVESTMENT FREEDOM — *60%*

Foreign and domestic capital are legally equal. Mongolia's laws support foreign direct investment in all sectors and businesses at whatever levels investors want, and investment is not screened. A major mining project with Canadian investors is expected to raise FDI significantly. Regulation is relatively straightforward, but individual agencies often hinder investment in some sectors. Domestic and foreign investors report similar abuses of inspections, permits, and licenses. Foreigners may own land but must register it. Residents and non-residents may hold foreign exchange accounts, subject to minimal restrictions. There are no restrictions on payments and transfers. Most credit and loan operations must be registered with the central bank.

FINANCIAL FREEDOM — *60%*

Mongolia's small financial system is dominated by banking. The Asian Development Bank invested $10 million in 2005 to help modernize the financial sector. The government imposes very few restraints on the flow of capital, and foreign investors may freely tap domestic capital markets. There were 16 commercial banks in 2006. Two banks were foreign-owned. One bank was wholly state-owned, and another was partly state-owned. State shares in banks have been reduced. Supervision is insufficient, and regulation is poorly enforced. Non-performing loans are a problem, and several banks are believed to be insolvent. The four largest banks control over 60 percent of assets. There are about six dozen smaller, largely unregulated non-bank lending institutions and 570 savings and credit unions. The government is refining regulation of the insurance sector, which included 16 companies in 2006. Capital markets are small and limited. The stock market was set up to facilitate privatization of state-owned enterprises but now functions as a regular exchange.

PROPERTY RIGHTS — *30%*

The enforcement of laws protecting private property is weak. Judges generally do not understand such commercial principles as the sanctity of contracts and regularly ignore the terms of contracts in their decisions. The legal system does recognize the concept of collaterized assets. There is no mortgage law. Pirated optical media are readily available and subject to spotty enforcement.

FREEDOM FROM CORRUPTION — *28%*

Corruption is perceived as widespread. Mongolia ranks 99th out of 163 countries in Transparency International's Corruption Perceptions Index for 2006. Corruption is both significant and growing. Allegations of public-sector corruption include cases involving cabinet-level officials.

LABOR FREEDOM — *62.4%*

Restrictive regulations impede employment opportunities and productivity growth. The non-salary cost of employing a worker can be high, but dismissing a redundant employee is costless. Regulations related to the number of work hours are not flexible.

MONTENEGRO

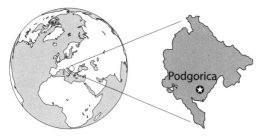

Podgorica

Rank: Not Ranked

Regional Rank: Not Ranked

Montenegro is a newly formed country and will receive an economic freedom score and ranking in future years when more reliable international data become available. This year, the country is being assessed for the first time in the *Index*.

BACKGROUND: Following a public referendum on May 21, 2006, the Republic of Montenegro officially declared its independence from Serbia on June 3, 2006. It has since become a member of the Organization for Security and Co-operation in Europe, the United Nations, the International Monetary Fund, the World Bank Group, and the Council of Europe. It is currently pursuing membership in the World Trade Organization, the European Union, and NATO. Having gradually pulled away from Serbia in the past decade, Montenegro introduced significant privatization and started using the German mark and then (despite not being an official member of the euro zone) the euro as its legal tender. Ongoing problems of particular importance include unemployment and the black market.

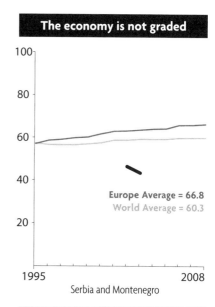

The economy is not graded

Europe Average = 66.8
World Average = 60.3

1995 — 2008
Serbia and Montenegro

QUICK FACTS

Population: 684,736

GDP (PPP): $3.4 billion
4.1% growth in 2005
5-r. comp. ann. growth n/a

$3,800 per capita

Unemployment: 27.7%

Inflation (CPI): 3.4%

FDI (net flow): n/a

Official Development Assistance:
Multilateral: None
Bilateral: None

External Debt: n/a

Exports: n/a
Primarily raw materials (except fuel), machinery and transport equipment, mineral fuels and lubricants

Imports: n/a
Primarily machinery, transport equipment, manufactures, food

2005 data unless otherwise noted.

How Do We Measure Economic Freedom? See Chapter 4 (page 39) for an explanation of the methodology or visit the *Index* Web site at *heritage.org/index*.

BUSINESS FREEDOM — NOT GRADED

Starting a business takes an average of 24 days, compared to the world average of 43 days. Obtaining a business license involves 19 procedures, which is the world average. Regulations can be inconsistent and non-transparent, and fees related to completing the relevant procedures are high.

TRADE FREEDOM — NOT GRADED

Progress has been made toward liberalizing the trade regime, but high tariffs, weak implementation of non-transparent standards and regulations, and corruption still add to the cost of trade. If Montenegro were graded, an additional 10 percentage points would be deducted from its trade freedom score to account for non-tariff barriers.

FISCAL FREEDOM — NOT GRADED

Montenegro enjoys competitive flat tax rates. The parliament passed a flat tax rate of 15 percent on individual income late in 2006. The corporate tax rate is a flat 9 percent. There is also a value-added tax (VAT), which Montenegro introduced in 2003.

GOVERNMENT SIZE — NOT GRADED

Total government expenditures, including consumption and transfer payments, are high. In the most recent year, government spending was estimated to be about 40.7 percent of GDP.

MONETARY FREEDOM — NOT GRADED

Inflation is low, averaging 1.8 percent between 2004 and 2006. State subsidies and price supports have been eliminated for most goods, and prices are determined by market forces. However, the government influences prices through state-owned enterprises; retains the right to control the prices of certain basic products; and regulates utility, energy, and transportation prices. If Montenegro were graded, an additional 10 percentage points would be deducted from its monetary freedom score to account for policies that distort domestic prices.

INVESTMENT FREEDOM — NOT GRADED

Foreign and domestic capital are equal. Montenegro's Foreign Investment Law incorporates protections like profit repatriation, loosened restrictions, and guarantees against expropriation. However, the business environment is still weak. As a new state, Montenegro faces challenges like excessive bureaucracy, red tape, and corruption. Privatization recently stalled with a halt in the sale of a major energy center, Pljevlja. Privatization of telecommunications and aluminum had contributed to a significant increase in foreign investment, as well as investments in real estate. Residents and non-residents may hold foreign exchange accounts, subject to central bank permission or conditions. Payments and transfers are subject to certain restrictions, and most capital transactions are subject to controls.

FINANCIAL FREEDOM — NOT GRADED

Montenegro's capital markets, though small and under-developed, are becoming more competitive. Montenegro joined the IMF and World Bank at the beginning of January 2007. Foreign banks' participation and investment are significant. There were 13 banks operating in Montenegro as of October 2006, almost all with private ownership. The government privatized the last bank with direct majority state ownership in 2005, selling its majority stake in Podgorica, the country's third-largest bank, to a French investor. A Hungarian bank purchased Crnogorska Komercijalna Banka, the dominant bank, in mid-2006. Growing competition has not yet significantly pushed down credit prices, which remain fairly high. Montenegro's securities sector is small, with its two stock exchanges playing only a small role as a financial tool.

PROPERTY RIGHTS — NOT GRADED

The constitution serves as the foundation of the legal system and creates an independent judiciary. Historically, the judicial system has been inefficient; judges are poorly trained. Sales of pirated optical media (DVDs, CDs, and software) and counterfeit trademarked goods (particularly sneakers and clothing) are fairly widespread. Procedures for enforcement of intellectual property rights are governed by recently enacted Laws on Civil Procedures.

FREEDOM FROM CORRUPTION — NOT GRADED

There is a widespread perception of government corruption in Montenegro, particularly in the executive and judicial branches and especially with regard to the privatization of state-owned firms. Conflict-of-interest legislation requiring the disclosure of government officials' salaries and property has not been fully implemented, and many officials refuse to comply. Organized crime, especially the smuggling of gasoline and cigarettes, has long been present in Montenegro.

LABOR FREEDOM — NOT GRADED

The non-salary cost of employing a worker can be high, but dismissing a redundant employee is not burdensome. Regulations related to the number of work hours can be rigid. Overall, the rigidity of employment creates a risk aversion for companies that would otherwise hire more people and grow.

MOROCCO

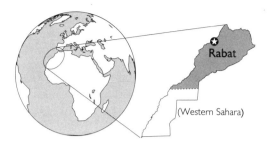

Rabat

(Western Sahara)

Rank: 98

Regional Rank: 12 of 17

Morocco's economy is 56.4 percent free, according to our 2008 assessment, which makes it the world's 98th freest economy. Its overall score is 0.8 percentage point lower than last year, partially reflecting deteriorated monetary freedom. Morocco is ranked 12th out of 17 countries in the Middle East/North Africa region, and its overall score is slightly lower than the regional average.

Morocco scores exceptionally well relative to the world average in two areas: business freedom and investment freedom. Inflation is low, but the kingdom still uses price supports for some goods. Despite regulatory obstacles, business formation is generally efficient. Foreign investment receives national treatment, but Morocco's bureaucracy provides its own *de facto* deterrent to foreign capital.

Morocco suffers from weak trade freedom, fiscal freedom, financial freedom, labor freedom, property rights, and freedom from corruption. The average tariff rate is high, and bureaucratic practices are opaque. The judiciary and the financial sector are inefficient and subject to substantial corruption (at least in the courts) and significant political interference from the king. The labor market is highly restrictive and one of the least free in the world.

BACKGROUND: The Arab constitutional monarchy of Morocco gained its independence from France in 1956 and became a close ally of the United States. King Mohammed VI has encouraged political and economic reform, the expansion of civil rights, and the elimination of corruption. Morocco has the world's largest phosphate reserves, a large tourist industry, and a growing manufacturing sector, but agriculture still accounts for about 20 percent of GDP and employs roughly 40 percent of the labor force. A free trade agreement between Morocco and the United States took effect in January 2006.

How Do We Measure Economic Freedom? See Chapter 4 (page 39) for an explanation of the methodology or visit the *Index* Web site at *heritage.org/index.*

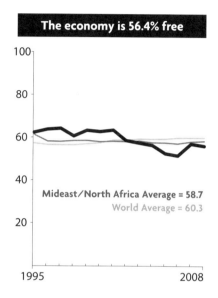

The economy is 56.4% free

Mideast/North Africa Average = 58.7
World Average = 60.3

1995   2008

QUICK FACTS

Population: 30.2 million

GDP (PPP): $137.4 billion
1.7% growth in 2005
3.7% 5-yr. comp. ann. growth
$4,555 per capita

Unemployment: 18.7%

Inflation (CPI): 1.0%

FDI (net flow): $2.8 billion

Official Development Assistance:
Multilateral: $318.3 million
Bilateral: $728.6 million (2.6% from the U.S.)

External Debt: $16.8 billion

Exports: $18.8 billion
Primarily clothing, fish, inorganic chemicals, transistors, crude minerals, fertilizers, petroleum products, fruits, vegetables

Imports: $22.7 billion
Primarily crude petroleum, textile fabric, telecommunications equipment, wheat, gas and electricity, transistors, plastics
2005 data unless otherwise noted.

MOROCCO'S TEN ECONOMIC FREEDOMS

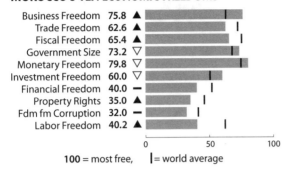

Business Freedom	75.8 ▲
Trade Freedom	62.6 ▲
Fiscal Freedom	65.4 ▲
Government Size	73.2 ▽
Monetary Freedom	79.8 ▽
Investment Freedom	60.0 ▽
Financial Freedom	40.0 —
Property Rights	35.0 ▲
Fdm fm Corruption	32.0 —
Labor Freedom	40.2 ▲

0   50   100

100 = most free, I = world average

BUSINESS FREEDOM — 75.8%

The overall freedom to start, operate, and close a business is relatively well protected by Morocco's regulatory environment. Starting a business takes less than half the world average of 43 days. Obtaining a business license takes less than the world average of 234 days. Bankruptcy proceedings are relatively easy and straightforward.

TRADE FREEDOM — 62.6%

Morocco's weighted average tariff rate was 13.7 percent in 2005. Prohibitive tariffs, inconsistent and opaque government procurement, non-transparent and arbitrary regulations and standards, import restrictions, service market access barriers, and weak enforcement of intellectual property rights add to the cost of trade. An additional 10 percentage points is deducted from Morocco's trade freedom score to account for non-tariff barriers.

FISCAL FREEDOM — 65.4%

In January 2007, the top income tax rate became 42 percent, down from 44 percent. The top corporate tax rate is 35 percent. Other taxes include a value-added tax (VAT) and a property tax. In the most recent year, overall tax revenue as a percentage of GDP was 21.8 percent.

GOVERNMENT SIZE — 73.2%

Total government expenditures, including consumption and transfer payments, are moderate. In the most recent year, government spending equaled 29.9 percent of GDP. The government has cut the public wage bill and trimmed subsidies to reduce spending.

MONETARY FREEDOM — 79.8%

Inflation is low, averaging 2.6 percent between 2004 and 2006. Relatively stable prices explain most of the monetary freedom score. Although price controls and subsidies are being phased out, the government influences prices through state-owned enterprises and utilities, including electricity; subsidizes fuel, health products, and educational supplies; and sets prices for staple commodities, including vegetable oil, sugar, flour, bread, and cereals. An additional 10 percentage points is deducted from Morocco's monetary freedom score to account for policies that distort domestic prices.

INVESTMENT FREEDOM — 60%

Foreign and locally owned investments are treated equally, and 100 percent foreign ownership is allowed in most sectors. Mining and ownership of agricultural land are not open to private investors. There is no screening requirement. The government has set up regional investment centers to decentralize and accelerate investment-related procedures. Incentives like free trade zones and cheaper land acquisition are available for some investments. New commercial courts have streamlined commercial law procedures. Residents and non-residents may hold foreign exchange accounts with some restrictions. Certain personal payments, transfer of interest, and travel payments are subject to approvals and requirements. Some capital transactions, including many capital and money market transactions and credit operations, require government approval.

FINANCIAL FREEDOM — 40%

Morocco's financial system is fairly well developed for the region but is still burdened by government influence, institutional weaknesses, poor supervision, and underdeveloped infrastructure. There are 17 commercial banks and 44 financing companies. Most private banks are partially owned by European banks. The state has declared its intention to privatize its large holdings in several banks. Several state-owned specialized banks together account for 43 percent of assets. The government still uses the banking system to influence domestic savings and finance government debt. Non-performing loans are a serious problem, particularly at publicly owned banks. The central bank has responded to some of these difficulties with measures involving risk assessment and claim reforms. Capital markets are relatively developed, with an ongoing campaign to increase modernization and transparency.

PROPERTY RIGHTS — 35%

The judiciary is influenced by the king and is slow to deal with cases, bankruptcy protection, and liquidation procedures or to enforce contracts. In recent years, strengthened property rights have encouraged a number of business start-ups. It remains to be seen whether new laws protecting intellectual property rights will be enforced effectively.

FREEDOM FROM CORRUPTION — 32%

Corruption is perceived as significant. Morocco ranks 79th out of 163 countries in Transparency International's Corruption Perceptions Index for 2006. Corruption exists in the executive, legislative, and (especially) judicial branches of government, and foreign firms have identified it as an obstacle to doing business.

LABOR FREEDOM — 40.2%

Restrictive employment regulations hinder employment opportunities and productivity growth. The non-salary cost of employing a worker is high, and the difficulty of hiring and laying off a worker creates a risk aversion for companies that would otherwise hire more people and grow. Morocco's labor freedom is among the lowest in the world.

MOZAMBIQUE

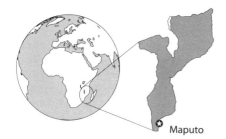

Maputo

Rank: 96

Regional Rank: 13 of 40

Mozambique's economy is 56.6 percent free, according to our 2008 assessment, which makes it the world's 96th freest economy. Its overall score is 0.7 percentage point higher than last year, partly reflecting the absence of meaningful reform. Mozambique is ranked 13th out of 40 countries in the sub-Saharan Africa region, and its overall score is slightly higher than the regional average.

Mozambique scores relatively well in government size and equals the world average in trade freedom, investment freedom, financial freedom, and monetary freedom. The top income and corporate tax rates are moderate, and overall tax revenue is low as a percentage of GDP. Inflation is fairly high, but the government does not generally distort market prices with subsidies.

Economic development has been hampered by weak labor freedom, property rights, freedom from corruption, and business freedom. The regulatory environment is a burden on business formation, most aspects of the labor market are inflexible, and judicial enforcement is subject to corruption and the political whims of the executive.

BACKGROUND: After Mozambique gained its independence in 1975, the Front for the Liberation of Mozambique (FRELIMO) established a one-party socialist state. One million people were killed in a 16-year civil war between FRELIMO and the Mozambican National Resistance (RENAMO) that ended in 1992. Mozambique held its first democratic elections in 1994 and since then has been a model for development and post-war recovery through economic liberalization, privatization, and stability. Economic growth averaged about 8 percent from 1994 to 2006, but the country remains very poor and needs additional reform, including a civil service overhaul and removal of regulatory barriers to business. Under President Armando Guebuza, inaugurated in 2005 after winning the 2004 election, labor reform and privatization have stalled. Over three-quarters of the population is engaged in small-scale agriculture. Infrastructure is poor, and HIV/AIDS is a serious problem.

How Do We Measure Economic Freedom? See Chapter 4 (page 39) for an explanation of the methodology or visit the *Index* Web site at *heritage.org/index*.

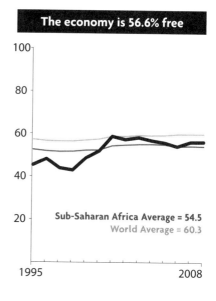

The economy is 56.6% free

Sub-Saharan Africa Average = 54.5
World Average = 60.3

1995 — 2008

QUICK FACTS

Population: 19.8 million

GDP (PPP): $24.6 billion
7.8% growth in 2005
7.9% 5-yr. comp. ann. growth
$1,242 per capita

Unemployment: 21.0% (1997 estimate)

Inflation (CPI): 6.4%

FDI (net flow): $108.0 million

Official Development Assistance:
Multilateral: $574.8 million
Bilateral: $784.1 million (12.2% from the U.S.)

External Debt: $5.1 billion

Exports: $2.1 billion
Primarily aluminum, prawns, cashews, cotton, sugar, citrus, timber, bulk electricity

Imports: $2.9 billion
Primarily machinery and equipment, vehicles, fuel, chemicals, metal products, foodstuffs, textiles

2005 data unless otherwise noted.

MOZAMBIQUE'S TEN ECONOMIC FREEDOMS

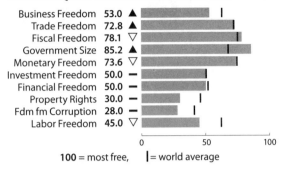

Business Freedom	53.0 ▲	
Trade Freedom	72.8 ▲	
Fiscal Freedom	78.1 ▽	
Government Size	85.2 ▲	
Monetary Freedom	73.6 ▽	
Investment Freedom	50.0 —	
Financial Freedom	50.0 —	
Property Rights	30.0 —	
Fdm fm Corruption	28.0 —	
Labor Freedom	45.0 ▽	

0   50   100

100 = most free, | = world average

BUSINESS FREEDOM — 53%

The overall freedom to start, operate, and close a business is restricted by Mozambique's regulatory environment. Starting a business takes an average of 29 days, compared to the world average of 43 days. Obtaining a business license takes more than the world average of 234 days, and fees are costly. Closing a business is difficult.

TRADE FREEDOM — 72.8%

Mozambique's weighted average tariff rate was 8.6 percent in 2005. Liberalization has progressed, but import restrictions, import taxes, import permits required for some goods, time-consuming and bureaucratic customs clearance, and corruption still add to the cost of trade. An additional 10 percentage points is deducted from Mozambique's trade freedom score to account for non-tariff barriers.

FISCAL FREEDOM — 78.1%

Mozambique has moderate tax rates. Both the top income tax rate and the top corporate tax rate are 32 percent. Other taxes include a value-added tax (VAT) and a tax on interest. In the most recent year, overall tax revenue as a percentage of GDP was 11.8 percent.

GOVERNMENT SIZE — 85.2%

Total government expenditures, including consumption and transfer payments, are moderate. In the most recent year, government spending equaled 22.2 percent of GDP. Privatization has transformed a state-dominated economy into one that is driven by the private sector, but progress has slowed.

MONETARY FREEDOM — 73.6%

Inflation is relatively high, averaging 11.5 percent between 2004 and 2006. Relatively unstable prices explain most of the monetary freedom score. The government influences prices through state-owned utilities, including electricity, telecommunications, ports, and transportation, and subsidizes passenger rail services. An additional 5 percentage points is deducted from Mozambique's monetary freedom score to account for policies that distort domestic prices.

INVESTMENT FREEDOM — 50%

Foreign and domestic capital are equal in most cases. Much of the economy is open to foreign investment, but outright private ownership of land is prohibited, and mining and management contracts are subject to specific performance requirements. All foreign and domestic investment must be approved. Larger investors receive far better bureaucratic service than do small and medium-size projects. Foreign investors have participated in Mozambique's fairly transparent privatization program, but major public utilities remain state-controlled. The judicial system is extremely slow. Mozambique allows repatriation of profits and retention of earned foreign exchange. Residents and non-residents may hold foreign exchange accounts. Payments and transfers are subject to maximum amounts, above which they must be approved by the central bank.

FINANCIAL FREEDOM — 50%

Mozambique's financial system has undergone liberalization since its near total nationalization in 1978 but remains small and dominated by banking. Supervision is insufficient. Non-performing loans led to a crisis in 2000–2001 but have been significantly reduced since then. In December 2006, there were nine commercial banks (all majority foreign-owned), one investment bank, two microfinance institutions, five credit and savings co-operatives, and three financial leasing companies. Banco Internacional de Moçambique, majority-owned by a Portuguese bank, is the largest bank and controls over 40 percent of total banking. The state retains shares in two large banks. Most banks concentrate their lending on large companies, but microfinance is expanding, and banking operations are reaching out to underserved areas. The small insurance sector is dominated by the state-owned insurance firm. Capital markets are very small, and the stock market mostly trades government debt.

PROPERTY RIGHTS — 30%

Property rights are weakly protected, and the judiciary is corrupt. There is a severe shortage of qualified legal personnel, and the backlog of cases is substantial. Enforcement of contracts and legal redress through the courts cannot be assured. Most commercial disputes are settled privately. Pirated and counterfeit copies of audio and videotapes, CDs/DVDs, software, and other goods are sold in Mozambique.

FREEDOM FROM CORRUPTION — 28%

Corruption is perceived as widespread. Mozambique ranks 99th out of 163 countries in Transparency International's Corruption Perceptions Index for 2006. Bribe-seeking by officials is endemic at every level. Frequent conflicts of interest between senior officials' public roles and private business interests are seldom investigated.

LABOR FREEDOM — 45%

Restrictive employment regulations hinder employment opportunities and productivity growth. The non-salary cost of employing a worker can be low, but the high cost of laying off a worker creates a risk aversion for companies that would otherwise hire more people and grow. Regulations on the number of work hours remain rigid.

NAMIBIA

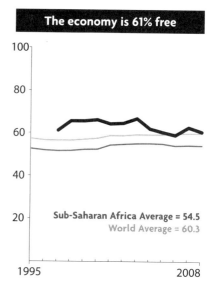

Windhoek

Namibia's economy is 61 percent free, according to our 2008 assessment, which makes it the world's 72nd freest economy. Its overall score is 2.1 percentage points lower than last year, reflecting worsened scores in six of the 10 economic freedoms. Namibia is ranked 6th out of 40 countries in the sub-Saharan Africa region, and its overall score is much higher than the regional average.

Namibia scores well in business freedom, trade freedom, and labor freedom. Starting a business takes longer than the world average, but licensing and bankruptcy procedures are simple. The average tariff rate is less than 1 percent. The labor market is highly flexible. Namibia's financial sector is small but developed for the region, and much of the banking industry is intertwined with South Africa's.

Investment freedom and property rights scores, however, are very low. Foreign investment is officially welcomed, but the government strongly encourages investors to form partnerships with local companies, and expropriation of white-owned farms is a serious deterrent. Corruption is not present to the degree found in the rest of the region.

BACKGROUND: Namibia became officially independent from South Africa in 1990, but the two countries remain closely linked, with over 80 percent of Namibia's imports originating in, and most exports going to, South Africa. Sam Nujoma, leader of the independence group SWAPO, was president from 1990 until 2005, when he was succeeded by Hifikepunye Pohamba. Namibia is rich in minerals, including uranium, diamonds, lead, silver, tin, tungsten, and zinc. Parts of the economy are modern and well developed, but a majority of Namibians engage in subsistence agriculture and herding. Despite a "willing seller, willing buyer" land redistribution policy, commercial farmers are under increasing pressure to sell. The government opposes privatization, and its Black Economic Empowerment policy requires foreign investors to partner with local BEE firms or trusts.

How Do We Measure Economic Freedom? See Chapter 4 (page 39) for an explanation of the methodology or visit the *Index* Web site at *heritage.org/index*.

The economy is 61% free

Sub-Saharan Africa Average = 54.5
World Average = 60.3

1995 — 2008

QUICK FACTS

Population: 2 million

GDP (PPP): $15.4 billion
4.2% growth in 2005
5.2% 5-yr. comp. ann. growth
$7,586 per capita

Unemployment: 5.3%

Inflation (CPI): 2.3%

FDI (net flow): $361.0 million

Official Development Assistance:
Multilateral: $35.8 million
Bilateral: $102.0 million (38.7% from the U.S.)

External Debt: $887.0 million

Exports: $2.3 billion (2004)
Primarily diamonds, copper, gold, zinc, lead, uranium, cattle, processed fish, karakul skins

Imports: $2.5 billion (2004)
Primarily foodstuffs, petroleum products and fuel, machinery and equipment, chemicals

2005 data unless otherwise noted.

NAMIBIA'S TEN ECONOMIC FREEDOMS

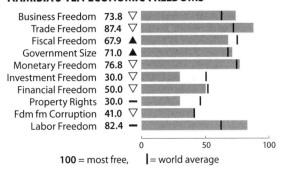

Business Freedom	73.8 ▽	
Trade Freedom	87.4 ▽	
Fiscal Freedom	67.9 ▲	
Government Size	71.0 ▲	
Monetary Freedom	76.8 ▽	
Investment Freedom	30.0 ▽	
Financial Freedom	50.0 ▽	
Property Rights	30.0 —	
Fdm fm Corruption	41.0 ▽	
Labor Freedom	82.4 —	

0   50   100

100 = most free,   ❙ = world average

BUSINESS FREEDOM — 73.8%
The overall freedom to start, operate, and close a business is relatively well protected by Namibia's regulatory environment. Starting a business takes an average of 99 days, compared to the world average of 43 days. Obtaining a business license takes less than the world average of 19 procedures and 234 days. Closing a business is relatively easy and not costly.

TRADE FREEDOM — 87.4%
Namibia's weighted average tariff rate was 1.3 percent in 2005. The trade regime is relatively open, but non-automatic import licensing regulations, import restrictions, and weak enforcement of intellectual property rights add to the cost of trade. An additional 10 percentage points is deducted from Namibia's trade freedom score to account for non-tariff barriers.

FISCAL FREEDOM — 67.9%
Namibia has burdensome tax rates. Both the top income tax rate and the top corporate tax rate are 35 percent. Other taxes include a value-added tax (VAT), a property transfer tax, and a vehicle tax. In the most recent year, overall tax revenue as a percentage of GDP was 27.6 percent.

GOVERNMENT SIZE — 71%
Total government expenditures, including consumption and transfer payments, are moderate. In the most recent year, government spending equaled 31.1 percent of GDP. Better spending management has helped to reduce the budget deficit to under 5 percent of GDP.

MONETARY FREEDOM — 76.8%
Inflation is relatively high, averaging 4.3 percent between 2004 and 2006. Relatively unstable prices explain most of the monetary freedom score. The government sets the prices of fuel products; influences prices through state-owned enterprises and utilities, including electricity, telecommunications, water, and transportation services; determines guideline prices for maize; and subsidizes agricultural production. An additional 10 percentage points is deducted from Namibia's monetary freedom score to account for policies that distort domestic prices.

INVESTMENT FREEDOM — 30%
National treatment is guaranteed for most sectors. For-eign-owned and non-productive farms are targets of land reform. Foreign investors are strongly encouraged to form partnerships with local businesses under the Black Economic Empowerment policy. Incentives like tax holidays are offered in Export Processing Zones, but this did not stop the largest foreign investment from announcing its closure in 2006. The government has halted privatization, declaring its intent to focus on commercialization and better management of state-run companies. Companies that are 75 percent or more foreign-owned are subject to exchange controls. Residents may hold foreign exchange accounts subject to prior approval and some restrictions. Non-residents may hold foreign currency accounts in certain areas. Capital transactions, transfers, and payments are subject to various restrictions. Investments abroad by residents are also restricted.

FINANCIAL FREEDOM — 50%
Namibia's small but sound financial sector is closely tied to South Africa's. There were four commercial banks at the end of 2005, all at least partly foreign-owned, and two asset management companies. The government owns the Agricultural Bank of Namibia, the Development Bank of Namibia, and the National Housing Enterprise and offers subsidized credits for subsistence farmers. There were eight life insurers in 2005. A 1995 law stating that at least 35 percent of funds received from the life insurance and pension sector must be invested in Namibian assets was altered in 2006 to lower the cap to 10 percent in dual-listed firms and 5 percent in unlisted Namibian companies. The Namibian Stock Exchange listed 27 companies at the end of 2005, mainly dual-listed with the South African exchange.

PROPERTY RIGHTS — 30%
Expropriating white-owned land is official policy. The government expropriated three large farms at the end of 2005 and by mid-2006 had begun to offer the land for resettlement. The lack of qualified magistrates, other court officials, and private attorneys causes a serious backlog of cases. Namibia lacks adequate mechanisms to address piracy and copyright violations.

FREEDOM FROM CORRUPTION — 41%
Corruption is perceived as significant. Namibia ranks 55th out of 163 countries in Transparency International's Corruption Perceptions Index for 2006. Despite efforts by the Anti-Corruption Commission, Office of the Ombudsman, and Office of the Auditor General, public corruption remains a problem.

LABOR FREEDOM — 82.4%
Flexible employment regulations enhance employment opportunities and productivity growth. The non-salary cost of employing a worker is very low, and dismissing a redundant employee is costless. Restrictions on the number of work hours are moderately flexible. Namibia's level of labor freedom is one of the world's highest.

NEPAL

Kathmandu

N epal's economy is 54.7 percent free, according to our
2008 assessment, which makes it the world's 112th free-
est economy. Its overall score is 0.4 percentage point lower
than last year. Nepal is ranked 19th out of 30 countries in
the Asia–Pacific region, and its overall score is lower than
the regional average.

Nepal enjoys high scores in fiscal freedom, government
size, and monetary freedom. Both the top income tax rate
and the top corporate tax rate are moderate, and overall
tax revenue is low as a percentage of GDP. Government
expenditures are also low. The government is working to
eliminate price controls.

As a developing nation with widespread civil unrest, Nepal
faces significant challenges. Investment freedom, financial freedom, trade freedom, property rights, and freedom
from corruption are weak. There are many restrictions on
foreign investment that put much of Nepal's economy off-
limits to foreign capital. These regulations are enforced
by an inefficient and corrupt bureaucracy. Property rights
are not secured by the judiciary, which is also subject to
substantial corruption and political influence.

BACKGROUND: Nepal's King Gyanendra relinquished the
throne and ceded power to a seven-party interim government in April 2006 in the face of pro-democracy street protests. The transition to a new government, which includes
negotiations between Maoist rebels and the country's
political parties, has been shaky. Against this backdrop,
economic development has stalled. Nepal attracts very
little foreign direct investment; its main industries are
agriculture and services.

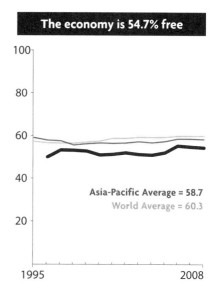

The economy is 54.7% free

Asia-Pacific Average = 58.7
World Average = 60.3

1995 — 2008

QUICK FACTS

Population: 27.1 million

GDP (PPP): $42.1 billion
2.7% growth in 2005
2.3% 5-yr. comp. ann. growth
$1,550 per capita

Unemployment: 42.0% (2004 estimate)

Inflation (CPI): 4.5%

FDI (net flow): $108.0 million

Official Development Assistance:
Multilateral: $139.5 million
Bilateral: $387.5 million (14.1% from the
U.S.)

External Debt: $3.3 billion

Exports: $1.3 billion
Primarily carpets, clothing, leather
goods, jute goods, grain

Imports: $2.7 billion
Primarily gold, machinery and equipment, petroleum products, fertilizer

2005 data unless otherwise noted.

How Do We Measure Economic Freedom? See Chapter
4 (page 39) for an explanation of the methodology or
visit the *Index* Web site at *heritage.org/index.*

NEPAL'S TEN ECONOMIC FREEDOMS

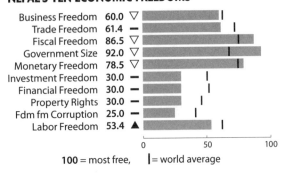

Business Freedom	60.0 ▽
Trade Freedom	61.4 —
Fiscal Freedom	86.5 ▽
Government Size	92.0 ▽
Monetary Freedom	78.5 ▽
Investment Freedom	30.0 —
Financial Freedom	30.0 —
Property Rights	30.0 —
Fdm fm Corruption	25.0 —
Labor Freedom	53.4 ▲

0   50   100

100 = most free, **❚ = world average**

BUSINESS FREEDOM — 60%

The overall freedom to start, operate, and close a business is limited by Nepal's regulatory environment. Starting a business takes an average of 31 days, compared to the world average of 43 days. Obtaining a business license takes more than the world average of 234 days. Bankruptcy proceedings are not straightforward and can be prolonged.

TRADE FREEDOM — 61.4%

Nepal's weighted average tariff rate was 14.3 percent in 2005. Nepal has one of the region's more open economies and continues to implement new reforms, but import bans, service market access barriers, import taxes, non-transparent regulations, and customs corruption add to the cost of trade. An additional 10 percentage points is deducted from Nepal's trade freedom score to account for non-tariff barriers.

FISCAL FREEDOM — 86.5%

Nepal has moderate tax rates. Both the top income tax rate and the top corporate tax rate are 25 percent. Other taxes include a value-added tax (VAT) and a property tax. In the most recent year, overall tax revenue as a percentage of GDP was 10.2 percent.

GOVERNMENT SIZE — 92%

Total government expenditures, including consumption and transfer payments, are low. In the most recent year, government spending equaled 16.3 percent of GDP. Procedural problems and weak political will have impeded the privatization of state-owned enterprises.

MONETARY FREEDOM — 78.5%

Inflation is relatively high, averaging 6.8 percent between 2004 and 2006. Relatively unstable prices explain most of the monetary freedom score. While most price controls have been eliminated, the government regulates the prices of petroleum products and telecommunications services and subsidizes companies in strategic sectors. An additional 5 percentage points is deducted from Nepal's monetary freedom score to account for policies that distort domestic prices.

INVESTMENT FREEDOM — 30%

Foreign ownership is permitted in such sectors as business and management consulting, accounting, engineer-ing, legal services, alcohol and cigarette production, travel and trekking agencies, telecommunications, civil aviation, and retail sales. Investment in defense is not allowed, but 100 percent foreign-owned companies are allowed in certain areas. Foreign investors complain about complex and opaque government procedures, as well as poor infrastructure, legal inconsistency, and political unrest. Privatization favors Nepalese investors if two proposals are equal. Residents may hold foreign exchange accounts in specific instances. Most non-residents may hold foreign exchange accounts. Most payments and transfers are subject to prior approval by the government. There are restrictions on most capital transactions, and all real estate transactions are subject to controls.

FINANCIAL FREEDOM — 30%

Nepal's financial system is dominated by banking and strongly influenced by the government. Financial supervision is insufficient, and anti-fraud efforts are lacking. Regulations are not transparent and fall short of international standards. In mid-2006, there were 18 commercial banks, 28 development banks, 67 finance companies, and 11 other development banks of a different category. The government owns one commercial bank and 40 percent of another. Government-controlled banks account for approximately 60 percent of lending and 50 percent of deposits. The central bank aims by 2008 to phase out forced credit activities whereby banks must lend a certain amount to government-designated projects. Foreign banks may own up to two-thirds of a joint venture but may not open a branch. There were 20 insurance companies in early 2006, of which three were foreign and the largest is majority-owned by the government. Capital markets are weak, and trading on the government-owned stock exchange is moribund.

PROPERTY RIGHTS — 30%

Nepal's judicial system suffers from corruption and inefficiency. Lower-level courts are vulnerable to political pressure, and bribery of judges and court staff is endemic. Weak protection of intellectual property rights has led to substantial levels of copyright piracy of optical media.

FREEDOM FROM CORRUPTION — 25%

Corruption is perceived as widespread. Nepal ranks 121st out of 163 countries in Transparency International's Corruption Perceptions Index for 2006. Foreign investors have identified corruption as an obstacle to maintaining and expanding direct investment, and there are frequent allegations of official corruption in the distribution of permits and approvals, the procurement of goods and services, and the award of contracts.

LABOR FREEDOM — 53.4%

Restrictive employment regulations impede employment opportunities and productivity growth. The non-salary cost of employing a worker is low, but the difficulty of laying off a worker creates a risk aversion for companies that would otherwise hire more people and grow.

THE NETHERLANDS

Amsterdam

The economy of the Netherlands is 76.8 percent free, according to our 2008 assessment, which makes it the world's 13th freest economy. Its overall score is 1.9 percentage points higher than last year, reflecting improved scores in five of the 10 economic freedoms. The Netherlands is ranked 6th out of 41 countries in the European region, and its overall score is much higher than the regional average.

The Netherlands enjoys very high levels of investment freedom, trade freedom, financial freedom, property rights, business freedom, freedom from corruption, and monetary freedom. The average tariff rate is low; non-tariff barriers include European Union subsidies. Business regulation is efficient. Virtually all commercial operations are simple and transparent. Inflation is low, and foreign investment is actively promoted. The financial sector is highly developed and has been a European banking hub for centuries. The judiciary, independent of politics and free of corruption, has an exemplary ability to protect property rights.

The Netherlands could do better in government size and fiscal freedom. Total government spending is almost half of GDP. The government has been working to liberalize the labor market, but impediments to reform, such as extensive unemployment benefits, still exist.

BACKGROUND: The Kingdom of the Netherlands is a wealthy country and home to a number of prominent multinational companies. Unemployment is low, and there are few restrictions on foreign direct investment. Rotterdam is by far Europe's largest port in terms of cargo tonnage and one of the largest ports in the world. A robust, modern agricultural sector exports high-quality foodstuffs, and other exports include metal manufactures and chemicals. As a founding member of the European Union, a key architect of the Treaty of Amsterdam, and an enthusiastic supporter of further European integration, the Netherlands stunned its fellow EU members by decisively rejecting the draft European Constitution in June 2005.

How Do We Measure Economic Freedom? See Chapter 4 (page 39) for an explanation of the methodology or visit the *Index* Web site at *heritage.org/index.*

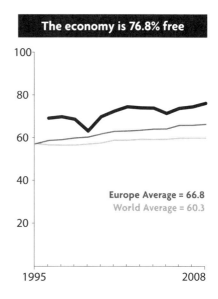

The economy is 76.8% free

Europe Average = 66.8
World Average = 60.3

1995 — 2008

QUICK FACTS

Population: 16.3 million

GDP (PPP): $533.4 billion
1.5% growth in 2005
1.0% 5-yr. comp. ann. growth
$32,684 per capita

Unemployment: 6.6%

Inflation (CPI): 1.5%

FDI (net flow): −$75.8 billion

Official Development Assistance:
Multilateral: None
Bilateral: None

External Debt: $1.9 trillion

Exports: $427.9 billion
Primarily machinery and equipment, chemicals, fuels, foodstuffs

Imports: $374.7 billion
Primarily machinery and transport equipment, chemicals, fuels, foodstuffs, clothing

2005 data unless otherwise noted.

THE NETHERLANDS' TEN ECONOMIC FREEDOMS

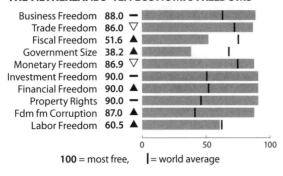

Business Freedom	88.0	▬
Trade Freedom	86.0	▽
Fiscal Freedom	51.6	▲
Government Size	38.2	▲
Monetary Freedom	86.9	▽
Investment Freedom	90.0	▬
Financial Freedom	90.0	▲
Property Rights	90.0	▬
Fdm fm Corruption	87.0	▲
Labor Freedom	60.5	▲

0   50   100

100 = most free, ▍ = world average

BUSINESS FREEDOM — 88%
The overall freedom to start, operate, and close a business is protected by the Netherlands' regulatory environment. Starting a business takes an average of 10 days, compared to the world average of 43 days. Obtaining a business license takes less than the world average of 19 procedures and 234 days. Closing a business is easy.

TRADE FREEDOM — 86%
The Netherlands' trade policy is the same as those of other members of the European Union. The common EU weighted average tariff rate was 2 percent in 2005. Non-tariff barriers reflected in EU policy include agricultural and manufacturing subsidies, import restrictions for some goods and services, market access restrictions in some service sectors, non-transparent and restrictive regulations and standards, and inconsistent customs administration across EU members. Supplementary biotechnology and pharmaceuticals rules exceed EU policy. Consequently, an additional 10 percentage points is deducted from the Netherlands' trade freedom score.

FISCAL FREEDOM — 51.6%
The Netherlands has high income tax rates and moderate corporate tax rates. The top income tax rate is 52 percent, and the top corporate tax rate was reduced to 25.5 percent effective January 2007. Other taxes include a value-added tax (VAT), a tax on insurance contracts, and a real estate tax. In the most recent year, overall tax revenue as a percentage of GDP was 38.2 percent.

GOVERNMENT SIZE — 38.2%
Total government expenditures, including consumption and transfer payments, are high. In the most recent year, government spending equaled 45.4 percent of GDP. Efforts to reform welfare spending have led to an improved budget balance.

MONETARY FREEDOM — 86.9%
The Netherlands is a member of the euro zone. Inflation is low, averaging 1.6 percent between 2004 and 2006. Relatively stable prices explain most of the monetary freedom score. As a participant in the EU's Common Agricultural Policy, the government subsidizes agricultural production, distorting the prices of agricultural products. The government also regulates energy prices, pharmaceutical prices,

and housing rents. An additional 5 percentage points is deducted from the Netherlands' monetary freedom score to account for these policies.

INVESTMENT FREEDOM — 90%
The Netherlands promotes foreign investment, except in railways, the national airport, and public broadcasting, with some of the world's most liberal policies, including fact-finding trips and consulting services. There is no screening, 100 percent foreign ownership is allowed in areas where foreign investment is permitted, and foreign investors receive national treatment. Commercial laws are straightforward. Environmental restrictions are tight, and restrictive changes in EU policy may dictate Dutch policies in the future. There are no restrictions on or barriers to current transfers, repatriation of profits, purchase of real estate, or access to foreign exchange. Capital transactions are not restricted but are subject to reporting requirements.

FINANCIAL FREEDOM — 90%
The financial system is subject to little government regulation. Dutch financial firms have an ever-expanding international reach and offer a variety of financial services, even real estate. Three conglomerates (ABN Amro, Rabobank, and ING Bank) account for about 75 percent of lending. There are few formal barriers to foreign banks, but foreign participation in retail banking is minimal due to intense competition and saturation. The government guarantees loans for small to medium-size enterprises that lack sufficient collateral. EU banks receive privileged treatment. Capital markets are well developed and partner with other international exchanges. Four Dutch companies account for almost 50 percent of total Amsterdam capitalization.

PROPERTY RIGHTS — 90%
Private property is secure, contracts are very secure, and the judiciary is sound. Citizens and foreigners purchasing real property receive equal treatment. Intellectual property rights are generally protected, but enforcement of anti-piracy laws and the piracy of optical disc media by organized criminal organizations are concerns.

FREEDOM FROM CORRUPTION — 87%
Corruption is perceived as minimal. The Netherlands ranks 9th out of 163 countries in Transparency International's Corruption Perceptions Index for 2006. Dutch law implementing the 1997 OECD anti-bribery convention makes corruption by Dutch businessmen in landing foreign contracts a penal offense, and bribes are no longer deductible for corporate tax purposes. Low-level law enforcement corruption is not believed to be widespread or systemic.

LABOR FREEDOM — 60.5%
Restrictive employment regulations hinder employment opportunities and productivity growth. The non-salary cost of employing a worker is high, and dismissing a redundant employee is relatively costly and difficult. Restrictions on the number of work hours are moderately flexible.

NEW ZEALAND

Wellington

New Zealand's economy is 80.2 percent free, according to our 2008 assessment, which makes it the world's 6th freest economy. Its overall score is 0.8 percentage point lower than last year, reflecting slightly lower scores in five of the 10 economic freedoms. New Zealand is ranked 4th out of 30 countries in the Asia–Pacific region, and its overall score is much higher than the regional average.

New Zealand rates highly in almost all areas of economic freedom but is most impressive in financial freedom, property rights, business freedom, labor freedom, and freedom from corruption. A globally competitive financial system based on market principles attracts many foreign banks, helped by low inflation and low tariff rates. A strong rule of law protects property rights, and New Zealand is one of the world's most corruption-free countries. Foreign and domestically owned businesses enjoy considerable flexibility in licensing, regulation, and employment practices.

New Zealand could do better in terms of government size and fiscal freedom. The top income tax rates, tax revenue, and government spending are fairly high, but the overall effect is eclipsed by the amount of economic freedom that has been established. New Zealand's economy is a global competitor and a regional model of economic freedom.

BACKGROUND: New Zealand is one of Asia's richest democracies. Following two decades of sound economic policies and structural reforms, it has transformed itself into a modern, flexible economy with one of the lowest unemployment rates of any member of the Organisation for Economic Co-operation and Development. Its export market is dominated by agricultural commodities. New Zealand relies heavily on international trade, and its openness has helped to boost exports of goods and services. Securing bilateral and regional free trade agreements is one of the government's major foreign policy goals, along with diversification of the economy into industrial goods.

How Do We Measure Economic Freedom? See Chapter 4 (page 39) for an explanation of the methodology or visit the *Index* Web site at *heritage.org/index*.

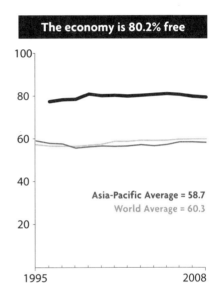

The economy is 80.2% free

Asia-Pacific Average = 58.7
World Average = 60.3

1995   2008

QUICK FACTS

Population: 4.1 million

GDP (PPP): $102.5 billion
2.1% growth in 2005
3.6% 5-yr. comp. ann. growth
$24,996 per capita

Unemployment: 3.7%

Inflation (CPI): 3.0%

FDI (net flow): $2.9 billion

Official Development Assistance:
Multilateral: None
Bilateral: None

External Debt: $47.0 billion

Exports: $30.5 billion
Primarily dairy products, meat, wood and wood products, fish, machinery

Imports: $32.9 billion
Primarily machinery and equipment, vehicles and aircraft, petroleum, electronics, textiles, plastics

2005 data unless otherwise noted.

NEW ZEALAND'S TEN ECONOMIC FREEDOMS

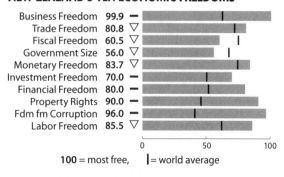

Business Freedom	99.9
Trade Freedom	80.8
Fiscal Freedom	60.5
Government Size	56.0
Monetary Freedom	83.7
Investment Freedom	70.0
Financial Freedom	80.0
Property Rights	90.0
Fdm fm Corruption	96.0
Labor Freedom	85.5

0   50   100

100 = most free, ❘ = world average

BUSINESS FREEDOM — 99.9%

The overall freedom to start, operate, and close a business is strongly protected by New Zealand's regulatory environment. Starting a business takes an average of 12 days, compared to the world average of 43 days. Obtaining a business license requires much less than the world average of 19 procedures and 234 days. Closing a business is very easy and straightforward.

TRADE FREEDOM — 80.8%

New Zealand's weighted average tariff rate was 4.6 percent in 2005. The trade regime is relatively open, but import restrictions, service market access barriers, import taxes and fees, restrictive sanitary and phytosanitary regulations, and issues involving the enforcement of intellectual property rights add to the cost of trade. An additional 10 percentage points is deducted from New Zealand's trade freedom score to account for non-tariff barriers.

FISCAL FREEDOM — 60.5%

New Zealand has high tax rates. The top income tax rate is 39 percent, and the top corporate tax rate is 33 percent, which is higher than those of most developing Asian countries. Other taxes include a value-added tax (VAT) and a tax on interest. In the most recent year, overall tax revenue as a percentage of GDP was 36.6 percent.

GOVERNMENT SIZE — 56%

Total government expenditures, including consumption and transfer payments, are high. In the most recent year, government spending equaled 38.3 percent of GDP. The state's role in the economy has been reduced, and spending management has been reasonably sound.

MONETARY FREEDOM — 83.7%

Inflation is moderate, averaging 3.2 percent between 2004 and 2006. Relatively unstable prices explain most of the monetary freedom score. There are no official price controls, but the government regulates the prices of utilities and subsidizes pharmaceuticals. An additional 5 percentage points is deducted from New Zealand's monetary freedom score to account for policies that distort domestic prices.

INVESTMENT FREEDOM — 70%

New Zealand encourages foreign investment. Foreign ownership is restricted in Telecom New Zealand, Air New Zealand, and fishing. Land and real estate purchases are subject to strong restrictions. Permits or licenses are needed for gold, coal, petroleum, or other minerals mining. Foreign investments involving acquisition of an existing business where foreign ownership would be 25 percent or greater or the investment exceeds NZ$50 million require the Overseas Investment Commission's approval. Incentives are offered to promote activity in information communications technologies as well as research and development. There are no restrictions on current transfers, repatriation of profits, or access to foreign exchange.

FINANCIAL FREEDOM — 80%

Regulation is minimal and transparent in accordance with international standards. The central bank is independent. There were 16 registered banks at the end of 2006. Foreign-owned banks account for approximately 90 percent of assets. The government owns Kiwibank Limited. New Zealand is a world leader in the use of electronic fund transfers and banking technology. Non-bank financial institutions may offer banking services, subject to normal restrictions. Mortgages represent over half of all lending. Regulations are different from ordinary banking supervision, requiring publicly available quarterly reports on risk and exposure. Capital markets are small but well developed, and stocks are actively traded. Insurance is lightly regulated, foreign participation is high, and the government is involved in the accident and earthquake sectors of the market. Capital markets are open to foreign participation.

PROPERTY RIGHTS — 90%

Private property is well protected. The judiciary is independent, and contracts are notably secure. Legislation has been proposed to bring the patent law into closer conformity with international standards by tightening the criteria for granting a patent. Manufacturers have expressed concern that parallel imports of "gray market" goods under New Zealand law will result in the importation of dated or unsuitable products.

FREEDOM FROM CORRUPTION — 96%

Corruption is perceived as almost nonexistent. New Zealand is ranked 1st out of 163 countries in Transparency International's Corruption Perceptions Index for 2006. New Zealand is renowned for its efforts to ensure transparent, competitive, and corruption-free government procurement. Stiff penalties against bribing government officials or accepting bribes are strictly enforced.

LABOR FREEDOM — 85.5%

Flexible employment regulations enhance employment opportunities and productivity growth. The non-salary cost of employing a worker is low, and dismissing a redundant employee is costless. Regulations related to the number of work hours are flexible. New Zealand's level of labor freedom is one of the highest in the world.

NICARAGUA

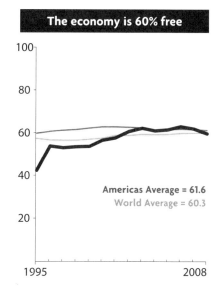

Managua

Rank: 81
Regional Rank: 19 of 29

Nicaragua's economy is 60 percent free, according to our 2008 assessment, which makes it the world's 81st freest economy. Its overall score is 2 percentage points lower than last year, one of the sharpest declines worldwide, reflecting lower scores in six of the 10 economic freedoms. Nicaragua is ranked 19th out of 29 countries in the Americas, and its overall score is slightly lower than the regional average.

Nicaragua enjoys relatively high scores in trade freedom, fiscal freedom, labor freedom, investment freedom, and government size. Personal and corporate tax rates are high, but overall tax revenue is low as a percentage of GDP. Government expenditures are also fairly low. The labor market is flexible. Foreign investment has been liberalized, and foreign capital is accorded equal treatment, although certain restrictions still exist.

Nicaragua's is weakest in property rights and freedom from corruption. The judicial system is inconsistent in contract enforcement and subject to political interference. Corruption has a negative impact on the economy. Business licensing procedures are difficult, but the government is working to streamline the regulatory process.

BACKGROUND: In the 1980s, the Sandinistas destroyed the economy and suppressed human rights. In November 2006, former Sandinista leader Daniel Ortega won the presidential election. Despite claims that he has shed his Marxism and converted to "fair markets" and democracy, he has shown little interest in restoring confiscated properties to their rightful owners or working for the rule of law. He is close to Venezuela's hard-left President Hugo Chávez and Bolivia's populist President Evo Morales. Nearly half of the workforce is unemployed or underemployed. The economy, which traditionally has depended heavily on coffee, seafood, and sugar exports, has been diversified to include minerals and *maquila* textiles. The Central America–Dominican Republic–United States Free Trade Agreement (CAFTA–DR) came into force in April 2006.

How Do We Measure Economic Freedom? See Chapter 4 (page 39) for an explanation of the methodology or visit the *Index* Web site at *heritage.org/index*.

The economy is 60% free

Americas Average = 61.6
World Average = 60.3

1995   2008

QUICK FACTS

Population: 5.1 million

GDP (PPP): $18.9 billion
4.0% growth in 2005
3.1% 5-yr. comp. ann. growth
$3,674 per capita

Unemployment: 6.5%

Inflation (CPI): 9.6%

FDI (net flow): $241.0 million

Official Development Assistance:
Multilateral: $286.2 million
Bilateral: $547.3 million (18.7% from the U.S.)

External Debt: $5.1 billion

Exports: $1.9 billion
Primarily coffee, beef, shrimp and lobster, tobacco, sugar, gold, peanuts

Imports: $3.3 billion
Primarily consumer goods, machinery and equipment, raw materials, petroleum products

2005 data unless otherwise noted.

NICARAGUA'S TEN ECONOMIC FREEDOMS

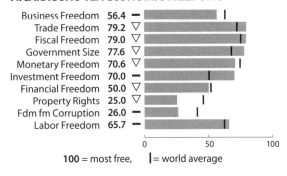

Business Freedom	56.4
Trade Freedom	79.2
Fiscal Freedom	79.0
Government Size	77.6
Monetary Freedom	70.6
Investment Freedom	70.0
Financial Freedom	50.0
Property Rights	25.0
Fdm fm Corruption	26.0
Labor Freedom	65.7

0   50   100

100 = most free, | = world average

BUSINESS FREEDOM — 56.4%

The overall freedom to start, operate, and close a business is limited by Nicaragua's regulatory environment. Starting a business takes an average of 39 days, compared to the world average of 43 days. Obtaining a business license requires less than the world average of 19 procedures and 234 days, but the cost is high. Closing a business is relatively easy.

TRADE FREEDOM — 79.2%

Nicaragua's weighted average tariff rate was 5.4 percent in 2005. The government has made progress in liberalizing the trade regime, but import restrictions, import taxes and fees, import licensing requirements for some goods, some restrictive technical standards, weak enforcement of intellectual property rights, corruption, and delays in customs clearance add to the cost of trade. An additional 10 percentage points is deducted from Nicaragua's trade freedom score to account for non-tariff barriers.

FISCAL FREEDOM — 79%

Nicaragua's tax rates are moderate. Both the top income tax rate and the top corporate tax rate are 30 percent. Other taxes include a value-added tax (VAT) and a capital gains tax. During the most recent year, overall tax revenue as a percentage of GDP was 17.4 percent.

GOVERNMENT SIZE — 77.6%

Total government expenditures, including consumption and transfer payments, are low. In the most recent year, government spending equaled 27.3 percent of GDP. The government has privatized telecommunications, but overall progress has been sluggish in recent years.

MONETARY FREEDOM — 70.6%

Inflation is relatively high, averaging 9.4 percent between 2004 and 2006. Unstable prices explain most of the monetary freedom score. Most price controls have been eliminated, but the government sets prices for pharmaceuticals, sugar, domestically produced soft drinks and cigarettes, and liquefied natural gas; regulates the retail price of butane gas and rates for electricity, energy, water, and telecommunications; and has a history of negotiating voluntary price restraints with domestic producers of important consumer goods. An additional 10 percentage points

is deducted from Nicaragua's monetary freedom score to account for policies that distort domestic prices.

INVESTMENT FREEDOM — 70%

Nicaragua has liberalized foreign investment. Investment is guaranteed equal treatment, is not screened, and faces no performance requirements. Investors may own and use property. The law grants investors repatriation of capital, quick resolution of disputes, and immediate remittance abroad of profits, and commercial arbitration procedures are codified, but poor protection of property rights and cumbersome procedures remain disincentives. Residents may hold foreign exchange accounts, but the only nonresidents who may hold such accounts are those with approved immigration status (such as diplomats). There are no controls or restrictions on payments and transfers and very few restrictions on capital transactions.

FINANCIAL FREEDOM — 50%

Nicaragua's financial system is underdeveloped and concentrated in urban areas. There are seven commercial banks and two finance companies. The 1998–2001 closing of three banks eliminated the state's last bank holdings. The system has been stabilizing since regulators intervened to liquidate four banks between November 2000 and March 2002 and reforms introduced international standards and revitalized the capital base. Many banking transactions take place in dollars. The insurance sector, once a state monopoly, is based primarily on insuring property and is now open to private investors. The state-owned firm remains the largest insurer and controls over half of the market. Capital markets are small, and the stock exchange trades primarily in government bonds, with five private companies listed as of February 2007.

PROPERTY RIGHTS — 25%

Protection of property rights is weak. Contracts are not strongly enforced, and the judiciary is politicized and subject to corruption. Protection of intellectual property rights is almost nonexistent. Estimates of optical media piracy range from 70 percent of DVDs sold to almost 100 percent of music CDs sold. Weak land title registries and the many unresolved land expropriation cases from the 1980s seriously undermine the security of real property interest.

FREEDOM FROM CORRUPTION — 26%

Corruption is perceived as widespread. Nicaragua ranks 111th out of 163 countries in Transparency International's Corruption Perceptions Index for 2006. Corruption and political deal-making, especially in the National Police and the judiciary, are viewed as pervasive.

LABOR FREEDOM — 65.7%

Relatively flexible employment regulations could be further improved to enhance employment opportunities and productivity growth. The non-salary cost of employing a worker is moderate, and dismissing a redundant employee is not costly. Regulations on the number of work hours remain rigid.

NIGER

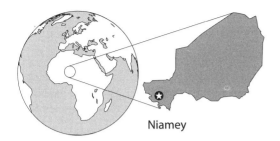

Niamey

Rank: 128

Regional Rank: 28 of 40

N iger's economy is 52.7 percent free, according to our 2008 assessment, which makes it the world's 128th freest economy. Its overall score is 0.4 percentage point lower than last year. Niger is ranked 28th out of 40 countries in the sub-Saharan Africa region, and its overall score is lower than the regional average.

Niger scores well in government size and monetary freedom. Total government expenditures equal roughly 20 percent of GDP. Although tax rates are high, overall tax revenue is low as a percentage of GDP. Inflation is low, and prices (except for petroleum) are set freely by the market.

Niger scores far below the world average in business freedom, labor freedom, financial freedom, property rights, and freedom from corruption. Starting a business takes less time than the world average, but the regulation constrains commercial operations. The labor market is one of the world's least free. The judicial system is not sufficiently independent and is subject to corruption.

BACKGROUND: Niger became independent in 1960, and a single-party civilian regime ruled until a military coup in 1974. The junta was pressured to institute a multi-party democratic system in the early 1990s. A new government established in 1991 oversaw the transition to civilian government in 1993. This government then fell in 1996, but a second coup in 1999 established another transitional government with a new constitution. Mamadou Tandja won the presidency in elections overseen by the transitional authority in 1999 and was re-elected in 2004. Niger is one of the world's poorest countries. Over 80 percent of the population engages in subsistence farming and herding, most economic activity is informal, infrastructure is poor, and drought leads to food shortages. Mineral resources, including uranium and gold, are substantial, and exploration for oil is underway. Niger has strong economic ties to Nigeria, a conduit to international markets.

How Do We Measure Economic Freedom? See Chapter 4 (page 39) for an explanation of the methodology or visit the *Index* Web site at *heritage.org/index*.

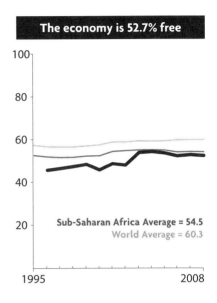

The economy is 52.7% free

Sub-Saharan Africa Average = 54.5
World Average = 60.3

1995   2008

QUICK FACTS

Population: 14.0 million

GDP (PPP): $10.9 billion
6.8% growth in 2005
3.4% 5-yr. comp. ann. growth
$781 per capita

Unemployment: n/a

Inflation (CPI): 7.8%

FDI (net flow): $9.0 million

Official Development Assistance:
Multilateral: $292.0 million
Bilateral: $272.5 million (11.2% from the U.S.)

External Debt: $2.0 billion

Exports: $530.1 million
Primarily uranium ore, livestock, cowpeas, onions

Imports: $852.0 million
Primarily foodstuffs, machinery, vehicles and parts, petroleum, cereals

2005 data unless otherwise noted.

NIGER'S TEN ECONOMIC FREEDOMS

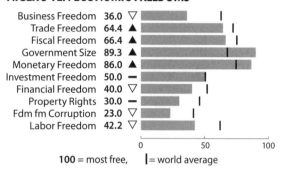

Business Freedom	36.0	▽
Trade Freedom	64.4	▲
Fiscal Freedom	66.4	▲
Government Size	89.3	▲
Monetary Freedom	86.0	▲
Investment Freedom	50.0	—
Financial Freedom	40.0	▽
Property Rights	30.0	—
Fdm fm Corruption	23.0	▽
Labor Freedom	42.2	▽

0   50   100

100 = most free, |= world average

BUSINESS FREEDOM — 36%

The overall freedom to start, operate, and close a business is significantly restricted by Niger's regulatory environment. Starting a business takes an average of 23 days, compared to the world average of 43 days. Obtaining all necessary business licenses takes more than the global average of 234 days, and fees are high. Closing a business can be a lengthy process.

TRADE FREEDOM — 64.4%

Niger's weighted average tariff rate was 12.8 percent in 2005. Import taxes, import licensing and certification regulations, inefficient and non-transparent customs implementation and regulation, and widespread corruption add to the cost of trade. An additional 10 percentage points is deducted from Niger's trade freedom score to account for non-tariff barriers.

FISCAL FREEDOM— 66.4%

Niger has high tax rates. The top income tax rate is 45 percent, and the top corporate tax rate is 35 percent. Other taxes include a value-added tax (VAT), a tax on interest, and an insurance tax. In the most recent year, overall tax revenue as a percentage of GDP was 10.7 percent.

GOVERNMENT SIZE — 89.3%

Total government expenditures, including consumption and transfer payments, are low. In the most recent year, government spending equaled 18.9 percent of GDP. The government has tried to be more prudent in managing spending, but results have been mixed. Privatization has been sluggish.

MONETARY FREEDOM — 86%

Inflation is low, averaging 2 percent between 2004 and 2006. Relatively stable prices explain most of the monetary freedom score. With the exception of petroleum products, the market sets prices, but the government does influence prices through state-owned utilities. Consequently, an additional 5 percentage points is deducted from Niger's monetary freedom score.

INVESTMENT FREEDOM — 50%

Foreign and domestic capital are legally equal. Investment is not screened, and all sectors are open except for national security purposes. Land ownership requires authorization.

Deterrents include a small economy, limited buying power, high transport costs, and bureaucracy. Foreign investment is relatively low for the region. Most of what is received involves the mining sector, especially uranium. Residents may hold foreign exchange accounts subject to some restrictions. Non-residents may hold foreign exchange accounts with prior approval. Payments and transfers to selected countries are subject to quantitative limits and approval. Some capital transactions to selected countries are subject to authorization. Real estate purchases by non-residents must be reported.

FINANCIAL FREEDOM — 40%

Niger's underdeveloped financial system is the weakest in the Economic Community of West African States. Credit is being reformed under a World Bank four-year plan. The Central Bank of West African States governs Niger's banking institutions and sets minimum reserve requirements. Four financial houses have been put in temporary arbitration as a result. Credit is allocated on market terms, but the cost is high, and credit generally is extended only to large businesses. The major commercial banks are Banque internationale pour l'Afrique au Niger, Societe nigerienne de Banque, Ecobank Niger, and Bank of Africa–Niger, which together control 87.5 percent of resources. Banks offer a limited number of financial instruments. The government is a shareholder in a number of financial institutions, but private banks and foreign banks account for most resources and deposits. Most capital market activity is centered in the regional stock exchange in the Ivory Coast, which also has a very small branch in Niger.

PROPERTY RIGHTS — 30%

Niger's judicial system is understaffed and subject to pressure from the executive. Corruption is fueled by low salaries and inadequate training programs. Despite an adequate legal regime for the protection of intellectual property rights, the government lacks the capacity and resources to enforce copyright violations, and counterfeit CDs and videocassettes are readily available in most cities.

FREEDOM FROM CORRUPTION — 23%

Corruption is perceived as pervasive. Niger ranks 138th out of 163 countries in Transparency International's Corruption Perceptions Index for 2006. Corruption in the executive and legislative branches is compounded by poorly financed and poorly trained law enforcement and weak administrative controls.

LABOR FREEDOM — 42.2%

Restrictive employment regulations hinder employment opportunities and productivity growth. The non-salary cost of employing a worker is high, and the difficulty of laying off a worker creates a risk aversion for companies that would otherwise hire more people and grow. Regulations on the number of work hours are very rigid.

NIGERIA

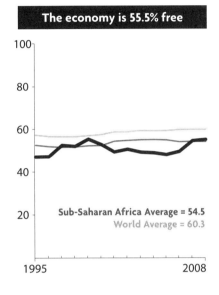

Abuja

Rank: 105

Regional Rank: 18 of 40

Nigeria's economy is 55.5 percent free, according to our 2008 assessment, which makes it the world's 105th freest economy. Its overall score is 0.5 percentage point lower than last year, reflecting worsened scores in two of the 10 economic freedoms. Nigeria is ranked 18th out of 40 countries in the sub-Saharan Africa region, and its overall score is slightly higher than the regional average.

Nigeria is above average only in labor freedom and fiscal freedom. Inflation is fairly high, but the government does not distort market prices with subsidies (except for rail transport). The labor market is fairly elastic.

Nigeria scores 10 percentage points below average in business freedom and financial freedom. Business licenses are subject to numerous delays, and similar regulatory excess hinders financial development. As a result, the economy is largely cash-based.

BACKGROUND: Independent since 1960, Nigeria has Africa's largest population, with 140 million people. It is the economic and political heavyweight of western Africa and increasingly has intervened politically and militarily in neighboring countries. A civilian government ruled until a 1966 military coup, followed (except for a brief period from 1979 to 1983) by a succession of military governments. Former General Olusegun Obasanjo, who oversaw the transition to civilian government in 1979, was elected president in 1999 and re-elected in 2003. Umaru Yar'Adua won what was widely considered to be a flawed election in 2007. Oil dominates the economy, accounting for about 25 percent of GDP, over 90 percent of exports, and over 70 percent of government revenue. Violence in the Delta region, the source of most of Nigeria's oil, disrupts production. The informal economy is extensive. Two-thirds of the population is engaged in agriculture. Economic reform has been slow. Corruption remains pervasive despite progress made by the Economic and Financial Crimes Commission.

How Do We Measure Economic Freedom? See Chapter 4 (page 39) for an explanation of the methodology or visit the *Index* Web site at *heritage.org/index*.

The economy is 55.5% free

100
80
60
40
20

Sub-Saharan Africa Average = 54.5
World Average = 60.3

1995   2008

QUICK FACTS

Population: 131.5 million

GDP (PPP): $148.3 billion
7.2% growth in 2005
6.3% 5-yr. comp. ann. growth
$1,128 per capita

Unemployment: 5.8%

Inflation (CPI): 17.8%

FDI (net flow): $3.2 billion

Official Development Assistance:
Multilateral: $495.9 million
Bilateral: $5.9 billion (2.0% from the U.S.)

External Debt: $22.2 billion

Exports: $52.2 billion
Primarily petroleum and petroleum products, cocoa, rubber

Imports: $24.6 billion
Primarily machinery, chemicals, transport equipment, manufactured goods, food and live animals

2005 data unless otherwise noted.

NIGERIA'S TEN ECONOMIC FREEDOMS

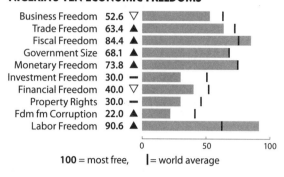

Business Freedom	52.6 ▽	
Trade Freedom	63.4 ▲	
Fiscal Freedom	84.4 ▲	
Government Size	68.1 ▲	
Monetary Freedom	73.8 ▲	
Investment Freedom	30.0 —	
Financial Freedom	40.0 ▽	
Property Rights	30.0 —	
Fdm fm Corruption	22.0 ▲	
Labor Freedom	90.6 ▲	

0   50   100

100 = most free, I = world average

BUSINESS FREEDOM — 52.6%

The overall freedom to start, operate, and close a business is limited by Nigeria's regulatory environment. Starting a business takes an average of 34 days, compared to the world average of 43 days. Obtaining a business license takes more than the world average of 234 days. Closing a business can be relatively easy.

TRADE FREEDOM — 63.4%

Nigeria's weighted average tariff rate was 10.8 percent in 2005. Trade liberalization has progressed, but prohibitive tariffs, heavy import fees, import and export taxes, import bans, export incentive programs, arbitrary regulations, export subsidies, weak enforcement of intellectual property rights, corruption, and inconsistent and non-transparent customs add to the cost of trade. An additional 15 percentage points is deducted from Nigeria's trade freedom score to account for non-tariff barriers.

FISCAL FREEDOM — 84.4%

Nigeria has moderate tax rates. The top income tax rate is 25 percent, and the top corporate tax rate is 30 percent. Other taxes include a value-added tax (VAT), a tax on interest, and a capital gains tax. Several bills passed in April 2007 affect tax administration. In the most recent year, overall tax revenue as a percentage of GDP was 6.2 percent.

GOVERNMENT SIZE — 68.1%

Total government expenditures, including consumption and transfer payments, are moderate. In the most recent year, government spending equaled 32.6 percent of GDP. Government involvement in the economy is still considerable. Privatization is behind schedule.

MONETARY FREEDOM — 73.8%

Inflation is high, averaging 11.2 percent between 2004 and 2006. Relatively unstable prices explain most of the monetary freedom score. With the exception of petroleum products, prices are set by the market. The government subsidizes agriculture and manufacturing and influences prices through state-owned enterprises and utilities. An additional 5 percentage points is deducted from Nigeria's monetary freedom score to account for policies that distort domestic prices.

INVESTMENT FREEDOM — 30%

Nigeria permits 100 percent foreign ownership except in petroleum and activities related to national security. Investment in banks, mining, gas, and insurance is subject to additional laws. Telecommunications and broadcasting have attracted interest since their recent deregulation. Disincentives include poor infrastructure, religious violence, confusing land ownership laws, arbitrary application of regulations, corruption, crime, and continuing abductions of foreign oil workers. Residents and non-residents may hold foreign exchange accounts. Some capital transactions are subject to documentation requirements and restrictions. Most payments and transfers must be conducted through banks.

FINANCIAL FREEDOM — 40%

Nigeria had 25 licensed banks in mid-2006, down from 89 because of a minimum capital requirement that forced many banks to merge or sell shares. Banks may offer a wide variety of services. Over 700 community banks focus on microfinance lending. Development of the banking sector is hindered by bureaucracy and a cash-based economy. Banks interact with a very limited portion of the population, and electronic procedures are only nascent. Foreign banks must acquire licenses from the central bank. The central bank introduced regulations at the end of 2006 mandating the rates at which it will lend and absorb money. The government owns six development banks and affects the allocation of credit under a scheme that requires banks to deposit 10 percent of their after-tax profits to fund its loan programs. There were approximately 100 insurance companies in late 2006. Capital markets are underdeveloped because of bureaucracy and the poor economic climate.

PROPERTY RIGHTS — 30%

Nigeria's judiciary suffers from corruption, delays, insufficient funding, a severe lack of available court facilities, a lack of computerized systems for document processing, and arbitrary adjournment of court sessions caused by power outages. One of the world's least efficient property registration systems makes acquiring and maintaining rights to real property difficult. Copyright, patent, and trademark enforcement is weak.

FREEDOM FROM CORRUPTION — 22%

Corruption is perceived as pervasive. Nigeria ranks 142nd out of 163 countries in Transparency International's Corruption Perceptions Index for 2006. Corruption is endemic at all levels of government and society, and the president, vice president, governors, and deputy governors are constitutionally immune from civil and criminal prosecution.

LABOR FREEDOM — 90.6%

Flexible employment regulations enhance employment opportunities and productivity growth. The non-salary cost of employing a worker is low, and dismissing a redundant employee is relatively costless and easy. Regulations related to the number of work hours are flexible. Nigeria enjoys one of the world's highest levels of labor freedom.

NORWAY

Oslo

Norway's economy is 69 percent free, according to our 2007 assessment, which makes it the world's 34th freest economy. Its overall score is 0.6 percentage point higher than last year, reflecting improvement in the investment climate and labor market flexibility. Norway is ranked 19th out of 41 countries in the European region, and its overall score is higher than the regional average.

Norway enjoys high levels of business freedom, trade freedom, property rights, and freedom from corruption. The average tariff rate is low, although some non-tariff barriers complicate trade. Starting a business takes only a few days, and the overall protection of business operations is high. Norway has an efficient, independent judiciary that protects property rights effectively, and corruption is negligible.

Norway has very low scores in terms of government size, fiscal freedom, and labor freedom. Government spending is high as a percentage of GDP. As in most other modern European welfare economies, the labor market is fairly rigid, but the government has been trying to introduce more flexibility into employment practices.

BACKGROUND: Norway has been an active member of NATO since 1949. Norwegian voters have twice rejected membership in the European Union in popular referenda, but Norway still benefits from close economic interaction with EU members under the European Economic Area agreement. The country's welfare state is largely subsidized by high taxes and oil revenues. The government is planning for the future depletion of finite energy resources by saving annual surpluses in investment funds outside of Norway. This fund is already the country's largest pension fund. Fisheries, metal, and oil are the most important economic sectors.

How Do We Measure Economic Freedom? See Chapter 4 (page 39) for an explanation of the methodology or visit the *Index* Web site at *heritage.org/index*.

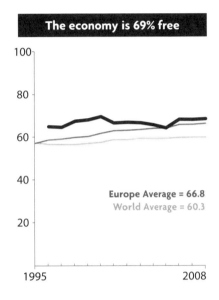

The economy is 69% free

Europe Average = 66.8
World Average = 60.3

QUICK FACTS

Population: 4.6 million

GDP (PPP): $191.5 billion
2.7% growth in 2005
2.3% 5-yr. comp. ann. growth
$41,420 per capita

Unemployment: 4.6%

Inflation (CPI): 1.6%

FDI (net flow): −$11.0 billion

Official Development Assistance:
Multilateral: None
Bilateral: None

External Debt: $350.3 billion

Exports: $133.0 billion
Primarily petroleum and petroleum products, machinery and equipment, metals, chemicals, ships, fish

Imports: $81.5 billion
Primarily machinery and equipment, chemicals, metals, foodstuffs

2005 data unless otherwise noted.

NORWAY'S TEN ECONOMIC FREEDOMS

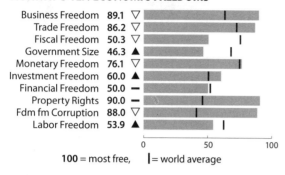

Business Freedom	89.1 ▽	
Trade Freedom	86.2 ▽	
Fiscal Freedom	50.3 ▽	
Government Size	46.3 ▲	
Monetary Freedom	76.1 ▽	
Investment Freedom	60.0 ▲	
Financial Freedom	50.0 ▬	
Property Rights	90.0 ▬	
Fdm fm Corruption	88.0 ▽	
Labor Freedom	53.9 ▲	

0   50   100

100 = most free, | = world average

BUSINESS FREEDOM — *89.1%*

The overall freedom to start, operate, and close a business is strongly protected by Norway's regulatory environment. Starting a business takes an average of 10 days, compared to the world average of 43 days. Obtaining a business license requires less than the world average of 19 procedures. Bankruptcy proceedings are simple and straightforward.

TRADE FREEDOM — *86.2%*

Norway's weighted average tariff rate was 1.9 percent in 2003. Although tariffs are relatively low, import bans and quotas, import licensing requirements, restrictive pharmaceutical and biotechnology policies, unpredictable tariff administration, agriculture and manufacturing subsidies, and inconsistent enforcement of intellectual property rights add to the cost of trade. An additional 10 percentage points is deducted from Norway's trade freedom score to account for non-tariff barriers.

FISCAL FREEDOM — *50.3%*

Norway has a high income tax rate and a moderate corporate tax rate. The top income tax rate is 47.8 percent, and the top corporate tax rate is 28 percent. Other taxes include a value-added tax (VAT) and a tax on net wealth. In the most recent year, overall tax revenue as a percentage of GDP was 43.6 percent.

GOVERNMENT SIZE — *46.3%*

Total government expenditures, including consumption and transfer payments, are high. In the most recent year, government spending equaled 42.3 percent of GDP. The government has focused on containing expensive welfare programs in recent years. The state still owns around 50 percent of all industries.

MONETARY FREEDOM — *76.1%*

Inflation is low, averaging 2 percent between 2004 and 2006. Stable prices explain most of the monetary freedom score. The government regulates prices for agriculture products, sets maximum prices for pharmaceuticals, influences prices through state-owned enterprises and utilities, and subsidizes agriculture and manufacturing. An additional 15 percentage points is deducted from Norway's monetary freedom score to account for policies that distort domestic prices.

INVESTMENT FREEDOM — *60%*

The government restricts investment in sectors in which it has a monopoly, such as financial services, mining, hydropower, property acquisition, and areas considered politically sensitive. Fishing and maritime transport are subject to nationality restrictions. Regulations, standards, and practices often marginally favor Norwegian, Scandinavian, and European Economic Area investors. Incentives are offered mainly for research in high technology and energy. Norway won a major case with the European Free Trade Association over its regional incentive tax system in mid-2006. Residents and non-residents may hold foreign exchange accounts. There are no restrictions on payments, transfers, or repatriation of profits.

FINANCIAL FREEDOM — *50%*

Supervision of the financial system is prudent, and regulations are largely consistent with international norms. Credit is allocated on market terms, and banks offer a wide array of services. There were eight foreign banks and three foreign subsidiary banks at the end of 2006. The government still owns 34 percent of Den Norske Bank, which accounts for 40 percent of assets. Acquisition of financial institutions that exceed certain thresholds must be approved by the Norwegian Financial Supervisory Authority. Half of a bank's board and corporate assembly must be nationals or permanent residents of Norway or an EEA nation. Insurance is dominated by private insurers and is integrated into the banking sector. The small stock exchange, in which the state and foreigners each hold about one-third of equity, is part of a Baltic/Nordic regional network and has announced its intention to strengthen oversight of the market.

PROPERTY RIGHTS — *90%*

Private property and contracts are secure, and the judiciary is sound. Norway adheres to key international agreements for the protection of intellectual property rights. Internet piracy and cable/satellite decoder and smart card piracy have risen, and enforcement of IPR protection is spotty. Imports of counterfeit or pirated goods are not expressly banned.

FREEDOM FROM CORRUPTION — *88%*

Corruption is perceived as minimal. Norway ranks 8th out of 163 countries in Transparency International's Corruption Perceptions Index for 2006. Corrupt activity by Norwegian or foreign officials is a criminal offense, and anti-corruption laws subject Norwegian nationals and companies who bribe officials in foreign countries to criminal penalties. Private-sector corruption usually involves bribery to influence purchasing decisions and sales of goods and services.

LABOR FREEDOM — *53.9 %*

Restrictive employment regulations hinder employment opportunities and productivity growth. The non-salary cost of employing a worker is moderate, but dismissing a redundant employee is relatively difficult and costly. Regulations related to the number of work hours are relatively rigid.

OMAN

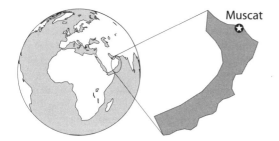

Muscat

Rank: 42

Regional Rank: 3 of 17

Oman's economy is 67.4 percent free, according to our 2008 assessment, which makes it the world's 42nd freest economy. Its overall score is 1.4 percentage points higher than last year, reflecting improved scores in three of the 10 economic freedoms. Oman is ranked 3rd freest among the 17 countries in the Middle East/North Africa region, and its overall score is higher than the regional average.

Oman's scores are higher than the world average in eight of the 10 economic freedoms and especially high in fiscal freedom, trade freedom, labor freedom, and freedom from corruption. There are no taxes on private income, and the highest corporate tax rate is 12 percent. There are significant non-tariff barriers to trade, but a free trade agreement signed with the United States in 2006 should lead to the easing of some restrictions. Corruption is low, particularly for a country that is not a democracy. The labor market is flexible, but foreign governments are forced to hire Omanis.

Oman could improve its trade freedom and limit its government size. Very high government spending is caused by a large state-owned energy sector.

BACKGROUND: The Arab monarchy of Oman has been trying to modernize its oil-dominated economy without diluting the ruling al-Said family's power. Oman is a relatively small oil producer, and production has declined steadily since 2001, but this decline has been offset by rising oil prices. To promote economic diversification, the government has sought to expand natural gas exports and develop gas-based industries. It has encouraged foreign investment in the petrochemical, electric power, telecommunications, and other industries. Dangerously high unemployment has led the government to place a high priority on "Omanization," or the replacement of foreign workers with local staff. A new free trade agreement reached with the U.S. in 2006 should spur further growth and opportunity.

How Do We Measure Economic Freedom? See Chapter 4 (page 39) for an explanation of the methodology or visit the *Index* Web site at *heritage.org/index*.

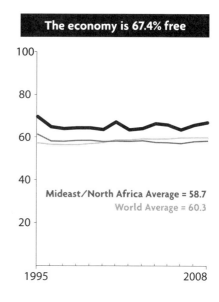

The economy is 67.4% free

Mideast/North Africa Average = 58.7
World Average = 60.3

QUICK FACTS

Population: 2.6 million

GDP (PPP): $52.8 billion
5.8% growth in 2005
3.9% 5-yr. comp. ann. growth
$20,099 per capita

Unemployment: 15% (2004 estimate)

Inflation (CPI): 1.9%

FDI (net flow): $671.0 million

Official Development Assistance:
Multilateral: $1.3 million
Bilateral: $36.6 million (12.3% from the U.S.)

External Debt: $3.5 billion

Exports: $19.5 billion
Primarily petroleum, re-exports, fish, metals, textiles

Imports: $11.1 billion
Primarily machinery and transport equipment, manufactured goods, food, livestock, lubricants

2005 data unless otherwise noted.

OMAN'S TEN ECONOMIC FREEDOMS

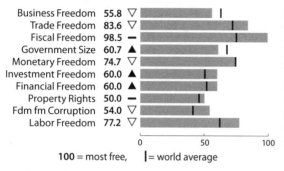

Business Freedom	55.8 ▽
Trade Freedom	83.6 ▽
Fiscal Freedom	98.5 —
Government Size	60.7 ▲
Monetary Freedom	74.7 ▽
Investment Freedom	60.0 ▲
Financial Freedom	60.0 ▲
Property Rights	50.0 ▲
Fdm fm Corruption	54.0 ▽
Labor Freedom	77.2 ▽

0   50   100

100 = most free, **|** = world average

BUSINESS FREEDOM — 55.8%

The overall freedom to start, operate, and close a business is limited by Oman's regulatory environment. Starting a business takes an average of 34 days, compared to the world average of 43 days. Obtaining a business license takes more than the world average of 234 days, and costs are high. Bankruptcy proceedings are lengthy.

TRADE FREEDOM — 83.6%

Oman's weighted average tariff rate was 3.2 percent in 2005. Prohibitive tariffs, import bans and restrictions, burdensome licensing requirements, subsidies, and protectionist government procurement policies add to the cost of trade. An additional 10 percentage points is deducted from Oman's trade freedom score to account for non-tariff barriers.

FISCAL FREEDOM — 98.5%

Oman has low tax rates. There is no income tax on individuals, and the top corporate tax rate is 12 percent. There is no consumption tax or value-added tax (VAT). In the most recent year, overall tax revenue as a percentage of GDP was 2.8 percent.

GOVERNMENT SIZE — 60.7%

Total government expenditures, including consumption and transfer payments, are high. In the most recent year, government spending equaled 36.2 percent of GDP. The state's involvement in the economy through public enterprises remains considerable.

MONETARY FREEDOM — 74.7%

Inflation is low, averaging 2.7 percent between 2004 and 2006. Stable prices explain most of the monetary freedom score. The government controls the prices of a range of core goods and services through an extensive subsidy system and influences prices through state-owned enterprises and utilities, including electricity and water. An additional 15 percentage points is deducted from Oman's monetary freedom score to account for policies that distort domestic prices.

INVESTMENT FREEDOM — 60%

The "Omanization" requirement that only Omanis may work in specified occupational categories is an impediment to foreign investment. The approval process for establishing a business can be difficult. Non-residents generally may not own land, but there are exceptions for citizens of Gulf Cooperation Council countries. The government allows 100 percent foreign ownership of certain companies, subject to its approval; 49 percent if the project is a certain size; and 65 percent if a lower-level approval is granted. Limited oil reserves have forced Oman to diversify its economy, with some successes. Residents and non-residents may hold foreign exchange accounts. Restrictions on payments, transactions, and transfers generally apply only to Israel.

FINANCIAL FREEDOM — 60%

The Central Bank of Oman regulates the financial sector. A 2000 banking law limited investments in foreign securities, raised capital requirements (raised again in 2005), and granted the central bank authority to reject candidates for senior positions in commercial banks. Since then, several banks have merged. The opening of Bank Sohar and the planned opening of the Oman Merchant Bank are signs of recovery from a 2001–2003 downturn. There are six domestic banks and nine foreign bank branches, as well as three specialized banks that provide housing and industrial loans to Omani citizens at favorable terms. Although most credit is offered at market rates, the government intervenes in credit markets through subsidized loans to promote investment. The central bank purchased a 35 percent stake in the National Bank of Oman in 2005. The Muscat Securities Market is very active and, unlike many other equity markets in the region, is open to foreign investors.

PROPERTY RIGHTS — 50%

The threat of expropriation is low, although the judiciary is subject to political influence. As of February 2006, foreigners may hold the title to homes inside specified tourism projects. Intellectual property laws on patents, copyrights, trademarks, industrial secrets, geographical indications, and integrated circuits are WTO-consistent, and enforcement has improved. Only the sultan can amend the laws, through royal decree.

FREEDOM FROM CORRUPTION — 54%

Corruption is perceived as present. Oman ranks 39th out of 163 countries in Transparency International's Corruption Perceptions Index for 2006. In 2005, several high-ranking government officials, including a member of the State Council, were sentenced to between three and five years in prison for bribery, misuse of public office, and breach of trust.

LABOR FREEDOM — 77.2%

Relatively flexible employment regulations could be further improved to enhance employment opportunities and productivity growth. The non-salary cost of employing a worker is low, and dismissing a redundant employee is not difficult. The labor laws enforce the "Omanization" policy that requires private-sector firms to meet quotas for hiring native Omani workers.

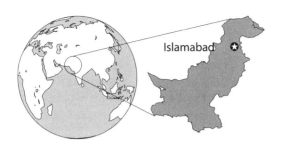

Islamabad

PAKISTAN

Rank: 93

Regional Rank: 16 of 30

Pakistan's economy is 56.8 percent free, according to our 2008 assessment, which makes it the world's 93rd freest economy. Its overall score is 1.7 percentage points lower than last year, reflecting worsened scores in six of the 10 economic freedoms. Pakistan is ranked 16th out of 30 countries in the Asia–Pacific region, and its overall score is slightly below the regional average.

Pakistan scores moderately well in fiscal freedom, business freedom, and labor freedom, but its only exceptionally high score is for limited government size. The corporate tax rate is high, but tax revenue and government spending are low relative to GDP. Commercial registration and licensing are historically inefficient, but efforts to liberalize the business climate are producing results. The labor market is flexible, although firing procedures are costly.

Pakistan has weak trade freedom, investment freedom, financial freedom, property rights, and freedom from corruption. Imports are subject to a high average tariff rate and burdensome non-tariff barriers. The judicial system does not protect property rights effectively because of a serious case backlog, understaffed facilities, and poor security. Serious corruption taints the judiciary and civil service, making Pakistan one of the most corrupt nations rated by the *Index*. Pakistan's financial market, though advanced for the region, is constrained by regulation and bureaucracy.

BACKGROUND: Pakistani President Pervez Musharraf, who took power in a bloodless coup in 1999, has faced ongoing political unrest and terrorism, especially in provinces bordering Afghanistan. President Musharraf has pledged to hold elections as early as 2008. Despite the political risk, Pakistan's economy grew strongly last year on the back of strength in the country's manufacturing sector and a pickup in foreign direct investment. The government is continuing to privatize key industries. Yet the country remains poor, and political risk deters more foreign investment.

How Do We Measure Economic Freedom? See Chapter 4 (page 39) for an explanation of the methodology or visit the *Index* Web site at *heritage.org/index*.

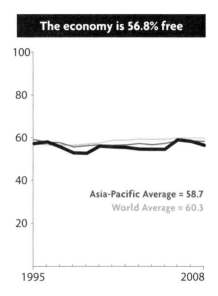

The economy is 56.8% free

Asia-Pacific Average = 58.7
World Average = 60.3

QUICK FACTS

Population: 155.8 million

GDP (PPP): $369.2 billion
8.0% growth in 2005
5.8% 5-yr. comp. ann. growth
$2,370 per capita

Unemployment: 6.6%

Inflation (CPI): 9.3%

FDI (net flow): $2.1 billion

Official Development Assistance:
Multilateral: $1.0 billion
Bilateral: $1.1 billion (35% from the U.S.)

External Debt: $33.7 billion

Exports: $19.1 billion
Primarily textiles, leather goods, manufactures, carpets and rugs

Imports: $29.0 billion
Primarily petroleum products, machinery, transportation equipment, iron and steel

2005 data unless otherwise noted.

PAKISTAN'S TEN ECONOMIC FREEDOMS

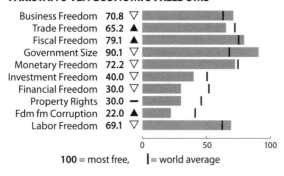

Business Freedom	70.8 ▽	
Trade Freedom	65.2 ▲	
Fiscal Freedom	79.1 ▲	
Government Size	90.1 ▽	
Monetary Freedom	72.2 ▽	
Investment Freedom	40.0 ▽	
Financial Freedom	30.0 ▽	
Property Rights	30.0 —	
Fdm fm Corruption	22.0 ▲	
Labor Freedom	69.1 ▽	

0   50   100

100 = most free, ▌= world average

BUSINESS FREEDOM — *70.8%*

The overall freedom to start, operate, and close a business is relatively well protected by Pakistan's regulatory environment. Starting a business takes an average of 24 days, compared to the world average of 43 days. Obtaining a business license takes less than the world average of 19 procedures and 234 days, but costs are high. Closing a business is relatively easy and straightforward.

TRADE FREEDOM — *65.2%*

Pakistan's weighted average tariff rate was 12.4 percent in 2005. Liberalization has progressed, but import bans and restrictions, import taxes, inconsistent standards administration, non-transparent government procurement, export subsidies, weak enforcement of intellectual property rights, and corruption add to the cost of trade. An additional 10 percentage points is deducted from Pakistan's trade freedom score to account for non-tariff barriers.

FISCAL FREEDOM — *79.1%*

Pakistan has implemented some tax cuts. The top income tax rate was reduced to 25 percent. The top corporate tax rate is 37 percent. Other taxes include a value-added tax (VAT) and a property tax. In the most recent year, overall tax revenue as a percentage of GDP was 10 percent.

GOVERNMENT SIZE — *90.1%*

Total government expenditures, including consumption and transfer payments, are low. In the most recent year, government spending equaled 18.2 percent of GDP. Privatization, including the sales of two major telecommunications and electricity enterprises, has advanced in recent years.

MONETARY FREEDOM — *72.2%*

Inflation is relatively high, averaging 7.9 percent between 2004 and 2006. Relatively unstable prices explain most of the monetary freedom score. The government controls pharmaceutical and fuel prices, subsidizes agriculture, and influences prices through state-owned enterprises and utilities, including electricity and water. An additional 10 percentage points is deducted from Pakistan's monetary freedom score to account for policies that distort domestic prices.

INVESTMENT FREEDOM — *40%*

Foreign capital is welcome. Foreign investors may own 100 percent of most businesses, except in arms and munitions, high explosives, currency and mint operations, radioactive substances, finance, and new non-industrial alcohol plants. Foreign ownership in agriculture is capped at 60 percent. Total foreign equity control is permitted in the services sector. The government requires a minimum initial investment in agriculture, infrastructure, and social services and maintains local content requirements for 16 items in the automobile and motorcycle industries. Deterrents include political violence, civil unrest, poor infrastructure, inconsistent and arbitrary regulation and enforcement, and a lack of coordination between the federal and regional governments. Restrictions on foreign exchange accounts include the need for government approval in some cases. Payments and transfers are subject to approval, quantitative limits, and other restrictions. Most capital transactions are not permitted or require government approval.

FINANCIAL FREEDOM — *30%*

Pakistan was supposed to have converted to an Islamic (interest-free) financial system system by 2001, but the Supreme Court is still considering a final judgment. Five domestic banks account for over 80 percent of assets. The government has a majority stake in the largest bank and controls several specialized banks; the three state-owned banks are saddled by non-performing loans. The central bank must approve all new domestic and foreign bank branches. New foreign banks must establish subsidiaries under 49 percent control rather than opening branches. Insurance is underdeveloped, and a state-owned firm controls over three-quarters of the life insurance market. Foreign investors may not own more than 51 percent of a life or general insurance company. Domestic insurance companies must meet their reinsurance needs in Pakistan. There are three stock exchanges, with the largest market based in Karachi.

PROPERTY RIGHTS — *30%*

Pakistan's judiciary, by law separate from the executive, remains hampered by ineffective implementation of the laws, poor security for judges and witnesses, sentencing delays, a huge backlog of cases, and corruption. The government closed down several pirate optical disc factories and beefed up enforcement of intellectual property rights in 2006.

FREEDOM FROM CORRUPTION — *22%*

Corruption is perceived as pervasive. Pakistan ranks 142nd out of 163 countries in Transparency International's Corruption Perceptions Index for 2006. Corruption among executive and legislative branch officials is viewed as widespread.

LABOR FREEDOM — *69.1%*

Relatively flexible employment regulations could be further improved to enhance employment opportunities and productivity growth. The non-salary cost of employing a worker is low, but the difficulty of laying off a worker creates a risk aversion for companies that would otherwise hire more people and grow.

PANAMA

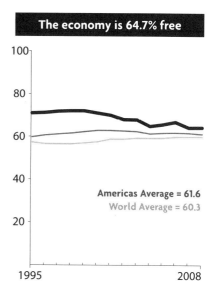

Panama City

Rank: 50
Regional Rank: 12 of 29

Panama's economy is 64.7 percent free, according to our 2008 assessment, which makes it the world's 50th freest economy. Its overall score is essentially unchanged from last year. Panama is ranked 12th out of 29 countries in the Americas, and its overall score is higher than the regional average.

Panama scores well in business freedom, financial freedom, investment freedom, and government size. Despite bureaucratic inefficiency, commercial operations are generally subject to clear rules. Personal and corporate income tax rates are moderate, and overall tax revenue is low as a percentage of GDP. Government expenditures are also fairly low. The law welcomes foreign capital and imposes only minor restrictions on investments. Panama is a regional financial hub and uses the U.S. dollar as its currency.

Panama suffers from weak property rights, labor freedom, and freedom from corruption. The judicial system is backlogged with cases, not committed to contract enforcement, and subject to political interference. There is significant corruption in the judiciary and civil service. Trade regulations are enforced inconsistently.

BACKGROUND: Since 1999, Panama has been solely responsible for operating the Panama Canal and has converted U.S. military bases in the former Canal Zone to commercial and tourism use. Martin Torrijos, son of the late dictator Omar Torrijos, was elected president in 2004 and has won voter approval to modernize the canal with construction of a third set of locks by 2014. Negotiations for the U.S.–Panama Trade Promotion Agreement were concluded in December 2006, and if ratified by both governments, this agreement, along with canal improvements, should promote economic growth and development. Panama's government-run education system is failing to prepare the country's youth for jobs in the service sector, which accounts for 80 percent of the economy.

How Do We Measure Economic Freedom? See Chapter 4 (page 39) for an explanation of the methodology or visit the *Index* Web site at *heritage.org/index.*

The economy is 64.7% free

Americas Average = 61.6
World Average = 60.3

1995 — 2008

QUICK FACTS

Population: 3.2 million

GDP (PPP): $24.6 billion
6.9% growth in 2005
5.2% 5-yr. comp. ann. growth
$7,605 per capita

Unemployment: 6.5%

Inflation (CPI): 2.9%

FDI (net flow): −$823 million

Official Development Assistance:
Multilateral: $11.2 million
Bilateral: $28.7 million (40.4% from the U.S.)

External Debt: $9.8 billion

Exports: $10.7 billion
Primarily bananas, shrimp, sugar, coffee, clothing

Imports: $10.6 billion
Primarily capital goods, foodstuffs, consumer goods, chemicals

2005 data unless otherwise noted.

PANAMA'S TEN ECONOMIC FREEDOMS

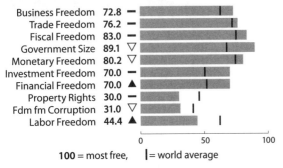

Business Freedom	72.8 —	
Trade Freedom	76.2 —	
Fiscal Freedom	83.0 —	
Government Size	89.1 ▽	
Monetary Freedom	80.2 ▽	
Investment Freedom	70.0 —	
Financial Freedom	70.0 ▲	
Property Rights	30.0 —	
Fdm fm Corruption	31.0 ▽	
Labor Freedom	44.4 ▲	

0   50   100

100 = most free, ▐ = world average

BUSINESS FREEDOM — 72.8%

The overall freedom to start, operate, and close a business is relatively well protected by Panama's regulatory environment. Starting a business takes an average of 19 days, compared to the world average of 43 days. Obtaining a business license takes less than the world average of 234 days. Closing a business can be lengthy and costly.

TRADE FREEDOM — 76.2%

Panama's weighted average tariff rate was 6.9 percent in 2005. Some high tariffs on agriculture products, import taxes, arbitrary and non-transparent import licensing, export subsidies, weak enforcement of intellectual property rights, and corruption add to the cost of trade. An additional 10 percentage points is deducted from Panama's trade freedom score to account for non-tariff barriers.

FISCAL FREEDOM — 83%

Panama has moderate income tax and corporate tax rates. The top income tax rate is 27 percent, and the top corporate tax rate is 30 percent. Other taxes include a value-added tax (VAT) and a transfer tax. In the most recent year, overall tax revenue as a percentage of GDP was 8.7 percent.

GOVERNMENT SIZE — 89.1%

Total government expenditures, including consumption and transfer payments, are low. In the most recent year, government spending equaled 19.1 percent of GDP. The state still dominates certain economic sectors, but private participation is also possible.

MONETARY FREEDOM — 80.2%

Panama has used the U.S. dollar as its legal tender since its founding in 1904. Inflation is relatively low, averaging 2.4 percent between 2004 and 2006. The government controls pharmaceutical and fuel prices, sets prices for a list of basic consumption items, and influences prices through state-owned enterprises and utilities, including electricity and water. An additional 10 percentage points is deducted from Panama's monetary freedom score to account for policies that distort domestic prices.

INVESTMENT FREEDOM — 70%

Panama's investment climate is superior to those of most of its neighbors, and most sectors are open to foreign investment. The government imposes some limitations on foreign ownership—for example, in the non-franchise retail and media sectors, where ownership must be Panamanian, and some professional sectors, such as medicine, law, and custom brokering. There is no government approval process, but investments must be registered. Except when applying for certain incentives, no minimum investment is required. Foreign investors may not purchase land within 10 kilometers of a national border or on an island. Residents and non-residents may hold foreign exchange accounts. There are no restrictions or controls on payments, transactions, transfers, repatriation of profits, or capital transactions.

FINANCIAL FREEDOM — 70%

Panama is a Latin American financial hub and home to many international companies and financial institutions. Because the U.S. dollar is legal tender, there is no central bank. An independent Banking Superintendency oversees the sector. A 1998 banking reform law brought regulations largely into compliance with international standards; Panama has since been removed from the OECD's tax haven and money-laundering blacklist. There are few restrictions on opening banks, and the government exercises little control over the allocation of credit. Foreign and domestic banks are treated equally, and one-third of the banking sector consists of foreign institutions. There were 84 operating banks at the beginning of 2007, of which two are state-owned and counted among the 10 largest. Capital markets are relatively sophisticated, although the stock market trades primarily in government debt, with about 100 listed companies.

PROPERTY RIGHTS — 30%

Panama's judiciary is constitutionally independent but influenced by the executive. Businesses do not trust the system as an objective, independent arbiter in legal or commercial disputes. Backlogs and corruption are severe. Enforcement of copyrights and trademarks, though still inadequate, is improving. Special intellectual property courts hear commercial cases alleging infringement, but redress remains slow.

FREEDOM FROM CORRUPTION — 31%

Corruption is perceived as widespread. Panama ranks 84th out of 163 countries in Transparency International's Corruption Perceptions Index for 2006. Corruption is viewed as having worsened during 2006, with political parties, the National Assembly, the police, and the judiciary the most corrupt government entities.

LABOR FREEDOM — 44.4%

Inflexible employment regulations hinder overall productivity growth and employment opportunities. The non-salary cost of employing a worker is high, and the rigidity of hiring and firing a worker creates a risk aversion for companies that would otherwise employ more people and grow. Regulations on the number of work hours are rigid.

PARAGUAY

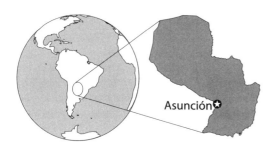

Asunción⦿

Rank: 77
Regional Rank: 16 of 29

Paraguay's economy is 60.5 percent free, according to our 2008 assessment, which makes it the world's 77th freest economy. Its overall score is 1.6 percentage points higher than last year, reflecting improvements in business freedom, property rights, and freedom from corruption. Paraguay is ranked 16th out of 29 countries in the Americas, and its overall score is slightly lower than the regional average.

Paraguay scores above average on half of the areas measured and especially well in terms of fiscal freedom and government size. Income and corporate tax rates are extremely low, and overall tax revenue is low as a percentage of GDP. Government spending is also low. Inflation is high and has increased, but most prices are set by the market.

Paraguay's business freedom, labor freedom, property rights, and freedom from corruption are weak. Opening a business is difficult, and regulations are enforced by an opaque bureaucracy. The labor system is one of the world's 20 most restricted. The government significantly influences the rule of law, and corruption is widespread.

BACKGROUND: President Nicanor Duarte Frutos, elected in 2003, will finish his five-year term in April 2008 and cannot succeed himself. Facing a likely challenge from populist former Bishop Fernando Lugo, Duarte has tried to move his conservative Colorado Party to the left by accepting assistance from Cuba's Fidel Castro and Venezuela's Hugo Chávez. Duarte's early success with fiscal and judicial reform later encountered strong opposition. Nearly half of all jobs are in agriculture (the major export earner), unemployment is high, and more than one-third of Paraguayans live below the poverty line. Improved security cooperation has resulted in reduced smuggling and closer scrutiny of suspected Middle Eastern terrorist–supported groups operating in the "Tri-border" area with Brazil and Argentina. Corruption continues to hinder the rule of law and maturation of democratic institutions.

How Do We Measure Economic Freedom? See Chapter 4 (page 39) for an explanation of the methodology or visit the *Index* Web site at *heritage.org/index.*

The economy is 60.5% free

Americas Average = 61.6
World Average = 60.3

1995   2008

QUICK FACTS

Population: 5.9 million

GDP (PPP): $27.4 billion
2.9% growth in 2005
2.7% 5-yr. comp. ann. growth
$4,642 per capita

Unemployment: 16.0%

Inflation (CPI): 6.8%

FDI (net flow): $215.0 million

Official Development Assistance:
Multilateral: $10.1 million
Bilateral: $105.2 million (10.2% from the U.S.)

External Debt: $3.1 billion

Exports: $3.9 billion
Primarily soybeans, feed, cotton, meat, edible oils, electricity, wood, leather

Imports: $4.1 billion
Primarily road vehicles, consumer goods, tobacco, petroleum products, electrical machinery

2005 data unless otherwise noted.

309

PARAGUAY'S TEN ECONOMIC FREEDOMS

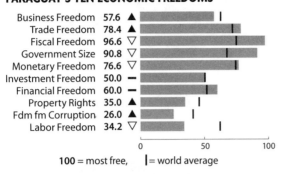

Business Freedom	57.6 ▲	
Trade Freedom	78.4 ▲	
Fiscal Freedom	96.6 ▽	
Government Size	90.8 ▽	
Monetary Freedom	76.6 ▽	
Investment Freedom	50.0 —	
Financial Freedom	60.0 —	
Property Rights	35.0 ▲	
Fdm fm Corruption	26.0 ▲	
Labor Freedom	34.2 ▽	

0   50   100

100 = most free,   ▮ = world average

BUSINESS FREEDOM — 57.6%

The overall freedom to start, operate, and close a business is limited by Paraguay's regulatory environment. Starting a business takes an average of 35 days, compared to the world average of 43 days. Obtaining a business license takes less than the world average of 19 procedures. Closing a business can be lengthy and difficult.

TRADE FREEDOM — 78.4%

Paraguay's weighted average tariff rate was 5.8 percent in 2005. Cumbersome customs procedures, import taxes, import fees, weak enforcement of intellectual property rights, and burdensome labeling requirements add to the cost of trade. Import restrictions and prohibitions are imposed for economic development and balance-of-payments purposes or to protect domestic industry. An additional 10 percentage points is deducted from Paraguay's trade freedom score to account for non-tariff barriers.

FISCAL FREEDOM — 96.6%

Paraguay has very low income tax rates. Both the top income tax and corporate tax rates are 10 percent. Other taxes include a value-added tax (VAT) and a property tax. In the most recent year, overall tax revenue as a percentage of GDP was 11.8 percent.

GOVERNMENT SIZE — 90.8%

Total government expenditures, including consumption and transfer payments, are low. In the most recent year, government spending equaled 17.5 percent of GDP. Reform and privatization of state-owned enterprises has been slow and uneven.

MONETARY FREEDOM — 76.6%

Inflation is relatively high, averaging 8.4 percent between 2004 and 2006. Relatively unstable prices explain most of the monetary freedom score. Most prices are set in the market, but the government controls the price of fuel and influences prices through state-owned enterprises and utilities, including electricity, telecommunications, transportation, and water. An additional 5 percentage points is deducted from Paraguay's monetary freedom score to account for policies that distort domestic prices.

INVESTMENT FREEDOM — 50%

Paraguay guarantees equal treatment to foreign inves-

tors, full repatriation of capital and profits, and (if necessary) international arbitration of disputes. Foreigners may not purchase land within 50 kilometers of the borders. Deterrents include legal insecurity, shortages of skilled labor, deficient infrastructure, and the absence of cheap and reliable transport. Land takeovers by squatters were suppressed to a lower level in 2005–2006. Privatization has been stalled by political opposition. Residents and non-residents may hold foreign exchange accounts. Most payments and transfers are permitted, except for certain financial sector transfers. Capital transactions are subject to minimal restrictions.

FINANCIAL FREEDOM — 60%

Several domestic financial crises have hurt the financial sector and have led the government to restructure the banking sector and improve oversight, but supervision still falls short of international standards. The central bank is not entirely independent. The state development bank is charged with channeling international institution loans to local banks and other financial institutions but is burdened with numerous non-performing loans. As of December 2006, there were 13 banks, 14 savings and loan companies, and 24 foreign-exchange firms. The two largest banks are foreign-owned, and foreign banks control 29 percent of assets and 40 percent of deposits. Any financial transaction may be conducted in foreign currency. There are 35 insurance companies, with the largest market being in car insurance. Capital markets are negligible, and trading on the small stock market is slight.

PROPERTY RIGHTS — 35%

Because of widespread judicial corruption, protection of property is extremely weak. Commercial and civil codes cover bankruptcy and give priority for claims first to employees, then to the state, and finally to private creditors. Acquiring title documents for land can take two years or more. Long recognized as a regional distribution and manufacturing center for illicit merchandise re-exported to Brazil, Paraguay has increased the seizure and destruction of counterfeit and pirated goods.

FREEDOM FROM CORRUPTION — 26%

Corruption is perceived as widespread, but there have been noteworthy improvements. Paraguay ranks 111th out of 163 countries in Transparency International's Corruption Perceptions Index for 2006. The current government has created a transparent, Internet-based procurement system, reformed the process for selecting prosecutors and judges, and appointed better officials to key posts. However, weak institutions still impede anti-corruption efforts.

LABOR FREEDOM — 34.2%

Restrictive regulations hinder employment opportunities and overall productivity growth. The non-salary cost of employing a worker is moderate, but the difficulty of laying off a worker creates a risk aversion for companies that would otherwise hire more people and grow. Regulations on the number of work hours remain rigid.

PERU

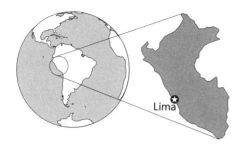

Lima

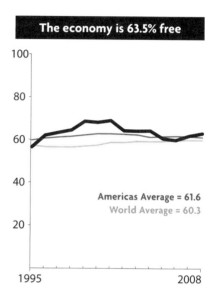

Rank: 55

Regional Rank: 13 of 29

Peru's economy is 63.5 percent free, according to our 2008 assessment, which makes it the world's 55th freest economy. Its overall score is 1 percentage point higher than last year, reflecting improved scores in five of the 10 economic freedoms. Peru is ranked 13th out of 29 countries in the Americas, and its overall score is higher than the regional average.

Peru scores above average in seven areas and is particularly strong in terms of government size. Personal income and corporate tax rates are moderate, and overall tax revenue is low as a percentage of GDP. Inflation is low, and prices are not significantly influenced by the state. Privatization is moving forward, particularly in infrastructure, and overall government expenditures are correspondingly low.

Peru faces significant challenges, particularly in labor freedom, property rights, and freedom from corruption. The slowness and unpredictability of the courts have led to allegations of corruption, but corruption is not as serious as it is in other countries in the region. Economic development is also impeded by a restrictive labor market that regulates costly employee dismissal procedures and inflexible weekly working hours.

BACKGROUND: Sound economic management under President Alejandro Toledo (2001–2006) resulted in annual economic growth of nearly 5 percent from 2002 to 2004. Trade liberalization, begun under Alberto Fujimori (1990–2000), has helped to reduce poverty, but half of all Peruvians are still considered poor. President Alan Garcia, elected to a second term in 2006, has continued most of Toledo's economic policies but, facing a Congress dominated by the opposition populist party, has not deepened the reforms. Nevertheless, economic growth has been impressive in recent years. Garcia has advocated for ratification of the U.S.–Peru Trade Promotion Agreement and has painted himself as the market-friendly alternative in the Andes to Venezuela's Hugo Chávez.

How Do We Measure Economic Freedom? See Chapter 4 (page 39) for an explanation of the methodology or visit the *Index* Web site at *heritage.org/index*.

The economy is 63.5% free

Americas Average = 61.6
World Average = 60.3

1995   2008

QUICK FACTS

Population: 28.0 million

GDP (PPP): $168.9 billion
6.4% growth in 2005
5.2% 5-yr. comp. ann. growth
$6,039 per capita

Unemployment: 7.6%

Inflation (CPI): 1.6%

FDI (net flow): $2.5 billion

Official Development Assistance:
Multilateral: $98.0 million
Bilateral: $554.4 million (18.4% from the U.S.)

External Debt: $28.7 billion

Exports: $19.4 billion
Primarily copper, gold, zinc, crude petroleum and petroleum products, coffee, potatoes, asparagus, textiles, guinea pigs

Imports: $15.2 billion
Primarily petroleum and petroleum products, plastics, machinery, vehicles, iron and steel, wheat, paper
2005 data unless otherwise noted.

PERU'S TEN ECONOMIC FREEDOMS

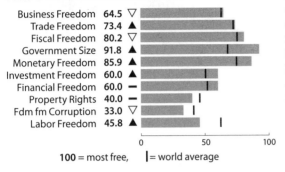

Business Freedom	64.5 ▽	
Trade Freedom	73.4 ▲	
Fiscal Freedom	80.2 ▽	
Government Size	91.8 ▲	
Monetary Freedom	85.9 ▲	
Investment Freedom	60.0 ▲	
Financial Freedom	60.0 —	
Property Rights	40.0 —	
Fdm fm Corruption	33.0 ▽	
Labor Freedom	45.8 ▲	

0   50   100

100 = most free, | = world average

BUSINESS FREEDOM — 64.5%

The overall freedom to start, operate, and close a business is relatively well protected by Peru's regulatory environment. Starting a business takes an average of 72 days, compared to the world average of 43 days. Obtaining a business license takes less than the world average of 234 days. Closing a business can be relatively lengthy.

TRADE FREEDOM — 73.4%

Peru's weighted average tariff rate was 8.7 percent in 2004. Variable import levies for certain agricultural goods to maintain minimum import prices, import restrictions, export and import taxes, restrictive labeling, sanitary and phytosanitary regulations, and weak enforcement of intellectual property rights add to the cost of trade. An additional 10 percentage points is deducted from Peru's trade freedom score to account for non-tariff barriers.

FISCAL FREEDOM — 80.2%

Peru has moderate income tax rates. Both the top income tax rate and the top corporate tax rate are 30 percent. Other taxes include a value-added tax (VAT), a real estate tax, and a vehicle tax. In the most recent year, overall tax revenue as a percentage of GDP was 13.6 percent.

GOVERNMENT SIZE — 91.8%

Total government expenditures, including consumption and transfer payments, are low. In the most recent year, government spending equaled 16.5 percent of GDP. Much of the progress in privatization has been in the infrastructure sector.

MONETARY FREEDOM — 85.9%

Inflation is relatively low, averaging 2.1 percent between 2004 and 2006. Relatively stable prices explain most of the monetary freedom score. Most prices are set in the market, but the government influences prices through regulation, state-owned enterprises, and utilities, and a special government fund is used to stabilize changes in fuel prices. An additional 5 percentage points is deducted from Peru's monetary freedom score to account for policies that distort domestic prices.

INVESTMENT FREEDOM — 60%

Peru provides national treatment. The "ProInversion" institution acts as a one-stop-shop for investors and privatization clearinghouse for natural resources and state companies. There is no screening process. Investments in domestic and foreign banking and in defense-related industries require prior approval, and investment in broadcast media and the purchase of land are restricted to Peruvian citizens. National air and water transportation are restricted to domestic operators. Peru limits the hiring of foreign employees. Privatization has been successful and transparent, with most assets being sold to foreign companies. Residents and non-residents may hold foreign exchange accounts. There are no restrictions or controls on payments, transactions, transfers, or repatriation of profits. Capital transactions face minimal restrictions.

FINANCIAL FREEDOM — 60%

Peru is open to foreign banks and insurance companies. The government has established capital requirements and has strengthened prudential standards and disclosure requirements. Credit is allocated on market terms, and foreign investors can obtain credit in the domestic market. As of mid-2007, there were 12 commercial banks (down from 26 in late 1998); seven municipal and rural savings banks; three government banks (the central bank, a deposit bank, and a development bank); and several dozen microfinance institutions and savings banks. The three largest commercial banks account for 74 percent of commercial loans. The insurance sector is small. Capital markets are centered on the small stock market and the pension system. Bisa de Valores de Lima, the stock exchange, was the developing world's best performing equities market in 2006, rising 188 percent.

PROPERTY RIGHTS — 40%

The judicial system is often extremely slow to hear cases and issue decisions. Allegations of corruption and outside interference are common. Copyright piracy is extensive, and enforcement of intellectual property rights laws is inadequate. Peruvian law does not provide for pipeline protection for patents or protection from parallel imports.

FREEDOM FROM CORRUPTION — 33%

Corruption is perceived as significant. Peru ranks 70th out of 163 countries in Transparency International's Corruption Perceptions Index for 2006. Government corruption is viewed as pervasive. Criminal charges for corruption and human rights violations have been brought against former President Fujimori.

LABOR FREEDOM — 45.8%

Inflexible employment regulations hinder overall productivity growth and employment opportunities. The non-salary cost of employing a worker is low, but the rigidity of hiring and firing a worker creates a risk aversion for companies that would otherwise hire more people and grow. Regulations related to the number of work hours remain inflexible.

THE PHILIPPINES

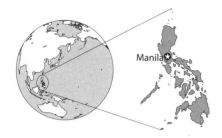

Manila

The economy of the Philippines is 56.9 percent free, according to our 2008 assessment, which makes it the world's 92nd freest economy. Its overall score is essentially unchanged from last year. The Philippines is ranked 15th out of 30 countries in the Asia–Pacific region, and its overall score is roughly equal to the regional average.

The Philippines scores relatively well in just two areas: trade freedom and government size. Fiscal freedom is average because income and corporate tax rates are burdensome, although overall tax revenue is low as a percentage of GDP. The average tariff rate is low, yet non-tariff barriers are significant. Total government expenditures in the Philippines are equal to roughly 20 percent of national GDP.

The Philippines is relatively weak in business freedom, investment freedom, property rights, and freedom from corruption. The government imposes both formal and non-formal barriers to foreign investment. Inflation is fairly high, and the government subsidizes the prices of several basic goods. The judicial system is weak and subject to extensive political influence. Organized crime is a major deterrent to the administration of justice, and bureaucratic corruption is extensive.

BACKGROUND: Current President of the Philippines Gloria Arroyo assumed the presidency of this democratic nation in 2001 after her predecessor's impeachment. She won re-election in 2004 and has weathered a number of impeachment attempts on her way toward restoring macroeconomic stability and bringing the government's budget deficit under control. Since 2002, the Philippines' GDP has grown about 5 percent annually, thanks to expansion of the service sector, increased agricultural output, and higher export demand. The economy remains heavily reliant on remittances from Filipinos working abroad and lacks adequate investments in infrastructure and education.

How Do We Measure Economic Freedom? See Chapter 4 (page 39) for an explanation of the methodology or visit the *Index* Web site at *heritage.org/index*.

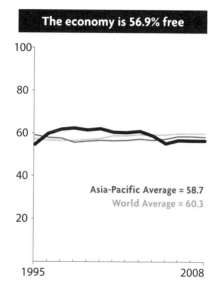

The economy is 56.9% free

Asia-Pacific Average = 58.7
World Average = 60.3

QUICK FACTS

Population: 83.1 million

GDP (PPP): $426.7 billion
5.0% growth in 2005
5.1% 5-yr. comp. ann. growth
$5,138 per capita

Unemployment: 8.7%

Inflation (CPI): 7.6%

FDI (net flow): $970.0 million

Official Development Assistance:
Multilateral: $61.0 million
Bilateral: $1.1 billion (11.5% from the U.S.)

External Debt: $61.5 billion

Exports: $44.7 billion
Primarily semiconductors and electronic products, transport equipment, garments, copper products, petroleum products, coconut oil, fruits

Imports: $53.6 billion
Primarily electronic products, mineral fuels, machinery and transport equipment, iron and steel, textile fabrics
2005 data unless otherwise noted.

THE PHILIPPINES' TEN ECONOMIC FREEDOMS

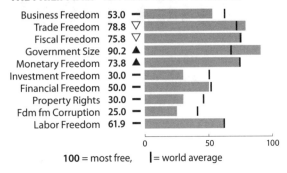

Business Freedom	53.0	—
Trade Freedom	78.8	▽
Fiscal Freedom	75.8	▽
Government Size	90.2	▲
Monetary Freedom	73.8	▲
Investment Freedom	30.0	—
Financial Freedom	50.0	—
Property Rights	30.0	—
Fdm fm Corruption	25.0	—
Labor Freedom	61.9	

0   50   100

100 = most free, | = world average

BUSINESS FREEDOM — 53%

The overall freedom to start, operate, and close a business is limited by the Philippines' regulatory environment. Starting a business takes an average of 58 days, compared to the world average of 43 days. Obtaining a business license takes less than the world average of 234 days. Closing a business can be difficult and lengthy.

TRADE FREEDOM — 78.8%

The Philippines' weighted average tariff rate was 3.1 percent in 2005. Import and export restrictions, quotas, service market access barriers, import and export taxes, burdensome import licensing requirements, restrictive and non-transparent standards, labeling and other regulations, domestic bias in government procurement, inconsistent and non-transparent customs valuation and administration, export subsidies, widespread corruption, and weak protection of intellectual property rights add to the cost of trade. An additional 15 percentage points is deducted from the Philippines' trade freedom score to account for non-tariff barriers.

FISCAL FREEDOM — 75.8%

The Philippines has burdensome tax rates. The top income tax rate is 32 percent, and the top corporate tax rate is 35 percent. Other taxes include a value-added tax (VAT) and a real property tax. In the most recent year, overall tax revenue as a percentage of GDP was 13 percent.

GOVERNMENT SIZE — 90.2%

Total government expenditures, including consumption and transfer payments, are low. In the most recent year, government spending equaled 18.1 percent of GDP. The government has tried to reform and privatize some public enterprises in recent years.

MONETARY FREEDOM — 73.8%

Inflation is high, averaging 6.5 percent between 2004 and 2006. Relatively unstable prices explain most of the monetary freedom score. The government influences prices through state-owned enterprises and utilities and controls the prices of electricity distribution, water, telecommunications, and most transportation services. Price ceilings are usually imposed only on basic commodities in emergencies, and presidential authority to impose controls to check inflation or ease social tension is rarely exercised. An additional 10 percentage points is deducted from the Philippines' monetary freedom score to account for policies that distort domestic prices.

INVESTMENT FREEDOM — 30%

Two negative lists restrict foreign investment and limit foreign involvement in numerous sectors: for example, 20 percent foreign equity in radio and communications, 30 percent in advertising, and 40 percent in utilities, deep-sea fishing, and education. Foreigners may not own land. Other deterrents include corruption, regulatory inconsistency, and recurring political instability. A December 2006 law mandating the use of certain biofuels will likely push energy costs for investors even higher. Residents and non-residents may hold foreign exchange accounts, but non-residents may do so only in certain circumstances. Payments, capital transactions, and transfers are subject to numerous restrictions, controls, quantitative limits, and authorizations.

FINANCIAL FREEDOM — 50%

Banking dominates the Philippines' relatively underdeveloped financial sector. The financial system is open to foreign competition, has higher capital standards, and is subject to improved oversight. Non-performing loans are declining. In late 2006, there were 17 expanded commercial banks (three foreign); 24 regular commercial banks (15 foreign); 85 thrift banks; and 746 rural and cooperative banks. Two large banks are state-owned, and one is partly state-owned. A small government Islamic bank serves Muslim citizens in the south. Credit is generally available at market terms, but the government requires banks to lend specified portions of their funds to preferred sectors. Foreign firms may fully own insurers and set up local subsidiaries. Capital markets are centered on the stock exchange, and personal information networks undermine regulations.

PROPERTY RIGHTS — 30%

The judicial system enforces the law weakly. Judges are nominally independent, but several were appointed strictly for political reasons and are corrupt. Organized crime is a strong deterrent to the administration of justice, and delays and uncertainty continue to concern investors. Despite some progress, enforcement of intellectual property rights remains problematic.

FREEDOM FROM CORRUPTION — 25%

Corruption is perceived as widespread. The Philippines ranks 121st out of 163 countries in Transparency International's Corruption Perceptions Index for 2006. Corruption is pervasive and long-standing. Enforcement of anti-corruption laws is inconsistent, and the public perception of judicial, executive, and legislative corruption remains high.

LABOR FREEDOM — 61.9%

Inflexible employment regulations hinder overall productivity growth and employment opportunities. The non-salary cost of employing a worker is low, but the rigidity of hiring and firing a worker creates a risk aversion for companies that would otherwise employ more people and grow.

POLAND

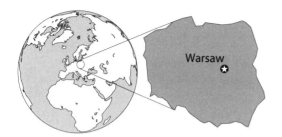

Warsaw

Rank: 83

Regional Rank: 35 of 41

Poland's economy is 59.5 percent free, according to our 2008 assessment, which makes it the world's 83rd freest economy. Its overall score is 2.1 percentage points higher than last year, reflecting improved scores in financial freedom and the investment climate. Poland is ranked 35th out of 41 countries in the European region, and its overall score is lower than the regional average.

Poland scores moderately above average in half of the areas measured: trade freedom, monetary freedom, investment freedom, financial freedom, and property rights. The average tariff rate is low, although non-tariff barriers include distortionary EU subsidies of agricultural and other goods. Inflation is also low.

Poland faces several economic challenges, as do other formerly Communist nations, but is progressing. It remains weak in government size, freedom from corruption, and labor freedom. The court system, though fairly reliable, is prone to inefficiency and sudden changes in laws or regulations. Foreign investment is generally welcome, but foreign ownership of companies in certain industries is limited. The financial sector is subject to government interference but is well regarded overall.

BACKGROUND: Poland's struggle for freedom from the Soviet Union ended in 1989 with Solidarity sweeping both the parliament and, the following year, the presidency. A pioneer among countries making the transition from Communism to free markets, Poland has managed to tame inflation as well as to achieve rapid real income growth and is now a member of the European Union. However, many problems, such as high unemployment, remain. Economic liberalization continues in some sectors, but other sectors, such as energy, remain subject to excessive government influence. Exports include foodstuffs, chemicals, steel, and transport equipment.

How Do We Measure Economic Freedom? See Chapter 4 (page 39) for an explanation of the methodology or visit the *Index* Web site at *heritage.org/index*.

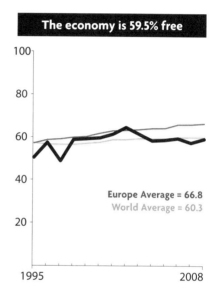

The economy is 59.5% free

Europe Average = 66.8
World Average = 60.3

1995   2008

QUICK FACTS

Population: 38.2 million

GDP (PPP): $528.5 billion
3.5% growth in 2005
3.5% 5-yr. comp. ann. growth
$13,847 per capita

Unemployment: 18.2%

Inflation (CPI): 2.1%

FDI (net flow): $6.3 billion

Official Development Assistance:
Multilateral: $1.1 billion (2004)
Bilateral: $433.0 million (1% from the U.S.) (2004)

External Debt: $98.8 billion

Exports: $112.6 billion
Primarily machinery and transport equipment, intermediate manufactured goods, miscellaneous manufactured goods

Imports: $113.5 billion
Primarily machinery and transport equipment, intermediate manufactured goods, chemicals, minerals, fuels, lubricants
2005 data unless otherwise noted.

315

POLAND'S TEN ECONOMIC FREEDOMS

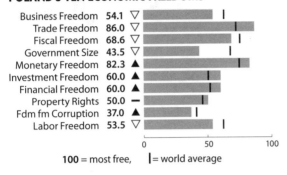

Business Freedom	54.1 ▽
Trade Freedom	86.0 ▽
Fiscal Freedom	68.6 ▽
Government Size	43.5 ▽
Monetary Freedom	82.3 ▲
Investment Freedom	60.0 ▲
Financial Freedom	60.0 ▲
Property Rights	50.0 —
Fdm fm Corruption	37.0 ▲
Labor Freedom	53.5 ▽

100 = most free, | = world average

BUSINESS FREEDOM — 54.1%

The overall freedom to start, operate, and close a business is limited by Poland's regulatory environment. Starting a business takes an average of 31 days, compared to the world average of 43 days. Obtaining a business license requires more than the world average of 19 procedures and 234 days. Closing a business can be lengthy.

TRADE FREEDOM — 86%

Poland's trade policy is the same as those of other members of the European Union. The common EU weighted average tariff rate was 2 percent in 2005. Non-tariff barriers reflected in EU policy include agricultural and manufacturing subsidies, import restrictions for some goods and services, market access restrictions in some service sectors, non-transparent and restrictive regulations and standards, and inconsistent customs administration across EU members. Biotechnology restrictions and pharmaceuticals regulation exceed general EU policy, and the enforcement of intellectual property rights remains problematic. Consequently, an additional 10 percentage points is deducted from Poland's trade freedom score.

FISCAL FREEDOM — 68.6%

Poland has a high income tax rate and a low corporate tax rate. The top income tax rate is 40 percent, and the top corporate tax rate is 19 percent. Other taxes include a value-added tax (VAT) and a property tax. In the most recent year, overall tax revenue as a percentage of GDP was 34.4 percent.

GOVERNMENT SIZE — 43.5%

Total government expenditures, including consumption and transfer payments, are high. In the most recent year, government spending equaled 43.4 percent of GDP. Privatization has reduced the state's role in the economy, increasing the private sector's contribution to over 70 percent of GDP, but progress more recently has been sluggish.

MONETARY FREEDOM — 82.3%

Inflation is relatively low, averaging 1.5 percent between 2004 and 2006. Relatively stable prices explain most of the monetary freedom score. As a participant in the EU's Common Agricultural Policy, the government subsidizes agricultural production, distorting the prices of agricultural products. The government also monitors utility rates and sets official prices for pharmaceutical and medical materials, taxi services, and any other goods or services required for the proper functioning of the economy. Consequently, an additional 10 percentage points is deducted from Poland's monetary freedom score.

INVESTMENT FREEDOM — 60%

Foreign capital is generally equal to domestic capital. The government does not screen investment and allows for 100 percent foreign ownership of domestic businesses, except for ceilings in some industries. Foreign capital is banned from gambling and limited to 49 percent in air transport and broadcasting. Foreign ownership of land is restricted. Poland's Law on Economic Freedom and EU membership increase its attractiveness to investors. Residents and non-residents may hold foreign exchange accounts, subject to certain restrictions. Payments, transactions, and transfers over a specified amount must be conducted through a domestic bank. Capital transactions with nations outside the EU are subject to restrictions and government approval.

FINANCIAL FREEDOM — 60%

Poland's financial system is open and well regulated, but government influence is considerable. Credit is available on market terms, and foreign investors can access domestic financial markets. Banking competition is intense. There were 54 banks at the end of 2005, 43 of which were foreign-controlled. Foreign banks control about 70 percent of assets. The government maintains majority control in four banks and provides low-interest loans to farmers and homeowners. The insurance sector has been growing, but privatization of the state-controlled company, which controls 50 percent of the market, has been slow. Capital markets and the stock exchange are expanding.

PROPERTY RIGHTS — 50%

Property rights are moderately well protected. The legal system protects and facilitates acquisition and disposition of all property rights. The judicial system is slow to resolve cases, however, and there can be unexpected changes in laws and regulations. Piracy of intellectual property continues despite government efforts to improve protection.

FREEDOM FROM CORRUPTION — 37%

Corruption is perceived as significant. Poland ranks 61st out of 163 countries in Transparency International's Corruption Perceptions Index for 2006. The government has established a central office to combat corruption, and the private sector is now paying greater attention to fighting it.

LABOR FREEDOM — 53.5%

Inflexible employment regulations hinder overall productivity growth and employment opportunities. The non-salary cost of employing a worker is high, and the rigidity of hiring and firing a worker creates a risk aversion for companies that would otherwise employ more people and grow.

PORTUGAL

Lisbon

Rank: 53

Regional Rank: 26 of 41

Portugal's economy is 64.3 percent free, according to our 2008 assessment, which makes it the world's 53rd freest economy. Its overall score is 0.2 percentage point lower than last year, reflecting worsened scores in four of the 10 economic freedoms. Portugal is ranked 26th freest out of 41 countries in the European region, and its overall score is slightly lower than the regional average.

Portugal enjoys very high levels of business freedom, trade freedom, investment freedom, property rights, and freedom from corruption. The average tariff rate is low, but non-tariff barriers include distortionary EU subsidies on agriculture and other goods. Business formation is efficient, although other commercial operations are often slowed by bureaucracy. Inflation is low, and the government actively promotes foreign investment. Case resolution is slower than the EU average, but the judiciary is independent and free of corruption.

Portugal has very low scores in government size, fiscal freedom, and labor freedom. Total government spending equals almost 50 percent of GDP, and the labor sector is highly restrictive in all areas, from maximum workweek hours to employment severance procedures.

BACKGROUND: After the 1974 "Revolution of the Carnations" that overthrew its long-running dictatorship, Portugal embarked on a course of rapid democratization and adopted a strong Euro-Atlantic outlook. It joined the European Union in 1986, liberalizing many parts of the economy and improving its infrastructure with the help of EU funds. However, Portugal has suffered in recent years from low educational achievement, sluggish growth, and fiscal imbalances. It also faces challenges from the loss of its comparative advantage in cheap labor following the accession of Central and Eastern European countries to the European Union. Portugal's main exports include agricultural produce, wood products (especially cork), and canned foods.

How Do We Measure Economic Freedom? See Chapter 4 (page 39) for an explanation of the methodology or visit the *Index* Web site at *heritage.org/index*.

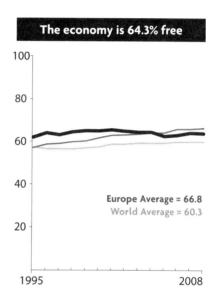

The economy is 64.3% free

Europe Average = 66.8
World Average = 60.3

1995 — 2008

QUICK FACTS

Population: 10.5 million

GDP (PPP): $215.3 billion
0.5% growth in 2005
0.5% 5-yr. comp. ann. growth
$20,410 per capita

Unemployment: 7.6%

Inflation (CPI): 2.1%

FDI (net flow): $2.0 billion

Official Development Assistance:
Multilateral: None
Bilateral: None

External Debt: $272.2 billion

Exports: $53.3 billion
Primarily clothing and footwear, machinery, chemicals, cork and paper products

Imports: $69.1 billion
Primarily machinery and transport equipment, chemicals, petroleum, textiles, agricultural products

2005 data unless otherwise noted.

PORTUGAL'S TEN ECONOMIC FREEDOMS

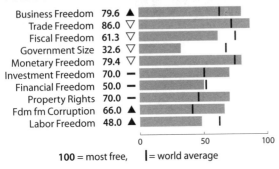

Business Freedom	79.6	▲
Trade Freedom	86.0	▽
Fiscal Freedom	61.3	▽
Government Size	32.6	▽
Monetary Freedom	79.4	▽
Investment Freedom	70.0	—
Financial Freedom	50.0	—
Property Rights	70.0	—
Fdm fm Corruption	66.0	▲
Labor Freedom	48.0	▲

0   50   100

100 = most free, | = world average

BUSINESS FREEDOM — 79.6%

The overall freedom to start, operate, and close a business is relatively well protected by Portugal's regulatory environment. Starting a business takes an average of seven days, compared to the world average of 43 days. Obtaining a business license requires more than the world average of 19 procedures and 234 days. Bankruptcy proceedings are fairly easy and straightforward.

TRADE FREEDOM — 86%

Portugal's trade policy is the same as those of other members of the European Union. The common EU weighted average tariff rate was 2 percent in 2005. Non-tariff barriers reflected in EU policy include agricultural and manufacturing subsidies, import restrictions for some goods and services, market access restrictions in some service sectors, nontransparent and restrictive regulations and standards, and inconsistent customs administration across EU members. Pharmaceutical regulations and non-transparent government procurement also add to the cost of trade. Consequently, an additional 10 percentage points is deducted from Portugal's trade freedom score.

FISCAL FREEDOM — 61.3%

Portugal has a high income tax rate and a moderate corporate tax rate. The top income tax rate is 42 percent, and the top corporate tax rate is 27.5 percent. Other taxes include a value-added tax (VAT), a property tax, and a vehicle tax. In the most recent year, overall tax revenue as a percentage of GDP was 36.3 percent.

GOVERNMENT SIZE — 32.6%

Total government expenditures, including consumption and transfer payments, are high. In the most recent year, government spending equaled 47.4 percent of GDP. The government has slowly pushed forward public administration reform as part of its effort to reduce the budget deficit.

MONETARY FREEDOM — 79.4%

Portugal is a member of the euro zone. Inflation is relatively low, averaging 2.8 percent between 2004 and 2006. Relatively stable prices explain most of the monetary freedom score. As a participant in the EU's Common Agricultural Policy, the government subsidizes agricultural production, distorting the prices of agricultural products. The government also influences prices through state-owned enterprises and utilities. Consequently, an additional 10 percentage points is deducted from Portugal's monetary freedom score.

INVESTMENT FREEDOM — 70%

Foreigners may invest in almost all sectors that are open to private enterprise. Non-EU investment in defense, water management, public-service telecommunications, railways, and maritime transportation requires approval; non-EU investment in regular air transport and television operations is also restricted. The government's "Simplex 2007" plan aims to simplify business investment and approval measures. Privatization of parts of the state airline, a utility, and a paper company are also scheduled. Residents and non-residents may hold foreign exchange accounts. There are no controls or restrictions on repatriation of profits, current transfers, payments for invisible transactions, or real estate transactions.

FINANCIAL FREEDOM — 50%

Financial institutions may offer a variety of services, and regulation by the central bank is improving. The sole remaining state-owned financial services firm, Caixa Geral de Depósitos (CGD), is Portugal's largest financial group. CGD and four large private banks account for about 80 percent of assets. Consolidation continued in 2006 with the merger of the largest and fourth-largest private banks. The government influences the allocation of credit through a program to assist small and medium-size enterprises. CGD also owns two of the three firms that dominate insurance. Capital markets and the stock market remain relatively small. The stock exchange participates in Euronext, the common trading platform linking the bourses of Paris, Brussels, and Amsterdam.

PROPERTY RIGHTS — 70%

The judiciary is independent. The court system is slow and deliberate, and the number of years it takes to resolve cases is well above the EU average. Portugal implements the WTO's Trade-Related Aspects of Intellectual Property Rights (TRIPS) and European intellectual property protection standards and has increased the penalties for violators.

FREEDOM FROM CORRUPTION — 66%

Corruption is perceived as present. Portugal ranks 26th out of 163 countries in Transparency International's Corruption Perceptions Index for 2006. Foreign firms no longer identify corruption as an obstacle to investment. Portugal has ratified the OECD Anti-bribery Convention and recently passed legislation to bring its criminal code into compliance with it.

LABOR FREEDOM — 48%

Inflexible employment regulations hinder overall productivity growth and employment opportunities. The non-salary cost of employing a worker is high, and the rigidity of hiring and firing a worker creates a risk aversion for companies that would otherwise employ more people. Regulations related to the number of work hours are not flexible.

QATAR

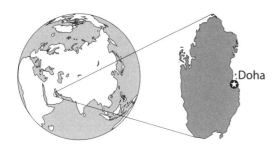

:Doha

Qatar's economy is 62.2 percent free, according to our 2008 assessment, which makes it the world's 66th freest economy. Its overall score is 0.7 percentage point lower than last year, reflecting worsened scores in two of the 10 economic freedoms. Qatar is ranked 8th out of 17 countries in the Middle East/North Africa region, and its overall score is higher than the regional average.

Qatar enjoys very high levels of freedom from corruption and fiscal freedom. There are no personal or corporate taxes on Qatari nationals, and overall tax revenue is very low as a percentage of GDP. Corruption is admirably low, particularly for a developing nation. Qatar's scores for property rights and government size are also above average.

Qatar has only one significant economic weakness relative to other economies: investment freedom. Investment in Qatar is hindered by rules that mandate the hiring of Qataris and limit the percentage of enterprises that foreigners may own.

BACKGROUND: Qatar has been ruled by the Al-Thani family ever since gaining its independence from Great Britain in 1971. Sheikh Hamad bin Khalifa al-Thani, who ousted his father in a bloodless coup in 1995, implemented a publicly approved constitution in 2005. The 2005 constitution cemented the country's social and economic progress through political reforms that include universal suffrage for adults over the age of 18, a completely independent judiciary, and increased transparency of government funding. The emir is pursuing a parliamentary election that is expected to grant direct legislative power to an advisory council elected by Qatari citizens. Despite efforts at diversification, the economy remains heavily dependent on oil and gas. Qatar recently overtook Indonesia to become the world's largest exporter of liquefied natural gas.

How Do We Measure Economic Freedom? See Chapter 4 (page 39) for an explanation of the methodology or visit the *Index* Web site at *heritage.org/index*.

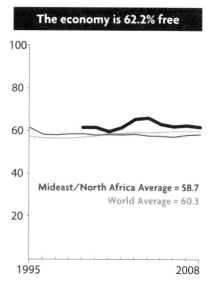

The economy is 62.2% free

Mideast/North Africa Average = 58.7
World Average = 60.3

1995 — 2008

QUICK FACTS

Population: 0.8 million

GDP (PPP): $29.6 billion
6.1% growth in 2005
9.2% 5-yr. comp. ann. growth
$33,637 per capita

Unemployment: 3.2%

Inflation (CPI): 8.8%

FDI (net flow): $1.1 billion

Official Development Assistance:
Multilateral: n/a
Bilateral: n/a

External Debt: $25.7 billion

Exports: $25.8 billion
Primarily liquefied natural gas, petroleum products, fertilizers, steel

Imports: $9.1 billion
Primarily machinery and transport equipment, food, chemicals

2005 data unless otherwise noted.

319

QATAR'S TEN ECONOMIC FREEDOMS

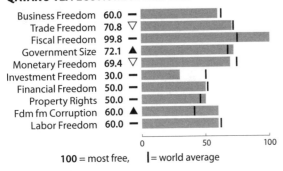

Business Freedom	60.0 —
Trade Freedom	70.8 ▽
Fiscal Freedom	99.8 —
Government Size	72.1 ▲
Monetary Freedom	69.4 ▽
Investment Freedom	30.0 —
Financial Freedom	50.0 —
Property Rights	50.0 —
Fdm fm Corruption	60.0 ▲
Labor Freedom	60.0 —

0   50   100

100 = most free, | = world average

BUSINESS FREEDOM — 60%

The overall freedom to start, operate, and close a business is somewhat restricted by Qatar's regulatory environment. The government has updated a number of commercial laws to enhance the business environment and further economic development, but bureaucracy and a lack of procurement transparency still challenge entrepreneurial activities.

TRADE FREEDOM — 70.8%

Qatar's average tariff rate was 9.6 percent in 2005. Prohibitive tariffs, import restrictions and bans, service market access barriers, import licensing requirements, restrictive sanitary and phytosanitary regulations, and non-transparent government procurement add to the cost of trade. An additional 10 percentage points is deducted from Qatar's trade freedom score to account for non-tariff barriers.

FISCAL FREEDOM — 99.8%

Qatar imposes no income taxes on individuals and no income tax on corporations that are wholly owned by Qatari nationals. The top corporate tax rate of 35 percent applies to foreign corporations operating in Qatar. Aside from customs duties, there are no other major taxes. In the most recent year, overall tax revenue as a percentage of GDP was 4.6 percent.

GOVERNMENT SIZE — 72.1%

Total government expenditures, including consumption and transfer payments, are high. In the most recent year, government spending equaled 30.5 percent of GDP. State involvement in the economy is still considerable despite some progress in privatization.

MONETARY FREEDOM — 69.4%

Inflation is high, averaging 10.6 percent between 2004 and 2006. Relatively unstable prices explain most of the monetary freedom score. The government influences prices through regulation, subsidies, and numerous state-owned enterprises and utilities. An additional 10 percentage points is deducted from Qatar's monetary freedom score to account for policies that distort domestic prices.

INVESTMENT FREEDOM — 30%

Qatar welcomes foreign investment but also tries to prevent Qatari firms from being swamped by experienced foreign firms. Full or majority foreign investment is permitted in agriculture, industry, health, education, tourism, and projects involved in the development of natural resources, and other sectors are capped at 49 percent foreign ownership, with prior approval. Foreign businesses must employ a local agent. Public transportation, steel, cement, and fuel distribution are not open to domestic or foreign investment and are controlled by semi-public companies. The government screens all major foreign investment in the oil and gas industry. Foreign companies may purchase land in certain areas. Residents and non-residents may hold foreign exchange accounts. There are no controls or restrictions on payments and transfers.

FINANCIAL FREEDOM — 50%

Supervision of Qatar's relatively open financial system is prudent, and regulation is largely consistent with international standards. A financial center opened in 2005 has attracted major financial firms and is intended to rival other regional financial hubs like Bahrain. There were 15 commercial banks as of February 2007; seven are Qatari-owned and control about 80 percent of assets. Five are commercial banks, and two are Islamic banks. The government owns 50 percent of Qatar National Bank, which holds nearly 50 percent of total deposits and handles most of the government's business. The government must approve foreign investment in banking and insurance and has shares in two prominent insurers. The Doha Securities Market has been opened to foreign investors, but their holdings are restricted to 25 percent of the issued capital of nearly all listed companies.

PROPERTY RIGHTS — 50%

Expropriation is not likely, but the judiciary is subject to inefficiencies and executive influence. The court system is slow, bureaucratic, and biased in favor of Qataris and the government. Successful raids, seizures, and prosecutions of violators of intellectual property rights have increased substantially, helping to reduce the level of piracy.

FREEDOM FROM CORRUPTION — 60%

Corruption is perceived as present. Qatar ranks 32nd out of 163 countries in Transparency International's Corruption Perceptions Index for 2006. There is no public access to government information, and little is available. Lack of clarity in government procurement is a concern. Qatar has no special commissions or institutions charged with eliminating corruption. It also lacks an independent auditing body outside the executive.

LABOR FREEDOM — 60%

Qatar's labor force consists primarily of expatriate workers whose role in the economy is vital. In general, flexible immigration and employment rules to enable the import of foreign labor are offered to foreign and Qatari investors as an incentive. Qatar has also tightened the administration of its manpower programs to control the flood of expatriate workers. The government does not mandate a minimum wage.

ROMANIA

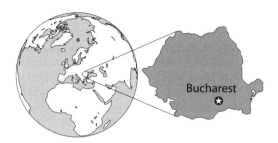

Romania's economy is 61.5 percent free, according to our 2008 assessment, which makes it the world's 68th freest economy. Its overall score is 0.3 percentage point higher than last year, reflecting improved scores in monetary freedom and the investment climate. Romania is ranked 30th out of 41 countries in the European region, and its overall score is below the regional average.

Romania enjoys high levels of business freedom, fiscal freedom, and trade freedom. The top income and corporate tax rates are a flat 16 percent, although overall tax revenue is fairly high as a percentage of GDP. Despite progress in lowering tariffs, non-tariff barriers remain significant. The financial system is consistent with international standards and has been enhanced by a recent reform and privatization program.

As one of the poorer European countries, Romania faces several economic challenges. Labor freedom, property rights, and freedom from corruption are weak. There is significant corruption in most areas of the bureaucracy, particularly the judiciary, which enforces commercial contracts only selectively.

BACKGROUND: Romania was under Soviet control until 1989. In preparation for joining the European Union, the government has been implementing economic reforms consistent with the Maastricht criteria. However, friction between Romania's two main governing coalition partners, the ruling Democratic Party (DP) and National Liberal Party (NLP), as well as within the DP and NLP parties themselves, has caused political deadlock more recently. Macroeconomic improvements have spurred the growth of the middle class and have helped to reduce poverty. Investment activity is expected to remain strong after accession to the EU, with new and modernized production facilities being launched, large public investment projects getting underway, and healthy inflows of foreign direct investment continuing.

How Do We Measure Economic Freedom? See Chapter 4 (page 39) for an explanation of the methodology or visit the *Index* Web site at *heritage.org/index*.

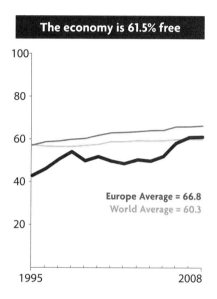

The economy is 61.5% free

Europe Average = 66.8
World Average = 60.3

1995 — 2008

QUICK FACTS

Population: 21.6 million

GDP (PPP): $196.0 billion
4.1% growth in 2005
5.7% 5-yr. comp. ann. growth
$9,060 per capita

Unemployment: 5.8%

Inflation (CPI): 9.0%

FDI (net flow): $6.4 billion

Official Development Assistance:
Multilateral: $706.0 million (2004)
Bilateral: $215.0 million (19% from the U.S.) (2004)

External Debt: $38.7 billion

Exports: $32.8 billion
Primarily textiles and footwear, metals and metal products, machinery and equipment, minerals and fuels, chemicals

Imports: $42.9 billion
Primarily machinery and equipment, fuels and minerals, chemicals, textile and products, metals, agricultural products
2005 data unless otherwise noted.

ROMANIA'S TEN ECONOMIC FREEDOMS

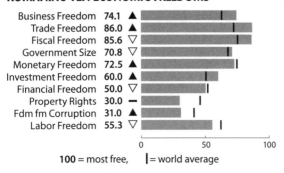

Business Freedom	74.1 ▲	
Trade Freedom	86.0 ▲	
Fiscal Freedom	85.6 ▽	
Government Size	70.8 ▽	
Monetary Freedom	72.5 ▲	
Investment Freedom	60.0 ▲	
Financial Freedom	50.0 ▽	
Property Rights	30.0 —	
Fdm fm Corruption	31.0 ▲	
Labor Freedom	55.3 ▽	

0   50   100

100 = most free,   l = world average

BUSINESS FREEDOM — 74.1%

The overall freedom to start, operate, and close a business is relatively well protected by Romania's regulatory environment. Starting a business takes an average of 14 days, compared to the world average of 43 days. Obtaining a business license takes about the same as the world average of 19 procedures and 234 days. Closing a business can be lengthy.

TRADE FREEDOM — 86%

Romania's trade policy is the same as those of other members of the European Union. The common EU weighted average tariff rate was 2 percent in 2005. Non-tariff barriers reflected in EU policy include agricultural and manufacturing subsidies, import restrictions for some goods and services, market access restrictions in some service sectors, non-transparent and restrictive regulations and standards, and inconsistent customs administration across EU members. Restrictions on biotechnology and sanitary and phytosanitary regulations exceed EU policy, and corruption and the enforcement of intellectual property rights are problems. Consequently, an additional 10 percentage points is deducted from Romania's trade freedom score.

FISCAL FREEDOM — 85.6%

Romania has low flat tax rates. Both the income tax rate and the corporate tax rate are a flat 16 percent. Other taxes include a value-added tax (VAT), a land tax, and a vehicle tax. In the most recent year, overall tax revenue as a percentage of GDP was 30.4 percent.

GOVERNMENT SIZE — 70.8%

Total government expenditures, including consumption and transfer payments, are moderate. In the most recent year, government spending equaled 31.2 percent of GDP. Most small and medium-sized public enterprises have been privatized, but privatization of large-scale companies has been sluggish.

MONETARY FREEDOM — 72.5%

Inflation is high, averaging 7.7 percent between 2004 and 2006. Relatively unstable prices explain most of the monetary freedom score. As a participant in the EU's Common Agricultural Policy, the government subsidizes agricultural production, distorting the prices of agricultural products. It also influences prices through regulation, subsidies, and state-owned enterprises and utilities. An additional 10 percentage points is deducted from Romania's monetary freedom score to account for these policies.

INVESTMENT FREEDOM — 60%

Foreign investment is officially welcome, but weak rule of law, regulatory unpredictability, and legislative fluctuations are deterrents. The government has simplified permit and licensing procedures, allows 100 percent foreign ownership of companies, and has begun the privatization of 41 industrial and energy companies. Residents and non-residents may hold foreign exchange accounts, subject to restrictions and government approval in some cases. All payments and transfers must be documented. Most restrictions on capital transactions have been removed, though derivative-based transactions still require approval.

FINANCIAL FREEDOM — 50%

Supervision and regulation are largely consistent with international standards. Significant reform and restructuring since 1998 includes privatization of many state-owned banks. Of Romania's 33 banks, 25 are foreign-controlled and accounted for 59 percent of assets in 2005. The five largest commercial banks control 60 percent of assets. As of December 2005, state-owned banks held less than 8 percent of assets, down from 75 percent in 1998. Privatization stalled in December 2006 when the state halted the sale of its majority stake in the State Savings Bank. Foreign insurers must partner with Romanians to enter the market. Capital markets are underdeveloped compared to those of other Eastern European countries, and most trading involves government debt.

PROPERTY RIGHTS — 30%

Investors often cite unpredictable changes in legislation as well as weak enforcement of contracts and the rule of law. The judicial system suffers from corruption, inefficiencies, lack of competence, and excessive workloads. Romania is a signatory to international conventions concerning intellectual property rights and has legislation protecting patents, trademarks, and copyrights, but enforcement is very weak.

FREEDOM FROM CORRUPTION — 31%

Corruption is perceived as widespread. Romania ranks 84th out of 163 countries in Transparency International's Corruption Perceptions Index for 2006. In 2006 the government continued to implement its Anticorruption Strategy, which includes (among other things) enforcement of laws and procedures to combat money laundering and tax evasion, but only low- and mid-level officials and functionaries have been prosecuted.

LABOR FREEDOM — 55.3%

Inflexible employment regulations hinder employment opportunities and overall productivity growth. The non-salary cost of employing a worker is very high, and the rigidity of hiring and firing a worker creates a risk aversion for companies that would otherwise employ more people and grow. Regulations related to the number of work hours are not flexible.

Moscow

RUSSIA

Russia's economy is 49.9 percent free, according to our 2008 assessment, which makes it the world's 134th freest economy. Its overall score is 2.5 percentage points lower than last year, one of the largest annual declines, caused by sharply lower scores in trade freedom and business freedom. Russia is ranked 40th out of 41 countries in the European region, and its overall score is much lower than the regional average.

Russia has weak or almost average scores in every area. The top individual income and corporate tax rates are relatively low at 13 percent and 24 percent, respectively, but overall tax revenue is relatively high as a percentage of GDP. The labor system is only partially flexible.

Russia's significant weaknesses lie in trade freedom, investment freedom, financial freedom, property rights, and freedom from corruption. Foreign investment in virtually all sectors faces official and unofficial hurdles, including bureaucratic inconsistency, corruption, and outright restrictions in lucrative sectors like energy. Corruption engenders a weak rule of law, which in turn reinforces the transience of property rights and arbitrary law enforcement.

BACKGROUND: After President Boris Yeltsin (1991–1999), Russia has moved to a more authoritarian "managed democracy" under President Vladimir Putin (2000–2008). The consumer economy is growing, bolstered by an emerging middle class, but Russia continues to depend heavily on sales of natural resources, especially oil and natural gas. State involvement in the economy is increasing through large state-controlled enterprises in energy, shipping, shipbuilding, and aerospace known as "national champions." Russia has almost paid off its debts and has a $400 billion hard currency reserve. The stock market was the best-performing of the world's emerging markets from 2000–2006. Although Russia aspires to join the World Trade Organization, weak intellectual property rights and protectionism in the natural resources sector are likely to make accession difficult.

How Do We Measure Economic Freedom? See Chapter 4 (page 39) for an explanation of the methodology or visit the *Index* Web site at *heritage.org/index*.

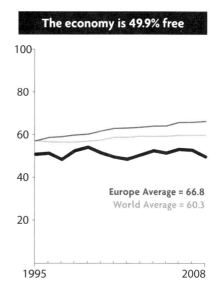

The economy is 49.9% free

Europe Average = 66.8
World Average = 60.3

1995   2008

QUICK FACTS

Population: 143.1 million

GDP (PPP): $1.6 trillion
6.4% growth in 2005
6.4% 5-yr. comp. ann. growth
$10,845 per capita

Unemployment: 7.6%

Inflation (CPI): 12.7%

FDI (net flow): $1.5 billion

Official Development Assistance:
Multilateral: n/a
Bilateral: n/a

External Debt: $229.0 billion

Exports: $268.1 billion
Primarily petroleum and petroleum products, natural gas, wood and wood products, metals, chemicals, civilian and military manufactures

Imports: $164.7 billion
Primarily machinery and equipment, consumer goods, medicines, meat, sugar, semifinished metal products
2005 data unless otherwise noted.

RUSSIA'S TEN ECONOMIC FREEDOMS

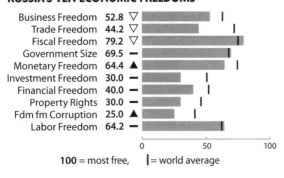

Business Freedom	52.8 ▽	
Trade Freedom	44.2 ▽	
Fiscal Freedom	79.2 ▽	
Government Size	69.5 —	
Monetary Freedom	64.4 ▲	
Investment Freedom	30.0 —	
Financial Freedom	40.0 —	
Property Rights	30.0 —	
Fdm fm Corruption	25.0 ▲	
Labor Freedom	64.2 —	

0   50   100

100 = most free,   I = world average

BUSINESS FREEDOM — 52.8%

The overall freedom to start, operate, and close a business is limited by Russia's regulatory environment. Bureaucratic obstacles are a particular problem for small businesses. Obtaining a business license is takes much more than the world average of 19 procedures and 234 days. Bankruptcy proceedings can be lengthy and difficult.

TRADE FREEDOM — 44.2%

Russia's weighted average tariff rate was 17.9 percent in 2005. Prohibitive tariffs, quotas, and service market access barriers; import and export restrictions; discriminatory import and export taxes, charges, and fees; non-transparent regulations and standards; discriminatory licensing, registration, and certification; complex and non-transparent customs valuation; customs fees; inefficient and arbitrary customs administration; subsidies; corruption; and weak enforcement of intellectual property rights add to the cost of trade. An additional 20 percentage points is deducted from Russia's trade freedom score to account for non-tariff barriers.

FISCAL FREEDOM — 79.2%

Russia has a low income tax rate and a moderate corporate tax rate. The individual income tax rate is a flat 13 percent, and the top corporate tax rate is 24 percent. Other taxes include a value-added tax (VAT), a property tax, and a transport tax. In the most recent year, overall tax revenue as a percentage of GDP was 36.6 percent.

GOVERNMENT SIZE — 69.5%

Total government expenditures, including consumption and transfer payments, are moderate. In the most recent year, government spending equaled 31.9 percent of GDP. Privatization has been hasty and inconsistent. State intervention in key sectors such as energy and mining has increased in recent years.

MONETARY FREEDOM — 64.4%

Inflation is high, averaging 10.5 percent between 2004 and 2006. Relatively unstable prices explain most of the monetary freedom score. The government influences prices through regulation, extensive subsidies, and numerous state-owned enterprises and utilities. An additional 15 percentage points is deducted from Russia's monetary freedom score to account for policies that distort domestic prices.

INVESTMENT FREEDOM — 30%

Foreign and domestic capital are legally equal, but the government tends to prefer joint ventures with the foreign company as a minority shareholder, especially in energy, and investment is restricted in many areas. Corruption, a politicized legal environment, crime, and bureaucracy are serious barriers. Residents and non-residents may hold foreign exchange accounts, subject to restrictions. Payments and transfers are also subject to restrictions.

FINANCIAL FREEDOM — 40%

Russia's financial system consists primarily of banking. Supervision and transparency are insufficient, though regulation improved in 2006. The 1,200 licensed and registered banks are generally small and undercapitalized, but consolidation is underway. Banking is dominated by two state-owned banks. Foreign banks may operate only as subsidiaries and must have a minimum number of Russian employees, and foreign investment is capped at 12 percent of total banking capital. There has not been much interest from foreign banks. There are about 920 insurance companies, and the state has a 25 percent stake in the largest insurer. Foreign insurers together may not control over 15 percent of the insurance market and are barred from life insurance. Capital markets are relatively small but growing and are dominated by energy companies.

PROPERTY RIGHTS — 30%

Protection of private property is weak. The judicial system is unpredictable, corrupt, and unable to handle technically sophisticated cases. Contracts are difficult to enforce, and an ancient antipathy to them continues to impede Russian integration into the West. Mortgage lending is in its initial stages. Violations of intellectual property rights continue to be a serious problem.

FREEDOM FROM CORRUPTION — 25%

Corruption is perceived as widespread. Russia ranks 121st out of 163 countries in Transparency International's Corruption Perceptions Index for 2006. Corruption remains pervasive, both in the number of instances and in the size of bribes sought. Manifestations also include misuse of budgetary resources, theft of government property, kickbacks in the procurement process, extortion, and official collusion in criminal acts. Customs officials are extremely inconsistent in their application of the law.

LABOR FREEDOM — 64.2%

Somewhat flexible employment regulations could be further improved to enhance overall productivity growth and employment opportunities. The non-salary cost of employing a worker is high, and the rigidity of hiring and firing a worker creates a risk aversion for companies that would otherwise employ more people and grow. Regulations related to the number of work hours are rigid.

Kigali ✪

RWANDA

R wanda's economy is 54.1 percent free, according to our 2008 assessment, which makes it the world's 116th freest economy. Its overall score is 1.7 percentage points higher than last year, reflecting improved scores in six of the 10 economic freedoms. Rwanda is ranked 22nd out of 40 countries in the sub-Saharan Africa region, and its overall score is slightly lower than the regional average.

Rwanda scores relatively well in fiscal freedom and government size. Personal and corporate income tax rates are moderately high, but overall tax revenue is relatively low as a percentage of GDP. The government recently reduced non-tariff barriers. Total government expenditures are slightly more than 25 percent of GDP, and state-owned businesses are not a large source of revenue.

Rwanda's scores for business freedom, investment freedom, financial freedom, property rights, and freedom from corruption are very low. Investment procedures have been streamlined, but political instability is still a major deterrent. The judicial system lacks enough qualified magistrates and independence, and legal procedures are subject to corruption. Inflation is high.

BACKGROUND: Following a 1961 referendum, the U.N. terminated Belgium's trusteeship and granted Rwanda independence in 1962. The military took power in 1973, and General Juvenal Habyarimana ruled for 20 years. Rwandan Tutsis, who had fled violence under the Hutu-dominated post-independence government, banded together as the Rwandan Patriotic Front (RPF) in 1990 and invaded Rwanda from Uganda. A 1992 cease-fire lasted until the plane carrying Habyarimana was shot down in 1994, sparking the genocide of up to 1 million Tutsis and moderate Hutus. The RPF seized power in 1994, ended the genocide, and ruled through a transition government until 2003, when Paul Kagame was elected president. Over 80 percent of Rwandans engage in subsistence agriculture supplemented by cash crops, particularly tea and coffee. The government has generally pursued a non-interventionist economic policy.

How Do We Measure Economic Freedom? See Chapter 4 (page 39) for an explanation of the methodology or visit the *Index* Web site at *heritage.org/index*.

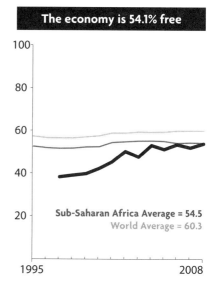

The economy is 54.1% free

Sub-Saharan Africa Average = 54.5
World Average = 60.3

1995 — 2008

QUICK FACTS

Population: 9.0 million

GDP (PPP): $10.9 billion
6.0% growth in 2005
5.0% 5-yr. comp. ann. growth
$1,206 per capita

Unemployment: n/a

Inflation (CPI): 9.2%

FDI (net flow): $7.0 million

Official Development Assistance:
Multilateral: $323.3 million
Bilateral: $304.9 million (20.7% from the U.S.)

External Debt: $1.5 billion

Exports: $257.2 million
Primarily coffee, tea, hides, tin ore

Imports: $659.0 million
Primarily foodstuffs, machinery and equipment, steel, petroleum products, cement and construction material

2005 data unless otherwise noted.

RWANDA'S TEN ECONOMIC FREEDOMS

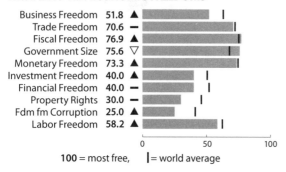

Business Freedom	51.8	▲
Trade Freedom	70.6	—
Fiscal Freedom	76.9	▲
Government Size	75.6	▽
Monetary Freedom	73.3	▲
Investment Freedom	40.0	▲
Financial Freedom	40.0	—
Property Rights	30.0	—
Fdm fm Corruption	25.0	▲
Labor Freedom	58.2	▲

0   50   100

100 = most free, | = world average

BUSINESS FREEDOM — *51.8%*

The overall freedom to start, operate, and close a business is restricted by Rwanda's regulatory environment. Starting a business takes an average of 16 days, compared to the world average of 43 days. Obtaining a business license takes less than the world average of 19 procedures and 234 days.

TRADE FREEDOM — *70.6%*

Rwanda's weighted average tariff rate was 9.7 percent in 2005. Liberalization of the trade regime has progressed, but prohibitive tariffs, import taxes, complex customs procedures, and lack of transparency in government procurement add to the cost of trade. An additional 10 percentage points is deducted from Rwanda's trade freedom score to account for non-tariff barriers.

FISCAL FREEDOM — *76.9%*

Rwanda has moderately high tax rates. The top income tax rate is 35 percent, and the top corporate tax rate is 30 percent. Other taxes include a value-added tax (VAT) and a property transfer tax. In the most recent year, overall tax revenue as a percentage of GDP was 13.6 percent.

GOVERNMENT SIZE — *75.6%*

Total government expenditures, including consumption and transfer payments, are moderate. In the most recent year, government spending equaled 28.5 percent of GDP. By the end of 2006, the government had privatized 70 out of 104 state-owned enterprises.

MONETARY FREEDOM — *73.3%*

Inflation is high, averaging 7 percent between 2004 and 2006. Relatively unstable prices explain most of the monetary freedom score. The government controls the prices of cement, electricity, water, telecommunications, petroleum, beer, and soft drinks and also influences prices through regulation and state-owned enterprises and utilities. An additional 10 percentage points is deducted from Rwanda's monetary freedom score to account for policies that distort domestic prices.

INVESTMENT FREEDOM — *40%*

There are no restrictions on investment in any sector, making Rwanda's investment regime one of the world's most liberal. Rwanda has adopted several initiatives, including a one-stop shop, but corruption, political instability (including the lingering issue of Hutu refugees in the neighboring Democratic Republic of Congo), and a nascent legal regime are persistent deterrents. The government liberalized its investment law in March 2006, facilitating regulatory requirements for investments. Commercial courts were created by law in December 2006, but none exists yet. Residents and non-residents may hold foreign exchange accounts if they provide supporting documentation. Payments and transfers are subject to authorizations, maximum allowances, and limits. Nearly all capital transactions require central bank approval.

FINANCIAL FREEDOM — *40%*

The small but growing financial sector is burdened by serious shortcomings in supervision, regulation, auditing, and oversight. The CEO of one of the largest banks, Banque du commerce, was embroiled in allegations of corruption and resigned in 2007. Non-performing loans are a problem for the financial sector, which consists primarily of small banks and microfinance institutions. There are eight commercial banks, the largest of which has a 50 percent stake controlled by the government (which the government officially intends to privatize). The government reduced its involvement in banking in 2004 when it sold off two majority bank holdings, but it remains extensively involved in the sector, according to the International Monetary Fund, and controls about 22 percent of total assets. There are four insurance companies in the insurance sector. The state owns the largest insurer, Sonarwa, and controls another insurance parastatal, and these two companies together account for a majority of the insurance market. There are no capital markets in Rwanda.

PROPERTY RIGHTS — *30%*

Rwanda's judiciary is government-influenced and suffers from inefficiency, a lack of resources, and corruption. A recently passed land law stipulates modalities of property registration, but no registries have been established. Despite adherence to key international agreements on intellectual property rights and adequate laws protecting IPR, sales of counterfeit goods and violations of pharmaceutical patents continue.

FREEDOM FROM CORRUPTION — *25%*

Corruption is perceived as widespread. Rwanda ranks 121st out of 163 countries in Transparency International's Corruption Perceptions Index for 2006. Experts regard corruption among public officials as "rampant." The authorities reportedly harass journalists who report on corruption in government.

LABOR FREEDOM — *58.2%*

Restrictive employment regulations hinder overall productivity growth. The non-salary cost of employing a worker is low, but dismissing a redundant employee can be difficult. Regulations relating to the number of work hours are rigid.

SAUDI ARABIA

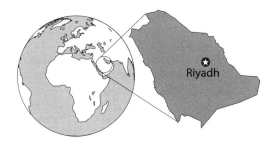

Saudi Arabia's economy is 62.8 percent free, according to our 2008 assessment, which makes it the world's 60th freest economy. Its overall score is 1.2 percentage points higher than last year, reflecting improved scores in four of the 10 economic freedoms. Saudi Arabia is ranked 6th out of 17 countries in the Middle East/North Africa region, and its overall score is above the regional average.

Saudi Arabia scores very well in fiscal freedom, labor freedom, and business freedom. Except for a mandatory 2.5 percent Islamic *zakat* charitable contribution, the government imposes no taxes on personal or corporate income. The labor market is flexible.

Saudi Arabia is weak in investment freedom, financial freedom, and freedom from corruption. As in many other Gulf oil states, high government spending is supported by a large state-owned energy sector. The monarchy has begun to liberalize aspects of foreign investment, but immense barriers remain in effect. Financial markets are distorted by government influence, and the legal system is similarly subject to political influence.

BACKGROUND: Saudi Arabia, the largest Persian Gulf oil kingdom, has been ruled as an absolute monarchy by the Saud dynasty ever since 1932, when it was founded by King Abdul Aziz al-Saud. Crown Prince Abdullah officially became monarch in August 2005 following the death of King Fahd. Saudi Arabia possesses roughly one-quarter of the world's oil reserves and, as the world's leading oil producer and exporter, plays a dominant role in the Organization of Petroleum Exporting Countries. Accession to the World Trade Organization in 2005 has led to gradual economic reforms, and the government has sought to attract foreign investment and promote diversification. The government's efforts to integrate Saudi Arabia more fully into the world economy have been opposed by Islamic extremists who have targeted Saudi oil facilities and foreign workers for terrorist attacks.

How Do We Measure Economic Freedom? See Chapter 4 (page 39) for an explanation of the methodology or visit the *Index* Web site at *heritage.org/index*.

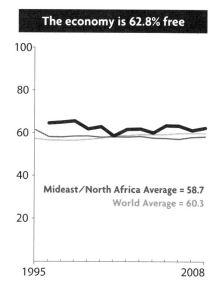

The economy is 62.8% free

Mideast/North Africa Average = 58.7
World Average = 60.3

1995 — 2008

QUICK FACTS

Population: 23.1 million

GDP (PPP): $363.2 billion
6.6% growth in 2005
4.9% 5-yr. comp. ann. growth
$15,711 per capita

Unemployment: 6.9%

Inflation (CPI): 0.7%

FDI (net flow): $3.4 billion

Official Development Assistance:
Multilateral: $2.0 million
Bilateral: $24.3 million (4.8% from the U.S.)

External Debt: $47.4 billion

Exports: $180.6 billion
Primarily petroleum and petroleum products

Imports: $79.3 billion
Primarily machinery and equipment, foodstuffs, chemicals, motor vehicles, textiles

2005 data unless otherwise noted.

SAUDI ARABIA'S TEN ECONOMIC FREEDOMS

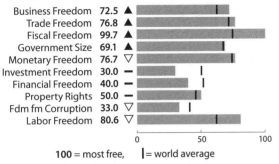

Business Freedom	72.5 ▲	
Trade Freedom	76.8 ▲	
Fiscal Freedom	99.7 ▲	
Government Size	69.1 ▲	
Monetary Freedom	76.7 ▽	
Investment Freedom	30.0 —	
Financial Freedom	40.0 —	
Property Rights	50.0 —	
Fdm fm Corruption	33.0 ▽	
Labor Freedom	80.6 ▽	

0   50   100

100 = most free,   I = world average

BUSINESS FREEDOM — 72.5%

The overall freedom to start, operate, and close a business is relatively well protected by Saudi Arabia's regulatory environment. Starting a business takes an average of 15 days, compared to the world average of 43 days. Obtaining a business license takes less than the world average of 19 procedures and 234 days. Bankruptcy proceedings are relatively straightforward.

TRADE FREEDOM — 76.8%

Saudi Arabia's weighted average tariff rate was 4.1 percent in 2005. Import bans, export controls, service market access barriers, non-transparent regulation and import licensing, domestic bias in government procurement, and weak protection of intellectual property rights add to the cost of trade. An additional 15 percentage points is deducted from Saudi Arabia's trade freedom score to account for non-tariff barriers.

FISCAL FREEDOM — 99.7%

Saudi Arabia has no income tax or corporate tax for Saudi nationals or citizens of the Gulf Cooperation Council (GCC). However, a fixed 2.5 percent religious tax (*zakat*) mandated by Islamic law is applied to Saudi and GCC individuals and corporations. Saudi Arabia has no value-added tax (VAT) or estate tax. In the most recent year, overall tax revenue as a percentage of GDP was 5.1 percent.

GOVERNMENT SIZE — 69.1%

Total government expenditures, including consumption and transfer payments, are high. In the most recent year, government spending equaled 32.1 percent of GDP. State participation in the economy remains substantial.

MONETARY FREEDOM — 76.7%

Inflation is low, averaging 1.7 percent between 2004 and 2006. Relatively stable prices explain most of the monetary freedom score. Islamic law forbids direct price controls, but the government influences prices across the economy through regulation, extensive subsidies, and state-owned enterprises and utilities, and a government purchasing agency controls prices for wheat and barley. An additional 15 percentage points is deducted from Saudi Arabia's monetary freedom score to account for policies that distort domestic prices.

INVESTMENT FREEDOM — 30%

Many sectors are still off-limits. Foreign investment projects require a license from the government, and most are joint ventures. Residents may hold foreign exchange accounts, but approval is required for non-residents. The SAGIA is the sole investment approval authority . In accordance with WTO accession, the government has heightened the allowable foreign equity in telecommunications and several other sectors. Regulations clarifying and liberalizing investment in insurance and tourism were issued in 2003 and 2006, respectively. There are no controls or restrictions on payments and transfers. Credit operations must be approved.

FINANCIAL FREEDOM — 40%

Financial markets are constrained by government influence, Islamic financial principles, and barriers to foreign participation, and services are insufficient. Banking-sector health is largely tied to oil earnings. Regulatory, supervisory, and accounting standards are generally consistent with international norms. Foreign ownership of financial institutions is limited. Of the 11 domestic commercial banks, four are locally owned, and two are Islamic banks. Seven banks are dual ventures with foreigners. The first Western bank began operations in 2005. At the end of 2006, there were 10 foreign branches. The government owns a majority of the largest domestic bank and 34 percent of the majority foreign-owned Gulf International Bank and offers subsidized credit to preferred sectors. All insurance companies must be locally registered and must operate according to the cooperative insurance principle. Insurance has undergone some liberalization. Capital markets are relatively well developed, and commercial banks may conduct transactions.

PROPERTY RIGHTS — 50%

Investors question the ability of Saudi courts to enforce contracts efficiently. The court system is slow, non-transparent, and influenced by the ruling elite. Laws on intellectual property rights are being revised to bring them in line with the WTO's Trade-Related Aspects of Intellectual Property Rights (TRIPS) agreement, but enforcement is weak, and procedures are inconsistent.

FREEDOM FROM CORRUPTION — 33%

Corruption is perceived as significant. Saudi Arabia ranks 70th out of 163 countries in Transparency International's Corruption Perceptions Index for 2006. Foreign firms view corruption as an obstacle to investment. Government procurement is often cited, as is *de facto* protection of businesses in which senior officials or elite individuals have a stake. Bribes, often disguised as "commissions," are reportedly commonplace.

LABOR FREEDOM — 80.6%

Flexible employment regulations enhance overall productivity growth and employment opportunities. The non-salary cost of employing a worker is low, and dismissing a redundant employee is not difficult. Regulations relating to the number of work hours are relatively flexible.

SENEGAL

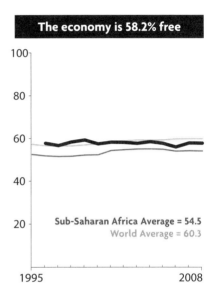

○ Dakar

Rank: 91

Regional Rank: 10 of 40

Senegal's economy is 58.2 percent free, according to our 2008 assessment, which makes it the world's 91st freest economy. Its overall score is essentially unchanged from last year. Senegal is ranked 10th out of 40 countries in the sub-Saharan Africa region, and its overall score is higher than the regional average.

Senegal scores well in government size, monetary freedom, and property rights, but the other seven measures score below the world average. Total government expenditures equal roughly 25 percent of GDP. Inflation is very low, and the market sets virtually all prices for consumer goods.

Business freedom, fiscal freedom, labor freedom, and freedom from corruption are weak. Starting a business takes more time than the world average, and the regulatory environment makes commercial operations more difficult. Tax rates are high, particularly the top income tax rate. The labor market is highly inelastic and one of the world's 20 least free. The judicial system does not have enough qualified magistrates or independence from the executive branch and is subject to corruption, as is much of the rest of Senegal's bureaucracy.

BACKGROUND: Senegal became independent in 1960 and is one of the few African countries never to have experienced a coup. Leopold Sedar Senghor was elected Senegal's first president and served until his retirement in 1980. His handpicked successor, Abdou Diouf, encouraged political pluralism and accepted his defeat by opposition candidate Abdoulaye Wade in the 2000 election. Wade was re-elected in 2007. Peace in the southern Casamance region is progressing fitfully. Senegal serves as a regional gateway and business center. It has limited natural resources, and agriculture and fishing occupy at least 60 percent of the population. Economic reforms aimed at liberalizing the economy are progressing slowly.

How Do We Measure Economic Freedom? See Chapter 4 (page 39) for an explanation of the methodology or visit the *Index* Web site at *heritage.org/index*.

The economy is 58.2% free

Sub-Saharan Africa Average = 54.5
World Average = 60.3

1995   2008

QUICK FACTS

Population: 11.7 million

GDP (PPP): $20.9 billion
5.5% growth in 2005
4.6% 5-yr. comp. ann. growth
$1,792 per capita

Unemployment: 48.0% (2001 estimate)

Inflation (CPI): 1.7%

FDI (net flow): $24.0 million

Official Development Assistance:
Multilateral: $345.0 million
Bilateral: $490.6 million (8.1% from the U.S.)

External Debt: $3.8 billion

Exports: $2.2 billion (2004)
Primarily fish, groundnuts (peanuts), petroleum products, phosphates, cotton

Imports: $3.2 billion (2004)
Primarily food and beverages, capital goods, fuels

2005 data unless otherwise noted.

SENEGAL'S TEN ECONOMIC FREEDOMS

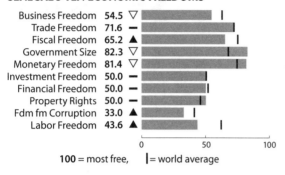

Business Freedom	54.5 ▽
Trade Freedom	71.6 ▬
Fiscal Freedom	65.2 ▲
Government Size	82.3 ▽
Monetary Freedom	81.4 ▽
Investment Freedom	50.0 ▬
Financial Freedom	50.0 ▬
Property Rights	50.0 ▬
Fdm fm Corruption	33.0 ▲
Labor Freedom	43.6 ▲

0   50   100

100 = most free, | = world average

BUSINESS FREEDOM — 54.5%

The overall freedom to start, operate, and close a business is restricted by Senegal's regulatory environment. Starting a business takes an average of 58 days, compared to the world average of 43 days. Obtaining business licenses takes less than the world average of 19 procedures and 234 days. Bankruptcy proceedings can be lengthy.

TRADE FREEDOM — 71.6%

Senegal's weighted average tariff rate was 9.2 percent in 2005. Significant import taxes and fees, non-transparent government procurement, inconsistent customs implementation, and corruption add to the cost of trade. An additional 10 percentage points is deducted from Senegal's trade freedom score to account for non-tariff barriers.

FISCAL FREEDOM — 65.2%

Senegal has high income tax rates but moderate corporate tax rates. The top income tax rate is 50 percent, and the top corporate tax rate is 25 percent, down from 33 percent. Other taxes include a value-added tax (VAT) and a vehicle tax. In the most recent year, overall tax revenue as a percentage of GDP was 18.8 percent.

GOVERNMENT SIZE — 82.3%

Total government expenditures, including consumption and transfer payments, are relatively low. In the most recent year, government spending equaled 24.3 percent of GDP. The government has fully or partially privatized large, strategic state-owned enterprises.

MONETARY FREEDOM — 81.4%

Inflation is low, averaging 1.9 percent between 2004 and 2006. Relatively stable prices explain most of the monetary freedom score. Many prices are freely determined, but the government controls the prices of pharmaceuticals and medical services and influences prices across the economy through state-owned enterprises and utilities. An additional 10 percentage points is deducted from Senegal's monetary freedom score to account for policies that distort domestic prices.

INVESTMENT FREEDOM — 50%

There is no legal discrimination against foreign investors, and 100 percent foreign ownership of businesses is permitted except for electricity, telecommunications, mining, and water. Unofficial barriers, such as corruption and judicial weakness, are substantial. Attractions include political stability, stable macroeconomic policies, modern telecommunications, and a bilateral investment agreement with the United States. There is a one-stop shop for investments, but its efficiency is limited. Privatization has been fairly successful, and the electricity distribution monopoly is the only major remaining business to be sold. The government must approve capital transfers to most countries. Other transfers are subject to requirements, controls, and authorization, depending on the transaction. Residents and non-residents must receive official approval to hold foreign exchange accounts.

FINANCIAL FREEDOM — 50%

Senegal's financial system is underdeveloped. The Central Bank of West African States, a central bank common to eight countries, governs Senegal's financial institutions. As of mid-2006, there were 13 commercial banks and three financial institutions. The largest banks are predominantly French-owned. Banking is highly concentrated, with three banks holding two-thirds of deposits. The government owns over 25 percent of the shares in seven banks, including a majority share in the agricultural bank. Most lending is carried out with only a few borrowers, and most services are concentrated in the capital. There are several microfinance institutions. Senegal participates in a small regional stock market based in the Ivory Coast, where the formerly state-owned telecommunications company is one of the major listings.

PROPERTY RIGHTS — 50%

Application of property title and land registration systems is uneven outside of urban areas. The housing finance market is underdeveloped, and few long-term mortgage financing vehicles exist. Senegal lacks commercial courts staffed with trained judges, so decisions can be arbitrary and inconsistent. An arbitration center administered by the Dakar Chamber of Commerce was established in 1998. Corruption is present in dispute settlement cases. Despite an adequate legal and regulatory framework, enforcement of intellectual property rights is weak to nonexistent.

FREEDOM FROM CORRUPTION — 33%

Corruption is perceived as significant. Senegal ranks 70th out of 163 countries in Transparency International's Corruption Perceptions Index for 2006. Corruption is a significant obstacle to economic development and competitiveness. There are credible allegations of corruption in government procurement, dispute settlement, and regulatory and enforcement agencies.

LABOR FREEDOM — 43.6%

Restrictive employment regulations hinder employment opportunities and overall productivity growth. The non-salary cost of employing a worker is high, and dismissing a redundant employee can be burdensome. Regulations related to the number of work hours are rigid. Senegal's labor freedom is one of the 20 lowest in the world.

SERBIA

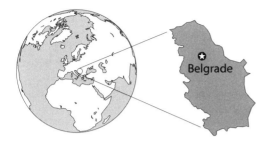
Belgrade

Rank: Not Ranked

Regional Rank: Not Ranked

Most of the economic freedom of Serbia cannot be properly graded because of the lack of reliable data. The last time Serbia was graded was in 2003, when it received a score of 39.5 percent.

Monetary freedom and trade freedom are weak. Inflation is high, particularly for a European country, and the government reserves the right to re-impose price supports that have been phased out in the past. Belgrade imposes a fairly high average tariff rate, although efforts are underway to liberalize the country's regulatory non-tariff barriers.

BACKGROUND: Following Montenegro's secession in May 2006, the National Assembly of Serbia declared Serbia the successor to the State Union of Serbia and Montenegro. After suffering from economic sanctions and NATO air strikes throughout the 1990s, Serbia eventually embarked on the long road to membership in the European Union by signing a Stability and Association Agreement in October 2005, but membership talks were suspended in May 2006 because of Serbia's failure to hand over indicted war criminal Ratko Mladic. The country continues to pursue economic reform to improve its situation, and the recent removal of the ultranationalists from the parliament has again repositioned Serbia toward the EU. The final status of Kosovo remains a potent political topic with the potential to destabilize future Euro–Serbian relations.

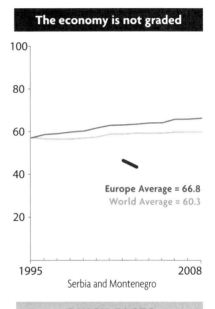

The economy is not graded

Europe Average = 66.8
World Average = 60.3

1995 — 2008

Serbia and Montenegro

QUICK FACTS

Population: 10.1 million

GDP (PPP): $44.8 billion
6.8% growth in 2005
5.3% 5-yr. comp. ann. growth
n/a
$4,400 per capita

Unemployment: 31.6%

Inflation (CPI): 15.5%

FDI (net flow): $1.3 billion

Official Development Assistance:
Multilateral: $280.9 million
Bilateral: $851.0 million (21.3% from the U.S.)

External Debt: $16.4 billion

Exports: $6.4 billion
Primarily manufactured goods, food and live animals, machinery and transport equipment

Imports: $10.6 billion
Primarily machinery, transport equipment, fuels and lubricants, manufactured goods
2005 data unless otherwise noted.

How Do We Measure Economic Freedom? See Chapter 4 (page 39) for an explanation of the methodology or visit the *Index* Web site at *heritage.org/index.*

BUSINESS FREEDOM — NOT GRADED

Starting a business takes an average of 23 days, compared to the world average of 43 days. Obtaining a business license takes slightly more than the world average of 19 procedures and 234 days, and costs are high. The enforcement of regulations can be inconsistent and non-transparent.

TRADE FREEDOM — NOT GRADED

Progress has been made toward liberalization, but some high tariffs, import restrictions, non-transparent regulations, and corruption add to the cost of trade. If Serbia were graded this year, an additional 10 percentage points would be deducted from its trade freedom score to account for non-tariff barriers.

FISCAL FREEDOM — NOT GRADED

Serbia has competitive tax rates for individual and corporate income. The individual income tax rate is 12 percent for salaries, and other personal income can be taxed at up to 20 percent. The corporate tax rate is a flat 10 percent. Other taxes include a value-added tax (VAT), introduced in 2005.

GOVERNMENT SIZE — NOT GRADED

Total government expenditures, including consumption and transfer payments, are high. In the most recent year, government spending was estimated to equal about 44.4 percent of GDP.

MONETARY FREEDOM — NOT GRADED

Inflation is high, averaging 13.6 percent between 2004 and 2006. The government can control the prices of certain basic products, including milk, bread, flour, and cooking oil; controls the prices of utilities, public transit, telecommunications services, and petroleum; and influences prices through numerous state-owned enterprises. If Serbia were graded this year, an additional 15 percentage points would be deducted from its monetary freedom score to account for policies that distort domestic prices.

INVESTMENT FREEDOM — NOT GRADED

Serbian law eliminates previous investment restrictions, provides for national treatment, permits transfer and repatriation of profits and dividends, guarantees against expropriation, and provides incentives. The industrial sector has not fully recovered from the 1999 bombing. Restructuring has been difficult, and the only significant and successful privatization has been in banking. Foreign direct investment has grown, but the high value of the dinar has hurt exports and made business relatively more expensive. The business environment is still fairly weak. Bureaucracy, red tape, and corruption are major impediments to existing enterprises and to the creation of new enterprises. Residents and non-residents may hold foreign exchange accounts, subject to central bank permission or conditions. Payments and transfers are subject to restrictions, and most capital transactions are subject to controls.

FINANCIAL FREEDOM — NOT GRADED

Serbia's financial system is relatively underdeveloped. Purchases of 5 percent or more in any bank must be approved by the central bank. Aggressive consolidation and privatization by the central bank since 2001 has helped to revive Serbia's moribund banking sector. In September 2006, Vojvodjanska Banka was sold to the National Bank of Greece. Banking is now dominated by foreign capital, and the number of banks has plummeted in the past five years. As of mid-2006, there were 37 banks:18 foreign-owned, 12 state-owned, and seven private Serbian banks. Insurance is dominated by state-owned insurers, although the government has announced its intention to privatize them. Capital markets are vigorous, and takeovers are common on the Belgrade Stock Exchange.

PROPERTY RIGHTS — NOT GRADED

The constitution of the Republic of Serbia creates an independent judiciary, but the judicial system is corrupt and inefficient. Judges are poorly trained, underpaid, and difficult to dismiss for incompetence. Central registries of land titles are typically not completely current, but the government is trying to modernize its cadastral system. Enforcement of intellectual property rights is governed by a recently enacted law on civil procedures.

FREEDOM FROM CORRUPTION — NOT GRADED

Corruption is perceived as widespread. Serbia ranks 90th out of 163 countries in Transparency International's Corruption Perceptions Index for 2006. The authorities are inconsistent in approaching official corruption, and investigations are often politically motivated. Demands for bribes are expected at all stages of a business transaction. A deeply rooted practice favors certain parties based on *veze* (connections). Organized criminal groups engage in money laundering and attempt to siphon off assets of previously politically connected tycoons.

LABOR FREEDOM — NOT GRADED

Relatively flexible employment regulations could be improved to enhance overall productivity growth and employment opportunities. The non-salary cost of employing a worker is moderate, and dismissing a redundant employee is not costly. Regulations related to the number of work hours are fairly flexible.

SIERRA LEONE

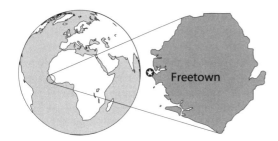

Freetown

Sierra Leone's economy is 48.9 percent free, according to our 2008 assessment, which makes it the world's 139th freest economy. Its overall score is 1.3 percentage points higher than last year, reflecting moderate improvement in five of the 10 economic freedoms. Sierra Leone is ranked 32nd out of 40 countries in the sub-Saharan Africa region, and its overall score is below the regional average.

Sierra Leone scores better than the world average in terms of government expenditures, which are low in formal terms, although this is not likely a sign of government efficiency. It is slightly above the world average in fiscal freedom because of weak tax revenue collection, not low tax rates.

Sierra Leone is recovering from a civil war and rates significantly below the world average in seven areas. The judicial system is riddled with corruption (as is virtually all of the civil service) and is often supplemented by traditional tribal courts in areas outside of the government's jurisdiction. The labor market is highly inflexible and one of the world's least free.

BACKGROUND: Sierra Leone became independent in 1961. Despite a series of military coups after the 1967 election, Siaka Stevens assumed office in 1968 and served until 1985. His successor was ousted by a coup in 1992. Popular pressure led to elections in 1996 that were won by Ahmad Tejan Kabbah, who was ousted in a coup, reinstated by Nigerian-led forces in 1998, and re-elected in 2002. Civil war with the Revolutionary United Front through the 1990s seriously damaged the infrastructure and economy but ended in 2002 with assistance from African, British, and U.N. peacekeepers. Mining accounts for 30 percent of GDP, and diamonds are the primary export. Agriculture accounts for over 50 percent of the economy, and two-thirds of the population engages in subsistence agriculture. Corruption is pervasive.

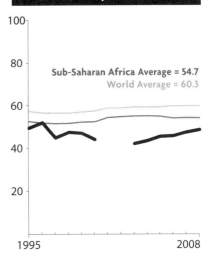

The economy is 48.9% free

Sub-Saharan Africa Average = 54.7
World Average = 60.3

1995 — 2008

QUICK FACTS

Population: 5.5 million

GDP (PPP): $4.5 billion
7.3% growth in 2005
12.6% 5-yr. comp. ann. growth
$806.0 per capita

Unemployment: n/a

Inflation (CPI): 12.1%

FDI (net flow): $27.0 million

Official Development Assistance:
Multilateral: $233.7 million
Bilateral: $132.4 million (15.8% from the U.S.)

External Debt: $1.7 billion

Exports: $263.1 million
Primarily diamonds, rutile, cocoa, coffee, fish

Imports: $452.3 million
Primarily foodstuffs, machinery and equipment, fuels and lubricants, chemicals
2005 data unless otherwise noted.

How Do We Measure Economic Freedom? See Chapter 4 (page 39) for an explanation of the methodology or visit the *Index* Web site at *heritage.org/index.*

SIERRA LEONE'S TEN ECONOMIC FREEDOMS

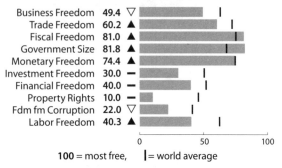

Business Freedom	49.4 ▽	
Trade Freedom	60.2 ▲	
Fiscal Freedom	81.0 ▲	
Government Size	81.8 ▲	
Monetary Freedom	74.4 ▲	
Investment Freedom	30.0 —	
Financial Freedom	40.0 —	
Property Rights	10.0 —	
Fdm fm Corruption	22.0 ▽	
Labor Freedom	40.3 ▲	

0   50   100

100 = most free, ▎= world average

BUSINESS FREEDOM — 49.4%

The overall freedom to start, operate, and close a business is restricted by Sierra Leone's regulatory environment. Starting a business takes an average of 26 days, compared to the world average of 43 days. Obtaining a business license takes much more than the world average of 19 procedures and 234 days. Bankruptcy proceedings are fairly straightforward but costly.

TRADE FREEDOM — 60.2%

The weighted average tariff rate in Sierra Leone was 14.9 percent in 2005. Liberalization of the trade regime is progressing, but import taxes and fees, non-transparent regulations, inefficient customs implementation, inadequate infrastructure, and corruption add to the cost of trade. An additional 10 percentage points is deducted from Sierra Leone's trade freedom score to account for non-tariff barriers.

FISCAL FREEDOM — 81%

Sierra Leone has relatively high tax rates. Both the top income tax rate and the top corporate tax rate are 30 percent, down from 35 percent. Other taxes include a vehicle tax and a tax on interest. In the most recent year, overall tax revenue as a percentage of GDP was 10 percent.

GOVERNMENT SIZE — 81.8%

Total government expenditures, including consumption and transfer payments, are moderate. In the most recent year, government spending equaled 24.6 percent of GDP. The budget deficit has been somewhat reduced, but better spending management is needed.

MONETARY FREEDOM — 74.4%

Inflation is high, averaging 10.6 percent between 2004 and 2006. Unstable prices explain most of the monetary freedom score. Most prices are freely set in the market, but the government influences prices through state-owned enterprises and utilities. An additional 5 percentage points is deducted from Sierra Leone's monetary freedom score to account for policies that distort domestic prices.

INVESTMENT FREEDOM — 30%

Businesses face a shortage of foreign exchange, corruption, devastated infrastructure, and uncertainty in the wake of the civil war. There is no screening, and foreign capital is legally equal to domestic capital. Non-citizens and foreign investors may not participate in certain economic activities. Foreigners may not own land. Clarifications of the 2005 investment law, which was intended to modernize existing regulations, are being developed. The judicial system is slow and prone to corruption. Residents and non-residents may hold foreign exchange accounts, subject to some restrictions. Payments and transfers face quantitative limits and certain approval requirements. Many capital transactions require the Bank of Sierra Leone's approval. Direct investment abroad by residents is prohibited.

FINANCIAL FREEDOM — 40%

During the civil war, Sierra Leone's financial system collapsed, and the major foreign banks (Barclay's and Standard Chartered) left the market. Sierra Leone is a member of the Economic Community of West African States, which promotes regional trade and economic integration. Poor enforcement of contracts discourages lending, and corruption is endemic. A substantial shadow market in U.S. dollars hinders efforts to combat money laundering. The banking sector includes the central bank, seven commercial banks, two discount houses, and four community banks and is becoming less sound. Non-performing loans have risen rapidly for four years. Foreign and domestic borrowers have access to credit at market rates, but banking services do not extend to rural areas. Government-owned banks account for a majority of assets, and the government's frequent bond auctions tend to crowd out credit to other markets. The government is setting up a stock market.

PROPERTY RIGHTS — 10%

Property is not secure. There is no land titling system, and judicial corruption is significant. Traditional tribal justice systems continue to serve as a supplement to the central government's judiciary, especially in rural areas. Optical discs and tapes of popular music and films are illegally copied and sold on a substantial scale.

FREEDOM FROM CORRUPTION — 22%

Corruption is perceived as pervasive. Sierra Leone ranks 142nd out of 163 countries in Transparency International's Corruption Perceptions Index for 2006. International companies cite corruption in all branches of government as an obstacle to investment. Official corruption is exacerbated by low civil service salaries and a lack of accountability.

LABOR FREEDOM — 40.3%

Inflexible employment regulations hinder overall productivity growth and employment opportunities. The non-salary cost of employing a worker is moderate, but the rigidity of hiring and firing a worker creates a risk aversion for companies that would otherwise employ more people and grow. Sierra Leone's labor freedom is among the world's 20 lowest.

SINGAPORE

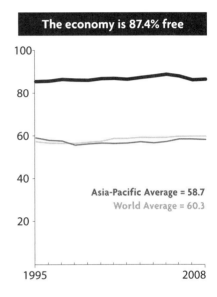
Singapore

Singapore's economy is 87.4 percent free, according to our 2008 assessment, which makes it the world's 2nd freest economy. Its overall score is slightly higher than last year, reflecting improved scores in five of the 10 economic freedoms. Singapore is ranked 2nd out of 30 countries in the Asia–Pacific region, and its overall score is much higher than the regional average.

Singapore is a world leader in all 10 areas of economic freedom. Virtually all commercial operations are performed with transparency and speed, and private enterprise has boomed. Inflation is low, and foreign investment is welcomed and given equal treatment. There are no tariffs. Singapore's legal system is efficient and highly protective of private property, and corruption is almost nonexistent. The labor market is highly flexible, and dismissing workers is costless.

Singapore could do slightly better in financial freedom, which at 50 percent is the only one of 10 economic freedoms below 80 percent. It is a world leader in foreign exchange transactions, and the government is promoting Singapore as a global financial hub, but state influence in the banking system persists.

BACKGROUND: Singapore, a city-state of 4.5 million, is the most well developed, prosperous country in Southeast Asia. While nominally a democracy, the island nation has been ruled by the People's Action Party since gaining its independence from Malaysia in 1965. Singapore boasts the freest economy in Southeast Asia, with a well-earned reputation for efficient administration and clean governance. While the service sector dominates the economy, the country is also a major manufacturer of electronics and chemicals. The most heavily trade-reliant country in the world, Singapore has led the global trend toward bilateral and multilateral free trade agreements.

How Do We Measure Economic Freedom? See Chapter 4 (page 39) for an explanation of the methodology or visit the *Index* Web site at *heritage.org/index*.

The economy is 87.4% free

Asia-Pacific Average = 58.7
World Average = 60.3

1995 — 2008

QUICK FACTS

Population: 4.3 million

GDP (PPP): $128.8 billion
6.6% growth in 2005
5.7% 5-yr. comp. ann. growth
$29,663 per capita

Unemployment: 3.1%

Inflation (CPI): 0.5%

FDI (net flow): $14.6 billion

Official Development Assistance:
Multilateral: $0.01 million
Bilateral: $9.1 million (0% from the U.S.)

External Debt: $24.3 billion

Exports: $283.6 billion
Primarily machinery and equipment (including electronics), consumer goods, mineral fuels, travel services, financial and insurance services

Imports: $248.6 billion
Primarily machinery and equipment, mineral fuels, financial services, foodstuffs
2005 data unless otherwise noted.

335

SINGAPORE'S TEN ECONOMIC FREEDOMS

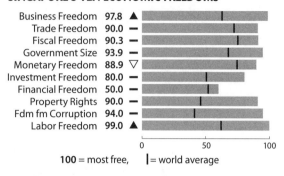

Business Freedom	97.8 ▲	
Trade Freedom	90.0 —	
Fiscal Freedom	90.3 —	
Government Size	93.9 —	
Monetary Freedom	88.9 ▽	
Investment Freedom	80.0 —	
Financial Freedom	50.0 —	
Property Rights	90.0 —	
Fdm fm Corruption	94.0 —	
Labor Freedom	99.0 ▲	

0   50   100

100 = most free,   **|= world average**

BUSINESS FREEDOM — *97.8%*

The overall freedom to start, operate, and close a business is strongly protected by Singapore's regulatory environment. Starting a business takes an average of five days, compared to the world average of 43 days. Obtaining a business license takes much less than the world average of 19 procedures and 234 days. Bankruptcy proceedings are easy and straightforward.

TRADE FREEDOM — *90%*

Singapore's weighted average tariff rate was zero percent in 2005. Tariffs are generally low, but import restrictions, import taxes, import licensing, export incentive programs, issues involving intellectual property rights, service market barriers, sanitary and phytosanitary rules, and non-transparent regulations add to the cost of trade. An additional 10 percentage points is deducted from Singapore's trade freedom score to account for non-tariff barriers.

FISCAL FREEDOM — *90.3%*

Singapore has low tax rates. The top income tax rate is 20 percent, and the top corporate tax rate is 20 percent, which will be reduced to 18 percent for the Year of Assessment 2008. Other taxes include a value-added tax (VAT) and a property tax. In the most recent year, overall tax revenue as a percentage of GDP was 12.9 percent.

GOVERNMENT SIZE — *93.9%*

Total government expenditures, including consumption and transfer payments, are low. In the most recent year, government spending equaled 14.4 percent of GDP. The state remains involved in the economy through Singapore's many government-linked companies.

MONETARY FREEDOM — *88.9%*

Inflation is low, averaging 0.9 percent between 2004 and 2006. Relatively stable prices explain most of the monetary freedom score. The government influences prices through regulation and state-supported enterprises and can impose controls as it deems necessary. An additional 5 percentage points is deducted from Singapore's monetary freedom score to account for policies that distort domestic prices.

INVESTMENT FREEDOM — *80%*

Foreign and domestic businesses are treated equally, there are no production or local content requirements, and near-ly all sectors are open to 100 percent foreign ownership. The government screens investment for incentive eligibility. Foreign investment is limited in broadcasting, newspaper services, foreign law firms and lawyers practicing in Singapore, and sectors dominated by government-linked companies. The government is trying to attract high-value-added manufacturing and services. Foreign ownership of certain landed properties is subject to approval. Residents and non-residents may hold foreign exchange accounts. There are no controls or requirements on current transfers, payments, or repatriation of profits.

FINANCIAL FREEDOM — *50%*

Singapore is among the top five foreign exchange trading centers. There were 109 commercial banks in mid-2006, 104 of them foreign. One of the three banking groups is the government-controlled Development Bank of Singapore (the largest domestic bank group and publicly listed), and two have significant government-held minority shares. Foreign banks now have greater freedom to open branches and offer services, but the government seeks to maintain the domestic bank share of deposits above 50 percent, and the majority of domestic bank board members must be Singapore citizens and residents. License quotas for full-service foreign banks were eliminated in July 2005, and the quota for U.S. wholesale banks was eliminated in January 2007. Foreign banks are allocated to three categories that specify the services they can provide; 48 merchant banks offer a range of investment-banking services. A free trade agreement with the U.S. has loosened restrictions on U.S. banks. Foreign firms compete aggressively in insurance, fund management, and venture capital. Capital markets are well developed, and the Singapore Exchange is increasing its ties with other Asian exchanges. A single institution regulates the securities exchanges.

PROPERTY RIGHTS — *90%*

The court system is efficient and protects private property. There is no expropriation, and contracts are secure. Singapore has one of Asia's strongest intellectual property rights regimes, and foreign and local entities may establish, operate, and dispose of their own enterprises.

FREEDOM FROM CORRUPTION — *94%*

Corruption is perceived as almost nonexistent. Singapore ranks 5th out of 163 countries in Transparency International's Corruption Perceptions Index for 2006. Singapore enforces strong anti-corruption laws. It is a crime for a citizen to bribe a foreign official or any other person, whether within or outside of Singapore.

LABOR FREEDOM — *99%*

Highly flexible employment regulations enhance overall productivity growth and employment opportunities. The non-salary cost of employing a worker is low, and dismissing a redundant employee is not burdensome. Regulations related to the number of work hours are very flexible.

SLOVAK REPUBLIC

Bratislava

The Slovak Republic's economy is 68.7 percent free, according to our 2008 assessment, which makes it the world's 35th freest economy. Its overall score is 0.3 percentage point higher than last year, reflecting improved scores in four of the 10 economic freedoms. The Slovak Republic is ranked 20th out of 41 countries in the European region, and its overall score is higher than the regional average.

The Slovak Republic has very high scores in most areas of economic freedom, especially investment freedom, trade freedom, financial freedom, and fiscal freedom. The average tariff rate is low, although non-tariff barriers include distortionary EU subsidies. Foreign investment is actively promoted, and foreigners are subject to remarkably few regulations in almost all areas of the economy. The financial sector has benefited significantly from an aggressive government privatization campaign.

The Slovak Republic is weak only in its score for government size. Total government spending equals almost two-fifths of GDP. The judiciary is independent of political influence, but cases take years to resolve, both for citizens and for foreign investors.

BACKGROUND: Slovakia became independent following its peaceful "Velvet Divorce" from the former Czechoslovakia in 1993. The reforms implemented by former Prime Minister Mikulas Dzurinda have led to low labor costs, low taxes, and political stability, making Slovakia one of Europe's most attractive economies, especially for automobile and other manufacturing. The 1996–2005 GDP average growth was about 4 percent. In 2006, real GDP growth was 8.3 percent, encouraged by strong exports and growing domestic demand. The current administration is not expected to modify previous reforms substantially, with the exception of increased government intervention in the health care sector. Slovakia's official target date for adoption of the euro is 2009, assuming that the Maastricht criteria can be met.

How Do We Measure Economic Freedom? See Chapter 4 (page 39) for an explanation of the methodology or visit the *Index* Web site at *heritage.org/index*.

The economy is 68.7% free

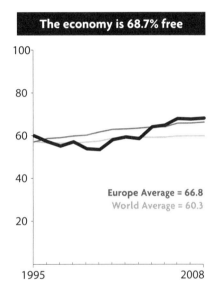

Europe Average = 66.8
World Average = 60.3

QUICK FACTS

Population: 5.4 million

GDP (PPP): $85.5 billion
6.0% growth in 2005
4.9% 5-yr. comp. ann. growth
$15,871 per capita

Unemployment: 11.7%

Inflation (CPI): 2.8%

FDI (net flow): $1.8 billion

Official Development Assistance:
Multilateral: $171.0 million (2004)
Bilateral: $64.0 million (2% from the U.S.) (2004)

External Debt: $23.7 billion

Exports: $32.0 billion
Primarily vehicles, machinery and electrical equipment, base metals, chemicals and minerals, plastics

Imports: $34.4 billion
Primarily machinery and transport equipment, intermediate manufactured goods, fuels, chemicals

2005 data unless otherwise noted.

SLOVAK REPUBLIC'S TEN ECONOMIC FREEDOMS

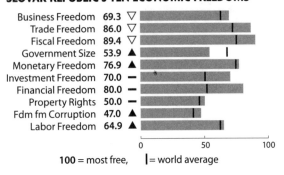

Business Freedom	69.3	▽
Trade Freedom	86.0	▽
Fiscal Freedom	89.4	▽
Government Size	53.9	▲
Monetary Freedom	76.9	▲
Investment Freedom	70.0	—
Financial Freedom	80.0	—
Property Rights	50.0	—
Fdm fm Corruption	47.0	▲
Labor Freedom	64.9	▲

0   50   100

100 = most free, | = world average

BUSINESS FREEDOM — 69.3%

The overall freedom to start, operate, and close a business is relatively well protected by the Slovak Republic's regulatory environment. Starting a business takes an average of 25 days, compared to the world average of 43 days. Obtaining a business license takes less than the world average of 19 procedures but can take more than the world average of 234 days. Closing a business can be difficult and time-consuming.

TRADE FREEDOM — 86%

The Slovak Republic's trade policy is the same as those of other members of the European Union. The common EU weighted average tariff rate was 2 percent in 2005. Non-tariff barriers reflected in EU policy include agricultural and manufacturing subsidies, import restrictions for some goods and services, market access restrictions in some service sectors, non-transparent and restrictive regulations and standards, and inconsistent customs administration across EU members. Pharmaceuticals regulation and non-transparent licensing procedures exceed general EU policy. Consequently, an additional 10 percentage points is deducted from the Slovak Republic's trade freedom score.

FISCAL FREEDOM — 89.4%

Both the income and corporate tax rates are a flat 19 percent. Other taxes include a value-added tax (VAT) and a property tax. In the most recent year, overall tax revenue as a percentage of GDP was 18.3 percent.

GOVERNMENT SIZE — 53.9%

Total government expenditures, including consumption and transfer payments, are high. In the most recent year, government spending equaled 39.2 percent of GDP. The state's role in the economy has been reduced.

MONETARY FREEDOM — 76.9%

Inflation is moderate, averaging 4.3 percent between 2004 and 2006. Relatively unstable prices explain most of the monetary freedom score. As a participant in the EU's Common Agricultural Policy, the government subsidizes agricultural production, distorting the prices of agricultural products. It also influences prices through regulation and state-owned enterprises and utilities. An additional 10 percentage points is deducted from the Slovak Republic's monetary freedom score to account for these policies.

INVESTMENT FREEDOM — 70%

There is no screening process, and full foreign ownership is permitted in some cases. The state owns railroad-rights-of-way, postal services, water supplies, and forestry companies. Privatization has encouraged foreign direct investment, but the government elected in mid-2006 has not encouraged privatization. Incentives are structured largely to encourage investment in less-developed regions. Residents may establish foreign exchange accounts when staying abroad or with permission of the National Bank of Slovakia. There are very few controls on capital transactions.

FINANCIAL FREEDOM — 80%

The government has implemented aggressive privatization and has adopted reforms to bring the financial sector into line with European standards. All financial service operations were brought under the central bank's regulatory aegis in January 2006. Interest rates have been liberalized, and credit limits have been abolished. The financial sector is dominated by banking. Most state-owned banks have been sold, and foreign capital controls 97 percent of the sector. The percentage of non-performing loans has declined for five years. The insurance sector is growing. Capital markets are small. Pension administration companies are required to invest at least 30 percent of their assets in Slovakia.

PROPERTY RIGHTS — 50%

The judiciary is independent and comparatively effective, although decisions can take years and corruption remains significant. The courts recognize and enforce foreign judgments, subject to the same delays. Secured interests in property and contractual rights are recognized and enforced. The mortgage market is growing, and the recording system is reliable. Intellectual property rights are protected under Slovak law and practice except for inadequate storage of proprietary data and improper registration of generic companies to produce drugs still under patent protection.

FREEDOM FROM CORRUPTION — 47%

Corruption is perceived as significant. The Slovak Republic ranks 49th out of 163 countries in Transparency International's Corruption Perceptions Index for 2006. Legislative and executive branch corruption especially affects health care, the judiciary, and education. The press has taken a more active role in reporting corruption. Slovakia is a signatory to the OECD Convention on Combating Bribery, and giving or accepting a bribe is a criminal act.

LABOR FREEDOM — 64.9%

Relatively flexible employment regulations could be further improved to enhance employment opportunities and overall productivity growth. The non-salary cost of employing a worker is high, but dismissing a redundant employee is not costly. Restrictions related to the number of work hours remain rigid.

SLOVENIA

Ljubljana

Slovenia's economy is 60.6 percent free, according to our 2008 assessment, which makes it the world's 75th freest economy. Its overall score is 0.4 percentage point higher than last year, mainly reflecting improved scores in fiscal freedom and freedom from corruption. Slovenia is ranked 33rd out of 41 countries in the European region, and its overall score is lower than the regional average.

Slovenia enjoys high levels of business freedom, investment freedom, trade freedom, and freedom from corruption. The average tariff rate is low, although non-tariff barriers include distortionary EU subsidies, and business regulations are transparent. Foreign investment is encouraged, and the streamlining of investment rules has left virtually no restrictions on foreign capital.

Slovenia is weak in terms of overall government size and has a relatively weak score in labor freedom. Total government spending equals more than two-fifths of GDP. Slovenia's labor market, like those of many other EU social democracies, remains very rigid.

BACKGROUND: As the first entity to secede from the former Yugoslavia in 1991, Slovenia largely managed to avoid the bloody conflict that followed Croatia's secession. As a result, Slovenia's relatively strong economic infrastructure was left intact, and its economy remains prosperous and stable. Slovenia joined both the European Union and NATO in 2004 as part of a broader strategy of integration into the Euro-Atlantic community. It also adopted the euro as its currency on January 1, 2007, in a smooth changeover. However, the government's approach to market-based reforms has been too cautious, and privatization and tax reform are needed sooner rather than later if Slovenia is to remain economically competitive.

How Do We Measure Economic Freedom? See Chapter 4 (page 39) for an explanation of the methodology or visit the *Index* Web site at *heritage.org/index*.

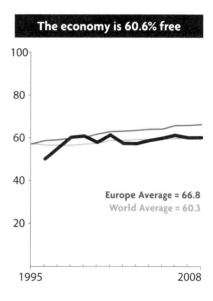

The economy is 60.6% free

Europe Average = 66.8
World Average = 60.3

1995 — 2008

QUICK FACTS

Population: 2.0 million

GDP (PPP): $44.6 billion
4.0% growth in 2005
3.6% 5-yr. comp. ann. growth
$22,273 per capita

Unemployment: 10.1%

Inflation (CPI): 2.5%

FDI (net flow): −$72.0 million

Official Development Assistance:
Multilateral: $58.0 million (2004)
Bilateral: $9.0 million (10% from the U.S.)

External Debt: $29.1 billion

Exports: $22.1 billion
Primarily manufactured goods, machinery and transport equipment, chemicals, food

Imports: $22.3 billion
Primarily machinery and transport equipment, manufactured goods, chemicals, fuels and lubricants, food

2005 data unless otherwise noted.

SLOVENIA'S TEN ECONOMIC FREEDOMS

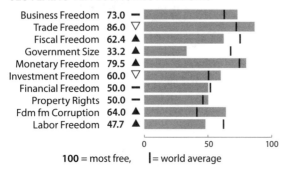

Business Freedom	73.0 —
Trade Freedom	86.0 ▽
Fiscal Freedom	62.4 ▲
Government Size	33.2 ▲
Monetary Freedom	79.5 ▲
Investment Freedom	60.0 ▽
Financial Freedom	50.0 —
Property Rights	50.0 —
Fdm fm Corruption	64.0 ▲
Labor Freedom	47.7 ▲

0   50   100

100 = most free, | = world average

BUSINESS FREEDOM — 73%

The overall freedom to start, operate, and close a business is relatively well protected by Slovenia's regulatory environment. Starting a business takes an average of 60 days, compared to the world average of 43 days. Obtaining a business license takes less than the world average of 19 procedures and 234 days. Bankruptcy proceedings are fairly simple and straightforward.

TRADE FREEDOM — 86%

Slovenia's trade policy is the same as those of other members of the European Union. The common EU weighted average tariff rate was 2 percent in 2005. Non-tariff barriers reflected in EU policy include agricultural and manufacturing subsidies, import restrictions for some goods and services, market access restrictions in some service sectors, non-transparent and restrictive regulations and standards, and inconsistent customs administration across EU members. Pharmaceutical and government procurement regulations exceed general EU policy. Consequently, an additional 10 percentage points is deducted from Slovenia's trade freedom score.

FISCAL FREEDOM — 62.4%

Slovenia has implemented tax cuts. The top income tax rate is 41 percent, down from 50 percent, and the top corporate tax rate is now a flat 23 percent. Other taxes include a value-added tax (VAT), a property transfer tax, and a tax on insurance. In the most recent year, overall tax revenue as a percentage of GDP was 39.4 percent.

GOVERNMENT SIZE — 33.2%

Total government expenditures, including consumption and transfer payments, are high. In the most recent year, government spending equaled 47.2 percent of GDP. Privatization of state-controlled companies has been sluggish.

MONETARY FREEDOM — 79.5%

Inflation is relatively low, averaging 2.7 percent between 2004 and 2006. Relatively stable prices explain most of the monetary freedom score. As a participant in the EU's Common Agricultural Policy, the government subsidizes agricultural production, distorting the prices of agricultural products. It also controls the prices of pharmaceuticals, oil, electricity, natural gas, and railway transport and influences other prices through regulation and state-

owned enterprises and utilities. An additional 10 percentage points is deducted from Slovenia's monetary freedom score to account for these policies.

INVESTMENT FREEDOM — 60%

Foreign investors receive national treatment, restrictions on portfolio investment have been abolished, and the government has streamlined the investment process. Most direct investment is unrestricted, but a license is needed to invest in the trading or producing of armaments or military equipment. A 2006 privatization task force did not see its ideas implemented, and several privatization programs were halted. Deterrents include an incomplete commercial legal code and official ambiguity about foreign investment. Residents and non-residents may hold foreign exchange accounts after proving their identity. There are no restrictions on payments and transfers. Nearly all restrictions on capital and money market instruments were removed in 2003.

FINANCIAL FREEDOM — 50%

Slovenia has been pursuing privatization and financial reform to meet EU standards. Banking is relatively well developed and sound. The top three banks account for a majority of assets. At the end of 2006, there were 20 banks, three savings institutions, and two subsidiaries of foreign banks. The government intends to sell its majority shares in the two largest banks but is unlikely to sell to a foreign company. The government also intends to sell its 85 percent of the largest insurer, Zavarovalnica Triglav, which dominates the general and life insurance markets. Capital markets are relatively small and centered on the Ljubljana Stock Exchange, which has grown rapidly.

PROPERTY RIGHTS — 50%

Private property is constitutionally guaranteed, but the courts are inadequately staffed and slow, and there are reports of corruption. Foreigners may own property. Comprehensive legislation to protect intellectual property reflects developments in the WTO's Trade-Related Aspects of Intellectual Property Rights (TRIPS) agreement and various EU directives, but foreign investors complain about enforcement delays. Prosecution of piracy is in the early stages.

FREEDOM FROM CORRUPTION — 64%

Corruption is perceived as present. Slovenia ranks 28th out of 163 countries in Transparency International's Corruption Perceptions Index for 2006. The public views corruption as widespread. The government has established an independent commission for the prevention of corruption.

LABOR FREEDOM — 47.7%

Inflexible employment regulations hinder overall productivity growth and employment opportunities. The non-salary cost of employing a worker is relatively high, and the rigidity of hiring and firing a worker creates a risk aversion for companies that would otherwise employ more people and grow. Regulations related to the number of work hours remain rigid.

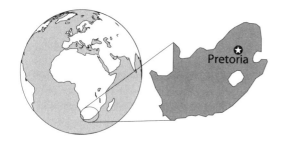

SOUTH AFRICA

Pretoria

South Africa's economy is 63.2 percent free, according to our 2008 assessment, which makes it the world's 57th freest economy. Its overall score is slightly lower than last year, reflecting worsened scores in three of the 10 economic freedoms. South Africa is ranked 4th out of 40 countries in the sub-Saharan Africa region, and its overall score is much higher than the regional average.

South Africa scores above average in seven areas. The government has been working to increase the transparency of commercial regulations. Income tax rates are high, but corporate taxes are moderate, and overall tax revenue is moderate as a percentage of GDP. Inflation is moderate, and the government subsidizes the market prices of only a few staple goods. The financial system is Africa's most advanced.

South Africa scores slightly below the world average in fiscal freedom and labor freedom. The judicial system is slow, and race laws and unclear regulation hamper foreign investment, but the legal environment is free from political interference and the threat of expropriation.

BACKGROUND: Two Boer republics and the British colonies of Cape and Natal formed the Union of South Africa in 1910, with whites retaining all political power. International pressure and popular uprisings led the apartheid government to lift bans on the African National Congress and other groups in 1990. Nelson Mandela won the first nonracial elections in 1994. Thabo Mbeki of the ANC won the 1999 election and was re-elected in 2004. The economic hub of sub-Saharan Africa, South Africa is in many ways two economies. Its mining, services, manufacturing, and agriculture sectors rival those in the developed world, but much of the population is poorly educated, and infrastructure and services remain inadequate. A decade of economic reform has helped growth rates. Crime, HIV/AIDS, and high unemployment remain serious problems.

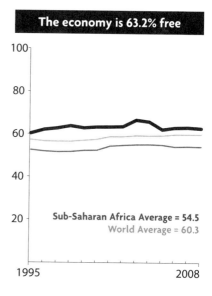

The economy is 63.2% free

Sub-Saharan Africa Average = 54.5
World Average = 60.3

1995 2008

QUICK FACTS

Population: 46.9 million

GDP (PPP): $520.9 billion
5.1% growth in 2005
4.2% 5-yr. comp. ann. growth
$11,110 per capita

Unemployment: 26.6%

Inflation (CPI): 3.4%

FDI (net flow): $6.3 billion

Official Development Assistance:
Multilateral: $213.5 million
Bilateral: $549.8 million (24.8% from the U.S.)

External Debt: $30.6 billion

Exports: $66.4 billion
Primarily gold, diamonds, platinum, other metals and minerals, machinery and equipment

Imports: $68.6 billion
Primarily machinery and equipment, chemicals, petroleum products, scientific instruments, foodstuffs

2005 data unless otherwise noted.

How Do We Measure Economic Freedom? See Chapter 4 (page 39) for an explanation of the methodology or visit the *Index* Web site at *heritage.org/index*.

SOUTH AFRICA'S TEN ECONOMIC FREEDOMS

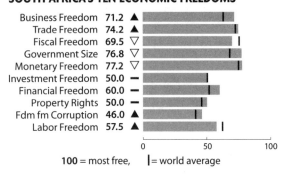

Business Freedom	71.2 ▲	
Trade Freedom	74.2 ▲	
Fiscal Freedom	69.5 ▽	
Government Size	76.8 ▽	
Monetary Freedom	77.2 ▽	
Investment Freedom	50.0 —	
Financial Freedom	60.0 —	
Property Rights	50.0 —	
Fdm fm Corruption	46.0 ▲	
Labor Freedom	57.5 ▲	

0   50   100

100 = most free, ▐ = world average

BUSINESS FREEDOM — 71.2%

The overall freedom to start, operate, and close a business is relatively well protected by South Africa's regulatory environment. Starting a business takes an average of 31 days, compared to the world average of 43 days. Obtaining a business license takes less than the world average of 19 procedures and 234 days. Closing a business is fairly simple and straightforward.

TRADE FREEDOM — 74.2%

South Africa's weighted average tariff rate was 5.4 percent in 2005. Import and export restrictions, service market barriers, burdensome technical standards, non-transparent and inefficient bureaucracy, excessive regulation, weak enforcement of intellectual property rights, inconsistent customs administration, and corruption add to the cost of trade. An additional 15 percentage points is deducted from South Africa's trade freedom score to account for non-tariff barriers.

FISCAL FREEDOM — 69.5%

South Africa has a high income tax rate and a moderate corporate tax rate. The top income tax rate is 40 percent, and the top corporate tax rate is 29 percent. Other taxes include a value-added tax (VAT), a property tax, and a capital gains tax. In the most recent year, overall tax revenue as a percentage of GDP was 24.6 percent.

GOVERNMENT SIZE — 76.8%

Total government expenditures, including consumption and transfer payments, are moderate. In the most recent year, government spending equaled 27.8 percent of GDP. The state still exerts monopolistic control of enterprises in some sectors.

MONETARY FREEDOM — 77.2%

Inflation is moderate, averaging 4.1 percent between 2004 and 2006. Relatively stable prices explain most of the monetary freedom score. Prices are generally set by the market, but the government controls the prices of petroleum products, coal, paraffin, and utilities and influences prices through regulation, state-owned enterprises, and support programs. An additional 10 percentage points is deducted from South Africa's monetary freedom score to account for policies that distort domestic prices.

INVESTMENT FREEDOM — 50%

South Africa permits foreign investment in most sectors, generally without restricting its form or extent. A $2.7 billion aluminum smelting project was announced by Canadian investors in November 2006. The Black Economic Empowerment strategy establishes targets for equity ownership, management, procurement, and employment equality for "historically disadvantaged" individuals. Unclear regulations, a very high crime rate, and rigid labor laws are disincentives. Residents may establish foreign exchange accounts through authorized dealers, subject to government approval and quantitative limits. Non-residents may hold them with authorized dealers. Many payments, capital transactions, and transfers are subject to restrictions, controls, quantitative limits, and prior approval.

FINANCIAL FREEDOM — 60%

Regulation is generally consistent with international standards and should be further improved by a new set of capital guidelines. Under the Financial Services Charter, banks must have 25 percent black ownership by 2010, direct a portion of after-tax profits to specific projects, and employ a fair representation of disadvantaged individuals in management. Banking is dominated by five large banks that account for 86 percent of operations and offer a full spectrum of services. Consolidation has reduced the number of domestic banks by 40 since 2001. There are many microfinance institutions, and many credit operations of traditionally disadvantaged black South Africans are outside of formal banks. There were 184 insurers as of mid-2006. Capital markets are well developed, and the JSE Securities Exchange is one of the world's 20 largest.

PROPERTY RIGHTS — 50%

The threat of expropriation is low. The judiciary is independent, and contracts are generally secure, but the courts are slow, understaffed, underfunded, and overburdened. Optical disc piracy is substantial, and end-use piracy is not a crime. The courts impose undue burdens and costs on rights holders pursuing infringement cases. The Medicines Control Council is notoriously inefficient and tardy with approvals.

FREEDOM FROM CORRUPTION — 46%

Corruption is perceived as significant. South Africa ranks 51st out of 163 countries in Transparency International's Corruption Perceptions Index for 2006. Official corruption, particularly in the police and the Department of Home Affairs, is viewed as widespread. South Africa is not a signatory of the OECD Convention on Combating Bribery but is a signatory of the U.N. Convention against Corruption.

LABOR FREEDOM — 57.5%

Inflexible employment regulations hinder overall productivity growth and employment opportunities. The non-salary cost of employing a worker is low, but the rigidity of hiring and firing a worker creates a risk aversion for companies that would otherwise employ more people and grow.

SPAIN

Madrid

Spain's economy is 69.7 percent free, according to our 2008 assessment, which makes it the world's 31st freest economy. Its overall score is slightly lower than last year. Spain is ranked 17th out of 41 countries in the European region, and its overall score is higher than the regional average.

Spain is notably strong in business freedom, trade freedom, investment freedom, financial freedom, property rights, and freedom from corruption. The average tariff rate is low, but non-tariff barriers include distortionary European Union subsidies on agriculture and other goods. The government has tried to streamline red tape and improve licensing procedures. Foreign investment is subject to few government restrictions. The judiciary is independent of politics, as in most other EU countries, but case resolution is extremely slow.

Spain is relatively weak in fiscal freedom, government size, and labor freedom. Total government spending equals almost two-fifths of GDP. The labor market is highly restrictive, from the number of workweek hours to employment severance procedures.

BACKGROUND: Many years of brisk growth characterized by strong job creation, structural reforms, and sound fiscal policy are a major part of the legacy of former Spanish Prime Minister José María Aznar's government (1996 to 2004). The current premier, José Luis Rodríguez Zapatero, won office in the wake of the pre-election al-Qaeda bombings in Madrid in 2004 on a promise that he would immediately withdraw Spanish troops from Operation Iraqi Freedom, but he did not reverse the Aznar reforms and continues to enjoy a buoyant economy on the back of Spain's economic liberalization. The key to continued growth lies in improving sluggish labor productivity and increasing Spain's ability to innovate, but Zapatero has not announced any major economic initiatives for the remainder of his term.

How Do We Measure Economic Freedom? See Chapter 4 (page 39) for an explanation of the methodology or visit the *Index* Web site at *heritage.org/index*.

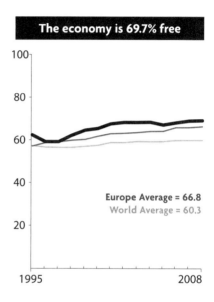

The economy is 69.7% free

Europe Average = 66.8
World Average = 60.3

1995   2008

QUICK FACTS

Population: 43.4 million

GDP (PPP): $1.2 trillion
  3.5% growth in 2005
  3.1% 5-yr. comp. ann. growth
  $27,169.2 per capita

Unemployment: 10.1%

Inflation (CPI): 3.4%

FDI (net flow): –$15.8 billion

Official Development Assistance:
Multilateral: None
Bilateral: None

External Debt: $1.6 trillion

Exports: $288.0 billion
Primarily machinery, motor vehicles, foodstuffs, pharmaceuticals, medicines, other consumer goods

Imports: $345.6 billion
Primarily machinery and equipment, fuels, chemicals, semifinished goods, foodstuffs, consumer goods, measuring and medical control instruments
2005 data unless otherwise noted.

SPAIN'S TEN ECONOMIC FREEDOMS

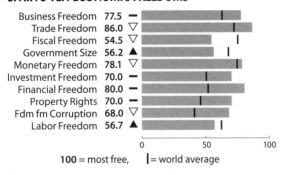

Business Freedom	77.5 ▬	
Trade Freedom	86.0 ▽	
Fiscal Freedom	54.5 ▽	
Government Size	56.2 ▲	
Monetary Freedom	78.1 ▽	
Investment Freedom	70.0 ▬	
Financial Freedom	80.0 ▬	
Property Rights	70.0 ▬	
Fdm fm Corruption	68.0 ▽	
Labor Freedom	56.7 ▲	

0   50   100

100 = most free,   **❙** = world average

BUSINESS FREEDOM — 77.5%

The overall freedom to start, operate, and close a business is relatively well protected by Spain's regulatory environment. Starting a business takes an average of 47 days, compared to the world average of 43 days. Obtaining a business license takes less than the world average of 19 procedures and 234 days. Bankruptcy proceedings are fairly easy and straightforward.

TRADE FREEDOM — 86%

Spain's trade policy is the same as those of other members of the European Union. The common EU weighted average tariff rate was 2 percent in 2005. Non-tariff barriers reflected in EU policy include agricultural and manufacturing subsidies, import restrictions for some goods and services, market access restrictions in some service sectors, nontransparent and restrictive regulations and standards, and inconsistent customs administration across EU members. Pharmaceutical and biotechnology regulations and service market access barriers exceed EU policy, and protection of intellectual property rights can be problematic. Consequently, an additional 10 percentage points is deducted from Spain's trade freedom score.

FISCAL FREEDOM — 54.5%

The top income tax rate is 43 percent, down from 45 percent, and the top corporate tax rate is 32.5 percent, down from 35 percent. Other taxes include a value-added tax (VAT), a property tax, and a transportation tax. In the most recent year, overall tax revenue as a percentage of GDP was 36.1 percent.

GOVERNMENT SIZE — 56.2%

Total government expenditures, including consumption and transfer payments, are moderate. In the most recent year, government spending equaled 38.2 percent of GDP. In comparison with other OECD countries, state involvement in the economy is low.

MONETARY FREEDOM — 78.1%

Spain is a member of the euro zone. Inflation is moderate, averaging 3.5 percent between 2004 and 2006. Nearly stable prices explain most of the monetary freedom score. As a participant in the EU's Common Agricultural Policy, the government subsidizes agricultural production, distorting the prices of agricultural products. It also controls the pric-

es of medicines and public transport and influences prices through regulation and state-owned enterprises and utilities. An additional 10 percentage points is deducted from Spain's monetary freedom score to account for these policies.

INVESTMENT FREEDOM — 70%

Foreign investment of up to 100 percent of equity is permitted, and capital movements are completely liberalized. National security–related activities require prior approval; other investments require after-the-fact notification of the Ministry of Finance. Foreign companies may bid on privatized assets, and privatization continues in telecommunications, tobacco, air transport, electricity, and petroleum. There are no restrictions or controls on resident or non-resident foreign exchange accounts, repatriation of profits, and proceeds from invisible transactions. Current transfers must be declared to deposit institutions. The Bank of Spain requires reporting on most credit and lending activities.

FINANCIAL FREEDOM — 80%

Spain is fully integrated into international financial markets, and its banks-to-inhabitants ratio is far above the EU average. There were 53 domestic credit entities in 2005. All commercial banks are privately owned, and Banco Santander Central Hispano and Banco Bilbao Vizcaya Argentaria account for almost a third of loans. Economic growth has greatly reduced non-performing loans. The government provides subsidized financing through modest credit institutions. There were 312 insurance companies at the end of 2005, and over a quarter of the sector was foreign-controlled. Capital markets are well developed and open to foreign investors.

PROPERTY RIGHTS — 70%

The judiciary is independent in practice, but bureaucratic obstacles are significant. Contracts are secure, although enforcement is very slow. Patent, copyright, and trademark laws approximate or exceed EU levels of intellectual property protection. Enforcement actions (especially private-sector initiatives) using Spain's new IPR legal framework have greatly increased the criminal and civil actions against intellectual property pirates.

FREEDOM FROM CORRUPTION — 68%

Corruption is perceived as minimal. Spain ranks 23rd out of 163 countries in Transparency International's Corruption Perceptions Index for 2006. Giving or accepting a bribe is a crime, and bribes are not tax-deductible for corporations or individuals. There is no obvious bias for or against foreign investors. Corruption is not an obstacle to investment.

LABOR FREEDOM — 56.7%

Inflexible employment regulations hinder overall productivity growth and employment opportunities. The non-salary cost of employing a worker is high, and the rigidity of hiring and firing a worker creates a risk aversion for companies that would otherwise employ more people and grow. Regulations related to the number of work hours are rigid.

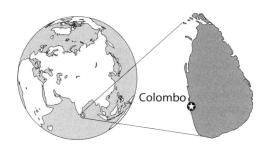

Colombo

SRI LANKA

S ri Lanka's economy is 58.3 percent free, according to our 2008 assessment, which makes it the world's 90th freest economy. Its overall score is 1 percentage point lower than last year. Sri Lanka is ranked 14th out of 30 countries in the Asia–Pacific region, and its overall score is slightly lower than the regional average.

Sri Lanka scores well in fiscal freedom and government size. Income and corporate tax rates are moderate, and overall tax revenue is relatively low as a percentage of GDP. Total government expenditures equal slightly more than one-fifth of GDP, and state-owned businesses generate a small portion of total tax revenue.

Sri Lanka scores poorly in investment freedom, financial freedom, monetary freedom, and freedom from corruption. The government generally welcomes foreign capital, but formal restrictions and the security situation are deterrents. The financial system is small but growing and would benefit from greater transparency. Inflation is high, and the government directly subsidizes a wide array of goods. The judicial system is not free of political interference and is subject to corruption as well as extensive delays.

BACKGROUND: Sri Lanka, a democratic island nation, has been engulfed in civil war for over two decades. Current President Mahinda Rajapakse, elected in November 2005, has countered Liberation Tigers of Tamil Eelam attacks with force; over the past year, the fighting has increased in scale and intensity. Despite that, the economy has grown between 6 percent and 7 percent annually in recent years. Textile and garments account for the majority of export growth, but Sri Lanka remains a poor nation where most people are employed in agricultural industries. The large Sri Lankan diaspora remit around $1 billion annually to their homeland.

How Do We Measure Economic Freedom? See Chapter 4 (page 39) for an explanation of the methodology or visit the *Index* Web site at *heritage.org/index*.

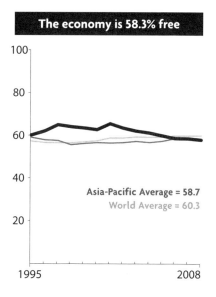

The economy is 58.3% free

Asia-Pacific Average = 58.7
World Average = 60.3

1995   2008

QUICK FACTS

Population: 19.6 million

GDP (PPP): $90.2 billion
6.0% growth in 2005
5.3% 5-yr. comp. ann. growth
$4,595 per capita

Unemployment: 7.7%

Inflation (CPI): 10.6%

FDI (net flow): $234.0 million

Official Development Assistance:
Multilateral: $370.1 million
Bilateral: $930.9 million (6.9% from the U.S.)

External Debt: $11.4 billion

Exports: $7.9 billion
Primarily textiles and apparel, tea and spices, diamonds, emeralds, rubies, coconut products, rubber manufactures, fish

Imports: $10.1 billion
Primarily textile fabrics, mineral products, petroleum, foodstuffs, machinery and transportation equipment
2005 data unless otherwise noted.

SRI LANKA'S TEN ECONOMIC FREEDOMS

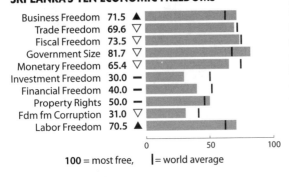

Business Freedom	71.5 ▲	
Trade Freedom	69.6 ▽	
Fiscal Freedom	73.5 ▽	
Government Size	81.7 ▽	
Monetary Freedom	65.4 ▽	
Investment Freedom	30.0 —	
Financial Freedom	40.0 —	
Property Rights	50.0 —	
Fdm fm Corruption	31.0 ▽	
Labor Freedom	70.5 ▲	

0   50   100

100 = most free, | = world average

BUSINESS FREEDOM — 71.5%

The overall freedom to start, operate, and close a business is relatively well protected by Sri Lanka's regulatory environment. Starting a business takes an average of 39 days, compared to the world average of 43 days. Obtaining a business license takes less than the world average of 234 days, but costs are high. Closing a business is relatively simple.

TRADE FREEDOM — 69.6%

Sri Lanka's weighted average tariff rate was 7.7 percent in 2005. Import bans and restrictions, export controls, service market barriers, restrictive import taxes, import fees, import licensing, restrictive standards, non-transparent government procurement, weak enforcement of intellectual property rights, export subsidies, and corruption add to the cost of trade. An additional 15 percentage points is deducted from Sri Lanka's trade freedom score to account for non-tariff barriers.

FISCAL FREEDOM — 73.5%

Sri Lanka has burdensome tax rates. The top income tax rate is 35 percent, and the top corporate tax rate is 35 percent, up from 32.5 percent. Other taxes include a value-added tax (VAT), a property tax, and a tax on interest. In the most recent year, overall tax revenue as a percentage of GDP was 14.2 percent.

GOVERNMENT SIZE — 81.7%

Total government expenditures, including consumption and transfer payments, are moderate. In the most recent year, government spending equaled 24.7 percent of GDP. Privatization has reduced government participation in manufacturing, but the state remains involved in such sectors as finance and utilities.

MONETARY FREEDOM — 65.4%

Inflation is high, averaging 9.6 percent between 2004 and 2006. Unstable prices explain most of the monetary freedom score. The government influences prices through regulation, state-owned enterprises, and subsidies for a wide array of goods. An additional 15 percentage points is deducted from Sri Lanka's monetary freedom score to account for policies that distort domestic prices.

INVESTMENT FREEDOM — 30%

Foreign investment, although generally welcomed, is prohibited in non-bank lending, pawnbroking, and retail trade with a capital investment of less than $1 million (with some exceptions). Investment in several sectors is screened and approved case-by-case when foreign equity exceeds 40 percent. Deterrents include the long-running civil war, bureaucratic inefficiency, and unpredictable economic policies. An intended one-stop shop lacks bureaucratic clout. Outward direct investment must be approved by the government. Residents and non-residents may hold foreign exchange accounts subject to requirements, including government approval in some cases. There are strict reporting requirements and limits on payments and transfers. Capital transactions are subject to many restrictions and government approval in some cases.

FINANCIAL FREEDOM — 40%

Sri Lanka's financial system is extensively government-influenced and growing rapidly. Regulations permit 100 percent foreign control of banks, insurance companies, and stockbrokerages. Reforms in 2004 helped to improve banking regulation and health. Regulations are largely consistent with international standards, but supervision and enforcement are insufficient. The central bank is not independent. The government influences the allocation of credit and uses half of domestic financial resources to finance government borrowing. Banking dominates the financial sector. The two largest commercial banks are state-owned, and the government opened a new development bank in 2006. The insurance sector is small, and the two largest companies control nearly three-fourths of the market. Capital markets are centered on the Colombo Stock Exchange, which is modern but relatively small and affected by the ongoing political violence.

PROPERTY RIGHTS — 50%

The judiciary is influenced by other branches of government, and extensive delays lead investors most often to pursue out-of-court settlements. Intellectual property rights come under both criminal and civil jurisdiction. International recording, software development, motion picture, clothing, and consumer product companies claim that lack of IPR protection damages their businesses.

FREEDOM FROM CORRUPTION — 31%

Corruption is perceived as significant. Sri Lanka ranks 84th out of 163 countries in Transparency International's Corruption Perceptions Index for 2006. Anti-corruption laws and regulations are unevenly enforced. The police and the judiciary are viewed as the most corrupt public institutions. Corruption in customs clearance enables wide-scale smuggling of certain consumer items.

LABOR FREEDOM — 70.5%

Relatively flexible employment regulations could be further improved to enhance overall productivity growth and employment opportunities. The non-salary cost of employing a worker is moderate, but the rigidity of hiring and firing a worker creates a risk aversion for companies that would otherwise employ more people and grow.

SUDAN

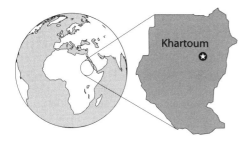

Khartoum ✪

Rank: Not Ranked

Regional Rank: Not Ranked

Most of Sudan's economic freedom cannot be graded because of the violence and genocide that have wracked the country in recent years. The last time Sudan was wholly graded was in 2000, when it received a score of 47.2 percent.

Trade freedom, monetary freedom, and freedom from corruption are all weak in Sudan. The average tariff rate is very high, and significant non-tariff barriers further impede trade. Inflation is also high, and the state subsidizes a wide array of goods. The government in Khartoum is riddled with corruption, and Sudan is one of the world's 20 most corrupt nations.

BACKGROUND: Sudan is Africa's largest country and has a long history of internal conflict. President Omar Hassan al-Bashir's government has ruled since a 1989 military coup. A January 2005 peace agreement ended the decades-long civil war between the government in Khartoum and the Sudan People's Liberation Movement/Army. In the western Darfur region, conflict between government-supported militia groups and rebels has resulted in 200,000 deaths and 2 million displaced persons. Sudan's economy is hindered by instability, poor infrastructure, economic mismanagement, and corruption. Until significant oil production began in 2000, the economy was predominantly agrarian, and most Sudanese remain engaged in agriculture.

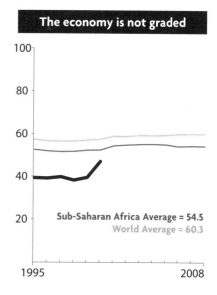

The economy is not graded

Sub-Saharan Africa Average = 54.5
World Average = 60.3

QUICK FACTS

Population: 36.2 million

GDP (PPP): $75.5 billion
8.6% growth in 2005
6.5% 5-yr. comp. ann. growth
$2,083 per capita

Unemployment: 18.7% (2002 estimate)

Inflation (CPI): 8.5%

FDI (net flow): $2.3 billion

Official Development Assistance:
Multilateral: $324.7 million
Bilateral: $1.5 billion (50.8% from the U.S.)

External Debt: $18.5 billion

Exports: $4.9 billion
Primarily oil and petroleum products, cotton, sesame, livestock, groundnuts, gum arabic, sugar

Imports: $7.8 billion
Primarily foodstuffs, manufactured goods, refinery and transport equipment, medicines and chemicals, textiles, wheat

2005 data unless otherwise noted.

How Do We Measure Economic Freedom? See Chapter 4 (page 39) for an explanation of the methodology or visit the *Index* Web site at *heritage.org/index*.

BUSINESS FREEDOM — NOT GRADED

Sudan's regulatory regime remains inconsistent, uneven, and non-transparent. Starting a business takes an average of 39 days, compared to the world average of 43 days. Obtaining a business license takes 271 days, compared to the world average of 234 days, and costs are high.

TRADE FREEDOM — NOT GRADED

Sudan's weighted average tariff rate was 19.6 percent in 2002. There has been some progress toward liberalizing the trade regime, but non-transparent regulations, discriminatory taxes, significant delays in customs clearance, inadequate infrastructure, and corruption add to the cost of trade. If Sudan were graded this year, an additional 15 percentage points would be deducted from its trade freedom score to account for non-tariff barriers.

FISCAL FREEDOM — NOT GRADED

Sudan has a low income tax rate but a burdensome corporate tax rate. The top income tax rate is 20 percent, and the top corporate tax rate is 35 percent. In the most recent year, overall tax revenue as a percentage of GDP was 5.9 percent.

GOVERNMENT SIZE — NOT GRADED

Total government expenditures, including consumption and transfer payments, are low. In the most recent year, government spending equaled 16.3 percent of GDP.

MONETARY FREEDOM — NOT GRADED

Inflation is high, averaging 7.6 percent between 2004 and 2006. The government influences prices through regulation, a wide range of subsidies, and state-owned enterprises and utilities, and petroleum products are subsidized and subject to price controls. If Sudan were graded this year, an additional 10 percentage points would be deducted from its monetary freedom score to account for policies that distort domestic prices.

INVESTMENT FREEDOM — NOT GRADED

Foreign and domestic investment are officially equal in most areas, but cumbersome regulations, political instability, and corruption are deterrents, as are the ongoing chaos and violence in Sudan's western Darfur province and the massive refugee problem. The government is seeking foreign investment for the privatization of state-owned enterprises, but SOEs are in such poor shape and the level of corruption is so high that investors do not find them an attractive prospect. Recent foreign investment inflows have been relatively high, probably as a result of the North–South peace agreement and high oil prices. All residents (but not public institutions) may hold foreign exchange accounts. Non-residents may hold foreign exchange accounts with government approval. Controls apply to all transactions involving capital market securities, money market instruments, credit operations, and outward direct investment.

FINANCIAL FREEDOM — NOT GRADED

Sudan's small financial system is underdeveloped and largely bound by Islamic financial principles, including a prohibition on charging interest, that are a legacy of the 1989 coup. Under the North–South peace agreement, banks operating in the South do not have to abide by Islamic principles. Supervision and regulation are weak. There are about 30 commercial banks, of which over half are completely or majority privately owned. One of the largest state-owned banks was sold in 2005. The government continues to direct the allocation of credit, and non-performing loans are a problem. As part of a restructuring agreement with the IMF, Sudan raised liquidity requirements in 2007. The insurance sector is small. Capital markets are very small and focused on trading bank shares on the Khartoum Stock Exchange.

PROPERTY RIGHTS — NOT GRADED

There is little respect for private property in Sudan. The government influences the judiciary, and the military and civil authorities do not follow due process to protect private property. There have been numerous disputes between the government and various churches involving confiscated church property but no reports of court-ordered property restitution or compensation. Better protection of intellectual property rights would permit increased food production and food security through biotechnology applications.

FREEDOM FROM CORRUPTION — NOT GRADED

Corruption is perceived as rampant. Sudan ranks 156th out of 163 countries in Transparency International's Corruption Perceptions Index for 2006. Relatives of high government officials often own companies that do business with the government and usually receive kickbacks for government business. Bribery of police is also a concern. There are no laws providing for public access to government information, and the government does not provide such access.

LABOR FREEDOM — NOT GRADED

The non-salary cost of employing a worker is moderate, but dismissing a redundant employee is burdensome and costly. Regulations related to the number of work hours are somewhat flexible.

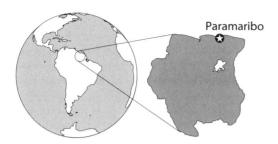

Paramaribo

SURINAME

Rank: 118

Regional Rank: 24 of 29

S uriname's economy is 53.9 percent free, according to our 2008 assessment, which makes it the world's 118th freest economy. Its overall score is 0.5 percentage point lower than last year. Suriname is ranked 24th out of 29 countries in the Americas, and its overall score is lower than the regional average.

Suriname scores strongly in only one area: labor freedom. The country's labor market is flexible, there is no minimum wage, and the non-salary costs of employment are low. Its scores for property rights and government size are above the world average.

Suriname is weak in most areas of economic freedom. Opening a business takes almost 15 times the world average time, and commercial operations are hamstrung by red tape. The government dominates economic activities. One central authority has been set up to coordinate foreign investment, but foreign investors still do not receive equal treatment under the law. Tax rates, inflation, and government spending are all high. Suriname's financial system is small, and the regulations that exist are antiquated. Banking is subject to substantial political interference. The judicial system is understaffed, and case backlogs are extensive.

BACKGROUND: Suriname has gone through five peaceful changes of government since becoming a presidential democracy in 1991, the most recent transfer occurring in 2000 with the election of current President Ronald Venetiaan. Suriname is rich in natural resources, especially timber and minerals, including bauxite, gold, nickel, and silver. Nevertheless, it remains one of the region's poorest and least-developed countries. Agriculture and mining together account for almost 20 percent of GDP. The public sector is the primary employer, with half of the total labor force on its payrolls. Fiscal budget deficits and inflation remain the most pressing economic problems.

How Do We Measure Economic Freedom? See Chapter 4 (page 39) for an explanation of the methodology or visit the *Index* Web site at *heritage.org/index.*

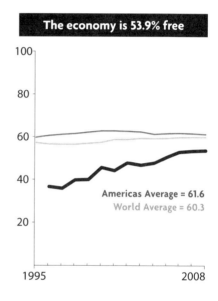

The economy is 53.9% free

Americas Average = 61.6
World Average = 60.3

1995   2008

QUICK FACTS

Population: 0.4 million

GDP (PPP): $3.5 billion
5.5% growth in 2005
5.5% 5-yr. comp. ann. growth
$7,722 per capita

Unemployment: 9.5% (2004)

Inflation (CPI): 9.9%

FDI (net flow): $41.0 million

Official Development Assistance:
Multilateral: $15.3 million
Bilateral: $33.6 million (2.6% from the U.S.)

External Debt: $504.3 million

Exports: $1.4 billion
Primarily alumina, crude oil, lumber, shrimp and fish, rice, bananas

Imports: $1.5 billion
Primarily capital equipment, petroleum, foodstuffs, cotton, consumer goods

2005 data unless otherwise noted.

SURINAME'S TEN ECONOMIC FREEDOMS

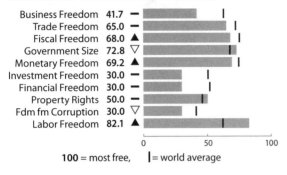

Business Freedom	41.7	—
Trade Freedom	65.0	—
Fiscal Freedom	68.0	▲
Government Size	72.8	▽
Monetary Freedom	69.2	▲
Investment Freedom	30.0	—
Financial Freedom	30.0	—
Property Rights	50.0	—
Fdm fm Corruption	30.0	▽
Labor Freedom	82.1	▲

0   50   100

100 = most free,   I = world average

BUSINESS FREEDOM — 41.7%

The overall freedom to start, operate, and close a business is very limited by Suriname's regulatory environment. Starting a business takes an average of 694 days, compared to the world average of 43 days. Obtaining a business license takes much more than the world average of 234 days. Bankruptcy proceedings are difficult and often prolonged.

TRADE FREEDOM — 65%

Suriname's weighted average tariff rate was 12.5 percent in 2000. The government has made progress toward liberalizing the trade regime, but non-transparent regulations and standards, import and export taxes, and import and export restrictions add to the cost of trade. An additional 10 percentage points is deducted from Suriname's trade freedom score to account for non-tariff barriers.

FISCAL FREEDOM — 68%

Suriname has high tax rates. The top income tax rate is 38 percent, and the top corporate tax rate is 36 percent. Other taxes include a property tax and a tax on dividends. In the most recent year, overall tax revenue as a percentage of GDP was 21.5 percent.

GOVERNMENT SIZE — 72.8%

Total government expenditures, including consumption and transfer payments, are high. In the most recent year, government spending equaled 30.1 percent of GDP. Despite efforts to restructure and privatize state-owned companies, direct state involvement in the economy through ownership and control remains considerable.

MONETARY FREEDOM — 69.2%

Inflation is high, averaging 10.8 percent between 2004 and 2006. Unstable prices explain most of the monetary freedom score. The government influences prices through regulation and state-owned enterprises and utilities, and prices of basic food items are controlled. An additional 10 percentage points is deducted from Suriname's monetary freedom score to account for policies that distort domestic prices.

INVESTMENT FREEDOM — 30%

The government has created InvestSur to process applications for investment requests, settle disputes, and help investors. The mixed success of InvestSur led the Chamber of Commerce later to open a one-stop shop for investment, also aimed at simplifying procedures. Foreign companies do not receive equal treatment. Investment is hindered by an unwieldy bureaucracy, a shortage of trained judges to handle commercial disputes, regulatory opacity, and local ambivalence about the necessity of foreign investment. Residents may hold foreign exchange accounts provided that the funds did not come from sales of real estate in Suriname. Non-residents may open foreign exchange accounts in U.S. dollars and with the approval of the Foreign Exchange Commission. Payments and transfers face various quantitative limits and approval requirements. Capital transactions involving outward remittances of foreign exchange require the Foreign Exchange Commission's approval.

FINANCIAL FREEDOM — 30%

Suriname's financial system is underdeveloped and subject to extensive government influence. Financial regulations are antiquated, and supervision is poor, which is reflected in ongoing concerns about money-laundering. There are eight banks, three of which controlled 87 percent of deposits in 2004. The state owns a majority of two of the three major banks. A large number of non-performing loans is a concern. The third major bank is owned by a parent company in Trinidad and Tobago. The state also owns three minor commercial banks, which are designated to be consolidated and their bad loans placed under the aegis of the government. The non-banking financial sector, including insurance and pension funds, is small and underdeveloped. Capital markets are slight and focused on the small stock market, which listed 11 companies as of June 2007.

PROPERTY RIGHTS — 50%

Private property is not well protected. There is a severe shortage of judges, and dispute settlement can be extremely time-consuming. Although Suriname has signed key international intellectual property rights treaties, in practice IPR protection is nonexistent since they have not been incorporated into domestic law. Suriname is a member of the World Trade Organization but has not ratified its Trade-Related Aspects of Intellectual Property Rights (TRIPS) agreement.

FREEDOM FROM CORRUPTION — 30%

Corruption is perceived as widespread. Suriname ranks 90th out of 163 countries in Transparency International's Corruption Perceptions Index for 2006. There is extensive corruption in the executive branch of the government, and a shortage of police personnel hampers investigations of fraud cases.

LABOR FREEDOM — 82.1%

Suriname's flexible employment regulations could enhance overall productivity growth and employment opportunities. The non-salary cost of employing a worker is low, but dismissing a redundant employee can be burdensome. There is no minimum wage.

SWAZILAND

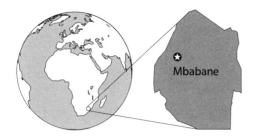

Swaziland's economy is 58.9 percent free, according to our 2008 assessment, which makes it the world's 86th freest economy. Its overall score is 1.7 percentage points lower than last year, reflecting lower scores in six of the 10 economic freedoms. Swaziland is ranked 8th out of 40 countries in the sub-Saharan Africa region, and its overall score is higher than the regional average.

Swaziland scores relatively well in business freedom, property rights, and labor freedom. Licensing procedures are simple, although opening an enterprise takes longer than the world average. The labor sector is flexible, but dismissing a redundant employee can be difficult.

Swaziland is weak in freedom from corruption and financial freedom. Inflation is fairly low, but subsidies distort the price of certain goods. Total government expenditures equal about a third of GDP. Corruption is widespread. The financial sector is extremely small and subject to political interference and unclear rules.

BACKGROUND: Swaziland became independent in 1968. Under the 2006 constitution, King Mswati III holds supreme executive, legislative, and judiciary powers. However, much authority is delegated to the prime minister, his cabinet, and traditional government structures. The king appoints 10 of the 65 seats in the House of Assembly (the others are elected through popular vote) and 20 members of the 30-seat Senate. Swaziland has one of the world's highest HIV/AIDS rates: an estimated 42 percent of adults in 2004. South Africa is the source of most imports and the destination for most exports. Most of the population is rural and engages in subsistence agriculture or herding. The cane sugar and soft-drink concentrate industries are the leading export earners and private-sector employers. Coal and diamonds are mined for export. Progress toward economic liberalization and privatization has been slow, and corruption remains a problem.

How Do We Measure Economic Freedom? See Chapter 4 (page 39) for an explanation of the methodology or visit the *Index* Web site at *heritage.org/index*.

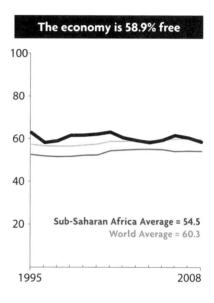

The economy is 58.9% free

Sub-Saharan Africa Average = 54.5
World Average = 60.3

1995 — 2008

QUICK FACTS

Population: 1.1 million

GDP (PPP): $5.5 billion
2.3% growth in 2005
2.6% 5-yr. comp. ann. growth
$4,824 per capita

Unemployment: 40.0%

Inflation (CPI): 4.8%

FDI (net flow): −$35 million

Official Development Assistance:
Multilateral: $32.2 million
Bilateral: $34.3 million (3.8% from the U.S.)

External Debt: $532.0 million

Exports: $2.1 billion
Primarily soft drink concentrates, sugar, wood pulp, cotton yarn, refrigerators, citrus, canned fruit

Imports: $2.2 billion
Primarily motor vehicles, machinery, transport equipment, foodstuffs, petroleum products, chemicals

2005 data unless otherwise noted.

SWAZILAND'S TEN ECONOMIC FREEDOMS

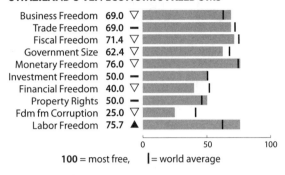

Business Freedom	69.0 ▽	
Trade Freedom	69.0 ▬	
Fiscal Freedom	71.4 ▽	
Government Size	62.4 ▽	
Monetary Freedom	76.0 ▽	
Investment Freedom	50.0 ▬	
Financial Freedom	40.0 ▽	
Property Rights	50.0 ▬	
Fdm fm Corruption	25.0 ▽	
Labor Freedom	75.7 ▲	

0   50   100

100 = most free, | = world average

BUSINESS FREEDOM — 69%

The overall freedom to start, operate, and close a business is relatively protected by Swaziland's regulatory environment. Starting a business takes an average of 61 days, compared to the world average of 43 days. Obtaining a business license takes less than the world average of 19 procedures and 234 days. Closing a business can be fairly easy and straightforward.

TRADE FREEDOM — 69%

Swaziland's weighted average tariff rate was 10.5 percent in 2005. Service market access barriers, select import permit requirements, import taxes, and weak enforcement of intellectual property rights add to the cost of trade. An additional 10 percentage points is deducted from Swaziland's trade freedom score to account for non-tariff barriers.

FISCAL FREEDOM — 71.4%

Swaziland has moderately high tax rates. The top income tax rate is 33 percent, and the top corporate tax rate is 30 percent. Other taxes include a real estate tax and a fuel tax. In the most recent year, overall tax revenue as a percentage of GDP was 29.5 percent.

GOVERNMENT SIZE — 62.4%

Total government expenditures, including consumption and transfer payments, are high. In the most recent year, government spending equaled 35.4 percent of GDP.

MONETARY FREEDOM — 76%

Inflation is moderate, averaging 4.9 percent between 2004 and 2006. Relatively unstable prices explain most of the monetary freedom score. The government influences prices through regulation and numerous state-owned enterprises and utilities, and government-administered prices account for approximately 16 percent of the consumer price index. An additional 10 percentage points is deducted from Swaziland's monetary freedom score to account for policies that distort domestic prices.

INVESTMENT FREEDOM — 50%

The foreign investment laws are not clear and are highly affected by government statements and decrees. Foreign investors are guided by an investment law from 1912, itself a derivative of a South African 1889 investment law, but the government has taken steps to codify some of these regulations and published a new National Export Strategy in 2006 to improve the business environment. A new industrial and investment policy was supposed to be released in 2007. All foreign workers must have permits, and the permit process can be time-consuming and cumbersome. Residents (with restrictions) and non-residents may hold foreign exchange accounts. Payments and transfers, while not usually restricted, are subject to quantitative limits and government approval in some cases. The central bank must approve most inward capital transfers. Most other capital transactions require documentation or face restrictions.

FINANCIAL FREEDOM — 40%

Swaziland's financial system is very small and subject to considerable government influence. As of late 2006, there were three foreign-owned private banks, a state-owned bank, a state-owned housing bank, and a few microfinance institutions. Supervision of banking is insufficient. The non-bank financial sector is dominated by the government. The government owns 41 percent of the Swaziland Royal Insurance Corporation, which has a monopoly on insurance, and controls the Royal Investment Trust, a profit-centered fund that has been criticized for allegedly being a vehicle for embezzlement. Two state-owned pension funds dominate the pension sector. Capital markets are slight and centered on the Swaziland Stock Exchange, which listed six companies in September 2006. There is also a small bond market, with six government and two corporate bonds listed.

PROPERTY RIGHTS — 50%

The judiciary suffers from inadequate training, low salaries, and a small budget. Delays are common, and the executive significantly influences decisions. Protection for patents, trademarks, and copyrights is inadequate. The government has acceded to the WTO's Trade-Related Aspects of Intellectual Property Rights (TRIPS) agreement but has not signed the World Intellectual Property Organization's Internet agreement.

FREEDOM FROM CORRUPTION — 25%

Corruption is perceived as widespread. Swaziland ranks 121st out of 163 countries in Transparency International's Corruption Perceptions Index for 2006. Corruption is viewed as widespread in the executive and legislative branches of government, and efforts to combat it are viewed as insufficient. Credible reports indicate that unqualified businesses were awarded contracts due to the owners' relationship with government officials.

LABOR FREEDOM — 75.7%

Relatively flexible employment regulations could be further improved to enhance overall productivity growth and employment opportunities. The non-salary cost of employing a worker is low, but the cost of laying off a worker creates a risk aversion for companies that would otherwise employ more people and grow.

SWEDEN

Sweden's economy is 70.4 percent free, according to our 2008 assessment, which makes it the world's 27th freest economy. Its overall score is 1.4 percentage points higher than last year, reflecting improvements in trade freedom and financial freedom. Sweden is ranked 14th out of 41 countries in the European region, and its overall score is higher than the regional average.

Sweden enjoys exceptionally high levels of investment freedom, financial freedom, property rights, business freedom, and freedom from corruption. Virtually all commercial operations are simple and transparent. Foreign investment is permitted without government approval, though capital is subject to restrictions in some areas. The financial sector is highly developed, and the Stockholm stock market is open to foreign investment. The judiciary, independent of politics and free of corruption, has an exemplary ability to protect property rights.

In contrast, Sweden has some of the lowest scores worldwide in fiscal freedom and government size. The top income tax rate of 60 percent is one of the highest in the world, and total government spending equals more than half of GDP. The labor market was highly regulated, but reforms have led to a score equal to the world average in labor freedom.

BACKGROUND: Renowned for its economic model of public–private partnerships, Sweden has enjoyed a buoyant economy since becoming a member of the European Union in 1995. Sweden relies heavily on international trade, with total trade accounting for more that 50 percent of GDP. Job creation in the private sector remains low, and as of this writing, this was seen as a possible catalyst for the removal of Göran Persson's Social Democratic–led coalition government in September 2006. Sweden's main exports include paper products, machinery and transport equipment, and chemicals.

How Do We Measure Economic Freedom? See Chapter 4 (page 39) for an explanation of the methodology or visit the *Index* Web site at *heritage.org/index*.

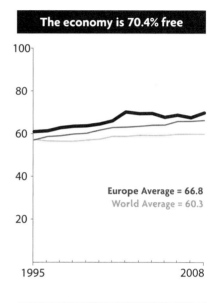

The economy is 70.4% free

Europe Average = 66.8
World Average = 60.3

QUICK FACTS

Population: 9.0 million

GDP (PPP): $293.5 billion
2.9% growth in 2005
2.7% 5-yr. comp. ann. growth
$32,525 per capita

Unemployment: 6.2%

Inflation (CPI): 0.8%

FDI (net flow): −$12.5 billion

Official Development Assistance:
Multilateral: None
Bilateral: None

External Debt: $598.2 billion

Exports: $178.1 billion
Primarily machinery, motor vehicles, paper products, pulp and wood, iron and steel products, chemicals

Imports: $150.4 billion
Primarily machinery, petroleum and petroleum products, chemicals, motor vehicles, iron and steel, foodstuffs, clothing

2005 data unless otherwise noted.

SWEDEN'S TEN ECONOMIC FREEDOMS

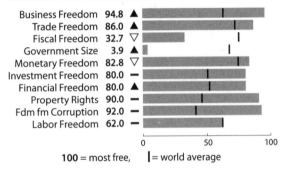

Business Freedom 94.8 ▲
Trade Freedom 86.0 ▲
Fiscal Freedom 32.7 ▽
Government Size 3.9 ▲
Monetary Freedom 82.8 ▽
Investment Freedom 80.0 —
Financial Freedom 80.0 ▲
Property Rights 90.0 —
Fdm fm Corruption 92.0 —
Labor Freedom 62.0 —

0   50   100

100 = most free, | = world average

BUSINESS FREEDOM — 94.8%

The overall freedom to start, operate, and close a business is strongly protected by Sweden's regulatory environment. Starting a business takes an average of 15 days, compared to the world average of 43 days. Obtaining a business license takes less than the world average of 19 procedures and 234 days. Bankruptcy proceedings are fairly easy and straightforward.

TRADE FREEDOM — 86%

Sweden's trade policy is the same as those of other members of the European Union. The common EU weighted average tariff rate was 2 percent in 2005. Non-tariff barriers reflected in EU policy include agricultural and manufacturing subsidies, import restrictions for some goods and services, market access restrictions in some service sectors, non-transparent and restrictive regulations and standards, and inconsistent customs administration across EU members. Sanitary and phytosanitary regulations are burdensome, and enforcement of intellectual property rights can be problematic. Consequently, an additional 10 percent is deducted from Sweden's trade freedom score.

FISCAL FREEDOM — 32.7%

Sweden has a very burdensome income tax rate and a moderate corporate tax rate. The top income tax rate is 60 percent, and the top corporate tax rate is 28 percent. Other taxes include a value-added tax (VAT) and a capital gains tax. In the most recent year, overall tax revenue as a percentage of GDP was 51.1 percent.

GOVERNMENT SIZE — 3.9%

Total government expenditures, including consumption and transfer payments, are very high. In the most recent year, government spending equaled 56.6 percent of GDP. Spending has been reduced from over 60 percent of GDP in the 1990s but is still one of the highest among OECD member countries.

MONETARY FREEDOM — 82.8%

Inflation is low, averaging 1.3 percent between 2004 and 2006. Stable prices explain most of the monetary freedom score. As a participant in the EU's Common Agricultural Policy, the government subsidizes agricultural production, distorting the prices of agricultural products. Prices are generally set by the market, but oligopolies may hin-

der competition, and the government influences prices through regulation and state-owned enterprises and utilities. An additional 10 percentage points is deducted from Sweden's monetary freedom score to account for policies that distort domestic prices.

INVESTMENT FREEDOM — 80%

Sweden has been encouraging foreign investment in industry. Foreign companies may purchase Swedish companies without government approval, although they are subject to controls in fishing, civil aviation, and transport and communications. Sweden is a world leader in telecommunications and electricity liberalization. Government monopoly prohibits investment in the retail sale of pharmaceuticals and alcoholic beverages. A complex network of permits and licenses applies to domestic and foreign firms. Residents and non-residents may hold foreign exchange accounts. There are no controls on payments and transfers or repatriation of profits. The purchase of real estate by non-residents may require a permit.

FINANCIAL FREEDOM — 80%

Regulation of the financial system is transparent and largely consistent with international norms. Banks offer a full range of financial services. There were 127 banks at the end of 2005: 26 Swedish, 28 foreign, and the rest savings banks or cooperative institutions. Nearly all commercial banks are privately owned and operated, and credit is allocated on market terms. Banking is highly concentrated, with four banks accounting for over 80 percent of assets. The government owns a mortgage company and several development funds and continues to offer concessional funds through various agencies. Foreign insurers are well represented in the insurance sector. The Stockholm Stock Exchange is modern, active, and open to domestic and foreign investment.

PROPERTY RIGHTS — 90%

The judiciary is independent and fair. Contracts are respected, and Swedish law generally provides adequate protection of all property rights, including intellectual property. As a member of the European Union, Sweden adheres to a series of multilateral conventions on industrial, intellectual, and commercial property.

FREEDOM FROM CORRUPTION — 92%

Corruption is perceived as almost nonexistent. Sweden ranks 6th out of 163 countries in Transparency International's Corruption Perceptions Index for 2006. Comprehensive laws on corruption are fully implemented, and Sweden has ratified the 1997 OECD Anti-bribery Convention. The constitution and law provide for public access to government information.

LABOR FREEDOM — 62%

Inflexible employment regulations hinder overall productivity growth and employment opportunities. The non-salary cost of employing a worker is high, and dismissing a redundant employee is costly and burdensome. Rigid regulations have contributed to slow job creation.

SWITZERLAND

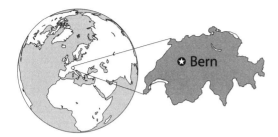

○ Bern

Switzerland's economy is 79.7 percent free, according to our 2008 assessment, which makes it the world's 9th freest economy. Its overall score is 1.6 percentage points higher than last year, reflecting improved scores in six of the 10 economic freedoms. Switzerland is ranked 2nd out of 41 countries in the European region, and its overall score is much higher than the regional average.

Switzerland has high levels of investment freedom, trade freedom, financial freedom, property rights, business freedom, and freedom from corruption. The average tariff rate is low, and commercial operations are protected by the regulatory environment and aided by a flexible labor market. Inflation is extremely low, and foreign investment is welcome and subject to only a few restrictions. The national financial sector leads the world and is both protective of privacy and open to foreign institutions. The judiciary, independent of politics, enforces contracts reliably. Corruption is virtually nonexistent.

Switzerland has relatively low scores in fiscal freedom and government size. As in many other European social democracies, personal income taxes can be burdensome, particularly at the provincial level. Total government spending equals more than a third of GDP.

BACKGROUND: Switzerland, one of the world's richest and most investment-friendly destinations, is a member of the World Trade Organization, the International Monetary Fund, the World Bank, and the Organisation for Economic Co-operation and Development. It is not a member of the European Union, even though it is at the geographical heart of Europe, and two referenda on EU membership have failed. Switzerland remains one of the world's most competitive economies and has particularly strong financial and banking sectors. Protectionism exists, particularly in agriculture.

Liechtenstein's economy is closely linked with Switzerland's, as the two economies share the same national currency, the Swiss franc.

How Do We Measure Economic Freedom? See Chapter 4 (page 39) for an explanation of the methodology or visit the *Index* Web site at *heritage.org/index*.

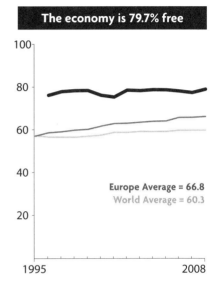

The economy is 79.7% free

Europe Average = 66.8
World Average = 60.3

1995 — 2008

QUICK FACTS

Population: 7.4 million

GDP (PPP): $265.0 billion
1.9% growth in 2005
1.1% 5-yr. comp. ann. growth
$35,633 per capita

Unemployment: 3.8%

Inflation (CPI): 1.2%

FDI (net flow): −$37.1 billion

Official Development Assistance:
Multilateral: None
Bilateral: None

External Debt: $1.1 trillion

Exports: $197.2 billion
Primarily machinery, chemicals, metals, watches, agricultural products, financial services, travel services

Imports: $171.5 billion
Primarily machinery, chemicals, vehicles, metals, agricultural products, textiles, financial services

2005 data unless otherwise noted.

SWITZERLAND'S TEN ECONOMIC FREEDOMS

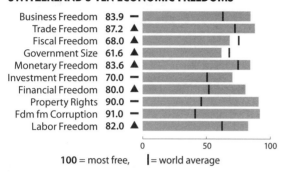

Business Freedom	83.9	—
Trade Freedom	87.2	▲
Fiscal Freedom	68.0	▲
Government Size	61.6	▲
Monetary Freedom	83.6	▲
Investment Freedom	70.0	—
Financial Freedom	80.0	▲
Property Rights	90.0	—
Fdm fm Corruption	91.0	—
Labor Freedom	82.0	▲

0   50   100

100 = most free, ❚ = world average

BUSINESS FREEDOM — *83.9%*

The overall freedom to start, operate, and close a business is well protected by Switzerland's regulatory environment. Starting a business takes an average of 20 days, compared to the world average of 43 days. Obtaining a business license takes less than the world average of 19 procedures and 234 days. Bankruptcy proceedings are relatively easy.

TRADE FREEDOM — *87.2%*

Switzerland's weighted average tariff rate was 1.4 percent in 2005. Prohibitive agriculture tariffs and quotas, restrictive biotechnology regulations, import taxes, export subsidies, and service market access barriers add to the cost of trade. An additional 10 percentage points is deducted from Switzerland's trade freedom score to account for non-tariff barriers.

FISCAL FREEDOM — *68%*

Taxation is more burdensome at the cantonal levels than it is at the federal level. The top federal income tax rate is 11.5 percent, but the combined top income tax rate (federal and sub-federal) can be as high as 42 percent, and the top corporate tax rate can be as high as 25 percent. Other taxes include a value-added tax (VAT), a property tax, and a vehicle tax. In the most recent year, overall tax revenue as a percentage of GDP was 29.2 percent.

GOVERNMENT SIZE — *61.6%*

Total government expenditures, including consumption and transfer payments, are high. In the most recent year, government spending equaled 35.8 percent of GDP. Direct government participation has been confined to public services such as post offices, railways, and defense.

MONETARY FREEDOM — *83.6%*

Inflation is low, averaging 1 percent between 2004 and 2006. Stable prices explain most of the monetary freedom score. Government measures influence the prices of agricultural goods and pharmaceutical products, and the government influences prices through regulation, subsidies, and state-owned utilities. An additional 10 percentage points is deducted from Switzerland's monetary freedom score to account for policies that distort domestic prices.

INVESTMENT FREEDOM — *70%*

Switzerland is generally open to foreign investment. Formal approval is not required, and screening applies only to real estate and national security–related investment. Hydroelectric and nuclear power are reserved for Swiss companies, and domestic air transport operators must be domiciled in Switzerland. Joint stock companies must have a majority of resident Swiss nationals on their boards. Cantons generally require 51 percent Swiss ownership in mining, and foreign ownership in petroleum exploitation must be less than 51 percent. Real estate purchases by non-residents must be approved by the canton in which the property is located. Residents and non-residents may hold foreign exchange accounts. There are no restrictions on repatriation of profits, payments for invisible transactions, or current transfers.

FINANCIAL FREEDOM — *80%*

Switzerland is a leading financial center with highly developed and well-regulated institutions. Credit, currency, and equity markets are open without restriction. The federal government is not a shareholder in the central bank but has appointment authority and approves its regulations. Banks offer a wide range of services, and credit is allocated on market terms. Banking secrecy has been loosened to prevent money laundering and tax evasion. There were 337 banks in 2005; the two biggest dominate the market and rank among the world's top 10 financial institutions. Savings deposits, mortgages, and lending to public authorities are offered by 24 province-owned banks. Approximately 44 percent of all banks are foreign-controlled. Insurance is well developed, and the state-owned postal service is a leader in the payments system and offers a variety of financial services. Capital markets are strong, and the stock exchange is Europe's fourth-largest.

PROPERTY RIGHTS — *90%*

The judiciary is independent, and contracts are secure. Switzerland has one of the world's best intellectual property–protection regimes for foreign and domestic rights holders. Most foreigners have the same rights as Swiss nationals when purchasing real property.

FREEDOM FROM CORRUPTION — *91%*

Corruption is perceived as almost nonexistent. Switzerland ranks 7th out of 163 countries in Transparency International's Corruption Perceptions Index for 2006. Corruption is not pervasive in any area of the economy, and enforcement procedures against domestic corruption are effective. Giving or accepting a bribe is subject to criminal and civil penalties, including imprisonment.

LABOR FREEDOM — *82%*

Flexible employment regulations enhance overall productivity growth and job creation. The non-salary cost of employing a worker is moderate, but dismissing a redundant employee can be costly. Switzerland's labor freedom is one of the highest in the world.

SYRIA

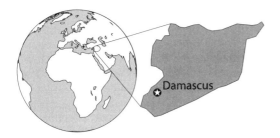

★ Damascus

Syria's economy is 46.6 percent free, according to our 2008 assessment, which makes it the world's 144th freest economy. Its overall score is 1.5 percentage points lower than last year, reflecting lower scores in four of the 10 economic freedoms. Syria is ranked 15th out of 17 countries in the Middle East/North Africa region, and its overall score is lower than the regional average.

Syria scores well in only one area: fiscal freedom. The top income tax is relatively low, and the corporate tax is moderate. Overall tax revenue is low as a percentage of GDP.

Syria is notably weak in trade freedom, investment freedom, financial freedom, property rights, and freedom from corruption. The government maintains a high average tariff rate, as well as non-tariff barriers such as an opaque regulatory process. Significant state influence in most areas of the economy taints the civil service and makes court rulings subject to the diktats of the Ba'athist government. This interference bleeds into the financial market, which is unsophisticated and dominated by the state. State expenditures are also high, and over half of Syria's revenue comes from state-owned businesses.

BACKGROUND: Syria has been ruled by the Assad regime ever since Minister of Defense Hafez al-Assad seized power in 1970. Assad was succeeded in 2000 by his son Bashar, who has failed to deliver on his promises to reform Syria's socialist economy. Foreign investment has been dampened by U.S. economic sanctions and Syria's growing isolation as a result of its involvement in the February 2005 assassination of former Lebanese Prime Minister Rafiq Hariri. Military withdrawal from Lebanon has deprived Syrian officials of substantial opportunities for graft and the smuggling of illicit goods.

How Do We Measure Economic Freedom? See Chapter 4 (page 39) for an explanation of the methodology or visit the *Index* Web site at *heritage.org/index*.

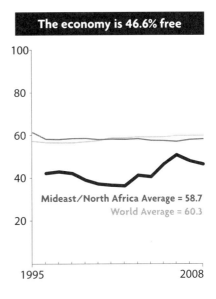

The economy is 46.6% free

Mideast/North Africa Average = 58.7
World Average = 60.3

1995   2008

QUICK FACTS

Population: 19.0 million

GDP (PPP): $72.5 billion
2.9% growth in 2005
2.5% 5-yr. comp. ann. growth
$3,808 per capita

Unemployment: 12.5%

Inflation (CPI): 7.2%

FDI (net flow): $500.0 million

Official Development Assistance:
Multilateral: $83.4 million
Bilateral: $92.0 million (0.4% from the U.S.)

External Debt: $6.5 billion

Exports: $9.8 billion
Primarily crude oil, petroleum products, fruits and vegetables, cotton fiber, clothing, meat and live animals, wheat

Imports: $107.2 billion
Primarily machinery and transport equipment, electric power machinery, food and livestock, metal and metal products, chemicals and chemical products, plastics
2005 data unless otherwise noted.

SYRIA'S TEN ECONOMIC FREEDOMS

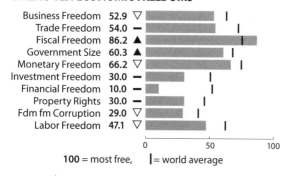

Business Freedom	52.9	▽
Trade Freedom	54.0	—
Fiscal Freedom	86.2	▲
Government Size	60.3	▲
Monetary Freedom	66.2	▽
Investment Freedom	30.0	—
Financial Freedom	10.0	—
Property Rights	30.0	—
Fdm fm Corruption	29.0	▽
Labor Freedom	47.1	▽

0   50   100

100 = most free, | = world average

BUSINESS FREEDOM — 52.9%

The overall freedom to start, operate, and close a business is restrained by Syria's regulatory environment. Starting a business takes about the world average of 43 days. Obtaining a business license requires slightly more than the world average of 19 procedures. Closing a business can be lengthy and burdensome.

TRADE FREEDOM — 54%

Syria's weighted average tariff rate was 15.5 percent in 2002. Prohibitive tariffs, import bans and restrictions, import taxes, non-transparent trade regulations, burdensome standards, a non-convertible currency, and corruption add to the cost of trade. An additional 15 percentage points is deducted from Syria's trade freedom score to account for non-tariff barriers.

FISCAL FREEDOM— 86.2%

Syria has a low income tax rate and a moderate corporate tax rate. The top income tax rate is 20 percent, and the top corporate tax rate was reduced to 28 percent in late 2006. Other taxes include a tax on insurance and a property transfer tax. In the most recent year, overall tax revenue as a percentage of GDP was 14 percent.

GOVERNMENT SIZE — 60.3%

Total government expenditures, including consumption and transfer payments, are moderate. In the most recent year, government spending equaled 36.4 percent of GDP. The state's direct role in the economy through public enterprises remains considerable.

MONETARY FREEDOM — 66.2%

Inflation is relatively high, averaging 8.8 percent between 2004 and 2006. Relatively high and unstable prices explain most of the monetary freedom score. The government controls prices for many goods; sets prices, provides subsidies, and controls marketing in the agricultural sector; influences prices through state-owned enterprises and utilities; and constrains private participation in manufacturing with input and output pricing limits. An additional 15 percentage points is deducted from Syria's monetary freedom score to account for policies that distort domestic prices.

INVESTMENT FREEDOM — 30%

Officially, foreigners may own 100 percent of a company. New laws guarantee against expropriation and permit repatriation. Gradual improvement in Syria's economic policies has led to some renewed EU interest in a Syria–EU Association Agreement. A new investment law approved in January 2007 allows foreigners to own the land under their investment and permits repatriation of capital and profits. Almost all sectors are open to foreign direct investment, except for power generation and distribution, air transport, port operation, water bottling, telephony, and oil and gas production and refining; A weak and arbitrary legal environment and regional political uncertainty are strong disincentives. Many capital transactions are subject to controls, and all foreign exchange and trade transactions require government approval.

FINANCIAL FREEDOM — 10%

Syria's financial system is subject to heavy state influence. Regulations are cumbersome and unclear, and interest rates are fixed by the government. State-owned banks account for 92 percent of private-sector lending, and the central bank is not independent. There were seven state banks in mid-2006, all serving a specialized market. When the sector opened in 2004, three private banks were licensed to operate in January, and three more were licensed to operate in June. Foreign banks have been allowed to establish offices in free trade zones since 2000, but only six, mostly Lebanese, have entered the country. A seventh, controlled by Bahraini capital, is scheduled to join the sector in 2007. Private banks must be 51 percent Syrian-owned, but this may change. The insurance sector is controlled almost entirely by a government-owned firm. Capital markets are negligible and restricted to small amounts of government debt. There is no stock market.

PROPERTY RIGHTS — 30%

Protection of property rights is weak. The government, political connections, and bribery influence court decisions. A new law promulgated early in 2007 permits foreigners to own or lease real property, but there is practically no legislation that protects intellectual property rights.

FREEDOM FROM CORRUPTION — 29%

Corruption is perceived as widespread. Syria ranks 93rd out of 163 countries in Transparency International's Corruption Perceptions Index for 2006. Even members of the regime are said to be alarmed at the level of corruption in the legislative, judicial, and executive branches of government.

LABOR FREEDOM — 47.1%

Inflexible employment regulations hinder overall productivity growth and employment opportunities. The non-salary cost of employing a worker is moderate, but the rigidity of hiring and firing a worker creates a risk aversion for companies that would otherwise employ more people and grow.

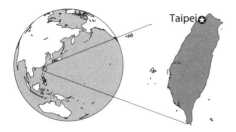

Taipei

TAIWAN

Taiwan's economy is 71 percent free, according to our 2008 assessment, which makes it the world's 25th freest economy. Its overall score is 0.8 percentage point higher than last year, reflecting improved scores in four of the 10 economic freedoms. Taiwan is ranked 6th out of 30 countries in the Asia–Pacific region, and its overall score is much higher than the regional average.

Taiwan has high scores for investment freedom, trade freedom, property rights, freedom from corruption, and government size. The average tariff rate, the inflation rate, and the level of corruption are all low. Although Taiwan's personal income tax is high, the corporate tax rate is moderate, and overall tax revenue is low as a percentage of GDP. Government spending is similarly low. Taiwan's investment climate is healthy, and 100 percent foreign ownership is permitted in most sectors. Property rights are protected by the judiciary, although there are minor problems with case delays and corruption associated with organized crime.

Taiwan has slightly lower than average scores in labor freedom and financial freedom. The country's labor market is not as flexible as it could be, and dismissing a redundant worker is costly.

BACKGROUND: Taiwan, Asia's fifth-largest economy, boasts one of the region's most dynamic democracies. In 2008, President Chen Shui-bian will step down, possibly shifting Taiwan toward a more moderate and open economic relationship with China. Taiwan is a modern, developed economy with a heavy emphasis on services, manufacturing, and high technology. The government has moved to liberalize its financial sector, allowing foreign investment in banks and gradually loosening capital controls, but more needs to be done to dismantle high trade barriers and further liberalize the economy.

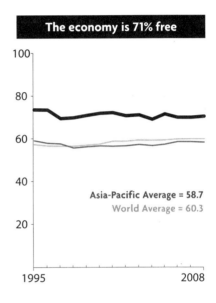

The economy is 71% free

Asia-Pacific Average = 58.7
World Average = 60.3

1995 — 2008

QUICK FACTS

Population: 22.9 million

GDP (PPP): $645.4 billion
4.0% growth in 2005
4.4% 5-yr. comp. ann. growth
$28,342 per capita

Unemployment: 4.1%

Inflation (CPI): 2.3%

FDI (net inflow): −$4.4 million

Official Development Assistance:
Multilateral: n/a
Bilateral: $16.7 million (3.8% from the U.S.) (2004)

External Debt: $93.1 million

Exports: $224.0 billion
Primarily computer products, electrical equipment, metals, textiles, plastics and rubber products, chemicals

Imports: $202.7 billion
Primarily machinery and electrical equipment, minerals, precision instruments

2005 data unless otherwise noted.

How Do We Measure Economic Freedom? See Chapter 4 (page 39) for an explanation of the methodology or visit the *Index* Web site at *heritage.org/index.*

TAIWAN'S TEN ECONOMIC FREEDOMS

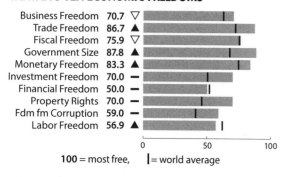

Business Freedom	70.7 ▽	
Trade Freedom	86.7 ▲	
Fiscal Freedom	75.9 ▽	
Government Size	87.8 ▲	
Monetary Freedom	83.3 ▲	
Investment Freedom	70.0 —	
Financial Freedom	50.0 —	
Property Rights	70.0 —	
Fdm fm Corruption	59.0 —	
Labor Freedom	56.9 ▲	

0   50   100

100 = most free, ▌= world average

BUSINESS FREEDOM — *70.7%*

The overall freedom to start, operate, and close a business is relatively well protected by Taiwan's regulatory environment. Starting a business takes an average of 48 days, compared to the world average of 43 days. Obtaining a business license requires more than the world average of 19 procedures. Bankruptcy proceedings are fairly easy and straightforward.

TRADE FREEDOM — *86.7%*

Taiwan's weighted average tariff rate was 1.67 percent in 2005. The government has been improving the trade regime, but import and export bans and restrictions, service market access barriers, tariff escalation, import taxes, import and export fees, burdensome standards and certification requirements, restrictive pharmaceutical regulations, cumbersome sanitary and phytosanitary rules, state trade in rice, and weak enforcement of intellectual property rights add to the cost of trade. An additional 10 percentage points is deducted from Taiwan's trade freedom score to account for non-tariff barriers.

FISCAL FREEDOM — *75.9%*

Taiwan has a high income tax rate and a moderate corporate tax rate. The top income tax rate is 40 percent, and the top corporate tax rate is 25 percent. Other taxes include a value-added tax (VAT) and a capital gains tax. In the most recent year, overall tax revenue as a percentage of GDP was 13.7 percent.

GOVERNMENT SIZE — *87.8%*

Total government expenditures, including consumption and transfer payments, are low. In the most recent year, government spending equaled 20.2 percent of GDP. Privatization and deregulation have reduced the government's role in the economy, but the state is still active in economic management.

MONETARY FREEDOM — *83.3%*

Inflation is low, averaging 1.1 percent between 2004 and 2006. Relatively stable prices explain most of the monetary freedom score. The government regulates the prices of pharmaceutical and medical products and influences prices through regulation, subsidies, and state-owned utilities. An additional 10 percentage points is deducted from Taiwan's monetary freedom score to account for policies that distort domestic prices.

INVESTMENT FREEDOM — *70%*

Foreign and domestic companies are equal under the law. Repatriation of profits is not restricted, and 100 percent ownership is permitted in most sectors. Investment is screened, but approval time is usually short. Taiwan has been widening the scope of sectors open to foreign investment since 2001. Foreign investment is prohibited in a handful of industries, such as agriculture, wireless broadcasting, coastal oil exploration, public utilities, and postal services, and limited in telecommunications, electricity transmission and distribution, and high-speed railway transportation. A three-year development program implemented in 2006 will encourage industrial investment in designated areas. Capital flows relating to portfolio investment are no longer restricted.

FINANCIAL FREEDOM — *50%*

Taiwan has liberalized its traditionally overregulated financial sector by, among other things, reducing many restrictions on financial activities, particularly those of foreign financial institutions. The collapse of the Rebar conglomerate in 2006 reportedly exposed weaknesses in supervisory institutions. A wide variety of financial instruments are available to foreign and domestic investors on market terms. Nine state-owned banks have been privatized since 1998, most recently in 2005. Four banks are state-controlled, including two of the three largest domestic banks, which together account for 16 percent of assets. State-run banks have not been consolidated to create Taiwan's largest bank as planned, and further consolidation seems to have been halted by labor protests and a lack of political will. Insurance is open to foreign competition. Capital markets are sophisticated, and the stock market is open to foreign participation, except for selected industries.

PROPERTY RIGHTS — *70%*

Property rights are generally protected, and the judiciary enforces contracts, although the court system is very slow. One of the judiciary's biggest problems is corruption associated with organized crime. Taiwan has tried to improve the protection of intellectual property rights but needs to expand efforts against pirated optical media, counterfeit pharmaceuticals, and counterfeit luxury goods.

FREEDOM FROM CORRUPTION — *59%*

Corruption is perceived as present. Taiwan ranks 34th out of 163 countries in Transparency International's Corruption Perceptions Index for 2006. There were allegations of government corruption in 2006, but the government continued to combat corruption in the executive and judicial branches.

LABOR FREEDOM — *56.9%*

Inflexible employment regulations hinder overall productivity growth. The non-salary cost of employing a worker is low, but dismissing a redundant employee is relatively costly and burdensome. Regulations related to the number of work hours are not flexible.

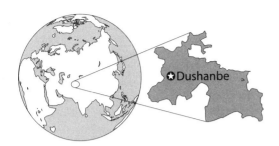

TAJIKISTAN

Tajikistan's economy is 54.5 percent free, according to our 2008 assessment, which makes it the world's 114th freest economy. Its overall score is 0.7 percentage point higher than last year, reflecting slightly improved scores in four of the 10 economic freedoms. Tajikistan is ranked 20th out of 30 countries in the Asia–Pacific region, and its overall score is lower than the regional average.

Tajikistan scores well in fiscal freedom, government size, and trade freedom. The government imposes low tax rates, including a 13 percent personal income rate. Total government expenditures are equal to about 20 percent of GDP.

Tajikistan's significant challenges are reflected in its significantly weaker than average scores in business freedom, monetary freedom, investment freedom, financial freedom, property rights, and freedom from corruption. The regulatory environment is not protective of business, and laws are both restrictive and inconsistent. Foreign investment faces many regulatory hurdles as well as outright corruption. Tajikistan is rated one of the world's 20 most corrupt nations, and corruption seeps into most aspects of official life, from the courts to customs.

BACKGROUND: Tajikistan gained its independence from the Soviet Union in 1991 and was wracked by civil war from 1992 to 1997. Since then, it has struggled with political and economic reforms. Poverty remains high, and drug trafficking and manufacturing are the most important major sources of income. Despite progress toward a market economy, the transition to a multi-party democracy and pluralism has been bumpy. Parliamentary elections in February 2005 failed to meet international standards, as did President Imomali Rahmonov's November 2006 reelection to a third term that will last until 2013. Rahmonov is consolidating his power by limiting political activity and tightening controls on civil society. Uneven implementation of structural reforms, weak governance, high unemployment, external debt, and drug trafficking have left the economy extremely fragile.

How Do We Measure Economic Freedom? See Chapter 4 (page 39) for an explanation of the methodology or visit the *Index* Web site at *heritage.org/index.*

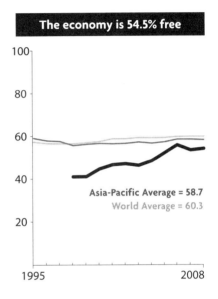

The economy is 54.5% free

Asia-Pacific Average = 58.7
World Average = 60.3

QUICK FACTS

Population: 6.5 million

GDP (PPP): $8.8 billion
6.7% growth in 2005
9.3% 5-yr. comp. ann. growth
$1,356 per capita

Unemployment: 12% (2004 estimate)

Inflation (CPI): 7.3%

FDI (net flow): $54.0 million

Official Development Assistance:
Multilateral: $144.2 million
Bilateral: $112.6 million (52% from the U.S.)

External Debt: $1.0 billion

Exports: $1.3 billion
Primarily aluminum, electricity, cotton, fruits, vegetable oil, textiles

Imports: $1.7 billion
Primarily electricity, petroleum products, aluminum oxide, machinery and equipment, foodstuffs

2005 data unless otherwise noted.

TAJIKISTAN'S TEN ECONOMIC FREEDOMS

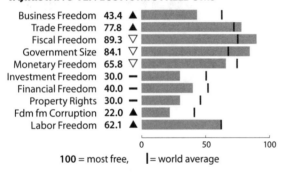

Business Freedom	43.4 ▲	
Trade Freedom	77.8 ▲	
Fiscal Freedom	89.3 ▽	
Government Size	84.1 ▽	
Monetary Freedom	65.8 ▽	
Investment Freedom	30.0 —	
Financial Freedom	40.0 —	
Property Rights	30.0 —	
Fdm fm Corruption	22.0 ▲	
Labor Freedom	62.1 ▲	

0   50   100

100 = most free, | = world average

BUSINESS FREEDOM — 43.4%

The overall freedom to start, operate, and close a business is restricted by Tajikistan's regulatory environment. Starting a business takes an average of 49 days, compared to the world average of 43 days. Obtaining a business license requires more than the world average 19 procedures, and costs are high. Closing a business is relatively protracted.

TRADE FREEDOM — 77.8%

Tajikistan's weighted average tariff rate was 6.1 percent in 2002. Some quotas, import bans and restrictions, non-transparent and poorly administered standards and certification requirements, inefficient and corrupt customs implementation, and weak enforcement of intellectual property rights add to the cost of trade. An additional 10 percentage points is deducted from Tajikistan's trade freedom score to account for non-tariff barriers.

FISCAL FREEDOM — 89.3%

Tajikistan has competitive tax rates. The top income tax rate is 13 percent, and the top corporate tax rate is 25 percent. Other taxes include a value-added tax (VAT) and a tax on immovable property. In the most recent year, overall tax revenue as a percentage of GDP was 16.6 percent.

GOVERNMENT SIZE — 84.1%

Total government expenditures, including consumption and transfer payments, are moderate. In the most recent year, government spending equaled 23 percent of GDP. The government is trying to improve spending management. Despite progress in privatizing small and medium-sized public enterprises, the private sector is developing slowly.

MONETARY FREEDOM — 65.8%

Inflation is high, averaging 9.2 percent between 2004 and 2006. Relatively unstable prices explain most of the monetary freedom score. The government influences prices through regulation, subsidies, and numerous state-owned enterprises and utilities. An additional 15 percentage points is deducted from Tajikistan's monetary freedom score to account for policies that distort domestic prices.

INVESTMENT FREEDOM — 30%

Corruption and a lack of transparency in government contracts and privatizations are among the substantial barriers to foreign investment. Investors face ownership restrictions and cumbersome procedures with regard to tax and business registration. The government has begun some large infrastructure projects that could improve the investment climate with foreign capital assistance. Remittance abroad of profits is allowed. Foreigners may purchase land under certain conditions. Residents (with some restrictions) and non-residents may hold foreign exchange accounts. Payments and transfers are subject to documentary requirements. Most capital transactions, including all direct investment transactions, require central bank approval.

FINANCIAL FREEDOM — 40%

Tajikistan's financial sector is small and underdeveloped. The government is trying to increase transparency and improve supervision and regulation. Consolidation has cut the banking sector by more than two-thirds since 1997; there were 12 domestic banks and the central bank at the end of 2005. The four largest banks, including a state-owned bank, control 80 percent of deposits. All banks, except for Amonat Bank (one of the four largest) are privately owned. Non-performing loans are decreasing. The opening of the banking sector to foreign competition has caused three foreign banks to enter the market since 2006. The small non-banking financial sector includes several small insurance companies and one pension fund. Capital markets are negligible, and a securities market has been established but was not yet functioning as of June 2007.

PROPERTY RIGHTS — 30%

Protection of private property is weak. Judicial corruption is widespread, and the courts are sensitive to pressure from the government and paramilitary groups. In 2006, the authorities revived a Soviet-era plan for the reconstruction of Dushanbe, the capital. In the process, they have threatened to expropriate the property of thousands of families. Many residents and small businesses already have been resettled on land of unequal value, often on the outskirts of the city's center. Tajikistan's weak enforcement regime lacks criminal penalties for violations of intellectual property rights.

FREEDOM FROM CORRUPTION — 22%

Corruption is perceived as pervasive. Tajikistan ranks 142nd out of 163 countries in Transparency International's Corruption Perceptions Index for 2006. Tajikistan is one of the world's poorest countries, and corruption, particularly bribery and nepotism, is endemic. There is no legal provision for regular citizens' public access to government information.

LABOR FREEDOM — 62.1%

Inflexible employment regulations hinder overall productivity growth and job creation. The non-salary cost of employing a worker is high, and the rigidity of hiring and firing a worker creates a risk aversion for companies that would otherwise employ more people and grow. Regulations related to the number of work hours are not flexible.

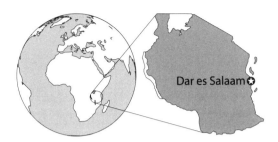

Dar es Salaam

TANZANIA

Tanzania's economy is 56.4 percent free, according to our 2008 assessment, which makes it the world's 97th freest economy. Its overall score is 0.4 percentage point lower than last year, reflecting worsened scores in four of the 10 economic freedoms. Tanzania is ranked 14th out of 40 countries in the sub-Saharan Africa region, and its overall score is slightly higher than the regional average.

Tanzania scores above the world average in fiscal freedom and government size. The top personal income and corporate tax rates are moderate, and overall tax revenue is relatively low as a percentage of GDP. Government expenditures are also fairly moderate.

Economic development is hurt by weak property rights, freedom from corruption, labor freedom, and business freedom. The overall regulatory environment is poor, and most business operations are seriously restricted. A slow civil service hurts trade freedom, as fairly high tariff rates are complemented by an inefficient customs service. As in many other sub-Saharan African nations, the judiciary is underdeveloped and subject to the political whims of the executive. The level of corruption is high, although not as high as it is in some other African nations.

BACKGROUND: The United Republic of Tanzania is composed of mainland Tanzania and the Zanzibar archipelago. Despite average growth of nearly 7 percent since 2001, it remains very poor. More than 80 percent of the population is rural, and agriculture accounts for nearly 50 percent of GDP. Tanzania's first president, Julius K. Nyerere, pursued a socialist economic policy that has hindered growth and development. Jakaya Kikwete won the 2005 election, succeeding Benjamin Mkapa. The historically state-led economy is becoming more market-based, and efforts to improve economic management and privatize public enterprises continue. The business and investment climate remains challenging, however, and the economy is hindered by corruption, poor infrastructure, and HIV/AIDS.

How Do We Measure Economic Freedom? See Chapter 4 (page 39) for an explanation of the methodology or visit the *Index* Web site at *heritage.org/index*.

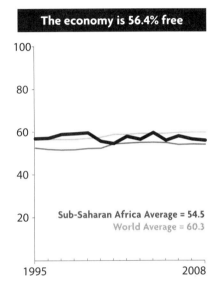

The economy is 56.4% free

Sub-Saharan Africa Average = 54.5
World Average = 60.3

1995   2008

QUICK FACTS

Population: 38.3 million

GDP (PPP): $28.5 billion
6.8% growth in 2005
6.6% 5-yr. comp. ann. growth
$744 per capita

Unemployment: 7.0%

Inflation (CPI): 4.4%

FDI (net flow): $473.0 million

Official Development Assistance:
Multilateral: $759.3 million
Bilateral: $889.1 million (12.2% from the U.S.)

External Debt: $7.8 billion

Exports: $2.9 billion
Primarily gold, coffee, cashew nuts, manufactures, cotton

Imports: $3.8 billion
Primarily consumer goods, machinery and transportation equipment, industrial raw materials, crude oil

2005 data unless otherwise noted.

TANZANIA'S TEN ECONOMIC FREEDOMS

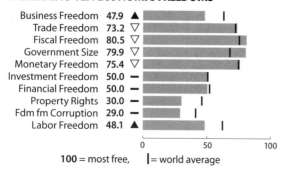

Business Freedom	47.9 ▲	
Trade Freedom	73.2 ▽	
Fiscal Freedom	80.5 ▽	
Government Size	79.9 ▽	
Monetary Freedom	75.4 ▽	
Investment Freedom	50.0 —	
Financial Freedom	50.0 —	
Property Rights	30.0 —	
Fdm fm Corruption	29.0 —	
Labor Freedom	48.1 ▲	

0   50   100

100 = most free, I = world average

BUSINESS FREEDOM — 47.9%

The overall freedom to start, operate, and close a business is very limited by Tanzania's regulatory environment. Starting a business takes an average of 29 days, compared to the world average of 43 days. Obtaining a business license takes more than the world average of 19 procedures and 234 days, and costs are high. Bankruptcy proceedings are fairly straightforward but relatively lengthy.

TRADE FREEDOM — 73.2%

Tanzania's weighted average tariff rate was 8.4 percent in 2005. Import and export bans and restrictions, import and export taxes and fees, prohibitive tariffs, import and export registration and licensing, and weak enforcement of intellectual property rights add to the cost of trade. An additional 10 percentage points is deducted from Tanzania's trade freedom score to account for non-tariff barriers.

FISCAL FREEDOM — 80.5%

Tanzania has moderate tax rates. Both the top income tax rate and the top corporate tax rate are 30 percent. Other taxes include a value-added tax (VAT), a property tax, and a tax on interest. In the most recent year, overall tax revenue as a percentage of GDP was 12.4 percent.

GOVERNMENT SIZE — 79.9%

Total government expenditures, including consumption and transfer payments, are low, but government spending has been rising for five years and in the most recent year equaled 25.9 percent of GDP. Privatization and restructuring of state-owned enterprises have progressed.

MONETARY FREEDOM — 75.4%

Inflation is relatively high, averaging 5.3 percent between 2004 and 2006. Relatively high and unstable prices explain most of the monetary freedom score. The government influences prices through regulation, subsidies, and state-owned enterprises and utilities. An additional 10 percentage points is deducted from Tanzania's monetary freedom score to account for policies that distort domestic prices.

INVESTMENT FREEDOM — 50%

There is no limit on foreign ownership or control, but foreign purchase of real estate in Tanzania and residents' purchase of real estate abroad must be approved by the government. Bureaucracy, poor infrastructure, and corrup-

tion are ongoing deterrents. Residents may hold foreign exchange accounts only for funds acquired outside of Tanzania; non-residents temporarily residing in Tanzania may also hold foreign exchange accounts. All foreign currency transfers from residents to non-residents must be approved by the central bank. Most capital transactions are subject to reporting requirements, and some are restricted.

FINANCIAL FREEDOM — 50%

Tanzania's financial system is relatively small and underdeveloped. There were 22 licensed banks in mid-2006. Credit is allocated largely at market rates. There are minimal restrictions on foreign banks, and international banks are expanding their operations. Privatization is ongoing. A controlling stake in the National Commercial Bank was sold to a foreign bank in 2001, and the government chose a consortium led by Rabobank of the Netherlands to buy 49 percent of the National Microfinance Bank in 2005. There are 11 non-bank financial institutions. The insurance sector is small. The state-owned National Insurance Corporation is the largest insurer and controls 25 percent of premiums. Capital markets are rudimentary. The Dar es Salaam Stock Exchange is open to foreign investors, but foreign ownership of listed companies is restricted to 60 percent. Due to the low number of stocks listed, there has been an effort to cross-list stocks with regional neighbors.

PROPERTY RIGHTS — 30%

The legal system is slow and subject to corruption. A commercial court has been established to improve the resolution of commercial disputes. Recent reforms have been aimed at establishing a reliable system of transferable property rights. Legislation conforms to international intellectual property rights conventions, including the WTO's Trade-Related Aspects of Intellectual Property Rights (TRIPS) agreement, and protects patents, copyrights, trademarks, and trade secrets, but violations are not seriously investigated, and courts lack experience and training in IPR issues.

FREEDOM FROM CORRUPTION — 29%

Corruption is perceived as widespread. Tanzania ranks 93rd out of 163 countries in Transparency International's Corruption Perceptions Index for 2006. Anti-corruption efforts include forming a presidential commission of inquiry, requiring that all top political leaders declare their assets, firing public servants for corrupt activity, and strengthening the Prevention of Corruption Bureau.

LABOR FREEDOM — 48.1%

Restrictive employment regulations hinder overall productivity growth and employment opportunities. The non-salary cost of employing a worker is moderate, but the rigidity of hiring and firing a worker creates a risk aversion for companies that would otherwise employ more people and grow.

THAILAND

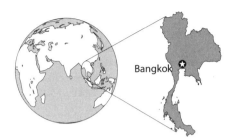

Bangkok

Thailand's economy is 63.5 percent free, according to our 2008 assessment, which makes it the world's 54th freest economy. Its overall score is 1.3 percentage points lower than last year, reflecting worsened scores in five of the 10 economic freedoms. Thailand is ranked 9th out of 30 countries in the Asia–Pacific region, and its overall score is higher than the regional average.

Thailand enjoys high scores for business freedom, government size, and especially labor freedom. Opening a business takes less time than the world average, and overall licensing procedures are simple and transparent. Government spending is also low as a percentage of GDP. Thailand's labor market is highly flexible, and firing a redundant worker is not difficult.

Thailand could do better in monetary freedom, investment freedom, and freedom from corruption. Though inflation is moderate, the government directly subsidizes the prices of a number of staple goods. Foreign investment is subject to a variety of serious restrictions that are not enforced uniformly. Corruption is significant, although not as extensive as it is in many neighboring countries.

BACKGROUND: Thailand's democratic government was overthrown by a military coup in September 2006, casting doubt on the trend of economic liberalization under previous administrations. Thailand had been known for its open economy and willingness to accept foreign direct investment. The economy was hit hard by the 1997–1998 Asian financial crisis, but economic reforms helped it to recover to pre-crisis levels by 2003. The current military-installed government has damaged Thailand's economy through a number of ill-considered actions, including the imposition of capital controls and the seizure of foreign pharmaceutical companies' drug patents.

How Do We Measure Economic Freedom? See Chapter 4 (page 39) for an explanation of the methodology or visit the *Index* Web site at *heritage.org/index*.

The economy is 63.5% free

Asia-Pacific Average = 58.7
World Average = 60.3

1995 — 2008

QUICK FACTS

Population: 64.2 million

GDP (PPP): $557.4 billion
4.5% growth in 2005
5.8% 5-yr. comp. ann. growth
$8,678 per capita

Unemployment: 1.8%

Inflation (CPI): 4.5%

FDI (net flow): $3.4 billion

Official Development Assistance:
Multilateral: $46.6 million
Bilateral: $838.8 million (2.2% from the U.S.)

External Debt: $52.3 billion

Exports: $133.6 billion
Primarily textiles and footwear, fishery products, rice, rubber, jewelry, automobiles, computers and electrical appliances

Imports: $129.8 billion
Primarily capital goods, intermediate goods and raw materials, consumer goods, fuels

2005 data unless otherwise noted.

THAILAND'S TEN ECONOMIC FREEDOMS

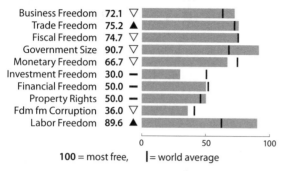

Business Freedom	72.1 ▽	
Trade Freedom	75.2 ▲	
Fiscal Freedom	74.7 ▽	
Government Size	90.7 ▽	
Monetary Freedom	66.7 ▽	
Investment Freedom	30.0 —	
Financial Freedom	50.0 —	
Property Rights	50.0 —	
Fdm fm Corruption	36.0 ▽	
Labor Freedom	89.6 ▲	

0   50   100

100 = most free,   **| = world average**

BUSINESS FREEDOM — 72.1%

The overall freedom to start, operate, and close a business is relatively well protected by Thailand's regulatory environment. Starting a business takes an average of 33 days, compared to the world average of 43 days. Obtaining a business license takes less than the world average of 19 procedures and 234 days. Bankruptcy proceedings are fairly easy and straightforward.

TRADE FREEDOM — 75.2%

Thailand's weighted average tariff rate was 4.9 percent in 2005. Import bans and restrictions, service market access barriers, complex import taxes and fees, prohibitive tariffs, burdensome standards and import licensing requirements, restrictive sanitary and phytosanitary rules, non-transparent government procurement, non-transparent and inefficient customs, export subsidies, and weak enforcement of intellectual property rights add to the cost of trade. An additional 15 percentage points is deducted from Thailand's trade freedom score to account for non-tariff barriers.

FISCAL FREEDOM — 74.7%

Thailand has burdensome tax rates. The top income tax rate is 37 percent, and the top corporate tax rate is 30 percent. Other taxes include a value-added tax (VAT) and a property tax. In the most recent year, overall tax revenue as a percentage of GDP was 16.3 percent.

GOVERNMENT SIZE — 90.7%

Total government expenditures, including consumption and transfer payments, are low. In the most recent year, government spending equaled 17.6 percent of GDP. Government intervention persists, and privatization has suffered several setbacks.

MONETARY FREEDOM — 66.7%

Inflation averaged 4.4 percent between 2004 and 2006. Relatively unstable prices explain most of the monetary freedom score. The economy-wide price freeze imposed after the 2006 coup is still in effect. The government can set price ceilings for basic goods and services and influences prices through regulation, subsidies, and state-owned utilities. An additional 20 percentage points is deducted from Thailand's monetary freedom score to account for policies that distort domestic prices.

INVESTMENT FREEDOM — 30%

The law permits 100 percent foreign ownership except in 32 service occupations, such as fishing, TV and radio outlets, farming, and newspapers, where foreign ownership is forbidden. Non-Thai businesses and citizens may own land only on government-approved industrial estates. Regulations are enforced inconsistently. A 2007 investment law addendum expanding the definition of a foreign company has caused several foreign firms to reduce their holdings. Privatization is slow. Residents and non-residents may hold foreign exchange accounts, subject to approval in some cases. Foreign exchange transactions, repatriation, some outward direct investments, and transactions involving capital market securities, bonds, debt securities, money market instruments, real estate, and short-term money securities are regulated and usually require government approval.

FINANCIAL FREEDOM — 50%

Financial regulation and supervision remain short of international standards. Credit is generally allocated on market terms. A December 2006 change in reporting standards for non-performing loans improved the health of many banks. In early 2007, there were 12 domestic commercial banks and 17 foreign banks. The government owns 56 percent of Krung Thai Bank, 48 percent of Siam City Bank, and 49 percent of BankThai, which are among the 10 largest domestic institutions. Foreign ownership is restricted in some cases. Roughly 100 insurance companies are registered, including many foreign firms, but new capital requirements should force consolidation. Capital markets are relatively well developed. The stock exchange is active and open to foreign investors.

PROPERTY RIGHTS — 50%

Private property is generally protected, but the legal process is slow, and litigants or third parties can affect judgments through extralegal means. Despite a Central Intellectual Property and International Trade Court, piracy (especially of optical media) continues. Under the Trade Secrets Act, the government can disclose trade secrets to protect any "public interest" not having commercial objectives, and there are concerns that approval-related data might not be protected against unfair commercial use.

FREEDOM FROM CORRUPTION — 36%

Corruption is perceived as significant. Thailand ranks 63rd out of 163 countries in Transparency International's Corruption Perceptions Index for 2006. Foreign and Thai companies continue to allege customs irregularities. The government is trying to make the evaluation of bids and awarding of contracts more transparent. Convictions of public officials on corruption-related charges are rare.

LABOR FREEDOM — 89.6%

Flexible employment regulations enhance overall productivity growth and employment opportunities. The non-salary cost of employing a worker is low, and dismissing a redundant employee is relatively costless. Regulations related to the number of work hours are quite flexible.

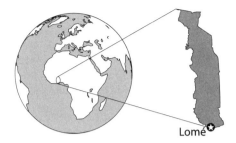

Lomé

TOGO

Rank: 140
Regional Rank: 33 of 40

Togo's economy is 48.8 percent free, according to our 2008 assessment, which makes it the world's 140th freest economy. Its overall score is 0.9 percentage point lower than last year, reflecting deteriorated scores in government spending and freedom from corruption. Togo is ranked 33rd out of 40 countries in the sub-Saharan Africa region, and its overall score is far below the regional average.

Togo scores best in monetary freedom and government size. Government spending is low, although this does not seem to be a sign of efficiency. Inflation is moderate, and petroleum is the only good that the government subsidizes directly.

Virtually all areas of economic freedom in Togo are heavily restricted. Opening a business takes longer than the world average, and commercial operations are hamstrung by red tape. Despite efforts at liberalization during the 1990s, foreign investment is allowed only in certain sectors. The judiciary is not free from political influence, and corruption pervades much of the economy. Formal and informal barriers to trade are high, and the financial system is rudimentary. Despite a smoothly functioning bureaucracy, extensive labor regulations make Togo one of the world's 20 least free labor markets.

BACKGROUND: Togo has an agrarian economy, and a majority of the population is engaged in subsistence agriculture. The principal exports are cotton and phosphates. Services are also important, particularly the re-export of goods through the Lomé port facility to landlocked states in the region. Following the death of President Gnassingbé Eyadéma in 2005, the military appointed his son, Faure Gnassingbé, to serve as president. After protests, international condemnation, and the imposition of sanctions, an election was held in April 2005. Gnassingbé won this election, but international pressure led him to establish a government of national unity with opposition party leader Edem Kodjo as prime minister.

How Do We Measure Economic Freedom? See Chapter 4 (page 39) for an explanation of the methodology or visit the *Index* Web site at *heritage.org/index*.

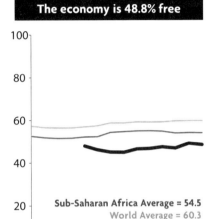

The economy is 48.8% free

Sub-Saharan Africa Average = 54.5
World Average = 60.3

1995   2008

QUICK FACTS

Population: 6.1 million

GDP (PPP): $9.3 billion
1.2% growth in 2005
2.1% 5-yr. comp. ann. growth
$1,506 per capita

Unemployment: n/a

Inflation (CPI): 6.8%

FDI (net flow): $59.0 million

Official Development Assistance:
Multilateral: $38.5 million
Bilateral: $65.0 million (4.6% from the U.S.)

External Debt: $1.7 billion

Exports: $751.0 million (2004)
Primarily re-exports, cotton, phosphates, coffee, cocoa

Imports: $1.1 billion (2004)
Primarily machinery and equipment, foodstuffs, petroleum products

2005 data unless otherwise noted.

TOGO'S TEN ECONOMIC FREEDOMS

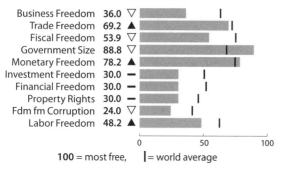

Business Freedom	36.0 ▽
Trade Freedom	69.2 ▲
Fiscal Freedom	53.9 ▽
Government Size	88.8 ▽
Monetary Freedom	78.2 ▲
Investment Freedom	30.0 —
Financial Freedom	30.0 —
Property Rights	30.0 —
Fdm fm Corruption	24.0 ▽
Labor Freedom	48.2 ▲

0   50   100

100 = most free, **|** = world average

BUSINESS FREEDOM — 36%

The overall freedom to start, operate, and close a business is very limited by Togo's regulatory environment. Starting a business takes an average of 53 days, compared to the world average of 43 days. Obtaining a business license takes more than the world average of 234 days, and costs are high.

TRADE FREEDOM — 69.2%

Togo's weighted average tariff rate was 10.4 percent in 2005. Import restrictions, numerous import taxes and fees, import permit requirements, complex customs valuation, export promotion programs, and weak enforcement of intellectual property rights add to the cost of trade. An additional 10 percentage points is deducted from Togo's trade freedom score to account for non-tariff barriers.

FISCAL FREEDOM — 53.9%

Togo has burdensome tax rates. The top income tax rate is 55 percent, and the top corporate tax rate is 37 percent. Other taxes include a value-added tax (VAT), a property tax, and a vehicle tax. In the most recent year, overall tax revenue as a percentage of GDP was 14.6 percent.

GOVERNMENT SIZE — 88.8%

Total government expenditures, including consumption and transfer payments, are moderate. In the most recent year, government spending equaled 19.3 percent of GDP. Spending management has been weak, and privatization has been sluggish in recent years.

MONETARY FREEDOM — 78.2%

Inflation is moderate, averaging 3.5 percent between 2004 and 2006. Relatively unstable prices explain most of the monetary freedom score. The government controls the prices of petroleum products and influences prices through regulation and state-owned enterprises and utilities. An additional 10 percentage points is deducted from Togo's monetary freedom score to account for policies that distort domestic prices.

INVESTMENT FREEDOM — 30%

Political unrest in the 1990s sharply dampened a tradition of strong foreign investment. This uncertainty negatively affects the bureaucracy and legal structures; there is an overall lack of administrative transparency. Investment is permitted only in certain sectors and is screened on a case-by-case basis. Purchases of real estate by non-residents for non-business purposes are subject to controls. Privatization in sectors like telecommunication, phosphates, and tourism is ongoing but hesitant. Residents and non-residents may hold foreign exchange accounts with prior government approval. Payments and transfers to certain countries are subject to authorization and quantitative limits in some cases. Most capital transactions are subject to controls or government approval.

FINANCIAL FREEDOM — 30%

Togo was once a local trading center, but government involvement has caused banking to deteriorate (particularly among the four state-owned banks) because of substantial levels of non-performing loans issued mainly to state-controlled companies. The Central Bank of West African States (BCEAO) governs Togo's financial institutions. Four of the eight commercial banks are state-controlled. Privatization of financial institutions has begun, but only one of the four state-owned banks has attracted private-sector interest. Two-thirds of the national savings bank was offered to the public in March 2005 as part of the institution's conversion into a commercial bank. The Banque Régionale de Solidarité opened in 2005, and the Banque sahelo-saharienne pour l'investissement et le commerce (a Libyan based regional bank) opened in mid-2006. Togo participates in a small regional stock market based in the Ivory Coast.

PROPERTY RIGHTS — 30%

The judicial system does not protect private property sufficiently and is subject to strong influence from the executive. Contracts are difficult to enforce. Protection of physical property is frequently contentious because of poorly defined inheritance laws and challenges to property transmission outcomes. Real and chattel property disputes are further complicated by judicial non-transparency, which often favors national entities.

FREEDOM FROM CORRUPTION — 24%

Corruption is perceived as widespread. Togo ranks 130th out of 163 countries in Transparency International's Corruption Perceptions Index for 2006. The executive and legislative branches are subject to corruption. Togo has a large informal market in pirated optical media, computer software, video and cassette recordings, and counterfeit beauty products. Government procurement contracts and dispute settlements are subject to bribery. Bribery of private or government officials, while technically a crime, is generally expected.

LABOR FREEDOM — 48.2%

Restrictive employment regulations hinder overall productivity growth and job creation. The non-salary cost of employing a worker is high, and the rigidity of hiring and firing a worker creates a risk aversion for companies that would otherwise employ more people and grow. Regulations related to the number of work hours are rigid.

TRINIDAD AND TOBAGO

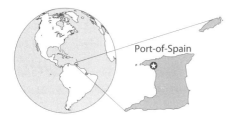

Port-of-Spain

Trinidad and Tobago's economy is 70.2 percent free, according to our 2008 assessment, which makes it the world's 29th freest economy. Its overall score is 1.1 percentage points lower than last year, reflecting worsened scores in four of the 10 economic freedoms. Trinidad and Tobago is ranked 6th out of 29 countries in the Americas, and its overall score is higher than the regional average.

Trinidad and Tobago scores well in fiscal freedom, government size, financial freedom, investment freedom, property rights, and labor freedom. Taxes have been simplified, and income and corporate rates have been lowered to 25 percent. Government expenditures equal about one-fourth of GDP. Foreign investment is welcome, and the financial market is generally transparent. Flexible labor regulations contribute to an elastic employment market. Property rights are secured by an independent judiciary, although there is a years-long backlog of cases.

Trinidad and Tobago is slightly weaker than average in monetary freedom and freedom from corruption. Regulation makes licensing procedures difficult, and enforcement is uneven. Although inflation is moderate, the government subsidizes the prices of several goods. Corruption is minimal for a developing nation.

BACKGROUND: Investor-friendly Trinidad and Tobago is the Americas' largest supplier of liquefied natural gas and has one of the largest economies in the Caribbean Community. Now a parliamentary democracy, the former British colony practices sound fiscal management and has embraced free-market policies. A stabilization fund exists to save windfall revenues when oil and gas prices are high so that expenses can be met when prices are low. Real GDP growth of 12 percent—attributed to market reforms, fiscal responsibility, tight monetary policy, and high world oil prices—was recorded in 2006. Exports include petrochemicals, and there is potential for growth in financial services. Trinidad and Tobago leads Caribbean integration efforts and supports the proposed Caribbean Single Market and Economy.

How Do We Measure Economic Freedom? See Chapter 4 (page 39) for an explanation of the methodology or visit the *Index* Web site at *heritage.org/index*.

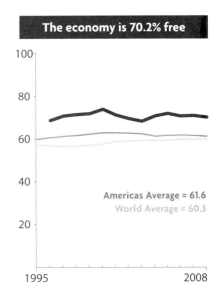

The economy is 70.2% free

Americas Average = 61.6
World Average = 60.3

1995 — 2008

QUICK FACTS

Population: 1.3 million

GDP (PPP): $19.1 billion
7.9% growth in 2005
9.7% 5-yr. comp. ann. growth
$14,603 per capita

Unemployment: 8.0%

Inflation (CPI): 6.9%

FDI (net flow): $980.0 million

Official Development Assistance:
Multilateral: $5.6 million
Bilateral: $6.1 million (8.3% from the U.S.)

External Debt: $2.7 billion

Exports: $7.3 billion (2004)
Primarily petroleum and petroleum products, chemicals, steel products, fertilizer, sugar, cocoa, coffee, citrus, flowers

Imports: $5.3 billion (2004)
Primarily machinery, transportation equipment, manufactured goods, food, live animals

2005 data unless otherwise noted.

369

TRINIDAD & TOBAGO'S TEN ECONOMIC FREEDOMS

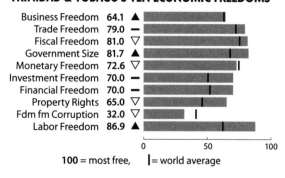

Business Freedom	64.1	▲
Trade Freedom	79.0	—
Fiscal Freedom	81.0	▽
Government Size	81.7	▲
Monetary Freedom	72.6	▽
Investment Freedom	70.0	—
Financial Freedom	70.0	—
Property Rights	65.0	▽
Fdm fm Corruption	32.0	▽
Labor Freedom	86.9	▲

0   50   100

100 = most free, ▌ **= world average**

BUSINESS FREEDOM — 64.1%

The overall freedom to start, operate, and close a business is limited by Trinidad and Tobago's regulatory environment. Starting a business takes an average of 53 days, compared to the world average of 43 days. Obtaining a business license takes slightly more than the world average of 19 procedures and 234 days. Bankruptcy proceedings are fairly easy and straightforward.

TRADE FREEDOM — 79%

The weighted average tariff rate in Trinidad and Tobago was 5.5 percent in 2003. Certain prohibitive tariffs, import taxes and fees, import and export licensing requirements, inefficient customs administration, and export support programs add to the cost of trade. An additional 10 percentage points is deducted from Trinidad and Tobago's trade freedom score to account for non-tariff barriers.

FISCAL FREEDOM — 81%

Trinidad and Tobago's tax system has been simplified through tax rate reductions in recent years. Both the top income tax rate and the standard corporate tax rate are 25 percent. Other taxes include a value-added tax (VAT) and a property tax. In the most recent year, overall tax revenue as a percentage of GDP was 25.4 percent.

GOVERNMENT SIZE — 81.7%

Total government expenditures, including consumption and transfer payments, are moderate. In the most recent year, government spending equaled 24.7 percent of GDP. Privatization has progressed considerably, and the government has focused on diversifying the economy to reduce dependence on the energy sector.

MONETARY FREEDOM — 72.6%

Inflation is high, averaging 7.5 percent between 2004 and 2006. Relatively unstable prices explain most of the monetary freedom score. The government retains price ceilings for a number of goods; controls prices for sugar, schoolbooks, and some pharmaceuticals; and influences prices through regulation, subsidies, and state-owned enterprises and utilities, including oil and gas. An additional 10 percentage points is deducted from Trinidad and Tobago's monetary freedom score to account for policies that distort domestic prices.

INVESTMENT FREEDOM — 70%

Foreign investment receives national treatment and is welcome in the privatization program. Foreign investment in private business is not subject to limitations, but a license is needed to purchase more than 30 percent of a publicly held business. Foreign ownership of land is restricted. The government is trying to improve the airport on Tobago and to construct a light rail system. There has been private investment in partially privatized state enterprises, and foreigners have been encouraged to bid. Industries like electric power and the postal service have been privatized. Residents and non-residents may hold foreign exchange accounts. There are no restrictions or controls on payments, transactions, transfers, or repatriation of profits.

FINANCIAL FREEDOM — 70%

Trinidad and Tobago's financial regulations and supervision are generally transparent and improving, and the level of non-performing loans has fallen to below 2 percent. There are no restrictions on foreign banks or foreign borrowers, and all banks may offer a wide range of services. There are six commercial banks, including one state-owned bank and several foreign banks. There were approximately 130 credit unions in 2006, encouraged by low competitiveness and tighter money-laundering controls on banks. The government announced measures to regulate credit unions in 2006. Insurance is dominated by a single large company. Capital markets are well developed but small and are centered on the stock exchange in Port-of-Spain.

PROPERTY RIGHTS — 65%

The judiciary is independent and fair, but cases are time-consuming, and the backlog is several years long. Legislation protecting intellectual property is among the hemisphere's most advanced, but enforcement is lax in some areas, particularly concerning copyright of music CDs and film DVDs, and prosecution for piracy is rare.

FREEDOM FROM CORRUPTION — 32%

Corruption is perceived as widespread. Trinidad and Tobago ranks 79th out of 163 countries in Transparency International's Corruption Perceptions Index for 2006. During 2006, bribery cases continued against a former minister of works and transport and a former minister of energy and energy industries, and the courts continued to hear a case that implicated the most senior members of the 1995–2001 government in embezzlement and bid-rigging on the Piarco Airport expansion project.

LABOR FREEDOM — 86.9%

Flexible employment regulations enhance overall productivity growth and employment opportunities. The non-salary cost of employing a worker is low, but dismissing a redundant employee can be relatively costly. Regulations related to the number of work hours are flexible.

TUNISIA

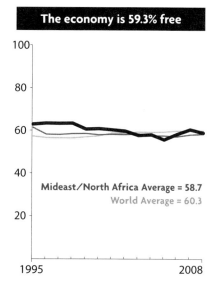

Tunis

Tunisia's economy is 59.3 percent free, according to our 2008 assessment, which makes it the world's 84th freest economy. Its overall score is 0.2 percentage point lower than last year, reflecting a deteriorated score in freedom from corruption. Tunisia is ranked 10th out of 17 countries in the Middle East/North Africa region, and its overall score is higher than the regional average.

Tunisia has high scores in business freedom and government size, which indicates a government limited in size and scope. Inflation is moderate, although the state can set prices in some circumstances. Tunisia maintains moderately high tax rates, but overall tax revenue is not particularly large as a percentage of GDP. There are regulatory obstacles, but businesses can be opened and closed without undue difficulty. The labor market is fairly flexible, and redundant workers can be fired without significant cost.

Tunisia faces challenges in labor freedom, investment freedom, and financial freedom. Protectionist economic policies have limited the opportunities for foreign investment. The financial sector is subject to heavy political influence, and much of its regulation and oversight falls short of international standards.

BACKGROUND: Tunisia gained its independence from France in 1956 and developed a socialist economy. President Zine al-Abidine Ben Ali has undertaken gradual free-market economic reforms since the early 1990s, including privatization of state-owned firms, simplification of the tax code, and more prudent fiscal restraint. The country's diverse economy includes significant agricultural, mining, energy, tourism, and manufacturing sectors. Tunisia's 1998 association agreement with the European Union, which has helped to create jobs and modernize the economy, was the first such agreement between the EU and a Maghreb country. The economy has also benefited from expanded trade and tourism.

How Do We Measure Economic Freedom? See Chapter 4 (page 39) for an explanation of the methodology or visit the *Index* Web site at *heritage.org/index*.

The economy is 59.3% free

Mideast/North Africa Average = 58.7
World Average = 60.3

1995 — 2008

QUICK FACTS

Population: 10.0 million

GDP (PPP): $84.0 billion
4.0% growth in 2005
4.3% 5-yr. comp. ann. growth
$8,371 per capita

Unemployment: 14.2%

Inflation (CPI): 2.0%

FDI (net flow): $770.0 million

Official Development Assistance:
Multilateral: $120.9 million
Bilateral: $428.7 million (0.03% from the U.S.)

External Debt: $17.8 billion

Exports: $14.5 billion
Primarily clothing, semi-finished goods and textiles, agricultural products, mechanical goods, phosphates and chemicals, hydrocarbons

Imports: $14.6 billion
Primarily textiles, machinery and equipment, hydrocarbons, chemicals, foodstuffs
2005 data unless otherwise noted.

TUNISIA'S TEN ECONOMIC FREEDOMS

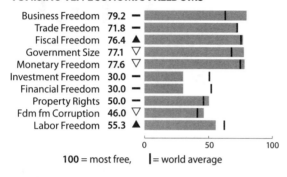

Business Freedom	79.2	—
Trade Freedom	71.8	—
Fiscal Freedom	76.4	▲
Government Size	77.1	▽
Monetary Freedom	77.6	▽
Investment Freedom	30.0	—
Financial Freedom	30.0	—
Property Rights	50.0	—
Fdm fm Corruption	46.0	▽
Labor Freedom	55.3	▲

0   50   100

100 = most free, | = world average

BUSINESS FREEDOM — 79.2%

The overall freedom to start, close, and operate a business is relatively well protected by Tunisia's regulatory environment. Starting a business takes an average of 11 days, compared to the world average of 43 days. Obtaining a business license takes much less than the world average of 234 days, although costs are fairly high. Bankruptcy proceedings are easy and straightforward.

TRADE FREEDOM — 71.8%

Tunisia's weighted average tariff rate was 9.1 percent in 2005. Import restrictions, some prohibitively high tariffs, import taxes and fees, import licensing requirements, export promotion programs, and inconsistent customs administration add to the cost of trade. An additional 10 percentage points is deducted from Tunisia's trade freedom score to account for non-tariff barriers.

FISCAL FREEDOM — 76.4%

Tunisia introduced a tax cut early in 2007. The top income tax rate is 35 percent, and the top corporate tax rate is 30 percent, down from 35 percent. Other taxes include a value-added tax (VAT) and a vehicle tax. In the most recent year, overall tax revenue as a percentage of GDP was 15.3 percent.

GOVERNMENT SIZE — 77.1%

Total government expenditures, including consumption and transfer payments, are moderate. In the most recent year, government spending equaled 27.6 percent of GDP. Privatization has been uneven and sluggish, and the state retains a large role in economic activities.

MONETARY FREEDOM — 77.6%

Inflation is moderate, averaging 3.8 percent between 2004 and 2006. Relatively unstable prices explain most of the monetary freedom score. The government can set prices for subsidized goods and influences prices through regulation, subsidies, and state-owned utilities and enterprises. An additional 10 percentage points is deducted from Tunisia's monetary freedom score to account for policies that distort domestic prices.

INVESTMENT FREEDOM — 30%

Tunisia restricts investment in some sectors to minimize the impact on domestic competitors. The Investment Code Law covers all major sectors except mining, energy, finance, and domestic trade. Foreign investment is screened. Foreign ownership of agricultural land is prohibited. The entry of French and Gulf capital indicates that discouragement of foreign investment in areas like restaurants, real estate, and retail distribution is moderating. The state telecommunications service privatized a major stake to a foreign investor in 2006. Non-tourism onshore companies with a capital share larger than 49 percent require government authorization. Residents and non-residents may hold foreign exchange accounts, subject to restrictions and approval. There are some controls, quantitative limits, and other restrictions on payments and transfers. There are many restrictions and controls on capital transactions.

FINANCIAL FREEDOM — 30%

Supervision and regulation are slowly being brought up to international standards but remain insufficient, although increased provisioning requirements have strengthened the banking environment. There are 14 commercial banks, six development banks, two merchant banks, and eight offshore banks. Five banks control 70 percent of deposits. The government sold its stake in two banks in 2002 and 2005 but remains the controlling shareholder in at least four banks that control 50 percent of assets. The percentage of non-performing loans remains high. State-mandated lending and the legal difficulty of settling with debtors have hindered financial development. The insurance sector is small, and the largest insurer is state-owned. Capital markets are nominal, but the stock market is active, although with little foreign participation.

PROPERTY RIGHTS — 50%

The executive branch is the supreme arbiter of events in the cabinet, government, judiciary, and military. Commercial cases take long to resolve and face complex legal procedures. Tunisia's intellectual property rights law is designed to meet the WTO's Trade-Related Aspects of Intellectual Property Rights (TRIPS) minimum standards. Copyright violations are not actively investigated by customs agents without a complaint by the copyright holder.

FREEDOM FROM CORRUPTION — 46%

Corruption is perceived as significant. Tunisia ranks 51st out of 163 countries in Transparency International's Corruption Perceptions Index for 2006. Corruption is less pervasive than in neighboring countries. Most foreigners involved in the Tunisian market have not identified corruption as a primary obstacle to direct investment. There are no laws to provide government documents to citizens.

LABOR FREEDOM — 55.3%

Somewhat flexible employment regulations could be improved to enhance overall productivity growth. The non-salary cost of employing a worker is high, and the rigidity of hiring and firing a worker creates a risk aversion for companies that would otherwise employ more people and grow.

TURKEY

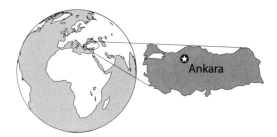

Ankara

Rank: 74

Regional Rank: 32 of 41

Turkey's economy is 60.8 percent free, according to our 2008 assessment, which makes it the world's 74th freest economy. Its overall score is 2.5 percentage points higher than last year, reflecting improved scores in more than half of the 10 economic freedoms. Turkey is ranked 32nd out of 41 countries in the European region, and its overall score is lower than the regional average.

Turkey is near the world average in most areas but has very strong trade freedom, with a low average tariff rate and some non-tariff barriers. The environment for young companies is business-friendly, although licensing and bankruptcy procedures are difficult. The top income and corporate tax rates are moderately high, and overall tax revenue is relatively moderate as a percentage of GDP. Property rights are well protected.

Turkey is very weak in labor freedom; laying off workers is difficult, and work rules are highly inefficient. Freedom from corruption, financial freedom, and monetary freedom score slightly below average. Inflation is fairly high, and the government distorts the prices of a variety of agricultural goods through direct subsidies. Total government expenditures equal more than a third of GDP. Corruption is not as serious as it is in some nearby Middle Eastern countries.

BACKGROUND: Ever since Mustafa Kemal Ataturk founded modern secular Turkey in 1923, the country has sought a more Western-oriented approach to policy, especially in its vigorous attempts to join the EU. In recent years, the government has sought with partial success to reverse decades of corruption, economic mismanagement, and authoritarian intervention with more market-based reforms. The public sector still dominates some industries. The EU agreed to start formal accession talks with Turkey in October 2005, but significant roadblocks make it appear that accession will take at least a decade. Principal exports include foodstuffs, textiles, clothing, iron, and steel.

How Do We Measure Economic Freedom? See Chapter 4 (page 39) for an explanation of the methodology or visit the *Index* Web site at *heritage.org/index*.

The economy is 60.8% free

Europe Average = 66.8
World Average = 60.3

1995 — 2008

QUICK FACTS

Population: 72.1 million

GDP (PPP): $605.9 billion
7.4% growth in 2005
7.5% 5-yr. comp. ann. growth
$8,407 per capita

Unemployment: 10.3%

Inflation (CPI): 8.2%

FDI (net flow): $8.6 billion

Official Development Assistance:
Multilateral: $429.8 million
Bilateral: $431.4 million (3.1% from the U.S.)

External Debt: $171.1 billion

Exports: $102.8 billion
Primarily apparel, foodstuffs, textiles, metal manufactures, transport equipment

Imports: $121.8 billion
Primarily machinery, chemicals, semi-finished goods, fuels, transport equipment

2005 data unless otherwise noted.

373

TURKEY'S TEN ECONOMIC FREEDOMS

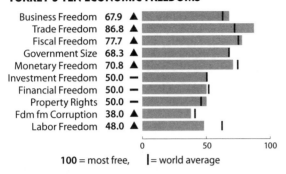

Business Freedom	67.9 ▲
Trade Freedom	86.8 ▲
Fiscal Freedom	77.7 ▲
Government Size	68.3 ▲
Monetary Freedom	70.8 ▲
Investment Freedom	50.0 —
Financial Freedom	50.0 —
Property Rights	50.0 —
Fdm fm Corruption	38.0 ▲
Labor Freedom	48.0 ▲

0   50   100

100 = most free, I = world average

BUSINESS FREEDOM — 67.9%

The overall freedom to start, operate, and close a business is relatively well protected by Turkey's regulatory environment. Starting a business takes an average of six days, compared to the world average of 43 days. Obtaining a business license requires more than the global average of 19 procedures but less than the world average of 234 days, and costs are relatively low. Bankruptcy proceedings can be burdensome and lengthy.

TRADE FREEDOM — 86.8%

Turkey's weighted average tariff rate was 1.6 percent in 2005. Service market access barriers, prohibitive tariffs for agriculture and food products, import taxes, restrictive import licensing requirements for food and agriculture products, non-transparent and arbitrary standards and regulations, export promotion programs, weak enforcement of intellectual property rights, and corruption add to the cost of trade. An additional 10 percentage points is deducted from Turkey's trade freedom score to account for non-tariff barriers.

FISCAL FREEDOM — 77.7%

Turkey has implemented lower tax rates. The top income tax rate is 35 percent, down from 40 percent, and the top corporate tax rate is 20 percent, down from 30 percent. Other taxes include a value-added tax (VAT), a property tax, and a tax on interest. In the most recent year, overall tax revenue as a percentage of GDP was 24.5 percent.

GOVERNMENT SIZE — 68.3%

Total government expenditures, including consumption and transfer payments, are moderate. In the most recent year, government spending equaled 32.5 percent of GDP. The ratio of public debt to GDP has been declining since 2001. Deregulation and privatization have somewhat reduced the role of the public sector.

MONETARY FREEDOM — 70.8%

Inflation is high, averaging 9.2 percent between 2004 and 2006. Unstable prices explain most of the monetary freedom score. The government sets prices for many agricultural products and pharmaceuticals and influences prices through regulation, subsidies, and state-owned utilities and enterprises. Municipalities fix ceilings on the retail price of bread. An additional 10 percentage points is deducted from Turkey's monetary freedom score to account for policies that distort domestic prices.

INVESTMENT FREEDOM — 50%

Foreign capital is legally equal to domestic capital. There are formal and informal barriers in broadcasting, aviation, maritime transportation, and value-added telecommunications services, and port facilities must be at least 51 percent Turkish-owned. The purchase of real estate by non-residents is restricted; foreign companies may acquire real estate through a Turkish legal entity or local partnership. Foreign investment is not screened. Procedures have been improved, but bureaucracy, a weak judicial system, and frequent changes in the legal environment remain deterrents. There were major privatizations in telecommunications, oil refining, and steel in 2005. Residents and non-residents may hold foreign exchange accounts. There are few restrictions on payments and transfers.

FINANCIAL FREEDOM — 50%

Following Turkey's 2000–2001 financial crisis, the government increased transparency, strengthened regulatory and accounting standards, and improved oversight. As of November 2006, there were three state-owned banks, controlling 30 percent of assets; 17 private domestic banks; and 13 majority foreign-owned banks, controlling 6 percent of assets. The five largest banks account for 60 percent of assets. Two of the 13 development and investment banks are majority foreign-controlled, and three are state-run. There were 24 non-life and 20 life/pension insurance companies in late 2006; foreign companies are not broadly represented. Capital markets are relatively small and dominated by government securities. The stock exchange is state-owned but autonomous.

PROPERTY RIGHTS — 50%

Property rights are generally enforced, but the courts are overburdened and slow, and judges are not well trained for commercial cases. The judiciary is subject to government influence. The intellectual property rights regime has improved, but insufficient protection of confidential pharmaceutical test data and high levels of piracy and counterfeiting of copyrighted and trademarked materials remain concerns.

FREEDOM FROM CORRUPTION — 38%

Corruption is perceived as significant. Turkey ranks 60th out of 163 countries in Transparency International's Corruption Perceptions Index for 2006. An independent public procurement board has the power to void contracts. The judicial system is viewed as susceptible to external influence and somewhat biased against outsiders.

LABOR FREEDOM — 48%

Inflexible employment regulations hinder overall productivity growth. The non-salary cost of employing a worker is high, and the rigidity of hiring and firing a worker creates a risk aversion for companies that would otherwise employ more people and grow. A recently enacted labor law allows employers increased flexibility.

TURKMENISTAN

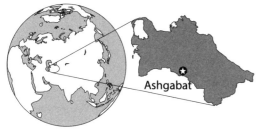

Ashgabat

Turkmenistan's economy is 43.4 percent free, according to our 2008 assessment, which makes it the world's 152nd freest economy. Its overall score is 0.3 percentage point higher than last year, partially reflecting improved freedom from corruption. Turkmenistan is ranked 28th out of 30 countries in the Asia–Pacific region, and its overall score is much lower than the regional average.

Turkmenistan scores relatively well in fiscal freedom, government size, and trade freedom. The top income tax is 10 percent, and the corporate tax is 20 percent. Government spending equals slightly more than one-fifth of GDP. Non-tariff barriers include cumbersome regulations, but the average tariff rate is low.

Turkmenistan has extremely low scores in business freedom, investment freedom, financial freedom, labor freedom, property rights, and freedom from corruption. Non-transparent regulation discourages local business and foreign investment. The financial market is unsophisticated, and most operations are dominated by the state. The judicial system is state-controlled, and corruption is pervasive. Inflation is fairly high, and the government subsidizes a wide array of goods. The labor market is highly inflexible, with the government providing most of the country's jobs.

BACKGROUND: Despite statistically high per capita wages and revenues, most of Turkmenistan's population is poor. The government, led until December 2006 by President Saparmurat Niyazov, is composed mainly of former Communists who have resisted reform, although newly elected President Gurbanguly Berdymnukhamidvo has hinted that some reform may be forthcoming. Turkmenistan's large external debt is due to low gas export prices and a heavy reliance on imports. The main exports are gas, oil, and oil products, which are sold primarily to Russia. Russian President Vladimir Putin recently signed an agreement to purchase Turkmenistan's gas and aid in exporting it, and the export price of Turkmen gas is expected to double. The other main industry, agriculture, is concentrated in cotton.

How Do We Measure Economic Freedom? See Chapter 4 (page 39) for an explanation of the methodology or visit the *Index* Web site at *heritage.org/index.*

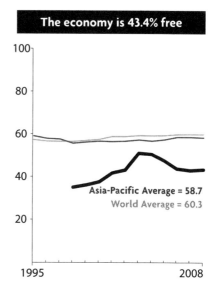

The economy is 43.4% free

Asia-Pacific Average = 58.7
World Average = 60.3

QUICK FACTS

Population: 4.8 million

GDP (PPP): $42.8 billion
9.0% growth in 2005
14.1% 5-yr. comp. ann. growth
$9,358 per capita

Unemployment: 60% (2004 estimate)

Inflation (CPI): 10.7%

FDI (net flow): $62.0 million

Official Development Assistance:
Multilateral: $5.3 million
Bilateral: $27.1 million (35.2% from the U.S.)

External Debt: $1.1 billion

Exports: $4.9 billion
Primarily gas, crude oil, petrochemicals, cotton fiber, textiles

Imports: $3.6 billion
Primarily machinery and equipment, chemicals, foodstuffs

2005 data unless otherwise noted.

TURKMENISTAN'S TEN ECONOMIC FREEDOMS

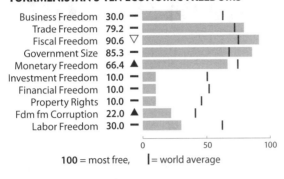

Business Freedom	30.0
Trade Freedom	79.2
Fiscal Freedom	90.6
Government Size	85.3
Monetary Freedom	66.4
Investment Freedom	10.0
Financial Freedom	10.0
Property Rights	10.0
Fdm fm Corruption	22.0
Labor Freedom	30.0

0   50   100

100 = most free, | = world average

BUSINESS FREEDOM — 30%

The overall freedom to start, operate, and close a business is very limited by Turkmenistan's regulatory environment. The system is non-transparent, enforcement is inconsistent, and businesses have difficulty getting copies of laws and regulations. Personal relations with government officials often help to determine how and when regulations are applied.

TRADE FREEDOM — 79.2%

Turkmenistan's weighted average tariff rate was 2.9 percent in 2002. Import and export bans and restrictions, prohibitive tariffs for agricultural and food products, import taxes and fees, import and export registration, subsidies, a non-convertible currency, and customs procedures that are bureaucratic, slow, and subject to corruption add to the cost of trade. An additional 15 percentage points is deducted from Turkmenistan's trade freedom score to account for non-tariff barriers.

FISCAL FREEDOM — 90.6%

Turkmenistan has low tax rates. The top income tax rate is 10 percent, and the top corporate tax rate is 20 percent. Other taxes include a value-added tax (VAT) and an excise tax. Important gaps in the available data include figures for government finance. In the most recent year, overall tax revenue as a percentage of GDP was 20.9 percent.

GOVERNMENT SIZE — 85.3%

Total government expenditures, including consumption and transfer payments, are moderate. In the most recent year, government spending was 22.1 percent of GDP. Economic reform has been very limited and uneven. Government intervention is pervasive, and privatization has stalled.

MONETARY FREEDOM — 66.4%

Inflation is high, averaging 8.6 percent between 2004 and 2006. Relatively unstable prices explain most of the monetary freedom score. Subsidies, price controls, and free provision of utilities underpin economic policy, and the government influences prices through numerous state-owned utilities and enterprises. An additional 15 percentage points is deducted from Turkmenistan's monetary freedom score to account for policies that distort domestic prices.

INVESTMENT FREEDOM — 10%

The government controls most of the economy and restricts foreign participation but has been somewhat supportive of foreign investment in energy, textiles, construction, and foodstuffs. Fully owned foreign companies may operate in the oil sector, and the one cellular company is Russian. Investors face currency and trade restrictions, and the state continues to interfere in privatized companies. The government chooses its investment partners selectively, and personal contact with high political officials is the best guarantor of approval. Privatization has been slow. Deficient rule of law, excessive and inconsistent regulation, and corruption are strong disincentives. Foreign exchange accounts require government approval, as do all payments and transfers. Capital transactions face restrictions and central bank approval in some cases.

FINANCIAL FREEDOM — 10%

Turkmenistan's financial system is subject to very heavy government influence. A financial crisis led the number of banks to fall from 67 to 12 in mid-2006. Many banks are insolvent by international standards, and the financial sector is dominated by state-owned or state-influenced institutions that are specialized by client; for example, Vneshekonombank handles foreign credit for the government, and Daikhan bank serves the agricultural sector. State-owned enterprises get an estimated 95 percent of all loans. The government directs credit allocation, often at subsidized rates. Most individuals hold their wealth in cash, preferably foreign currency. The central bank is not independent. Private enterprises have little access to credit. International accounting standards were adopted in 2002. There are no significant non-bank financial institutions, and the state-owned insurance company is the sole insurer. There is no private capital market.

PROPERTY RIGHTS — 10%

The legal system does not strongly enforce contracts and rights. Laws are poorly developed, and judicial employees and judges are poorly trained and open to bribery. Ownership rights are limited. Laws designed to protect intellectual property rights are implemented arbitrarily or not at all. Pirated copies of copyrighted and trademarked materials like videos, cassette tapes, and literature are freely copied and sold.

FREEDOM FROM CORRUPTION — 22%

Corruption is perceived as pervasive. Turkmenistan ranks 142nd out of 163 countries in Transparency International's Corruption Perceptions Index for 2006. The magnitude of the problem is evident from the existence of patronage networks, a lack of transparency and accountability mechanisms, and fear of government reprisal. Observers allege that authorities have used anti-corruption campaigns to remove potential rivals.

LABOR FREEDOM — 30%

Highly inflexible employment regulations hinder overall productivity growth and employment opportunities. The government provides the majority of jobs and mandates minimum wages.

UGANDA

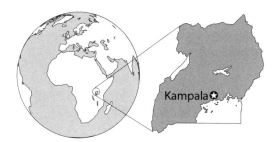

Kampala

Rank: 52

Regional Rank: 3 of 40

Uganda's economy is 64.4 percent free, according to our 2008 assessment, which makes it the world's 52nd freest economy. Its overall score is 0.7 percentage point higher than last year, reflecting improved scores in four of the 10 economic freedoms. Uganda is ranked 3rd out of 40 countries in the sub-Saharan Africa region, and its overall score is much higher than the regional average.

Uganda scores well in fiscal freedom, government size, financial freedom, and labor freedom. The top income and corporate tax rates are moderate, and overall tax revenues are not large as a percentage of GDP. Government expenditures are fairly low. The small financial sector is dominated by banking. The labor sector is elastic in work hours and workforce flexibility.

Uganda is weaker in freedom from corruption, property rights, and business freedom. Commercial licensing is burdensome, and regulations are enforced inconsistently. Closing a business is difficult. Uganda opened its first commercial court several years ago, but most investors seek settlements or outside arbitration. Corruption is a problem.

BACKGROUND: Uganda remains poor despite market reforms that contributed to economic growth averaging over 6 percent annually during the past decade. Under the "abstinence, be faithful, and condoms" (ABC) program, HIV prevalence fell to 6.5 percent in 2005 from 18 percent in the 1990s. Milton Obote, who led Uganda to independence in 1962 as prime minister, suspended the constitution in 1966 and was ousted in 1971 by Idi Amin Dada, under whom Uganda experienced economic decline and social disintegration. Tanzanian forces ousted Amin in 1979. Yoweri Museveni, president since leading a successful insurgency in 1986, was elected to a third five-year term in 2006. The agricultural sector employs most Ugandans and accounted for over one-third of GDP in 2004. A 20-year conflict with the rebel Lord's Resistance Army has created a human rights catastrophe in northern Uganda.

How Do We Measure Economic Freedom? See Chapter 4 (page 39) for an explanation of the methodology or visit the *Index* Web site at *heritage.org/index*.

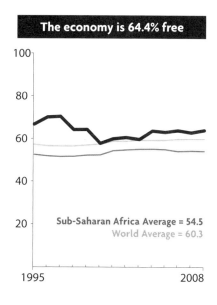

The economy is 64.4% free

Sub-Saharan Africa Average = 54.5
World Average = 60.3

1995   2008

QUICK FACTS

Population: 28.8 million

GDP (PPP): $41.9 billion
6.7% growth in 2005
5.9% 5-yr. comp. ann. growth
$1,454 per capita

Unemployment: 0.7%

Inflation (CPI): 8.0%

FDI (net flow): $258.0 million

Official Development Assistance:
Multilateral: $605.8 million
Bilateral: $713.9 million (34% from the U.S.)

External Debt: $4.5 billion

Exports: $1.3 billion
Primarily coffee, fish and fish products, tea, cotton, flowers, horticultural products, gold

Imports: $2.6 billion
Primarily capital equipment, vehicles, petroleum, medical supplies, cereals

2005 data unless otherwise noted.

377

UGANDA'S TEN ECONOMIC FREEDOMS

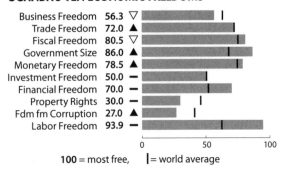

Business Freedom 56.3 ▽
Trade Freedom 72.0 ▲
Fiscal Freedom 80.5 ▽
Government Size 86.0 ▲
Monetary Freedom 78.5 ▲
Investment Freedom 50.0 —
Financial Freedom 70.0 —
Property Rights 30.0 —
Fdm fm Corruption 27.0 ▲
Labor Freedom 93.9 —

0   50   100

100 = most free, | = world average

BUSINESS FREEDOM — 56.3%

The overall freedom to start, operate, and close a business is limited by Uganda's regulatory environment. Starting a business takes an average of 28 days, compared to the world average of 43 days. Obtaining a business license takes less than the world average of 19 procedures and 234 days, but costs are high. Bankruptcy proceedings are fairly straightforward but costly.

TRADE FREEDOM — 72%

Uganda's weighted average tariff rate was 9 percent in 2005. The government has made progress in liberalizing the trade regime, but import and export restrictions, some high tariffs, import and export taxes and fees, inefficient and non-transparent regulation and customs, export promotion programs, weak enforcement of intellectual property rights, and corruption add to the cost of trade. An additional 10 percentage points is deducted from Uganda's trade freedom score to account for non-tariff barriers.

FISCAL FREEDOM — 80.5%

Uganda has moderate tax rates. Both the top income tax rate and the top corporate tax rate are 30 percent. Other taxes include a value-added tax (VAT), a property tax, and a vehicle tax. In the most recent year, overall tax revenue as a percentage of GDP was 12.1 percent.

GOVERNMENT SIZE — 86%

Total government expenditures, including consumption and transfer payments, are low. Spending management is reasonably sound. In the most recent year, government spending equaled 21.6 percent of GDP. Many state-owned companies have been privatized or divested.

MONETARY FREEDOM — 78.5%

Inflation is relatively high, averaging 6.8 percent between 2004 and 2006. Relatively unstable prices explain most of the monetary freedom score. The government influences prices through state-owned utilities and enterprises. An additional 5 percentage points is deducted from Uganda's monetary freedom score to account for policies that distort domestic prices.

INVESTMENT FREEDOM — 50%

Foreign investment is allowed in privatized industries. Despite presidential recognition that foreign investment is desirable, corruption has not been significantly reduced. Foreign investors may form 100 percent foreign-owned companies and majority or minority joint ventures with local investors and may acquire or take over domestic enterprises. Uganda's reformed commercial legal system is far faster at case resolution than the rest of the country's legal system. Foreign investors, however, do not receive equal treatment, especially for performance obligations. A slow registry and complex regulations make land acquisition difficult. Residents and non-residents may hold foreign exchange accounts. There are no restrictions or controls on payments, transactions, or transfers.

FINANCIAL FREEDOM — 70%

Uganda's small financial system is dominated by banking. The banking industry generally is sound and well capitalized, with a relatively small level of non-performing loans. The central bank has tightened supervision and increased regulatory requirements since several bank closures in the late 1990s. A new regulatory law bringing Uganda in line with international financial regulatory standards was adopted in 2004. Most banks are foreign-owned, and five of them dominate the sector. New banks are not allowed unless they offer completely new financial services or take over existing banks. The insurance sector is small, and the state-owned National Insurance Company is undergoing privatization. Capital markets are relatively small and underdeveloped, though more private companies are being listed.

PROPERTY RIGHTS — 30%

Uganda opened its first commercial court about six years ago, but a shortage of judges and funding drives most commercial cases to outside arbitration or settlement. The judiciary suffers from corruption. Domestic private entities may own and dispose of property and other businesses. Foreign private entities share these rights, but there are restrictions in land ownership. Ugandan laws generally protect intellectual property in theory but rarely act as a deterrent to counterfeiters and pirates.

FREEDOM FROM CORRUPTION — 27%

Corruption is perceived as widespread. Uganda ranks 105th out of 163 countries in Transparency International's Corruption Perceptions Index for 2006. In addition to demands for and acceptance of bribes, bureaucratic apathy and ignorance of rules within public organizations also contribute to perceptions of corruption. Foreign businesses are not specifically targeted for bribes and payoffs, but they report some difficulties due to lack of transparency and possible collusion between competing business interests and government officials.

LABOR FREEDOM — 93.9%

Highly flexible employment regulations enhance overall productivity growth and employment opportunities. The non-salary cost of employing a worker is low, and dismissing a redundant employee is not difficult. Regulations related to the number of work hours are flexible.

UKRAINE

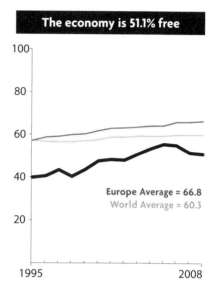

Kiev

Rank: 133

Regional Rank: 39 of 41

Ukraine's economy is 51.1 percent free, according to our 2008 assessment, which makes it the world's 133rd freest economy. Its overall score is 0.6 percentage point lower than last year. Ukraine is ranked 39th out of 41 countries in the European region, and its overall score is much lower than the regional average.

Ukraine scores moderately well in trade freedom and fiscal freedom. The average tariff rate is low, although complex regulations are significant. The top personal income and corporate tax rates are relatively low, and overall revenue from taxes is not high as a percentage of GDP.

Ukraine is very weak in business freedom, government size, monetary freedom, investment freedom, property rights, and freedom from corruption. Inflation is high, and government expenditures equal nearly two-fifths of GDP. While foreign investment is officially welcomed, corruption and regulations are deterrents to capital. The judiciary does not always enforce contracts and is tarnished with corruption. Corruption is a major problem throughout the civil service, and bureaucratic inefficiency makes many commercial operations difficult.

BACKGROUND: Ukraine gained its independence after the collapse of the Soviet Union in 1991. Promises of more market openness and economic reform after Ukraine's 2004 "Orange Revolution" have fallen short, and infighting between President Victor Yushchenko and Prime Minister Victor Yanukovich has generated instability. Prominent sectors of the economy include services, mining, metals, and manufacturing. The agricultural sector is strong but overregulated through quotas and tariffs on grain exports. Ukraine has benefited heavily from recent increases in the prices of metals. Despite lucrative opportunities for foreign direct investment, economic progress in the near term may be slowed by persistent corruption, steadily increasing gas prices, deteriorating infrastructure, and political uncertainty.

How Do We Measure Economic Freedom? See Chapter 4 (page 39) for an explanation of the methodology or visit the *Index* Web site at *heritage.org/index*.

The economy is 51.1% free

Europe Average = 66.8
World Average = 60.3

1995 — 2008

QUICK FACTS

Population: 47.1 million

GDP (PPP): $322.4 billion
2.7% growth in 2005
7.3% 5-yr. comp. ann. growth
$6,848 per capita

Unemployment: 3.2%

Inflation (CPI): 13.5%

FDI (net flow): $7.5 billion

Official Development Assistance:
Multilateral: $116.8 million
Bilateral: $308.3 million (39.8% from the U.S.)

External Debt: $33.3 billion

Exports: $44.4 billion
Primarily ferrous and nonferrous metals, fuel and petroleum products, chemicals, machinery and transport equipment, food products

Imports: $43.7 billion
Primarily energy, machinery and equipment, chemicals

2005 data unless otherwise noted.

UKRAINE'S TEN ECONOMIC FREEDOMS

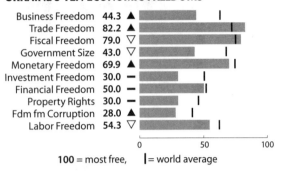

Business Freedom	44.3 ▲	
Trade Freedom	82.2 ▲	
Fiscal Freedom	79.0 ▽	
Government Size	43.0 ▽	
Monetary Freedom	69.9 ▲	
Investment Freedom	30.0 —	
Financial Freedom	50.0 —	
Property Rights	30.0 —	
Fdm fm Corruption	28.0 ▲	
Labor Freedom	54.3 ▽	

0   50   100

100 = most free,   I = world average

BUSINESS FREEDOM — 44.3%

The overall freedom to start, operate, and close a business is limited by Ukraine's regulatory environment. Starting a business takes an average of 27 days, compared to the world average of 43 days. Obtaining a business license takes more than the world average of 19 procedures and 234 days, and costs are high. Bankruptcy proceedings are relatively straightforward.

TRADE FREEDOM — 82.2%

Ukraine's weighted average tariff rate was 3.9 percent in 2002. Some export restrictions, service market access barriers, import taxes and fees, import licensing requirements, restrictive sanitary and phytosanitary regulations, complex standards and certification regulations, non-transparent government procurement, and weak enforcement of intellectual property rights add to the cost of trade. An additional 10 percentage points is deducted from Ukraine's trade freedom score to account for non-tariff barriers.

FISCAL FREEDOM — 79%

Ukraine has low tax rates. The top income tax rate changed from a flat 13 percent to 15 percent in January 2007, and the top corporate tax rate is 25 percent. Other taxes include a value-added tax (VAT), a land tax, and a vehicle tax. In the most recent year, overall tax revenue as a percentage of GDP was 35.4 percent.

GOVERNMENT SIZE — 43%

Total government expenditures, including consumption and transfer payments, are high. In the most recent year, government spending equaled 43.6 percent of GDP. The government has privatized over 80 percent of its public enterprises, but the economy is still shackled by government intervention in the private sector.

MONETARY FREEDOM — 69.9%

Inflation is high, averaging 10.1 percent between 2004 and 2006. Relatively unstable prices explain most of the monetary freedom score. The executive branch can establish high minimum prices for goods and services, and the government influences prices through regulation and state-owned enterprises and utilities. An additional 10 percentage points is deducted from Ukraine's monetary freedom score to account for policies that distort domestic prices.

INVESTMENT FREEDOM — 30%

The laws provide equal treatment with some restrictions in publishing, broadcasting, energy, and insurance. Foreign investment in weapons manufacturing and alcoholic spirits is prohibited. Complex regulations and corruption are major deterrents. Contracts are not always honored by the legal system. The current government is unwilling to continue its predecessor's re-examination of old, allegedly tainted privatization deals. Resident and non-resident foreign exchange accounts are subject to restrictions and government approval in some cases. Payments and transfers are subject to various requirements and quantitative limits. Some capital transactions are subject to controls and licenses.

FINANCIAL FREEDOM — 50%

Financial regulation and supervision are weak, although central bank policies and regulatory improvements have increased banking soundness. Banks may offer a wide range of services. Most of the 166 licensed banks as of January 2007 are very small. Two banks are state-owned, and the 10 largest banks account for over half of net assets. Foreign bank branches are not permitted, but 100 foreign-owned subsidiaries operate on par with domestic banks. The insurance sector is small, and foreign insurers are subject to more restrictions than domestic insurers. Capital markets are underdeveloped and poorly regulated but have been growing. Poor corporate governance weakens stock market transparency.

PROPERTY RIGHTS — 30%

Protection of property is weak. The judiciary is subject to executive branch and criminal pressure, and corruption is significant. Contracts are not well enforced, and expropriation is possible. A number of initiatives to develop a mortgage market have resulted in a strong increase in the number of mortgages and laid the legislative and administrative groundwork for a functioning market. Ukraine is a major trans-shipment point, storage location, and market for illegal optical media produced in Russia and elsewhere.

FREEDOM FROM CORRUPTION — 28%

Corruption is perceived as widespread. Ukraine ranks 99th out of 163 countries in Transparency International's Corruption Perceptions Index for 2006. Corruption pervades all levels of society and government and all spheres of economic activity. Low public-sector salaries fuel corruption in local administrative bodies such as the highway police and tax administration as well as in the education system.

LABOR FREEDOM — 54.3%

Inflexible employment regulations hinder overall productivity growth and employment opportunities. The non-salary cost of employing a worker is very high, and the rigidity of hiring and firing a worker creates a risk aversion for companies that would otherwise employ more people and grow.

UNITED ARAB EMIRATES

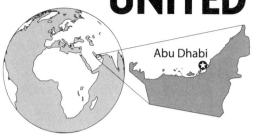

Abu Dhabi

The economy of the United Arab Emirates (UAE) is 62.8 percent free, according to our 2008 assessment, which makes it the world's 63rd freest economy. Its overall score is 0.1 percentage point lower than last year, reflecting worsened scores in three of the 10 economic freedoms. The UAE is ranked 7th out of 17 countries in the Middle East/North Africa region, and its overall score is higher than the regional average.

The UAE scores above the world average in fiscal freedom, labor freedom, freedom from corruption, government size, and trade freedom. The average tariff rate is not high, but general import licenses are issued only to nationals. Individual emirates impose their own corporate taxes, but there are no income or corporate taxes at the federal level. The labor market is highly flexible, and there is no minimum wage. The level of corruption is admirably low for a developing nation.

The UAE is weak in business freedom, investment freedom, financial freedom, and property rights. Foreign investment is restricted, and majority Emirati ownership is mandated even in the free zones. The UAE is a regional financial hub, but its financial sector is subject to considerable government interference. The courts are dominated by the UAE's rulers.

BACKGROUND: The United Arab Emirates is a federation of seven Arab monarchies (Abu Dhabi, Ajman, Dubai, Fujairah, Ras Al-Khaimah, Sharjah, and Umm al-Qaiwain) that became independent from Great Britain in 1971. Abu Dhabi accounts for about 90 percent of UAE oil production and has taken a leading role in political and economic decision-making, but many economic policy decisions are made by the rulers of the individual emirates. Dubai has developed into the UAE's foremost center of finance, commerce, transportation, and tourism. UAE nationals continue to rely heavily on a bloated public sector for employment, subsidized services, and government handouts.

How Do We Measure Economic Freedom? See Chapter 4 (page 39) for an explanation of the methodology or visit the *Index* Web site at *heritage.org/index*.

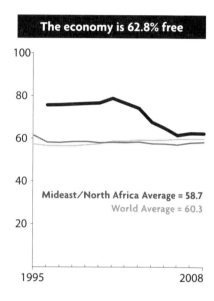

The economy is 62.8% free

Mideast/North Africa Average = 58.7
World Average = 60.3

QUICK FACTS

Population: 4.5 million

GDP (PPP): $115.7 billion
8.5% growth in 2005
8.1% 5-yr. comp. ann. growth
$25,514 per capita

Unemployment: 2.4% (2001)

Inflation (CPI): 7.8%

FDI (net flow): $5.3 billion

Official Development Assistance:
Multilateral: n/a
Bilateral: n/a

External Debt: $39.1 billion

Exports: $117.2 billion
Primarily crude oil, natural gas, re-exports, dried fish, dates

Imports: $74.5 billion
Primarily machinery and transport equipment, chemicals, food

2005 data unless otherwise noted.

UAE'S TEN ECONOMIC FREEDOMS

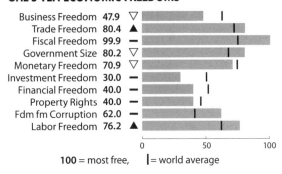

Business Freedom	47.9	▽
Trade Freedom	80.4	▲
Fiscal Freedom	99.9	—
Government Size	80.2	▽
Monetary Freedom	70.9	▽
Investment Freedom	30.0	—
Financial Freedom	40.0	—
Property Rights	40.0	—
Fdm fm Corruption	62.0	—
Labor Freedom	76.2	▲

0   50   100

100 = most free, | = world average

BUSINESS FREEDOM — 47.9%

The overall freedom to start, operate, and close a business is limited by the UAE's regulatory environment. Starting a business takes an average of 62 days, compared to the world average of 43 days. The minimum capital requirement to launch a business is costly. Obtaining a business license takes less than the world average of 234 days. Bankruptcy proceedings are lengthy and cumbersome.

TRADE FREEDOM — 80.4%

The weighted average tariff rate in the UAE was 4.8 percent in 2005. Import restrictions, service market access barriers, non-transparent standards, sanitary and phytosanitary regulations, and inconsistent government procurement add to the cost of trade; only firms with a trade license may engage in importation; and only majority-owned UAE firms may obtain such a license (except for goods imported into free zones). An additional 10 percentage points is deducted from the UAE's trade freedom score to account for non-tariff barriers.

FISCAL FREEDOM — 99.9%

The UAE has no income tax and no federal-level corporate tax, but there are different corporate tax rates in some emirates (for example, corporate tax rates of 55 percent for foreign oil companies and 20 percent for foreign banks). There is no value-added tax or general sales tax. In the most recent year, overall tax revenue as a percentage of GDP was 2.1 percent.

GOVERNMENT SIZE — 80.2%

Total government expenditures, including consumption and transfer payments, are moderate. In the most recent year, government spending equaled 25.7 percent of GDP. The state remains significantly involved in the economy through regulation and state-owned enterprises.

MONETARY FREEDOM — 70.9%

Inflation is high, averaging 9.1 percent between 2004 and 2006. Relatively unstable prices explain most of the monetary freedom score. The government influences prices through regulation, subsidies, and numerous state-owned enterprises and utilities, including oil, gas, electricity, and telecommunications. An additional 10 percentage points is deducted from the UAE's monetary freedom score to account for policies that distort domestic prices.

INVESTMENT FREEDOM — 30%

Foreign investors do not receive national treatment. Except for companies in the free zones, at least 51 percent of a business must be owned by a UAE national. Distribution of goods must be through an Emirati partner, although "liberalized goods" may be imported without the agent's approval. Non–Gulf Cooperation Council nationals may not own land. There are no controls or requirements on current transfers, access to foreign exchange, or repatriation of profits.

FINANCIAL FREEDOM — 40%

Financial supervision has been strengthened. There are 21 Emirati banks (some with federal or local government ownership), 25 foreign bank entities, two investment banks, and about 50 representative bank offices. Six major banks account for 70 percent of assets. Rising oil revenues have improved the health of the financial sector. Domestic banks offer a full range of services. Islamic banking systems are increasingly prominent. The central bank, under WTO mandates, has announced that it will issue licenses for new foreign bank branches, not issued since the mid-1980s. There is a 20 percent tax on foreign bank profits. The government has also announced that it will reopen the insurance sector, closed to new foreign entries since 1989. Capital markets are relatively developed. The two stock markets are open to foreign investment, but foreign ownership of listed companies is limited to 49 percent, and some companies prohibit foreign ownership.

PROPERTY RIGHTS — 40%

The ruling families exercise considerable influence on the judiciary. Incompetence and corruption are rarely challenged. All land in Abu Dhabi, largest of the seven emirates, is government-owned. Mortgages have been introduced for select Dubai-based five-star property developments and are otherwise generally unavailable. The UAE leads the region in protecting intellectual property rights.

FREEDOM FROM CORRUPTION — 62%

Corruption is perceived as present. The UAE ranks 31st out of 163 countries in Transparency International's Corruption Perceptions Index for 2006. A February 2005 Abu Dhabi police study citing "rampant" bribery, nepotism, embezzlement, and abuse of power throughout local administrations prompted the government to establish special anti-corruption sections to investigate and prosecute violators.

LABOR FREEDOM — 76.2%

Relatively flexible employment regulations could be further improved to enhance overall productivity growth and job creation. The non-salary cost of employing a worker is moderate, but dismissing a redundant employee is relatively costly. Regulations related to the number of work hours are not flexible. There is no minimum wage.

UNITED KINGDOM

London

The economy of the United Kingdom (U.K.) is 79.5 percent free, according to our 2008 assessment, which makes it the world's 10th freest economy. Its overall score is 0.5 percentage point lower than last year, reflecting worsened scores in four of the 10 economic freedoms. The U.K. is ranked 3rd out of 41 countries in the European region, and its overall score is much higher than the regional average.

The U.K. scores extraordinarily well in investment freedom, trade freedom, financial freedom, property rights, business freedom, and freedom from corruption. The average tariff rate is low, despite distortionary EU agricultural tariffs, and business regulation is efficient. Almost all commercial operations are simple and transparent, and support for private enterprise is a world model. Inflation is fairly low, and the business climate attracts foreign investment. The financial sector is a world hub. The judiciary is independent and highly trained. Corruption is almost nonexistent, and the labor market is notably flexible.

The U.K. scores far below the world average in government size and fiscal freedom. Total government spending equals more than two-fifths of GDP, and tax revenue and rates are very high.

BACKGROUND: Since the market reforms instituted by Prime Minister Margaret Thatcher in the 1980s, the United Kingdom has experienced steady economic growth and has outpaced other large EU economies. Under the Labour governments of Tony Blair, Britain promoted an open, global economic outlook and made stability a priority. The Bank of England's independence contributes much to macroeconomic stability. The City of London remains one of the world's leading centers of commerce and should continue to grow. The U.K. is now the world's top destination for foreign direct investment. As with most other Western European countries, Britain faces demographic challenges. Reform of public services, especially the National Health Service, is necessary but politically very sensitive.

How Do We Measure Economic Freedom? See Chapter 4 (page 39) for an explanation of the methodology or visit the *Index* Web site at *heritage.org/index*.

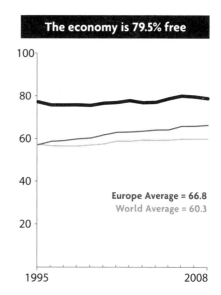

The economy is 79.5% free

Europe Average = 66.8
World Average = 60.3

1995 — 2008

QUICK FACTS

Population: 60.2 million

GDP (PPP): $2.0 trillion
1.9% growth in 2005
2.5% 5-yr. comp. ann. growth
$33,238 per capita

Unemployment: 4.7%

Inflation (CPI): 2.0%

FDI (net flow): $63.4 billion

Official Development Assistance:
Multilateral: None
Bilateral: None

External Debt: $8.3 trillion

Exports: $587.5 billion
Primarily manufactured goods, fuels, chemicals, food, beverages, tobacco, financial and insurance services

Imports: $669.8 billion
Primarily manufactured goods, machinery, fuels, foodstuffs, financial services, communications

2005 data unless otherwise noted.

UNITED KINGDOM'S TEN ECONOMIC FREEDOMS

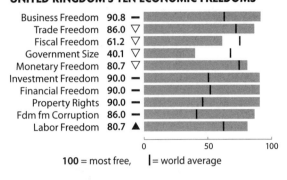

Business Freedom	90.8	—
Trade Freedom	86.0	▽
Fiscal Freedom	61.2	▽
Government Size	40.1	▽
Monetary Freedom	80.7	▽
Investment Freedom	90.0	—
Financial Freedom	90.0	—
Property Rights	90.0	—
Fdm fm Corruption	86.0	—
Labor Freedom	80.7	▲

100 = most free, **|** = world average

BUSINESS FREEDOM — *90.8%*

The overall freedom to start, operate, and close a business is strongly protected by the U.K.'s regulatory environment. Starting a business takes an average of 13 days, compared to the world average of 43 days. Obtaining a business license takes less than the world average of 234 days and is not costly. Bankruptcy proceedings are easy and straightforward.

TRADE FREEDOM — *86%*

The U.K.'s trade policy is the same as those of other members of the European Union. The common EU weighted average tariff rate was 2 percent in 2005. Non-tariff barriers reflected in EU policy include agricultural and manufacturing subsidies, import restrictions for some goods and services, market access restrictions in some service sectors, non-transparent and restrictive regulations and standards, and inconsistent customs administration across EU members. Consequently, an additional 10 percentage points is deducted from the U.K.'s trade freedom score.

FISCAL FREEDOM — *61.2%*

The U.K. has a high income tax rate and a moderate corporate tax rate. The top income tax rate is 40 percent, and the top corporate tax rate is 30 percent. Other taxes include a value-added tax (VAT), an environmental tax, and a capital gains tax. In the most recent year, overall tax revenue as a percentage of GDP was 37.2 percent.

GOVERNMENT SIZE — *40.1%*

Total government expenditures, including consumption and transfer payments, are very high. Government spending has been rising since the 1990s and in the most recent year equaled 44.7 percent of GDP.

MONETARY FREEDOM — *80.7%*

Inflation is low, averaging 2.1 percent between 2004 and 2006. Relatively stable prices explain most of the monetary freedom score. As a participant in the EU's Common Agricultural Policy, the government subsidizes agricultural production, distorting the prices of agricultural products. Prices are generally set by market forces, but pharmaceutical prices are capped, and the government influences prices through regulation and state-owned utilities. An additional 10 percentage points is deducted from the U.K.'s monetary freedom score to account for these policies.

INVESTMENT FREEDOM — *90%*

Foreign investors receive the same treatment as domestic businesses. Capital markets are deep and sophisticated, macroeconomic fundamentals are strong, and the labor market is relatively flexible. The U.K. was the largest receiver of foreign direct investment in 2005. The government rarely blocks foreign acquisitions, and foreigners may buy land. The promotion of competition and privatization has been a policy of the past two governments. Registered companies must have at least one U.K.-resident director. Residents and non-residents may hold foreign exchange accounts. Payments and proceeds on invisible transactions and current transfers are not subject to restrictions, and profits can be repatriated freely.

FINANCIAL FREEDOM — *90%*

The U.K.'s financial system offers all forms of financial services. Credit is allocated on market terms. Supervision is prudent, regulations are transparent, and oversight is maintained by an independent institution. The banking sector is the world's third-largest. In March 2006, there were 252 foreign-controlled banks, 75 British banks, and several credit unions. There are no government banks, but some government agencies provide grants and financing, and the Post Office provides some personal banking services. More banks are offering Islamic-friendly services. The central bank manages interest rates through direct market intervention. The insurance market is the world's third largest. Most large foreign insurers are represented, and many account for significant market shares. The London Stock Exchange is one of the world's largest exchanges.

PROPERTY RIGHTS — *90%*

Property rights are respected and enforced. Contracts are secure. The legal system protects intellectual property rights. Violations of IPR statutes are viewed as serious crimes that threaten the economy and consumers. The National Intellectual Property Crime Strategy includes training for enforcers and those engaged in combating counterfeiting and piracy.

FREEDOM FROM CORRUPTION — *86%*

Corruption is perceived as minimal. The United Kingdom ranks 11th out of 163 countries in Transparency International's Corruption Perceptions Index for 2006. Bribery of domestic or foreign public officials is a criminal offense, and corrupt payments are not tax-deductible. Foreign investors generally do not view official corruption as a factor in doing business.

LABOR FREEDOM — *80.7%*

Flexible employment regulations enhance overall productivity growth and employment opportunities. The non-salary cost of employing a worker is moderate, but dismissing a redundant employee is not burdensome. Regulations related to the number of work hours are quite flexible.

2008 Index of Economic Freedom

UNITED STATES

The economy of the United States is 80.6 percent free, according to our 2008 assessment, which makes it the world's 5th freest economy. Its overall score is 0.3 percentage point lower than last year, reflecting minor declines in four of the 10 economic freedoms. The United States is ranked 1st out of 29 countries in the Americas, and its overall score is much higher than the regional average.

The United States scores higher than the world average in eight areas and 30–40 percentage points higher in five: business freedom, investment freedom, financial freedom, property rights, and freedom from corruption. Foreign investment is subject to the same rules as domestic capital. Financial markets are open to foreign competition and are the world's most dynamic and modern. The judiciary is independent and of high quality.

America could do better in its scores for fiscal freedom and government size, which are 7 and 8 points below average, respectively. Total government spending equals more than a third of GDP. Corporate and personal taxes are moderately high and are getting relatively higher as other advanced economies reform with lower tax rates.

BACKGROUND: The United States is the world's dominant economy. With over two centuries of a fundamentally free, constitutionally protected economy, America benefits from its massive scale and intrastate competition. Trade barriers among the 50 states are unconstitutional, for example, allowing for the free movement of goods and labor. However, there have been troubling developments in recent years. Property rights have been threatened by the Supreme Court's 2005 ruling in *Kelo v. City of New London*. Congress has been active in raising the minimum wage, which has harmed labor freedom, but inactive in lowering corporate tax rates, unlike most other advanced economies. Most alarming, America's major political parties have been unwilling to curb growing government expenditures, particularly public entitlements.

How Do We Measure Economic Freedom? See Chapter 4 (page 39) for an explanation of the methodology or visit the *Index* Web site at *heritage.org/index*.

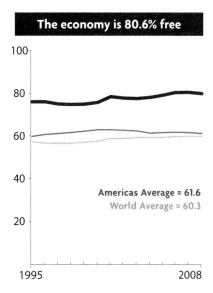

The economy is 80.6% free

Americas Average = 61.6
World Average = 60.3

1995   2008

QUICK FACTS

Population: 296.4 million

GDP (PPP): $12.4 trillion
3.2% growth in 2005
2.8% 5-yr. comp. ann. growth
$41,890 per capita

Unemployment: 5.1%

Inflation (CPI): 3.4%

FDI (net inflow): $112.2 billion

Official Development Assistance:
Multilateral: None
Bilateral: None

External Debt: $10.0 trillion

Exports: $1.3 trillion
Primarily agricultural products, transistors, aircraft, motor vehicle parts, computers, telecommunications equipment, automobiles, medicines, financial services

Imports: $2.0 trillion
Primarily agricultural products, industrial supplies, computers, telecommunications equipment, motor vehicle parts
2005 data unless otherwise noted.

385

UNITED STATES' TEN ECONOMIC FREEDOMS

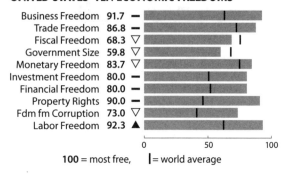

Business Freedom	91.7	—
Trade Freedom	86.8	—
Fiscal Freedom	68.3	▽
Government Size	59.8	▽
Monetary Freedom	83.7	▽
Investment Freedom	80.0	—
Financial Freedom	80.0	—
Property Rights	90.0	—
Fdm fm Corruption	73.0	▽
Labor Freedom	92.3	▲

0   50   100

100 = most free, | = world average

BUSINESS FREEDOM — 91.7%

The overall freedom to start, operate, and close a business is strongly protected by the U.S. regulatory environment. Starting a business takes an average of six days, compared to the world average of 43 days. Obtaining a business license takes much less than the world average of 19 procedures and 234 days. Bankruptcy proceedings are very easy and straightforward.

TRADE FREEDOM — 86.8%

The weighted average U.S. tariff rate was 1.6 percent in 2005. High out-of-quota tariffs, anti-dumping provisions, countervailing duties, some export controls, service market access restrictions, and export promotion programs and subsidies add to the cost of trade. An additional 10 percentage points is deducted from the U.S. trade freedom score to account for non-tariff barriers.

FISCAL FREEDOM — 68.3%

U.S. tax rates are burdensome. Both the top income tax rate and the top corporate tax rate are 35 percent. Other taxes include a property tax, an estate tax, and excise taxes. In the most recent year, overall tax revenue as a percentage of GDP was 26.8 percent.

GOVERNMENT SIZE — 59.8%

Total government expenditures, including consumption and transfer payments, are high. Government spending has been rising and in the most recent year equaled 36.6 percent of GDP.

MONETARY FREEDOM — 83.7%

Inflation is moderate, averaging 3.2 percent between 2004 and 2006. Relatively moderate and unstable prices explain most of the monetary freedom score. Price controls apply to some regulated monopolies; certain states and localities control residential rents; Hawaii caps gasoline prices; and the government influences prices through subsidies, particularly for the agricultural sector, dairy products, and some forms of transportation. An additional 5 percentage points is deducted from the U.S. monetary freedom score to account for policies that distort domestic prices.

INVESTMENT FREEDOM — 80%

Foreign and domestic enterprises are legally equal, and foreign investors are not required to register with or seek approval from the federal government. Foreign investment in banking, mining, defense contracting, certain energy-related industries, fishing, shipping, communications, and aviation is restricted. The government also restricts foreign acquisitions that might impair national security. There are no controls or requirements on currency transfers, access to foreign exchange, or repatriation of profits. Purchase of real estate is unrestricted on a national level, but the purchase of agricultural land by foreign nationals or companies must be reported to the government.

FINANCIAL FREEDOM — 80%

The U.S. has the world's most dynamic and developed financial markets. Reform in 1999 permitted a wider range of services and eliminated barriers to entry and barriers between commercial banks, insurance companies, and securities firms. Regulations are generally straightforward and consistent with international standards, although concerns have been raised about the intrusive nature and cost of the 2002 Sarbanes–Oxley Act. The instability of the housing market in late 2006 and ongoing concern about sub-prime lending could affect financial stability. Foreign financial institutions and domestic banks are subject to the same restrictions. There were 7,549 banking and thrift institutions in mid-2005. The Federal National Mortgage Association and Federal Home Mortgage Loan Corporation account for about half of home mortgages. Foreign participation in equities and insurance is substantial and competitive.

PROPERTY RIGHTS — 90%

Property rights are guaranteed. Contracts are very secure, and the judiciary is independent and of high quality. The courts recognize foreign arbitration and court rulings. Individual states' land-ownership limitations do not normally affect foreigners seeking property for commercial or manufacturing purposes. A well-developed licensing system protects patents, trademarks, and copyrights, and laws protecting intellectual property rights are strictly enforced.

FREEDOM FROM CORRUPTION — 73%

Corruption is perceived as minimal. The U.S. ranks 20th out of 163 countries in Transparency International's Corruption Perceptions Index for 2006. The U.S. is a leader in fighting corruption domestically and overseas. In 1977, it became the first country to pass a law making bribery of foreign officials a crime. The corruption perceptions score apparently was influenced by a series of scandals involving both U.S. corporations as well as members of Congress in recent years, highlighting some relatively few incidents of special interests' attempts to buy more access and influence.

LABOR FREEDOM — 92.3%

The labor market operates under highly flexible employment regulations that enhance overall productivity growth and employment opportunities. The non-salary cost of employing a worker is low, and dismissing a redundant employee is not burdensome.

URUGUAY

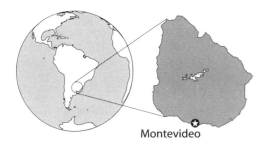

Montevideo

Uruguay's economy is 68.1 percent free, according to our 2008 assessment, which makes it the world's 40th freest economy. Its overall score is 0.7 percentage point lower than last year, reflecting worsened scores in five of the 10 economic freedoms. Uruguay is ranked 8th out of 29 countries in the Americas, and its overall score is higher than the regional average.

Uruguay has high levels of investment freedom, trade freedom, property rights, freedom from corruption, and fiscal freedom. The average tariff rate is fairly low, though non-tariff barriers are extensive, and business regulation is relatively simple. There is no personal income tax, and GDP per capita is Latin America's fourth-highest. Foreign investment is permitted in almost all sectors, and the government has never expropriated foreign capital. The judiciary is independent and corruption-free but can be subject to bureaucratic delays. The labor market is flexible.

Uruguay has a low financial freedom score but is average or above average in other areas. The small financial system is subject to heavy government influence.

BACKGROUND: Under President Tabare Vazquez, elected in 2005, Uruguay is trying to emerge from the shadows of Brazil and Argentina. Uruguay is a founding member of MERCOSUR (the Southern Cone Common Market), which has produced disappointing results. The government is increasingly trade-friendly. In January 2007, Uruguay signed a Trade and Investment Framework Agreement with the United States, its major trading partner, but pursuit of a free trade agreement with the U.S. has been stymied by other MERCOSUR members. The economy is based largely on beef and wool exports, but wood and software are gaining export market shares. Although privatization is viewed with suspicion, private firms have been permitted in some sectors, such as cellular, port operations, insurance, and mortgage banking. Further privatization is needed in telecommunications, energy, and public utilities.

How Do We Measure Economic Freedom? See Chapter 4 (page 39) for an explanation of the methodology or visit the *Index* Web site at *heritage.org/index.*

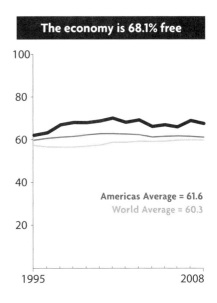

The economy is 68.1% free

Americas Average = 61.6
World Average = 60.3

1995 — 2008

QUICK FACTS

Population: 3.5 million

GDP (PPP): $34.5 billion
6.6% growth in 2005
2.0% 5-yr. comp. ann. growth
$9,962 per capita

Unemployment: 12.0%

Inflation (CPI): 4.7%

FDI (net flow): $605.0 million

Official Development Assistance:
Multilateral: $14.5 million
Bilateral: $27.4 million (2.8% from the U.S.)

External Debt: $14.6 billion

Exports: $5.1 billion
Primarily meat, rice, leather products, wool, fish, dairy products

Imports: $4.6 billion
Primarily machinery, chemicals, road vehicles, crude petroleum

2005 data unless otherwise noted.

URUGUAY'S TEN ECONOMIC FREEDOMS

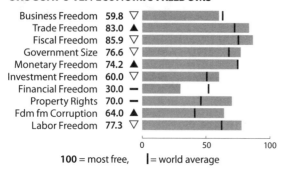

Business Freedom	59.8 ▽	
Trade Freedom	83.0 ▲	
Fiscal Freedom	85.9 ▽	
Government Size	76.6 ▽	
Monetary Freedom	74.2 ▲	
Investment Freedom	60.0 ▽	
Financial Freedom	30.0 —	
Property Rights	70.0 —	
Fdm fm Corruption	64.0 ▲	
Labor Freedom	77.3 ▽	

0   50   100

100 = most free, ▌**= world average**

BUSINESS FREEDOM — 59.8%

The overall freedom to start, operate, and close a business is limited by Uruguay's regulatory environment. Starting a business takes an average of 44 days, compared to the world average of 43 days. Obtaining a business license requires more than the world average of 19 procedures. Closing a business is fairly easy and straightforward.

TRADE FREEDOM — 83%

Uruguay's weighted average tariff rate was 3.5 percent in 2005. Import bans and restrictions, import taxes and fees, import licensing requirements, and customs delays add to the cost of trade. An additional 10 percentage points is deducted from Uruguay's trade freedom score to account for non-tariff barriers.

FISCAL FREEDOM — 85.9%

Uruguay imposes no income tax, but the social security contribution can be as high as 24.1 percent. The top corporate tax rate is 30 percent. Other taxes include a value-added tax (VAT), a capital tax, and a property transfer tax. In the most recent year, overall tax revenue as a percentage of GDP was 22.5 percent.

GOVERNMENT SIZE — 76.6%

Total government expenditures, including consumption and transfer payments, are moderate. In the most recent year, government spending equaled 27.9 percent of GDP. The state retains considerable control of the economy though its monopoly stances.

MONETARY FREEDOM — 74.2%

Inflation is high, averaging 6.2 percent between 2004 and 2006. Relatively unstable prices explain most of the monetary freedom score. Uruguay has eliminated most price controls, but the executive branch fixes prices of certain staples, including milk, and the government influences prices through regulation and numerous state-owned enterprises and utilities, including energy, petroleum products, and telecommunications. An additional 10 percentage points is deducted from Uruguay's monetary freedom score to account for policies that distort domestic prices.

INVESTMENT FREEDOM — 60%

Foreign and domestic capital are treated equally, except for a few sectors. Foreign investors face few restrictions outside of state-monopoly sectors. Uruguay has traditionally met its commitments to foreign investors and has never confiscated foreign capital. State monopolies include electricity, hydrocarbons, railroads, some minerals, port administration, and telecommunications, and some are allowed to forge private partnerships. Privatization is not widely popular, and progress has been mixed. Certain government tenders favor local services. Residents and non-residents may hold foreign exchange accounts. There are no restrictions or controls on payments, transactions, transfers, or repatriation of profits. Non-residents may purchase real estate.

FINANCIAL FREEDOM — 30%

Uruguay's small financial system is subject to heavy government influence. Reform has progressed slowly since a financial crisis that led to the closing of four major banks, and consolidation is resisted by labor unions. In January 2007, the banking system included the central bank, three state-owned banks, 23 private banks, and 15 other financial institutions. The state-owned Banco de la República Oriental del Uruguay is the largest bank, and the state-owned Banco Hipotecario del Uruguay is the leading mortgage lender. The two largest banks comprised 55 percent of financial assets. Most private banks are foreign bank branches. Significant dollarization in the banking sector is a potentially destabilizing factor. The government-owned Banco de Seguros del Estadoize dominates the insurance sector, accounting for over half of the market. Capital markets are underdeveloped and concentrated in government debt. The two stock exchanges listed 26 firms in 2007, and trading is negligible.

PROPERTY RIGHTS — 70%

Private property is generally secure, and expropriation is unlikely. Contracts are enforced, although the judiciary tends to be slow. The government has established a Settlement and Arbitration Center to improve investment relations. Regulations protecting copyrights appear to be working, but protection of confidential test data from unfair commercial use, as required by the WTO's Trade-Related Aspects of Intellectual Property Rights (TRIPS) agreement, remains inadequate. Aggressive anti-piracy campaigns have led to several successful prosecutions.

FREEDOM FROM CORRUPTION — 64%

Corruption is perceived as present. Uruguay ranks 28th out of 163 countries in Transparency International's Corruption Perceptions Index for 2006. Although Uruguay has strong laws to prevent bribery and other corrupt practices, public surveys indicate a widespread perception of public-sector corruption. Foreign firms have not identified corruption as an obstacle to investment.

LABOR FREEDOM — 77.3%

Relatively flexible employment regulations enhance overall productivity growth. The non-salary cost of employing a worker is low, and dismissing a redundant employee is relatively easy. Regulations related to the number of work hours are not quite flexible.

UZBEKISTAN

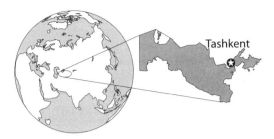
Tashkent

Uzbekistan's economy is 52.3 percent free, according to our 2008 assessment, which makes it the world's 130th freest economy. Its overall score is 0.3 percentage point higher than last year. Uzbekistan is ranked 24th out of 30 countries in the Asia–Pacific region, and its overall score is lower than the regional average.

Uzbekistan has relatively high levels of fiscal freedom, business freedom, and labor freedom. The top personal income tax rate is moderate, the top corporate tax rate is low, and overall tax revenue equals little more than 20 percent of GDP. The labor market is flexible. Licensing and bankruptcy procedures are costly, but opening a business is easy, and the average tariff rate is moderate.

Uzbekistan is weaker in monetary freedom, investment freedom, financial freedom, property rights, and freedom from corruption. Inflation is disastrous, and the government controls the prices of a variety of goods through state monopolies. Foreign investment is officially welcome, but opaque bureaucracy and political interference are disincentives. The courts are subject to political interference, and corruption is pervasive throughout the civil service.

BACKGROUND: Uzbekistan achieved independence from the Soviet Union in 1991 after more than 120 years of Russian imperial and Soviet rule. President Islam Karimov has ruled since the late 1980s and since the violent May 2005 Islamist insurrection in Andijan has intensified the repression of opponents. In 2005, Uzbekistan changed its political orientation from Washington to Moscow and closed the U.S. Air Force base in Karshi–Khanabad. Uzbekistan relies heavily on natural gas, gold, and cotton as sources of revenue. Privatization is expected to remain sluggish because of the absence of the rule of law, an uninviting investment environment, and the government's reluctance to relinquish its majority interest in strategic enterprises.

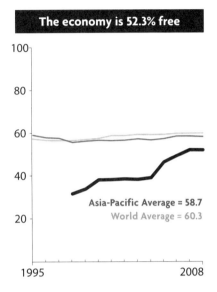

The economy is 52.3% free

Asia-Pacific Average = 58.7
World Average = 60.3

1995   2008

QUICK FACTS

Population: 26.2 million

GDP (PPP): $54.0 billion
7.0% growth in 2005
5.7% 5-yr. comp. ann. growth
$2,063 per capita

Unemployment: 3.0%

Inflation (CPI): 21.0%

FDI (net flow): $45.0 million

Official Development Assistance:
Multilateral: $31.5 million
Bilateral: $148.2 million (25.3% from the U.S.)

External Debt: $4.2 billion

Exports: $5.4 billion
Primarily cotton, gold, energy products, mineral fertilizers, ferrous and nonferrous metals, textiles, food products, machinery, automobiles

Imports: $4.1 billion
Primarily machinery and equipment, foodstuffs, chemicals, ferrous and non-ferrous metals

2005 data unless otherwise noted.

How Do We Measure Economic Freedom? See Chapter 4 (page 39) for an explanation of the methodology or visit the *Index* Web site at *heritage.org/index*.

UZBEKISTAN'S TEN ECONOMIC FREEDOMS

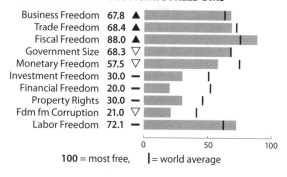

Business Freedom	67.8 ▲	
Trade Freedom	68.4 ▲	
Fiscal Freedom	88.0 ▲	
Government Size	68.3 ▽	
Monetary Freedom	57.5 ▽	
Investment Freedom	30.0 —	
Financial Freedom	20.0 —	
Property Rights	30.0 —	
Fdm fm Corruption	21.0 ▽	
Labor Freedom	72.1 —	

0   50   100

100 = most free, ▌= world average

BUSINESS FREEDOM — *67.8%*

The overall freedom to start, operate, and close a business is relatively well protected by Uzbekistan's regulatory environment. Starting a business takes an average of 13 days, compared to the world average of 43 days. Obtaining a business license takes more than the world average of 19 procedures and 234 days. Closing a business is lengthy.

TRADE FREEDOM — *68.4%*

Uzbekistan's weighted average tariff rate was 5.8 percent in 2001. Service market access barriers, high tariffs, discriminatory import taxes and fees, excessive import licensing requirements, currency controls, non-transparent and burdensome standards and certification regulations, non-transparent government procurement, export subsidies, weak enforcement of intellectual property rights, corruption, and inefficient customs implementation add to the cost of trade. An additional 20 percentage points is deducted from Uzbekistan's trade freedom score to account for non-tariff barriers.

FISCAL FREEDOM — *88%*

Uzbekistan has implemented moderate tax cuts. The top income tax rate is 25 percent, and the top corporate tax rate is 10 percent, effective in 2007. Other taxes include a value-added tax (VAT) and a property tax. In the most recent year, overall tax revenue as a percentage of GDP was 21.8 percent.

GOVERNMENT SIZE — *68.3%*

Total government expenditures, including consumption and transfer payments, are moderate. In the most recent year, government spending equaled 32.5 percent of GDP. Extensive state control of the economy still hinders development of the private sector and privatization of large state-owned enterprises.

MONETARY FREEDOM — *57.5%*

Inflation is very high, averaging 18.9 percent between 2004 and 2006. Unstable prices explain most of the monetary freedom score. The government influences prices through regulation, subsidies, and state-owned enterprises and utilities. It controls prices primarily by declaring companies or certain products national or regional monopolies, which automatically requires official review and approval of prices for such products. An additional 15 percentage points is deducted from Uzbekistan's monetary freedom score to account for policies that distort domestic prices.

INVESTMENT FREEDOM — *30%*

Officially, all sectors are open to foreign investment except for industries the government deems "strategic." In practice, investors face such barriers as cumbersome procedures, the threat of expropriation, uncertain and arbitrary regulation, corruption, and political unrest and violence. The government repealed tax breaks for all foreign companies in mid-2006, ending several firms' operations. Residents and non-residents may hold foreign exchange accounts, subject to some restrictions. Payments and transfers face quantitative limits and *bona fide* tests. Some capital transactions, including credit operations and real estate transactions, are subject to controls.

FINANCIAL FREEDOM — *20%*

Uzbekistan's underdeveloped financial sector is subject to heavy government intervention. Foreigners regard banks as technically insolvent. In late 2005, there were 29 banks, most of them privately owned. The five largest banks account for over 80 percent of assets; the largest state-owned bank itself controls 65 percent. Government-controlled banks support the government's economic priorities through subsidized loans offered to specific sectors. The government uses the banking system to collect and enforce taxes by freezing the accounts of those who are believed to be evading taxes. Foreign banks may operate only in a subsidiary status, and all routine banking operations require government permission. The insurance sector is minimal. Uzbek law grants state-owned companies a monopoly over certain forms of insurance. Capital markets are virtually nonexistent, and the stock market is very small. Listed stocks are mainly owned by employees and similar insiders.

PROPERTY RIGHTS — *30%*

The government influences the judiciary. Judicial procedures fall short of international standards, corruption is extensive, and expropriation is possible. Uzbekistan has no general system for registration of liens on chattel property. Pirated audiotapes, compact discs, videotapes, and other optical media are sold freely.

FREEDOM FROM CORRUPTION — *21%*

Corruption is perceived as pervasive. Uzbekistan ranks 151st out of 163 countries in Transparency International's Corruption Perceptions Index for 2006. Foreign-owned businesses view corruption as one of the largest obstacles to foreign direct investment. The law does not forbid government officials from acting as "consultants," a common method of extracting payment.

LABOR FREEDOM — *72.1%*

Relatively flexible employment regulations could be further improved to enhance overall productivity growth and job creation. The non-salary cost of employing a worker is high, but dismissing a redundant employee is relatively costless. Regulations related to the number of work hours remain somewhat rigid.

VENEZUELA

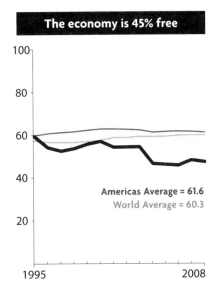

Caracas

Venezuela's economy is 45 percent free, according to our 2008 assessment, which makes it the world's 146th freest economy. Its overall score is 2.9 percentage points lower than last year, mainly reflecting worsened property rights and labor freedom. Venezuela is ranked 28th out of 29 countries in the Americas, and its overall score is much lower than the regional average.

Venezuela scores better than the world average in terms of government expenditures, which are low in formal terms. The top income and corporate taxes are relatively high, but overall tax revenue is low as a percentage of GDP.

Venezuela is weak in labor freedom, as well as extremely weak in financial freedom, investment freedom, monetary freedom, property rights, and freedom from corruption. Regulation is burdensome and confusing. The judiciary is heavily influenced by the government and does not enforce contracts well. The financial market is vulnerable to political interference. Pervasive corruption and the likelihood of expropriation deter foreign investment. Inflation is extremely high, and the government has the power to set prices.

BACKGROUND: Since 1998, President Hugo Chávez has pursued a military buildup, hobbled political opponents through electoral manipulation, imposed foreign exchange controls, undermined speech and property rights, and politicized the state oil company that dominates the economy. Last year, Chávez confiscated control from private-sector oil companies and nationalized the largest electricity supplier and the biggest telephone company. He is spending billions on an international, anti-American petro-diplomacy campaign and propping up the regime of his mentor, Cuban dictator Fidel Castro. Coupled with import and price controls, these policies hurt the lower-income groups that Chávez promises to help. Venezuela has one of the world's highest inflation rates. Price controls on food, medicines, and basic services discourage private production and result in shortages.

How Do We Measure Economic Freedom? See Chapter 4 (page 39) for an explanation of the methodology or visit the *Index* Web site at *heritage.org/index.*

The economy is 45% free

Americas Average = 61.6
World Average = 60.3

1995 — 2008

QUICK FACTS

Population: 26.6 million

GDP (PPP): $176.3 billion
10.3% growth in 2005
2.3% 5-yr. comp. ann. growth
$6,632 per capita

Unemployment: 14.0%

Inflation (CPI): 15.9%

FDI (net flow): $1.5 billion

Official Development Assistance:
Multilateral: $27.1 million
Bilateral: $38.0 million (23.6% from the U.S.)

External Debt: $44.2 billion

Exports: $56.8 billion
Primarily petroleum, bauxite and aluminum, steel, chemicals, agricultural products, basic manufactures

Imports: $29.4 billion
Primarily raw materials, machinery and equipment, transport equipment, construction materials

2005 data unless otherwise noted.

VENEZUELA'S TEN ECONOMIC FREEDOMS

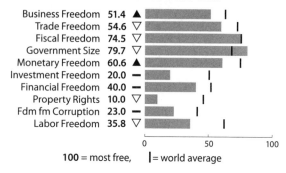

Business Freedom	51.4 ▲	
Trade Freedom	54.6 ▽	
Fiscal Freedom	74.5 ▽	
Government Size	79.7 ▽	
Monetary Freedom	60.6 ▲	
Investment Freedom	20.0 ▬	
Financial Freedom	40.0 ▬	
Property Rights	10.0 ▽	
Fdm fm Corruption	23.0 ▬	
Labor Freedom	35.8 ▽	

0   50   100

100 = most free, | = world average

BUSINESS FREEDOM — 51.4%

The overall freedom to start, operate, and close a business is seriously restricted by Venezuela's regulatory environment. Starting a business takes an average of 141 days, compared to the world average of 43 days. Obtaining a business license takes more than the world average of 234 days. Closing a business can be burdensome and lengthy.

TRADE FREEDOM — 54.6%

Venezuela's weighted average tariff rate was 12.7 percent in 2005. Import bans and restrictions, service market access barriers, import taxes, import licensing requirements, non-transparent and discriminatory administration of tariff rate quotas, non-transparent government procurement, currency controls, non-transparent standards and labeling regulations, export subsidies, weak enforcement of intellectual property rights, and customs inefficiency add to the cost of trade. An additional 20 percentage points is deducted from Venezuela's trade freedom score to account for non-tariff barriers.

FISCAL FREEDOM — 74.5%

Venezuela has burdensome tax rates. Both the top income tax rate and the top corporate tax rate are 34 percent. Other taxes include a value-added tax (VAT) and a property tax. In the most recent year, overall tax revenue as a percentage of GDP was 15.3 percent.

GOVERNMENT SIZE — 79.7%

Total government expenditures, including consumption and transfer payments, are moderate. In the most recent year, government spending equaled 26 percent of GDP. The government's economic policy has become increasingly interventionist.

MONETARY FREEDOM — 60.6%

Inflation is high, averaging 14.9 percent between 2004 and 2006. Relatively unstable prices explain most of the monetary freedom score. The government controls most prices through regulation, subsidies, and numerous state-owned enterprises and utilities and uses a non-legislated system of guaranteed minimum prices to protect agricultural producers. An additional 15 percentage points is deducted from Venezuela's monetary freedom score to account for policies that distort domestic prices.

INVESTMENT FREEDOM — 20%

The government restricts certain types of investment and requires that some professions be licensed. Foreign equity participation in media companies is limited to 20 percent, and the number of foreign workers that foreign companies may hire is limited. In January 2007, the government announced that it would nationalize companies in the electricity, telecommunications, and petroleum sectors. Planned revision of commercial regulations indicates that state involvement in "strategic" sectors like oil, petrochemicals, mining, and aluminum will increase. The government controls foreign exchange and fixes the exchange rate. Special regulations exist for foreign investment, remittances, foreign private debt, imports, exports, insurance and reinsurance, and the airline industry.

FINANCIAL FREEDOM — 40%

Venezuela's financial system is subject to growing government influence. At the end of 2006, there were 48 private and 10 public banking institutions. Foreign banks may acquire existing banks, create wholly owned foreign banks, or establish branches. There were eight foreign-controlled banks in 2005, down from 12 in 2004. Financial institutions are increasingly directed to provide credit in accordance with government requirements. Recent signs indicate that the government will impose a profit limit on banks or transfer government funds to state-controlled institutions. Maximum and minimum levels for lending and deposit interest rates were established in 2005. Foreigners are active in the insurance sector, which included 49 companies in mid-2006. Capital markets are relatively small. Foreign companies may participate in capital markets and may buy shares in Venezuelan companies directly or on the stock exchange.

PROPERTY RIGHTS — 10%

The right to hold and accumulate private property was further eroded in 2007 by changes in the constitution, nationalization, and expropriations. The judiciary is controlled by the executive, politically inconvenient contracts are abrogated, and the legal system discriminates against or in favor of investors from certain foreign countries. Pirated music, movies, and software are readily available.

FREEDOM FROM CORRUPTION — 23%

Corruption is perceived as pervasive. Venezuela ranks 138th out of 163 countries in Transparency International's Corruption Perceptions Index for 2006. Government tenders are vulnerable because the process frequently lacks transparency. Critics allege that price and exchange controls, as well as kickbacks on major weapons purchases, are sources of corruption.

LABOR FREEDOM — 35.8%

Highly inflexible employment regulations hinder overall productivity growth and job creation. The non-salary cost of employing a worker is moderate, but the rigidity of hiring and firing a worker creates a risk aversion for companies that would otherwise employ more people and grow. Regulations related to the number of work hours remain inflexible.

VIETNAM

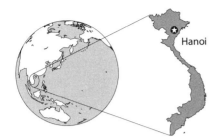

Hanoi

Vietnam's economy is 49.8 percent free, according to our 2008 assessment, which makes it the world's 135th freest economy. Its overall score is 0.4 percentage point better than last year, mainly reflecting an improvement in trade freedom. Vietnam is ranked 25th out of 30 countries in the Asia–Pacific region, and its overall score is lower than the regional average.

Vietnam's score on government size is above the world average. Total government expenditures equal about a fourth of GDP, which is relatively low compared to other countries. Yet weakness in all other areas suggests that this is not because of bureaucratic efficiency. The government imposes high personal tax rates, but overall tax revenue is not so large.

Vietnam has weak investment freedom, financial freedom, property rights, and freedom from corruption. Although it is undergoing reform, the financial sector is neither well regulated nor independent of the government. Despite some progress made, foreign investment is subject to an array of opaque regulations and cannot be guaranteed legally. The judiciary is subject to political influence, and commercial cases often take years to reach resolution. Corruption is a serious problem in the legal system, as well as for the civil service as a whole.

BACKGROUND: The Socialist Republic of Vietnam continues to reform its economy while maintaining a single-party state. Vietnam now boasts the fastest-growing economy in Southeast Asia, averaging over 7 percent growth annually. Since economic reform began in 1986, progress has been steady if slow, culminating most recently in Vietnam's January 2007 accession to the World Trade Organization. Agriculture accounts for the bulk of employment, although the services and manufacturing industries account for a large share of GDP. The state-owned sector represents 31 percent of GDP, and four state-owned banks control over 70 percent of all lending.

How Do We Measure Economic Freedom? See Chapter 4 (page 39) for an explanation of the methodology or visit the *Index* Web site at *heritage.org/index.*

The economy is 49.8% free

Asia-Pacific Average = 58.7
World Average = 60.3

1995 — 2008

QUICK FACTS

Population: 83.1 million

GDP (PPP): $255.3 billion
8.4% growth in 2005
7.7% 5-yr. comp. ann. growth
$3,071 per capita

Unemployment: 2.0%

Inflation (CPI): 8.3%

FDI (net flow): $2.0 billion

Official Development Assistance:
Multilateral: $715.9 million
Bilateral: $1.4 billion (2.2% from the U.S.)

External Debt: $19.3 billion

Exports: $36.6 billion
Primarily crude oil, marine products, rice, coffee, rubber, tea, garments, shoes

Imports: $38.6 billion
Primarily machinery and equipment, petroleum products, fertilizer, steel products, raw cotton, grain, cement, motorcycles

2005 data unless otherwise noted.

VIETNAM'S TEN ECONOMIC FREEDOMS

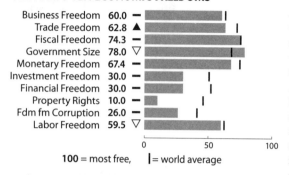

Business Freedom	60.0 —	
Trade Freedom	62.8 ▲	
Fiscal Freedom	74.3 —	
Government Size	78.0 ▽	
Monetary Freedom	67.4 —	
Investment Freedom	30.0 —	
Financial Freedom	30.0 —	
Property Rights	10.0 —	
Fdm fm Corruption	26.0 —	
Labor Freedom	59.5 ▽	

0   50   100

100 = most free, ∣ = world average

BUSINESS FREEDOM — 60%

The overall freedom to start, operate, and close a business is limited by Vietnam's regulatory environment. Starting a business takes an average of 50 days, compared to the world average of 43 days. Obtaining a business license takes less than the world average of 19 procedures and 234 days. Bankruptcy proceedings can be burdensome and lengthy.

TRADE FREEDOM — 62.8%

Vietnam's weighted average tariff rate was 13.6 percent in 2005. The government has made progress toward liberalizing the trade regime, but import bans and restrictions, service market access barriers, import taxes, import licensing requirements, non-transparent regulations, state trade in some commodities, weak enforcement of intellectual property rights, corruption, and customs inconsistency add to the cost of trade. An additional 10 percentage points is deducted from Vietnam's trade freedom score to account for non-tariff barriers.

FISCAL FREEDOM — 74.3%

Vietnam has a high income tax rate and a moderate corporate tax rate. The top income tax rate is 40 percent, and the top corporate tax rate is 28 percent. Other taxes include a value-added tax (VAT) and a business licensing tax. In the most recent year, overall tax revenue as a percentage of GDP was 13.5 percent.

GOVERNMENT SIZE — 78%

Total government expenditures, including consumption and transfer payments, are moderate. In the most recent year, government spending equaled 27.1 percent of GDP. There has been modest progress in restructuring state-owned enterprises in recent years.

MONETARY FREEDOM — 67.4%

Inflation is high, averaging 7.7 percent between 2004 and 2006. Unstable prices explain most of the monetary freedom score. The government controls prices to stem inflation and influences prices through regulation, subsidies, and state-owned enterprises and utilities. An additional 15 percentage points is deducted from Vietnam's monetary freedom score to account for policies that distort domestic prices.

INVESTMENT FREEDOM — 30%

As the government moves from a state-controlled economy to a market economy, complex and unclear barriers are common. The courts cannot enforce commercial rules, and the employment of foreign workers is limited. Foreigners may not own land but may lease it from the government. A mid-2006 investment law sought to solidify systemic and legal guarantees for foreign capital. Residents and non-residents may hold foreign exchange accounts, subject to restrictions and some government approvals. Payments and transfers are subject to restrictions. Most transactions in money market and capital instruments, derivatives, commercial credits, and direct investments are prohibited or require government approval.

FINANCIAL FREEDOM — 30%

Despite reform efforts, the government remains heavily involved in the financial sector. Regulations, supervision, and transparency fall short of international standards, and the state banks' rate of non-performing loans is estimated to be far higher than reported. The central bank is not independent. There are 37 joint-stock commercial banks, five state-owned commercial banks, four joint-venture banks, 35 foreign-invested branches, and 43 representative offices. The four primary state-owned banks control 70 percent of lending. Foreign banks may now open 100 percent-owned subsidiaries, branches, or representative offices and provide almost all of the services provided by Vietnamese banks. Lending by state banks is still used as an arm of government policy, particularly with subsidized interest rates and debt relief to farmers and large state-owned enterprises. The insurance sector is small, and the largest insurer is state-owned. Capital markets are very small. Trading on the first stock market, founded in 2000, has been light.

PROPERTY RIGHTS — 10%

The rudiments of a system that protects and facilitates property rights have been established, but laws and enforcement mechanisms need to be developed. The judiciary is not independent. Corruption among judges and court clerks is common. Contracts are weakly enforced, and resolution of disputes can take years. All land belongs to the state. Infringement of intellectual property rights is widespread, and enforcement in IPR cases is problematic.

FREEDOM FROM CORRUPTION — 26%

Corruption is perceived as widespread. Vietnam ranks 111th out of 163 countries in Transparency International's Corruption Perceptions Index for 2006. Foreign and domestic private-sector firms view official corruption and inefficient bureaucracy as serious problems.

LABOR FREEDOM — 59.5%

Inflexible employment regulations hinder overall productivity growth and employment opportunities. The non-salary cost of employing a worker is moderate, but the rigidity of hiring and firing a worker creates a risk aversion for companies that would otherwise employ more people and grow.

YEMEN

Sanaa

Yemen's economy is 52.8 percent free, according to our 2008 assessment, which makes it the world's 125th freest economy. Its overall score is 0.4 percentage point lower than last year, reflecting slightly worsened scores in monetary freedom and labor freedom. Yemen is ranked 14th out of 17 countries in the Middle East/North Africa region, and its overall score is lower than the regional average.

Yemen scores well in fiscal freedom and labor freedom. The top income tax is relatively low, but the corporate tax rate is more burdensome. Overall tax revenue is low as a percentage of GDP. The labor market is relatively flexible.

Yemen faces major challenges in financial freedom, monetary freedom, government size, property rights, and freedom from corruption. The regulatory process is opaque, and court rulings are subject to the demands of the government. Political interference bleeds into the financial market, which is unsophisticated, dominated by the state, and not subject to standard oversight and international regulations. Corruption is prevalent throughout the civil service. Inflation is high, although the government directly subsidizes only a few goods. State expenditures equal almost two-fifths of GDP.

BACKGROUND: Yemen, in addition to being a poor country with few natural resources, is politically unstable. President Ali Abdallah Saleh's government continues to face intermittent challenges from some of the country's often unruly tribes and Islamic radicals, who oppose economic reform and cooperation with the United States in the war against terrorism. Saleh's government has placed economic reforms on the back burner while it has waged war against Islamic extremists. In recent years, the economy has been hurt by declining oil production, terrorist attacks, and kidnappings, which have undermined tourism and foreign investment. The government has taken some steps to combat corruption it, but it needs to do more.

How Do We Measure Economic Freedom? See Chapter 4 (page 39) for an explanation of the methodology or visit the *Index* Web site at *heritage.org/index*.

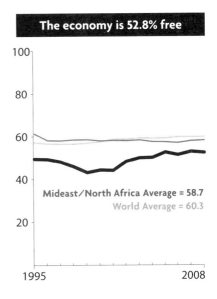

The economy is 52.8% free

Mideast/North Africa Average = 58.7
World Average = 60.3

1995 — 2008

QUICK FACTS

Population: 21.0 million

GDP (PPP): $19.5 billion
3.7% growth in 2005
3.3% 5-yr. comp. ann. growth
$930 per capita

Unemployment: 35.0% (2003 estimate)

Inflation (CPI): 11.8%

FDI (net flow): −$266.0 million

Official Development Assistance:
Multilateral: $200.8 million
Bilateral: $242.5 million (7.4% from the U.S.)

External Debt: $5.4 billion

Exports: $6.8 billion
Primarily crude oil, coffee, dried and salted fish

Imports: $5.3 billion
Primarily food and live animals, machinery and equipment, chemicals

2005 data unless otherwise noted.

YEMEN'S TEN ECONOMIC FREEDOMS

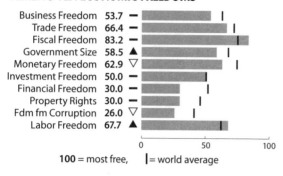

Business Freedom	53.7	—
Trade Freedom	66.4	—
Fiscal Freedom	83.2	—
Government Size	58.5	▲
Monetary Freedom	62.9	▽
Investment Freedom	50.0	—
Financial Freedom	30.0	—
Property Rights	30.0	—
Fdm fm Corruption	26.0	▽
Labor Freedom	67.7	▲

0   50   100

100 = most free,   **▌= world average**

BUSINESS FREEDOM — 53.7%

The overall freedom to start, operate, and close a business is restrained by Yemen's regulatory environment. Starting a business takes an average of 63 days, compared to the world average of 43 days. Obtaining a business license takes less than the world average of 19 procedures and 234 days. Bankruptcy proceedings are relatively straightforward.

TRADE FREEDOM — 66.4%

Yemen's weighted average tariff rate was 11.8 percent in 2000. Some import bans and restrictions, import taxes, import licensing requirements, weak enforcement of intellectual property rights, inefficient customs administration, and corruption add to the cost of trade. An additional 10 percentage points is deducted from Yemen's trade freedom score to account for non-tariff barriers.

FISCAL FREEDOM — 83.2%

Yemen has a low income tax rate but a burdensome corporate tax rate. The top income tax rate is 20 percent, and the top corporate tax rate is 35 percent. Other taxes include a property tax and a fuel tax. In the most recent year, overall tax revenue as a percentage of GDP was 7.4 percent.

GOVERNMENT SIZE — 58.5%

Total government expenditures, including consumption and transfer payments, are high. In the most recent year, government spending equaled 37.2 percent of GDP. Yemen depends heavily on foreign private oil companies that have production-sharing agreements with the government.

MONETARY FREEDOM — 62.9%

Inflation is high, averaging 18.4 percent between 2004 and 2006. Unstable prices explain most of the monetary freedom score. The government controls the prices of pharmaceuticals and petroleum products and influences prices through regulation, subsidies, and state-owned enterprises and utilities. An additional 10 percentage points is deducted from Yemen's monetary freedom score to account for policies that distort domestic prices.

INVESTMENT FREEDOM — 50%

The government officially permits foreign investment in most sectors, grants equal treatment to domestic and foreign investors, and intends to turn the General Investment Authority into a one-stop shop for investors. Foreign investment in the exploration for and production of oil, gas, and minerals is subject to production-sharing agreements. Foreign investment is not permitted in the arms and explosive materials industries, industries that could cause environmental disasters, or wholesale and retail imports. Though political unrest and civil violence are deterrents, Yemen appears to have attracted some regional investment enthusiasm and political support since its presidential election in late 2006. Foreign exchange accounts are permitted. There are no restrictions on payments and transfers, and capital transactions are subject to few restrictions. Corruption is significant.

FINANCIAL FREEDOM — 30%

Yemen's financial system is small, underdeveloped, and dominated by the state. Financial regulation remains insufficient, but the government is taking some steps to improve certain regulations like capital requirements. Non-performing loans are a problem. Of the 16 commercial banks (including four Islamic banks) in October 2006, nine were private domestic banks, five were foreign banks, and two were state-owned banks. Two state-owned development banks lend to the agriculture and housing sectors. The state wholly owns the country's largest bank, the National Bank of Yemen, and owns a majority of the Yemen Bank for Reconstruction and Development. Efforts to privatize these banks have foundered. A second plan, to combine them into a single institution, has also stalled. The Embassy of Yemen reports that the state is a very small shareholder in three other private banks. Commercial lending is limited to a small circle of clients, party because of legal inability to collect on overdue debts. The insurance sector is small, capital markets are negligible, and there is no stock market.

PROPERTY RIGHTS — 30%

The judiciary is subject to government pressure and corruption. Contracts are weakly enforced. Foreigners may own property, but foreign firms must operate through Yemeni agents. Protection of intellectual property rights is inadequate.

FREEDOM FROM CORRUPTION — 26%

Corruption is perceived as widespread. Yemen ranks 111th out of 163 countries in Transparency International's Corruption Perceptions Index for 2006. Government officials and members of parliament are presumed to benefit from insider arrangements and embezzlement. Procurement is a regular source of corruption in the executive branch.

LABOR FREEDOM — 67.7%

Relatively flexible employment regulations could be further improved to enhance overall productivity growth and job creation. The non-salary cost of employing a worker is low, but dismissing a redundant employee can be burdensome. Regulations related to the number of work hours remain rigid.

ZAMBIA

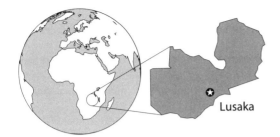

Lusaka

Rank: 99
Regional Rank: 15 of 40

Zambia's economy is 56.4 percent free, according to our 2008 assessment, which makes it the world's 99th freest economy. Its overall score is 0.8 percentage point lower than last year, mainly reflecting a much-worsened score in labor freedom. Zambia is ranked 15th out of 40 countries in the sub-Saharan Africa region, and its overall score is slightly higher than the regional average.

Zambia scores better than the world average only in terms of government expenditures, which are low in formal terms. This is likely a sign of government weakness, not efficiency. Personal and corporate tax rates are moderately high, but overall tax revenue is relatively low as a percentage of GDP. Total government expenditures equal about one-fourth of national GDP.

All of Zambia's other scores are equal to or below the world average. The judicial process is slow, and many courts cannot arbitrate commercial suits effectively. Corruption is widespread. The regulatory environment hinders business activity, and labor regulations are especially difficult. The government has streamlined foreign investment procedures, but capital is still subject to extensive restrictions.

BACKGROUND: The former British protectorate of Northern Rhodesia became the independent Republic of Zambia in 1964. Popular demand for multi-party democracy led President Kenneth Kaunda, who had ruled since independence, to remove restrictions on political parties. Multi-party elections were held in 1991 for the first time since the 1960s. Current President Levy Mwanawasa's anti-corruption effort won a major victory when a British court convicted his predecessor of corruption. Falling copper prices led to steadily declining income from 1974 to 1990. Economic reform began in the 1990s, but much needs to be done to improve governance and enhance the business climate. Copper is the biggest export, but mining contributes only 12 percent to GDP. Subsistence agriculture is the main employer. HIV/AIDS is a significant problem.

How Do We Measure Economic Freedom? See Chapter 4 (page 39) for an explanation of the methodology or visit the *Index* Web site at *heritage.org/index*.

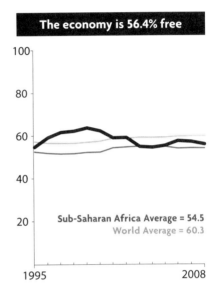

The economy is 56.4% free

Sub-Saharan Africa Average = 54.5
World Average = 60.3

1995   2008

QUICK FACTS

Population: 11.7 million

GDP (PPP): $11.9 billion
5.2% growth in 2005
4.7% 5-yr. comp. ann. growth
$1,023 per capita

Unemployment: 50.0% (2000 estimate)

Inflation (CPI): 18.3%

FDI (net flow): $259.0 million

Official Development Assistance:
Multilateral: $422.7 million
Bilateral: $1.5 billion (8.5% from the U.S.)

External Debt: $5.7 billion

Exports: $3.9 billion
Primarily copper, cobalt, electricity, tobacco, flowers, cotton

Imports: $3.1 billion
Primarily machinery, transportation equipment, petroleum products, electricity, fertilizer, foodstuffs, clothing

2005 data unless otherwise noted.

ZAMBIA'S TEN ECONOMIC FREEDOMS

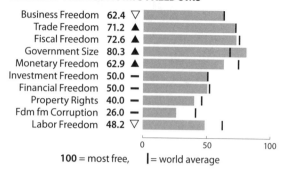

Business Freedom	62.4 ▽	
Trade Freedom	71.2 ▲	
Fiscal Freedom	72.6 ▲	
Government Size	80.3 ▲	
Monetary Freedom	62.9 ▲	
Investment Freedom	50.0 —	
Financial Freedom	50.0 —	
Property Rights	40.0 —	
Fdm fm Corruption	26.0 —	
Labor Freedom	48.2 ▽	

0   50   100

100 = most free, **|** = world average

BUSINESS FREEDOM — 62.4%

The overall freedom to start, operate, and close a business is restricted by Zambia's regulatory environment. Starting a business takes an average of 33 days, compared to the world average of 43 days. Obtaining a business license takes more than the world average of 234 days, and costs are high. Closing a business is relatively straightforward.

TRADE FREEDOM — 71.2%

Zambia's weighted average tariff rate was 9.4 percent in 2005. Import restrictions, import taxes, import certification, export licensing requirements, and corruption add to the cost of trade. An additional 10 percentage points is deducted from Zambia's trade freedom score to account for non-tariff barriers.

FISCAL FREEDOM — 72.6%

Zambia has burdensome tax rates. The top income tax rate is 35 percent, and the top corporate tax rate is 35 percent. Other taxes include a value-added tax (VAT), a tax on services, and a property transfer tax. In the most recent year, overall tax revenue as a percentage of GDP was 17 percent.

GOVERNMENT SIZE — 80.3%

Total government expenditures, including consumption and transfer payments, are moderate. In the most recent year, government spending equaled 25.6 percent of GDP. Progress in improving spending management and restructuring the public sector has been mixed.

MONETARY FREEDOM — 62.9%

Inflation is high, averaging 12.2 percent between 2004 and 2006. Relatively unstable prices explain most of the monetary freedom score. The government subsidizes agricultural input products and influences prices through state-owned enterprises and utilities. An additional 15 percentage points is deducted from Zambia's monetary freedom score to account for policies that distort domestic prices.

INVESTMENT FREEDOM — 50%

Zambia's positive approach to foreign investment is dampened by corruption. The Zambian Investment Center is a one-stop resource for international investors. An investment board screens all investments for which incentives are requested. Investments in communications, banking, tourism, transport, mining, health, education, and aviation are subject to additional regulations and approvals. The retail sector is closed to foreigners. Privatization of certain sectors like electricity and telecommunications stalled in 2003. Red tape is extensive, and corruption remains common despite government efforts. Residents and non-residents may hold foreign exchange accounts. There are no controls on payments, transfers, capital transactions, or repatriation of profits.

FINANCIAL FREEDOM — 50%

Zambia's financial sector is small and dominated by banking. Zambia has one of Southern Africa's more liberal banking regimes. Banking supervision and regulation have improved. There were 11 commercial banks in August 2006, including several majority foreign-owned banks. The poor loan repayment records of many borrowers and difficulty in seizing loan collateral have led banks to invest in government debt and to remain highly risk-averse. The legal climate does not easily support creditor claims on collateral, and lengthy trials are common. Zambia is creating a credit assistance program to build a wider network of reliable potential borrowers. The insurance market is open to competition. Privatization of the state-owned Zambia State Insurance Corporation has stalled with little investor interest. Though participation is increasing, capital markets remain very small. There are no restrictions on foreign investment in the stock exchange.

PROPERTY RIGHTS — 40%

Zambia's judicial system suffers from inefficiency, government influence, and a lack of resources. Contracts are weakly enforced, and courts are relatively inexperienced in commercial litigation. Despite constitutional and legal protections, customary law and practice place women in a subordinate status with respect to property, inheritance, and marriage. Trademark protection is adequate, but copyright protection is limited and does not cover computer applications. It takes at least four months to patent an item or process.

FREEDOM FROM CORRUPTION — 26%

Corruption is perceived as widespread. Zambia ranks 111th out of 163 countries in Transparency International's Corruption Perceptions Index for 2006. Controls over government funds and property are often weak, investigative units lack authority and personnel, and officials dealing with the public frequently demand illicit payments with impunity. The government has no clear policy for the disposal of confiscated assets, and a lack of transparency surrounds the liquidation of assets seized in the recent government campaign against corruption.

LABOR FREEDOM — 48.2%

Rigid employment regulations hamper overall productivity growth and employment opportunities. The non-salary cost of employing a worker is low, but the rigidity of hiring and firing a worker creates a risk aversion for companies that would otherwise employ more people and grow.

ZIMBABWE

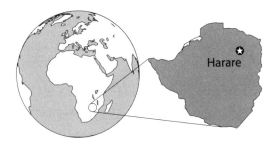

Harare

Rank: 155

Regional Rank: 40 of 40

Zimbabwe's economy is 29.8 percent free, according to our 2008 assessment, which makes it the world's 155th freest economy. Its overall score is 2 percentage points lower than last year, reflecting worsened scores in four of the 10 economic freedoms. Zimbabwe is ranked 40th out of 40 countries in the sub-Saharan Africa region, and its overall score is much lower than the regional average.

Zimbabwe has transformed itself from the "breadbasket of Africa" into a starving, destitute tyranny. All areas of economic freedom score below or far below the world average.

The average tariff rate is high, and non-tariff barriers are embedded in the labyrinthine customs service. National expenditures are also high. State influence in most areas is stifling, and expropriation is common as the executive pushes forward its economic plan of resource redistribution by angry mob. Political interference has wrecked the once-prosperous financial market, and the state makes a point of not welcoming foreign investment. Inflation is crippling, and the government directly subsidizes a wide array of goods.

BACKGROUND: The white minority government of the self-governing British colony of Rhodesia declared its independence in 1965. International sanctions and increasingly destructive attacks by armed African nationalist guerrilla groups in the 1970s led the Rhodesian government to agree to majority rule. The country became the independent nation of Zimbabwe under majority rule in 1980. President Robert Mugabe, who led one of the major African nationalist groups (the Zimbabwe African National Union, or ZANU), won the 1980 election and has been in power since then. When it became independent, Zimbabwe had extensive natural resources, a diversified economy, a well developed infrastructure, and an advanced financial sector. Economic mismanagement and political repression designed to strengthen Mugabe's hold on power have led to chaos and severe economic decline since 2000. Many Zimbabweans have fled to neighboring countries.

How Do We Measure Economic Freedom? See Chapter 4 (page 39) for an explanation of the methodology or visit the *Index* Web site at *heritage.org/index*.

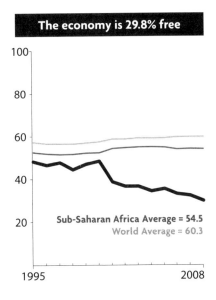

The economy is 29.8% free

Sub-Saharan Africa Average = 54.5
World Average = 60.3

1995   2008

QUICK FACTS

Population: 13.0 million

GDP (PPP): $26.5 billion
−5.3% growth in 2005
−6.0% 5-yr. comp. ann. growth
$2,038 per capita

Unemployment: 80.0%

Inflation (CPI): 237.8%

FDI (net flow): $102.0 million

Official Development Assistance:
Multilateral: $198.3 million
Bilateral: $180.2 million (18.5% from the U.S.)

External Debt: $4.3 billion

Exports: $1.6 billion
Primarily cotton, tobacco, gold, ferroalloys, textiles, clothing

Imports: $2.1 billion
Primarily machinery and transport equipment, other manufactures, chemicals, fuels

2005 data unless otherwise noted.

ZIMBABWE'S TEN ECONOMIC FREEDOMS

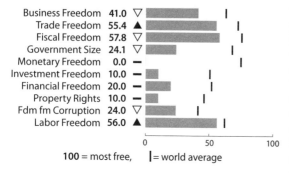

Business Freedom	41.0 ▽	
Trade Freedom	55.4 ▲	
Fiscal Freedom	57.8 ▽	
Government Size	24.1 ▽	
Monetary Freedom	0.0 —	
Investment Freedom	10.0 —	
Financial Freedom	20.0 —	
Property Rights	10.0 —	
Fdm fm Corruption	24.0 ▽	
Labor Freedom	56.0 ▲	

0   50   100

100 = most free, | = world average

BUSINESS FREEDOM — *41%*

The overall freedom to start, operate, and close a business is seriously restricted by Zimbabwe's regulatory environment. Starting a business takes more than twice the world average of 43 days. Obtaining a business license takes much more than the world average of 234 days. Closing a business is relatively difficult and costly.

TRADE FREEDOM — *55.4%*

Zimbabwe's weighted average tariff rate was 7.3 percent in 2003. Import bans and restrictions, import taxes, government controls on export and domestic trading of major agricultural commodities, and customs corruption add to the cost of trade. An additional 10 percentage points is deducted from Zimbabwe's trade freedom score to account for non-tariff barriers.

FISCAL FREEDOM — *57.8%*

Zimbabwe has burdensome tax rates. The top income tax rate is 47.5 percent, and the top corporate tax rate is 30 percent. Other taxes include a 3 percent AIDS surcharge on all taxes, a value-added tax (VAT), and a capital gains tax. In the most recent year, overall tax revenue as a percentage of GDP was 32.6 percent.

GOVERNMENT SIZE — *24.1%*

Total government expenditures, including consumption and transfer payments, are very high. In the most recent year, government spending equaled 50.3 percent of GDP. Privatization has stalled, and the government remains highly interventionist.

MONETARY FREEDOM — *0%*

Inflation is high, averaging 766.1 percent between 2004 and 2006. Unstable prices explain most of the monetary freedom score. The government sets price ceilings for essential commodities such as agricultural seeds, bread, maize meal, sugar, beef, stock feeds, and fertilizer; controls the prices of basic goods and food staples; influences prices through subsidies and state-owned enterprises and utilities; and has begun to arrest traders for not complying with orders to cut prices on a range of products. An additional 15 percentage points is deducted from Zimbabwe's monetary freedom score to account for policies that distort domestic prices.

INVESTMENT FREEDOM — *10%*

The government will consider foreign investment up to 100 percent in high-priority projects but applies pressure for eventual majority ownership by Zimbabweans and stresses the importance of investment from Asian countries, especially China and Malaysia, rather than Western countries. The government's hostility toward foreign investment encourages cronyism and corruption. Expropriation is very common. Formal investment agreements with other countries have not prevented the seizure of land owned by foreign nationals. Privatization has stalled with slightly over 10 percent of targeted concerns privatized. Foreign exchange accounts are subject to government approval and restrictions. Payments and transfers are subject to government approval and numerous restrictions, and all outward capital transactions are controlled.

FINANCIAL FREEDOM — *20%*

Government intervention, lack of adequate supervision, and repeated crises have severely damaged a once relatively sophisticated financial system. Several banks that collapsed were placed under Reserve Bank of Zimbabwe (RBZ) control in 2004 during reconsolidation. The government has used the RBZ to finance deficit spending and direct loans to state-owned enterprises. Many banks are illiquid, but the government has begun to tighten regulations and impose stricter capitalization requirements. The government also owns a savings bank and a development bank devoted to financing specific sectors. The insurance sector is small. The stock market is small and subject to wide speculative swings. A lack of options elsewhere in the economy led to significant upturns in the stock market over the past year. Foreign participation in the bond market or ownership of any locally listed company is capped.

PROPERTY RIGHTS — *10%*

The executive branch exerts strong influence on the judiciary and openly challenges court outcomes when they run afoul of government action. Corruption and expropriation are common. The ongoing redistribution of expropriated, white-owned, commercial farms substantially favors the ruling elite and continues to lack transparency.

FREEDOM FROM CORRUPTION — *24%*

Corruption is perceived as pervasive. Zimbabwe ranks 130th out of 163 countries in Transparency International's Corruption Perceptions Index for 2006. Top officials handpick multiple farms and register them in the names of family members to evade the official one-farm policy, and the government allows individuals aligned with top officials to seize land not designated for acquisition.

LABOR FREEDOM — *56%*

Restrictive employment regulations hinder overall productivity growth. The non-salary cost of employing a worker is low, but the difficulty of laying off a worker creates a risk aversion for companies that would otherwise hire more people and grow.

Appendix

Index of Economic Freedom Scores, 1995–2008

Country	1995	1996	1997	1998	1999	2000	2001	2002	2003	2004	2005	2006	2007	2008
Albania	49.7	53.8	54.8	53.9	53.4	53.6	56.6	56.8	56.8	58.5	58.7	61.4	62.4	63.3
Algeria	55.7	54.5	54.9	55.8	57.2	56.8	57.3	61.0	57.7	58.1	53.2	55.3	55.0	55.7
Angola	27.4	24.4	24.2	24.9	23.7	24.3	*	*	*	*	*	43.9	45.2	47.1
Argentina	68.0	74.7	73.3	70.9	70.6	70.0	68.6	65.7	56.3	53.9	53.4	54.6	55.0	55.1
Armenia	*	42.2	46.7	49.6	56.4	63.0	66.4	68.0	67.3	70.3	70.3	75.0	69.4	70.3
Australia	74.1	74.0	75.5	75.6	76.4	77.1	77.4	77.3	77.4	77.9	78.6	79.4	81.1	82.0
Austria	70.0	68.9	65.2	65.4	64.0	68.4	68.1	67.4	67.6	67.6	66.6	69.7	70.1	70.0
Azerbaijan	*	30.0	34.0	43.1	47.4	49.8	50.3	53.3	54.1	53.4	54.9	53.4	54.8	55.3
Bahamas, The	71.8	74.0	74.5	74.5	74.7	73.9	74.8	74.4	73.5	72.1	72.6	72.3	72.0	71.1
Bahrain	84.0	84.2	81.7	81.2	80.8	81.2	82.5	82.2	81.9	81.7	76.2	73.6	71.2	72.2
Bangladesh	38.7	51.1	49.9	52.1	50.0	48.9	51.2	51.9	49.3	50.0	47.6	54.2	48.0	44.9
Barbados	*	62.3	64.5	67.9	66.7	69.5	71.5	73.6	71.3	69.4	70.1	71.9	70.0	71.3
Belarus	40.4	38.7	39.8	38.0	35.4	41.3	38.0	39.0	39.7	43.1	46.6	46.8	46.4	44.7
Belgium	*	66.0	64.6	64.7	62.9	63.5	63.8	67.6	68.1	68.7	68.8	71.5	72.4	71.5
Belize	62.9	61.6	64.3	59.1	60.7	63.3	65.9	65.6	63.5	62.8	64.4	64.6	63.2	62.8
Benin	*	54.5	61.3	61.7	60.6	61.5	60.1	57.3	54.9	54.6	51.9	53.9	55.0	55.0
Bolivia	56.8	65.2	61.8	68.8	65.6	65.0	68.0	65.1	64.3	64.5	59.0	58.7	54.4	53.2
Bosnia and Herzegovina	*	*	*	29.4	29.4	45.1	36.6	37.4	40.6	44.7	49.3	55.6	54.3	53.7
Botswana	56.8	61.6	59.1	62.8	62.9	65.8	66.8	66.2	68.6	69.9	70.4	69.2	68.5	68.6
Brazil	51.4	48.1	52.6	52.3	61.3	61.1	61.9	61.5	63.4	62.0	62.0	60.9	56.1	55.9
Bulgaria	50.0	48.6	47.6	45.7	46.2	47.3	51.9	57.1	57.0	59.2	61.5	63.4	62.0	62.9
Burkina Faso	*	49.4	54.0	54.5	55.0	55.7	56.7	58.8	58.9	58.0	56.7	55.8	55.1	55.6
Burma (Myanmar)	*	45.1	45.4	45.7	46.4	47.9	46.1	45.5	44.9	43.6	40.5	40.0	41.0	39.5
Burundi	*	*	45.4	44.7	41.1	42.6	*	*	*	*	*	48.7	47.1	46.3
Cambodia	*	*	52.8	59.8	59.9	59.3	59.6	60.7	63.7	61.1	60.2	56.9	56.1	56.2
Cameroon	51.3	45.7	44.6	48.0	50.3	49.9	53.3	52.8	52.7	52.3	52.4	54.3	55.4	54.0
Canada	69.4	70.3	67.9	68.5	69.3	70.5	71.2	74.6	74.8	75.3	75.9	77.5	78.1	80.2
Cape Verde	*	49.7	47.7	48.0	50.7	51.9	56.3	57.6	56.1	58.1	58.5	59.2	57.1	58.4
Central African Republic	*	*	*	*	*	*	*	59.8	60.0	57.5	56.1	53.9	50.3	48.2

Index of Economic Freedom Scores, 1995–2008

Country	1995	1996	1997	1998	1999	2000	2001	2002	2003	2004	2005	2006	2007	2008
Chad	*	*	45.1	46.6	47.2	46.8	46.4	49.2	52.6	53.1	51.6	49.8	50.0	47.7
Chile	71.2	72.6	75.9	74.9	74.1	74.7	75.1	77.8	76.0	76.9	78.6	79.3	79.0	79.8
China, People's Republic of	52.0	51.3	51.7	53.1	54.8	56.4	52.6	52.8	52.6	52.5	53.6	53.4	51.8	52.8
Colombia	64.5	64.3	66.4	65.5	65.3	63.3	65.6	64.2	64.2	61.2	59.6	60.1	59.7	61.9
Congo, (Democratic Republic of)	41.4	39.5	39.5	40.6	34.0	34.8	*	*	*	*	*	*	*	*
Congo, Republic of	*	40.3	42.2	33.8	41.6	40.6	44.3	45.3	47.7	45.9	46.1	43.7	44.4	45.2
Costa Rica	68.0	66.4	65.6	65.6	67.4	68.4	67.6	67.5	67.0	66.4	66.8	66.4	64.6	64.8
Croatia	*	48.0	46.7	51.7	53.1	53.6	50.7	51.1	53.3	53.1	52.6	54.1	53.9	54.6
Cuba	27.8	27.8	27.8	28.2	29.7	31.3	31.6	32.4	35.1	34.4	35.5	29.3	28.6	27.5
Cyprus	*	67.7	67.9	68.2	67.8	67.2	71.0	73.0	73.3	74.1	71.9	71.8	71.7	71.3
Czech Republic	67.8	68.1	63.3	68.4	69.7	68.6	70.2	66.5	67.5	67.0	66.2	66.8	67.8	68.5
Denmark	*	67.3	67.5	67.5	68.1	68.3	68.3	71.1	73.2	72.4	72.9	75.4	77.0	79.2
Djibouti	*	*	54.5	55.9	57.1	55.1	58.3	57.8	55.7	55.6	56.6	54.3	53.5	52.3
Dominican Republic	55.8	58.1	53.5	58.1	58.1	59.0	59.1	58.6	57.8	54.6	55.2	57.1	57.7	58.5
Ecuador	57.7	60.1	61.0	62.8	62.9	59.8	55.1	53.1	54.1	54.4	53.5	54.8	55.6	55.4
Egypt	45.7	52.0	54.5	55.8	58.0	51.7	51.5	54.1	55.3	55.5	54.5	53.9	55.1	59.2
El Salvador	69.1	70.1	70.5	70.2	75.1	76.3	73.0	73.0	71.5	71.2	72.5	70.5	69.8	69.2
Equatorial Guinea	*	*	*	*	45.1	45.6	47.9	46.4	53.1	53.3	54.2	52.4	54.1	52.5
Estonia	65.2	65.4	69.1	72.5	73.8	69.9	76.1	77.6	77.7	77.4	75.3	74.9	78.0	77.8
Ethiopia	42.6	45.9	48.1	49.2	46.7	50.2	48.9	49.8	48.8	54.5	52.1	51.7	54.4	53.2
Fiji	54.7	57.4	58.0	58.2	58.4	57.8	53.7	53.9	54.7	58.0	56.7	58.1	60.6	61.5
Finland	*	63.7	65.2	63.5	63.9	64.3	69.7	73.6	73.7	73.4	71.7	73.3	74.2	74.8
France	64.4	63.7	59.1	58.9	59.1	57.4	58.0	58.0	59.2	60.9	61.4	61.9	62.8	65.4
Gabon	57.5	55.7	58.8	59.2	60.5	58.2	55.0	58.0	58.7	57.1	54.3	55.5	54.2	53.6
Gambia, The	*	*	52.9	53.4	52.1	52.7	56.6	57.7	56.3	55.3	56.1	57.1	57.4	56.6
Georgia	*	44.1	46.5	47.9	52.5	54.3	58.3	56.7	58.6	58.9	58.1	63.5	69.3	69.2
Germany	69.8	69.1	67.5	64.3	65.6	65.7	69.5	70.4	69.7	69.5	68.6	71.4	71.5	71.2
Ghana	55.6	57.7	51.1	51.5	52.3	58.1	58.0	57.2	58.2	59.1	56.5	55.3	57.3	56.7
Greece	61.2	60.5	59.6	60.6	61.0	61.0	63.4	59.1	58.8	59.1	58.0	59.7	58.3	60.1

Index of Economic Freedom Scores, 1995–2008

Country	1995	1996	1997	1998	1999	2000	2001	2002	2003	2004	2005	2006	2007	2008
Guatemala	62.0	63.7	65.7	65.8	66.2	64.3	65.1	62.3	62.3	59.6	60.5	60.1	61.3	60.5
Guinea	59.4	58.5	52.9	61.0	59.4	58.2	58.4	52.9	54.6	56.1	57.6	52.9	54.5	52.8
Guinea–Bissau	*	*	*	*	33.5	34.7	42.5	42.3	43.1	42.6	44.6	47.2	46.8	45.1
Guyana	45.7	50.1	53.2	52.7	53.3	52.4	53.3	54.3	50.3	53.0	57.5	57.2	54.3	49.4
Haiti	43.0	41.0	45.8	45.7	45.9	45.7	47.1	47.9	50.6	51.2	48.7	49.2	51.4	48.9
Honduras	57.0	56.6	56.0	56.2	56.7	57.6	57.0	58.7	60.4	55.3	57.2	58.7	60.4	60.2
Hong Kong	88.6	90.5	88.6	88.0	88.5	89.5	89.9	89.4	89.8	90.0	90.2	89.3	90.6	90.3
Hungary	55.2	56.8	55.3	56.9	59.6	64.4	65.6	64.5	63.0	62.7	63.3	64.7	64.4	67.2
Iceland	*	*	70.5	71.2	71.4	74.0	73.4	73.1	73.5	72.1	76.9	76.5	76.7	76.5
India	45.1	47.4	49.7	49.7	50.2	47.4	49.0	51.2	51.2	51.5	54.2	52.4	54.1	54.2
Indonesia	54.9	61.0	62.0	63.4	61.5	55.2	52.5	54.8	55.8	52.1	54.3	52.7	53.9	53.9
Iran	*	36.1	34.5	36.0	36.8	36.1	35.9	36.4	43.2	42.8	48.3	44.1	44.1	44.0
Iraq	*	17.2	17.2	17.2	17.2	17.2	17.2	15.6	*	*	*	*	*	*
Ireland	68.5	68.5	72.6	73.7	74.6	76.1	81.2	80.5	80.9	80.3	78.6	82.1	82.6	82.4
Israel	61.5	62.0	62.7	68.0	68.3	65.5	66.1	66.9	62.7	61.4	62.9	64.2	64.6	66.1
Italy	61.2	60.8	58.1	59.1	61.6	61.9	63.0	63.6	64.3	64.2	62.9	61.9	62.7	62.5
Ivory Coast	53.4	49.9	50.5	51.3	51.7	50.2	54.8	57.3	56.7	57.8	56.3	57.2	56.0	54.9
Jamaica	64.4	66.7	67.7	67.1	64.7	65.5	63.7	61.7	67.0	66.7	67.6	66.9	66.0	66.2
Japan	75.1	72.6	70.3	70.2	69.1	70.7	70.9	66.7	67.6	64.3	66.4	72.8	72.2	72.5
Jordan	62.7	60.8	63.6	66.8	67.4	67.5	68.3	66.2	65.3	66.1	65.9	62.7	63.5	63.0
Kazakhstan	*	*	*	41.7	47.3	50.4	51.8	52.4	52.3	49.7	53.5	59.7	59.1	60.5
Kenya	54.5	56.4	60.1	58.4	58.2	59.7	57.6	58.2	58.6	57.7	58.5	60.0	59.9	59.6
Korea, Democratic Republic of (North Korea)	8.9	8.9	8.9	8.9	8.9	8.9	8.9	8.9	8.9	8.9	8.0	4.0	3.0	3.0
Korea, Republic of (South Korea)	72.0	73.0	69.8	73.3	69.7	69.7	69.1	69.5	68.3	67.8	66.3	66.9	67.2	67.9
Kuwait	*	66.1	64.8	66.3	69.5	69.7	68.2	65.4	66.7	63.6	64.7	66.7	66.6	68.3
Kyrgyz Republic	*	*	*	51.8	54.8	55.7	53.7	51.7	56.8	58.1	57.1	61.0	60.3	61.1
Laos	*	38.5	35.1	35.2	35.2	36.8	33.5	36.8	41.0	42.0	43.4	46.4	49.2	49.2
Latvia	*	55.0	62.4	63.4	64.2	63.4	66.4	65.0	66.0	67.4	65.8	67.2	68.3	68.3
Lebanon	*	63.2	63.9	59.0	59.1	56.1	61.0	57.1	56.7	56.9	58.1	58.4	61.4	60.9

Index of Economic Freedom Scores, 1995–2008

Country	1995	1996	1997	1998	1999	2000	2001	2002	2003	2004	2005	2006	2007	2008
Lesotho	*	47.0	47.2	48.4	48.2	48.4	50.6	48.9	52.0	50.3	54.3	54.6	53.1	51.9
Libya	*	31.7	28.9	32.0	32.3	34.7	34.0	35.4	34.6	31.5	32.8	33.2	37.0	38.7
Lithuania	*	49.7	57.3	59.4	61.5	61.9	65.5	66.1	69.7	72.4	70.7	71.8	71.5	70.8
Luxembourg	*	72.5	72.8	72.7	72.4	76.4	80.1	79.4	79.9	78.9	78.1	76.1	75.3	75.2
Macedonia	*	*	*	*	*	*	*	58.0	60.1	56.8	57.0	59.6	60.7	61.1
Madagascar	51.6	52.2	53.8	51.8	52.8	54.4	53.9	56.8	62.8	60.9	63.3	61.1	61.1	62.4
Malawi	54.7	56.2	53.4	54.1	54.0	57.4	56.2	56.9	53.2	53.6	54.9	56.5	54.0	53.8
Malaysia	71.9	69.9	66.8	68.2	68.9	66.0	60.2	60.1	61.1	59.9	63.6	62.3	64.5	64.5
Mali	52.4	57.0	56.4	57.3	58.4	60.3	60.1	61.1	58.6	56.6	55.9	54.1	54.7	55.5
Malta	56.3	55.8	57.9	61.2	59.3	58.3	62.9	62.2	61.1	63.3	68.9	67.3	66.1	66.0
Mauritania	*	45.5	47.0	43.7	42.8	46.0	48.5	52.5	59.0	61.8	59.3	55.6	53.6	55.0
Mauritius	*	*	*	*	70.7	67.2	66.4	67.7	64.4	64.3	66.2	67.5	69.2	72.3
Mexico	63.1	61.2	57.1	57.9	58.5	59.3	60.6	63.0	65.3	66.0	66.0	64.9	66.3	66.4
Moldova	33.0	52.5	48.9	53.5	56.1	59.6	54.9	57.4	60.0	57.1	57.0	58.3	59.2	58.4
Mongolia	47.8	47.4	52.9	57.3	58.6	58.5	56.0	56.7	57.7	56.5	59.1	61.8	59.8	62.8
Morocco	62.8	64.3	64.7	61.1	63.8	63.2	63.9	59.0	57.8	56.7	52.8	52.3	57.2	56.4
Montenegro	*	*	*	*	*	*	*	*	*	*	*	*	*	*
Mozambique	45.5	48.4	44.0	43.0	48.9	52.2	59.2	57.7	58.6	57.2	56.2	53.1	55.9	56.6
Namibia	*	*	61.6	66.1	66.1	66.7	64.8	65.1	67.3	62.4	60.8	60.3	63.2	61.0
Nepal	*	50.3	53.6	53.5	53.1	51.3	51.6	52.3	51.5	51.2	52.3	54.5	55.1	54.7
Netherlands, The	*	69.7	70.4	69.2	63.6	70.4	73.0	75.1	74.6	74.5	72.0	74.8	74.9	76.8
New Zealand	*	78.1	79.0	79.2	81.7	80.9	81.1	80.7	81.1	81.5	81.9	81.7	81.0	80.2
Nicaragua	42.5	54.1	53.3	53.8	54.0	56.9	58.0	61.1	62.6	61.4	61.9	63.1	61.9	60.0
Niger	*	*	46.6	47.5	48.6	45.9	48.9	48.2	54.2	54.6	53.9	52.4	53.1	52.7
Nigeria	47.3	47.4	52.8	52.3	55.7	53.1	49.6	50.9	49.5	49.2	48.3	48.4	56.0	55.5
Norway	*	65.4	65.1	68.0	68.6	70.1	67.1	67.4	67.2	66.2	64.7	68.5	68.4	69.0
Oman	70.2	65.4	64.5	64.9	64.9	64.1	67.7	64.0	64.6	66.9	66.3	63.9	66.1	67.4
Pakistan	57.6	58.4	56.0	53.2	53.0	56.4	56.0	55.8	55.0	54.9	54.9	59.3	58.5	56.8
Panama	71.6	71.8	72.4	72.6	72.6	71.6	70.6	68.5	68.4	65.3	66.1	65.5	64.6	64.7

Index of Economic Freedom Scores, 1995–2008

Country	1995	1996	1997	1998	1999	2000	2001	2002	2003	2004	2005	2006	2007	2008
Paraguay	65.9	67.1	67.3	65.2	63.7	64.0	60.3	59.6	58.2	56.7	54.1	56.3	58.9	60.5
Peru	56.9	62.5	63.8	65.0	69.2	68.7	69.6	64.8	64.6	64.7	61.0	60.3	62.5	63.5
Philippines, The	55.0	60.2	62.2	62.8	61.9	62.5	60.9	60.7	61.3	59.1	55.5	57.2	56.9	56.9
Poland	50.7	57.8	49.0	59.2	59.6	60.0	61.8	65.0	61.8	58.7	59.0	58.6	57.4	59.5
Portugal	62.4	64.5	63.6	65.0	65.6	65.5	66.0	65.4	64.9	64.9	62.9	63.4	64.5	64.3
Qatar	*	*	*	*	62.0	62.0	60.0	61.9	65.9	66.5	63.5	56.4	62.9	62.2
Romania	42.9	46.2	50.8	54.4	50.1	52.1	50.0	48.7	50.6	50.0	52.2	58.2	61.2	61.5
Russia	51.1	51.6	48.6	52.8	54.5	51.8	49.8	48.7	50.8	52.8	51.7	52.7	52.5	49.9
Rwanda	*	*	38.3	39.1	39.8	42.3	45.4	50.4	47.8	53.3	51.4	52.8	52.4	54.1
Saudi Arabia	*	68.3	68.7	69.3	65.5	66.5	62.2	65.3	63.2	60.4	63.8	63.8	61.6	62.8
Senegal	*	58.2	58.1	59.7	60.6	58.9	58.7	58.6	58.1	58.9	58.1	56.2	58.1	58.2
Serbia	*	*	*	*	*	*	*	*	*	*	*	*	*	*
Serbia and Montenegro	*	*	*	*	*	*	*	46.6	43.5	*	*	*	*	*
Sierra Leone	49.8	52.3	45.0	47.7	47.2	44.2	*	*	42.2	43.6	45.6	45.8	47.6	48.9
Singapore	86.3	86.5	87.3	87.0	86.9	87.7	87.8	87.4	88.2	88.9	89.7	89.1	87.2	87.4
Slovak Republic	60.4	57.6	55.5	57.5	54.2	53.8	58.5	59.8	59.0	64.6	65.4	68.7	68.4	68.7
Slovenia	*	50.4	55.6	60.7	61.3	58.3	61.8	57.8	57.7	59.2	60.3	62.4	60.2	60.6
South Africa	60.7	62.5	63.2	64.3	63.3	63.7	63.8	64.0	67.1	66.3	62.6	63.5	63.4	63.2
Spain	62.8	59.6	59.6	62.6	65.1	65.9	68.1	68.8	68.8	68.9	67.6	68.9	69.9	69.7
Sri Lanka	60.6	62.5	65.5	64.6	64.0	63.2	66.0	64.0	62.5	61.6	60.3	58.6	59.3	58.3
Sudan	39.4	39.2	39.9	38.3	39.6	47.2	*	*	*	*	*	*	*	*
Suriname	*	36.7	35.9	39.9	40.1	45.8	44.3	48.0	46.9	47.9	50.8	54.7	54.4	53.9
Swaziland	63.3	58.6	59.4	62.0	62.1	62.6	63.6	60.9	59.6	58.6	59.7	61.8	60.6	58.9
Sweden	61.4	61.8	63.3	64.0	64.2	65.1	66.6	70.8	70.1	70.1	68.3	70.6	69.0	70.4
Switzerland	*	76.8	78.6	79.0	79.1	76.8	76.0	79.3	79.0	79.5	79.4	79.0	78.1	79.7
Syria	*	42.3	43.0	42.2	39.0	37.2	36.6	36.3	41.3	40.6	46.6	51.0	48.1	46.6
Taiwan	74.2	74.1	70.0	70.4	71.5	72.5	72.8	71.3	71.7	69.6	72.1	70.4	70.2	71.0
Tajikistan	*	*	*	41.1	41.2	44.8	46.8	47.3	46.5	48.7	52.5	52.7	53.8	54.5
Tanzania	57.3	57.5	59.3	59.6	60.1	56.0	54.9	58.3	56.9	60.1	56.4	58.5	56.8	56.4

Index of Economic Freedom Scores, 1995–2008

Country	1995	1996	1997	1998	1999	2000	2001	2002	2003	2004	2005	2006	2007	2008
Thailand	71.3	71.1	66.1	57.3	66.9	66.6	68.9	69.1	65.8	63.7	64.0	64.5	64.8	63.5
Togo	*	*	*	*	48.2	46.4	45.3	45.2	46.8	47.0	47.8	47.3	49.7	48.8
Trinidad and Tobago	*	69.2	71.3	72.0	72.4	74.5	71.8	70.1	68.8	71.3	72.5	71.2	71.4	70.2
Tunisia	63.4	63.9	63.8	53.9	61.1	61.3	60.8	60.2	58.1	58.4	56.0	56.8	59.6	59.3
Turkey	58.4	56.7	60.8	60.9	59.2	63.4	60.6	54.2	51.9	52.8	51.3	57.8	58.2	60.8
Turkmenistan	*	*	*	35.0	36.1	37.6	41.8	43.2	51.3	50.7	47.6	43.8	43.0	43.4
Uganda	67.3	70.7	71.0	54.7	64.8	58.2	60.4	61.1	60.1	64.1	63.5	64.5	63.7	64.4
Ukraine	39.9	40.6	43.5	40.4	43.7	47.8	48.5	48.2	51.1	53.7	55.8	54.6	51.6	51.1
United Arab Emirates	*	71.6	71.9	72.2	71.5	74.2	74.9	73.6	73.4	67.2	65.5	62.4	62.8	62.8
United Kingdom	77.9	76.4	76.4	76.5	76.2	77.3	77.6	78.5	77.5	77.7	79.4	80.6	80.0	79.5
United States	76.7	76.7	75.6	75.4	75.5	76.4	79.1	78.4	78.2	78.7	79.8	81.1	80.9	80.6
Uruguay	62.5	63.7	67.5	58.6	68.5	69.3	70.7	68.7	69.8	66.7	67.5	65.8	68.8	68.1
Uzbekistan	*	*	*	31.5	33.8	38.1	38.2	38.5	38.3	39.1	46.5	49.2	52.0	52.3
Venezuela	59.8	54.5	52.8	54.0	56.1	57.4	54.6	54.7	54.8	46.7	46.3	45.0	47.9	45.0
Vietnam	41.7	40.2	38.6	40.4	42.7	43.7	44.3	45.6	46.2	46.1	46.8	50.1	49.4	49.8
Yemen	49.8	49.6	48.4	46.1	43.3	44.5	44.3	48.6	50.3	50.5	53.0	51.8	53.2	52.8
Zambia	55.1	59.6	62.1	62.7	64.2	62.8	59.5	59.6	55.3	54.9	55.8	57.6	57.2	56.4
Zimbabwe	48.5	46.7	48.0	44.6	47.2	48.7	38.8	36.7	36.7	34.4	35.5	33.4	31.9	29.8

*Not graded

Source: Kim R. Holmes, Edwin J. Feulner, and Mary Anastasia O'Grady, 2008 Index of Economic Freedom (Washington, D.C.: The Heritage Foundation and Dow Jones & Company, Inc., 2008), at www.heritage.org/index.

Major Works Cited

The following sources provided the basis for the country factor analyses in the 2008 *Index of Economic Freedom*. In addition, the authors and analysts of the various elements of the *Index* relied on supporting documentation and information from various government agencies and sites on the Internet, news reports and journal articles, and official responses to inquiries. All statistical and other information received from government sources was verified with independent, internationally recognized nongovernmental sources as well.

African Development Bank, *Selected Statistics on African Countries 2007*; available at *www.afdb. org/pls/portal/docs/PAGE/ADB_ADMIN_PG/DOCUMENTS/STATISTICS/SELECTED%202007_ WEB_0.PDF.*

Asian Development Bank, *Key Indicators 2006: Measuring Policy Effectiveness in Health and Education*; available at *www.adb.org/Documents/Books/Key_Indicators/2006/default.asp.*

——, *Key Indicators 2007: Inequality in Asia*; available at *www.adb.org/Documents/Books/Key_ Indicators/2007/default.asp.*

Central Intelligence Agency, *The World Factbook 2007*; available at *www.cia.gov/library/ publications/the-world-factbook/index.html.*

Country statistical agencies, central banks, and ministries of finance, economy, and trade; available at *www.un.org/Depts/unsd/gs_natstat.htm; www.census.gov/main/www/stat_int.html* and *www.bis.org/cbanks.htm.*

Deloitte, *Country Snapshots*; available at *www.deloitte.com/dtt/section_node/ 0,1042,sid%253D11410,00.html.*

Economist Intelligence Unit Limited, *Country Profile*, London, U.K., 2005–2007.

———, *EIU Country Report*, London, U.K., 1996–2007.

———, *Country Commerce*, London, U.K., 2005–2007.

Ernst & Young International, Ltd., *The Global Executive*, New York, N.Y., 2005–2007.

———, *Worldwide Corporate Tax Guide*, New York, N.Y., 2004–2006.

———, direct correspondence with Country Office.

European Bank for Reconstruction and Development, *Country Strategies*, 2005–2007; available at *www.ebrd.org/about/strategy/index.htm#country*.

Inter-American Development Bank; available at *www.iadb.org*.

International Monetary Fund, *Annual Report on Exchange Arrangements and Exchange Restrictions, 2005*, Washington, D.C., September 2005.

———, *Article IV Staff Reports*, various countries, Washington, D.C., 2002–2007; available at *www.imf.org/external/ns/cs.aspx?id=51*.

———, *International Financial Statistics Online*, Washington, D.C., 2007; available by subscription at *http://ifs.apdi.net/imf/logon.aspx*.

———, *Selected Issues and Statistical Appendix*, various countries, Washington, D.C., 2001–2007.

———, *World Economic Outlook: Spillovers and Cycles in the Global Economy*, Washington, D.C., April 2007; available at *www.imf.org/external/pubs/ft/weo/2007/01/index.htm*.

———, *Country Information*; available at *www.imf.org/external/country/index.htm*.

Organisation for Economic Co-operation and Development, *OECD Economic Outlook*, No. 78 (December 2005) and No. 81 (May 2007).

———, *OECD Statistics*; available at *www.oecd.org/statsportal/0,3352,en_2825_293564_1_1_1_1_1,00.html*.

———, OECD Web site; available at *www.oecd.org/home*.

Transparency International, *The Corruption Perceptions Index*, Berlin, Germany, 1999–2006; available at *www.transparency.org/policy_research/surveys_indices/cpi*.

United Nations, *National Accounts*; available at *http://unstats.un.org/unsd/nationalaccount/nadefault.htm*.

———, *National Accounts Main Aggregates Database*; available at *http://unstats.un.org/unsd/snaama/Introduction.asp*.

United States Department of Commerce, *Country Commercial Guides*, Washington, D.C., 2004–2007; available at *www.buyusainfo.net/adsearch.cfm?search_type=int&loadnav=no*.

United States Department of State, *Country Reports on Human Rights Practices for 2006*, released by the Bureau of Democracy, Human Rights, and Labor, March 2007; available at *www.state.gov/g/drl/rls/hrrpt/2006/*.

———, *Investment Climate Statements: 2007*, released by the Bureau of Economic and Business Affairs, February 2007; available at *www.state.gov/e/eeb/ifd/2007/*.

United States Trade Representative, Office of the, *2007 National Trade Estimate Report on Foreign Trade Barriers*, Washington, D.C., 2007; available at *www.ustr.gov/Document_Library/Reports_Publications/2007/2007_NTE_Report/Section_Index.html?ht=*.

World Bank, *World Bank World Development Indicators Online*, Washington, D.C., 2007; available by subscription at *http://publications.worldbank.org/WDI/*.

———, *Doing Business*, 2004–2008; available at *www.doingbusiness.org/*.

World Trade Organization, *Trade Policy Reviews*, 1995–2007; available at *www.wto.org/english/tratop_e/tpr_e/tpr_e.htm*.